Ca ping, aravan
& Holiday Parks

Foreword

Thank you for thinking of Britain for your next holiday and welcome to this official guide to hundreds of our country's camping and caravan parks. We hope that 2010 will again benefit from the British passion for holidays at home as millions discover the many special places and surprising experiences that this country has to offer.

As anyone who has spent time with us will know, we have a range of enviable tourism assets, from stunning landscapes to vibrant, multicultural cities. Our rich history of tradition, heritage and culture lives beside modern design, music, theatre and architecture. And a tour of sites around Britain can be an ideal way to experience that diversity.

Exploring all that Britain has to offer has never been easier, thanks to this latest guide and never more affordable. You also want to be assured of a quality experience that exceeds your expectations and choosing one of our 'star-rated' parks will help. After all, who else will have checked them out before you check in.

A holiday at home offers an unrivalled social season and a calendar of unbeatable events – from Royal Ascot to Cowes Week, Edinburgh Tattoo to the Chelsea Flower Show. British destinations have inspired some of the world's greatest authors and poets, and produced number one musicians, leading fashion designers and award-winning actors, as well as sporting legends and iconic characters from Harry Potter to James Bond.

Take the time to discover the very best places to pitch your tent or park your caravan throughout England, Scotland, Wales and Northern Ireland and you'll find an enormous variety of experiences. You'll also realise just how easily every corner of Britain can be explored – even on a short break.

I wish you a memorable stay.

Christopher Rodrigues
Chairman, VisitBritain

Contents

How to use this guide

This official **VisitBritain** guide is packed with information from where to stay, to how to get there and what to see and do. In fact, everything you need to know to enjoy Britain.

Choose from a wide range of quality-assessed places to stay to suit all budgets and tastes. This guide contains a comprehensive listing of touring, camping and holiday parks, and holiday villages participating in the British-Graded Holiday Parks Scheme.

Each park is visited annually by a professional assessor who applies nationally agreed standards so that you can book with confidence knowing your accommodation has been checked and rated for quality.

Check out the places to visit in each region, from towns and cities to spectacular coast and countryside, plus historic homes,

castles and great family attractions! Maps show accommodation locations, selected destinations and some of the National Cycle Networks. For even more ideas go online at **visitbritain.com**

Regional tourism contacts and tourist information centres are listed – Contact them for further information. You'll also find events, travel information, maps and useful indexes.

Accommodation entries explained

Each accommodation entry contains detailed information to help you decide if it is right for you. This has been provided by proprietors and our aim is to ensure that it is as objective and factual as possible.

NOTTINGHAM, Nottinghamshire Map ref 4C2   SAT NAV NG12 2LU

National Water Sports Centre Caravan & Camping Park
Adbolton Lane, Holme Pierrepont, Nottingham NG12 2LU
t 01159 824 721 e nwsccampsite@nottscc.gov.uk
nwscnotts.com ONLINE MAP GUEST REVIEWS LAST MINUTE OFFERS

(52)   £10.00–£13.00
(52)   £13.00–£15.00
(360)   £7.00–£13.00
52 touring pitches

Special Promotions Available Upon Request. Electric hook-up available for £4.00.

Set in a 270 Acre country park the National Water Sports Centre is just 3 miles from Nottingham City Centre with local bus and train services. At the main centre activities available include, white water rafting, water skiing, windsurfing and canoeing along with great walks and good cycling too.

open All year
payment credit/debit cards, cash, cheques

directions 3 Miles From City Centre on A52. (Please See Website)

General   Leisure

Sample Enhanced Entry

1 Listing under town or village with map reference

2 Rating (and/or) Award where applicable

3 Prices per pitch per night for touring pitches; per unit per week for static holiday units

4 Establishment name, address, telephone and email

5 Website information

6 Satellite navigation

7 Accessible rating where applicable

8 Walkers, cyclists, pets and families welcome where applicable

9 Payment accepted

10 At-a-glance facility symbols

11 Accommodation details

12 Travel directions

At the end of each regional section you will find a listing of every Park in England assessed under the British Holiday Parks Scheme.

The information includes brief contact details for each place to stay, together with its star rating and classification. The listing also shows if an establishment has a National Accessible rating or participates in the Welcome schemes: Cyclists Welcome, Walkers Welcome, Welcome Pets! and Families Welcome (see page 7 for further information).

More detailed information on all the places shown in bold can be found in the main 'Where to Stay' sections (where parks have paid to have their details included). To find these entries please refer to the park index at the back of this guide.

Key to symbols

Information about many of the accommodation services and facilities is given in the form of symbols.

Pitches/Units

- Caravans (number of pitches and rates)
- Motor caravans (number of pitches and rates)
- Tents (number of pitches and rates)
- Caravan holiday homes (number of pitches and rates)
- Log cabins/lodges (number of units and rates)
- Chalets/villas (number of units and rates)

Leisure

- Swimming pool – indoor
- Swimming pool – outdoor
- Clubhouse with bar
- Regular evening entertainment
- Games room
- Outdoor play area
- Tennis court(s)
- Riding/pony-trekking nearby
- Fishing nearby
- Access to golf
- Cycle hire on site/nearby

General

- Overnight holding area
- Motor home pitches reserved for day trips off-site
- Electrical hook-up points
- Calor Gas/Camping Gaz purchase/exchange service
- Chemical toilet disposal point
- Motor home waste disposal point
- Showers
- Public telephone
- Laundry facilities
- Food shop on site
- Restaurant on site
- Pets welcome by arrangement
- Prior booking recommended in summer
- Wi-Fi
- Internet access

National Accessible Scheme

The National Accessible Scheme includes standards for hearing and visual impairment as well as mobility impairment – see pages 8-9 for further information.

Welcome schemes

Walkers, cyclists, families and pet owners are warmly welcomed where you see these signs – see page 7 for further information.

Visitor Attraction Quality Assurance
Participating attractions are visited annually by a professional assessor. High standards in welcome, hospitality, services, presentation; standards of toilets, shop and café, where provided, must be achieved to receive these awards.

A special welcome

To help make your selection of accommodation easier VisitBritain h̶
four special Welcome schemes which accommodation in England can b̶
assessed to. Owners participating in these schemes go the extra mile to
welcome walkers, cyclists, families or pet owners and provide additional
facilities and services to make your stay even more comfortable.

Families Welcome

If you are searching for a great family break look out for the Families Welcome sign. The
sign indicates that the proprietor offers additional facilities and services catering for a
range of ages and family units. For families with young children, the accommodation
will have special facilities such as cots and highchairs, storage for push-chairs and
somewhere to heat baby food or milk. Where meals are provided, children's choices
will be clearly indicated, with healthy options available.They'll also have information on
local walks, attractions, activities or events suitable for children, as well as local child-
friendly pubs and restaurants. Not all accommodation is able to cater for all ages or
combinations of family units, so do check when you book.

Welcome Pets!

Want to travel with your faithful companion? Look out for accommodation displaying
the Welcome Pets! sign. Participants in this scheme go out of their way to meet the
needs of guests bringing dogs, cats and/or small birds. In addition to providing water
and food bowls, torches or nightlights, spare leads and pet washing facilities, they'll buy
in food on request, and offer toys, treats and bedding. They'll also have information on
pet-friendly attractions, pubs, restaurants and recreation. Of course, not everyone is able
to offer suitable facilities for every pet, so do check if there are any restrictions on the
type, size and number of animals when you book.

Walkers Welcome

If walking is your passion seek out accommodation participating in the Walkers
Welcome scheme. Facilities include a place for drying clothes and boots, maps and
books for reference and a first-aid kit. Packed breakfasts and lunch are available
on request in hotels and guesthouses, and you have the option to pre-order basic
groceries in self-catering accommodation. A wide range of information is provided
including public transport, weather, local restaurants and attractions, details of the
nearest bank and all night chemists.

Cyclists Welcome

If you like to explore by bike, seek out accommodation displaying the Cyclists Welcome
symbol. Facilities include a lockable undercover area and a place to dry outdoor
clothing and footwear, an evening meal if there are no eating facilities available within
one mile, and a packed breakfast or lunch on request. Information is also provided on
cycle hire and cycle repair shops, maps and books for reference, weather and details of
the nearest bank and all night chemists and more.

For further information go online at enjoyengland.com/quality

National Accessible Scheme

Finding suitable accommodation is not always easy, especially if you have to seek out rooms with level entry or large print menus. Use the National Accessible Scheme to help you make your choice.

Proprietors of accommodation taking part in the National Accessible Scheme have gone out of their way to ensure a comfortable stay for guests with special hearing, visual or mobility needs. These exceptional places are full of extra touches to make everyone's visit trouble-free, from handrails, ramps and step-free entrances (ideal for buggies too) to level-access showers and colour contrast in the bathrooms. Members of staff may have attended a disability awareness course and will know what assistance will really be appreciated.

Appropriate National Accessible Scheme symbols are included in the guide entries (shown opposite). If you have additional needs or special requirements, we strongly recommend that you make sure these can

be met by your chosen establishment before you confirm your reservation. The index at the back of the guide gives a list of accommodation that have received a National Accessible rating.

For the widest possible selection of places to stay, OpenBritain 2010 is the new guide to accessible accommodation in Britain. Packed with Hotels, B&B's, Self Catering and Caravan and Camping sites – OpenBritain is the perfect accessible travel planner. Available from all good bookstores or direct from Tourism for All priced £9.99 (plus £4.50 P&P)

The criteria VisitEngland and national/regional tourism organisations have adopted do not necessarily conform to British Standards or to Building Regulations. They reflect what the organisations understand to be acceptable to meet the practical needs of guests with mobility or sensory impairments and encourage the industry to increase access to all.

You can also search for NAS accredited accommodation at **www.enjoyengland.com/stay**

Click '**Advanced search options**' and scroll down to use the '**Suitability**' filter to view accommodation suitable for your level of access needs.

Additional help and guidance on accessible tourism can be obtained from the national charity Tourism for All:

Tourism for All

Tourism for All c/o Vitalise
Shap Road Industrial Estate
Kendal LA9 6NZ

Information helpline 0845 124 9971
Reservations 0845 124 9973
(lines open 9-5 Mon-Fri)
F 01539 735567
E info@tourismforall.org.uk
W http://www.tourismforall.org.uk

England

Mobility Impairment Symbols

 Typically suitable for a person with sufficient mobility to climb a flight of steps but who would benefit from fixtures and fittings to aid balance.

 Typically suitable for a person with restricted walking ability and for those who may need to use a wheelchair some of the time and can negotiate a maximum of three steps.

 Typically suitable for a person who depends on the use of a wheelchair and transfers unaided to and from the wheelchair in a seated position. This person may be an independent traveller.

 Typically suitable for a person who depends on the use of a wheelchair and needs assistance when transferring to and from the wheelchair in a seated position.

 Access Exceptional is awarded to establishments that meet the requirements of independent wheelchair users or assisted wheelchair users shown above and also fulfil more demanding requirements with reference to the British Standards BS8300:2001.

Visual Impairment Symbols

 Typically provides key additional services and facilities to meet the needs of visually impaired guests.

 Typically provides a higher level of additional services and facilities to meet the needs of visually impaired guests.

Hearing Impairment Symbols

 Typically provides key additional services and facilities to meet the needs of guests with hearing impairment.

 Typically provides a higher level of additional services and facilities to meet the needs of guests with hearing impairment.

The Guide - out Nov 09

OpenBritain is the title of a new guide and website to accessible places to stay and visit that has been created by the merger of two major disability charities' guides - Easy Access Britain published by Tourism for All, and Where to Stay and There and Back published by RADAR.

The new guide is now the definitive guide for people with mobility, sight or hearing impairments, packed with easy to use information - from where to stay, how to get there and what to see and do once you are there. In short, everything you need to explore and enjoy Britain to the full.

Basis of Entries in OpenBritain

Accommodation in the guide must be either inspected under the National Accessible Scheme (NAS), operated by VisitEngland, or under those operated by VisitScotland, VisitLondon or other regional scheme, OR accommodations, attractions, or services who have joined OpenBritain on a self-assessed basis, and are subject to random checks. The former offer a higher level of assurance and will be clearly flagged.

The Website **OPENBRITAIN.NET**

Using the easy to use searchable database and interactive map, the OpenBritain.net website provides the online one stop solution for the traveller with access needs.

The website is full of useful information to help you choose the most suitable accommodation for your own individual needs, as well as useful information about suitable places to visit, eat and drink.

OpenBritain.net also provides you with the opportunity to share your own travel and accommodation experiences by adding your personal reviews to the site using the Forum and Blog. Experiences (both good and bad) can then be shared with others.

The definitive guide to accessible Britain

OPEN BRITAIN 2010

The definitive guide to accessible Britain

Only £9.99+p&p

To pre-order your copy of OpenBritain 2010:

- Use the online pre-order form on www.openbritain.net

- ☎ Call 01603 813740 and speak to one of our friendly staff

From November 2009 OpenBritain will be available from all good bookshops.

ISBN 978-0-85101-442-5

At last!

A definitive **one-stop-shop** to accessible Britain & a nationally recognised symbol for disabled access information

If you have access needs, OpenBritain is the only guide you need to plan holidays and book stress free travel throughout the UK.

- Over 1000 places to stay which have been assessed or audited for quality and accessibility
- Ideas for great days out
- National and regional access contacts
- Travel and holiday resources
- Index for mobility, hearing and visual needs
- Published by Tourism For All UK and Radar

Peace of mind with Star Ratings

Most camping and caravan parks in Britain have a star rating from one of the four assessing bodies – VisitEngland, VisitScotland, VisitWales or the AA. They all assess to the same national standards so you can expect comparable services, facilities and quality standards at each star rating.

All the parks in this guide are checked annually by national tourist board assessors. So when you see the star rating sign you can be confident that we've checked it out.

The national standards are based on our research of consumer expectations. The independent assessors decide the type (classification) of park – for example if it's a 'touring park', 'holiday park', 'holiday village', etc. – and award a star rating based on over fifty separate aspects, from landscaping and layout to maintenance, customer care and, most importantly, cleanliness.

The Quality Rose sign helps you choose with confidence knowing that the park has been thoroughly checked out before you check in.

Accommodation Types

Always look at or ask for the type of accommodation as each offers a very distinct experience. The parks you'll find in this guide are:

Camping Park – these sites only have pitches available for tents.

Touring Park – sites for your own caravan, motor home or tent.

Holiday Park – sites where you can hire a caravan holiday home for a short break or longer holiday, or even buy your own holiday home. Sites range from small, rural sites to larger parks with added extras, such as a swimming pool.

Many of the above parks will offer a combination of these classifications.

Holiday Villages – usually comprise a variety of types of accommodation, with the majority in custom-built rooms, chalets, for example. The option to book on a bed and breakfast, or dinner, bed and breakfast basis is normally available. A range of facilities, entertainment and activities are also provided which may, or may not, be included in the tariff. Holiday Villages must meet minimum requirements for provision and quality of facilities and services, including fixtures, fittings, furnishings, décor and any other extra facilities.

Forest Holiday Village – a holiday village situated in a forest setting with conservation and sustainable tourism being a key feature. Usually offer a variety of accommodation, often purpose built, and with a range of entertainment, activities and facilities on site free of charge or at extra cost.

Star ratings are based on a combination of range of facilities, level of service offered and quality - if a park offers facilities required to achieve a certain star rating but does not achieve the quality score required for that rating, a lower star rating is awarded.

A random check is made of a sample of accommodation provided for hire (caravans, chalets, etc) but the quality of the accommodation itself is not included in the grading assessment.

Holiday Villages are assessed under a separate rating scheme (for details see enjoyEngland.com).

Also included in this guide **Bunkhouses and Camping Barns** – safe, budget-priced, short-term accommodation for individuals and groups.

The more stars, the higher the quality and the greater the range of facilities and level of service:

★ One-Star
Park must be clean with good standards of maintenance and customer care.

★ ★ Two-Star
As above plus improved level of landscaping, lighting, maintenance and refuse disposal. May be less expensive than more highly rated parks.

★ ★ ★ Three-Star
This represents the industry standard as most parks fall within this category. The range of facilities may vary from park to park, but they will be of good standard and will be well maintained.

★ ★ ★ ★ Four-Star
These parks rank among the industry's best and provide careful attention to detail in the provision of all services and facilities.

★ ★ ★ ★ ★ Five-Star
The highest level of customer care provided. All facilities will be maintained in pristine condition in attractive surroundings.

Caravan Holiday Home Award Scheme

VisitBritain and VisitScotland run award schemes for individual holiday caravan homes on highly graded caravan parks. In addition to complying with standards for Holiday Parks, these exceptional caravans must have a shower or bath, toilet, mains electricity and water heating (at no extra charge) and a fridge (many also have a colour TV).

Award-winning parks listed in this guide show the relevant logo by their entry.

What to expect

Star ratings

Parks are required to meet progressively higher standards of quality as they move up the scale from one to five stars:

ONE-STAR   Acceptable   ★

To achieve this grade, the park must be clean with good standards of maintenance and customer care.

TWO-STAR   Good   ★★

All the above points plus an improved level of landscaping, lighting, refuse disposal and maintenance. May be less expensive than more highly rated parks.

THREE-STAR   Very Good   ★★★

Most parks fall within this category; three stars represent the industry standard. The range of facilities provided may vary from park to park, but they will be of a very good standard and will be well maintained.

FOUR-STAR   Excellent   ★★★★

You can expect careful attention to detail in the provision of all services and facilities. Four star parks rank among the industry's best.

FIVE-STAR   Exceptional   ★★★★★

The highest levels of customer care will be provided. All facilities will be maintained in pristine condition in attractive surroundings.

picnic **2 HOURS**

country walk **1 AFTERNOON**

riverside cottage **1 WEEK**

train ride **90 MINUTES**

pony trekking **3 HOURS**

fishing **1 MORNING**

There are 112 Saturdays, Sundays and Bank Holidays each year.
So why not make the most of them by getting out and about and enjoying England.
For hundreds of money saving offers and ideas visit **enjoyEngland.com**

ENJOY EVERY MINUTE, enjoyEngland.com

Enjoy England Awards for Excellence

Enjoy England awards for Excellence are all about telling the world what a fantastic place England is to visit, whether it's for a day trip, a weekend break or a fortnight's holiday.

Organised by VisitBritain and sponsored by The Caravan Club, The Enjoy England Awards for Excellence are the annual accolades for English tourism, recognizing the best places to stay and visit. Now in their 21st year, the Awards are known throughout the industry, promoting healthy competition and high standards. Competition is fierce, and entries are submitted to regional tourism organizations across England before being short-listed for the national finals, culminating in an Awards ceremony held in April each year.

There are seventeen catagories, from visitor attractions and hotels to self-catering accommodation and caravan parks. This year's winners include a Norwegian inspired lodge in Hexham, a spectacular Stately Home in Leeds, Bed & Breakfast in a Castle in Cumbria and a Michelin 'Bib Gourmand' country inn and pub in East Yorkshire. Seek them out and experience them for yourself – you won't be disappointed.

The complete list of winners can be found online at **www.enjoyengland.com**

This year's Caravan Holiday Park of the Year gold winner is Hidden Valley Park, in Devon. Nestled amid 27 acres of countryside, it is the only park in the region to offer luxury touring facilities all year round. Hidden Valley provides a range of superbly maintained pitches for caravans, motor homes and campers as well as a three-bedroom self-catering chalet sleeping up to five people. Three years of investment has led to exciting new developments including the addition of premier pitches with space for a car, a caravan and a generous garden; a new therapy room; an upgraded amenities block with under-floor heating and thermostatically controlled showers and an eco store to complement an existing coffee shop. Hidden Valley has a sustainable water treatment system, nature events, green tariff electricity, local community recycling and has won the Gold David Bellamy Award for eight consecutive years.

Judges described the park as 'an outstanding touring site catering for both caravanners and tent tourers, with an excellent commitment to the environment and a standard of customer care which all tourism businesses should aim to emulate'. www.hiddenvalleypark.com

Caravan Holiday Park of the Year 2009

GOLD WINNER

Hidden Valley Touring & Camping Park, Ilfracombe, Devon ★ ★ ★ ★ ★

SILVER WINNERS

Parkcliffe Caravan Park, Camping & Caravan Estate, Windermere, Cumbria ★ ★ ★ ★ ★

Seafield Caravan Park, Seahouses, Northumberland ★ ★ ★ ★ ★

Historic Houses & Gardens

Castles and Heritage Sites

2010

HUDSONS

All you need for fabulous days out

Enjoy your UK holidays more with The Caravan Club

Choose from 200 superb Club Sites in the finest locations

Troutbeck Head Caravan Club Site, one of The Club's eight sites in Cumbria

With the UK's increasing popularity as a holiday destination, there's no better way to discover Britain & Ireland's beauty and heritage than by staying at one of The Caravan Club's 200 quality Club Sites.

Caravan Club Sites are renowned for their excellence. With most of those graded achieving 4 or 5 stars from VisitBritain, you can be sure of consistently high standards.

And with over 40 Club Sites open all year, you can enjoy superb touring all year round.

You can be assured of excellent facilities and a friendly welcome from our Resident Wardens. Why not discover the best of Britain this year?

Why choose a Caravan Club Site?

- Choice of superb locations throughout Britain & Ireland
- Sites are immaculately maintained
- Most Club Sites are in peaceful settings, ideal for a relaxing holiday
- Care for the local environment and wildlife is paramount

Clumber Park Caravan Club Site, Nottinghamshire

Call today for your FREE Site Guide on 0800 521 161 quoting VB10

Trewethett Caravan Club Site, Cornwall

You don't have to be a member to stay on most Caravan Club Sites but members save £7 per night on pitch fees!

For Caravan Club Site details and locations visit www.caravanclub.co.uk

THE CARAVAN CLUB

A Club with a conscience

Sustainable tourism, carbon footprint, green initiatives are all buzzwords of the moment, but for The Caravan Club it's nothing new. And we take our responsibilities seriously. We promote and encourage initiatives across our sites, we protect and enhance the local environment and ensure visitors get the most from their surroundings.

Here's a glimpse of some of the work we are doing and what you can do to be a green and responsible traveller.

The Club, supported by its members, is making a positive and united contribution to sustainable tourism. Enjoy caravanning at our sites and help make sure that future generations can, too.

What we are doing

Sustainable tourism initiatives

Across our sites we promote and implement many sustainable tourism initiatives. These include:

- Employing energy consultants to ensure we are using gas and electricity most efficiently and at the right price.
- Using biodegradable and environment-friendly products across the Sites Network.
- Building with timber from sustainable resources (timber is FSC certified from a sustainable source and we often use green oak or other timber cladding).
- Shredding tree prunings on Club Sites and using the material there.

across our network. This includes leaving tree stumps to provide excellent stag beetle habitat, providing nest boxes and bird feeding stations, and planting bluebells and foxgloves.

Ground-breaking eco-friendly initiatives

New to The Caravan Club network is Poolsbrook. Forming part of a large, recently created country park on the site of a former colliery, Poolsbrook is nestled in a rich-in-biodiversity landscape. The Club has been involved in the site's development from the outset and has incorporated a range of exciting sustainable resources and energy-saving features including:

- Geothermal energy
- Solar panels
- Grey water recycling
- Heat recovery ventilation
- A wind turbine

All these initiatives are monitored on display panels in the site reception, so visitors are able to see how they are contributing to minimise the effect on the environment. This is a ground-breaking project for The Club and should be heralded as a blueprint for caravan sites of the future.

What you can do

Buy local produce – not only are you supporting the community (each year visitors to our sites contribute nearly £180 million to local economies in the UK), but products are more likely to be less energy-intensive in their production. You'll also savour an authentic taste of the region.

Recycle waste on site or nearby, including the rubbish from a picnic, and buy products with minimal packaging.

Appreciate nature, from wildflower meadows to butterflies, birds and beetles and get involved with our Boosting Biodiversity programme.

Save energy – be mindful of how often you use the laundry room, turn off stand-by appliances, take a shorter shower.

Reduce your carbon footprint where possible and try to incorporate 'car-free' days into your holiday. Catch a bus or take a walking city tour; cycling is also a great environmentally friendly way to get around and keep you fit.

Recycle guide books – once you've finished your trip, pass on your brochures and leaflets to other travellers.

Have respect for the natural balance of the environment and the local culture, and take personal responsibility for your actions and their impact on the people and places you visit – so that you and others can enjoy the same thing again.

- Trialling a number of eco-friendly systems: wind and solar energy trials, a rainwater recovery system that avoids flushing drinking-quality water down the toilet, photovoltaic roof tiles, solar panels, ground source heat recovery.
- Using low-energy lamps where possible.

The natural environment

We've planted more than 500,000 trees in the last ten years so that sites are fully screened and carefully landscaped. And our commitment to the natural environment means birds and wildlife find a welcome habitat. On and around your base you might enjoy seasonal sightings of deer, robins, finches and tits. We're proud to have teamed up with the Royal Society for the Protection of Birds as the Species Champion of the song thrush, an endangered bird that likes the thick hedgerows, open farmland and native woodland on many Club Sites.

Our expanding Boosting Biodiversity programme – now on 40 sites – is another way in which we help safeguard the environment and encourage guests to enjoy the natural world around them. We conduct biodiversity appraisals using professional ecologists and follow a biodiversity action plan

THE GOOD FOOD GUIDE

The selection of restaurant reviews in this VisitBritain guide have been taken from the highly respected *The Good Food Guide 2010*.

Written and compiled from scratch each year, *The Good Food Guide* is Britain's longest-running and best-selling restaurant guide. It includes reviews of the very best dining experiences in the UK, from the Cornish coast and the Channel Islands to the Scottish Highlands and Northern Ireland, and covers a wide range of establishments from great value pubs ideal for Sunday lunch with friends, to perfect venues for that once-in-a-lifetime blow-out meal.

Every entry is based on genuine reader feedback, all inspections are anonymous and the Guide does not accept any sponsorship, advertising or free meals.

Inside *The Good Food Guide 2010* you will find:

✻ Over 1,200 reviews

✻ Great value eateries and budget tips

✻ High-end dining and places to treat yourself

✻ Foodie features including trends to watch and interviews with top chefs

✻ £50 of money-off vouchers to use at restaurants around the UK

✻ The latest recommendations from our readers

...it's meticulous

Daily Telegraph

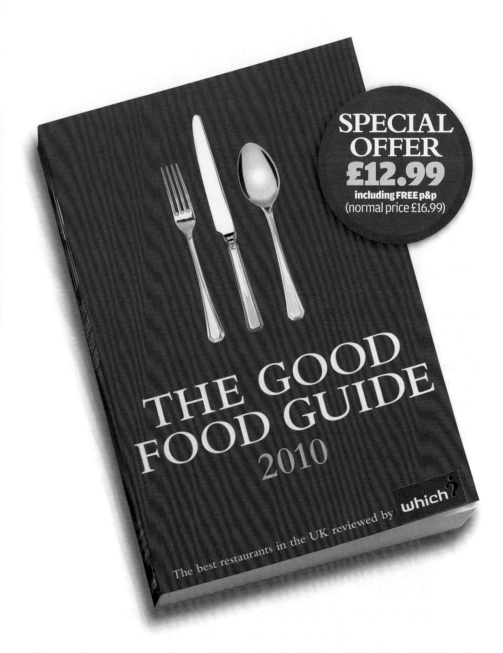

SPECIAL
OFFER
£12.99
including **FREE** p&p
(normal price £16.99)

THE GOOD
FOOD GUIDE
2010

The best restaurants in the UK reviewed by **which?**

To order your copy of *The Good Food Guide 2010* at the special offer price of £12.99 including FREE p&p (normal price £16.99), please call 01903 828557 and quote GFGV10.

Offer is valid to 31st December 2010.

ISBN: 978 1 84490 066 4 | 624 pages | Full colour, including maps for each region

David Bellamy Conservation Award

'These well-deserved awards are a signpost to parks which are making real achievements in protecting our environment. Go there and experience wrap-around nature … you could be amazed at what you find!' says Professor David Bellamy.

More than 600 gold, silver and bronze parks were named this year in the David Bellamy Conservation Awards, organised in conjunction with the British Holiday and Home Parks Association.

These parks are recognised for their commitment to conservation and the environment through their management of landscaping, recycling policies, waste management, the cultivation of flora and fauna and the creation of habitats designed to encourage a variety of wildlife onto the park. Links with the local community and the use of local materials are also important considerations.

Parks wishing to enter for a David Bellamy Conservation Award must complete a detailed questionnaire covering different aspects of their environmental policies, and describe what positive conservation steps they have taken. The park must also undergo an independent audit from a local wildlife or conservation body which is familiar with the area. Final assessments and the appropriate level of any award are then made personally by Professor Bellamy.

An index of award-winning parks featured in the regional pages of this guide can be found on page 428.

Over **100** **award-winning** camp sites

The **Camping** and **Caravanning** **Club**
The Friendly Club

Cannock Club Site

If you love camping as much as we do, you'll love staying on one of The Camping and Caravanning Club's 109 UK Club Sites. Each of our sites are in great locations and are an ideal base for exploring the UK.

There's just one thing: once you've discovered the friendly welcome, the excellent facilities and clean, safe surroundings, you'll probably want to join anyway!

To book your adventure or to join The Club

call **0845 130 7633**

quoting code **2744** or visit
www.thefriendlyclub.co.uk

- More choice of highly maintained, regularly inspected sites
- Friendly sites that are clean and safe, so great for families
- Preferential rates – recoup your membership fee in just 6 nights' stay
- Reduced site fees for 55's and over and special deals for families
- Exclusive Member Services including specialist insurance and advice.

View of St. Michael's Mount, linked to the mainland by a causeway exposed at low tide, Marazion, Cornwall, England.

South West England

Cornwall, Isles of Scilly, Devon, Dorset,
Gloucestershire, Somerset, Wiltshire

South West England

A region of contrasts. Wherever you go, you will see spectacular scenery, wonderful countryside and beautiful coastlines offering everything from lively resorts, long safe, sandy beaches to rugged, dramatic cliffs guarding secluded coves and picturesque fishing villages. The South West is a glorious region, each county offering its own unique charm.

Majestic cathedrals grace cities like Salisbury, Gloucester, Wells, Truro and Exeter. The City of Bath boasts elegant Georgian splendour and famous Roman remains. Maritime history features strongly in Plymouth, the departure port for Sir Francis Drake and the Pilgrim Fathers.

The South West has a wealth of prehistoric sites, stone circles, villages with thatched, cob cottages and riverside walks with country pubs. The area has a wonderful choice of stately homes, many with glorious landscape gardens. There are also a multitude of great gardens, all different in character and content, just waiting to be explored. But for wild landscape with wide open spaces and stunning views the National Parks, Exmoor and Dartmoor are in Somerset and Devon. Nearly all of the charming Cotswolds, an Area of Outstanding Natural Beauty, is in the South West region. The magical Royal Forest of Dean can be found on the western side of Gloucestershire and the New Forest in Hampshire.

Bristol is the largest city in the South West offering a unique blend of fascinating history and exciting new attractions and home to the wonderful Aarnolfini, a leading centre for contemporary arts. After a regeneration programme, the harbourside and old warehouses now offer a fabulous choice of restaurants and wine bars alongside some fabulous attractions such as At-Bristol which has huge 3D-cinema screen and a living rainforest. Bristol is now 'the' place to visit.

Off the coast of the South West region are the Isles of Scilly, warmed by the Gulf Stream, a group of over a hundred islands only 28 miles off the tip of Lands end, Cornwall. Take a boat (only 20 mins) or helicopter trip to the five inhabited islands: St Mary's, Tresco, St Martin's, St Agnes and Bryher and then fast speedboat to over 100 more islands waiting to be explored.

Cornwall & Isles of Scilly

The Cathedral city of Truro is Cornwall's only city and main shopping centre. In the late 18th century, Truro was celebrated for its splendid architecture and today the city's famous Lemon Street is considered one of the finest examples of a Georgian street in England.

North Cornwall

Sixty miles of dramatic Heritage Coastline, pounded by the Atlantic coast, the sandy beaches attract surfers. There is much to explore in the hidden coves, pretty fishing villages, wooded river valleys, bustling market towns and the beguiling beauty of Bodmin Moor.

St Ives

St Ives is famous for surfing, blue flag beaches, individual art galleries, studios and craft shops. On a grander scale, modern art is on display at the architecturally impressive Tate St Ives and nearby is the Barbara Hepworth Museum and Sculpture Garden.

Padstow & Rock

Padstow is a working fishing port but great for a holiday too. There is plenty of harbour life, great restaurants and a beach nearby at Harbour Cove to relax on, or take a ferry trip across the Camel Estuary to Rock. Inappropriately named for such a sandy beach, Rock is often referred to as 'Chelsea-on-Sea' with expensive real estate to match. Rock, because of its sheltered waters, is best known for sailing and water-based pursuits.

South Cornwall

Gentler than the north, South Cornwall has golden beaches, unspoilt bays and picturesque fishing villages with colour-washed cottages, much painted by the artists that have flocked to the area for over a hundred years.

The Roseland Peninsula

A beautiful, unspoilt area that delivers breathtaking scenery, tranquil beaches and activities to suit all ages - few places can compare. An Area of Outstanding Natural Beauty there are many secret creeks, superb coastal and country walks, pretty fishing and rural villages, plus, a huge variety of sailing and other marine activities.

Falmouth

Falmouth's natural harbour is the third largest deep-water harbour in the world, the traditional gateway to the Atlantic, and one of the world's great sailing harbours. The world-class National Maritime Museum Cornwall houses the small boat collection and offers unique and interactive displays of boats and their place in people's lives.

Fowey

Fowey is not only an historic town but also a commercial seaport. Designated as an Area of Outstanding Natural Beauty, Fowey has much to offer with something for everyone. A natural harbour, it is a haven for yachtsmen.

Isles of Scilly

The islands have some of the best beaches in Britain, white sandy coves, exposed granite headlands, lagoons and important moorland sites. Take your choice from sailing, canoeing, windsurfing, horse riding, sea fishing, coastal walking and cycling or even diving with seals!

Devon

Exeter, the county capital for culture, leisure and shopping, is a vibrant city brimming with character and steeped in ancient history. Exeter today offers visitors a magnificent Gothic Cathedral with a delightful mix of high-quality attractions, restaurants and shops in a setting of architectural splendour.

South Devon

Known as the English Riviera it has been one of Europe's most popular destinations since the late 18th century. At that time, visitors remarked on the 22 miles of breathtaking coastal landscape and beautiful beaches, attributes which continue to attract discerning holidaymakers to the area today.

Famed for its palm trees and lush vegetation, the area is blessed with its very own micro-climate which means that visitors can be assured of agreeable weather throughout the year. Short, mild winters give way to long, balmy summers, allowing the area's sub-tropical plant life to flourish.

The English Riviera encompasses **Torquay**, the busy cosmopolitan resort and a favourite amongst affluent jet set and the fun-loving traveller alike. The stylish Harbourside area has developed into a real Riviera café culture that is complimented by a glitzy marina, lively nightlife and specialist shopping opportunities. **Paignton**, the perfect family holiday town boasting unrivalled stretches of sandy beaches and endless activities for the young and young at heart. Finally, **Brixham** offers a more sedate option and generations have fallen in love with this quaint attractive port and working harbour, with its colourful fishing cottages and quaint winding streets.

Visitors of all ages will be enthralled by the award-winning Kent's Cavern and Babbacombe Model Village, while Living Coasts and Occombe Farm join Paignton Zoo as must-sees for animal lovers. Variety is also very much alive with a choice of six theatres offering something to suit everyone.

North Devon

There are few places in Britain that can lay claim to such a wonderful combination of stunning landscapes. A coastline of spectacular cliffs, secret coves and golden beaches together with a hinterland of wild moorland, sparkling river valleys and lush rolling hills makes North Devon and Exmoor a very special place.

UNESCO recently gave world-wide acknowledgement to the North Devon landscape by designating it as the UK's first new-style Biosphere Reserve – an area of international importance because of its diversity and abundance of rare plants and continuous human use from ancient times.

There are varied opportunities for outdoor activities – walking, horse-riding, cycling, and golf or you can take to the water and enjoy surfing, fishing, windsurfing, sailing or a simple boat trip. Countryside and coastal areas can be enjoyed via extensive walking and cycling trails including the Tarka and Ruby Trails.

Town and village centres and local markets give the region a distinctive flavour with the variety of food, drink, arts and crafts. An exciting calendar of events including street carnivals, beer festivals and concerts for every musical taste ensures there is something for everyone.

Main centres are Woolacombe, Ilfracombe, Barnstaple, Bideford, Westward Ho!, Croyde, Lynton & Lynmouth, South Molton, Torrington, Holsworthy, Combe Martin and Lundy Island.

Dorset

Dorchester, the county town in southern central Dorset, is deep in the heart of Thomas Hardy's Wessex. Hardy based many of his novels in Dorset and *'Casterbridge'* is based on Hardy's home town of Dorchester.

Bournemouth

A world-class resort that has everything you need for a perfect holiday or short break, and where there's a host of sights and activities within easy reach. Relax on award-winning beaches, with seven miles of golden sand fringing the clear blue sea. Wander through the exquisite parks and gardens, or explore the many fascinating boutiques and larger department stores.

Christchurch

A beautiful Saxon market town with a magnificent 900-year-old Priory Church, situated on the spectacular Dorset coast; close to lively Bournemouth and the tranquillity of the New Forest. Its Saxon charm and fascinating heritage, combined with beautiful floral displays make it an ideal location for a short break, day trip or as a base to discover the hidden treasures of rural Dorset and the New Forest.

Jurassic Coast World Heritage Site

From Studland Bay in Dorset to Orcombe Rocks in Devon the Jurassic Coast gives a unique insight into life in the past through the rocks exposed along the 95 miles of beautiful coastline. 185 million years of Earth history for you to explore. Walk along the coast and walk through time! Discover the Mesozoic Era, a time when dinosaurs

ruled the Earth! The Jurassic is represented between Pinhay in Devon and Kimmeridge in Dorset, providing a complete record of every stage of the Jurassic period and exceptional fossils. Marine reptiles continue to be found, including new species. A remarkable new specimen of Scelidosauras dinosaur and many other fossils, often exceptionally preserved, make this coast a world-class venue for palaeontology.

Lyme Regis

Lyme Regis is a picturesque seaside town set in an Area of Outstanding Natural Beauty, on the border where Dorset meets Devon. It's a narrow tangle of streets and shops that find their way to the famous 13th-century Cobb harbour. The Cobb has been a haven for shipping from the time it was built and is famous for being the landing place of the Duke of Monmouth prior to the Pitchfork Rebellion at Sedgemoor in 1685. It was made famous as the location of the film *'The French Lieutenant's Woman'*, from the book by resident local author John Fowles.

Poole

World renowned for its award-winning beaches, beautiful harbour, sailing and the pottery outlet shop that bears the name of the town, Poole is known as the St Tropez of the south coast. Poole harbour, the second largest natural habour in the world, has five unique islands, including Brownsea Island, and offers fabulous scenery, wonderful wildlife and exhilarating watersports. Much of the town's history is visible on the quay, one of Poole's major tourist attractions. The exciting Cockle Trail guides visitors around the old town's mix of Georgian and medieval buildings bringing to life Poole's romantic seafaring and trading history.

Gloucestershire

The magnificent Norman cathedral lies at the heart of the city of Gloucester, monument to the finest craftsmanship with its extraordinary fan-vaulted cloisters. In the historic Gloucester Docks, 15 Victorian warehouses stand as proud guardians to Britain's most inland port.

Bath

The gold city of Bath, developed around the hot spring waters discovered by the Romans, has been welcoming visitors for over 2,000 years. A designated UNESCO World Heritage Site and one of Britain's Heritage Cities, Bath is home to some of the finest architectural sights in Europe plus wonderful shopping and restaurant opportunities.

Bourton-on-the-Water

Often referred to as the 'Venice of the Cotswolds' because the River Windrush runs right through the centre. The combination of this clear sparkling water and the attractive low bridges crossing it create a charming scene. The Model Village (a mini replica of the village itself) opened in 1937 and can be found behind the Old New Inn.

Cheltenham Spa

Considered the most complete Regency town in England, the 'town within a park' offers beautiful parks and gardens, tree-lined avenues and colourful floral displays. Described as 'the Festival town of England', Cheltenham hosts an annual programme of major sporting and cultural events, including internationally acclaimed music and literature festivals, cricket and horse racing, including the famous Cheltenham Gold Cup - the highlight of the National Hunt Festival.

Chipping Campden

Called the 'flower of the villages of all England', Chipping Campden is truly unspoilt; it has many beautiful buildings and an impressive 15th-century church. The long and flowing main street gives this typical Cotswold market town its shape and style.

Forest of Dean

The Royal Forest of Dean is one of England's few remaining ancient forests, covering 27,000 acres of woodland. Designated as a National Forest Park in 1938, this 'Queen of Forests' boasts a spectacular range of natural beauty combined with an aura of magic and mystery that has been the inspiration for many great artists and writers including Tolkien and JK Rowling.

Tewkesbury

Tewkesbury is dominated by the 12th-century Abbey and renowned as having one of the best medieval black and white townscapes in the country.

The Cotswolds

The Cotswolds is a designated Area of Outstanding Natural Beauty, recognised as a unique environment, with some of England's finest countryside. It is protected as a special landscape of national importance and lies between Gloucester, Stratford-Upon-Avon, Oxford and Bath. Attracting visitors all year round it is a fascinating place to explore, with something for everyone to enjoy. There are charming villages, historic towns, impressive churches, rolling countryside and glorious gardens. Walking, cycling and horse riding are popular pursuits. There are internationally important beech and yew woods, giving sensational seasonal colour.

Some of the smaller towns are certainly worth a visit: Biddlestone, Painswick or Woodstock. Northleach is famous for its magnificent chuch, St Peter and Paul considered by some to be the 'Cathedral of the Cotswolds'.

Somerset

Taunton, the county capital, lies in the spectacular Vale of Taunton Deane between the Quantock and Blackdown Hills. It combines relics of its dramatic past with the buzz and efficiency of a modern county town. The town has many fine architectural features, attractive back streets, parks and gardens.

Burnham-on-Sea

Burnham-on-Sea is a traditional seaside resort, famous for its unique nine-legged lighthouse and seven miles of sandy beach. Burnham has all the ingredients for a traditional English seaside holiday; donkey rides, ice creams, a jetty for launching boats and pier pavilion. Burnham has a fine esplanade and seafront overlooking Bridgwater Bay and the distant Welsh coast.

Cheddar and Cheddar Gorge

View the magnificent limestone gorge carved into the southern slopes of the Mendip hills above the village of Cheddar. Reaching 500 feet in places, the sides of the ravine boast the highest inland cliffs in the country and can be viewed from the road running through the base of the gorge or from footpaths along the cliff tops. At the lower end of the gorge are riverside walks, tea rooms and gift shops and the famous Showcaves, a series of labyrinthine underground chambers. Cheddar cheese is known throughout the world, its manufacture originating at farms in the region. You can watch traditional Cheddar cheese making at the Cheddar Gorge Cheese Company in the lower Gorge.

Minehead

A traditional family seaside resort with a long sandy beach. As well as a lively seafront there are quieter areas with lime-washed thatched cottages and a harbour. The 630-mile South West Coast Path, the longest of the National Tails, begins in Minehead.

Wells

Nestling in the Mendip Hills is Wells, England's smallest city with a beautiful cathedral. Probably the finest national example of early English architecture, Wells Cathedral was largely built between the 12th and 14th centuries, but was itself a successor to a 7th-century church, founded by the Saxon King Ina. The cathedral is famed for its magnificent west front, featuring over 300 statues and carvings; the inverted scissor arches of the nave, and one of the oldest working mechanical clocks (dated about 1390). The wells, which gave the city its name are now contained within the grounds of the Bishop's Palace, which is regulary open to the public.

Weston Super Mare

Weston-super-Mare is a great seaside resort. The wide sweep of Weston Bay has miles of clean sandy beach, traditional seaside attractions and beautiful countryside and coastline to explore. Despite the devastating fire on the Grand Pier, a brand new state of the art pavilion is being built and is due to re-open in the summer of 2010 but worth checking before visiting. Weston beach has a designated area for kite buggies, small land yachts and kite boards, while jet skiers, power boat users and other boats can launch from Knightstone slipway.

Wookey Hole

Carved out under the limestone Mendip Hills over millions of years by the mysterious River Axe, Wookey Hole Caves have become a popular visitor attraction, featuring magnificent underground chambers and pools, where spectacular light and sound effects bring the caves' natural wonder to life. Cave diving expeditions since 1935 have revealed 25 caverns, but there are surely more that remain unexplored.

Wiltshire

Trowbridge is situated on the River Biss in the west of the county. The crucial part the woollen trade played in the town's development is told in the fascinating museum based in the last woollen mill which closed its doors in 1982.

Chippenham

Chippenham, founded over 1,000 years ago, was the Royal Hunting Lodge for Alfred the Great from where he pursued his fight against the invading Danes. In the Middle Ages corn mills made way for the prosperous wool trade and famous cheese market. West of Chippenham are the exquisite 'picture postcard' villages of Castle Combe, National Trust Lacock, and Biddestone, complete with village green and duck pond.

Cricklade

Cricklade is the only Wiltshire town on the young River Thames. Nearby is the Cotswold Water Park, Britain's largest with 132 lakes which offer peaceful walks and exciting water sports.

Devizes

Half an hour from Bath, Salisbury and Swindon, Devizes makes an ideal day out destination. The town's rich history makes it a treasure in the heart of Wiltshire. Dating back to the 11th century, Devizes is filled with history, from its medieval street plan and Norman churches to Georgian architecture and the Kennet and Avon canal. The canal cuts through the town and no visit would be complete without seeing the Caen Hill lock flight, a staircase of 29 locks. More on the heritage of the canal can be found at the Canal Museum.

Marlborough

Marlborough lies in the valley of the River Kennet between the ancient Savernake Forest and the Marlborough Downs. Each end of the high street is capped by a church; at the west end the 15th-century St Peter's, and to the east (behind the Town Hall) the Church of St Mary's. Other notable buildings in the high street include the splendid Merchant's House, built during the Cromwell period and now restored as a 17th-century town house. Marlborough's high street is reputedly one of the widest streets in Britain.

Salisbury

Nestling in the very heart of rural southern England, Salisbury is every bit the classic English city. It combines the charm of a medieval city with the vibrancy of modern life, where high street names and modern café culture intermingle with independent shops and traditional English pubs. A visit to the cathedral is a must. Built between 1220 and 1258, the cathedral boasts the tallest spire in Britain, which rises elegantly above the sweeping lawns of the tranquil cathedral close. Within the close, you can enjoy award-winning museums and graceful period homes as you wander peacefully around the relaxed setting.

Swindon

A vibrant, growing town where the West Country meets the Cotswolds. Discover Swindon – theatre, fabulous restaurants, fashionable bars and premier nightclubs. Visit delightful villages and beautiful countryside, or STEAM where the history of the Great Western Railway is brought to life.   Shop till you drop in the town centre, the McArthurGlen Designer Outlet centre, or at the small curiosity shops in Old Town. If sport's your thing there's plenty on offer from ice-skating to horse riding; the choice is yours. Swindon is within easy distance of London, Bath and Salisbury.

Wilton

Wilton, the ancient capital of Wessex, is a quintessential English market town with a history spanning more than 2,000 years. The town gave its name to Wiltshire and the famous Wilton Carpets which are still made there today.

Where to Go

 Attractions with this sign participate in the **Visitor Attraction Quality Assurance Scheme** (see page 6) which recognises high standards in all aspects of the visitor experience.

ENTERTAINMENT & CULTURE

Brunel's s.s. Great Britain
Bristol, City of Bristol, BS1 6TY
(0117) 926 0680
www.ssgreatbritain.org
Experience life aboard Brunel's famous steam ship, the Victorian forerunner of all modern shipping.

City Sightseeing Tours
Bristol, City of Bristol, BS1 4AH
0870 444 0654
www.city-sightseeing.com
Open top bus tours with guides and headphones around the City of Bristol. Service runs daily throughout the Summer months.

Falmouth Art Gallery
Falmouth, Cornwall, TR11 2RT
(01326) 313863
www.falmouthartgallery.com
Family-friendly exhibitions, internationally acclaimed artists and one of the best collections in the Southwest featuring Pre-Raphaelites and British Impressionists.

Fashion Museum
Bath, Somerset, BA1 2QH
(01225) 477173
www.fashionmuseum.co.uk
A world-class collection of contemporary and historical dress, housed in the Georgian Assembly Rooms.

Roman Baths
Bath, Somerset, BA1 1LZ
(01225) 477785
www.romanbaths.co.uk
Stunning Roman Baths and Temple of Sulis Minerva. Computer reconstructions bring your experience to life.

STEAM - Museum of the Great Western Railway
Swindon, Wiltshire, SN2 2TA
(01793) 466646
www.swindon.gov.uk/steam
The remarkable story of the GWR. Sights sounds, footplate access and detailed reconstructions.

Tate St Ives
St Ives, Cornwall, TR26 1TG
(01736) 796226
www.tate.org.uk/stives
Catch exhibitions of top international, modern and contemporary art in this striking gallery overlooking Porthmeor Beach.

The Jane Austen Centre
Bath, Somerset, BA1 2NT
(01225) 443000
www.janeausten.co.uk
Celebrate Bath's most famous resident with this snapshot of the Regency life that inspired her.

The Tank Museum
Wareham, Dorset, BH20 6JG
(01929) 405096
www.tankmuseum.org
The world's finest display of armoured fighting vehicles. Experimental vehicles, interactive displays, disabled access and facilities.
Dogs not accepted.

Victoria Art Gallery
Bath, Somerset, BA2 4AT
(01225) 477232
www.victoriagal.org.uk
Permanent collection of 15th–21stC British and European fine and decorative art. Also major touring exhibitions.

Wookey Hole
Wells, Somerset, BA5 1BB
(01749) 672243
www.wookey.co.uk
Spectacular caves, a working Victorian paper mill, maze and Cave Diving Museum.

FAMILY FUN

Brean Leisure Park
Brean, Somerset, TA8 2QY
(01278) 751595
www.brean.com
Fun park with over 30 rides and attractions from roundabouts to rollercoasters. Pool complex with 5 waterslides, golf course, garden centre, bars & restaurants.

Cornwall's Crealy Great Adventure Park
Wadebridge, Cornwall, PL27 7RA
(01841) 540276
www.crealy-Cornwall.co.uk
Maximum magical fun and unforgettable adventures. Discover Cornwall's all-weather family attraction.

Explore-At-Bristol
Bristol, City of Bristol, BS1 5DB
0845 345 1235
www.at-bristol.org.uk
An exciting science adventure: interactive exhibits, special exhibitions. Tour the night sky in the Planetarium.

HERITAGE

Avon Valley Railway
Bristol, Gloucestershire, BS30 6HD
(0117) 932 5538
www.avonvalleyrailway.org
Travel back in time on this 2.5 mile steam railway. Locomotives and rolling stock collection.

Dartmouth Castle
Dartmouth, Devon, TQ6 0JN
(01803) 833588
www.english-heritage.org.uk/dartmouth
One of the first castles built with artillery in mind, strategically positioned at the water's edge.

Gloucester Cathedral
Gloucester, Gloucestershire, GL1 2LR
(01452) 528095
www.gloucestercathedral.org.uk
An architectural gem made of honey-coloured limestone with crypt, cloisters and chapter house in its precincts.

Gloucestershire-Warwickshire Railway
Cheltenham, Gloucestershire, GL50 4SH
(01242) 621405
www.gwsr.com
Steam and diesel heritage railway, running from Cheltenham to Winchcombe and Toddington. Trips, galas, events.

Old Sarum
Tisbury, Wiltshire, SP3 6RR
(01747) 870487
www.english-heritage.org.uk/oldsarum
An Iron Age hill fort settled by Romans, Saxons and Normans. Earthworks cover 56 acres.

Old Wardour Castle
Salisbury, Wiltshire SP1 3SD
(01722) 335398
www.english-heritage.org.uk/oldwardour
Unusual hexagonal ruins of a 14thC castle. The serene lakeside scene hides a bloodthirsty past!

Portland Castle
Portland, Dorset DT5 1AZ
(01305) 820539
www.english-heritage.org.uk/portland
A well-preserved coastal fort built by Henry VIII to defend Weymouth harbour against possible French and Spanish attack. Exhibition: 400 years of the castle's history.

Salisbury Cathedral
Salisbury, Wiltshire, SP1 2EJ
(01722) 555120
www.salisburycathedral.org.uk
Come and celebrate the 750th anniversary of the cathedral's dedication (1258). Exciting calendar of events.

Stonehenge
Amesbury, Wiltshire, SP4 7DE
0870 333 1181
www.english-heritage.org.uk/stonehenge
Ceremonial centre or astronomical calendar? See what you make of this iconic monument built c3000–1600 BC.

Swanage Railway
Swanage, Dorset, BH19 1HB
(01929) 425800
www.swanagerailway.co.uk
Visit the seaside by steam train: Norden to Swanage six miles, passing Corfe Castle. Jurassic Coast adventure.

West Somerset Railway
Minehead, Somerset, TA24 5BG
(01643) 704996
www.west-Somerset-railway.co.uk
Country's longest heritage railway. Twenty mile trips: Bishops Lydeard via Quantocks and coast to Minehead.

NATURE & WILDLIFE

Abbotsbury Swannery
Abbotsbury, Dorset, DT3 4JG
(01305) 871858
www.abbotsbury-tourism.co.uk
Watch up to 1,000 swans during nesting and hatching time. Feeding: noon and 4 pm. No dogs.

Bristol Zoo Gardens
Bristol, City of Bristol, BS8 3HA
(0117) 974 7399
www.bristolzoo.org.uk
See the world's smallest tortoise or largest ape – amongst a rich, diverse range of species.

Cheddar Caves
Cheddar, Somerset, BS27 3QF
(01934) 742343
www.cheddarcaves.co.uk/
A major tourist attraction, with plenty to do above and below ground. Outstanding Natural Beauty, where you'll find many rare species. The Cathedral-like caves and Britain's biggest Gorge are million-year-old Ice Age river beds.

Dairyland Farm World
Newquay, Cornwall, TR8 5AA
(01872) 510246
www.dairylandfarmworld.com
Farm park, country life museum and adventure playground. See 120 cows milked in Clarabelle's space-age orbiter!

Eden Project
St Austell, Cornwall, PL24 2SG
(01726) 811911
www.edenproject.com
Enter the giant biomes and immerse yourself in a living theatre of exotic plants and people. Children's play areas, story telling, workshops.

Hidcote Manor Garden
Chipping Campden, Gloucestershire, GL55 6LR
(01386) 438333
www.nationaltrust.org.uk/hidcote
Celebrated Arts and Crafts style garden featuring rare trees and shrubs, herbaceous borders, unusual plants.

Horseworld
Bristol, Somerset, BS14 0QJ
(01275) 540173
www.horseworld.org.uk
Meet friendly horses, ponies and donkeys. Touch and groom areas, pony rides, adventure playground and shows.

Living Coasts
Torquay, DEVON, TQ1 2BG
(01803) 202470
www.livingcoasts.org.uk
Loud, loveable penguins, playful fur seals, bright puffins, waders, sea ducks – see them all here.

Longleat
Longleat, Wiltshire, BA12 7NW
(01985) 844400
www.longleat.co.uk
From safari park to Elizabethan stately home, mazes to simulator rides, there's something for everyone.

Lost Gardens of Heligan
St Austell, Cornwall, PL26 6EN
(01726) 845100
www.heligan.com
Recently voted 'The Nation's Favourite Garden' by BBC Gardeners' World viewers, the award-winning restoration of Heligan's productive gardens is only one of many features which combine to create a destination with a breadth of interest.

Monkey World - Ape Rescue Centre
Wareham, Dorset, BH20 6HH
(01929) 462537
www.monkeyworld.org
Rescued chimps in large natural enclosures, also lemurs, macaques and orangutans. Pets encounter and restaurants.

Newquay Zoo
Newquay, Cornwall, TR7 2LZ
(01637) 873342
www.newquayzoo.org.uk
Encounter hundreds of animals, from Pygmy Marmosets to African lions. Talks/feeding times throughout the day.

Noah's Ark Zoo Farm
Bristol, Somerset, BS48 1PG
(01275) 852606
www.noahsarkzoofarm.co.uk
Varied zoo on a working farm. Exotic birds, reptiles, monkeys, zebra. Educational animal shows and mazes.

Painswick Rococo Garden
Stroud, Gloucestershire, GL6 6TH
(01452) 813204
www.rococogarden.org.uk
An 18thC Rococo garden set in a hidden combe, with garden buildings, vistas and woodland paths.

Springfields Fun Park and Pony Centre
St Columb, Cornwall, TR9 6HU
(01637) 881224
www.springfieldsponycentre.co.uk
Create magical memories with indoor/outdoor family fun - giant play barn, pony rides, pets' corner, go-karts.

Stourhead House and Garden
Stourton, Wiltshire, BA12 6QD
(01747) 841152
www.nationaltrust.org.uk/stourhead
World-renowned 18thC English landcape garden 'paradise'. Palladian mansion with Chippendale furniture and Regency library.

Westonbirt, the National Arboretum
Tetbury, Gloucestershire, GL8 8QS
(01666) 880220
www.forestry.gov.uk/westonbirt
Wander 600 acres featuring the finest tree collections. Beautiful spring flowers, stunning autumn colour. Events.

Weymouth Sea Life Park and Marine Sanctuary
Weymouth, Dorset, DT4 7SX
(01305) 788255
www.sealifeeurope.com/local/index.php?loc=weymouth
From May 2009 Weymouth SEA LIFE Park launches its new feature - Crocodile Creek! "Embark on a safari style log flume adventure and come face to face with crocodiles!" Sea Life houses an amazing array of the world's most fascinating marine l

RELAXING & PAMPERING

Thermae Bath Spa
Bath, Somerset, BA1 1SJ
0844 888 0844
www.thermaebathspa.com
Bathe in natural hot waters, as the Romans and Celts did over 2,000 years ago.

Events 2010

Autumn Walking Week
Gurnsey / Jersey
www.jersey.com/walking
September

Bath Comedy Festival
Bath
www.bathcomedyfestival.co.uk
1st-12th April

Bath International Music Festival
Bath
www.bathmusicfest.org.uk/
28th May - 12th June

Battle of Flowers Carnival
Jersey
www.battleofflowers.com
August

Bristol Harbour Festival
Bristol
www.bristolharbourfestival.co.uk/
July-August

Cheese Rolling
Brockworth
www.cheese-rolling.co.uk/
31st May

GoldCoast Oceanfest
North Devon
www.goldcoastoceanfest.co.uk
18th-20th June

Great Dorset Steam Fair
Blandford Forum
www.gdsf.co.uk
September

Jane Austen Festival
Bath
www.janeausten.co.uk/festival/
17th - 26th September

Jersey International Air Display
Jersey
www.jerseyairdisplay.org.uk
September

Liberation Day
Guernsey
www.floralguernsey.gg
9th May

National Hunt Festival
Prestbury Park
www.cheltenham.co.uk/festival/the_festival.html
16th-19th March

Royal International Air Tattoo
www.airtattoo.com
17th-18th July

Spirit of the Sea
Weymouth
www.spiritofthesea.org.uk
July

Spring Floral Festival Week
Guernsey
www.floralguernsey.gg
17th-25th April

Summer Solstice
Amesbury
www.english-heritage.org.uk/summersolstice
June

The Bath and West Show
Shepton Mallet
www.bathandwest.co.uk
May

The Times Cheltenham Literature Festival
Cheltenham
October

Where to Eat

The South West England region has great places to eat. The restaurant reviews on these pages are just a small selection from the highly respected *The Good Food Guide 2010*. Please see pages 20–21 for further information on the guide and details of a Special Offer for our readers.

CHANNEL ISLANDS

Longueville Manor

Country-house dining from the kitchen garden
St Saviour, Jersey, JE2 7WF
Tel no: (01534) 725501
www.longuevillemanor.com
Modern British | £55

Guide regular Longueville has been in the Lewis family for half a century, and remains a beacon of grand country-house elegance and solicitude. It was built in the 14th century and is surrounded by 15 acres of woodland and grounds – including a Victorian kitchen garden – and is run with sympathetic warmth and professionalism. Chef Andrew Baird has clocked up a fair few years here (his third decade is upon us), and the results are there for all to see, in cooking that takes its cue from the seasons and its influences from modern French modes. Poached sea bass is teamed with crab gratin in one main course, while meatier options might be loin and shoulder of lamb with flageolets and baby vegetables, or marrow-crusted Angus fillet with braised cheek and béarnaise. Top and tail with inventive dishes such as grilled scallops, belly pork, trompettes, honey and five-spice, and pineapple wrap with riz au lait, pannacotta and kiwi. The Taste of Jersey menu is worth the punt, incorporating perhaps crab, halibut and pork from the vicinity, with Longueville's own honey in the form of a soufflé. The monster wine list is a delight – it doesn't just concentrate lazily on France, but has fine, authoritative selections from Italy, New Zealand and South America too. An excellent glass selection starts at £4.75.

Chef/s: Andrew Baird. **Open:** all week L 12 to 2, D 7 to 10. **Meals:** Set L £17 (2 courses) to £20.50. Set D £47.50 (2 courses) to £55. Sun Set L £30. **Service:** service included. **Details:** Cards accepted. 60 seats. 35 seats outside. Separate bar. No music. No mobile phones. Wheelchair access. Children allowed. Car parking.

CORNWALL

Blas Burgerworks

Feel-good organic burger bar
The Warren, St Ives, TR26 2EA
Tel no: (01736) 797272
www.blasburgerworks.co.uk
Burgers | £15

There's a cheerful, feel-good atmosphere in this alternative backstreet burger bar, fuelled by the sheer enthusiasm for what the owners do. With just four communal tables (made from reclaimed wood) you may have to wait for a seat, and it's best to check opening times in winter, but readers are full of praise for burgers made from 100% organic Cornish beef and free-range chicken. There's chargrilled fish from sustainable stocks, too, and locally made ice cream to finish. House wine is £13.50.

Chef/s: Sally Cuckson and Marie Dixon. **Open:** Tue to Sun D 6 to 10 (Mon in summer). **Closed:** Mid Nov to mid Dec and early Feb. **Meals:** alc (main courses £8 to £10). **Service:** not inc. **Details:** Cards accepted. Wheelchair access. Music. Children allowed.

Paul Ainsworth at No. 6

Affordable, accomplished food
6 Middle Street, Padstow, PL28 8AP
Tel no: (01841) 532093
www.number6inpadstow.co.uk
Modern British | £30

Paul Ainsworth now owns the restaurant in which he has cooked for four years. He's changed the style of operation by simplifying the menu, making the carte more affordable and introducing 'bargain lunches'. 'Big improvement' appears to be the consensus. The restaurant (especially service) and the consistency of the cooking needs to settle down a little, but you can eat dishes of a very high standard at prices that won't break the bank. There is superb bread – four different flavoured rolls – and starters of scallops with maple-glazed chicken wings and a 'swipe of celeriac' or mussels with pearl barley in a vegetable broth. Fine main course dishes are the pork belly with a 'beautifully made' black pudding sausage roll, apple compote and crackling, served, at one meal, with a copper pot of purple sprouting broccoli on the side, and mackerel atop a broth of cockles, chorizo and chickpeas. The sweets – more erratic – are fashionable: slices of Alphonse mango with pistachio ice cream and madeleines, and chocolate moelleux with peanut butter ice cream. On the global wine list 10 house recommendations begin with French vin du pays at £14 (£3.75 a glass).

Chef/s: Paul Ainsworth and John Walton. **Open:** Tue to Sat L 12 to 2.30, D 6 to 10. **Closed:** Sun (except L in summer), Mon, 23 to 26 Dec, 5 to 26 Jan. **Meals:** alc (main courses £13 to £20). Set L £10 (2 courses) to £13.50. **Service:** not inc. **Details:** Cards accepted. 42 seats. No mobile phones. Wheelchair access. Music. Children allowed.

DEVON

Gidleigh Park

Assured cooking in a blissful setting
Chagford, TQ13 8HH
Tel no: (01647) 432367
www.gidleigh.com
Modern European | £46

When dinner hour arrives, Gidleigh Park's blissful edge-of-the-moor location, extensive grounds and rumbling river are locked out in the blackness. The smart half-timbered exterior disappears with them, and the focus is on the series of wood-panelled dining rooms, which have an ambience that some guests find 'superb' and others 'dreary'. In truth, a lot depends on whether fellow occupants of these small salons are hushed or exuberant in their enjoyment of Michael Caines' precise modern cooking. Though new dishes do arrive (pastry, particularly, is evolving nicely) menus cleave closely to a repertoire of studiously local protein with tried-and-true garnishes. This matters less than it might, not

only because the place screams 'treat' but also because Caines' magpie tendencies make his classic dishes a lively proposition. Thai purée and lemongrass foam, which serve as the baubles on Cornish sea bass, might abut a ballottine of foie gras with melting Madeira jelly and truffle salad, while fennel purée and tapenade jus add mild exotica to a main course of Dartmoor lamb with boulangère potatoes. Cheese, sliced or spooned from the trolley with knowledge and great good humour, is another strength, as are soufflés – perhaps pistachio or prune and Armagnac – so light they're fit to be inhaled. Staff, who must linger in the corridor while their charges butter their bread ('flaky' black olive and tomato is a favourite), are sharp-eyed, proper and mindful of boundaries: over-familiarity is unlikely to be a problem here. A commitment to quality is clear, however, especially when the delights of the 950-bin cellar are being communicated by members of a young but expert wine team. The thinking drinker will find lots to discuss and more to be tempted by, including plenty of French classics, an extensive selection of halves, and a couple of good French ciders. Wine flights may be the relatively easy option, but include both heavenly and interesting matches, and bottle entry level is £28.

Chef/s: Michael Caines. **Open:** all week L 12 to 2.30, D 7 to 9.45. **Meals:** Set L £38 (2 courses) to £46. Set D £105 (3 courses). Tasting menu £120 (7 courses). **Service:** not inc. **Details:** Cards accepted. 52 seats. Separate bar. No music. No mobile phones. Wheelchair access. Car parking.

Oyster Shack

Milburn Orchard Farm, Stakes Hill,
Bigbury-on-Sea, TQ7 4BE
Tel no: (01548) 810876
www.oystershack.co.uk
Seafood

The Shack is a valuable local resource and an agreeable stopover for visitors with absolutely fresh seafood the main attraction, although it may receive plain or elaborately creamy treatment. Expect oysters, lobsters hot and cold and whole Salcombe crabs (£22), as well as baked haddock with soft herb crust and home-dried tomato chutney (£15.95) and local trout with creamy curried mussels. House wine from £14.30. Open all week. A second branch is at Hannaford's Landing, 11-13 Island Street, Salcombe; tel (01548) 843596.

DORSET

Plumber Manor

Country-house dynasty
Sturminster Newton, DT10 2AF
Tel no: (01258) 472507
www.plumbermanor.com
British | £30

Like a vintage Rolls-Royce, Plumber Manor has had just one careful owner – namely the Prideaux-Brune family, who have been its custodians since Jacobean times. Englishness is in its bones, right down to the ancestral portraits and black Labradors padding about. Brian Prideaux-Brune has no truck with culinary fashion, but channels his energies into producing chicken with lemon and tarragon, salmon with pink peppercorns and other Anglo-French staples. Dinner might begin with grilled goats' cheese and blackcurrant vinaigrette or moules marinière, while supplements such as seared scallops with minted pea purée followed by venison with red cabbage keep the regulars interested. The reputable wine list has good-value drinking from £16.
Chef/s: Brian Prideaux-Brune. **Open:** Sun L12 to 2, all week D 7 to 9. **Closed:** Feb. **Meals:** Set D £26 (2 courses) to £30. Sun L £23. **Service:** not inc. **Details:** Cards accepted. 65 seats. Separate bar. No music. Wheelchair access. Children allowed. Car parking.

Sienna Restaurant

Engaging intimacy and big aspirations
36 High West Street, Dorchester, DT1 1UP
Tel no: (01305) 250022
www.siennarestaurant.co.uk
Modern British | £39

Russell and Elena Brown's converted shop may be small but it makes a big impact – although it feels more like a tidy 'family bistro' than a restaurant with serious aspirations. Homely touches, colourful flower arrangements and artwork set the scene, and Elena's friendly presence out front adds to the mood of engaging intimacy. In the kitchen, Russell manages to 'wring the maximum flavour' out of carefully sourced seasonal ingredients, and his menus are cleverly contrived showcases for what one reader called 'insightful combinations' – witness pan-fried fillet of brill with a tiger prawn and mushroom tartlet, Jerusalem artichoke velouté and sherry reduction. To start, breast of wood pigeon with roasted beetroot, Puy lentils and horseradish follows the calendar, while in-tune desserts show their class with the likes of pear and maple syrup sponge pudding with a pear and ginger smoothie and crème fraîche ice cream. The carefully chosen, 50 -bin wine list has house selections from £15.95 (£10.80 a decanter).
Chef/s: Russell Brown. **Open:** Tue to Sat L 12 to 2, D 7 to 9. **Closed:** Sun, Mon, 2 weeks spring and autumn. **Meals:** Set L £21.50 (2 courses) to £24.50. Set D £32.50 (2 courses) to £39. Tasting menu £48.50 (6 courses). **Service:** not inc. **Details:** Cards accepted. 15 seats. Air-con. No mobile phones. Music.

BRISTOL

Casamia

Ambitious young chefs aiming high
38 High Street, Westbury on Trym, Bristol, BS9 3DZ
Tel no: (0117) 9592884
www.casamiarestaurant.co.uk
Italian | £28

The unassuming entrance gives nothing away. First impressions are of a low-key neighbourhood restaurant, the neat décor suggesting something a little more traditional than the reality – a glance at the menu should put the uninitiated in the picture. Peter and Jonray Sanchez-Iglesias go about their business with deadly serious intent, their creative and complex ideas mostly executed with considerable intricacy and consummate flair. Their menu descriptions remain in the listing style and the deconstruction of classic dishes is a recurring theme: Caesar salad as a starter and tiramisu at dessert stage have both worked well. However one reporter felt that a proper pesto might have been better than the deconstructed version (basil jelly, piles of parmesan and pine nuts) that accompanied roast organic lamb. But in general what appears on the plate has purpose and vigour – as

salmon poached in olive oil, with peas, pancetta, rock hyssop and wild mushroom proved for one visitor. Desserts are equally palette-broadening (and 'really good'), with plenty of textural complexity and delicate nuances – as in, say, dark chocolate tart with walnuts and beetroot ice cream. The set lunch has been described as 'extremely good value for the quality involved'. The wine list is mostly Italian with a good selection by the glass from £4.

Chef/s: Jonray and Peter Sanchez-Iglesias. **Open:** Wed to Sat L 12.30 to 2.30, Tue to Sat D 7 to 9.30. **Closed:** 25 and 26 Dec, bank hols. **Meals:** Set L £15 (2 courses) to £20. Set D £23 (2 courses) to £28. Tasting menu £30 (6 courses) to £45 (10 courses). **Service:** not inc. **Details:** Cards accepted. 40 seats. 10 seats outside. Separate bar. No mobile phones. Wheelchair access. Music.

The Albion

Punchy pub food with a big heart
Boyces Avenue, Clifton Village, Bristol, BS8 4AA
Tel no: (0117) 9733522
www.thealbionclifton.co.uk
Modern British | £28

This listed 17th century inn was transformed from grotty student boozer to foodie-friendly 'public house and dining rooms' in a trademark gastropub reclamation – and it has never looked back. Exposed wood floors, heritage colours and a brick fireplace set just the right tone for punchy food with a big heart. You can eat in the bar or in the more formal upstairs dining room from a menu that avoids purple prose in favour of terse, no-nonsense descriptions: pig's head, white dandelion and capers, then lamb's offal and polenta or lemon sole and brown shrimps, with custard tart and rhubarb or blood orange sorbet and vodka to finish. The results on the plate are suitably emphatic, and the wine list backs things up with a lively global selection from £15 (£3.90 a glass).

Chef/s: Jake Platt. **Open:** Tue to Sun L 12 to 3,Tue to Sat D 7 to 10. **Closed:** 25 and 26 Dec, 1 Jan. **Meals:** alc (main courses £11 to £19). Set D £24 (2 courses) to £30. **Service:** 10% (optional). **Details:** Cards accepted. 60 seats. 40 seats outside. Wheelchair access. Music. Children allowed.

Little Barwick House

Meticulously polished restaurant-with-rooms
Barwick, BA22 9TD
Tel no: (01935) 423902
www.littlebarwickhouse.co.uk
Modern British | £38

Tim and Emma Ford's 18th century dower house continues to enchant visitors with its disarmingly serene outlook and ever-so-English sense of decorum. Set in three acres of distracting gardens and grounds (complete with an ancient cedar tree on the lawn) it glides along as a meticulously polished restaurant-with-rooms. Much depends on the output of Tim Ford's kitchen and his fruitful connections with the local food network: dependable supplies mean he can change his menu each day and keep everyone interested. Game always get a good outing in season, perhaps pink-roasted pigeon with braised lentils and spiced plums or saddle of wild rabbit with wild mushroom risotto and Calvados sauce. For those who fancy fish, the West Country ports provide red mullet (grilled and served with sun-blush tomatoes and basil dressing), sea bass (with white wine and chive sauce) and more besides. Unwavering consistency and highly skilled execution are also the hallmarks of finely crafted desserts such as exotic mango mousse and coconut pannacotta with marinated pineapple and passion fruit sorbet. Otherwise there are West Country farmhouse cheeses with quince paste for a savoury finale. The glorious global wine list is a prestigious, impeccably groomed selection that is aimed at connoisseurs and everyday quaffers alike. Top-end Aussies and Californians challenge the aristocratic French classics, and there are half-bottles in abundance. Six house recommendations start at £17.95 (£5.95 a glass).

Chef/s: Tim Ford. **Open:** Wed to Sun L 12 to 2, Tue to Sat D 7 to 9. **Closed:** Mon, 3 weeks from 25 Dec. **Meals:** Set L £20.95 (2 courses) to £24.95. Set Sun L £27.95. Set D £32.95 (2 courses) to £37.95. **Service:** not inc. **Details:** Cards accepted. 40 seats. Air-con. Separate bar. No music. No mobile phones. Children allowed. Car parking.

The Lord Poulett Arms

Vivid flavours in a revitalised pub
High Street, Hinton St George, TA17 8SE
Tel no: (01460) 73149
www.lordpoulettarms.com
Gastropub | £24

Steve Hill and Michelle Paynton have breathed new life into this lovely hamstone pub in one of Somerset's most enchanting villages. Visitors now lap up its gentrified, rural chic interior, as well as partaking of outdoor pleasures in the fragrant herb garden, wildflower meadow and lavender-edged boules 'piste'. The menu covers a lot of ground and the kitchen generates vivid flavours in dishes such as beetroot

and satsuma salad with goats' cheese and sour cherry vinaigrette or cumin and apple-glazed pork belly with spinach and polenta-crusted potatoes. There are also a few whiffs of the orient about, say, citrus-cured salmon with pomegranate, grapefruit and pickled ginger or Malaysian fish stew with rice noodles. Desserts pack an exotic punch with the likes of orange and cardamom crème brûlée accompanied by spiced shortbread. House wines start at £12.
Chef/s: Gary Coughlan. **Open:** all week L 12 to 2, D 7 to 9. **Closed:** 25 and 26 Dec, 1 Jan. **Meals:** alc (main courses £11 to £24). Set Sun L £16 (2 courses) to £19. **Service:** not inc. **Details:** Cards accepted. 70 seats. 40 seats outside. Separate bar. No music. Wheelchair access. Children allowed. Car parking.

WILTSHIRE

Bybrook Restaurant
Modern country-house cuisine
The Manor House Hotel, Castle Combe, SN14 7HR
Tel no: (01249) 782206
www.manorhouse.co.uk
Modern European | £52
At the heart of the medieval village of Castle Combe, the Manor House has stood in one form or another since the 14th century. It is surrounded by as many acres of woodland and park as there are days in the year, and a championship golf course is a powerful draw for the swingers. The cooking in the chandeliered

Bybrook restaurant exercises its own attractive powers in the hands of Richard Davies, who offers a highly refined style of country-house cuisine in the modern British mould. An appetiser cup of foamy soup, and a shot-glass of foamy pre-dessert, are therefore de rigueur, but in between lie some more substantial dishes. Sautéed Skye scallops appear on butternut squash purée with slivers of chorizo and diced poached pear to create a well-conceived assemblage of flavours. Micuit salmon with goose foie gras, apple and celeriac has become a signature starter. Mains might go down the familiar route of wrapping monkfish in Parma ham, or partnering slow-cooked cannon of lamb with honey-glazed swede and a soubise of caramelised onion. Warm, sticky almond and banana financier sponge with creamy rum and raisin ice cream is a nice way to finish. The wine list majors in big names and mature vintages, with glass prices from £7.
Chef/s: Richard Davies. **Open:** Sun to Fri L 12.30 to 2, all week D 7 to 9.30 (10 Sat). **Meals:** Set L £17 (2 courses) to £21. Set D £30 (2 courses) to £52. Sun L £27.50. **Service:** not inc. **Details:** Cards accepted. 55 seats. 15 seats outside. Separate bar. No mobile phones. Wheelchair access. Music. Children allowed. Car parking.

Helen Browning at the Royal Oak
Country pub with charm and chat
Cues Lane, Bishopstone, SN6 8PP
Tel no: (01793) 790481
www.royaloakbishopstone.co.uk
British | £25
Here's a proper country pub, off a narrow country road, down an even narrower one, full of books, chalkboard menus and things for the kids to do. Helen Browning's organic Eastbrook Farm provides pork, beef, eggs and much of the fruit and veg. Lunch is a simple affair – an organic burger with beetroot julienne and triple-cooked chips or a big fat fishcake of grey mullet, perhaps, with a dessert of properly runny Seville orange posset. In the evenings, the menu stretches its legs a little into a three-course format that might progress from pancakes with air-dried ham and turnip purée, through ribeye steak with mash and salad, to silky-smooth chocolate tart. Service is all charm and chat, and a short wine list does its job succinctly, from £4 a glass.
Chef/s: Jasper Ayckroyd. **Open:** all week L 12 to 2.30 (4 Sat, Sun), D 6.30 to 9.30 (8.30 Sun). **Meals:** alc (main courses £9 to £20). **Service:** not inc. **Details:** Cards accepted. 40 seats. 20 seats outside. Music. Children allowed. Car parking.

Content brought to you by **The Good Food Guide 2010.** Please see pages 20–21 for further details.

Tourist Information Centres

When you arrive at your destination, visit an Official Partner Tourist Information Centre for quality assured help with accommodation and information about local attractions and events, or email your request before you go. To search for attractions and Tourist Information Centres on the move just text INFO to 62233, and a web link will be sent to your mobile phone. To find a Tourist Information Centre by region visit enjoyEngland.com/find-tic.

AVEBURY	Avebury Chapel Centre	01672 539425	all.tic's@kennet.gov.uk
BATH	Abbey Chambers	0906 711 2000	tourism@bathtourism.co.uk
BODMIN	Shire Hall	01208 76616	bodmintic@visit.org.uk
BOURTON-ON-THE-WATER	Victoria Street	01451 820211	bourtonvic@btconnect.com
BRIDPORT	47 South Street	01308 424901	bridport.tic@westdorset-dc.gov.uk
BRISTOL: HARBOURSIDE	Wildwalk @Bristol	0906 711 2191	ticharbourside@destinationbristol.co.uk
BRIXHAM	The Old Market House	01803 211 211	holiday@torbay.gov.uk
BUDE	Bude Visitor Centre	01288 354240	budetic@visitbude.info
BURNHAM-ON-SEA	South Esplanade	01278 787852	burnham.tic@sedgemoor.gov.uk
CAMELFORD	North Cornwall Museum	01840 212954	manager@camelfordtic.eclipse.co.uk
CARTGATE	South Somerset TIC	01935 829333	cartgate.tic@southsomerset.gov.uk
CHEDDAR	The Gorge	01934 744071	cheddar.tic@sedgemoor.gov.uk
CHELTENHAM	Municipal Offices	01242 522878	info@cheltenham.gov.uk
CHIPPENHAM	Yelde Hall	01249 665970	tourism@chippenham.gov.uk
CHIPPING CAMPDEN	The Old Police Station	01386 841206	information@visitchippingcampden.com
CHRISTCHURCH	49 High Street	01202 471780	enquiries@christchurchtourism.info
CIRENCESTER	Corn Hall	01285 654180	cirencestervic@cotswold.gov.uk
COLEFORD	High Street	01594 812388	tourism@fdean.gov.uk
CORSHAM	Arnold House	01249 714660	enquiries@corshamheritage.org.uk
DEVIZES	Cromwell House	01380 729408	all.tic's@kennet.gov.uk
DORCHESTER	11 Antelope Walk	01305 267992	dorchester.tic@westdorset-dc.gov.uk
FALMOUTH	11 Market Strand	01326 312300	info@falmouthtic.co.uk
FOWEY	5 South Street	01726 833616	info@fowey.co.uk
FROME	The Round Tower	01373 467271	frome.tic@ukonline.co.uk

GLASTONBURY	The Tribunal	01458 832954	glastonbury.tic@ukonline.co.uk
GLOUCESTER	28 Southgate Street	01452 396572	tourism@gloucester.gov.uk
LOOE	The Guildhall	01503 262072	looetic@btconnect.com
LYME REGIS	Guildhall Cottage	01297 442138	lymeregis.tic@westdorset-dc.gov.uk
MALMESBURY	Town Hall	01666 823748	tic@malmesbury.gov.uk
MORETON-IN-MARCH	High Street	01608 650881	moreton@cotswold.gov.uk
PADSTOW & WADEBRIDGE	Red Brick Building	01841 533449	padstowtic@btconnect.com
PAIGNTON	The Esplanade	01803 211 211	holiday@torbay.gov.uk
PENZANCE	Station Road	01736 362207	pztic@penwith.gov.uk
PLYMOUTH	Plymouth Mayflower Centre	01752 306330	barbicantic@plymouth.gov.uk
SALISBURY	Fish Row	01722 334956	visitorinfo@salisbury.gov.uk
SHEPTON MALLET	70 High Street	01749 345258	sheptonmallet.tic@ukonline.co.uk
SHERBORNE	3 Tilton Court	01935 815341	sherborne.tic@westdorset-dc.gov.uk
SOMERSET VISITOR CENTRE	Sedgemoor Services	01934 750833	somersetvisitorcentre@somerset.gov.uk
ST AUSTELL	Southbourne Road	01726 879 500	tic@cornish-riviera.co.uk
ST IVES	The Guildhall	01736 796297	ivtic@penwith.gov.uk
STOW-ON-THE-WOLD	Hollis House	01451 831082	stowvic@cotswold.gov.uk
STREET	Clarks Village	01458 447384	street.tic@ukonline.co.uk
STROUD	Subscription Rooms	01453 760960	tic@stroud.gov.uk
SWANAGE	The White House	01929 422885	mail@swanage.gov.uk
SWINDON	37 Regent Street	01793 530328	infocentre@swindon.gov.uk
TAUNTON	The Library	01823 336344	tauntontic@tauntondeane.gov.uk
TETBURY	33 Church Street	01666 503552	tourism@tetbury.org
TEWKESBURY	100 Church Street	01684 855043	tewkesburytic@tewkesburybc.gov.uk
TORQUAY	The Tourist Centre	01803 211 211	holiday@torbay.gov.uk
TRURO	Municipal Building	01872 274555	tic@truro.gov.uk
WAREHAM	Holy Trinity Church	01929 552740	tic@purbeck-dc.gov.uk
WARMINSTER	Central Car Park	01985 218548	visitwarminster@btconnect.com
WELLS	Town Hall	01749 672552	touristinfo@wells.gov.uk
WESTON-SUPER-MARE	Beach Lawns	01934 888800	westontouristinfo@n-somerset.gov.uk
WEYMOUTH	The King's Statue	01305 785747	tic@weymouth.gov.uk
WINCHCOMBE	Town Hall	01242 602925	winchcombetic@tewkesbury.gov.uk
YEOVIL	Hendford	01935 845946/7	yeoviltic@southsomerset.gov.uk

Regional Contacts and Information

For more information on accommodation, attractions, activities, events and holidays in South West England, contact one of the following regional or local tourism organisations. Their websites have a wealth of information and many produce free publications to help you get the most out of your visit.

Visit the following websites for further information on South West England or call 01392 360050:

• visitsouthwest.co.uk
• swcp.org.uk
• accessiblesouthwest.co.uk

Publications available from South West Tourism:

• The Trencherman's Guide to Top Restaurants in South West England
• Adventure South West
  Your ultimate activity and adventure guide.
• World Heritage Map
  Discover our World Heritage.

Where to Stay

Entries appear alphabetically by town name in each county. A key to symbols appears on page 6. Maps start on page 394. A listing of all Enjoy England assessed accommodation appears at the end of the region.

BLACKWATER, Cornwall Map ref 1B3

SAT NAV TR4 8HR

Trevarth Holiday Park
Blackwater, Truro TR4 8HR
e **trevarth@lineone.net**
w **trevarth.co.uk**

(30)	£11.00–£16.50
(30)	£11.00–£16.50
(30)	£11.00–£16.50
(20)	£150.00–£595.00

30 touring pitches

Luxury caravan holiday homes, touring and camping. A small, quiet park conveniently situated for north- and south-coast resorts. Level touring and tent pitches with electric hook-up.

open April to October
payment credit/debit cards, cash, cheques

directions Leave A30 at Chiverton roundabout (signed St Agnes). At the next roundabout take the road to Blackwater. Park on right after 200 m.

General ▢ ◖ ◭ ☼ ▣ ⚲ ⚑ ☐ ☎ ⚐ Leisure ∪ ⚲ ⟋ ⚓ ⚍

Looking for something else?

You can also buy a copy of our popular guide 'Hotels' including country house and town house hotels, metro and budget hotels, serviced apartments, restaurants with rooms and Spas in England 2010. Now available in good bookshops and online at **enjoyenglanddirect.com**
£10.99

holidays and **short breaks** at one of Darwin's award winning parks in the beautiful South West

family holidays from £7.00 pppn*

whether you're looking for a fun filled family holiday or a quiet, relaxing short break, **Darwin Holiday Parks** can offer you outstanding value and stunning locations throughout the UK

The range of facilities include**
- ✓ Camping & Caravan Pitches
- ✓ Motor Home Facilities & Lodges
- ✓ Seasonal Pitches Available
- ✓ Holiday Homes for Sale
- ✓ Kid's Activities & Playgrounds

- ✓ Shops, Bars & Restaurants
- ✓ Family Entertainment
- ✓ Swimming Pools
- ✓ Olympic BMX Track
- ✓ Dedicated Rally & Festival Areas
- ✓ Modern Toilet & Wash Facilities

🌐 www.darwinholidays.co.uk

✉ enquiries@darwinholidays.co.uk

darwin
holiday parks

* Offer price liable to change. Please see website for details. Not all parks quality rated.
** See website for individual park site facilities. Darwin Holiday Parks are managed by Darwin Contract Management Ltd. ©

BUDE, Cornwall Map ref 1B2   SAT NAV EX23 0NA

Budemeadows Touring Park
Widemouth Bay, Bude EX23 0NA
t (01288) 361646 f (01288) 361646 e holiday@budemeadows.com
w **budemeadows.com** ONLINE MAP GUEST REVIEWS LAST MINUTE OFFERS

⊞ (145)	£13.00–£25.00
⊞ (145)	£13.00–£25.00
▲ (145)	£13.00–£25.00
145 touring pitches	

Family run site providing a superb centre for surfing, scenery and sightseeing. All usual facilities including heated pool, licensed bar, shop, launderette, playground. Well kept and maintained grounds. **directions** Signposted on A39, 3 miles south of Bude. Look for signs after turning to Widemouth Bay. Full directions available on our website. **open** All year **payment** credit/debit cards, cash, cheques

General ⟨icons⟩ Leisure ⟨icons⟩

BUDE, Cornwall Map ref 1B2   SAT NAV EX23 9HW

Sandymouth Holiday Park
Sandymouth Holiday Park, Stibb, Bude EX23 9HW
t (01288) 352563 f (01288) 354822 e reception@sandymouthbay.co.uk
w **sandymouthbay.co.uk** ONLINE MAP ONLINE BOOKING LAST MINUTE OFFERS

⊞ (23)	£20.00–£30.00
⊞	£20.00–£30.00
▲ (50)	£13.00–£24.00
⊞ (6)	£222–£917
⊞ (1)	£379–£1049
⊟ (129)	£192.00–£924.00
23 touring pitches	

SPECIAL PROMOTIONS
Various promotions for certain times of the year. Call us or visit website.

Sandymouth is privately owned, set in 24 acres of immaculately maintained parkland on North Cornwalls Atlantic Coast. One mile from Sandymouth Bay beach, with stunning rural and sea views. Facilities include heated indoor pool, Black Pearl Adventure play area, Waves Cafe, Ocean Bar, launderette, mini market, family amusements, friendly staff.

open March to November
payment credit/debit cards, cash, cheques

directions On M5 from north, exit jct 27. Travel on A361/A39 towards Bude. Just past the village of Kilkhampton, take right-hand turning signposted Sandymouth.

General ⟨icons⟩ X
Leisure ⟨icons⟩

BUDE, Cornwall Map ref 1C2   SAT NAV EX23 0LP

Upper Lynstone Caravan Park
Lynstone Road, Bude EX23 0LP
t (01288) 352017 f (01288) 359034 e reception@upperlynstone.co.uk
w **upperlynstone.co.uk**

⊞	£10.50–£17.50
⊞	£10.50–£17.50
▲	£10.50–£17.50
⊟ (20)	£185.00–£498.00
65 touring pitches	

A quiet family-run park just 0.75 miles from the sandy beach and town centre. Enjoy the beauty of the coastal path from our site. Spacious camping and electric hook-up pitches. Modern, well-equipped caravans for hire. Families and couples only. **directions** Half a mile south of Bude on coastal road to Widemouth Bay. Signposted. **open** Easter to October **payment** credit/debit cards, cash, cheques

General ⟨icons⟩ Leisure ⟨icons⟩

BUDE, Cornwall Map ref 1B2   SAT NAV EX23 9HJ

Wooda Farm Holiday Park
Poughill, Bude, Cornwall EX23 9HJ
t (01288) 352069 f (01288) 355258 e enquiries@wooda.co.uk
w **wooda.co.uk**

🚐 (50)	£14.00–£28.00
🚎 (50)	£14.00–£28.00
⚊ (40)	£14.00–£23.00
🏠 (55)	£200.00–£770.00
60 touring pitches	

Stunning views over Bude Bay and countryside; 1.5 miles from safe, sandy beaches. Family-owned and run with excellent facilities for touring and camping and luxury holiday homes for hire. Activities include fishing, sports barn, tennis court, woodland walks, golf. An ideal base for touring the delights of Devon and Cornwall.

open April to October   **directions** Please contact us for directions
payment credit/debit cards, cash, cheques

General ♿ 🖥 ♒ 🐕 🔧 🏢 🏠 ☀ 📧 🚿 🍴 👕 ⦿ ✕   Leisure ▶ ∪ ✎ 🐎 ✒ ♦ ⛰

FOWEY, Cornwall Map ref 1B3   SAT NAV PL23 1JU

Penhale Caravan & Camping Park
Fowey PL23 1JU
t (01726) 833425 f (01726) 833425 e info@penhale-fowey.co.uk
w **penhale-fowey.co.uk**

🚐 (35)	£50.00
🚎 (16)	£8.00–£18.00
⚊ (56)	£8.00–£18.00
🏠 (10)	£195.00–£535.00
56 touring pitches	

Friendly, uncrowded park, lovely views over St Austell Bay. In Area of Outstanding Natural Beauty. David Bellamy Bronze Award. Choice of caravans for hire. Touring pitches, electric hook-ups and free showers. **directions** From A30 west from Lostwithiel, on A390 turn left after 1 mile onto B3269, after 3 miles turn right onto A3082. Penhale 600 yds on left. **payment** cash, cheques

General 🖥 🐕 🏢 🏠 ☀ 📧 ⦿ 🍴   Leisure ∪ ✒ ♦

For **key to symbols** see page 6

FOWEY, Cornwall Map ref 1B3 — SAT NAV PL23 1LZ

Penmarlam Caravan & Camping Park

Bodinnick By Fowey, Fowey PL23 1LZ
t (01726) 870088 **f** (01726) 870082 **e** info@penmarlampark.co.uk
w **penmarlampark.co.uk** ONLINE MAP ONLINE BOOKING

🚐 (65)   £12.00–£22.50
🚐 (65)   £12.00–£22.50
⛺ (65)   £12.00–£22.50
65 touring pitches

A quiet, grassy site on the Fowey Estuary, an Area of Outstanding Natural Beauty. Choose from our lawned, sheltered field or enjoy breathtaking views from the upper field. Shop and off-licence, immaculately clean heated amenity block, electric hook-ups and serviced pitches, Wi-Fi internet access, boat launching and storage adjacent.

open April to October
payment credit/debit cards, cash, cheques, euros

directions A38 Dowballs bypass, roundabout take A390 (St Austell). In East Taphouse, left onto B3359 (Looe Polperro). After 5 miles, right (Bodinnick Fowey). 5 miles on right.

General ⟨symbols⟩   Leisure ⟨symbols⟩

HAYLE, Cornwall Map ref 1B3 — SAT NAV TR27 5AW

Beachside Holiday Park

Phillack, Hayle TR27 5AW
t (01736) 753080 **f** (01736) 757252 **e** enquiry@beachside.demon.co.uk
w **beachside.co.uk** ONLINE MAP LAST MINUTE OFFERS

🚐   £9.00–£27.50
🚐   £9.00–£27.50
⛺   £9.00–£27.50
🏠 (117)   £145–£815
84 touring pitches

Beachside is a family holiday park amidst sand dunes beside the sea in the famous St Ives Bay. Our location is ideal for the beach and for touring the whole of West Cornwall. **directions** Please contact us for directions **open** Easter to End October **payment** credit/debit cards, cash, cheques

General ⟨symbols⟩   Leisure ⟨symbols⟩

HAYLE, Cornwall Map ref 1B3 — SAT NAV TR27 5BH

St Ives Bay Holiday Park

73 Loggans Road, Upton Towans, Hayle TR27 5BH
t (01736) 752274 **f** (01736) 754523 **e** stivesbay@btconnect.com
w **stivesbay.co.uk** GUEST REVIEWS ONLINE BOOKING

🚐 (250)   £10.00–£31.00
🚐 (250)   £10.00–£31.00
⛺ (250)   £10.00–£31.00
🏠 (4)   £469–£1399
🏠 (150)   £148–£674
🏠 (250)   £139.00–£839.00
250 touring pitches

Magnificent location in dunes overlooking huge sandy beach. Caravans, chalets and camping. Many units and pitches with sea views. Open Easter to October. **directions** Take first Hayle exit from A30 going West. Turn immediately left at Lidl. Park entrance 500 meters on left. **payment** credit/debit cards, cash, cheques

General ⟨symbols⟩   Leisure ⟨symbols⟩

HELSTON, Cornwall Map ref 1B3   SAT NAV TR13 9NN

HOLIDAY, TOURING & CAMPING PARK

Poldown Camping & Caravan Park
Carleen, Breage, Helston TR13 9NN
t (01326) 574560 e stay@poldown.co.uk
w **poldown.co.uk** ONLINE MAP ONLINE BOOKING LAST MINUTE OFFERS

(13)	£9.00–£14.25	
(13)	£9.00–£14.25	
(13)	£9.00–£14.25	
(7)	£130.00–£495.00	
13 touring pitches		

Small and pretty countryside site. Peace and quiet guaranteed. Within easy reach of West Cornwall's beaches, walks and attractions. Very good touring facilities. Modern holiday caravans. **directions** From Helston Penzance for 0.5 mile, right direction Camborne 2nd left direction Carleen. From A30 wait for Camborne exit, follow Helston, 2 miles before Helston right direction Carleen. **payment** cash, cheques, euros

General   Leisure

LANDRAKE, Cornwall Map ref 1C2   SAT NAV PL12 5AF

TOURING & CAMPING PARK

Dolbeare Caravan & Camping Park
Landrake, Saltash PL12 5AF
t (01752) 851332 f (01752) 547871 e reception@dolbeare.co.uk
w **dolbeare.co.uk** ONLINE MAP GUEST REVIEWS ONLINE BOOKING LAST MINUTE OFFERS

(60)	£13.90–£19.80	
(60)	£13.90–£19.80	
(20)	£3.50–£19.80	
60 touring pitches		

Voted Regional Winner by Practical Caravan in their Top 100 parks awards for 2009. Great park, refurbished amenities, hardstanding pitches set amidst Cornish countryside. One mile A38. Warm welcome awaits. **directions** From M5 follow A38 and over Tamar Bridge. At Landrake, turn right just under footbridge and follow signs. One mile from A38. **open** All year **payment** credit/debit cards, cash

WALKERS ☑ CYCLISTS ☑
WALKERS ☑ CYCLISTS ☑

General   Leisure

LANIVET, Cornwall Map ref 1B2   SAT NAV PL30 5HD

HOLIDAY PARK

Kernow Caravan Park
Clann Lane, Lanivet, Bodmin PL30 5HD
t (01208) 831343

(6)	£150.00–£490.00

SPECIAL PROMOTIONS
Weekend and mini-breaks subject to availability. The garden adjacent to caravan park is available to visitors.

Kernow Caravan Park is quiet and peaceful, in a tranquil setting run by a Cornish family. An ideal touring location to visit Eden Project, Heligan Lost Gardens, Lanhydrock, Camel Trail, Saints Way or Wenford Steam Railway. A few minutes' walk from Lanivet village shop, pub, fish and chip restaurant.

open March to October
payment cash, cheques

directions Leave A30 Innis Downs roundabout. Follow sign to Lanivet 0.75 miles. Left in village centre, opposite shop. Along Clann Lane 300 m left into concrete drive.

General   Leisure

LOOE, Cornwall Map ref 1C2

SAT NAV PL13 2JR

Tencreek Hoilday Park
Polperro Road, Looe PL13 2JR
t (01503) 262447 f (01503) 262760 e reception@tencreek.co.uk
w **dolphinholidays.co.uk** ONLINE BOOKING LAST MINUTE OFFERS

(100)	£9.50–£18.90
(40)	£9.50–£18.90
(100)	£9.50–£18.90
(100)	£125.00–£497.00
240 touring pitches	

Lying close to the South Cornwall coast, in a rural but not isolated position, Tencreek Holiday Park has panoramic coastal and countryside views. Tencreek is the closest park to Looe. **directions** A38 from Tamar bridge. Left at roundabout. follow Looe signs. Right onto A387, becomes B3253. Through Looe towards Polperro. Tencreek 1.25 miles from Looe bridge. **open** All year **payment** credit/debit cards, cash, cheques

General 🔲🔲🐕🔧🔲🔲🔲🔲🔲🔲🔲🔲🔲✗ Leisure ▶🔲🔲🔲🔲🔲🔲🔲🔲🔲🔲

LUXULYAN, Cornwall Map ref 1B2

SAT NAV PL30 5EQ

Croft Farm Holiday Park
Luxulyan, Bodmin, Cornwall PL30 5EQ
t (01726) 850228 f (01726) 850498 e lynpick@ukonline.co.uk
w **croftfarm.co.uk** LAST MINUTE OFFERS

	£10.50–£15.50
	£10.50–£15.50
	£10.50–£15.50
(11)	£168.00–£575.00
52 touring pitches	

A beautifully secluded holiday park, situated just 1 mile from Eden Project. A peaceful, friendly base from which to explore Cornwall. Statics & cottages for rent. **directions** A30, follow Eden Project. Eden left, Luxulyan. 1 mile left. A380 right after level crossing St Blazey. T-junction right, Luxulyan. T-junction right, 500 yds left. **open** 21st March to 21st January **payment** credit/debit cards, cash, cheques

General 🔲🐕🔧🔲🔲🔲🔲🔲🔲🔲 Leisure 🔲🔲🔲

MEVAGISSEY, Cornwall Map ref 1B3

SAT NAV PL26 6LL

Seaview International
Boswinger, Gorran, St Austell PL26 6LL
t (01726) 843425 f (01726) 843358 e holidays@seaviewinternational.com
w **seaviewinternational.com** ONLINE BOOKING LAST MINUTE OFFERS

(189)	£7.00–£30.00
(189)	£7.00–£30.00
(189)	£7.00–£30.00
(38)	£149.00–£999.00
189 touring pitches	

AA's Best Campsite 4 Times, 3.5 miles west of Mevagissy. Parkland setting with breathtaking, panoramic coastal view. Luxury caravans and pitches, Heligan, Eden, Maritime museum all close. **directions** From St Austell roundabout take B3273 to Mevagissy, at brow of hill before village turn right follow signs for Gorran and then brown Seaview signs. **open** Mid-March to October **payment** credit/debit cards, cash, cheques

General 🔲🔲🐕🔧🔲🔲🔲🔲🔲🔲🔲🔲🔲 Leisure ▶🔲🔲🔲🔲🔲🔲🔲

NEWQUAY, Cornwall Map ref 1B2

SAT NAV TR7 3NH

Porth Beach Tourist Park
Porth, Newquay TR7 3NH
t (01637) 876531 f (01637) 871227 e info@porthbeach.co.uk
w **porthbeach.co.uk** ONLINE MAP LAST MINUTE OFFERS

	£13.00–£27.00
	£14.00–£30.00
	£11.00–£35.00
(18)	£280.00–£690.00
200 touring pitches	

Situated only 100 m from beautiful Porth Beach the park has superb pitches, excellent award-winning facilities and brand new luxury caravans in a quiet valley location. Families and couples only. **directions** A30 then A392 Newquay Road. At Quintrell Downs roundabout follow signs for Porth. Turn right at Porth Four Turnings, park is 0.5 miles on. **open** March to November **payment** credit/debit cards, cash, cheques

General 🔲🔧🔲🔲🔲🔲🔲🔲🔲🔲🔲 Leisure 🔲🔲🔲🔲

NEWQUAY, Cornwall Map ref 1B2 — SAT NAV TR8 4NY

Hendra Holiday Park

Hendra Holiday Park, Lane, Newquay TR8 4NY
t (01637) 875778 **f** (01637) 879017 **e** enquiries@hendra-holidays.com
w hendra-holidays.com ONLINE MAP GUEST REVIEWS LAST MINUTE OFFERS

(378) £10.75–£19.00
(378) £10.75–£19.00
(170) £10.75–£19.00
(254) £200.00–£1050.00
378 touring pitches

SPECIAL PROMOTIONS
See website for offers, 3/4-night short breaks, caravans for all budgets and our range of touring/camping options.

Award-winning Hendra is ideal for families and couples offering superb-quality holiday homes and touring/camping pitches. With entertainment, indoor and outdoor play areas, amusements, children's club, cafes and restaurant, and Oasis Fun Pool complex. An ideal location for exploring Cornwall - you'll have your best holiday ever!

open Easter to October
payment credit/debit cards, cash, cheques, euros

directions Take the M5 south to Exeter, then A30 westbound. Stay on A30 until you see Newquay signposted. We are on the A392 into Newquay.

General
Leisure

NEWQUAY, Cornwall Map ref 1B2 — SAT NAV TR8 5QJ

Newperran Holiday Park

Rejerrah, Newquay TR8 5QJ
t (01872) 572407 **f** (01872) 571254 **e** holidays@newperran.co.uk
w newperran.co.uk ONLINE MAP GUEST REVIEWS ONLINE BOOKING LAST MINUTE OFFERS

£9.00–£15.70
£9.00–£15.70
£9.00–£15.70
(5) £235.00–£660.00
395 touring pitches

SPECIAL PROMOTIONS
3 night short breaks from £99 - £125 in our luxury caravans.

Peaceful family holiday park renowned for its spacious perimeter pitching, with breathtaking open countryside and sea views. Modern facilities including brand new shower blocks and spectacular outdoor swimming pool. Caravans, motor homes and tents welcome, Holiday caravans for hire. Call for a free brochure.

open Easter to October
payment credit/debit cards, cash, cheques

directions Take the A30 signposted Redruth, turn right onto the B3285 Perranporth. At the T junction Goonhavern turn right A3075, Newperran is 500 meters on left.

General
Leisure

NEWQUAY, Cornwall Map ref 1B2

SAT NAV TR8 4PE

Riverside Holiday Park
Lane, Newquay TR8 4PE
t (01637) 873617 e info@riversideholidaypark.co.uk
w **riversideholidaypark.co.uk**

🚐 £13.00–£17.00
🚐 (19) £200.00–£700.00
60 touring pitches

Peaceful riverside family park. 2 miles to Newquay. Sheltered, level touring pitches, luxury lodges and caravans. Covered, heated pool and bar. **directions** Please contact us for directions **open** Easter to October **payment** credit/debit cards, cash, cheques

General 🗑🐕🏊🎱📶☼🔌🚻🚿✕ Leisure ▶∪🚲♨🎾🏆🎣⛰

NEWQUAY, Cornwall Map ref 1B2

SAT NAV TR8 4JF

Trekenning Tourist Park
Trekenning, Newquay TR8 4JF
t (01637) 880462 f (01637) 880462 e holidays@trekenning.co.uk
w **trekenning.co.uk** ONLINE MAP

🚐 (63) £15.00–£20.00
🚐 (2) £15.00–£20.00
⛺ (12) £12.00–£17.00
75 touring pitches

Set in beautiful Cornish countryside and only a 10 minute drive from Cornwall's finest beaches and attractions. A must for caravanners and campers. Great for surfing and rambling nearby. **directions** Travel along A30 to Indian Queens turnoff A39. At next roundabout turn right for Wadebridge. At Trekenning roundabout turn left, camp on left. **open** All year **payment** credit/debit cards, cash, cheques

General 🗑🐕🏊🎱📶☼🔌🚻🚿✕ Leisure ▶∪🚲♨🎾🏆🎵🎣⛰

NEWQUAY, Cornwall Map ref 1B2

SAT NAV TR8 4JN

Treloy Touring Park
Newquay TR8 4JN
t (01637) 872063 f (01637) 876279 e treloy.tp@btconnect.com
w **treloy.co.uk** ONLINE MAP

🚐 (200) £10.00–£14.70
🚐 (200) £10.00–£14.70
⛺ (200) £10.00–£14.70
200 touring pitches

SPECIAL PROMOTIONS
Free-night offers early and late season. Conditions apply.

A family-run park catering exclusively for touring caravans, tents and motor homes. We aim to offer fun and enjoyable holidays for families and couples, in a pleasant, relaxed setting with clean modern facilities. Nearby is Treloy Golf Club and driving range. Coarse fishing available at Porth Reservoir, 1 mile away.

open Easter to Mid September
payment credit/debit cards, cash

directions Leave A30 at Highgate Hill, take 3rd exit (Newquay). At Halloon roundabout take A39 Wadebridge (3rd exit). Then Trekenning roundabout 1st left, Treloy 4 miles.

General 🗑📶🐕🏊🎱📶☼♿🔌🚻🚿🎮✕
Leisure ▶∪♨🎾🏆🎵🎣⛰

PADSTOW, Cornwall Map ref 1B2   SAT NAV PL28 8SL

Mother Ivey's Bay Caravan Park (Camping)
Mother Ivey's Bay Caravan Park, Trevose Head, Padstow PL28 8SL
t (01841) 520990 f (01841) 520550 e info@motheriveysbay.com
w **motheriveysbay.com** ONLINE MAP

🚐 (118)	£11.74–£46.98
🚏 (118)	£11.74–£46.98
▲ (124)	£11.74–£46.98
🏠 (50)	£200.64–£1125.53
126 touring pitches	

5 Star holiday park situated on the coast with spectacular sea views and our own private sandy beach, perfect for traditional family holidays, with luxurious holiday caravans and separate touring area **directions** 4 miles west of Padstow, signed from St Merryn on the B3276 Padstow to Newquay coast road. On Trevose Head. **open** April to October **payment** credit/debit cards, cash, cheques

General 🖥 📶 🐕 🏋 📱 🏠 ☀ 🍴 🎮 🛒 🏧 Leisure ▶ ∪ 🚵 ⚓ 🏔

PADSTOW, Cornwall Map ref 1B2   SAT NAV PL28 8LE

Padstow Touring Park
Padstow, Cornwall PL28 8LE
t (01841) 532061 e mail@padstowtouringpark.co.uk
w **padstowtouringpark.co.uk**

🚐 (180)	£10.00–£15.50
🚏 (180)	£10.00–£15.50
▲ (180)	£10.00–£15.50
180 touring pitches	

Located 1 mile from Padstow with footpath access. Quiet family park with panoramic views. Sandy beaches 2 miles. Three modern amenity blocks, one underfloor heated. Some en-suite pitches. Easy access. **directions** Situated off the main road (B3274/A389) in to Padstow, approx 1 mile before Padstow. **open** All year **payment** credit/debit cards, cash, cheques

General 🖥 📶 🐕 🏋 📱 🏠 ☀ 🍴 🎮 🛒 🏧 Leisure ∪ 🚵 ⚓ 🏔

PENZANCE, Cornwall Map ref 1A3   SAT NAV TR19 6BZ

Tower Park Caravans & Camping
Tower Park Caravans & Camping, St Buryan, Penzance, Cornwall TR19 6BZ
t (01736) 810286 f (01736) 810286 e enquiries@towerparkcamping.co.uk
w **towerparkcamping.co.uk** ONLINE MAP LAST MINUTE OFFERS

🚐	£12.50–£17.00
🚏	£12.50–£17.00
▲	£9.50–£13.50
🏠 (5)	£170.00–£440.00
102 touring pitches	

Famiy-run campsite ideally situated for beaches, coast path and Minack Theatre. Level pitches for tents and tourers, yurts and static caravans for hire. **directions** From the A30 Lands End road, fork left onto the B3283 signposted St Buryan. On entering the village, turn right. Site is 300 yds from village. **open** March to October **payment** credit/debit cards, cash, cheques

General 🖥 🐕 🏋 🏠 ☀ 🍴 🎮 🛒 Leisure ▶ ∪ ⚓ 🎣 🏔

Looking for something else?

You can also buy a copy of our popular guide 'B&B' including guest accommodation, B&B's, guest houses, farmhouses, inns, and campus and hostel accommodation in England 2010.

Now available in good bookshops and online at **enjoyenglanddirect.com**

£11.99

PORTHTOWAN, Cornwall Map ref 1B3
SAT NAV TR4 8TY

enjoyEngland.com
★★★★
TOURING & CAMPING PARK

Porthtowan Tourist Park
Mile Hill, Porthtowan, Truro, Cornwall TR4 8TY
t (01209) 890256 f (01209) 890256 e admin@porthtowantouristpark.co.uk
w **porthtowantouristpark.co.uk**

🚐 (35)   £9.00–£16.00
🚎 (10)   £9.00–£16.00
⛺ (35)   £9.00–£16.00
80 touring pitches

SPECIAL PROMOTIONS
Off-peak special offers -
book in advance for seven
nights or more and get one
night free.

This quiet, family-run park offers plenty of space and level pitches. Superb new toilet/laundry facilities with family rooms. Close to a sandy surfing beach, coastal path and Portreath to Devoran cycle trail. An excellent base from which to discover the delights of Cornwall. David Bellamy Silver Conservation Award.

open April to September
payment credit/debit cards, cash, cheques

directions From A30, take 3rd exit off the roundabout signed Redruth/Porthtowan. Follow this road for 2 miles. Turn right at T-junction. Site on left after 0.5 miles.

General 🅿 🐕 ⛐ 🏪 🌂 ☀ ♿ 📶 📷 ☎
Leisure ∪ 🚲 🎣 🎿 🔍 ⚜

PORTREATH, Cornwall Map ref 1B3
SAT NAV TR16 4HT

enjoyEngland.com
★★★
TOURING & CAMPING PARK

Cambrose Touring Park
Portreath Road, Redruth TR16 4HT
t (01209) 890747 f (01209) 891665 e cambrosetouringpark@supanet.com
w **cambrosetouringpark.co.uk**

🚐 (60)   £9.00–£15.00
🚎 (60)   £9.00–£15.00
⛺ (60)   £9.00–£15.00
60 touring pitches

Six acres of well-sheltered land in a valley. Excellent suntrap. Most roads are tarmac finished. Facilities for the disabled. **directions** From Redruth take B3300 to Portreath passing treasure park on left 0.25 mile take road on the right (Porthtowan) Cambrose 100 yds on left. **open** April to October **payment** credit/debit cards, cash, cheques

General 🅿 🐕 ⛐ 🏪 🌂 ☀ ♿ 📷 ☎   Leisure ∪ 🚲 🎣 🎿 🔍 ⚜

PORTREATH, Cornwall Map ref 1B3 — SAT NAV TR16 4JQ

Tehidy Holiday Park

Harris Mill, Near Portreath, Cornwall TR16 4JQ
t (01209) 216489 f (01209) 213555 e holiday@tehidy.co.uk
w **tehidy.co.uk** ONLINE MAP GUEST REVIEWS ONLINE BOOKING LAST MINUTE OFFERS

(38)	£10.00–£16.00
(3)	£10.00–£16.00
(35)	£10.00–£14.00
	£265–£590
(20)	£140.00–£490.00

Holiday Park of the Year 2008 - Shires Magazine. David Bellamy Gold Award 2008. Camping, holiday caravans and cottages nestled in a wooded valley. Near broad sandy beaches and hidden coves. An ideal base for exploring Cornwall. Children's play area, shop/off licence, payphone, games room. Modern, clean showers with laundrette.

open March to November
payment credit/debit cards, cash, cheques

directions Exit A30 to Redruth/ Porthtowan. Right to Porthtowan. 300 m left at crossroads. Straight on over B3300 (Portreath)crossroads. Past Cornish Arms. Site 500 m on left.

General
Leisure

REDRUTH, Cornwall Map ref 1B3 — SAT NAV TR16 6LP

Lanyon Holiday Park

Loscombe Lane, Four Lanes, Redruth TR16 6LP
t (01209) 313474 e info@lanyonholidaypark.co.uk
w **lanyonholidaypark.co.uk** ONLINE MAP GUEST REVIEWS ONLINE BOOKING LAST MINUTE OFFERS

(25)	£10.00–£16.00
(25)	£10.00–£16.00
(50)	£10.00–£16.00
(16)	£230.00–£580.00
25 touring pitches	

High-quality park, distant views to the coast. All are large, most with hedged boundary, ideal for RVs. Modern amenity block with free hot water. Covered, heated swimming pool, games room, children's play area, bar/restaurant. **directions** Off A30 at Redruth, follow signs toward, Helston B3297. At Four Lanes, right at Pencoys Village Hall (Loscombe Lane), park 500 m on left. **payment** credit/debit cards, cash, cheques

General   Leisure

ROSUDGEON, Cornwall Map ref 1B3

SAT NAV TR20 9AU

Kenneggy Cove Holiday Park

Higher Kenneggy, Rosudgeon, Penzance TR20 9AU
t (01736) 763453 e enquiries@kenneggycove.co.uk
w **kenneggycove.co.uk**

🚐 (25) £14.50–£23.00
🚛 (25) £14.50–£23.00
🅰 (50) £10.00–£23.00
🏕 (9) £275.00–£530.00
50 touring pitches

SPECIAL PROMOTIONS
No single-sex groups or
large parties.

Flat, lawned pitches in a beautiful garden setting with panoramic sea views. Twelve minutes' walk to South West Coast Path and secluded, sandy beach. Home-made breakfasts available. Please note: this is a quiet site, operating a policy of no noise between 2200 and 0800. German and French spoken.

open 15 May to 3 October
payment cash, cheques, euros

directions Halfway between Penzance and Helston on A394. At Helston end of Rosudgeon turn south down lane towards sea. Kenneggy is at end of the lane.

General 🔲 ♈ 🐕 📱 🎇 ☼ 🚿 💷 🏧 🛒 ♿
Leisure ► ∪ 🚴 🥊 ⛰

RUAN MINOR, Cornwall Map ref 1B3

SAT NAV TR12 7LZ

Silver Sands Holiday Park

Gwendreath, Kennack Sands, Helston TR12 7LZ
t (01326) 290631 e enquiries@silversandsholidaypark.co.uk
w **silversandsholidaypark.co.uk**

🚐 (16) £14.00–£19.50
🚛 (14) £14.00–£19.50
🅰 (20) £12.00–£17.00
🏕 (16) £147.00–£497.00
34 touring pitches

Silver Sands is a family-run holiday park set in 9 acres of landscaped grounds with large emplacemants separated by hedges a short woodland walk away is Kennack sands. **directions** A3083 from Helston past RNAS Culdrose, left onto B3293 (St Keverne). Right turn after passing Goonhilly satellite station. Left after 1.5 miles to Gwendreath. **open** Easter to middle of September
payment credit/debit cards, cash, cheques, euros

General 🔲 ♊ ♈ 🐕 📱 🎇 ☼ 🚿 🛒 ♿ Leisure ► ∪ 🥊 ⛰

ST AGNES, Cornwall Map ref 1B3 SAT NAV TR5 0NU

Beacon Cottage Farm Touring Park
Beacon Drive, St Agnes TR5 0NU
t (01872) 552347 e beaconcottagefarm@lineone.net
w **beaconcottagefarmholidays.co.uk** ONLINE MAP GUEST REVIEWS LAST MINUTE OFFERS

(69)	£15.00–£21.00
(69)	£15.00–£21.00
(69)	£15.00–£21.00
	£285–£750
69 touring pitches	

Peaceful, secluded park on a working family farm in an Area of Outstanding Natural Beauty and Heritage Coast. Pitches in six small, landscaped paddocks. Beautiful sea views, lovely walks, 10 minutes' walk to sandy beach. Ideal location for touring Cornwall. **directions** From A30 take B3277 to St Agnes at mini roundabout turn left and follow signs to park. **open** April to October **payment** credit/debit cards, cash, cheques

General 🖥📶🐕🔌📷☀🎲🚲🐾🚰🚻🎱 Leisure ∪🚲🎣⛰

ST JUST IN ROSELAND, Cornwall Map ref 1B3 SAT NAV TR2 5JF

Trethem Mill Touring Park
St Just in Roseland, Nr St Mawes, Truro, Cornwall TR2 5JF
t (01872) 580504 f (01872) 580968 e reception@trethem.com
w **trethem.com** ONLINE MAP

(84)	£15.00–£22.00
(55)	£15.00–£22.00
(30)	£15.00–£22.00
84 touring pitches	

We offer peace and tranquillity with an exceptional standard of facilities. Cornwall Tourism Awards: 'Consistent winners offering consistent quality.' Say hello to a new experience. **directions** A3078 towards Tregony/St Mawes, over Tregony bridge. After 5 miles follow brown caravan and camping signs from Trewithian. Site 2 miles beyond on right-hand side. **open** April to mid-October **payment** credit/debit cards, cash

General 🖥📶🐕🔌📷☀🚰🐾🚰🚻🎱 Leisure ∪🚲🎣⛰

ST MERRYN, Cornwall Map ref 1B2 SAT NAV PL28 8PR

Trevean Farm Caravan & Camping park
St Merryn, Padstow PL28 8PR
t (01841) 520772 f (01841) 520722 e trevean.info@virgin.net

	£8.00–£13.00
	£8.00–£13.00
	£8.00–£13.00
(3)	£175.00–£480.00
70 touring pitches	

Small, pleasant farm site, 1 mile from the sea. Ideally situated for beaches, walking and many visitor attractions. **directions** From St Merryn crossroads take B3276 towards Newquay. Take first left after approx 3/4 mile. We are along this road on right. **open** Easter to October **payment** cash, cheques, euros

General 🖥🐕🔌📷☀🚰🐾🚰🚻 Leisure ∪🎣⛰

Looking for something else?
You can also buy a copy of our popular guide 'B&B' including guest accommodation, B&B's, guest houses, farmhouses, inns, and campus and hostel accommodation in England 2010.

Now available in good bookshops and online at **enjoyenglanddirect.com**

£11.99

TINTAGEL, Cornwall Map ref 1B2 SAT NAV PL34 0BQ

Trewethett Farm Caravan Club Site

Trethevy, Tintagel PL34 0BQ
t (01840) 770222 f (01840) 779066 e uksitesbookingservice@caravanclub.co.uk
w **caravanclub.co.uk**

🚐 (142) £14.00–£26.90
🚐 (142) £14.00–£26.90
142 touring pitches

SPECIAL PROMOTIONS
Special member rates mean
you can save your
membership subscription in
less than a week. Visit our
website to find out more.

The views from here are breathtaking as the site
boasts a cliff top setting, overlooking Bossiney
Cove with its safe and sandy beach. The coastal
path borders the site and there are spectacular
walks to enjoy. Tintagel is a popular coastal
resort with shops, bars and restaurants aplenty.

open March to November
payment credit/debit cards, cash, cheques

directions From A30 onto A395 signposted
Camelford. Right onto A39 signposted Bude. Left
just before transmitter. Right onto B3266
signposted Boscastle. Left onto B3263. Site
entrance is on the right in about 2 miles.

General 🗑 ⚙ 🕱 🔌 ☼ 🔱 🖃 📶
Leisure ▶ ✦

TRURO, Cornwall Map ref 1B3 SAT NAV TR4 8PF

Killiwerris Touring Park

Killiwerris, Penstraze, Truro, Cornwall TR4 8PF
t 01872 561356 e killiwerris@aol.com
w **killiwerris.co.uk** ONLINE MAP

🚐 £13.50–£17.50
🚐 (20) £13.50–£17.50
20 touring pitches

Killiwerris is a small, friendly site which caters exclusively for adults.
It is centrally situated near Truro an ideal base for exploring all of
Cornwall. Open all year. **directions** Please contact us for directions
open All year **payment** cash, cheques

General 🗑 🕱 🔌 ☼ 🔱 🖃 📶 Leisure ▶ ∪ ⚲ ✦

OFFICIAL TOURIST BOARD GUIDE
Self Catering 2010

Looking for something else?

You can also buy a copy of our popular guide
'Self Catering' including self-catering holiday homes,
approved caravan holiday homes, boat accommodation
and holiday cottage agencies in England 2010.

Now available in good bookshops and online at
enjoyenglanddirect.com

£11.99

WATERGATE BAY NEWQUAY, Cornwall Map ref 1B2
SAT NAV TR8 4AD

Watergate Bay Touring Park
Tregurrian, Newquay, Cornwall TR8 4AD
t (01637) 860387 f 0871 661 7549 e email@watergatebaytouringpark.co.uk
w **watergatebaytouringpark.co.uk** ONLINE MAP GUEST REVIEWS

(171)	£10.00–£18.00
(171)	£10.00–£18.00
(171)	£10.00–£18.00
(2)	£200.00–£550.00
171 touring pitches	

Half mile from Watergate Bays sand, surf and cliff walks. Rural Location in an Area of Outstanding Natural Beauty. Personally run & supervised by resident owners. Heated pool, tennis courts, games room, shop/cafe, licenced clubroom, free entertainment including kids club, kids play area.

open March to end of October
payment credit/debit cards, cash, cheques

directions From A30 follow signs for Newquay then airport. After passing the airport, turn left onto the B3276. Park 0.5 mile on right

General 🔌▢♋🐕🎱🛖🔥☼🔌🚲🔌👕🅦✕
Leisure ∪✎♪↝☂♫🔍🏔

ISLES OF SCILLY, Isles of Scilly Map ref 1A3
SAT NAV TR22 0PL

Troytown Farm Campsite
Troytown Farm, St Agnes, Isles of Scilly TR22 0PL
t (01720) 422360 e enquiries@troytown.co.uk
w **troytown.co.uk** ONLINE MAP LAST MINUTE OFFERS

(A)	£7.00–£9.00

A stunning location, on the waters edge of remote St Agnes, with panoramic atlantic views, taking in the Bishop Rock Lighthouse, rugged western rocks and other islands. Farm produce available. **directions** Fly or sail from the mainland to St Marys, then a short crossing to St Agnes. The campsite is a short walk from the quay. **open** Feb to Nov **payment** credit/debit cards, cash, cheques

General ▢🐕🎱🔥☼🅖 **Leisure** ♪

BRAUNTON, Devon Map ref 1C1
SAT NAV EX33 1HB

Lobb Fields Caravan and Camping Park
West Meadow Road, Braunton EX33 1HG
t (01271) 812090 f (01271) 812090 e info@lobbfields.com
w **lobbfields.com**

(100)	£9.00–£26.00
(40)	£9.00–£26.00
(40)	£8.00–£26.00
180 touring pitches	

Fourteen-acre grassy park with panoramic views across the Taw Estuary. Situated 1 mile from Braunton centre on B3231 and 1.5 miles from Saunton beach and Biosphere reserve. **directions** Please contact us for directions **open** March to October **payment** credit/debit cards, cash, cheques

General 🔌▢🐕🛖🔥☼🔌🔌👕🅦 **Leisure** ∪🚲♪🏔

BRIXHAM, Devon Map ref 1D2

Galmpton Touring Park

Greenway Road, Galmpton, Brixham TQ5 0EP
t (01803) 842066 f (01803) 844458 e galmptontouringpark@hotmail.com
w **galmptontouringpark.co.uk** ONLINE MAP

(60)	£12.00–£18.70
(10)	£12.00–£18.70
(60)	£12.00–£18.70
(4)	£220–£560
120 touring pitches	

SPECIAL PROMOTIONS
Off-peak reductions.

Overlooking the River Dart with superb views from pitches. A quiet base for families and couples to explore Torbay and South Devon. Sorry no dogs peak season. We also have 2 Self-catering cottages available throughout the year.

open Easter to September
payment credit/debit cards, cash, cheques

directions Take A380 Torbay ring road then A379 towards Brixham. Take 2nd right to Galmpton Park through village to park. Site signposted. Careful using SatNav.

General 🔌 🐕 🚿 ⛺ 🔥 ☼ ♨ 🛒 📶 ☎
Leisure 🏊 ⛰

BRIXHAM, Devon Map ref 1D2

Hillhead Caravan Club Site

Hillhead, Brixham TQ5 0HH
t (01803) 853204
w **caravanclub.co.uk**

(239)	£14.90–£35.00
(239)	£14.90–£35.00
239 touring pitches	

SPECIAL PROMOTIONS
Special member rates mean you can save your membership subscription in less than a week. Visit our website to find out more.

Set in 22 acres of Devon countryside with many pitches affording stunning views. There's plenty of entertainment on site – an outdoor heated swimming pool, skateboard ramp and indoor complex housing a games room, shop, restaurant and bar. There's also evening entertainment. Brixham is less than 2 miles away.

open March 2010 to January 2011
payment credit/debit cards, cash, cheques

directions Right off A380 (Newton Abbot). 3 miles onto ring road (Brixham). 7 miles turn right, A3022. In 0.75 miles, right onto A379. 2 miles keep left onto B3025. Site entrance on left

General 🔌 🍴 🐕 🚿 ⛺ 🔥 ☼ 🛒 📶 ☎ 🏧 ✕
Leisure 🎣 🎾 ♪ ⚽ ⛰

DAWLISH, Devon Map ref 1D2

Cofton Country Holidays

Starcross, Nr Dawlish, Devon EX6 8RP
t (01626) 890111 f (01626) 891572 e info@coftonholidays.co.uk
w **coftonholidays.co.uk** ONLINE MAP LAST MINUTE OFFERS

🚐 (450)	£13.00–£26.00	
🚐 (450)	£13.00–£26.00	
⛺ (450)	£13.00–£26.00	
🏠 (17)	£265–£840	
🚐 (66)	£180.00–£705.00	

450 touring pitches

SPECIAL PROMOTIONS
Save £2 per night during low, mid and high season. Advance bookings only, minimum 3 nights stay. Senior Citizens discounts.

A glorious corner of Devon. Family-run holiday park in 30 acres of delightful parkland. Some of the finest pitches in South Devon, many with superb countryside views. Limited hard-standing and super pitches available. David Bellamy Gold Conservation Award. Two minutes from Dawlish Warrens Blue Flag beach.

open All year
payment credit/debit cards, cash, cheques

directions Leave M5 at junction 30, take A379 towards Dawlish. After passing through harbour village of Cockwood, park is on the left after half a mile.

General 🔲 💧 🐕 🚲 🏢 🏧 ☼ ❄ 📷 🅿 🚻 🛒 ✕
Leisure 🏊 🎣 🏓 🎱 🚶 ⛰

DAWLISH, Devon Map ref 1D2

Welcome Family Holiday Park

Welcome Family Holiday Park, Dawlish Warren, Dawlish EX7 0PH
t 08451 65 62 65 f (01626) 868988 e fun@welcomefamily.co.uk
w **welcomefamily.co.uk** ONLINE MAP GUEST REVIEWS LAST MINUTE OFFERS

🏠 (33)	£36–£128
🏠 (60)	£94–£111
🚐 (140)	£13.00–£94.00

SPECIAL PROMOTIONS
Please see our website:
www.welcomefamily.co.uk
for last minute offers!

Four indoor heated fun pools, entertainment 7 days and nights, Spanish-style lodges, bungalows and all-electric caravans set in award-winning gardens, a short level walk to the Sandy Blue-flag Beach and Nature reserve. Fantastic local attractions. Over 2 out of 3 come back to Welcome Family: Where the fun always shines!

open Easter to Autumn Half-term
payment credit/debit cards, cash, cheques

directions By train to Dawlish or Dawlish Warren. By Car to M5 to Exeter, exit Junction 30. Take A379 to Dawlish, turn off to Dawlish Warren.

General 🔲 🐕 🚲 🏢 🏧 ☼ ✕
Leisure ⛳ 🚵 🏊 🎣 🏓 🎱 🎵 🚶

EXMOUTH, Devon Map ref 1D2

SAT NAV EX5 1EA

Webbers Caravan & Camping Park

Castle lane, Woodbury, Exeter EX5 1EA
t (01395) 232276 f (01395) 233389 e reception@webberspark.co.uk
w **webberspark.co.uk**

⊟ (40)	£13.00–£19.00
⊟ (40)	£13.00–£19.00
▲ (40)	£13.00–£19.00
⊟ (10)	£145.00–£510.00

120 touring pitches

SPECIAL PROMOTIONS
Tents/tourers/motorhomes: 2
people, 1 week, low season
£70.00.

Set in a tranquil corner of East Devon, this quiet, family-run park has breathtaking views of Dartmoor and the Exe Estuary. Just a short distance from Woodbury Common, with some 3,000 acres of unspoilt open heathland to roam. Relax, and enjoy this outstanding piece of countryside.

open Mid-March to End October
payment credit/debit cards, cash, cheques

directions Leave M5 jct 30 and follow A376 Exmouth. At second roundabout take B3179 Budleigh Salterton. At Woodbury village centre turn left, follow brown signs.

General ⊟ ⊁ ⅄ ◨ ⋒ ☼ ⊡ ⊕ ⊙ ☎ ⊞ **Leisure** ► ∪ ⤸ ⚠

HOLSWORTHY, Devon Map ref 1C2

SAT NAV EX22 7JB

Noteworthy Caravan and Campsite

Bude Road, Holsworthy EX22 7JB
t (01409) 253731 f (01409) 253731 e enquiries@noteworthy-devon.co.uk
w **noteworthy-devon.co.uk**

⊟ (5)	£4.00–£6.00
⊟ (5)	£4.00–£6.00
▲ (15)	£4.00–£6.00
⊟	£150.00–£400.00

Rural caravan and camping site, self-contained park on the Devon/Cornwall border. 4 miles Holsworthy, 6 miles Bude. **directions** Please contact us for directions **payment** cash

General ⊁ ◨ ⋒ ☼ ⇱ ⊕ ☎ **Leisure** ⚠

ILFRACOMBE, Devon Map ref 1C1

SAT NAV EX34 8NU

Hidden Valley Touring & Camping Park

West Down, Ilfracombe EX34 8NU
t (01271) 813837 **f** (01271) 814041 **e** relax@hiddenvalleypark.com
w **hiddenvalleypark.com** LAST MINUTE OFFERS

⊕ (115)	£15.00–£40.00
⊞ (60)	£15.00–£40.00
▲ (55)	£15.00–£40.00
⊞ (1)	£245–£895

115 touring pitches

SPECIAL PROMOTIONS
Look on our website for our
special offers and events.

National Caravan Park of the Year 2009 - a warm welcome awaits at this beautiful owner-run touring park set in a picturesque wooded valley with superb facilities. Sheltered, level pitches amidst peaceful surroundings, with a therapy suite, shop, coffee shop and acres of walks. Ideally located for exploring coast and countryside.

open All year
payment credit/debit cards, cash, cheques

directions M5 jct 27 follow A361 to Barnstaple, through Barnstaple on A361, signed towards Ilfracombe. We are directly off the A361, 3.5 miles from Braunton, on left.

General 🖥 ⊕ 🐕 ⚊ ▥ 🐾 ☼ ⊠ 🗨 🖰 🐾 ⊕ ✕
Leisure ► ∪ 🚲 ✦ ⚊

KENTISBEARE, Devon Map ref 1D2

SAT NAV EX15 2DT

Forest Glade Holiday Park

Forest Glade, Near Kentisbeare, Cullompton EX15 2DT
t (01404) 841381 **f** (01404) 841593 **e** enquiries@forest-glade.co.uk
w **forest-glade.co.uk** ONLINE MAP LAST MINUTE OFFERS

⊕	£13.50–£19.00
⊞	£13.50–£19.00
▲	£11.50–£15.00
⊞ (26)	£200.00–£475.00

80 touring pitches

Free indoor heated pool on small, family-owned park surrounded by forest with deer. Large, flat, sheltered pitches. Modern six berth holiday homes for hire. **directions** From Honiton, take Dunkeswell road, follow Forest Glade signs. From M5, A373, 2.5 miles at Keepers Cottage inn then 2.5 miles on Sheldon road. **open** Mid-March to end of October **payment** credit/debit cards, cash, cheques

General 🖥 ⊕ 🐕 ⚊ ▥ 🐾 ☼ ⊠ 🗨 🖰 🐾 ⊞ Leisure ∪ ⚲ 🚲 ✦ 🐟 ✦ ⚊

MODBURY, Devon Map ref 1C3

SAT NAV PL21 0SH

Broad Park Caravan Club Site

Higher East Leigh, Modbury, Ivybridge PL21 0SH
t (01548) 830714 **e** enquiries@caravanclub.co.uk
w **caravanclub.co.uk**

CARAVAN CLUB

⊕ (112)	£12.20–£25.30
⊞ (112)	£12.20–£25.30

112 touring pitches

Situated between moor and sea, this makes a splendid base from which to explore South Devon. Head for Dartmoor, or seek out the small villages of the South Hams. **directions** From B3027 (signposted Modbury), site on left after 1 mile. **open** March to November **payment** credit/debit cards, cash, cheques

General 🖥 ▥ 🐾 ⊠ 🗨 🖰 ⊞ Leisure ⚊

MORTEHOE, Devon Map ref 1C1   SAT NAV EX34 7EG

North Morte Farm Caravan & Camping Park

North Morte Road, Mortehoe, Woolacombe EX34 7EG
t (01271) 870381 **f** (01271) 870115 **e** info@northmortefarm.co.uk
w northmortefarm.co.uk

🚐 (25)	£13.00–£20.50
🚍	£12.00–£19.50
🛆 (150)	£12.00–£17.00
🚎 (24)	£230.00–£580.00

Set in beautiful countryside overlooking Rockham Bay, close to village of Mortehoe, and Woolacombe. **directions** Please contact us for directions **open** April to September **payment** credit/debit cards, cash

General 🔲 🐕 ⚡ 🔋 🔦 ☼ 🔌 🚰 🚻 💧   **Leisure** ♨ 🎣 🏔

MORTEHOE, Devon Map ref 1C1   SAT NAV EX34 7EJ

Warcombe Farm Camping Park

Station Road, Mortehoe, Devon EX34 7EJ
t (01271) 870690 **f** (01271) 871070 **e** info@warcombefarm.co.uk
w warcombefarm.co.uk   GUEST REVIEWS ONLINE BOOKING

🚐	£12.50–£30.00
🚍	£12.50–£30.00
🛆	£10.50–£30.00
260 touring pitches	

We invite you to relax on our five star park which has luxurious facilities, beautiful grounds and sea views. We aim to offer the best family camping experience from the moment you arrive. Spotless facilities, excellent play area and coarse fishing lake. Close to the beaches and Devons natural treasures.

open Contact us for details
payment credit/debit cards, cash

directions From Barnstaple follow the signs for Ilfracombe and then head towards Woolacombe and then head towards Mortehoe, the park is the first on the right.

General 🛁 🔲 🐕 ⚡ 🔋 🔦 ☼ 🔌 🚰 🚻 💧   **Leisure** 🎣 🏔

NEWTON ABBOT, Devon Map ref 1D2   SAT NAV TQ12 6DD

enjoyEngland.com

★★★★★
TOURING &
CAMPING PARK

Dornafield Touring Park

Two Mile Oak, Newton Abbot TQ12 6DD
t (01803) 812732 **f** (01803) 812032 **e** enquiries@dornafield.com
w dornafield.com ONLINE BOOKING

🚐 (119)   £13.50–£25.00
🚏 (119)   £13.50–£25.00
⛺ (16)   £13.50–£24.00
135 touring pitches

SPECIAL PROMOTIONS
Early- and late-season
bookings. Book for 7 days
and pay only for 5. Details
on request.

Beautiful 14thC farmhouse located in 30 acres of glorious South Devon countryside. So quiet and peaceful, yet so convenient for Torbay and Dartmoor. Superb facilities to suit the discerning caravanner, including many hardstanding, all-service pitches. Shop, games room, adventure play area, tennis and golf close by. Our brochure is only a phone call away.

open All year
payment credit/debit cards, cash, cheques

directions Take A381 Newton Abbot to Totnes road. In 2.5 miles at Two Mile Oak Inn turn right. In 0.5 miles 1st turn to left. Site 200 yds on right.

General 🔌 ⓦ 🐕 🛒 📼 📻 ☼ 📺 🛏 📞 🚻 ♿
Leisure ► ◔ ● ⚴

PAIGNTON, Devon Map ref 1D2   SAT NAV TQ4 7JE

enjoyEngland.com

★★★★★
HOLIDAY, TOURING
& CAMPING PARK

Beverley Holidays

Goodrington Road, Paignton TQ4 7JE
t (01803) 661971 **f** (01803) 845427 **e** info@beverley-holidays.co.uk
w beverley-holidays.co.uk ONLINE MAP ONLINE BOOKING LAST MINUTE OFFERS

🚐   £15.50–£38.50
🚏   £15.50–£38.50
⛺   £13.00–£32.50
🏠   £265–£1415
🏕 (189)   £120.00–£950.00
175 touring pitches

SPECIAL PROMOTIONS
Special discounts touring
plus for over-50s and
under-5s in holiday
caravans. Specific dates
apply.

Superb luxury holiday park overlooking Torbay with fabulous sea views. South West Tourism 'Caravan Park of the Year' 2007/2008. David Bellamy Gold Conservation Award. Indoor/outdoor pools, tennis, gym, crazy golf, playground, restaurant, bar, shop, plus golf, watersports, and unlimited coastal walks nearby. Less than 1 mile to the beach.

open All year
payment credit/debit cards, cash

directions Follow the A380/A3022 from the English Riviera roundabout towards Brixham for 5.6 miles. Turn left into Goodrington Road at the traffic lights at the garage.

General 🚗 🔌 ⓦ 🛒 📼 📻 ☼ 📺 📞 🚻 ♿ ✕
Leisure ► ◔ ⚲ ♨ ⚷ 🎣 🎵 ● ⚴

PAIGNTON, Devon Map ref 1D2 — SAT NAV TQ9 6RN

Higher Well Farm Holiday Park
Waddeton Road, Stoke Gabriel, Totnes TQ9 6RN
t (01803) 782289 e higherwell@talk21.com
w **higherwellfarmholidaypark.co.uk** ONLINE MAP

🚐 (80)	£9.50–£15.50
🚐 (80)	£9.50–£15.50
⛺ (80)	£9.50–£15.50
🏠 (18)	£165.00–£500.00
80 touring pitches	

Secluded farm park with static caravans and separate area welcoming touring caravans, tents and motor homes. Within 1 mile of Stoke Gabriel and the River Dart. 4 miles to Paignton. **directions** Please contact us for directions **payment** credit/debit cards, cash, cheques

General 🗐 🐕 🛁 🛈 🐾 ☼ 🚲 🔌 🛒 🚻 WP Leisure ▶

PAIGNTON, Devon Map ref 1D2 — SAT NAV TQ4 7PF

Whitehill Country Park
Stoke Road, Paignton TQ4 7PF
t (01803) 782338 f (01803) 782722 e info@whitehill-park.co.uk
w **whitehill-park.co.uk** ONLINE MAP ONLINE BOOKING LAST MINUTE OFFERS

🚐	£15.00–£28.50
🚐	£15.00–£28.50
⛺	£13.00–£26.00
🏠 (60)	£160.00–£640.00
260 touring pitches	

SPECIAL PROMOTIONS
Over-50s discount 1 Apr–14 May, 5 June–10 July & 4 Sept–24 Sept.

Beautifully situated in rolling Devon countryside yet within easy reach of the sea, the bright lights of Torbay, and Dartmoor. Outdoor swimming pool, play area, craft room, table tennis, amusements, cycle and walking trails, bar and restaurant.

open Easter to September
payment credit/debit cards, cash

directions From the A358 Totnes Road, turn left at the Parker's Arms. We are 1 mile along towards Stoke Gabriel.

General 🔥 🗐 🛁 🛈 🐾 ☼ 🔌 🛒 🚻 ✕
Leisure ⚓ 🎱 🔍 ⛰

PLYMOUTH, Devon Map ref 1C2   SAT NAV PL9 0AE

Plymouth Sound Caravan Club Site

Bovisand Lane, Down Thomas, Plymouth PL9 0AE
t (01752) 862325
w caravanclub.co.uk

THE
CARAVAN
CLUB

🚐 (58)   £8.10–£19.20
🚃 (58)   £8.10–£19.20
58 touring pitches

SPECIAL PROMOTIONS
Special member rates mean
you can save your
membership subscription in
less than a week. Visit our
website to find out more.

Within easy reach of the historic port, set on a
headland outside Plymouth with superb views
over the Sound and close to the South West
Coastal Footpath, the Plym Valley Cycleway and
lovely beaches. Children will love the ice rink
and Atlantis pool at the Plymouth Pavilions.

open March to October
payment credit/debit cards, cash, cheques

directions Turn right at village signposted Down
Thomas into Bovisand Lane. Site on right.

General 🐕 🔌 ⬦ ⓦ🄿
Leisure ⚑

SALCOMBE, Devon Map ref 1C3   SAT NAV TQ7 3DY

Bolberry House Farm Caravan & Camping

Bolberry, Malborough, Kingsbridge TQ7 3DY
t (01548) 561251 f (01548) 561251 e enquiries@bolberryparks co.uk
w bolberryparks.co.uk

🚐 (20)   £11.00–£20.00
🚃 (20)   £11.00–£12.00
⛺ (50)   £7.00–£20.00
🚐   £160.00–£530.00
70 touring pitches

SPECIAL PROMOTIONS
Special rates, low season for
couples only, over-50s –
from £65 per week (incl
electric). Outdoor and indoor
swimming pools and tennis
nearby. Caravan prices are
for 2 adults and 2 children.

Beautiful coastal area, our friendly family-run park is situated between the sailing paradise of
Salcombe and the old fishing village of Hope Cove. It is peaceful and mostly level with good
facilities. Children's play area. Good access to coastal footpaths. Sandy beaches nearby. Small shop
(high season only).

open April to October
payment cash, cheques

directions A381 from Totnes to Kingsbridge.
Between Kingsbridge and Salcombe at
Malborough take sharp right through the village
follow signs to Bolberry which is approx. 1 mile.

General 🗑 🐕 🛁 🏪 🚿 ☀ 🖥 🛒 🔌 ☎ Leisure ⚑ ⋃ ⚓ ⟁

SHALDON, Devon Map ref 1D2 SAT NAV TQ14 0BG

HOLIDAY, TOURING & CAMPING PARK

🚐 (20)	£25.00–£39.00
🚏 (20)	£19.00–£31.00
⛺ (200)	£15.00–£25.00
🏠 (29)	£129–£790
🏡 (22)	£222.00–£726.00

Coast View Holiday Park
Torquay Road, Shaldon, Teignmouth TQ14 0BG
t (01626) 872392 f (01626) 872719 e info@coastview.co.uk
w **coastview.co.uk** LAST MINUTE OFFERS

Coast View Holiday Park boasts some of the best scenery in South Devon. A variety of accommodation including chalet/caravan hire, and camping and touring. **directions** A38 from Exeter, A380 towards Torquay, A381 Teignmouth turnoff, right at the lights over Shaldon bridge, proceed up hill, we are on the right. **open** March to October **payment** credit/debit cards, cash, cheques, euros

General 🔥 🗄 👤 🐕 🛒 🏕 📶 ☀ 🔌 🛗 🏪 ✕ Leisure 🎣 🐟 🍺 🎵 🎯

SHIRWELL, Devon Map ref 1C1 SAT NAV EX31 4JJ

TOURING PARK

🚐 (20)	£10.00–£16.00
🚏 (20)	£10.00–£16.00
⛺ (20)	£6.00–£12.00
20 touring pitches	

Brightly Cott Barton
Brightlycott Barton, shirwell, Barnstaple EX31 4JJ
t (01271) 850330 e friend.brightlycott@virgin.net
w **brightlycottbarton.co.uk** ONLINE MAP GUEST REVIEWS

Quiet, family-run site with excellent panoramic views. New ablution block (2006) with good laundry and washing facilities. 7 miles from nearest beach and close to Exmoor. 2.5 miles NE of Barnstaple **directions** Juntion 27 off M5 onto A361 straight into Barnstaple and take A39 signposted Lynton. Coming out of town pass hospital on right next campsite on A39 **open** 15th March to 15th November **payment** cash, cheques, euros

General 🗄 🐕 🏕 ☀ 🔌 🏪 📶 Leisure 🏇 ⛳ 🚴 🎣 🔥 🏔

SIDBURY, Devon Map ref 1D2 SAT NAV EX10 0QQ

TOURING PARK

🚐 (117)	£12.20–£25.30
🚏 (117)	£12.20–£25.30
117 touring pitches	

Putts Corner Caravan Club Site
Putts Corner, Sidbury, Sidmouth EX10 0QQ
t (01404) 42875
w **caravanclub.co.uk**

THE CARAVAN CLUB

A quiet site in pretty surroundings, with a private path to the local pub. Bluebells create a sea of blue in spring, followed by foxgloves **directions** From M5 jct 25, A375 signposted Sidmouth. Turn right at Hare and Hounds onto B3174. In about 0.25 miles turn right into site entrance. **open** March to November **payment** credit/debit cards, cash, cheques

General 🗄 🐕 🏕 📶 🔌 🛗 🏪 Leisure 🏔

TAVISTOCK, Devon Map ref 1C2 SAT NAV PL19 9LS

HOLIDAY, TOURING & CAMPING PARK

ROSE AWARD CARAVAN HOLIDAY PARK

🚐 (40)	£11.50–£18.00
🚏 (40)	£11.50–£18.00
⛺ (40)	£11.50–£16.50
🏠	£308–£525
🏡 (14)	£235.00–£460.00
120 touring pitches	

Harford Bridge Holiday Park
Harford Bridge, Peter Tavy, Tavistock PL19 9LS
t (01822) 810349 f (01822) 810028 e enquiry@harfordbridge.co.uk
w **harfordbridge.co.uk**

Beautiful park set in Dartmoor with level riverside and other spacious camping including electric hook-up & fully serviced pitches. Luxury, self-catering caravan holiday homes for hire; open all year. **directions** M5 onto A30 to Sourton Cross; take A386 Tavistock Road. 2 miles north of Tavistock take Peter Tavy turn off, entrance 200 yrds on left. **open** All year **payment** credit/debit cards, cash, cheques

General 🗄 👤 🐕 🏕 📶 ☀ 🍴 🔌 🛗 🏪 📶 Leisure 🏇 ⛳ 🎣 🚴 🔥 🏔

TAVISTOCK, Devon Map ref 1C2

Langstone Manor Holiday Park

Moortown, Tavistock, Devon PL19 9JZ
t 01822 613371 f (01822) 613371 e jane@langstonemanor.co.uk
w **langstonemanor.co.uk** ONLINE MAP

🚐 (15)   £13.00–£15.00
🚎 (15)   £13.00–£15.00
🅰 (15)   £13.00–£15.00
🚐 (7)   £170.00–£465.00
45 touring pitches

SPECIAL PROMOTIONS
£25 discount for 2-week
booking in holiday homes.
20% discount for 2 people
sharing on weekly bookings
in holiday accommodation
(off-peak).

Fantastic location with direct access onto moor
offering great walks straight from the park.
Peaceful site with beautiful views of the
surrounding moorland. Level pitches, some
hardstanding with four star facilites. The
Langstone Bar provides evening meals or a
place to relax after a day out. A warm welcome
awaits!

open March 15th to Oct 15th for camping and
15th Nov for self-catering
payment credit/debit cards, cash, cheques

directions Take the B3357 Princetown road from
Tavistock. After approx 1.5 miles, signs to
Langstone Manor. Turn right, go over cattle grid,
up hill, left following signs.

General 🔲 🛠 🏕 🥘 ☼ 🔌 💷 🚻 WP ✗
Leisure ⚑ ∪ 🚲 ⚓ 🍴 🎣 ⛰

TEIGNGRACE, Devon Map ref 1D2

Twelve Oaks Farm Caravan Park

Teigngrace, Newton Abbot TQ12 6QT
t (01626) 352769 f (01626) 352769 e info@twelveoaksfarm.co.uk
w **twelveoaksfarm.co.uk** ONLINE BOOKING

🚐 (25)   £9.00–£15.00
🚎 (25)   £9.00–£15.00
🅰   £9.00–£15.00
25 touring pitches

A working farm specialising in Charolais beef cattle. Friendly,
personal service. Luxury showers and toilets, heated swimming
pool. Coarse fishing. **directions** Please contact us for directions
open All year **payment** credit/debit cards, cash, cheques

General 🔲 🛠 🐾 🥘 ☼ 🔌 💷 🚻 WP   Leisure ∪ 🚲 ⚓ 🎣

TOTNES, Devon Map ref 1D2

Broadleigh Farm Park

Coombe House Lane, Stoke Gabriel, Totnes TQ9 6PU
t (01803) 782110 f (01803) 782422 e enquiries@broadleighfarm.co.uk
w **broadleighfarm.co.uk** ONLINE MAP

🚐   £11.50–£19.50
🚎   £11.50–£19.50
🅰   £11.50–£19.50
85 touring pitches

Situated in beautiful South Hams village of Stoke Gabriel close to
River Dart and Torbay's wonderful, safe beaches. Many local walks.
Bus stop at end of lane. Dartmoor within easy reach. **directions**
Please contact us for directions **open** March to October **payment**
cash, cheques

General 🔲 📶 🛠 🥘 ☼ 🔌 💷 🚻 WP   Leisure ⚑ ∪ ⚓

TOTNES, Devon Map ref 1D2

SAT NAV TQ9 5AL

TOURING PARK

Steamer Quay Caravan Club Site

Steamer Quay Road, Totnes TQ9 5AL
t (01803) 862738
w caravanclub.co.uk

£9.30–£21.00
£9.30–£21.00
40 touring pitches

A quiet, green and pleasantly open site with pastoral views, yet within a short walk of the bustling centre of Totnes with its good pubs and restaurants. **directions** From Totnes cross railway bridge and turn right at roundabout. In 300 yards turn left over bridge and right into Seymour Road. Turn right.

General

WEMBURY, Devon Map ref 1C3

SAT NAV PL9 0DZ

HOLIDAY PARK

Churchwood Valley Holiday Cabins

Churchwood Valley, Wembury Bay, Nr Plymouth PL9 0DZ
t (01752) 862382 **f** (01752) 863274 **e** churchwoodvalley@btconnect.com
w churchwoodvalley.com ONLINE MAP LAST MINUTE OFFERS

(56) £250–£845

A peaceful Park set in a beautiful wooded valley, close to beach, coastal walks and glorious countryside. Comfortable timber cabins/ lodges, each with a secluded patio. Wildlife abounds. Pets welcome **directions** From A38 take A379 Plymouth-Kingsbridge road to Elburton, then follow signs to Langdon Court Hotel, drive past hotel entrance and follow Churchwood signs. **open** Mid-March to Mid-January **payment** credit/debit cards, cash, cheques

General Leisure

WEST DOWN, Devon Map ref 1C1

SAT NAV EX34 8NE

TOURING PARK

Brook Lea

Brook Lea Caravan Club Site, West Down, Ilfracombe EX34 8NE
t (01271) 862848
w caravanclub.co.uk

£8.00–£15.00
£8.00–£15.00
100 touring pitches

SPECIAL PROMOTIONS
All-inclusive fee for a standard pitch (including electricity) is £8 per night for 2 adults and all children. Additional fees for extra adults and non-member supplement applies

Situated 3 miles inland from Ilfracombe and the North Devon coast, this has superb views to west and north coasts and inland to Dartmoor. Ideal base for beach lovers and walkers with Woolacombe beach and the footpaths of Exmoor close by.

open March to October
payment credit/debit cards, cash

directions From A361 at Mullacott roundabout turn right onto A3123, in about 0.75 miles turn right at caravan sign (signposted West Down). Site on left in 1 mile.

General

ALDERHOLT, Dorset Map ref 2B3

SAT NAV SP6 3EG

Hill Cottage Farm Camping and Caravan Park

Sandleheath Road, Alderholt, Fordingbridge SP6 3EG
t (01425) 650513 f (01425) 652339 e hillcottagefarmcaravansite@supanet.com
w **hillcottagefarmcampingandcaravanpark.co.uk** ONLINE MAP

🚐 (35)	£18.00–£22.00
🚍 (35)	£18.00–£22.00
▲ (50)	£12.00–£20.00
35 touring pitches	

Listed in Top 100 Parks (Practical Caravan). Edge of New Forest, Dorset/Hants border. Small lakes for fishing, camping field. Rallies welcome with access to function room. Excellent facilities.
directions From Fordingbridge take B3078 to Alderholt for 2 miles. On sharp left hand bend take a right, we are 0.5 mile on left. **open** March to November **payment** credit/debit cards, cash, cheques

General 🗊 📶 🐾 🛋 🏠 ☼ 🎱 🛢 🔌 🛒 🚽 🛁 ⚙ Leisure ∪ 🚲 🎣 🎯 ⚓

BERE REGIS, Dorset Map ref 2B3

SAT NAV BH20 7LP

Rowlands Wait Touring Park

Rye Hill, Bere Regis, Wareham, Wareham BH20 7LP
t (01929) 472727 f (01929) 472727 e enquiries@rowlandswait.co.uk
w **www.rowlandswait.co.uk** ONLINE MAP

🚐 (71)	£14.00–£18.00
🚍 (71)	£14.00–£18.00
▲ (71)	£12.00–£15.00
71 touring pitches	

Set in an Area of Outstanding Natural Beauty. Modern amenity block with family/disabled facilities. Centrally situated for many attractions and places of interest. Direct access to heathland, ideal for walkers, cyclists, couples, families and nature lovers. Open winter by arrangement.

open March to October
payment credit/debit cards, cash

directions At Bere Regis follow signs to Wool/Bovington. Rowlands Wait is 0.75 miles (1.2 km) from the village, top of the hill on the right.

General 🗊 🐾 🛢 🏠 ☼ 🛢 🔌 🛒 🚽 🛁 ⚙ Leisure ▶ ∪ 🚲 🎣 🎯 ⚓

BLANDFORD FORUM, Dorset Map ref 2B3 SAT NAV DT11 9AD

The Inside Park

Fairmile Road, Blandford Forum DT11 9AD
t (01258) 453719 e mail@theinsidepark.co.uk
w **theinsidepark.co.uk** ONLINE MAP

🚐	£13.00–£22.00
🚏	£13.00–£22.00
⛺	£13.00–£22.00

125 touring pitches

Secluded park and woodland with facilities built into 18thC stable and coach house. Ideal location for touring the county. 1.5 miles south west of Blandford on road to Winterborne Stickland. Country walks, cycling, wildlife, large play area, family-friendly camping.

open April to October
payment credit/debit cards, cash, cheques

directions Please contact us for directions

General 🔲 🐕 🚻 🏕 🔥 ☼ ♨ 🎣 🔄 ☕ 🍴 Leisure ∪ 🚣 🎣 ⛰

BOURNEMOUTH, Dorset Map ref 2B3 SAT NAV BH23 2PQ

Meadow Bank Holidays

Stour Way, Christchurch BH23 2PQ
t (01202) 483597 f (01202) 483878 e enquiries@meadowbank-holidays.co.uk
w **meadowbank-holidays.co.uk** ONLINE MAP LAST MINUTE OFFERS

🚐	(41)	£9.00–£29.00
🚏	(41)	£9.00–£29.00
🏠	(136)	£157.00–£915.00

41 touring pitches

Meadowbank Holidays operate Bournemouth's closest holiday caravan and touring park. We are superbly located on the beautiful River Stour and provide a wonderful relaxing environment for a peaceful, carefree holiday or break visiting the superb local beaches, New Forest or the famous Jurassic Coast.

open March to October
payment credit/debit cards, cash, cheques

directions A35 from Christchurch, west 1.5 miles, turn right at Crooked Beam Restaurant into The Grove, site 3rd left.

General 🔲 🚻 🏕 🔥 ☼ 🔄 ☕ 🍴 📺 Leisure ▶ ∪ 🚴 🚣 🎣 ⛰

BRIDPORT, Dorset Map ref 2A3   SAT NAV DT6 4PT

Freshwater Beach Holiday Park
Burton Bradstock, Bridport DT6 4PT
t (01308) 897317 f (01308) 897336 e office@freshwaterbeach.co.uk
w **freshwaterbeach.co.uk** ONLINE MAP LAST MINUTE OFFERS

🚐 (350)   £13.00–£35.00
🚐 (50)   £13.00–£35.00
⛺ (100)   £13.00–£35.00
🚐 (60)   £180.00–£820.00
500 touring pitches

SPECIAL PROMOTIONS
Pitch prices include up to 6
people and club
membership.

Family park with a large touring and camping field. Own private beach on Dorset's spectacular World Heritage Coastline. Surrounded by countryside and within easy reach of Dorset's features and attractions. Free nightly family entertainment (Spring BH–mid-September) and children's activities. Horse and pony rides, donkey derby, beach fishing, cliff and seaside walks.

open Mid-March to mid-November
payment credit/debit cards, cash, cheques

directions From Bridport take B3157, situated 2 miles on the right.

General 📱🏕🐾🐾🏛🔥☀️🎱🎮🛢🍴📶✖️ Leisure ▶👤🎵🏊🍷🎵🎣⛰

BRIDPORT, Dorset Map ref 2A3   SAT NAV DT6 6JX

Golden Cap Holiday Park
Seatown, Chideock, Bridport DT6 6JX
t (01308) 422139 f (01308) 425672 e holidays@wdlh.co.uk
w **wdlh.co.uk** ONLINE MAP GUEST REVIEWS LAST MINUTE OFFERS

🚐   £13.25–£28.00
🚐   £13.25–£28.00
⛺ (159)   £13.25–£22.00
🚐 (21)   £215.00–£600.00
108 touring pitches

One hundred metres from beach overlooked by Dorset's highest cliff top - Golden Cap - surrounded by countryside on this Heritage Coast. **directions** Follow A35 to Chideock, in village turn off opposite the church into Duck Street signposted for Seatown. Follow narrow road towards sea, park on left. **open** March to November **payment** credit/debit cards, cash, cheques

General 📱📶🏕🐾🏛🔥☀️🎮🛢🍴📶 Leisure ▶🚲🏊⛰

BRIDPORT, Dorset Map ref 2A3   SAT NAV DT6 6AR

Highlands End Holiday Park
Eype, Bridport, Dorset DT6 6AR
t (01308) 422139 f (01308) 425672 e holidays@wdlh.co.uk
w **wdlh.co.uk** ONLINE MAP GUEST REVIEWS LAST MINUTE OFFERS

THE
CARAVAN
CLUB

🚐   £13.70–£24.50
🚐   £13.70–£24.50
⛺ (80)   £10.50–£22.50
🚐 (21)   £274.00–£588.00
120 touring pitches

Quiet, select, family park overlooking sea with exceptional views of Heritage Coast and Lyme Bay. Indoor swimming pool. **directions** Please contact us for directions **open** March to November **payment** credit/debit cards, cash, cheques

General 📱📶🏕🐾🏛🔥☀️🎮🛢🍴📶✖️ Leisure ▶🎱🏊🍷🎣⛰

CHARMOUTH, Dorset Map ref 1D2
SAT NAV DT6 6QL

Manor Farm Holiday Centre
The Street, Charmouth, Bridport DT6 6QL
t (01297) 560226 f (01297) 560429 e enq@manorfarmholidaycentre.co.uk
w **manorfarmholidaycentre.co.uk**

(300)	£12.00–£24.00
(300)	£12.00–£24.00
(300)	£12.00–£24.00
(6)	£200.00–£650.00

300 touring pitches

Large, open site in Area of Outstanding Natural Beauty close to the sea. From east end of Charmouth bypass, come into Charmouth and the site is 0.75 miles on the right. **directions** Please contact us for directions **open** All year **payment** credit/debit cards, cash, cheques

General 🄳 🕈 🐾 🖬 🄮 🝔 ☼ 🔲 🛒 🖰 🛎 🅰 ✕ **Leisure** ► ∪ ♪ ⚲ 🎭 🎵 🔍 ⚱

CHARMOUTH, Dorset Map ref 1D2
SAT NAV DT6 6QS

Seadown Holiday Park
Bridge Road, Charmouth, Bridport DT6 6QS
t (01297) 560154 f (01297) 561130 e bookings@seadownholidaypark.co.uk
w **seadowncaravanpark.co.uk** LAST MINUTE OFFERS

(40)	£12.00–£18.00
(10)	£12.00–£18.00
(10)	£12.00–£18.00
(68)	£185.00–£555.00

60 touring pitches

Quiet, family-run park which runs alongside the River Char. It has its own direct access to Charmouth's famous fossil beach, which is situated on the World Heritage Coastline. **directions** Please contact us for directions **open** Mid-March to end of October **payment** credit/debit cards, cash, cheques

General 🄳 🐾 🖬 🝔 ☼ 🔲 🝔 🖰 🛎 🅰 **Leisure** ∪ ♪ ⚱

CHRISTCHURCH, Dorset Map ref 2B3
SAT NAV BH23 8JE

Harrow Wood Farm Caravan Park
Poplar Lane, Bransgore, Christchurch BH23 8JE
t (01425) 672487 f (01425) 672487 e harrowwood@caravan-sites.co.uk
w **caravan-sites.co.uk/pages/harrowwood.htm**

(60)	£14.00–£24.00
(60)	£14.00–£24.00
(14)	£14.00–£20.00

60 touring pitches

Quiet site bordered by woods and meadows. Take A35 from Lyndhurst, after approximately 11 miles turn right at Cat and Fiddle pub, site approximately 1.5 miles into Bransgore, first right after school. **directions** Please contact us for directions **open** 1 March to 6 January **payment** credit/debit cards, cash, cheques

General ♿ 🄳 🕈 🖬 🝔 ☼ 🔲 🖰 🛎 🅰 **Leisure** ► ∪ 🚲 ♪

CORFE CASTLE, Dorset Map ref 2B3   SAT NAV BH20 5DS

Norden Farm Campsite
Norden Farm, Corfe Castle BH20 5DS
t (01929) 480098 e nordenfarm@fsmail.net
w **nordenfarm.com**

🚐	£13.00–£23.00
🚍	£13.00–£20.00
▲ (90)	£13.00–£22.00

52 touring pitches

SPECIAL PROMOTIONS
5% discount for 7 nights or more throughout season

Level fields on working farm site in the beautiful Purbeck Valley. Excellent toilet/shower facilities. Good family location. Set away from main road but with easy access. Family-run business with adjoining farm shop and bed and breakfast.

open March to October
payment credit/debit cards, cash, cheques

directions A351 Wareham to Corfe Castle, follow signs for Norden Park'n'Ride and look for us on right-hand side as castle comes into view.

General 🔲 ⛺ 🔧 📶 ☀ 🔌 📠 ♿ Leisure ► ∪ ⚓ ⛰

DORCHESTER, Dorset Map ref 2B3   SAT NAV DT2 7TR

Giant's Head Caravan & Camping Park
Old Sherborne Road, Dorchester DT2 7TR
t (01300) 341242 e holidays@giantshead.co.uk
w **giantshead.co.uk** ONLINE BOOKING

🚐	(50)	£7.00–£14.00
🚍	(50)	£7.00–£14.00
▲	(50)	£7.00–£14.00
⌂	(3)	£165–£275

50 touring pitches

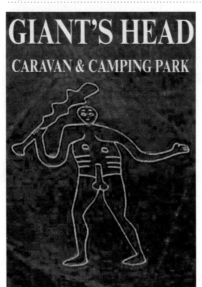

Two miles north-east of Cerne Abbas, 3 miles south of Middlemarsh, 8 miles from Dorchester.

payment cash, cheques

directions Please contact us for directions

General 🔲 ⛺ 📶 🔌 ♿ 🔌 📠 ♿
Leisure ► ⚓

LYME REGIS, Dorset Map ref 1D2 — SAT NAV DT7 3XW

Shrubbery Touring Park

Rousdon, Lyme Regis DT7 3XW
t (01297) 442227 f (01297) 442227 e info@shrubberypark.co.uk
w **shrubberypark.co.uk** GUEST REVIEWS

£10.25–£15.25
£10.25–£15.25
£10.25–£15.25
120 touring pitches

Ten acre level site, on the Devon & Dorset border. Pitches for tents, motor vans & caravans. Electric Hook-ups. Spacious modern shower blocks. Large children's play area. Crazy golf. Dog Walking Area. Rallies welcome. Off peak special offers.

open Mid-March to End October
payment credit/debit cards, cash, cheques

directions 3 miles west of Lyme Regis on the A3052 Coast Road

General ☐ ♀ ⚡ ⛺ ⟁ ☼ ⚏ ⚐ ⟳ ♀ Leisure ⚏

POOLE, Dorset Map ref 2B3 — SAT NAV BH16 6JB

South Lytchett Manor Caravan & Camping Park

Dorchester Road, Poole, Dorset BH16 6JB
t (01202) 622577 e info@southlytchettmanor.co.uk
w **southlytchettmanor.co.uk** ONLINE MAP GUEST REVIEWS LAST MINUTE OFFERS

(120) £13.00–£22.75
(120) £13.00–£22.75
(30) £13.00–£22.75
150 touring pitches

Situated in 20 acres of stunning parkland. Just 3 miles from Poole. Within walking distance of 2 village pubs with restaurants. Bus service at gates to Poole and Heritage Coastline. **directions** Follow signs towards Poole from the A31. Continue on A35 signposted Dorchester. Right at the Bakers Arms roundabout Lytchett Minster, on left 300 outside village. **open** 1st March to 2nd January
payment credit/debit cards, cash, cheques, euros

General ♿ ☐ ♁ ♀ ⚡ ⛺ ⟁ ☼ ⚐ ⟳ ♀ 🚐 Leisure ▶ ∪ ♿ ⚓ ♦ ⚏

SWANAGE, Dorset Map ref 2B3

Haycraft Caravan Club Site

Haycrafts Lane, Swanage BH19 3EB
t (01929) 480572
w **caravanclub.co.uk**

🚐 (53)   £14.00–£26.90
🚍 (53)   £14.00–£26.90
53 touring pitches

SPECIAL PROMOTIONS
Special member rates mean
you can save your
membership subscription in
less than a week. Visit our
website to find out more.

Peaceful site located 5 miles from Swanage, with its safe, sandy beach. Spectacular cliff-top walks, Corfe Castle, Lulworth Cove and Durdle Door within easy reach. There are numerous public footpaths and coastal walks nearby. The Swanage Railway is a favourite with young and old alike.

open March to November
payment credit/debit cards, cash, cheques

directions Midway between Corfe Castle and Swanage. Take A351 from Wareham to Swanage, at Harmans Cross turn right into Haycrafts Lane, site 0.5 miles on the left.

General 🖥 🐕 🛖 🎪 ☼ 🎮 🛅 🚻 🅿
Leisure ▶ 🏊

WAREHAM, Dorset Map ref 2B3

The Lookout Holiday Park

Corfe Road, Stoborough, Wareham BH20 5AZ
t (01929) 552546 f (01929) 556662 e enquiries@caravan-sites.co.uk
w **caravan-sites.co.uk**

🚐   £15.00–£28.00
🚍   £15.00–£28.00
⛺   £11.00–£24.00
🏠   £189.00–£607.00

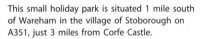

This small holiday park is situated 1 mile south of Wareham in the village of Stoborough on A351, just 3 miles from Corfe Castle.

open All year
payment credit/debit cards, cash, cheques

directions Please contact us for directions

General 🖥 ♿ 🛒 🛖 🎪 ☼ 🎮 🛅 🚻
Leisure 🎣 ⛰

WAREHAM, Dorset Map ref 2B3
SAT NAV BH20 6AW

Luckford Wood Farm Caravan & Camping Park
Luckford Wood House, East Stoke, Wareham BH20 6AW
t (01929) 463098 (07888719002) e luckfordleisure@hotmail.co.uk
w **luckfordleisure.co.uk** ONLINE MAP ONLINE BOOKING

🚐 (40)	£8.00–£20.00
🚎 (40)	£8.00–£20.00
🛖 (40)	£8.00–£20.00
🏠 (1)	£280–£350
40 touring pitches	

SPECIAL PROMOTIONS
Low season 3 night mid week stay £4.50 per person. 5 night stays £4 per person per night.

Old-fashioned camping around a camp fire with a relaxed, traditional feel, with mod cons. Central position makes Luckford Wood an ideal location for you to enjoy the Jurassic Coastline, wonderful beaches and bays, coastal and inland walks, many exciting places to explore. Country-house accommodation available. Telephone for details.

open March to October
payment credit/debit cards, cash, cheques

directions A352 west for 1 mile. B3070, 1 mile to East Stoke. Turn right into Holme Lane, 1 mile. Entrance to our site on right-hand side. Observe sign and flags.

General 🐕 🏕 ☼ 🛱 📞 ♿ Leisure ► ∪ 🚵 ✴

WEYMOUTH, Dorset Map ref 2B3
SAT NAV DT2 8BE

Crossways Caravan Club Site
Crossways, Dorchester DT2 8BE
t (01305) 852032
w **caravanclub.co.uk**

THE CARAVAN CLUB

🚐 (120)	£10.60–£23.60
🚎 (120)	£10.60–£23.60
120 touring pitches	

Set in 35 acres of woodland. Dorchester is nearby, also Weymouth's award-winning, sandy beach. Visit Lawrence of Arabia's house at Cloud's Hill. If you want to leave the car behind for the day, the railway station is just 5 minutes' walk from the site. **directions** North from A35 or south from A352, join B3390. Site on right within 1 mile. Entrance to site by forecourt of filling station. **open** April to October **payment** credit/debit cards, cash, cheques

General 🔋 ⚡ 🏕 ☼ 🚐 📞 🚿 ♿ 🚐 Leisure ⛰

WIMBORNE MINSTER, Dorset Map ref 2B3

SAT NAV BH21 4HW

Wilksworth Farm Caravan Park

Cranborne Road, Furzehill, Wimborne BH21 4HW
t (01202) 885467 e rayandwendy@wilksworthfarmcaravanpark.co.uk
w **wilksworthfarmcaravanpark.co.uk** ONLINE MAP LAST MINUTE OFFERS

⊕ (60)	£16.00–£26.00
⊕ (60)	£16.00–£26.00
Å (25)	£16.00–£26.00
85 touring pitches	

SPECIAL PROMOTIONS
7-night booking outside
peak times - 1 night free.
Monday-Thursday outside of
peak times - £15 pitch fee
per night.

Wilksworth Farm caravan Park is a five star, premier park surrounding a grade 2 star listed farmhouse once belonging to Henry VIII and listed in the Doomsday Book. Newly refurbished swimming pool and children's pool, a large children's adventure play area, Tea Room and modern, fully refurbished toilet block.

open April to October
payment credit/debit cards, cash, cheques

directions 1 mile north of Wimborne on B3078 (Cranborne Road).

General ▢ ♔ ♞ ☏ ⋒ ⋔ ☼ ▣ ☎ ⚑ ♻ ♟ ✕
Leisure ∪ ♺ ↗ ⚘ ♦ ⚒

WOOL, Dorset Map ref 2B3

SAT NAV BH20 6HG

Whitemead Caravan Park

East Burton Road, Wool, Wareham BH20 6HG
t (01929) 462241 f (01929) 462241 e whitemeadcp@aol.com
w **whitemeadcaravanpark.co.uk**

⊕ (95)	£9.50–£16.25
⊕ (95)	£9.50–£16.25
Å (95)	£9.50–£16.25
95 touring pitches	

Within easy reach of beaches and beautiful countryside, this friendly site is maintained to a high standard of cleanliness. Turn west off the A352 near Wool level crossing. **directions** Turn west off A352, Wareham–Dorchester Road,along East Burton Road, by Wool level crossing. We are along this road on the right. **open** 15 March to 31 October **payment** cash, cheques

General ▢ ♔ ♞ ☏ ⋔ ☼ ▣ ♻ ♟ ♟ Leisure ↗ ♦ ⚒

BRISTOL, Gloucestershire Map ref 2A2   SAT NAV BS1 6XG

TOURING PARK

THE
CARAVAN
CLUB

Baltic Wharf Caravan Club Site
Cumberland Road, Southville, Bristol BS1 6XG
t (0117) 926 8030 f (0117) 926 8030 e enquiries@caravanclub.co.uk
w **caravanclub.co.uk**

🚐 (55)   £14.90–£28.90
🚎 (55)   £14.90–£28.90
55 touring pitches

SPECIAL PROMOTIONS
Special member rates mean
you can save your
membership subscription in
less than a week. Visit our
website to find out more.

A waterside site, right in the heart of Bristol's
beautifully redeveloped dockland. Linked in the
summer by a river ferry to the city centre. For
families there is the zoo and Downs Park; a safe
place for young children to play in and an ideal
picnic spot.

open All year
payment credit/debit cards, cash, cheques

directions M5 jct 18, A4, under bridge. Left lane
follow Historic Harbour/SS Great Britain, into
Hotwells Road. Right lane at lights, left lane after
pedestrian crossing. Over bridge, site on left.

General 🖥 📱 🏕 ☼ 🔌 🗜 🚰 🆆🅿
Leisure ▶

DRYBROOK, Gloucestershire Map ref 2B1   SAT NAV GL17 9HW

TOURING &
CAMPING PARK

Greenway Farm Caravan & Camping Park
Puddlebrook Road, Hawthorns, Drybrook GL17 9HW
t (01594) 544877 e admin@greenwayfarm.org
w **greenwayfarm.org** ONLINE MAP GUEST REVIEWS

🚐 (20)   £16.00–£20.00
🚎 (20)   £16.00–£20.00
⛺ (35)   £13.00–£17.00
55 touring pitches

David and Lorraine welcome you to Greenway Farm, a smallholding
of 5 acres with beautiful views and woodland walks within 100 yds.
Relax in the heart of the Forest. **directions** A40 Gloucester to Ross.
1.5 miles after Lea, left turn signposted Drybrook. A40 Ross to
Gloucester. 1.5 miles after Weston, right turn, signposted Drybrook.
payment credit/debit cards, cash, cheques

General 🖥 🐕 📱 🏕 ☼ 🚗 🔌 🗜 🚰 🆆🅿 ✕   Leisure 🚲 🏌 ⛰

MORETON-IN-MARSH, Gloucestershire Map ref 2B1 — SAT NAV GL56 0BT

Moreton-in-Marsh Caravan Club Site
Bourton Road, Moreton-in-Marsh GL56 0BT
t (01608) 650519
w **caravanclub.co.uk**

🚐 (183) £14.90–£28.30
🚐 (183) £14.90–£28.30
183 touring pitches

SPECIAL PROMOTIONS
Special member rates mean
you can save your
membership subscription in
less than a week. Visit our
website to find out more.

An attractive, well-wooded site within easy walking distance of the market town of Moreton-in-Marsh. On-site facilities include crazy golf, volleyball and boules. Large dog-walking area. The site is within easy walking distance of town with its many interesting shops and Tuesday street market.

payment credit/debit cards, cash, cheques

directions From Moreton-in-Marsh on A44 the site entrance is on the right 250 yds past the end of the speed limit sign.

General
Leisure

TEWKESBURY, Gloucestershire Map ref 2B1 — SAT NAV GL20 5PG

Tewkesbury Abbey Caravan Club Site
Gander Lane, Tewkesbury GL20 5PG
t (01684) 294035 e natalie.tiller@caravanclub.co.uk
w **caravanclub.co.uk**

🚐 (157) £12.20–£25.10
🚐 (157) £12.20–£25.10
157 touring pitches

SPECIAL PROMOTIONS
Special member rates mean
you can save your
membership subscription in
less than a week. Visit our
website to find out more.

Located only a short walk away from the old town, it is almost in the shadow of the ancient Abbey, with superb mature trees screening it. There are many historic buildings, interesting walks and excellent museums. Take a boat cruise on the river to explore the Avon.

open April to November
payment credit/debit cards, cash, cheques

directions From M5 leave by exit 9 onto A438. In about 3 miles in town centre, at cross-junction turn right. After 200 yds turn left into Gander Lane. From M50 leave by exit 1 on A38. For details on other routes visit caravanclub.co.uk.

General
Leisure

BREAN, Somerset Map ref 1D1   SAT NAV TA8 2RB

HOLIDAY VILLAGE

Holiday Resort Unity
Coast Road, Brean Sands, Brean TA8 2RB
t (01278) 751235 f (01278) 751539 e admin@hru.co.uk
w **hru.co.uk** ONLINE MAP GUEST REVIEWS ONLINE BOOKING LAST MINUTE OFFERS

🚐	£7.50–£30.00
🚐	£7.50–£30.00
Å (69)	£6.00–£27.00
🏠 (169)	£194.00–£730.00
385 touring pitches	

Pitches for caravans, motorhomes and tents. Lodges, villas, caravans and tents for hire. Entertainment, pools with 4 waterslides. Fun Park, children's club, fishing, golf. Specials from £8.50 per night. **directions** Off Junction 22 of M5. Follow Brown and White Tourist Board Signs from motorway towards Burnham On Sea and North heading for Berrow and Brean. **open** Feb to Nov plus New Year **payment** credit/debit cards

General 🔥 📶 🛜 🔭 🛒 🐕 🔥 ☼ 🍴 🛗 🅿 🚐 ✕ Leisure ▶ U 🚲 ♪ ⌖ ⌕ 🍷 🎵 ◆ 🎣

BREAN, Somerset Map ref 1D1   SAT NAV TA8 2SE

HOLIDAY, TOURING & CAMPING PARK

Northam Farm Touring Park
South Road, Brean TA8 2SE
t (01278) 751244 f (01278) 751150 e enquiries@northamfarm.co.uk
w **northamfarm.co.uk** ONLINE MAP

🚐 (350)	£7.25–£22.50
🚐 (350)	£7.25–£22.50
Å (150)	£7.25–£19.00
450 touring pitches	

An attractive touring park situated 200 m from a sandy beach. 30-acre park offering children's outdoor play areas, fishing lake, cafe, mini-supermarket, launderette, dog walks, hardstanding and grass pitches. **directions** M5 jct 22. Follow signs to Burnham-on-Sea, Brean. Continue through Brean and Northam Farm is on the right, 0.5 miles past Brean Leisure Park. **open** March to October **payment** credit/debit cards, cash, cheques

General 🛜 🐕 🔥 ☼ 🍴 🛗 🅿 🚐 ✕ Leisure U ♪ 🎣

BREAN, Somerset Map ref 1D1   SAT NAV TA8 2RP

HOLIDAY, TOURING & CAMPING PARK

Warren Farm Holiday Centre
Warren Road, Brean Sands, Brean TA8 2RP
t (01278) 751227 f (01278) 751033 e enquiries@warren-farm.co.uk
w **warren-farm.co.uk** ONLINE MAP GUEST REVIEWS

🚐	£7.00–£16.00
🚐	£7.00–£16.00
Å	£7.00–£16.00
🏠 (11)	£180.00–£510.00
575 touring pitches	

Our large, family-run holiday park is close to the beach and is divided into several fields, each with their own designated facilities. Pitches are spacious and level and enjoy panoramic views of the Mendip Hills and Brean Down. There is a large indoor play area, a bar and restaurant.

open April to October   **directions** Please contact us for directions
payment credit/debit cards, cash, cheques

General 🔥 📶 🛜 🔭 🛒 🐕 🔥 ☼ 🍴 🛗 🅿 🚐 ✕ Leisure ▶ U 🚲 ♪ 🍷 🎵 ◆ 🎣

BURNHAM-ON-SEA, Somerset Map ref 1D1

Lakeside Holiday Park
Westfield Road, Burnham-on-Sea TA8 2AE
t (01278) 792222 **f** (01278) 795592 **e** booking-enquiries@btconnect.com
w **lakesideholidays.co.uk** ONLINE MAP LAST MINUTE OFFERS

(89)   £167.00–£630.00

Close to 7 mile long beach, town centre and beautiful countryside. Super complex, brilliant family entertainment, even private tree-lined coarse fishing lake. **directions** From M25 J22, follow B3140 into Burnham and towards Berrow/Bream - turn right opposite swimming pool into Westfield Road. **open** Easter to 31st October **payment** credit/debit cards, cash

General ⬜ 🐾 🏠 ☀ ✕   Leisure ∪ ⚡ ♪ ⟨ ♨ ♫ ♣ ⚒

CROWCOMBE, Somerset Map ref 1D1

Quantock Orchard Caravan Park
Flaxpool, Crowcombe, Taunton, Somerset TA4 4AW
t (01984) 618618 **f** (01984) 618618 **e** member@flaxpool.freeserve.co.uk
w **quantock-orchard.co.uk** ONLINE MAP GUEST REVIEWS LAST MINUTE OFFERS

(31)   £13.00–£25.00
(19)   £13.00–£25.00
(19)   £13.00–£25.00
(8)   £35.00–£85.00
69 touring pitches

Award-winning campsite with superb panoramic views of the Quantock Hills; open all year, fully heated toilet and shower block; tastefully landscaped with several stunning holiday homes for hire. **directions** On the A358 between Williton and Taunton. Behind Flaxpool Garage. **open** All year **payment** credit/debit cards, cash

General ⚡ ⬜ 🐕 🏋 🏠 🐾 ☀ 🚲 ⚡ ⟳ 🚻 ⚏   Leisure ⟶ ∪ ⚡ ♪ ⟨ ♣ ⚒

DULVERTON, Somerset Map ref 1D1

Exmoor House Caravan Club Site
Oldberry, Dulverton TA22 9HL
t (01398) 323268
w **caravanclub.co.uk**

THE CARAVAN CLUB

(64)   £12.20–£25.30
(64)   £12.20–£25.30
64 touring pitches

Very quiet and secluded, in the heart of Lorna Doone country. Shops and pubs within walking distance, Exmoor is on the doorstep. Leave your car behind and explore this walker's paradise. **directions** From M5 jct 27, B3222 to Dulverton, left over river bridge, 200 yds on. Note: 2 narrow hump bridges on B3222, approach carefully. **open** March to November **payment** credit/debit cards, cash, cheques

General ⬜ 🐕 🏠 🏠 ⚡ ⟳ 🚻 ⚏

DULVERTON, Somerset Map ref 1D1

SAT NAV TA22 9BE

Lakeside Caravan Club Site

Higher Grants, Exebridge, Dulverton TA22 9BE
t (01398) 324068 e enquiries@caravanclub.co.uk
w **caravanclub.co.uk**

THE
CARAVAN
CLUB

(80) £14.00–£26.90
(80) £14.00–£26.90
80 touring pitches

SPECIAL PROMOTIONS
Special member rates mean
you can save your
membership subscription in
less than a week. Visit our
website to find out more.

Recently redeveloped, Lakeside has splendid
new facilities and all pitches (now level) boast
superb views of surrounding hills and the Exe
Valley. Within easy reach of the National Park
and Lorna Doone country.

open March to November
payment credit/debit cards, cash, cheques

directions From A396 site on left within 2.5
miles.

General 🔲 🐕 📶 📷 🔌 💧 🚾
Leisure 🎵

PORLOCK, Somerset Map ref 1D1

SAT NAV TA24 8HT

Burrowhayes Farm Caravan and Camping Site and Riding Stables

West Luccombe, Porlock TA24 8HT
t (01643) 862463 e info@burrowhayes.co.uk
w **burrowhayes.co.uk**

(54) £10.00–£17.00
(54) £10.00–£17.00
(66) £10.00–£15.00
(19) £170.00–£400.00
120 touring pitches

Popular family site in delightful National Trust
setting on Exmoor, just 2 miles from the Coast.
Surrounding moors and woods provide a
walker's paradise. Children can play and explore
safely. Riding stables offer pony-trekking for all
abilities. Heated shower block with disabled and
baby-changing facilities, laundrette and pot
wash.

open Mid-March to end of October
payment credit/debit cards, cash, cheques

directions From Minehead, A39 towards Porlock
1st left after Allerford to Horner and West
Luccombe; Burrowhayes is 0.25 miles along on
right before hump-backed bridge.

General 🔲 🐕 ⚡ 📶 📷 ☀ 🔌 💧 🐕 🚾
Leisure ∪ 🎵

PORLOCK, Somerset Map ref 1D1   SAT NAV TA24 8ND

Porlock Caravan Park
High Bank, Porlock TA24 8ND
t (01643) 862269 f (01643) 862269 e info@porlockcaravanpark.co.uk
w **porlockcaravanpark.co.uk**

🚐	£12.00–£18.50
🚙	£12.00–£16.00
⛺	£11.00–£14.50
🏠 (9)	£300.00–£550.00
40 touring pitches	

Select high-quality park situated within walking distance of quaint village of Porlock. Luxury holiday homes for hire, touring caravans motor homes and tents welcome. **directions** A39 from Minehead, in Porlock village take B3225 to Porlock Weir, site signposted **open** March to October **payment** credit/debit cards, cash, cheques

General 🖥 ♻ 🐕 🏕 📷 ☼ 🔌 🌣 🚻   Leisure ▶ ∪ ⚓ ✒

TAUNTON, Somerset Map ref 1D1   SAT NAV TA3 5NW

Ashe Farm Caravan and Campsite
Ashe Farm Caravan and Campsite, Thornfalcon TA3 5NW
t (01823) 443764 f (01823) 443372 e info@ashefarm.co.uk
w **ashefarm.co.uk** ONLINE MAP

🚐 (20)	£10.00–£13.00
🚙 (10)	£10.00–£12.00
⛺ (10)	£10.00–£12.00
🏠 (3)	£120.00–£200.00
30 touring pitches	

Quiet farm site, lovely views, easy access. Central for touring. Easy reach coast and hills. Family run and informal. **directions** Leave M5 at Jnt 25, take A358 eastwards for 2.5 miles, turn right at Nags Head pub towards West Hatch. Site 0.25 mile on RHS. **open** 1st April to 31st October **payment** cash, cheques

General 🖥 🐕 📷 ☼ 🚲 🔌 🚻   Leisure ▶ ✎ ✒ ⛰

TAUNTON, Somerset Map ref 1D1   SAT NAV TA3 7EA

Holly Bush Park
B3170, Taunton TA3 7EA
t (01823) 421515 e info@hollybushpark.com
w **hollybushpark.com**

🚐 (30)	£14.00–£18.00
🚙 (30)	£14.00–£18.00
⛺ (10)	£12.00–£16.00
40 touring pitches	

Map image

A small, clean, quiet and friendly park. Ideal for walking, relaxing or touring. Excellent local inn 150 yds. Opposite woodlands and in an Area of Outstanding Natural Beauty. **directions** M5 junction 25 follow signs for racecourse on B3170- 3 miles after Corfe turn right at crossroads then next right then park on left. **open** All year **payment** credit/debit cards, cash, cheques

General 🖥 🐕 🛒 🏕 📷 ☼ 🚲 🔌 🌣 🚻   Leisure ▶ ∪

or **key to symbols** see page 6

UPTON, Somerset Map ref 1D1 — SAT NAV TA4 2DB

Lowtrow Cross Caravan & Camping Site

Lowtrow Cross, Upton TA4 2DB
t (01398) 371199 e lowtrowcross@aol.com
w **lowtrowcross.co.uk** ONLINE MAP

🚐 (10)	£10.50–£16.50
🚎 (5)	£10.50–£16.50
⛺ (12)	£10.50–£16.50
🏠 (2)	£185.00–£285.00

Small, quiet, ADULTS ONLY site nestling in the Brendon Hills close to Wimbleball Lake on the edge of Exmoor. 2 well-equipped static caravans for hire. Free use of microwave and freezer onsite. Traditonal Inn adjacent to site. Spotlessly clean refurbished shower block. Wonderful local walks. Well-behaved dogs welcome.

open Easter to end of October
payment credit/debit cards, cash, cheques

directions Exit M5 jnc.25 follow signs Minehead A358 turn left onto B3224 continue onto B3190. Exit M5 jnc.27 onto A361 through Bampton turn left onto B3190.

General 🔧🚿♿🐕🚻🏪📮☀🎯🔌📞🛒♨
Leisure 🏊

WATERROW, Somerset Map ref 1D1 — SAT NAV TA4 2AZ

Waterrow Touring Park

B3227, Wiveliscombe, Nr Taunton, Somerset TA4 2AZ
t (01984) 623464 f (01984) 624280 e waterrowpark@yahoo.co.uk
w **waterrowpark.co.uk**

🚐 (38)	£14.00–£22.00
🚎 (38)	£14.00–£22.00
⛺ (7)	£14.00–£22.00
🏠 (1)	£300.00–£425.00

45 touring pitches

A gently sloping, grassy site with landscaped hardstandings in the peaceful Tone Valley. An ideal base from which to explore this beautiful unspoilt area. One holiday caravan for hire. Adults only. **directions** M5 Junction 25, A358 round Taunton. B3227 (sp Barnstaple) past Wiveliscombe to Waterrow. Park is 500 yds after The Rock Inn. **open** All year **payment** credit/debit cards, cash, cheques

General 🚿♿🐕🏪📮☀🎯🔌🛒♨📶 Leisure 🏊

WESTON-SUPER-MARE, Somerset Map ref 1D1 — SAT NAV BS22 9UJ

Country View Holiday Park

29 Sand Road, Sand Bay, Weston-super-Mare BS22 9UJ
t (01934) 627595 e info@cvhp.co.uk
w **cvhp.co.uk**

🚐 (90)	£12.00–£22.00
🚎 (90)	£12.00–£22.00
⛺ (30)	£12.00–£22.00

120 touring pitches

Country View is a beautifully kept site surrounded by countryside and just 200 yds from the Sand Bay beach. Heated pool, bar, shop and children's play area. Fantastic new toilet and shower facilities. New and used holiday homes for sale. **directions** Exit 21 of M5 follow signs for Sand Bay along Queensway into Lower Norton Lane and take right into Sand Road. **open** March to January **payment** credit/debit cards, cash, cheques

General 🚿🐕🚻🏪📮☀🎯🔌🛒♨📶 Leisure ▶♿🎣🏊🎾🍽🔍🎮

WESTON-SUPER-MARE, Somerset Map ref 1D1   SAT NAV BS24 0JQ

Dulhorn Farm Holiday Park
Weston Road, Lympsham, Weston Super Mare BS24 0JQ
t (01934) 750298 f (01934) 750913 e dfhp@btconnect.com
w **dulhornfarmholidayfarm.co.uk**

🚐	£10.00–£20.00
🚐 (8)	£10.00–£20.00
⛺ (16)	£8.00–£20.00
🏠 (5)	£148–£398
68 touring pitches	

A family site on a working farm set in the countryside, approximately four miles from the beach, midway between Weston and Burnham. Ideal for touring. Easily accessible from M5. **directions** M5 Junction 22, then North on A38, at next rounabout A370 towards Weston-Super-Mare, 1.5 miles on left. **open** March to October **payment** credit/debit cards, cash, cheques

General 🖥 ⛑ 🐕 🛉 📶 ☼ 🍴 ♨ ⌚ ♿ 🚿 ♨ Leisure ∪ 🏊 ⚓

WINSFORD, Somerset Map ref 1D1   SAT NAV TA24 7JL

Halse Farm Caravan & Tent Park
Halse Farm Caravan & Tent Park, Winsford, Exmoor, Somerset TA24 7JL
t (01643) 851259 f (01643) 851592 e brit@halsefarm.co.uk
w **halsefarm.co.uk** ONLINE MAP

🚐	£12.00–£16.00
🚐 (22)	£12.00–£16.00
⛺ (22)	£12.00–£16.00
44 touring pitches	

Exmoor National Park, small, peaceful, working farm with spectacular views. Paradise for walkers and country lovers. David Bellamy Gold Conservation Award. One mile to Winsford with shop, Thatched pub, Tea gardens. **directions** Signposted from A396. In Winsford turn left and bear left past Royal Oak Inn. One mile up hill. Entrance immediately after cattle grid on left. **open** 19 March to 31 October. **payment** credit/debit cards, cash, cheques

General 🖥 ⛑ 🛉 📶 ☼ 🍴 ♨ ⌚ ♿ 🚿 Leisure ∪ 🏊 ⚓

YEOVIL, Somerset Map ref 2A3   SAT NAV BA22 7JH

Long Hazel Park
High Street, Sparkford, Yeovil, Somerset BA22 7JH
t (01963) 440002 f (01963) 440002 e longhazelpark@hotmail.com
w **sparkford.f9.co.uk/lhi.htm** ONLINE MAP

🚐 (30)	£18.00
🚐 (30)	£18.00
⛺ (20)	£18.00
🏠 (1)	£400–£800
🚐 (1)	£250.00–£500.00
50 touring pitches	

Adult Only Park in village location just off the A303T. Level, landscaped grounds. Hardstandings, full disabled facilities. Lodges for sale/hire. Pub/restaurant, shop, services and bus stop 200m. **directions** From Hazlegrove Services follow brown and white tourist signs into High Street. We are on the left-hand side just past the 30mph speed limit signs. **open** All year **payment** cash, cheques, euros

General ♿ 🖥 ⌀ ⛑ 🛉 📶 ☼ ♨ ⌚ ♿ 🚿 Leisure ▶ ∪ 🚴 🏊

LACOCK, Wiltshire Map ref 2B2   SAT NAV SN15 2LP

Piccadilly Caravan Park Ltd
Folly Lane (West), Lacock, Chippenham SN15 2LP
t (01249) 730260 e piccadillylacock@aol.com

🚐 (39)	£15.00–£17.00
🚐 (39)	£15.00–£17.00
⛺ (4)	£15.00–£17.00
43 touring pitches	

This well-maintained and peaceful site stands in open countryside 0.5 miles from the historic National Trust village of Lacock. **directions** Turn off A350 between Chippenham and Melksham, into Folly Lane West signposted Gastard and with Caravan symbol. **open** April to October **payment** cash, cheques

General 🖥 ⛑ 🛉 📶 ☼ ♨ ⌚ ♿ 🚿 Leisure 🏊 ⚓

WARMINSTER, Wiltshire Map ref 2B2

SAT NAV BA12 7NL

Longleat Caravan Club Site
Longleat, Warminster BA12 7NL
t (01985) 844663 f (01342) 410258 e enquiries@caravanclub.co.uk
w **caravanclub.co.uk**

THE
**CARAVAN
CLUB**

🚐 (165) £14.90–£28.90
🚎 (165) £14.90–£28.90
165 touring pitches

Close to Longleat House, this is the only site where you can hear lions roar at night! Cafés, pubs and restaurants within walking distance. Non-members welcome. **directions** Take A362, signed for Frome, 0.5 miles at roundabout turn left (1st exit) onto Longleat Estate. Through toll booths, follow caravan and camping pennant signs for 1 mile. **open** March to November **payment** credit/debit cards, cash, cheques

General 🔲 📶 🐕 📫 🏪 ☀ 🔌 🔄 🕑 🚻 🆚 **Leisure** ⛰

All Assessed Accommodation

Cornwall

BLACKWATER

Trevarth Holiday Park ★★★★
Holiday, Touring & Camping Park
ROSE AWARD
Blackwater, Truro
TR4 8HR
e trevarth@lineone.net
w trevarth.co.uk

BODMIN

Bodmin Camping and Caravanning Club Site ★★★★
Touring & Camping Park
Old Callywith Road, Bodmin
PL31 2DZ
t (01208) 73834
w campingandcaravanningclub.co.uk/bodmin

Ruthern Valley Holidays ★★★★
Holiday, Touring & Camping Park
Ruthern Bridge, Bodmin
PL30 5LU
t (01208) 831395

BOSSINEY

Ocean Cove Caravan Park
★★★★★ *Holiday Park*
Old Borough Farm, Bossiney, Tintagel
PL34 0AZ
t (01288) 770325
e andy.tweddle@haulfryn.co.uk
w ocean-cove.co.uk

BUDE

Bude Holiday Park (Cranstar Holidays) ★★★
Holiday, Touring & Camping Park
Maer Lane, Bude
EX23 9EE
t (01288) 355955
e enquiries@budeholidaypark.co.uk
w budeholidaypark.co.uk

Budemeadows Touring Park
★★★★★ *Touring Park*
Widemouth Bay, Bude
EX23 0NA
t (01288) 361646
e holiday@budemeadows.com
w budemeadows.com

Penhalt Farm Holiday Park ★★★
Touring & Camping Park
Poundstock, Bude
EX23 0DG
t (01288) 361210
e denandjennie@penhaltfarm.fsnet.co.uk
w penhaltfarm.co.uk

Sandymouth Holiday Park
★★★★★ *Holiday & Touring Park*
ROSE AWARD
Sandymouth Holiday Park, Stibb, Bude
EX23 9HW
t (01288) 352563
e reception@sandymouthbay.co.uk
w sandymouthbay.co.uk

Upper Lynstone Caravan Park
★★★★
Holiday, Touring & Camping Park
Lynstone Road, Bude
EX23 0LP
t (01288) 352017
e reception@upperlynstone.co.uk
w upperlynstone.co.uk

Wooda Farm Holiday Park
★★★★★ *Holiday & Touring Park*
Poughill, Bude, Cornwall
EX23 9HJ
t (01288) 352069
e enquiries@wooda.co.uk
w wooda.co.uk

CAMELFORD

Juliots Well Holiday Park ★★★
Holiday, Touring & Camping Park
Camelford
PL32 9RF
t (01840) 213302
e juliotswell@breaksincornwall.com
w juliotswell.com

Lanteglos Hotel & Villas Ltd
★★★★ *Holiday Village*
Camelford, Camelford
PL32 9RF
t (01840) 213551

CARDINHAM

Gwel-an-nans Farm ★★★★
Touring & Camping Park
Little Downs, Cardinham, Bodmin
PL30 4EF
e info@gwelannans.co.uk

CARNON DOWNS

Carnon Downs Caravan & Camping Park ★★★★★
Touring & Camping Park
Carnon Downs, Truro
TR3 6JJ
t (01872) 862283
e info@carnon-downs-caravanpark.co.uk
w carnon-downs-caravanpark.co.uk

CHACEWATER

Chacewater Park ★★★★
Touring & Camping Park
Cox Hill, Chacewater, Truro
TR4 8LY
t (01209) 820762
e enquiries@chacewaterpark.co.uk
w chacewaterpark.co.uk

CONNOR DOWNS

Higher Trevaskis Park ★★★★
Touring & Camping Park
Gwinear Road, Connor Downs, Hayle
TR27 5JQ
t (01209) 831736
w visitcornwall.com/site/places-to-stay/higher-trevaskis-park-p120603

CRACKINGTON HAVEN

Hentervene ★★★
Holiday, Touring & Camping Park
Crackington Haven, Nr Boscastle, Bude
EX23 0LF
t (01840) 230365
e contact@hentervene.co.uk
w hentervene.co.uk

DOBWALLS

Hoburne Doublebois ★★★★★
Holiday Park
Dobwalls, Liskeard
PL14 6LD
t (01579) 320049
e enquiries@hoburne.com
w hoburne.com

DOUBLEBOIS

ine Green Caravan Park ★★★★
Touring & Camping Park
oublebois, Dobwalls, Liskeard
L14 6LE
t (01579) 320183
e mary.ruhleman@btinternet.com
w pinegreenpark.co.uk

FALMOUTH

ennance Mill Farm ★★★
oliday & Camping Park
laenporth, Falmouth
R11 5HJ
t (01326) 317431
e pennancemill@amserve.com
w pennancemill.co.uk

FOWEY

**enhale Caravan & Camping Park
★★**
oliday, Touring & Camping Park
owey
L23 1JU
t (01726) 833425
e info@penhale-fowey.co.uk
w penhale-fowey.co.uk

**enmarlam Caravan & Camping
ark ★★★★**
Touring & Camping Park
odinnick By Fowey, Fowey
L23 1LZ
t (01726) 870088
e info@penmarlampark.co.uk
w penmarlampark.co.uk

GOONHAVERN

**enrose Farm Touring Park
★★★**
oliday, Touring & Camping Park
enrose Farm Touring Park,
oonhavern, Truro
R4 9QF
t (01872) 573185

erran Springs Holiday Park
oliday, Touring & Camping Park
oonhavern, Truro
R4 9QG
t (01872) 540568
e info@perransprings.co.uk
w perransprings.co.uk

HAYLE

tlantic Coast Holiday Park
oliday, Touring & Camping Park
3 Upton Towans, Hayle
R27 5BL
t (01736) 752071
e enquiries@atlanticcoastpark.co.uk
w atlanticcoastpark.co.uk

eachside Holiday Park ★★★★
oliday, Touring & Camping Park
hillack, Hayle
R27 5AW
t (01736) 753080
e enquiry@beachside.demon.co.uk
w beachside.co.uk

**hurchtown Farm Caravan and
amping ★★★★**
ouring & Camping Park
withian, Hayle
R27 5BX
t (01736) 753219
e caravanning@churchtownfarmg
withian.fsnet.co.uk
w churchtownfarm.org.uk

**aven Riviere Sands Holiday Park
★★★ *Holiday Park* ROSE AWARD**
iviere Towans, Hayle
R27 5AX
t (01736) 752132
e carla.tarpey@bourne-leisure.co.uk
w havenholidays.com/rivieresands

St Ives Bay Holiday Park ★★★★
Holiday, Touring & Camping Park
73 Loggans Road, Upton Towans,
Hayle
TR27 5BH
t (01736) 752274
e stivesbay@btconnect.com
w stivesbay.co.uk

HELSTON

**Poldown Camping & Caravan
Park ★★★★**
Holiday, Touring & Camping Park
Carleen, Breage, Helston
TR13 9NN
t (01326) 574560
e stay@poldown.co.uk
w poldown.co.uk

Sea Acres Holiday Park ★★★★
Holiday Park ROSE AWARD
Kennack Sands
TR12 7LT
t 0871 641 0191
e enquiries@parkdeanholidays.co.
uk
w parkdeanholidays.co.uk/?e=1227

Seaview Holiday Park ★★★
Holiday Park
Gwendreath, Ruan Minor, Helston
TR12 7LZ
t (01326) 290635
e reception@seaviewcaravanpark.
com
w seaviewcaravanpark.com

HOLYWELL BAY

The Meadow ★★★
Holiday, Touring & Camping Park
The Meadow, Holywell Bay,
Newquay
TR8 5PP
t (01872) 572752
w holywellbeachholidays.co.uk

ILLOGAN

Portreath Camping Barn
Bunkhouse
Nance Farm, Illogan, Redruth
TR16 4QX
t (01209) 842244
e mary.alway@btinternet.com

KILKHAMPTON

Penstowe Park Holiday Village
★★★★ *Holiday Village*
Penstowe Holiday Village,
Kilkhampton, Bude
EX23 9QY
t (01288) 321354
e enquiries@penstoweholidays.co.uk
w penstoweholidays.co.uk

LAND'S END

**Cardinney Caravan & Camping
Park ★★★★**
Touring & Camping Park
Near Crows-an-Wra, St Buryan,
Penzance
TR19 6HX
t (01736) 810880
e cardinney@btinternet.com
w cardinney-camping-park.co.uk

LANDRAKE

**Dolbeare Caravan & Camping
Park ★★★★★**
Touring & Camping Park
Landrake, Saltash
PL12 5AF
t (01752) 851332
e reception@dolbeare.co.uk
w dolbeare.co.uk

LANIVET

Kernow Caravan Park ★★★
Holiday Park
Clann Lane, Lanivet, Bodmin
PL30 5HD
t (01208) 831343

LOOE

Looe Bay Holiday Park ★★★★
Holiday Park ROSE AWARD
Looe Bay Holiday Park, St Martins,
Looe
PL13 1NX
t 0870 444 7774
e bookings@weststarholidays.co.uk
w weststarholidays.co.uk/ic

Seaview Holiday Village ★★★★
Holiday Park
Polperro, Looe
PL13 2JE
t (01503) 272335
e reception@seaviewholidayvillage.
co.uk
w seaviewholidayvillage.co.uk

Tencreek Hoilday Park ★★★★
Holiday, Touring & Camping Park
Polperro Road, Looe
PL13 2JR
t (01503) 262447
e reception@tencreek.co.uk
w dolphinholidays.co.uk

**Tregoad Park Quality Family
Touring Site ★★★★**
Holiday, Touring & Camping Park
St Martins, Looe
PL13 1PB
t (01503) 262718
e info@tregoadpark.co.uk
w tregoadpark.co.uk

LUXULYAN

Croft Farm Holiday Park ★★★★
Holiday, Touring & Camping Park
Luxulyan, Bodmin, Cornwall
PL30 5EQ
t (01726) 850228
e lynpick@ukonline.co.uk
w croftfarm.co.uk

MARAZION

Mounts Bay Caravan Park
★★★★ *Holiday Park*
ROSE AWARD
Green Lane, Marazion, Penzance
TR17 0HQ
t (01736) 710307
e reception@mountsbay-carav
anpark.co.uk
w mountsbay-caravanpark.co.uk

Wayfarers Caravan Park ★★★★
Holiday, Touring & Camping Park
Relubbus Lane, St Hilary, Penzance
TR20 9EF
t (01736) 763326
e elaine@wayfarerspark.co.uk
w wayfarerspark.co.uk

MAWGAN PORTH

Marver Holiday Park ★★
Holiday, Touring & Camping Park
Marver Chalets, Mawgan Porth,
Newquay
TR8 4BB
t (01637) 860493
e familyholidays@aol.com
w marverholidaypark.co.uk

**Sun Haven Valley Country
Holiday Park ★★★★★**
Holiday, Touring & Camping Park
ROSE AWARD
Mawgan Porth, Near Padstow
TR8 4BQ
t (01637) 860373
e visitcornwall@sunhavenvalley.
com
w sunhavenvalley.com

MEVAGISSEY

Seaview International ★★★★★
Holiday, Touring & Camping Park
ROSE AWARD
Boswinger, Gorran, St Austell
PL26 6LL
t (01726) 843425
e holidays@seaviewinternational.
com
w seaviewinternational.com

MULLION

Mullion Holiday Park ★★★★
Holiday, Touring & Camping Park
ROSE AWARD
Ruan Minor, Helston
TR12 7LJ
t 0870 444 5344

NANCLEDRA

Higher Chellew ★★★★
Touring & Camping Park
Nancledra, Penzance
TR20 8BD
t (01736) 364532
e higherchellew@btinternet.com
w higherchellewcamping.co.uk

NEWQUAY

Crantock Beach Holiday Park
★★★★ *Holiday Park* ROSE AWARD
Crantock, Newquay
TR8 5RH
t 0871 641 0191
e enquiries@parkdeanholidays.co.
uk
w parkdeanholidays.co.uk/?e=1227

Hendra Holiday Park ★★★★★
Holiday, Touring & Camping Park
ROSE AWARD
Hendra Holiday Park, Lane,
Newquay
TR8 4NY
t (01637) 875778
e enquiries@hendra-holidays.com
w hendra-holidays.com

Holywell Bay Holiday Park
★★★★
Holiday, Touring & Camping Park
ROSE AWARD
Holywell Bay, Newquay
TR8 5PR
t 0871 641 0191
e enquiries@parkdeanholidays.co.
uk
w parkdeanholidays.co.uk/?e=1227

Mawgan Porth Holiday Park
★★★★★ *Holiday Park*
Mawgan Porth, Newquay
TR8 4BD
t (01637) 860322
e mawganporth@btconnect.com
w mawganporth.co.uk

Nancolleth Caravan Gardens
★★★★ *Holiday Park*
Summercourt, Newquay
TR8 4PN
t (01872) 510236
e nancolleth@summercourt.
freeserve.co.uk
w nancolleth.co.uk

Newperran Holiday Park ★★★★★
Holiday Park ROSE AWARD
Rejerrah, Newquay
TR8 5QJ
t (01872) 572407
e holidays@newperran.co.uk
w newperran.co.uk

Newquay Holiday Park ★★★★
Holiday Park ROSE AWARD
Newquay
TR8 4HS
t 0871 641 0191
e enquiries@parkdeanholidays.co.
uk
w parkdeanholidays.co.uk/e=1227

Porth Beach Tourist Park ★★★★
Holiday, Touring & Camping Park
ROSE AWARD
Porth, Newquay
TR7 3NH
t (01637) 876531
e info@porthbeach.co.uk
w porthbeach.co.uk

Riverside Holiday Park ★★★★
Holiday, Touring & Camping Park
Lane, Newquay
TR8 4PE
t (01637) 873617
e info@riversideholidaypark.co.uk
w riversideholidaypark.co.uk

Smugglers Haven ★★★
Holiday, Touring & Camping Park
Trevelgue Road, Porth, Newquay,
Cornwall
TR8 4AS

Trekenning Tourist Park ★★★★
Holiday, Touring & Camping Park
Trekenning, Newquay
TR8 4JF
t (01637) 880462
e holidays@trekenning.co.uk
w trekenning.co.uk

Treloy Touring Park ★★★★
Touring & Camping Park
Newquay
TR8 4JN
t (01637) 872063
e treloy.tp@btconnect.com
w treloy.co.uk

Trenance Holiday Park ★★★★
Holiday, Touring & Camping Park
Edgcumbe Avenue, Newquay
TR7 2JY
t (01637) 873447
e enquiries@trenanceholidaypark.
co.uk
w trenanceholidaypark.co.uk

Trethiggey Touring Park ★★★★
Holiday, Touring & Camping Park
ROSE AWARD
Quintrell Downs, Newquay
TR8 4QR
t (01637) 877672
e enquiries@trethiggey.co.uk
w trethiggey.co.uk

Trevella Caravan & Camping Park
★★★★★ *Holiday Park*
ROSE AWARD
Crantock, Newquay
TR8 5EW
t (01637) 830308
e holidays@trevella.co.uk
w trevella.co.uk

Trevornick Holiday Park ★★★★★
Holiday Park
Holywell Bay, Newquay, Cornwall
TR8 5PW
t (01637) 830531
e info@trevornick.co.uk
w trevornick.co.uk

PADSTOW

**Carnevas Farm Holiday Park
(Camping)** ★★★★
Holiday, Touring & Camping Park
ROSE AWARD
Carnevas Farm, St Merryn, Padstow
PL28 8PN
t (01841) 520230
e carnevascampsite@aol.com
w carnevasholidaypark.co.uk

The Laurels ★★★★
Touring & Camping Park
Padstow Road, Whitecross,
Wadebridge, Wadebridge
PL27 7JQ
t (01209) 313474
e jamierielly@btconnect.com
w thelaurelsholidaypark.co.uk

**Mother Ivey's Bay Caravan Park
(Camping)** ★★★★★
Holiday, Touring & Camping Park
ROSE AWARD
Mother Ivey's Bay Caravan Park,
Trevose Head, Padstow
PL28 8SL
t (01841) 520990
e info@motheriveysbay.com
w motheriveysbay.com

Padstow Touring Park ★★★★
Touring & Camping Park
Padstow, Cornwall
PL28 8LE
t (01841) 532061
e mail@padstowtouringpark.co.uk
w padstowtouringpark.co.uk

PAR

Par Sands Holiday Park ★★★★
Holiday Park ROSE AWARD
Par Beach, Par
PL24 2AS
t (01726) 812868
e holidays@parsands.co.uk
w parsands.co.uk

PENTEWAN

Pentewan Sands Holiday Park
★★★★
Holiday, Touring & Camping Park
ROSE AWARD
Mevagissey, St Austell
PL26 6BT
t (01726) 843485
e info@pentewan.co.uk
w pentewan.co.uk

PENZANCE

Tower Park Caravans & Camping
★★★★
Holiday, Touring & Camping Park
Tower Park Caravans & Camping, St
Buryan, Penzance, Cornwall
TR19 6BZ
t (01736) 810286
e enquiries@towerparkcamping.co.
uk
w towerparkcamping.co.uk

PERRANPORTH

Haven Perran Sands Holiday Park
★★★★
Holiday, Touring & Camping Park
ROSE AWARD
Perran Sands Holiday Park,
Perranporth
TR6 0AQ
t 0870 405 0144
e lisa.spickett@bourne-leisure.co.uk
w perransands-park.co.uk

POLGOOTH

**St Margarets Park Holiday
Bungalows** ★★★★★ *Holiday Park*
Tregongeeves Lane, Polgooth, St
Austell
PL26 7AX
t (01726) 74283
e reception@stmargaretsholidays.
co.uk
w stmargaretsholidays.co.uk

POLRUAN-BY-FOWEY

**Polruan Holidays Camping &
Caravanning** ★★★★
Holiday, Touring & Camping Park
Polruan-by-Fowey, Fowey
PL23 1QH
t (01726) 870263
e polholiday@aol.com
w polruanholidays.co.uk

POLZEATH

Polzeath Beach Holiday Park
★★★★ *Holiday Park*
Trenant Nook, Polzeath, Wadebridge
PL27 6ST
t (01208) 863320
e info@polzeathbeachholidaypark.
com
w polzeathbeachholidaypark.com

Valley Caravan Park ★★
Holiday, Touring & Camping Park
Polzeath, Wadebridge
PL27 6SS
t (01208) 862391
e martin@valleycaravanpark.co.uk
w valleycaravanpark.co.uk

PORTH

Trevelgue Holiday Park ★★★
Holiday, Touring & Camping Park
Porth, Newquay
TR8 4AS
t (01637) 870493
e stuart.cranstar@btconnect.com
w trevelgue.co.uk

PORTHTOWAN

Porthtowan Tourist Park ★★★★
Touring & Camping Park
Mile Hill, Porthtowan, Truro,
Cornwall
TR4 8TY
t (01209) 890256
e admin@porthtowantouristpark.co.
uk
w porthtowantouristpark.co.uk

PORTREATH

Cambrose Touring Park ★★★
Touring & Camping Park
Portreath Road, Redruth
TR16 4HT
t (01209) 890747
e cambrosetouringpark@supanet.
com
w cambrosetouringpark.co.uk

Gwel an Mor Luxury Lodges
★★★★★ *Village*
Tregea Hill, Portreath, Redruth
TR16 4PE
t (01209) 842354
e enquiries@gwelanmor.com
w gwelanmor.com

Tehidy Holiday Park ★★★★
Holiday, Touring & Camping Park
Harris Mill, Near Portreath, Cornwall
TR16 4JQ
t (01209) 216489
e holiday@tehidy.co.uk
w tehidy.co.uk

PRAA SANDS

The Old Farm ★★★★
Holiday, Touring & Camping Park
Lower Pentreath Caravan &
Campsite, Lower Pentreath,
Penzance
TR20 9TL
t (01736) 763221
e info@theoldfarmpraasands.co.uk
w theoldfarmpraasands.co.uk

REDRUTH

Lanyon Holiday Park ★★★★
Holiday, Touring & Camping Park
Loscombe Lane, Four Lanes,
Redruth
TR16 6LP
t (01209) 313474
e info@lanyonholidaypark.co.uk
w lanyonholidaypark.co.uk

RELUBBUS

River Valley Country Park
★★★★★ *Holiday Park*
Relubbus, Penzance
TR20 9ER
t (01736) 763398
e rivervalley@surfbay.dircon.co.uk
w surfbayholidays.co.uk

ROSUDGEON

Kenneggy Cove Holiday Park
★★★★
Holiday, Touring & Camping Park
ROSE AWARD
Higher Kenneggy, Rosudgeon,
Penzance
TR20 9AU
t (01736) 763453
e enquiries@kenneggycove.co.uk
w kenneggycove.co.uk

RUAN MINOR

Silver Sands Holiday Park ★★★★
Holiday, Touring & Camping Park
Gwendreath, Kennack Sands,
Helston
TR12 7LZ
t (01326) 290631
e enquiries@silversandsholidaypark.
co.uk
w silversandsholidaypark.co.uk

SALTASH

St Mellion International Resort
★★★★★ *Holiday Village*
St Mellion, Saltash, Cornwall
PL12 6SD

ST AGNES

**Beacon Cottage Farm Touring
Park** ★★★★
Touring & Camping Park
Beacon Drive, St Agnes
TR5 0NU
t (01872) 552347
e beaconcottagefarm@lineone.net
w beaconcottagefarmholidays.co.uk
📷

ST AUSTELL

Carlyon Bay Caravan & Camping
★★★★★ *Touring & Camping Park*
Cypress Avenue, Carlyon Bay, St
Austell
PL25 3RE
t (01726) 812735
e holidays@carlyonbay.net
w carlyonbay.net

River Valley Holiday Park
★★★★★
Holiday, Touring & Camping Park
Pentewan Road, St Austell
PL26 7AP
t (01726) 73533
e rivervalley@tesco.net
w cornwall-holidays.co.uk

Sun Valley Holiday Park ★★★★★
Holiday, Touring & Camping Park
ROSE AWARD
Pentewan road, St Austell
PL26 6DJ
t (01726) 843266
e reception@sunvalleyholidays.co.
uk
w sunvalleyholidays.co.uk

**Trencreek Farm Country Holiday
Park** ★★★★
Holiday, Touring & Camping Park
Hewaswater, St Austell
PL26 7JG
t (01726) 882540
e reception@trencreek.co.uk
w surfbayholidays.co.uk

ST BURYAN

**Sennen Cove Camping and
Caravanning Club Site** ★★★★
Touring & Camping Park
Higher Tregiffian Farm, St Buryan,
Penzance
TR19 6JB
t (01736) 871588
w campingandcaravanningclub.co.
uk/sennencove

ST EWE

**Heligan Woods Camping &
Caravan Park** ★★★★★
Holiday, Touring & Camping Park
ROSE AWARD
Mevagissey
PL26 6BT
t (01726) 843485
e info@pentewan.co.uk
w pentewan.co.uk

ST GENNYS

**Bude Camping and Caravanning
Club Site** ★★★★
Touring & Camping Park
St Gennys, Bude
EX23 0BG
t (01840) 230650
w campingandcaravanningclub.co.
uk/bude

ST IVES

Ayr Holiday Park ★★★★
Holiday, Touring & Camping Park
ROSE AWARD
Higher Ayr, St Ives
TR26 1EJ
t (01736) 795855
e recept@ayrholidaypark.co.uk
w ayrholidaypark.co.uk

Little Trevarrack Holiday Park
★★★★ *Touring & Camping Park*
Laity Lane, Carbis Bay, St Ives
TR26 3HW
t (01736) 797580
e info@littletrevarrack.co.uk
w littletrevarrack.co.uk

olmanter Touring Park ★★★★★
ouring & Camping Park
alsetown, St Ives
R26 3LX
(01736) 795640
reception@polmanter.co.uk
w polmanter.co.uk

revalgan Touring Park ★★★★
ouring & Camping Park
t Ives
R26 3BJ
(01736) 792048
recept@trevalgantouringpark.co.
uk
w trevalgantouringpark.co.uk

ST JUST-IN-PENWITH

oselands Caravan Park ★★★★
oliday, Touring & Camping Park
owran, St Just, Lands End
R19 7RS
(01736) 788571
camping@roseland84.freeserve.
co.uk
w roselands.co.uk

ST JUST IN ROSELAND

rethem Mill Touring Park
★★★★ *Touring & Camping Park*
: Just in Roseland, Nr St Mawes,
ruro, Cornwall
R2 5JF
(01872) 580504
reception@trethem.com
w trethem.com

ST MERRYN

rethias Farm Caravan Park ★★★
ouring Park
rethias, St Merryn, Padstow
_28 8PL
(01841) 520323

revean Farm Caravan &
amping park ★★★★
oliday, Touring & Camping Park
: Merryn, Padstow
_28 8PR
(01841) 520772
trevean.info@virgin.net

ST MINVER

inham Farm Caravan and
amping Park ★★★★
oliday, Touring & Camping Park
t Minver, Wadebridge
_27 6RH
(01208) 812878
info@dinhamfarm.co.uk
w dinhamfarm.co.uk

ittle Dinham Woodland Caravan
ark ★★★★ *Holiday Park*
: Minver, Nr Rock, Wadebridge
L27 6RH
(01208) 812538
littledinham@hotmail.com
w littledinham.co.uk

t Minver Holiday Park ★★★★
oliday, Touring & Camping Park
OSE AWARD
t Minver, Wadebridge
L27 6RR
0871 641 0191
enquiries@parkdeanholidays.co.
uk
w parkdeanholidays.co.uk/?e=1227

ST TUDY

lengar Manor Country Park
★★★★ *Holiday Park*
t Tudy, Bodmin
°L30 3PL
(01208) 850382
holidays@hengarmanor.co.uk
w hengarmanor.co.uk

Michaelstow Manor Holiday Park
★★★★ *Holiday Park*
Michaelstow, St Tudy, Bodmin
L30 3PB
(01208) 850244
michaelstow@eclipse.co.uk
w michaelstow-holidays.co.uk

TINTAGEL

Trewethett Farm Caravan Club
Site ★★★★★
Touring & Camping Park
Trethevy, Tintagel
PL34 0BQ
t (01840) 770222
e uksitesbookingservice@carav
anclub.co.uk
w caravanclub.co.uk

TREGURRIAN

Tregurrian Camping and
Caravanning Club Site ★★★★
Touring & Camping Park
Tregurrian, Newquay
TR8 4AE
t (01637) 860448
w campingandcaravanningclub.co.
uk/tregurrian

TRURO

Killiwerris Touring Park
Touring Park
Killiwerris, Penstraze, Truro, Cornwall
TR4 8PF
t 01872 561356
e killiwerris@aol.com
w killiwerris.co.uk

Summer Valley Touring Park
★★★★ *Touring Park*
Shortlanesend, Truro
TR4 9DW
t (01872) 277878
e res@summervalley.co.uk
w summervalley.co.uk

VERYAN

Veryan Camping and Caravanning
Club Site ★★★★
Touring & Camping Park
Tretheake Manor Caravan Park,
Veryan, Truro
TR2 5PP
t (01872) 501658
w campingandcaravanningclub.co.
uk/veryan

WADEBRIDGE

Little Bodieve Holiday Park
(Camping) ★★★★
Holiday, Touring & Camping Park
Bodieve Road, Wadebridge
PL27 6EG
t (01208) 812323
e berry@littlebodieveholidaypark.
fsnet.co.uk
w littlebodieve.co.uk

WATERGATE BAY NEWQUAY

Watergate Bay Touring Park
★★★★
Holiday, Touring & Camping Park
Tregurrian, Newquay, Cornwall
TR8 4AD
t (01637) 860387
e email@watergatebaytouringpark.
co.uk
w watergatebaytouringpark.co.uk

WHITE CROSS

White Acres Country Park
★★★★★ *Holiday Park*
ROSE AWARD
Whitecross, Newquay
TR8 4LW
t 0871 641 0191
e enquiries@parkdeanholidays.co.
uk
w parkdeanholidays.co.uk

Isles of Scilly

ISLES OF SCILLY

St. Martin's Campsite ★★★★
Camping Park
Middle Town, Stmartins
TR25 0QN
t (01720) 422888
e bmgillett@btinternet.com
w stmartinscampsite.co.uk

Troytown Farm Campsite ★★★
Camping Park
Troytown Farm, St Agnes, Isles of
Scilly
TR22 0PL
t (01720) 422360
e enquiries@troytown.co.uk
w troytown.co.uk

Devon

ASHBURTON

Parkers Farm Holiday Park
★★★★
Holiday, Touring & Camping Park
Higher Mead Farm, Ashburton
TQ13 7LJ
t (01364) 654869
e parkersfarm@btconnect.com
w parkersfarm.co.uk

Parkers Farm Park ★★★★
Holiday Park
Parkers Farm - Self Catering & Park,
The Rockery, Ashburton
TQ13 7LH
t (01364) 653008
e parkerscottages@btconnect.com
w parkersfarm.co.uk

River Dart Adventures ★★★★
Touring & Camping Park
Holne Park, Ashburton, Newton
Abbot
TQ13 7NP
t (01364) 652511
e enquires@riverdart.co.uk
w riverdart.co.uk

AXMINSTER

Andrewshayes Caravan Park
★★★★ *Holiday Park*
Dalwood, Axminster
EX13 7DY
t (01404) 831225
e enquiries@andrewshayes.co.uk
w andrewshayes.co.uk

Hunters Moon Country Estate
★★★★
Holiday, Touring & Camping Park
Hawkchurch, Axminster
EX13 5UL
t (01297) 678402
w ukparks.co.uk/huntersmoon

BARNSTAPLE

Kentisbury Grange ★★★★
Holiday, Touring & Camping Park
Kentisbury, Barnstaple
EX31 4NL
t (01271) 883454
e info@kentisburygrange.co.uk
w kentisburygrange.co.uk

BERRY HEAD

Landscove Holiday Village ★★★
Holiday Park
Gillard Road, Brixham
TQ5 9EP
t 0870 442 9750
e bookings@landscove.biz
w southdevonholidays.biz

BERRYNARBOR

Sandaway Beach Holiday Park
★★★★ *Holiday Park* **ROSE AWARD**
Berrynarbor, Ilfracombe
EX34 9ST
t (01271) 866766
e stay@johnfowlerholidays.com
w johnfowlerholidays.com

BIDEFORD

Bideford Bay Holiday Park ★★★★
Holiday Park **ROSE AWARD**
Bucks Cross, Bideford
EX39 5DU
t 0871 664 9707
e holidaysales.bidefordbay@park-
resorts.com
w park-resorts.com

BOVISAND

Bovisand Lodge Estate Ltd
★★★★ *Holiday Park* **ROSE AWARD**
Bovisand Lodge, Bovisand,
Plymouth
PL9 0AA
t (01752) 403554
e stay@bovisand.com
w bovisand.com

BRATTON CLOVELLY

South Breazle Holidays ★★★★
Holiday, Touring & Camping Park
South Breazle Holidays, Bratton
Clovelly
EX20 4JS
t (01837) 871752
e louise@southbreazleholidays.co.
uk
w southbreazleholidays.co.uk

BRAUNTON

Lobb Fields Caravan and
Camping Park ★★★★
Touring & Camping Park
West Meadow Road, Braunton
EX33 1HG
t (01271) 812090
e info@lobbfields.com
w lobbfields.com

BRIDESTOWE

Fox & Hounds *Camping Barn*
Fox & Hounds Hotel, Bridestowe,
Okehampton
EX20 4HF
t (01822) 820206
e info@foxandhoundshotel.com
w foxandhoundshotel.com

BRIXHAM

Brixham Holiday Park ★★★★
Holiday Park
Fishcombe Road, Brixham
TQ5 8RB
t (01803) 853324
e enquiries@brixhamholpk.fsnet.co.
uk
w brixhamholidaypark.co.uk

Galmpton Touring Park ★★★★
Touring & Camping Park
Greenway Road, Galmpton, Brixham
TQ5 0EP
t (01803) 842066
e galmptontouringpark@hotmail.
com
w galmptontouringpark.co.uk

Hillhead Caravan Club Site
★★★★★ *Touring & Camping Park*
Hillhead, Brixham
TQ5 0HH
t (01803) 853204
w caravanclub.co.uk

Riviera Bay Holiday Centre
★★★★ *Holiday Park*
Mudstone Lane, Brixham
TQ5 9EJ
t (01803) 856335
e info@rivierabay.biz
w rivierabay.biz

CHUDLEIGH

Finlake Holiday Park ★★★★★
Holiday Park
Chudleigh, Newton Abbot
TQ13 0EJ
t (01626) 853833
e finlake@haulfryn.co.uk
w finlake.co.uk

Holmans Wood Holiday Park
★★★★
Holiday, Touring & Camping Park
Harcombe Cross, Chudleigh,
Newton Abbot
TQ13 0DZ
t (01626) 853785
e enquiries@holmanswood.co.uk
w holmanswood.co.uk

COMBE MARTIN

Newberry Valley Park ★★★★
Touring & Camping Park
Newberry Farm, Woodlands,
Ilfracombe
EX34 0AT
t   (01271) 882334
e   enq@newberrycampsite.co.uk
w newberrycampsite.co.uk

Stowford Farm Meadows ★★★★
Touring & Camping Park
Combe Martin, Ilfracombe
EX34 0PW
t   (01271) 882476
e   enquiries@stowford.co.uk
w stowford.co.uk

CROCKERNWELL

Barley Camping Caravan Meadow Park ★★★★
Touring & Camping Park
Crockernwell, Exeter, Devon
EX6 6NR

CROYDE

Croyde Bay Holiday Village (Unison) ★★★★ *Holiday Village*
Croyde, Braunton
EX33 1QB
t   (01271) 890890
w croydeunison.co.uk

CROYDE BAY

Ruda Holiday Park ★★★★
Holiday, Touring & Camping Park
ROSE AWARD
Croyde Bay, Braunton
EX33 1NY
t   0871 641 0410
e   enquiries@parkdeanholidays.co.uk
w parkdeanholidays.co.uk

DAWLISH

Cofton Country Holidays ★★★★
Holiday, Touring & Camping Park
ROSE AWARD
Starcross, Nr Dawlish, Devon
EX6 8RP
t   (01626) 890111
e   info@coftonholidays.co.uk
w coftonholidays.co.uk

Dawlish Sands Holiday Park
★★★★ *Holiday Park*
Warren Road, Dawlish Warren,
Dawlish
EX7 0PG
t   (01626) 862038

**Golden Sands Holiday Park
★★★★**
Holiday, Touring & Camping Park
Week Lane, Dawlish Warren,
Dawlish
EX7 0LZ
t   (01626) 863099
e   info@goldensands.co.uk
w goldensands.co.uk

Lady's Mile Touring and Camping Park ★★★★
Holiday, Touring & Camping Park
ROSE AWARD
Exeter Road, Dawlish
EX7 0LX
t   (01626) 863411
e   info@ladysmile.co.uk
w ladysmile.co.uk

Leadstone Camping ★★★
Touring & Camping Park
Warren Road, Dawlish
EX7 0NG
t   (01626) 864411
e   post@leadstonecamping.co.uk
w leadstonecamping.co.uk

Oakcliff Holiday Park ★★★★
Holiday Park ROSE AWARD
Mount Pleasant Road, Dawlish
Warren, Dawlish
EX7 0ND
t   (01626) 863347
e   info@oakcliff.co.uk
w oakcliff.co.uk

Peppermint Park ★★★★
Holiday, Touring & Camping Park
Warren Road, Dawlish Warren,
Dawlish
EX7 0PQ
t   (01626) 863436
e   info@peppermintpark.co.uk
w peppermintpark.co.uk

**Welcome Family Holiday Park
★★★★** *Holiday Park* ROSE AWARD
Welcome Family Holiday Park,
Dawlish Warren, Dawlish
EX7 0PH
t   08451 65 62 65
e   fun@welcomefamily.co.uk
w welcomefamily.co.uk

DAWLISH WARREN

Hazelwood Park ★★★
Holiday Park
Warren Road, Hazelwood Park,
Dawlish Warren, Dawlish
EX7 0PF
t   (01626) 862955
w hazelwood.co.uk

DREWSTEIGNTON

**Woodland Springs Touring Park
★★★★** *Touring & Camping Park*
Venton, Drewsteignton
EX6 6PG
t   (01647) 231695
e   enquiries@woodlandsprings.co.uk
w woodlandsprings.co.uk

EAST WORLINGTON

**Yeatheridge Farm Caravan Park
★★★★** *Touring & Camping Park*
East Worlington, Crediton
EX17 4TN
t   (01884) 860330

EXMOUTH

**Webbers Caravan & Camping
Park ★★★★★**
Holiday, Touring & Camping Park
Castle Lane, Woodbury, Exeter
EX5 1EA
t   (01395) 232276
e   reception@webberspark.co.uk
w webberspark.co.uk

GREAT TORRINGTON

**Smytham Manor Holiday Park
★★★★** *Holiday & Touring Park*
Little Torrington, Torrington
EX38 8PU
t   (01805) 622110
e   info@smytham.co.uk
w smytham.co.uk

HOLSWORTHY

**Noteworthy Caravan and
Campsite ★★**
Holiday, Touring & Camping Park
Bude Road, Holsworthy
EX22 7JB
t   (01409) 253731
e   enquiries@noteworthy-devon.co.uk
w noteworthy-devon.co.uk

HORN'S CROSS

Steart Farm Touring Park ★★★
Touring & Camping Park
Horns Cross, Bideford
EX39 5DW
t   (01237) 431836
e   steartenquiries@btconnect.com

ILFRACOMBE

Beachside Holiday Park ★★★★★
Holiday Park
33 Beach Road, Hele, Ilfracombe
EX34 9QZ
t   (01271) 863006
e   enquiries@beachsidepark.co.uk
w beachsidepark.co.uk

Hele Valley Holiday Park ★★★★
Holiday, Touring & Camping Park
ROSE AWARD
Hele Bay, Ilfracombe
EX34 9RD
t   (01271) 862460
e   holidays@helevalley.co.uk
w helevalley.co.uk

**Hidden Valley Touring & Camping
Park ★★★★★**
Touring & Camping Park
EXCELLENCE AWARD
West Down, Ilfracombe
EX34 8NU
t   (01271) 813837
e   relax@hiddenvalleypark.com
w hiddenvalleypark.com

Mullacott *Bunkhouse*
Mullacott Farm, Mullacott Cross,
Ilfracombe
EX34 8NA
t   (01271) 866877
e   relax@mullacottfarm.co.uk
w mullacottfarm.co.uk

Mullacott Park ★★★★
Holiday Park ROSE AWARD
Mullacott Cross, Ilfracombe
EX34 8NB
t   (01271) 866212
e   info@mullacottpark.co.uk
w mullacottpark.co.uk

IPPLEPEN

Ross Park ★★★★★
Touring & Camping Park
Moor Road, Ipplepen, Newton
Abbot
TQ12 5TT
t   (01803) 812983
e   enquiries@rossparkcaravanpark.co.uk
w rossparkcaravanpark.co.uk

Woodville Touring Park ★★★★
Touring Park
Totnes Road, Ipplepen, Newton
Abbot
TQ12 5TN
t   (01803) 812240
e   woodvillepark@lineone.net
w caravan-sitefinder.co.uk/sthwest/devon/woodville.html

KENNFORD

**Exeter Racecourse Caravan Club
Site ★★★** *Touring & Camping Park*
Kennford, Exeter
EX6 7XS
t   (01392) 832107
e   enquiries@caravanclub.co.uk
w caravanclub.co.uk

KENTISBEARE

Forest Glade Holiday Park ★★★★
Holiday & Touring Park
ROSE AWARD
Forest Glade, Near Kentisbeare,
Cullompton
EX15 2DT
t   (01404) 841381
e   enquiries@forest-glade.co.uk
w forest-glade.co.uk

KINGSBRIDGE

**Challaborough Bay Holiday Park
★★★★** *Holiday Park* ROSE AWARD
Challaborough Beach, Kingsbridge
TQ7 4HU
t   0871 641 0191
e   enquiries@parkdeanholidays.co.uk
w parkdeanholidays.co.uk

LYNTON

**Channel View Caravan and
Camping Park ★★★★**
Holiday & Touring Park
ROSE AWARD
Manor Farm, Lynton
EX35 6LD
t   (01598) 753349
e   relax@channel-view.co.uk
w channel-view.co.uk

**Lynton Camping and Caravanning
Club Site ★★★**
Touring & Camping Park
Lynton, Lynton
EX35 6JS
t   (01598) 752379
w campingandcaravanningclub.co.uk/lynton

MANATON

Great Houndtor *Camping Barn*
Manaton, Newton Abbot
TQ13 9UW
t   (01647) 221202

MARLDON

Widend Touring Park ★★★★
Holiday, Touring & Camping Park
Totnes Road, Marldon, Paignton
TQ3 1RT
t   (01803) 550116

MODBURY

**Broad Park Caravan Club Site
★★★★** *Touring Park*
Higher East Leigh, Modbury,
Ivybridge
PL21 0SH
t   (01548) 830714
e   enquiries@caravanclub.co.uk
w caravanclub.co.uk

**Camping & Caravanning Club Site
- California Cross ★★★★**
Touring & Camping Park
Modbury, Ivybridge
PL21 0SG
t   (01548) 821297
w campingandcaravanningclub.co.uk

Moor View Touring Park ★★★★
Touring & Camping Park
Modbury, Ivybridge
PL21 0SG
t   (01548) 821485
e   moorview@tinyworld.co.uk
w moorviewtouringpark.co.uk

**Pennymoor Camping & Caravan
Park ★★★★**
Holiday, Touring & Camping Park
Modbury, Ivybridge
PL21 0SB
t   (01548) 830542
w pennymoor-camping.co.uk

MORTEHOE

**Easewell Farm Holiday Park &
Golf Club ★★★**
Holiday, Touring & Camping Park
Mortehoe, Woolacombe, Devon
EX34 7EH
t   (01271) 870343
e   goodtimes@woolacombe.com
w woolacombe.com

**North Morte Farm Caravan &
Camping Park ★★★★**
Holiday, Touring & Camping Park
North Morte Road, Mortehoe,
Woolacombe
EX34 7EG
t   (01271) 870381
e   info@northmortefarm.co.uk
w northmortefarm.co.uk

**Twitchen House Holiday Park
★★★★**
Holiday, Touring & Camping Park
Mortehoe Station Road, Mortehoe,
Devon
EX34 7ES
t   (01271) 870343
e   goodtimes@woolacombe.com
w woolacombe.com

**Warcombe Farm Camping Park
★★★★★** *Touring & Camping Park*
Station Road, Mortehoe, Devon
EX34 7EJ
t   (01271) 870690
e   info@warcombefarm.co.uk
w warcombefarm.co.uk

NEWTON ABBOT

⋯ornafield Touring Park ★★★★★
⋯ouring & Camping Park
⋯wo Mile Oak, Newton Abbot
⋯Q12 6DD
t (01803) 812732
e enquiries@dornafield.com
w dornafield.com

NORTH MOLTON

⋯iverside Caravan Park ★★★★
⋯ouring & Camping Park
⋯Marsh lane, North Molton Road,
⋯outh Molton
⋯X36 3HQ
t (01769) 579269
e relax@exmoorriverside.co.uk
w exmoorriverside.co.uk

OTTERTON

⋯adram Bay Holiday Centre
★★★
⋯oliday, Touring & Camping Park
⋯OSE AWARD
⋯tterton, Budleigh Salterton
⋯X9 7BX
t (01395) 568398
e welcome@ladrambay.co.uk
w ladrambay.co.uk

PAIGNTON

⋯shvale Holiday Park ★★★★
⋯oliday Park
⋯oodrington Road, Paignton
⋯Q4 7JD
t (01803) 843887
e info@beverley-holidays.co.uk
w beverley-holidays.co.uk

⋯everley Holidays ★★★★★
⋯oliday, Touring & Camping Park
⋯oodrington Road, Paignton
⋯Q4 7JE
t (01803) 661971
e info@beverley-holidays.co.uk
w beverley-holidays.co.uk

⋯igher Well Farm Holiday Park
★★★
⋯oliday, Touring & Camping Park
⋯Waddeton Road, Stoke Gabriel,
⋯otnes
⋯Q9 6RN
t (01803) 782289
e higherwell@talk21.com
w higherwellfarmholidaypark.co.uk

⋯oburne Torbay ★★★★
⋯oliday & Touring Park
⋯OSE AWARD
⋯range Road, Paignton
⋯Q4 7JP
t (01803) 558010
e torbay@hoburne.com
w hoburne.com

⋯arine Park Holiday Centre
★★★ *Holiday & Touring Park*
⋯range Road, Paignton
⋯Q4 7JR
t (01803) 843887
e info@beverley-holidays.co.uk
w beverley-holidays.co.uk

⋯aterside Holiday Park ★★★★
⋯oliday Park
⋯hree Beaches, Dartmouth Road,
⋯aignton
⋯Q4 6NS
t (01803) 842400
w watersidepark.co.uk

⋯hitehill Country Park ★★★★
⋯oliday, Touring & Camping Park
⋯toke Road, Paignton
⋯Q4 7PF
t (01803) 782338
e info@whitehill-park.co.uk
w whitehill-park.co.uk

PLYMOUTH

⋯lymouth Sound Caravan Club
⋯ite ★★★★★ *Touring Park*
⋯ovisand Lane, Down Thomas,
⋯lymouth
⋯L9 0AE
t (01752) 862325
w caravanclub.co.uk

POSTBRIDGE

Runnage *Camping Barn*
Runnage Farm, Postbridge,
Yelverton
PL20 6TN
t (01822) 880222
e christine@runnagecampingbarns.
fsnet.co.uk
w runnagecampingbarns.co.uk

ROUSDON

Pinewood Holiday Homes
★★★★★ *Holiday Park*
Sidmouth Road, Rousdon, Lyme
Regis
DT7 3RD
t (01297) 22055
e info@pinewood.uk.net
w pinewood.uk.net

SALCOMBE

Bolberry House Farm Caravan &
Camping ★★★
Holiday, Touring & Camping Park
Bolberry, Malborough, Kingsbridge
TQ7 3DY
t (01548) 561251
e enquiries@bolberryparks.co.uk
w bolberryparks.co.uk

Higher Rew Touring Caravan &
Camping Park ★★★★
Touring & Camping Park
Higher Rew, Malborough,
Kingsbridge
TQ7 3DW
t (01548) 842681
e enquiries@higherrew.co.uk
w higherrew.co.uk

SALCOMBE REGIS

Kings Down Tail Caravan &
Camping Park ★★★★
Touring & Camping Park
Salcombe Regis, Sidmouth, Devon
EX10 0PD
t (01297) 680313 and fax
e info@kingsdowntail.co.uk
w kingsdowntail.co.uk

SANDY BAY

Devon Cliffs Holiday Park
★★★★★ *Holiday & Touring Park*
ROSE AWARD
Sandy Bay, Exmouth
EX8 5BT
t (01395) 226226
e john.ball@bourne-leisure.co.uk
w devoncliffs-park.co.uk

SEATON

Axe Vale Caravan Park ★★★★
Holiday Park
Colyford Road, Seaton
EX12 2DF
t 0800 068816
e info@axevale.co.uk
w axevale.co.uk

SHALDON

Coast View Holiday Park ★★★★
Holiday, Touring & Camping Park
Torquay Road, Shaldon, Teignmouth
TQ14 0BG
t (01626) 872392
e info@coastview.co.uk
w coastview.co.uk

Devon Valley Holiday Village
★★★★ *Holiday Park* **ROSE AWARD**
Coombe Road, Ringmore,
Teignmouth
TQ14 0EY
t 0870 442 9750
e info@devonvalley.biz
w southdevonholidays.biz

SHIRWELL

Brightly Cott Barton ★★★
Touring Park
Brightlycott Barton, shirwell,
Barnstaple
EX31 4JJ
t (01271) 850330
e friend.brightlycott@virgin.net
w brightlycottbarton.co.uk

SIDBURY

Putts Corner Caravan Club Site
★★★★ *Touring Park*
Putts Corner, Sidbury, Sidmouth
EX10 0QQ
t (01404) 42875
w caravanclub.co.uk

SIDMOUTH

Salcombe Regis Camping and
Caravan Park ★★★★★
Holiday, Touring & Camping Park
ROSE AWARD
Salcombe Regis, Sidmouth
EX10 0JH
t (01395) 514303
e info@salcombe-regis.co.uk
w salcombe-regis.co.uk

SLAPTON

Slapton Sands Camping and
Caravanning Club Site ★★★★
Touring & Camping Park
Middlegrounds, Sands Road,
Slapton, Kingsbridge
TQ7 2QW
t (01548) 580538
w campingandcaravanningclub.co.
uk/slaptonsands

STOKE FLEMING

Dartmouth Camping and
Caravanning Club Site ★★★★
Touring & Camping Park
Dartmouth Road, Stoke Fleming,
Dartmouth
TQ6 0RF
t (01803) 770253
w campingandcaravanningclub.co.
uk/dartmouth

TAVISTOCK

Harford Bridge Holiday Park
★★★★
Holiday, Touring & Camping Park
ROSE AWARD
Harford Bridge, Peter Tavy,
Tavistock
PL19 9LS
t (01822) 810349
e enquiry@harfordbridge.co.uk
w harfordbridge.co.uk

Langstone Manor Holiday Park
★★★★
Holiday, Touring & Camping Park
ROSE AWARD
Moortown, Tavistock, Devon
PL19 9JZ
t 01822 613371
e jane@langstonemanor.co.uk
w langstonemanor.co.uk

Tavistock Camping and
Caravanning Club Site ★★★★
Touring & Camping Park
Higher Longford, Moorstop,
Tavistock, Devon
PL19 9LQ
w campingandcaravanningclub.co.
uk/

Woodovis Park ★★★★★
Holiday, Touring & Camping Park
ROSE AWARD
Gulworthy, Tavistock
PL19 8NY
t (01822) 832968
e info@woodovis.com
w woodovis.com

TEIGNGRACE

Twelve Oaks Farm Caravan Park
★★★★ *Touring & Camping Park*
Teigngrace, Newton Abbot
TQ12 6QT
t (01626) 352769
e info@twelveoaksfarm.co.uk
w twelveoaksfarm.co.uk

TORQUAY

TLH Leisure Resort ★★★★
Holiday Village
Derwent Hotel, 22-28 Belgrave
Road, Torquay
TQ2 5HT
t (01803) 400500
e rooms@tlh.co.uk
w tlh.co.uk

Torquay Holiday Park ★★★★
Holiday Park **ROSE AWARD**
Kingskerswell Road, Torquay
TQ2 8JU
t 0871 641 0410
e enquiries@parkdeanholidays.co.
uk
w parkdeanholidays.co.uk/?e=1072

Widdicombe Farm Touring Park
★★★★
Holiday, Touring & Camping Park
Marldon, Paignton
TQ3 1ST
t (01803) 558325
e enquiries@torquaytouring.co.uk
w torquaytouring.co.uk

TOTNES

Broadleigh Farm Park ★★★★
Touring & Camping Park
Coombe House Lane, Stoke Gabriel,
Totnes
TQ9 6PU
t (01803) 782110
e enquiries@broadleighfarm.co.uk
w broadleighfarm.co.uk

Steamer Quay Caravan Club Site
★★★ *Touring Park*
Steamer Quay Road, Totnes
TQ9 5AL
t (01803) 862738
w caravanclub.co.uk

UMBERLEIGH

Umberleigh Camping and
Caravanning Club Site ★★★★
Touring & Camping Park
Over Weir, Umberleigh, Umberleigh
EX37 9DU
t (01769) 560009
w campingandcaravanningclub.co.
uk/umberleigh

WEMBURY

Churchwood Valley Holiday
Cabins ★★★★ *Holiday Park*
Churchwood Valley, Wembury Bay,
Nr Plymouth
PL9 0DZ
t (01752) 862382
e churchwoodvalley@btconnect.
com
w churchwoodvalley.com

WEST DOWN

Brook Lea ★★★★ *Touring Park*
Brook Lea Caravan Club Site, West
Down, Ilfracombe
EX34 8NE
t (01271) 862848
w caravanclub.co.uk

WESTON

Oakdown Touring and Holiday
Caravan Park ★★★★★
Holiday & Touring Park
ROSE AWARD
Gatedown lane, Nr Weston,
Sidmouth
EX10 0PT
t (01297) 680387
e enquiries@oakdown.co.uk
w oakdown.co.uk

WESTWARD HO!

Beachside Holiday Park ★★★★
Holiday Park
Merley Road, Westward Ho!,
Bideford
EX39 1JX
t   0845 601 2541
e   beachside@surfbay.dircon.co.uk
w beachsideholidays.co.uk

Surf Bay Holiday Park ★★★★
Holiday Park **ROSE AWARD**
Golf Links Road, Westward Ho!,
Bideford
EX39 1HD
t   0845 601132
e   surfbayholidaypark@surfbay.
dircon.co.uk
w surfbay.co.uk

WOODBURY

Castle Brake Holiday Park ★★★★
Holiday, Touring & Camping Park
ROSE AWARD
Castle Lane, Woodbury, Exeter
EX5 1HA
t   (01395) 232431
e   reception@castlebrake.co.uk
w castlebrake.co.uk

WOOLACOMBE

Golden Coast Holiday Park
★★★★ *Holiday Park*
Station Road, Woolacombe, Devon
EX34 7HW
t   (01271) 870343
e   goodtimes@woolacombe.com
w woolacombe.com

**Woolacombe Bay Holiday Parks
(Cleavelhouse House)** ★★★★
Holiday, Touring & Camping Park
Woolacombe, Devon
EX34 7HW
t   (01271) 870343
e   goodtimes@woolacombe.com
w woolacombe.com

Woolacombe Bay Holiday Village
★★★★
Holiday, Touring & Camping Park
Sandy Lane, Woolacombe, Devon
EX34 7AH
t   (01271) 870343
e   goodtimes@woolacombe.com
w woolacombe.com

Woolacombe Sands Holiday Park
★★★★
Holiday, Touring & Camping Park
Beach Road, Woolacombe
EX34 7AF
t   (01271) 870569
e   lifesabeach@woolacombe-sands.
co.uk
w woolacombe-sands.co.uk

Dorset

ALDERHOLT

**Hill Cottage Farm Camping and
Caravan Park** ★★★★
Touring & Camping Park
Sandleheath Road, Alderholt,
Fordingbridge
SP6 3EG
t   (01425) 650513
e   hillcottagefarmcaravansite@
supanet.com
w hillcottagefarmcampingandcarav
anpark.co.uk

BERE REGIS

Rowlands Wait Touring Park
★★★ *Touring & Camping Park*
Rye Hill, Bere Regis, Wareham,
Wareham
BH20 7LP
t   (01929) 472727
e   enquiries@rowlandswait.co.uk
w www.rowlandswait.co.uk

BLANDFORD FORUM

The Inside Park ★★★★
Touring & Camping Park
Fairmile Road, Blandford Forum
DT11 9AD
t   (01258) 453719
e   mail@theinsidepark.co.uk
w theinsidepark.co.uk

BOURNEMOUTH

Meadow Bank Holidays ★★★★★
Holiday & Touring Park
ROSE AWARD
Stour Way, Christchurch
BH23 2PQ
t   (01202) 483597
e   enquiries@meadowbank-holidays.
co.uk
w meadowbank-holidays.co.uk

BRIDPORT

**Bingham Grange Touring &
Camping Park** ★★★★
Touring & Camping Park
Binghams Farm, Melplash, Bridport
DT6 3TT
t   (01308) 488234
e   enquiries@binghamsfarm.co.uk
w binghamsfarm.co.uk

Eype House Caravan Park Ltd
★★★
Holiday, Touring & Camping Park
Eype, Bridport
DT6 6AL
t   (01308) 424903
e   enquiries@eypehouse.co.uk
w eypehouse.co.uk

Freshwater Beach Holiday Park
★★★★
Holiday, Touring & Camping Park
Burton Bradstock, Bridport
DT6 4PT
t   (01308) 897317
e   office@freshwaterbeach.co.uk
w freshwaterbeach.co.uk

Golden Cap Holiday Park
★★★★★
Holiday, Touring & Camping Park
ROSE AWARD
Seatown, Chideock, Bridport
DT6 6JX
t   (01308) 422139
e   holidays@wdlh.co.uk
w wdlh.co.uk

Highlands End Holiday Park
★★★★★
Holiday, Touring & Camping Park
ROSE AWARD
Eype, Bridport, Dorset
DT6 6AR
t   (01308) 422139
e   holidays@wdlh.co.uk
w wdlh.co.uk

BURTON BRADSTOCK

Coastal Caravan Park ★★★
Holiday, Touring & Camping Park
Annings Lane, Burton Bradstock,
Bridport
DT6 4QP
t   (01308) 422139
e   coastal@wdlh.co.uk
w wdlh.co.uk

CHARMOUTH

**Charmouth Camping and
Caravanning Club Site** ★★★★★
Touring & Camping Park
Monkton Wyld, Bridport
DT6 6DB
t   (01297) 32965
w campingandcaravanningclub.co.
uk/charmouth

Dolphins River Park ★★★★
Holiday Park
Berne Lane, Charmouth, Bridport
DT6 6RD
t   0800 074 6375
e   info@dolphinsriverpark.co.uk
w dolphinsriverpark.co.uk

Manor Farm Holiday Centre ★★★
Holiday, Touring & Camping Park
The Street, Charmouth, Bridport
DT6 6QL
t   (01297) 560226
e   enq@manorfarmholidaycentre.co.
uk
w manorfarmholidaycentre.co.uk

Newlands Holidays ★★★★★
Holiday, Touring & Camping Park
Newlands Holiday Park, Charmouth,
Bridport
DT6 6RB
t   (01297) 560259
e   enq@newlandsholidays.co.uk
w newlandsholidays.co.uk

Seadown Holiday Park ★★★★★
Holiday, Touring & Camping Park
Bridge Road, Charmouth, Bridport
DT6 6QS
t   (01297) 560154
e   bookings@seadownholidaypark.
co.uk
w seadowncaravanpark.co.uk

**Wood Farm Caravan and
Camping Park** ★★★★★
Holiday, Touring & Camping Park
Charmouth, Bridport
DT6 6BT
t   (01297) 560697
e   holidays@woodfarm.co.uk
w woodfarm.co.uk

CHICKERELL

Bagwell Farm Touring Park
★★★★ *Touring & Camping Park*
Knights in The Bottom, Chickerell,
Weymouth
DT3 4EA
t   (01305) 782575
e   enquiries@bagwellfarm.co.uk
w bagwellfarm.co.uk

CHRISTCHURCH

Harrow Wood Farm Caravan Park
★★★ *Touring & Camping Park*
Poplar Lane, Bransgore, Christchurch
BH23 8JE
t   (01425) 672487
e   harrowwood@caravan-sites.co.uk
w caravan-sites.co.uk/pages/harro
wwood.htm

Hoburne Park ★★★★★
Holiday Park **ROSE AWARD**
Hoburne Lane, Christchurch
BH23 4HU
t   (01425) 273379
e   enquiries@hoburne.com
w hoburne.com

Sandhills Holiday Park ★★★
Holiday Park
Mudeford, Christchurch
BH23 4AL
t   (01425) 274584

CORFE CASTLE

Norden Farm Campsite ★★
Touring & Camping Park
Norden Farm, Corfe Castle
BH20 5DS
t   (01929) 480098
e   nordenfarm@fsmail.net
w nordenfarm.com

DORCHESTER

**Giant's Head Caravan & Camping
Park** ★★ *Touring & Camping Park*
Old Sherborne Road, Dorchester
DT2 7TR
t   (01300) 341242
e   holidays@giantshead.co.uk
w giantshead.co.uk

Morn Gate Caravan Park ★★★★
Holiday Park
Bridport Road, Dorchester
DT2 9DS
t   (01305) 889284
e   morngate@ukonline.co.uk
w morngate.co.uk

HAMWORTHY

Rockley Park Holiday Park
★★★★★
Holiday, Touring & Camping Park
ROSE AWARD
Napier Road, Poole
BH15 4LZ
t   (01202) 679393
e   enquiries@british-holidays.co.uk
w british-holidays.co.uk

HIGHCLIFFE

Cobb's Holiday Park ★★★★
Holiday Park **ROSE AWARD**
32 Gordon Road, Highcliffe-on-Sea,
Christchurch
BH23 5HN
t   (01425) 273301
e   enquiries@cobbsholidaypark.co.
uk
w cobbsholidaypark.co.uk

HOLTON HEATH

Sandford Holiday Park ★★★★
Holiday, Touring & Camping Park
Organford Road, Holton Heath,
Poole
BH16 6JZ
t   0870 444 7774
e   bookings@parkdean.com
w parkdean.com

LYME REGIS

Shrubbery Touring Park ★★★★
Touring & Camping Park
Rousdon, Lyme Regis
DT7 3XW
t   (01297) 442227
e   info@shrubberypark.co.uk
w shrubberypark.co.uk

MORETON

**Moreton Camping and
Caravanning Club Site** ★★★★
Touring & Camping Park
Moreton, Moreton, Dorchester
DT2 8BB
t   (01305) 853801
w campingandcaravanningclub.co.
uk/moreton

OSMINGTON

White Horse Holiday Park ★★★
Holiday Park
Osmington Hill, Osmington,
Weymouth
DT3 6ED
t   (01305) 832164
e   hols@whitehorsepark.co.uk
w whitehorsepark.co.uk

OWERMOIGNE

Sandyholme Holiday Park ★★★★
Holiday, Touring & Camping Park
Moreton Road, Owermoigne,
Dorchester
DT2 8HZ
t   (01305) 852677
e   sandyholme@wdlh.co.uk
w wdlh.co.uk

POOLE

**South Lytchett Manor Caravan &
Camping Park** ★★★★
Holiday, Touring & Camping Park
Dorchester Road, Poole, Dorset
BH16 6JB
t   (01202) 622577
e   info@southlytchettmanor.co.uk
w southlytchettmanor.co.uk

PORTLAND

Cove Holiday Park ★★★★★
Holiday Park
Pennsylvania Road, Portland
DT5 1HU
t   (01305) 821286
e   enquiries@coveholidaypark.co.uk
w coveholidaypark.co.uk

PRESTON

Weymouth Bay Holiday Park
★★★ *Holiday Park*
Preston Road, Preston, Weymouth
DT3 6BQ
t (01305) 832271
w haven.com/weymouthbay

SIXPENNY HANDLEY

**Church Farm Caravan & Camping
Park** ★★★ *Touring & Camping Park*
High Street, Sixpenny Handley,
Salisbury
SP5 5ND
t (01725) 552563
e churchfarmcandcpark@yahoo.co.
uk
w churchfarmcandcpark.co.uk

ST LEONARDS

Back-of-Beyond Touring Park
★★★ *Touring & Camping Park*
Ringwood Road, St Leonards,
Ringwood
BH24 2SB
t (01202) 876968
e melandsuepike@aol.com
w backofbeyondtouringpark.co.uk

Oakdene Forest Park ★★★★
Holiday Park
St Leonards, Ringwood
BH24 2RZ
t (01590) 648331
e holidays@shorefield.co.uk
w shorefield.co.uk

SWANAGE

Haycraft Caravan Club Site
★★★★ *Touring Park*
Haycrafts Lane, Swanage
BH19 3EB
t (01929) 480572
w caravanclub.co.uk

Swanage Bay View Holiday Park
★★★ *Holiday Park*
Panorama Road, Swanage
BH19 2QS
t (01929) 422130
e info@swanagebayviewholida
ypark.co.uk
w swanagebayviewholidaypark.co.
uk

Ulwell Cottage Caravan Park
★★★
Holiday, Touring & Camping Park
Ulwell, Swanage
BH19 3DG
t (01929) 422823
e enq@ulwellcottagepark.co.uk
w ulwellcottagepark.co.uk

Ulwell Farm Caravan Park ★★★
Holiday Park
Ulwell, Swanage
BH19 3DG
t (01929) 422825
e ulwell.farm@virgin.net
w ukparks.co.uk/ulwellfarm

WAREHAM

Birchwood Tourist Park ★★★★
Touring & Camping Park
Bere Road, Coldharbour, Wareham
BH20 7PA
t (01929) 554763
e birchwoodtouristpark@hotmail.
com

The Lookout Holiday Park ★★★★
Holiday, Touring & Camping Park
ROSE AWARD
Corfe Road, Stoborough, Wareham
BH20 5AZ
t (01929) 552546
e enquiries@caravan-sites.co.uk
w caravan-sites.co.uk

**Luckford Wood Farm Caravan &
Camping Park** ★
Touring & Camping Park
Luckford Wood House, East Stoke,
Wareham
BH20 6AW
t (01929) 463098 (07888719002)
e luckfordleisure@hotmail.com
w luckfordleisure.co.uk

Wareham Forest Tourist Park
★★★★ *Touring & Camping Park*
Bere Road, North Trigon, Wareham
BH20 7NZ
t (01929) 551393
e holiday@wareham-forest.co.uk
w wareham-forest.co.uk

WARMWELL

Warmwell Caravan Park ★★★★
Holiday, Touring & Camping Park
Warmwell, Dorchester
DT2 8JD
t (01305) 852313
e stay@warmwellcaravanpark.co.uk
w warmwellcaravanpark.co.uk

Warmwell Leisure Resort ★★★★
Holiday Park **ROSE AWARD**
Warmwell, Dorchester
DT2 8JE
t 0871 641 0191
e enquiries@parkdeanholidays.co.
uk
w parkdeanholidays.co.uk/?e=1072

WEST BAY

West Bay Holiday Park ★★★★
Holiday, Touring & Camping Park
ROSE AWARD
West Bay, Bridport
DT6 4HB
t 0871 641 0191
e enquiries@parkdeanholidays.co.
uk
w parkdeanholidays.co.uk/?e=1072

WEST BEXINGTON

Gorselands Caravan Park ★★★★
Holiday Park
West Bexington Road, West
Bexington
DT2 9DJ
t (01308) 897232
e info@gorselands.co.uk
w gorselands.co.uk

WEST LULWORTH

Durdle Door Holiday Park ★★★
Holiday, Touring & Camping Park
West Lulworth, Wareham
BH20 5PU
t (01929) 400200
e durdle.door@lulworth.com
w lulworth.co.uk

WEYMOUTH

Chesil Beach Holiday Park
★★★★★ *Holiday Park*
ROSE AWARD
Chesil Beach, Portland Road,
Weymouth
DT4 9AG
t (01305) 773233
e info@chesilholidays.co.uk
w chesilholidays.co.uk

Crossways Caravan Club Site
★★★★ *Touring Park*
Crossways, Dorchester
DT2 8BE
t (01305) 852032
w caravanclub.co.uk

East Fleet Farm Touring Park
★★★★ *Touring & Camping Park*
Chickerell, Weymouth
DT3 4DW
t (01305) 785768
e enquiries@eastfleet.co.uk
w eastfleet.co.uk

Littlesea Holiday Park ★★★★★
Holiday, Touring & Camping Park
ROSE AWARD
Lynch Lane, Weymouth
DT4 9DT
t (01305) 774414
e david.bennett@bourne-leisure.co.
uk
w littlesea-park.co.uk

Seaview Holiday Park ★★★★
Holiday, Touring & Camping Park
Preston, Weymouth
DT3 6DZ
t (01305) 833037
w haven.com/seaview

Waterside Holiday Park ★★★★★
Holiday & Touring Park
ROSE AWARD
Bowleaze Coveway, Weymouth
DT3 6PP
t (01305) 833103
e info@watersideholidays.co.uk
w watersideholidays.co.uk

WIMBORNE MINSTER

Merley Court Touring Park
★★★★★ *Touring & Camping Park*
Merley Court, Merley, Wimborne
BH21 3AA
t (01590) 648331
e holidays@shorefield.co.uk
w shorefield.co.uk

Wilksworth Farm Caravan Park
★★★★★ *Touring & Camping Park*
Cranborne Road, Furzehill,
Wimborne
BH21 4HW
t (01202) 885467
e rayandwendy@wilksworthfarmc
aravanpark.co.uk
w wilksworthfarmcaravanpark.co.uk

WOODLANDS

**Verwood, New Forest Camping
and Caravanning Club Site** ★★★
Touring & Camping Park
Sutton Hill Camping Site, Sutton,
Wimborne
BH21 8NQ
t (01202) 822763
w campingandcaravanningclub.co.
uk/verwood

WOOL

Whitemead Caravan Park ★★★★
Touring & Camping Park
East Burton Road, Wool, Wareham
BH20 6HG
t (01929) 462241
e whitemeadcp@aol.com
w whitemeadcaravanpark.co.uk

Gloucestershire

BRISTOL

Baltic Wharf Caravan Club Site
★★★★ *Touring Park*
Cumberland Road, Southville, Bristol
BS1 6XG
t (0117) 926 8030
e enquiries@caravanclub.co.uk
w caravanclub.co.uk

CHELTENHAM

**Cheltenham Racecourse Caravan
Club Site** ★★★ *Touring Park*
Prestbury Park, Evesham Road,
Prestbury, Cheltenham
GL50 4SH
t (01242) 523102
e debby.towers@caravanclub.co.uk
w caravanclub.co.uk

CHRISTCHURCH

**Woodland Caravan and Camping
Site** ★★★ *Touring Park*
Bracelands Drive, Christchurch,
Coleford
GL16 7NN
t (01594) 837258
e fod.site@forestholidays.co.uk
w forestholidays.co.uk

COLEFORD

Braceland Adventure Centre
Bunkhouse
Christchurch, Coleford
GL16 7NP
t (01594) 833820
e alison839@btinternet.com
w bracelandadventurecentre.co.uk

Bracelands Campsite ★★★
Touring & Camping Park
Bracelands Drive, Christchurch,
Coleford
GL16 7NN
t 0845 130 8224
w forestholidays.co.uk

Christchurch Campsite ★★★
Touring & Camping Park
Bracelands Drive, Christchurch,
Coleford
GL16 7NN
t 0845 130 8224
w forestholidays.co.uk

DRYBROOK

**Greenway Farm Caravan &
Camping Park** ★★★★★
Puddlebrook Road, Hawthorns,
Drybrook
GL17 9HW
t (01594) 544877
e admin@greenwayfarm.org
w greenwayfarm.org

MORETON-IN-MARSH

**Moreton-in-Marsh Caravan Club
Site** ★★★★★ *Touring Park*
Bourton Road, Moreton-in-Marsh
GL56 0BT
t (01608) 650519
w caravanclub.co.uk

PERROTTS BROOK

Mayfield Touring Park ★★★★
Touring Park
Cheltenham Road, Bagendon,
Christchurch
GL7 7BH
t (01285) 831301
e mayfield-park@cirencester.fsbus
iness.co.uk
w mayfieldpark.co.uk

SOUTH CERNEY

Hoburne Cotswold ★★★★
Holiday Park
Broadway Lane, South Cerney,
Christchurch
GL7 5UQ
t (01285) 860216
e cotswold@hoburne.com
w hoburne.com

TEWKESBURY

Croft Farm Waterpark ★★★
Holiday & Touring Park
Croft Farm, Bredons Hardwick, Nr
Tewkesbury
GL20 7EE
t (01684) 772321
e enquiries@croftfarmleisure.com
w croftfarmleisure.com

**Tewkesbury Abbey Caravan Club
Site** ★★★★★
Touring & Camping Park
Gander Lane, Tewkesbury
GL20 5PG
t (01684) 294035
e natalie.tiller@caravanclub.co.uk
w caravanclub.co.uk

WINCHCOMBE

**Winchcombe Camping and
Caravanning Club Site** ★★★★
Touring & Camping Park
Brooklands Farm, Alderton,
Tewkesbury
GL20 8NX
t (01242) 620259
w campingandcaravanningclub.co.
uk/winchcombe

Somerset

BATH

Newton Mill Camping ★★★★
Touring & Camping Park
Newton Road, Bath
BA2 9JF
t (01225) 333909
e newtonmill@hotmail.com
w campinginbath.co.uk

BEETHAM

Five Acres Caravan Club Site
★★★★ *Touring Park*
Giants Grave Road, Nr Chard
TA20 3QA
t (01460) 234519
w caravanclub.co.uk

BISHOP SUTTON

Bath Chew Valley Caravan Park
★★★★ *Touring Park*
Ham Lane, Bishop Sutton, Bristol
BS39 5TZ
t (01275) 332127
e enquiries@bathchewvalley.co.uk
w bathchewvalley.co.uk

BLUE ANCHOR

Hoburne Blue Anchor ★★★★
Holiday & Touring Park
ROSE AWARD
Carhampton Road, Blue Anchor
TA24 6JT
t (01643) 821360
e enquiries@hoburne.com
w hoburne.com

BREAN

Diamond Farm ★★★
Touring & Camping Park
Weston Road, Brean
TA8 2RL
t (01278) 751263
e trevor@diamondfarm42.freeserve.co.uk
w diamondfarm.co.uk

Dolphin Caravan Park ★★★★★
Holiday Park
Coast Road, Brean
TA8 2QY
t (01278) 751258
w dolphincaravanpark.co.uk

Holiday Resort Unity ★★★★
Holiday Village
Coast Road, Brean Sands, Brean
TA8 2RB
t (01278) 751235
e admin@hru.co.uk
w hru.co.uk

Northam Farm Touring Park
★★★★
Holiday, Touring & Camping Park
South Road, Brean
TA8 2SE
t (01278) 751244
e enquiries@northamfarm.co.uk
w northamfarm.co.uk

Warren farm - Isis and Wyndham Park ★★★★ *Holiday Park*
ROSE AWARD
Warren Road, Brean Sands,
Burnham-on-Sea
TA8 2RP
t (01278) 751227
e enquiries@warren-farm.co.uk
w warren-farm.co.uk

Warren Farm Holiday Centre
★★★★
Holiday, Touring & Camping Park
Warren Road, Brean Sands, Brean
TA8 2RP
t (01278) 751227
e enquiries@warren-farm.co.uk
w warren-farm.co.uk

BURNHAM-ON-SEA

Burnham-on-Sea Holiday Village
★★★★
Holiday, Touring & Camping Park
Marine Drive, Burnham-on-Sea
TA8 1LA
t (01278) 783391
e enquiries@british-holidays.co.uk
w british-holidays.co.uk

Home Farm Holiday Park
★★★★★ *Holiday & Touring Park*
Stoddens Lane, Nr Highbridge
TA9 4HD
t (01278) 788888
e office@homefarmholidaypark.co.uk
w homefarmholidaypark.co.uk

Lakeside Holiday Park ★★★★
Holiday Park
Westfield Road, Burnham-on-Sea
TA8 2AE
t (01278) 792222
e booking-enquiries@btconnect.com
w lakesideholidays.co.uk

The Retreat Caravan Park
★★★★★ *Holiday Park*
Berrow Road, Burnham-on-Sea
TA8 2ES
t 07007 387328
e roger@retreat.uk.com
w retreatcaravanpark.co.uk

CHARD

Alpine Grove Touring Park
★★★★ *Touring Park*
Alpine Grove Touring Park, Forton
TA20 4HD
t (01460) 63479
e stay@alpinegrovetouringpark.com
w alpinegrovetouringpark.com

CHEDDAR

Broadway House Holiday Touring Caravan and Camping Park
Holiday, Touring & Camping Park
Axbridge Road, Cheddar
BS27 3DB
t (01934) 742610
e info@broadwayhouse.uk.com
w broadwayhouse.uk.com

Cheddar, Mendip Heights Camping and Caravanning Club Site ★★★★
Touring & Camping Park
Townsend, Priddy, Wells
BA5 3BP
t (01749) 870241
e cheddar@campingandcaravanningclub.co.uk
w campingandcaravanningclub.co.uk/cheddar

Cheddar Bridge Touring Park
★★★★
Holiday, Touring & Camping Park
Draycott Road, Cheddar
BS27 3RJ
t (01934) 743048
e enquiries@cheddarbridge.co.uk
w cheddarbridge.co.uk/

CROWCOMBE

Quantock Orchard Caravan Park
★★★★★
Holiday, Touring & Camping Park
Flaxpool, Crowcombe, Taunton,
Somerset
TA4 4AW
t (01984) 618618
e member@flaxpool.freeserve.co.uk
w quantock-orchard.co.uk

DONIFORD

Doniford Bay Holiday Park
★★★★ *Holiday Park*
Sea Lane, Doniford
TA23 0TJ
t (01984) 632423
e doniford.bay@bourne-leisure.co.uk
w donifordbay-park.co.uk

Sunnybank Caravan Park
★★★★★ *Holiday Park*
Sunny Bank Holiday Caravan Park,
Watchet
TA23 0UD
t (01984) 632237
e mail@sunnybankcp.co.uk
w sunnybankcp.co.uk

DULVERTON

Exmoor House Caravan Club Site
★★★★ *Touring Park*
Oldberry, Dulverton
TA22 9HL
t (01398) 323268
w caravanclub.co.uk

Lakeside Caravan Club Site
★★★★★ *Touring Park*
Higher Grants, Exebridge, Dulverton
TA22 9BE
t (01398) 324068
e enquiries@caravanclub.co.uk
w caravanclub.co.uk

Northcombe *Bunkhouse*
Northcombe Farm, Nr Dulverton
TA22 9JH
t (01398) 323602
e sally@northcombecampingbarns.fsnet.co.uk

EAST HUNTSPILL

Cripps Farm Caravan Park ★★★★
Holiday & Touring Park
Merry Lane, East Huntspill,
Highbridge
TA9 3PS
t (01278) 783762
e gharris@gotadsl.co.uk
w crippsfarm.co.uk

Westhill Farm Caravan Park ★★
Holiday, Touring & Camping Park
Catherine Street, East Huntspill,
Highbridge
TA9 3PX
t (01278) 786326
e westhillfarm@sky.com
w westhillfarmcaravanpark.co.uk

GLASTONBURY

The Old Oaks Touring Park
★★★★★ *Touring & Camping Park*
Wick Lane, Glastonbury
BA6 8JS
t (01458) 831437
e info@theoldoaks.co.uk
w theoldoaks.co.uk

HIGHBRIDGE

Greenacre Place Touring Caravan Park and Holiday Cottage ★★★★
Touring Park
Bristol Road, Highbridge
TA9 4HA
t (01278) 785227
e info@greenacreplace.com
w greenacreplace.com

KEWSTOKE

Ardnave Holiday Park ★★★
Holiday & Touring Park
Crookes Lane, Kewstoke, Weston-super-Mare
BS22 9XJ
t (01934) 622319
e enquiries@ardnaveholidaypark.co.uk
w ardnaveholidaypark.co.uk

Kewside Caravans ★★
Holiday Park
Crookes Lane, Weston-super-Mare
BS22 9XF
t (01934) 521486

LANGPORT

Bowdens Crest Caravan and Camping Park ★★★★
Holiday, Touring & Camping Park
Bowdens, Langport
TA10 0DD
t (01458) 250553
e bowcrest@btconnect.com
w bowdenscrest.co.uk

MARTOCK

Southfork Caravan Park ★★★★★
Holiday, Touring & Camping Park
ROSE AWARD
Parrett Works, Martock
TA12 6AE
t (01935) 825661
e southforkcaravans@btconnect.com
w southforkcaravans.co.uk

MINEHEAD

Beeches Holiday Park ★★★★
Holiday Park **ROSE AWARD**
Blue Anchor Bay, Nr Minehead
TA24 6JW
t (01984) 640391
e info@beeches-park.co.uk
w beeches-park.co.uk

Butlins Skyline Holiday Park
Minehead ★★★
Holiday, Touring & Camping Park
Warren Road, Minehead
TA24 5SH
w butlins.com

Butlins Skyline Ltd ★★★★
Holiday Village
Warren Road, Minehead
TA24 5SH
t (01643) 703331
e minehead.hbs@bourne-leisure.co.uk
w butlins.com

Minehead Camping and Caravanning Club Site ★★★★
Camping Park
North Hill, Minehead
TA24 5LB
t (01643) 704138
w campingandcaravanningclub.co.uk/minehead

MUCHELNEY

Thorney Lakes and Caravan Park
★★★ *Touring & Camping Park*
Thorney Lakes, Nr Langport
TA10 0DW
t (01458) 250811
e enquiries@thorneylakes.co.uk
w thorneylakes.co.uk

POOLE

Cadeside Caravan Club Site
★★★★ *Touring Park*
Nynehead Road, Nynehead
TA21 9HN
t (01823) 663103
e enquiries@caravanclub.co.uk
w caravanclub.co.uk

PORLOCK

Burrowhayes Farm Caravan and Camping Site and Riding Stables
★★★★
Holiday, Touring & Camping Park
West Luccombe, Porlock
TA24 8HT
t (01643) 862463
e info@burrowhayes.co.uk
w burrowhayes.co.uk

Porlock Caravan Park ★★★★
Holiday, Touring & Camping Park
ROSE AWARD
High Bank, Porlock
TA24 8ND
t (01643) 862269
e info@porlockcaravanpark.co.uk
w porlockcaravanpark.co.uk

REDHILL

Brook Lodge Farm Touring Caravan and Tent Park ★★★
Touring & Camping Park
Brook Lodge Farm, Cowslip Green,
Nr Churchill
BS40 5RB
t (01934) 862311
e brooklodgefarm@aol.com
w brooklodgefarm.com

RODNEY STOKE

Bucklegrove Caravan & Camping Park ★★★★
Holiday, Touring & Camping Park
ROSE AWARD
Wells Road, Nr Cheddar
BS27 3UZ
t (01749) 870261
w bucklegrove.co.uk

SIMONSBATH

The Pinkery Centre *Bunkhouse*
Simonsbath, Minehead
TA24 7LL
t (01643) 831437

TAUNTON

she Farm Caravan and Campsite
★★ *Touring & Camping Park*
she Farm Caravan and Campsite,
hornfalcon
3 5NW
t (01823) 443764
e info@ashefarm.co.uk
w ashefarm.co.uk

olly Bush Park ★★★★
ouring & Camping Park
3170, Taunton
3 7EA
t (01823) 421515
e info@hollybushpark.com
w hollybushpark.com

UPTON

**owtrow Cross Caravan &
amping Site** ★★★★
oliday, Touring & Camping Park
wtrow Cross, Upton
4 2DB
t (01398) 371199
e lowtrowcross@aol.com
w lowtrowcross.co.uk

WATERROW

aterrow Touring Park ★★★★★
ouring & Camping Park
3227, Wiveliscombe, Nr Taunton,
merset
4 2AZ
t (01984) 623464
e waterrowpark@yahoo.co.uk
w waterrowpark.co.uk

WELLINGTON

eenacres Touring Park ★★★★
oliday, Touring & Camping Park
aywards Lane, Chelston,
ellington, Somerset
21 9PH

WESTON-SUPER-MARE

arefree Holiday Park ★★★★★
oliday Park
2 Beach Road, Kewstoke, Weston-
uper-Mare
22 9UZ
t (01934) 624541
e crichardson@hotmail.co.uk

Country View Holiday Park
★★★★
Holiday, Touring & Camping Park
29 Sand Road, Sand Bay, Weston-
super-Mare
BS22 9UJ
t (01934) 627595
e info@cvhp.co.uk
w cvhp.co.uk

Dulhorn Farm Holiday Park
★★★★ *Touring & Camping Park*
Weston Road, Lympsham, Weston
Super Mare
BS24 0JQ
t (01934) 750298
e dfhp@btconnect.com
w dulhornfarmholidayfarm.co.uk

Sand Bay Holiday Village ★★★
Holiday Village
67 Beach Road, Kewstoke, Weston-
super-Mare
BS22 9UR
t (01934) 428200
e cro@hollybushhotels.co.uk
w sandbayholidayvillage.co.uk

Weston-super-Mare Camping and
Caravanning Club Site ★★★
Touring Park
West End Farm, Locking, Weston-
super-Mare
BS24 8RH
t (01934) 822548

WEST QUANTOXHEAD

St Audries Bay ★★★★
Holiday & Touring Park
West Quantoxhead, Nr Williton
TA4 4DY
t (01984) 632515
e info@staudriesbay.co.uk
w staudriesbay.co.uk

WINCANTON

Wincanton Racecourse Campsite
★★★ *Touring & Camping Park*
Old Hill, Wincanton
BA9 8BJ
t (01963) 34276
e enquiries@caravanclub.co.uk
w caravanclub.co.uk

WINSFORD

Halse Farm Caravan & Tent Park
★★★★ *Touring & Camping Park*
Halse Farm Caravan & Tent Park,
Winsford, Exmoor, Somerset
TA24 7JL
t (01643) 851259
e brit@halsefarm.co.uk
w halsefarm.co.uk

YEOVIL

Long Hazel Park ★★★★
Holiday, Touring & Camping Park
High Street, Sparkford, Yeovil,
Somerset
BA22 7JH
t (01963) 440002
e longhazelpark@hotmail.com
w sparkford.f9.co.uk/lhi.htm

Wiltshire

CLYFFE PYPARD

The Goddard Arms *Bunkhouse*
Clyffe Pypard
SN4 7PY
t (01793) 731386
e clyffepypard@yha.org.uk

COOMBE BISSETT

Summerlands Caravan Park ★★★
Touring & Camping Park
College Farm, Rockbourne Road,
Coombe Bissett, Salisbury
SP5 4LP
t (01722) 718259
e summerlands-park@compaqnet.
co.uk
w summerlands-park.com

KINGTON LANGLEY

Plough Lane Caravan Site
★★★★★ *Touring Park*
Plough Lane, Kington Langley,
Chippenham
SN15 5PS
t (01249) 750146
e ploughlane@lineone.net
w ploughlane.co.uk

LACOCK

Piccadilly Caravan Park Ltd
★★★★★ *Touring & Camping Park*
Folly Lane (West), Lacock,
Chippenham
SN15 2LP
t (01249) 730260
e piccadillylacock@aol.com

LONGLEAT

Center Parcs Longleat Forest
★★★★★ *Forest Holiday Village*
Longleat, Warminster
BA12 7PU
t 0870 067 3030
w centerparcs.co.uk/villages/
longleat/index.jsp

MARLBOROUGH

Postern Hill Caravan and
Camping Site ★★★
Touring & Camping Park
Postern Hill, Marlborough,
Marlborough
SN8 4ND
t (01672) 515195
e posternhill.site@forestholidays.co.
uk
w forestholidays.co.uk

OARE

Hill-View Park ★★★
Touring & Camping Park
Sunnyhill Lane, Oare, Marlborough
SN8 4JG
t (01672) 563151

ORCHESTON

Stonehenge Touring Park ★★★
Touring & Camping Park
Stonehenge Park, Orcheston,
Salisbury
SP3 4SH
t (01980) 620304
e stay@stonehengetouringpark.
com
w stonehengetouringpark.com

SALISBURY

Salisbury Camping and
Caravanning Club Site ★★★★
Touring & Camping Park
Castle Road, Salisbury, Salisbury
SP1 3RR
t (01722) 320713
w campingandcaravanningclub.co.
uk/salisbury

SEEND

Devizes Camping and
Caravanning Club Site ★★★★
Touring & Camping Park
Sells Green, Seend, Melksham
SN12 6RN
t (01380) 828839
w campingandcaravanningclub.co.
uk/devizes

WARMINSTER

Longleat Caravan Club Site
★★★★★ *Touring Park*
Longleat, Warminster
BA12 7NL
t (01985) 844663
e enquiries@caravanclub.co.uk
w caravanclub.co.uk

The Royal Pavilion at night, Brighton, East Sussex, England.

South East England

Berkshire, Buckinghamshire, Hampshire, Isle of Wight,
Kent, Oxfordshire, Surrey, Sussex

South East England

South East England is a region rich in experiences with coast and countryside. It has something to offer every age group. Visit the historic houses and marvel at the wonderful interiors. Relax in the tranquil settings of some of the most beautiful gardens and parks. Stroll through the streets, villages, towns and cities and experience the splendid architectural heritage on offer.

Buckinghamshire has The Chiltern Hills, River Thames and some of the finest stately homes and heritage sites. Berkshire is a great destination providing something to keep the whole family entertained, Legoland Windsor, Ascot Racecourse, and the royal residence, Windsor Castle.

The rolling hills and riverside walks of Hampshire are waiting to be discovered, whilst the Isle of Wight has all the elements needed for a perfect break. Often referred to as 'The Garden of England', Kent has rolling hills, green valleys and miles of open landscape; perfect English countryside! Or you could enjoy the charm of the Oxfordshire Cotswolds, with its breathtaking scenery,

chocolate box villages and busy market towns. Oxford, the 'city of dreaming spires' has much to inspire!

Just 16 miles from London, Surrey is an interesting yet relaxing escape, steeped in history, with market towns and an excellent range of attractions. Sussex offers a diverse variety of destinations from vibrant and colourful Brighton in the East to chic Chichester in the West.

The South East Region really does have everything to suit all tastes and budgets.

Berkshire

Reading in Royal Berkshire has the excitement of a modern city, and the charm of English countryside. There's lots to do – shopping in one of the country's top ten retail capitals, walking along the Thames Path and Ridgeway National Trails, or enjoying the nightlife.

Ascot

A leading venue for flat and National Hunt racing Ascot racecourse is a popular venue both for the serious horseracing fraternity and those who like to dress-up, particularly for the Royal Ascot meeting in June, and have a 'flutter'.

Burnham Beeches

Burnham, mentioned in the Domesday Book, is home to Burnham Beeches which are considered to be one of the finest woodland tracts anywhere in Britain. Once it was a huge forest that almost covered the whole of the county. Today, there are well signposted walks through various habitats that are home to a wide range of flora and fauna, birds and even bats. Peaceful and relaxing Burnham Beeches is at its best in autumn, but delightful at any time of year.

Cookham

Cookham is a popular Thameside resort boasting fine restaurants and inns, an ideal destination to visit. The Bel and the Dragon, dating from 1417, is said to be one of the oldest licensed public houses in England. The artist Sir Stanley Spencer (1891–1959) lived in Cookham until his death. Spencer used the village scenery as the background in many of his paintings and the Stanley Spencer Gallery, housed in the Methodist Chapel he attended, shows a fine exhibition of his work.

Newbury

Alongside the Kennet & Avon Canal, Newbury has a bustling high street with interesting shops and a monthly farmer's market, crammed full with delicious, local produce. Wander along the canal path to Victoria Park, admire the swans or join a boat trip. Don't miss the renowned Comedy Festival in July. Donnington Castle, all that is left is the gatehouse, overlooks the town and visitors are attracted by the views. Just outside the town is the internationally renowned Newbury Racecourse positioned in a stunning setting and boasting fantastic hospitality.

Pangbourne

Nestling alongside the River Thames, Pangbourne has been the subject of much literary inspiration. Kenneth Grahame, author of 'Wind in the Willows', lived in the town and The Swan Public House is referred to in Jerome K. Jerome's 'Three Men in a Boat'. Today Pangbourne is still a charming place, full of character, with individual shops, pubs and cafes, an ideal place to potter. Close by is splendid Basildon Park, a National Trust property, recently used in the filming of Pride and Prejudice.

Windsor

The historic and regal town of Windsor is a familiar site to fans of the British Monarchy, it is a town which hides hundreds of exciting stories that are just waiting to be discovered. Why not explore the world's largest inhabited castle and watch the changing of the guard. Take a tour of Eton College, once home to Princes William and Harry. Alternatively have some fun and adventure at Legoland, one of the UK's Top Twenty Visitor attractions.

Buckinghamshire

Aylesbury, the county town of Buckinghamshire, is a lively market town steeped in history. Located at the foot of the Chiltern Hills and in the heart of the rich agricultural Vale of Aylesbury.

Buckingham

Dating back to the 7th-century, the ancient town of Buckingham contains some fine Georgian buildings, a distinctive Old Gaol and an imposing Town Hall. Nearby is Stowe Landscape Gardens, one of the finest Georgian landscape gardens in Britain and Silverstone Motor Racing Circuit.

Milton Keynes

There are not many cities in Europe where you can go shopping, snow-boarding, water-skiing and sailing – then catch a west-end show at the popular and successful MK theatre. Milton Keynes is fast becoming the UK's extreme sports capital. Xscape is the ultimate leisure complex where you can practice skiing and snow-boarding on the slopes of the UK's longest indoor real-snow slope, or try your hand at mountaineering on the indoor climbing wall. But if it's water sports you're after then head to Willen Lake where Whitecap Leisure offers you the opportunity to go water-skiing and wakeboarding on the UK's longest cable tow. If extreme shopping is your passion, visit The Centre: MK which extends over 3 miles with over 200 retail outlets, restaurants and cafés. The adjacent Theatre District also offers a wide choice of restaurants

and bars and is home to the UK's most successful regional theatre, MK Theatre; and the MK Gallery, which hosts around 10 free exhibitions every year.

Hambleden

Hambleden is one of the county's prettiest villages, in one of the Chiltern's prettiest valleys. Lord Cardigan, of Light Brigade fame, was born in the Manor House and his sea chest which accompanied him to the Crimea is on display in the beautiful old church. Charming brick and flint cottages surround a perfectly preserved village square with chestnut tree and village pump… just the Smithy is missing! Head for the Thames for Hambleden Mill and Weir which was first constructed in early 15th-century.

Marlow

Marlow is a charming historic town situated on the River Thames and surrounded by beautiful countryside, with the Chiltern Hills to the north. Being a thriving community only about 30 miles west of the centre of London and with good communications by road and rail, it is popular destination. It is the perfect place to enjoy the peace and tranquility of the river, shopping with a difference, walking around historical buildings, taking part in the many sports and leisure activities or eating and drinking in the numerous cafés, restaurants and pubs.

Wendover

Picturesque Wendover, renowned for fine eating places and antique shops, nestles into the edge of the Chiltern Hills. The Ridgeway National trail leads through Wendover Woods up to Coombe Hill, and 33 miles of footpaths surround the town.

Hampshire

Best known for its 11th-century Cathedral, Great Hall and Winchester College, Winchester is England's ancient capital and former seat of King Alfred the Great. Home of good food, birthplace of cricket, resting place of author Jane Austen, Winchester has interesting historic charm and much to offer visitors.

Alresford

A vision of pastel perfection, Alresford is a handsome Georgian town of colour-washed houses, riverside walks, specialist shops and the UK's capital of watercress farming. The town's history is punctuated with fires, despite the abundance of water in the area, and the buildings that today rose from the ashes of the great fires of the 17th century. The Mid-Hants Railway, known locally as the Watercress Line, can be found here. Hop on board one of the powerful steam locomotives for the 10 mile trip to Alton.

Alton

A thriving country market town, with a fascinating history, Alton was built around a wealthy Saxon settlement and had the most valuable recorded market in the Doomsday Book. The 11th-century St Lawrence Church was the scene of the civil war 'Battle of Alton' and still bears the scars. At one time the town was notorious for the brutal murder of 'Sweet Fanny Adams'. Today the town is a delightful mix of historic buildings, modern shops, and arcades. Tuesday is market day, and the town hosts many markets and fairs throughout the year.

New Forest

The forest has changed little since William the Conqueror gave it his special protection over 900 years ago. The unique landscape has been moulded by centuries of grazing by commoner's animals. You can still see their ponies eating by the roadside, pigs foraging for beechnuts, and donkeys ambling along the streets. Most of the forest is made up of endless open heathland. In spring and autumn it is spectacular – a purple carpet of heather speckled with vibrant yellow splashes of gorse. It is in these seasons that visitors will find uncluttered roads and a forest all their own.

Portsmouth

At the heart of the city is Portsmouth Historic Dockyard. Here you can explore Lord Nelson's flagship, HMS Victory and tour Queen Victoria's battleship, HMS Warrior 1860. You can see Henry VIII's Mary Rose and trace the history of the Royal Navy at the Royal Naval Museum. Then come right up to date with 'Action Stations' an interactive attraction on today's navy.

Southampton

The historic city of Southampton is fast becoming one of the most popular leisure and cultural destinations in the south. The city's Maritime Museum tells the story of this important port and is home to the Titanic Exhibition where visitors can re-live the ill-fated story of this famous ship.

Isle of Wight

Less than one mile from the mainland, take a step back to a more tranquil time with rolling hills, cliff-top walks, charming thatched villages and glorious beaches. Osborne House, a magnificent Italianate villa was built for Queen Victoria and it was here she chose to retire to grieve when her beloved husband died in 1861.

Ryde

The festival town of Ryde boasts Britain's oldest carnival, traditionally held at the end of summer. Ryde has 6 miles of glorious sandy beaches and shallow coastal waters, ideal for swimming.

Sandown

A firm favourite with families seeking a traditional seaside holiday. The magnificent sandy beach slopes gently into the sea, ideal for paddling and swimming. There are all kinds of watersports and attractions including amusements on the pier.

Shanklin

Shanklin is a resort of great charm with a beautiful sandy beach, excellent swimming and sunbathing. Lush and verdant Shanklin Chine, with its unique microclimate, is home to an unusual range of flora and fauna, as well as a couple of waterfalls.

Brading

Standing on the western bank of the River Yar in the east of the island, this ancient little town is pleasantly built on a hillside below Brading Down within an Area of Outstanding Natural Beauty (AONB). Rolling green hills dropping down to the sea, breathtaking views and plenty of attractions including the Roman villa and Waxworks.

Cowes

A Mecca for yachtsman, Cowes hosts many national and international events. The narrow pedestrianised high street is bursting with interesting boutiques, antique shops and much more. The high-speed ferry to Southampton departs from adjacent Fountain Quay.

Wootton Bridge

A charming country village on the north coast of the island. The Creek is used by yachtsmen and boaters whilst the Millpond is home to herons, egrets and kingfishers, with the surrounding countryside home to red squirrels.

How To Get There

Wightlink and Red Funnel Isle of Wight Ferries operate the ferry service between the England mainland and the Isle of Wight, sailing the Southampton to Cowes, Portsmouth to Fishbourne, Lymington to Yarmouth and Portsmouth to Ryde routes.

Kent

Surrounded by a gentle landscape of orchards and hop gardens, Maidstone, Kent's thriving County Town, combines a wealth of historical attractions with arts, culture and superb shopping. Situated on the River Medway halfway between Dover and London the town is a great place to shop and visit.

Broadstairs

Unpretentious and unspoilt, Broadstairs unpacks a suitcase full of quiet charm. The town was a holiday home for Charles Dickens and continues to court its guests with a delightful mix of beautiful bays, maritime history and tiny, character-packed streets. Book shops, restaurants, craft shops and souvenir shops vie for attention and a mix of cottages and Victorian homes add to Broadstairs' old-world feel. Glorious Viking Bay is a wide sweep of golden sand basking against a backdrop of cliffs and picturesque Victorian and Edwardian architecture.

Deal

Enjoy a leisurely stroll along the unspoilt promenade and newly restored Pier. Step back in time and explore the maze of narrow streets and alleys where smugglers would try and evade King George's men. Henry VIII liked Deal so much he built three castles, only two remain, Deal with its distinctive 'Tudor Rose' shape and Walmer which is now an elegant stately home with beautiful gardens.

Faversham

Voted 'Best market town in Kent' by Country Life Magazine, Faversham is a destination that exudes old world charm. Found in the North of the county, between the stunning natural landscapes of the Downs and Kent Mashes, it is a town steeped in history with no less than 475 listed properties. Many of the English historical eras, can be found represented throughout the area, with some buildings dating back to the Medieval period.

Herne Bay

The resort town of Herne Bay proudly flies the 2007 Quality Coast Award flag over its safe clean beaches. The resort is a popular destination for water sports, wind surfing, sailing, zapcats racing and jet skiing but is still suitable for sandcastles, swimming and excellent fishing too. Popular wildlife sailing trips leave most days to see seals and dolphins in their natural habitat. At Wildwood on nearby Herne Common, land-dwelling wildlife such as wolves, beavers, badgers and otters may be seen.

Rochester

Rochester is home to England's second oldest Cathedral and sits proudly next to its inseparable twin Rochester Castle with the tallest Keep in the land. The Victorian High Street was the inspiration to Charles Dickens for three of his books, '*Great Expectations*', '*The Pickwick Papers*' and '*Mystery of Edwin Drood*'.

Tunbridge Wells

Ever since the discovery of the Chalybeate Spring 400 years ago, visitors have been going to Royal Tunbridge Wells. A magnet for the gentry and members of the Georgian Royal family, Tunbridge Wells became one of the most fashionable destinations of the 18th-century. The elegance and atmosphere of this bygone era still remains today.

Oxfordshire

Oxford is known as the 'city of the dreaming spires'. The golden-stone university buildings include some of England's most impressive architecture, notably the Bodleian Library, Sir Christopher Wren's Sheldonian Theatre, and the Radcliffe Camera. Looking at these beautiful buildings, it's no surprise that Oxford is one of Britain's Heritage Cities Attractions.

Banbury

Banbury is an historic market town famous for its Cross, Cakes and 'Ride a Cock Horse to Banbury Cross' Nursery Rhyme. Banbury is a vibrant mix of the traditional and historic against a backdrop of modern living. The narrow streets and hidden lanes of Banbury form part of a historic town trail and guided walks are available from June–September. New developments such as the Banbury Museum & Tooley's Boatyard and the Castle Quay Shopping Centre have regenerated the Oxford Canal as it flows through the heart of the town.

Dorchester on Thames

A charming, riverside, Oxfordshire village, 5 miles from Wallingford and 9 miles from Oxford, Dorchester-on-Thames is steeped in history. Close

to an Iron Age hill fort, it was formerly a Celtic market centre and a Roman town, but it was the advent of Christianity that truly put Dorchester-on-Thames on the map. St Birinus baptised the Saxon King Cynegils in 635 and established an Episcopal see that covered most of England. Dorchester today is a village of interesting and charming buildings, reflecting many architectural styles, and was recently a location for the Television series 'Midsommer Murders'.

Cotswolds

Classified as an Area of Outstanding Natural Beauty, the Oxfordshire Cotswolds is a beautiful representation of quintessential England. Every which way you turn you will find sweeping landscapes and picture postcard villages that both captivate and charm, making it the popular tourist haven that it is today.

White Horse Country

Lying between the Ridgeway and the River Thames, the White Horse Country stretches from the edge of Oxford to the threshold of the Cotswolds. Its enchanting landscape is marked by a mysterious pagan past – the name of the Vale comes from the oldest chalk figure in Britain dating back over 3,000 years. Wander through the peaceful tranquil countryside to untouched stretches of the River Thames, waterside pubs, pretty villages and elegant country homes. White Horse Country has a network of footpaths that connect two nature trails – the prehistoric Ridgeway slips across open downland and the Thames Path leads you onto lush willowy walks.

Surrey

Set in the rolling hills of Surrey, Guildford, is the vibrant historic county town, with cobbled high street and riverside walks. It also has excellent shopping and entertainment. Full of history, visit the castle keep, the 15th-century Guildhall and a wealth of other interesting buildings.

Cobham

A delightful town with a village feel, situated on the banks of the River Mole. Cobham offers interesting shopping and good eateries. The ancient parish church of St Andrews retains much of its character including a Norman tower, 16th-century brasses and stained glass windows designed by Edward Burne-Jones. The beautifully restored Cobham Mill and Cobham Bus Museum are fascinating visits. Painshill Park's wonderful 18th-century parkland, lake and follies are a 'Living Work of Art' where visitors can enjoy fantastic views across Surrey.

Cranleigh

Reputed to be the largest village in England, Cranleigh takes its name from the craneries at two nearby estates, which were reputed to have bred cranes as delicacies for the King. The crane has since become the village symbol, adorning monuments in the town. Running through Cranleigh, the Downslink, connecting the North and South Downs, runs through the village along 61 acres of former railway line and adjacent embankments and cuttings. It is one of the country's long distance bridleways, as well as a designated Public Open Space, following a level route through woodland, wetland and agricultural land. Way-marked by signs, and with seating en-route, the link is popular with cyclists, horse-riders and walkers alike.

Dorking

Dorking is a market town in the best tradition of English rural towns. Wander the delightful high street with varying architecture, from timber-framed medieval inns to much grander Victorian and Edwardian buildings. Browse the many antique shops on West Street, Friday is market day. Dorking has literary links; Daniel Defoe and EM Forster lived in the town and it inspired Charles Dickens to write 'Pickwick Papers'. The composer Ralph Vaughan Williams grew up here.

The Surrey Hills

The Surrey Hills Area of Outstanding Natural Beauty (AONB) is one of 37 nationally protected landscapes in England, and was one of the first landscapes to be designated an AONB in 1958, with its beauty being considered equivalent to that of a National Park. This nationally treasured landscape stretches across a quarter of the county of Surrey and includes the chalk slopes of the North Downs from Farnham in the west to Oxted in the east and extends south to the deeply wooded Greensand Hills which rise in Haslemere. The Surrey Hills are not only rich in wildlife, woodland, attractive market towns and villages but also provide some of the best walking in southern England. There is always plenty to do in a county where old traditions and institutions such as royal residences, cream teas and cricket rub shoulders with modern architecture, contemporary theatre, international horse racing (including the world-renowned Epsom Derby held each year in June), excellent sporting facilities and state-of-the-art theme parks.

Sussex

Lewes is the county town of East Sussex. The remains of the Norman castle dominate the medieval streets, tiny alleyways, and old English churches. Lewes is home to the handsome townhouse of Anne of Cleves (fourth wife of King Henry VIII). Chichester is the county town of West Sussex. Take a walk along the circular walls for fine views of the city.

East Sussex

What makes the perfect holiday? For some, it's walking in peaceful countryside, for others it's visiting historic houses or museums, or serious shopping. Whatever your choice, East Sussex has a unique mix of unspoilt countryside, narrow cobbled town streets, medieval cottages and fairytale castles, glorious gardens and picturesque old villages.

Brighton

Brighton is more than the seaside, more than the city and the mix is more than double the fun. Fashionable, funky and loaded with style, Brighton & Hove has everything; a royal palace, elegant Regency architecture, museums, plus laid-back beach life and superb shopping – all this on the south coast just 49 minutes from central London.

Rye

Perched on a hill, the medieval town of Rye is the sort of place you thought existed only in your imagination. Almost suspended in time, Rye's unhurried atmosphere and enchanting streets draw visitors with their warm welcome. It's small enough to make you feel at home but holds enough secret treasures to entice you to stay.

West Sussex

West Sussex lies on the southern coast of England combining stunning seascapes and the rolling South Downs, an (AONB). An inspirational setting to the likes of poet William Blake, painter John Constable and novelist H G Wells, this beautiful rural county remains an unspoilt and unexplored part of England.

Arundel

The picturesque town of Arundel is dominated by the stunning Norman Arundel Castle and the Gothic cathedral. The town is relaxed and friendly with cobbled streets, specialist shops and tea rooms. Straddling the River Arun, the sleepy little town nestles between the rolling South Downs and the glistening sea.

Chichester

Brimming with arts and culture and steeped in 2,000 years of history, the cathedral city of Chichester is situated between the gorgeous rolling hills of the South Downs and the seclusion and tranquillity of the harbour. The area boasts four impressive historic houses - Petworth House, Uppark, Goodwood House and Stansted Park.

Winnie The Pooh Country

An AONB, Ashdown Forest is the single largest tract of open land in the South East. A walker's paradise, visitors are free to walk wherever they like over the 6,500 acres of the Forest. Over the years the Forest has provided the setting and inspiration for many stories including some Sherlock Holmes novels written by Sir Arthur Conan Doyle, whilst AA Milne captured the imagination of children across the world by writing about his son, Christopher Robin and his friendship with a certain Pooh Bear.

Where to Go

Attractions with this sign participate in the **Visitor Attraction Quality Assurance Scheme** (see page 6) which recognises high standards in all aspects of the vistor experience.

ENTERTAINMENT & CULTURE

Ascot Racecourse
Ascot, Berkshire, SL5 7JX
0870 727 1234
www.ascot.co.uk
Founded in 1711 and recently redeveloped, Ascot stages quality flat and jump racing all year round.

Canterbury Tales
Canterbury, Kent, CT1 2TG
(01227) 479227
www.canterburytales.org.uk
Follow Chaucer's colourful medieval pilgrims, journeying to St Thomas Becket's shrine at Canterbury. Audiovisual fun.

Chichester Festival Theatre
Chichester, West Sussex, PO19 6AP
(01243) 781312
www.cft.org.uk
Positioned in the beautiful surroundings of Oaklands Park, Chichester Festival Theatre is one of the United Kingdom's flagship theatres, with a dazzling international reputation for producing an annual festival.

Dinosaur Isle
Sandown, Isle of Wight, PO36 8QA
(01983) 404344
www.dinosaurisle.com
Step back through fossilized time and meet life sized replicas of dinosaurs, including animatronic Neovenator.

Goodwood Racecourse
Chichester, West Sussex, PO18 0PX
(01243) 755022
www.goodwood.co.uk
Horse racing, motor sports, golf, events. Goodwood House contains notable art.

Mercedes-Benz World
Weybridge, Surrey, KT13 0SL
0870 400 4000
www.mercedes-benzworld.co.uk
A world that is all Mercedes-Benz. Thrilling driving experiences, fascinating attractions, fun for kids. Fine dining, exciting events and classic cars too.

Milestones
Basingstoke, Hampshire, RG21 6YR
(01256) 477766
www.milestones-museum.com
Revisit Victorian times and the 1930s, along atmospheric streets with shops, pub and village green.

National Motor Museum
Beaulieu, Brockenhurst, Hampshire, SO42 7ZN
(01590) 612345
www.beaulieu.co.uk
Over 250 exhibits trace our motoring history. Also Palace House, Wheels Experience and Beaulieu Abbey ruins.

Roald Dahl Museum and Story Centre
Great Missenden, Buckinghamshire, HP16 0AL
(01494) 892192
www.roalddahlmuseum.org
Discover the life behind so many well-loved books. Lots of activities for children aged 6–12.

FAMILY FUN

Blackgang Chine
Chale, Isle of Wight, PO38 2HN
(01983) 730330
www.blackgangchine.com
Explore the water gardens, dinosaur park, maze, Nurseryland, Smugglerland, Fantasyland, Rumpus Mansion and Cliffhanger.

INTECH Science Centre & Planetarium
Winchester, Hampshire, SO21 1HX
(01962) 863791
www.intech-uk.com
Experience the worlds of science, technology, engineering and mathematics brought to life. Suits all ages.

LEGOLAND® Windsor
Windsor,Berkshire, SL4 4AY,
0870 504 0404
www.legoland.co.uk
Family park with hands-on activities, over 50 interactive rides, themed playscapes and countless LEGO bricks.

Paultons Park
Romsey, Hampshire, SO51 6AL
(023) 8081 4442
www.paultonspark.co.uk
Over 50 attractions. Big and small rides, play areas, exotic birds and gardens.

Thorpe Park
Chertsey, Surrey, KT16 8PN
0870 444 4466
www.thorpepark.com
Get a fix of high-adrenalin adventure with Slammer, Nemesis Inferno, Colossus and much more.

HERITAGE

1066 Battle Abbey and Battlefield
Battle, East Sussex, TN33 0AD
(01424) 773792
www.english-heritage.org.uk
William the Conqueror's abbey commemorates the fallen. Interactives recreate the Battle of Hastings. Battlefield audio tours.

Arundel Castle and Gardens
Arundel, West Sussex, BN18 9AB
(01903) 882173
www.arundelcastle.org
Fortified castle and family home since 1067. Priceless collections and marvellous interiors.

Blenheim Palace
Woodstock, Oxfordshire, OX20 1PX
(01993) 811091
www.blenheimpalace.com
Seat of the Duke of Marlborough, birthplace of Winston Churchill. Superb furnishings. Capability Brown parkland.

Bluebell Railway
Uckfield, East Sussex, TN22 3QL
(01825) 720800
www.bluebell-railway.co.uk
Take an 18-mile round trip through open countryside. Steam engines dating from 1870s to 1950s.

Brighton Pier
Brighton, East Sussex, BN2 1TW
(01273) 609361
www.brightonpier.co.uk
Enjoy Brighton's landmark Victorian pier: fairground attractions, Palace of Fun arcade, slot machines and eateries.

Buckinghamshire Railway Centre
Quainton, Buckinghamshire, HP22 4BY
(01296) 655720
www.bucksrailcentre.org
Large collection of railway relics, steam locomotives, carriages and equipment. Steam train rides certain days.

Carisbrooke Castle
Newport, Isle of Wight, PO30 1XY
(01983) 522107
www.english-heritage.org.uk/carisbrooke
Imposing Norman castle where Charles I was imprisoned. Includes a well with a treadwheel worked by donkeys.

Chichester Cathedral
Chichester, West Sussex, PO19 1RP
(01243) 782595
www.chichestercathedral.org.uk
Ancient and modern glories: Norman architecture, St Richard's Shrine, works by Sutherland, Chagall, Piper. Tours.

Chinnor & Princes Risborough Railway
Chinnor, Oxfordshire, OX39 4ER
(01844) 353535
www.chinnorrailway.co.uk
Steam and heritage diesel rides on 3.5 miles of ex-GWR branch line. Duration of journey approximately 45 minutes affording outstanding views across the Vale of Aylesbury.

Didcot Railway Centre
Didcot, Oxfordshire, OX11 7NJ
(01235) 817200
www.didcotrailwaycentre.org.uk
The golden age of the Great Western Railway. Steam locomotives, trains, Brunel's broad-gauge railway and relics.

Hever Castle and Gardens
Edenbridge, Kent, TN8 7NG
(01732) 865224
www.hevercastle.co.uk
The magical, double moated childhood home of Anne Boleyn. Splendidly furnished rooms and breathtaking award-winning gardens.

Isle of Wight Steam Railway
Havenstreet, Isle of Wight, PO33 4DS
(01983) 882204
www.iwsteamrailway.co.uk
Beautifully restored Victorian & Edwardian carriages and locomotives accurately re-create the bygone age of steam train travel on the Isle of Wight.

Jane Austen's House
Hampshire, GU34 1SD
(01420) 83262
www.jane-austens-house-museum.org.uk
Austen's home from 1809–17, where she wrote or revised her six famous novels. Letters, pictures, memorabilia.

Kent & East Sussex Railway
Tenterden, Kent, TN30 6HE
(01580) 765155
www.kesr.org.uk
Full size heritage railway. Restored Edwardian stations at Tenterden and Northiam, and 14 steam engines.

Knole
Sevenoaks, Kent, TN15 0RP
www.nationaltrust.org.uk/knole
Intriguing treasure house with links to royalty, Vita Sackville-West and Virginia Woolf. Magnificent deer park.

Leeds Castle
Maidstone, Kent, ME17 1PL
(01622) 765400
www.leeds-castle.com
Experience 1,000 years of history at this castle set on two islands in a lake.

Loseley Park
Guildford, Surrey, GU3 1HS
(01483) 405112
www.loseley-park.com
Delightful, 'lived-in' ancestral home of the More-Molyneux family, built in the 1560s. Stunning walled garden.

Mapledurham House
Mapledurham, Oxfordshire, RG4 7TR
(0118) 972 3350
www.mapledurham.co.uk
An Elizabethan manor house alongside the River Thames, containing paintings, oak staircases, and moulded ceilings. Home to the Blount family for over 500 years.

Mid-Hants Railway 'Watercress Line'
Alresford, Hampshire, SO24 9JG
(01962) 733810
www.watercressline.co.uk
Ten miles of preserved steam railway taking passengers between Alton and Alresford.

Osborne House
East Cowes, Isle of Wight, PO32 6JX
(01983) 200022
www.english-heritage.org.uk/osbornehouse
Visit Queen Victoria and Prince Albert's seaside holiday home. Victorian carriage rides, gardens, exhibition and shop.

Oxford Castle Unlocked
Oxford, Oxfordshire, OX1 1AY
(01865) 260666
www.oxfordcastleunlocked.co.uk
For the first time in 1,000 years, the secrets of Oxford Castle have been 'unlocked', revealing episodes of violence, executions, great escapes, betrayal and even romance. Visit Oxford Castle and uncover the secrets for yourself.

Portsmouth Historic Dockyard
Portsmouth, Hampshire, PO1 3LJ
(023) 9283 9766
www.historicdockyard.co.uk
Home to the famous ships HMS Victory, Mary Rose and HMS Warrior.

Royal Pavilion
Brighton, East Sussex, BN1 1EE
(01273) 290900
www.royalpavilion.org.uk
Be dazzled by King George IV's Indian style seaside residence, decorated inside in Chinese style.

Spinnaker Tower
Portsmouth, Hampshire, PO1 3TT
(023) 9285 7520
www.spinnakertower.co.uk
Enjoy spectacular views from this elegant tower soaring 170 m above Portsmouth Harbour. Waterside cafe bar.

The Historic Dockyard Chatham
Chatham, Kent, ME4 4TZ
(01634) 823807
www.thedockyard.co.uk
Four centuries of maritime heritage. Includes 18thC adventure, WWII destroyer, Cold War submarine and RNLI exhibition.

Waddesdon Manor
Aylesbury, Buckinghamshire, HP18 0JH
(01296) 653226
www.waddesdon.org.uk
View the Rothschild Collection of art treasures and breathtaking gardens at this French Renaissance-style chateau. A National Trust property.

Winchester Cathedral
Winchester, Hampshire, SO23 9LS
(01962) 857200
www.winchester-cathedral.org.uk
Magnificent medieval cathedral with soaring Gothic nave and Jane Austen's tomb.

Windsor Castle
Windsor, Berkshire, SL4 1NJ
(020) 7766 7304
www.royalcollection.org.uk
The world's largest inhabited castle, a royal residence since the 11thC. State apartments and Queen Mary's Doll's House.

NATURE & WILDLIFE

Cotswold Wildlife Park & Gardens
Burford, Oxfordshire, OX18 4JW
(01993) 823006
www.cotswoldwildlifepark.co.uk
Spot animals from around the world. Extensive gardens and woodland, narrow gauge railway, picnic areas.

Exbury Gardens and Steam Railway
Exbury, Hampshire, SO45 1AZ
(023) 8089 1203
www.exbury.co.uk
Vast woodland garden featuring the Rothschild collection of rhododendrons, azaleas, camellias, magnolias. Narrow-gauge steam railway.

Goodnestone Park Gardens
Canterbury, Kent, CT3 1PL
(01304) 840107
www.goodnestoneparkgardens.co.uk
Explore 14 acres of 18thC parkland with Jane Austen connections. Old fashioned roses, walled garden.

Groombridge Place and The Enchanted Forest
Royal Tunbridge Wells, Kent, TN3 9QG
(01892) 861444
www.groombridge.co.uk
Award-winning gardens featuring traditional and 17thC walled gardens, with exciting mysteries in the ancient woodland.

Marwell Wildlife
Winchester, Hampshire, SO21 1JH
(01962) 777407
www.marwell.org.uk
Meet 200-plus species of animals in 100 acres of countryside. New Australian bush walk.

Painshill Park
Cobham, Surrey, KT11 1JE
(01932) 868113
www.painshill.co.uk
Restored and renovated 160-acre 18thC park. Folly buildings, period plantings, American Roots exhibition, children's trails and events.

RHS Garden Wisley
Woking, Surrey, GU23 6QB
0845 260 9000
www.rhs.org.uk/wisley
Wisley demonstrates best gardening practices for every season, in over 240 wonderful acres. Plant centre and restaurant.

The Hop Farm Country Park
Paddock Wood, Kent, TN12 6PY
(01622) 872068
www.thehopfarm.co.uk
Visit a once working hop farm. Victorian oast houses, shire horses, interactive museum, play areas.

University of Oxford Botanic Garden
Oxford, Oxfordshire, OX1 4AZ
(01865) 286690
www.botanic-garden.ox.ac.uk
Britain's oldest botanic garden with glasshouses, over 6,000 species of plants, rock and water gardens.

OUTDOOR ACTIVITIES

French Brothers Ltd
Windsor, Berkshire, SL4 5JH
(01753) 851900
www.boat-trips.co.uk
Great choice of public trips on weather-proof vessels from Windsor, Runnymede, Maidenhead and Wallingford.

Hobbs of Henley
Henley-on-Thames, Oxfordshire RG9 1AZ
(01491) 572035
www.hobbsofhenley.com
Self-drive boat hire available 10:00-17:00. Charter available for weddings, parties and corporate events.

Events 2010

Alltech FEI European Jumping & Dressage Championships
Windsor
www.alltechwindsoreuropeans.com/
August

Banbury and District Show
Banbury
www.banbury.gov.uk
June

Brighton Festival
Brighton
www.brightonfestival.org
1st–23rd May

British Science Festival
Guildford
www.britishsciencefestival.org
September

Cowes Week
Cowes
www.cowesweek.co.uk
August

Eastbourne International Airshow
Eastbourne
www.eastbourneairshow.com/
August

Emsworth Seafood Week
Emsworth
www.emsworthfoodfestival.co.uk
October

Festive Fair – Leeds Castle
Maidstone
www.leeds-castle.co.uk
November

Goodwood Festival of Speed
Chichester
www.goodwood.co.uk
July

Goodwood Revival Festival
Chichester
www.goodwood.co.uk
September

Great Gardening Show at Loseley Park
Guidford
www.greatgardeningshow.co.uk
July

Guildford Summer Festival
Guildford
www.guildfordsummerfestival.co.uk
June–August

Henley Royal Regatta
Henley-on-Thames
www.hrr.co.uk
30th Jun–4th July

Isle of Wight Garlic Festival
Newchurch
www.garlic-festival.co.uk
August

Isle of Wight Walking Festival
Isle of Wight
www.isleofwightwalkingfestival.co.uk
8th–23rd May

Kent County Show
Maidstone
www.kentshowground.co.uk
July

Littlehampton Bonfire Celebrations
Littlehampton
www.lbs.me.uk
October

Marlow Town Regatta & Festival
Marlow
www.marlowtownregatta.org.uk
12th–13th June

Medieval Spectacular at Appuldurcombe House
Ventnor
www.appuldurcombe.co.uk
July

New Forest and Hampshire Show
Brockenhurst
www.newforestshow.co.uk
July

Royal Ascot
Ascot
www.ascot.co.uk
June

Royal Windsor Horse Show
Windsor
www.rwhs.co.uk
May

Southampton Boat Show
Southampton
www.southamptonboatshow.com
September

Surrey County Show
Guildford
www.surreycountyshow.co.uk
31st May

The Royal County of Berkshire Show
Hermitage
www.newburyshowground.co.uk
September

Windsor Castle Royal Tattoo
Windsor
www.windsortattoo.com
12th–15th May

Where to Eat

The South East England region has great places to eat. The restaurant reviews on these pages are just a small selection from the highly respected *The Good Food Guide 2010*. Please see pages 20–21 for further information on the guide and details of a Special Offer for our readers.

BERKSHIRE

Pot Kiln
Rooted in the countryside
Frilsham, RG18 0XX
Tel no: (01635) 201366
www.potkiln.co.uk
Gastropub | £26

Surrounded by woods and meadows, the 300 year-old Pot Kiln is Berkshire rusticity personified. Fittingly, TV chef/landlord Mike Robinson is keen on local, country flavours and his menus have a gutsy edge. Some new dishes have impressed of late – including onion tarte Tatin with goat's cheese and pesto, and devilled chicken livers on toast. Elsewhere, expect anything from confit pork belly with braised red cabbage to Braeburn apple crumble. Real ales are taken seriously, and wines start at £12.95.

Chef/s: Mike Robinson. **Open:** all week L 12 to 2 (2.30 Sun), Mon to Sat D 7 to 9. **Closed:** Sun D and Tue in winter, 25 Dec. **Meals:** alc (main courses £13 to £17). Set L £14.50 (2 courses) to £19.50. **Service:** 10% (optional).
Details: Cards accepted. 48 seats. 80 seats outside. Separate bar. No music. No mobile phones. Wheelchair access. Children allowed. Car parking.

The Royal Oak
Upper tier pub food
Paley Street, SL6 3JN
Tel no: (01628) 620541
www.theroyaloakpaleystreet.com
British | £35

'The welcome was warm and genuine, the menu interesting and well-balanced, and overall this was just a fab evening out,' was the verdict of one reporter who had clearly enjoyed a dinner at this beamed village pub a little off the M4. Owned by Sir Michael Parkinson and his son Nick, the place is a haven of old-school comfort, with sofas to sink into and artwork on the walls. It also boasts a hugely accomplished chef in Dominic Chapman, whose menus reflect a fondness for traditional British food, conscientiously sourced and prepared with obvious care and skill. Smoked haddock soup comes with a poached egg to create vivid impact while main courses are full of nostalgic appeal, running from oxtail and kidney pudding to grilled lemon sole with chips. They also find room for the odd idea from beyond these shores – perhaps roast halibut with spiced aubergine, cucumber and mint. Desserts bring it all back home with Cambridge burnt cream or lemon posset, and there are fine British cheeses too. A great choice of 13 wines by the glass leads off a diverse and fascinating list of quality drinking, with a wealth of options at the affordable end of the spectrum. Prices start at £17.

Chef/s: Dominic Chapman. **Open:** all week L 12 to 3 (4 Sun), Mon to Sat D 6.30 to 9.30 (10 Fri, Sat). **Closed:** 25 Dec **Meals:** alc (main courses £12 to £25). Set L £15 (2 courses) to £19.95. Set D £25 (3 courses). **Service:** 12.5% (optional).
Details: Cards accepted. 46 seats. 20 seats outside. Air-con. Separate bar. Music. Children allowed. Car parking.

BUCKINGHAMSHIRE

Hand & Flowers

Modern feet-on-the-ground cooking

26 West Street, Marlow, SL7 2BP
Tel no: (01628) 482277
www.thehandandflowers.co.uk
Modern British | £36

Some readers have been critical of the Kerridiges' smart roadside pub-cum-restaurant with rooms, but inspectors and other readers remain firm – this is a restaurant of high local repute. With low, beamed ceilings, evening candles and simple but comfortable décor, it is the setting for modern cooking with its feet on the ground – even the fish and chips served in the bar at lunchtime is a cut above the norm. A couple directed here by word of mouth were glad they took the advice: their red mullet soup came with toasted fennel grissini, crispy squid and 'layers of flavour', while the main course, slow-cooked beef with 'an incredibly light' bone marrow bread pudding, pomme galette and braising juices was a dish of strong appeal. Others might enjoy terrine of Old Spot pork and bacon with hot pickled pineapple or fillet of sea bream with braised Puy lentils, smoked butter, mussels and parsley. Appealing desserts include warm pistachio sponge cake with melon sorbet and marzipan or lavender pannacotta with heather honey, honeycomb and whisky. 'Welcome, service and ambience are fantastic' and the wine list opens at £16.

Chef/s: Tom Kerridge. **Open:** all week L 12 to 2.30 (Sun 3), Mon to Sat D 7 to 9.30. **Closed:** 24 to 26 Dec, L 31 Dec, D 1 Jan. **Meals:** alc (main courses £16 to £20). **Service:** not inc. **Details:** Cards accepted. 50 seats. 20 seats outside. Wheelchair access. Music. Children allowed. Car parking.

La Petite Auberge

French cooking with charm and cheer

107 High Street, Great Missenden, HP16 0BB
Tel no: (01494) 865370
www.lapetiteauberge.co.uk
French | £34

Hubert Martel's French bistro does exactly what is required, as confirmed by the couple who report, 'we continue to come back to this restaurant year after year and we are very rarely disappointed'. Crab and tiger prawn gratin sauced with brandy, turbot with anchovies in caper sauce, beef fillet in grain mustard: these are the kinds of dishes, capably executed, that first lured the British across the Channel. They are served with impeccable charm and cheer and, what's more, you can ease gently to a halt with a slice of caramelised lemon tart. The all-French drinking extends from a good Muscadet at £15.50 to Henriot rosé champagne and Pineau des Charentes for the desserts.

Chef/s: Hubert Martel. **Open:** Mon to Sat D 7 to 10. **Closed:** 2 weeks Christmas, 2 weeks Easter. **Meals:** alc

(main courses £17 to £19). **Service:** not inc. **Details:** Cards accepted. 30 seats. No music. No mobile phones. Wheelchair access. Children allowed.

HAMPSHIRE

Caracoli

15 Broad Street, Alresford, SO24 9AR
Tel no: (01962) 738730
www.caracoli.co.uk
Global

Caracoli 'bridges a gap in the food market – in between a tea shop and a bistro'. Fresh, local and quality are bywords, with a 'truly excellent range of home-baked cakes and pastries and good coffee' bolstering the short, daily-changing lunch menu. Typical dishes might include local watercress and trout rillettes served with house hazelnut brioche (£6), or perhaps smoked duck salad with apple, Manchego and chives (£6.50). Sunday brunch is a draw too. Wines start at £12. Open all week.

Marco Pierre White's Yew Tree

Smart country inn

Hollington Cross, Andover Road,
Highclere, RG20 9SE
Tel no: (01635) 253360
www.theyewtree.net
Classic British/French | £30

Marco Pierre White, master of all he surveys, owns this rambling roadside inn by the junction of a narrow lane with the busy A343. The day-to-day running of the kitchen is down to Neil Thornley, who does a sound job in interpreting the MPW classics-based style. The appeal of the long and relatively unchanging menu (some of it in gastronomic franglais) is not hard to find. It delivers good renditions of dishes that soothe rather than challenge. The straightforwardness of the cooking is another confidence-booster, as the repertoire runs from Morecambe Bay potted shrimps via omelette Arnold Bennett, to Wheeler's of St James's fish pie. Another element at work is the comfort factor, which produces parfait of foie gras en gelée, for example, alongside ribeye steak au poivre (or with béarnaise sauce), and British classics like shepherd's pie, braised oxtail and kidney pudding, and rice pudding. Raspberry soufflé is, however, the star turn at dessert. Service is on the ball and the two-page wine list nicely judged, with bottles starting at £15.50 and good choice under £25. France is the focus, although the New World is more than just name-checked.

Chef/s: Neil Thornley. **Open:** all week, L 12 to 2.30 (3 Sun), D 6 to 9.30 (9 Sun). **Closed:** 25 and 26 Dec D, 1 Jan D. **Meals:** alc (main courses £14 to £20). Set L £13.50 (2 courses) to £19.50. Set D Sun £19.50 (2 courses) to £22.95. **Service:** not inc. **Details:** Cards accepted. 70 seats. 30 seats outside. Separate bar. Wheelchair access. Music. Children allowed. Car parking.

Sportsman

Sophisticated cooking in a no-frills pub
Faversham Road, Seasalter, Whitstable, CT5 4BP
Tel no: (01227) 273370
www.thesportsmanseasalter.co.uk
Modern British | £30

In the somewhat bracing setting of the Seasalter coastal grazing marshes stands this simple pub with bare tables, paper napkins and basic cutlery, the simplicity of the setting giving no indication of the quality of the cooking to come. For here the brilliant, idiosyncratic Steve Harris cooks with an instinctive use of the best ingredients. From a winter menu might come a warm rock oyster with homemade chorizo, a little nibble of herring, apple jelly and cream, incredibly moreish pork scratchings and a few slices of own-cured ham. To follow, a trio of scallop dishes: with seaweed butter; with tomato powder and lardo (a delicacy made from pork fat); as a carpaccio topped with smoked brill roe and sorrel. Satisfaction, too, in the form of a superb turbot, its flavour complemented by home-smoked pork belly and a sensational vin jaune sauce. At other times and other meals there have been exemplary roast rack and shank of local lamb and an exquisite banana parfait with hazelnuts, caramel and chocolate sorbet. Attention to the best ingredients extends to bread ('the focaccia in particular'), butter (which is churned on the premises) and the wine – a fairly priced mix of France and New World with the vast majority under £25.
Chef/s: Stephen Harris and Dan Flavel. **Open:** Tue to Sun L 12 to 2.30, Tue to Sat D 7 to 9. **Closed:** Mon, 25 to 26 Dec. **Meals:** alc (main courses £11 to £22). **Service:** not inc. **Details:** Cards accepted. 50 seats. Music. Children allowed. Car parking.

The Allotment

A gem of a find
9 High Street, Dover, CT16 1DP
Tel no: (01304) 214467
www.theallotmentdover.com
Modern British | £24

The best food in Dover is served behind the pretty vine-patterned stained-glass window of a former wine shop. It is an idiosyncratic, informal all-day café-restaurant with an open-plan kitchen-cum-dining room, thoroughly good-humoured service from owner David Flynn and a menu that moves with the seasons. There is no standing on ceremony, yet the food can impress. The style is unmistakably modern British brasserie: fresh soups such as a thick, satisfying carrot, prawns with garlic and chilli and 21-day aged sirloin of beef. Vegetables and salads emphasise the theme, although there's a Mediterranean flavour to some dishes, such as an impressive Andalucian lamb with

couscous. The breakfast menu is worth exploring, too. With a succinct list of modern wines (from £14) it's 'an absolute gem of a find'.
Chef/s: David Flynn. **Open:** Tue to Sat 8.30am to 11pm. **Closed:** Mon, Sun, 24 Dec to 17 Jan. **Meals:** alc (main courses £8 to £17). **Service:** not inc. **Details:** Cards accepted. 26 seats. 26 seats outside. Wheelchair access. Music. Children allowed.

Crooked Billet

Newlands Lane, Stoke Row, RG9 5PU
Tel no: (01491) 681048
www.thecrookedbillet.co.uk
British

'A delight!', exclaimed one reader about this famously idiosyncratic Oxfordshire gem. Out in the middle of nowhere, it maintains a high profile – thanks to numerous film and TV appearances – and crowds come from all over to revel in its classy bohemian atmosphere, fine food and offbeat music events. Local flavours and eclectic ideas fill the handwritten menu, which embraces everything from aubergine polenta cakes with spinach dumpling (£7) to quince Bakewell tart (£5), via venison steak with haggis, roast figs and juniper sauce (£20). Global wines from £16.75. Open all week.

The Sir Charles Napier

Irresistible and original old charmer
Sprigg's Alley, Chinnor, OX39 4BX
Tel no: (01494) 483011
www.sircharlesnapier.co.uk
Modern European | £34

'If ever there was a place that regenerated the spirit, it's the Napier – a deliciously irresistible, quirky piece of gloryland high up in the Chilterns', enthused one fan about this consistent Guide veteran. Its lovable eccentricity, animal sculptures and surreal *objets d'art* continue to charm the pants off everyone, and – as ever – owner Julie Griffiths remains the life and soul of the party. The food is potently seasonal, carefully rendered and convincing, with game a noticeably strong suit – perhaps thick slices of pitch perfect venison with red onion tarte Tatin or 'deeply autumnal' breast of mallard with confit leg, beetroot purée and quince. Fish also shines, witness a memorable 'miniature' of caramelised scallops with teardrops of carrot purée, sultana and hazelnut dressing. Desserts are a treat, whether it's a jokey combo of banana crème brûlée with chocolate doughnuts and toffee popcorn or refreshing mango parfait with Kaffir lime and grapefruit sorbet. The wine list also comes up trumps: it's a deeply considered, creative global selection with France, Australia and California leading the way and house recommendations from £15.95.

Chef/s: Sam Hughes. **Open:** Tue to Sun L 11.30 to 2.30 (3.30 Sun), Tue to Sat D 6 to 9.30 (10 Sat). **Closed:** Mon, 25 to 27 Dec. **Meals:** alc (main courses £17 to £27). Set L Tue to Fri £15.50 (2 courses). Set D Tue to Fri £16.50 (2 courses). **Service:** 12.5% (optional). **Details:** Cards accepted. 70 seats. 70 seats outside. Air-con. Separate bar. Wheelchair access. Music. Children allowed. Car parking.

SURREY

Frère Jacques
Upbeat waterfront brasserie
10-12 Riverside Walk, Kingston-Upon-Thames,
KT1 1QN
www.frerejacques.co.uk
French | £27

On warm summer days there's a touch of the Med at this well-established French-themed brasserie beside the Thames and Kingston Bridge. With red-clothed tables and front terrace it's a perfect spot to watch the world go by. All the seasons are covered though, with further tables beneath a permanent awning and an unstuffy, cheerful dining area inside. The kitchen delivers accomplished Gallic classics (from moules marinière to tarte Tatin) alongside more challenging choices (oven roasted monkfish wrapped in bacon and steamed with dill-infused potatoes, wilted spinach and a shellfish and mussel bisque). An optional fixed-price menu and accessible wines (from £14.25) continue the upbeat form.

Chef/s: Gerhard Peleschka. **Open:** all week L 12 to 5, D 6 to 11. **Closed:** 25 and 26 Dec, 1 Jan. **Meals:** alc (main courses £12 to £18). Set L £12 (2 courses) to £16. **Service:** 12.5% (optional). **Details:** Cards accepted. 52 seats. 48 seats outside. Air-con. Wheelchair access. Music. Children allowed.

EAST SUSSEX

Coach & Horses
Charming, upbeat country pub
School Lane, Danehill, RH17 7JF
Tel no: (01825) 740369
www.coachandhorses.danehill.biz
Gastropub | £25

Ian and Catherine Philpotts have created an upbeat rural pub brimming with charm and character. Overlooking the South Downs, it has stayed true to its roots with roaring fires and real ales in the interlinked bars, while a converted stable makes a suitably rustic dining room. Local sourcing is the foundation of the menus: game liver parfait with redcurrant and rosemary jam, and potted smoked haddock with sauce gribiche, perhaps, followed by confit leg of local rabbit or baked fillets of gurnard with smoked bacon and *fines herbes* risotto. The tidy wine list promises sound drinking from £12.75.

Chef/s: Lee Cobb. **Open:** all week L 12 to 2 (Sat 2.30, Sun 3), Mon to Sat D 7 to 9 (Fri and Sat 9.30). **Meals:** alc

(main courses £11 to £19). **Service:** not inc. **Details:** Cards accepted. 60 seats. 70 seats outside. Separate bar. Wheelchair access. Music. Children allowed. Car parking.

The Restaurant at Drakes
Sophisticated high-end cooking
43-44 Marine Parade, Brighton, BN2 1PE
Tel no: (01273) 696934
www.drakesofbrighton.com
Modern European | £43

Andrew MacKenzie remains at the stoves of this restaurant at the stylish modern hotel on the eastern side of the Brighton seafront. Olive-green banquettes and lowlighting create an atmospheric evening ambience. The culinary approach is high-end, the menus casually multilingual (if erratically spelt), and much of what turns up impresses for both conception and sheer, burnished technique. A gently rich main course of pan-roasted halibut on jet-black squid-ink risotto comes topped with a homemade pasta frisbee of lobster; Oxford beef ribeye is topped with a juice-drenched bundle of braised cheek in a deep, authoritative red wine sauce. A starter of red mullet terrine was less impressive – fridgey and under-seasoned, though it was partially saved by blobs of excellent tapenade. When pre-dessert and petits fours are both unremittingly chococentric, there seems little point in ordering a chocolate dessert – but the nougatine wafers sandwiching white chocolate mousse with malt custard and anglaise sauces was the real deal. Chilean house wines are £16 a bottle, £4 a glass.

Chef/s: Andrew MacKenzie. **Open:** all week L 12.30 to 2 (Sun 2.30), D 7 to 10. **Meals:** alc (main courses £15 to £25). Set L £15 (2 courses) to £20. Sun L £25. **Service:** 12.5% (optional). **Details:** Cards accepted. 45 seats. Air-con. Separate bar. No mobile phones. Music.

WEST SUSSEX

East Beach Café
Stunning building with buzzy menus
Sea Road, Littlehampton, BN17 5GB
Tel no: (01903) 731903
www.eastbeachcafe.co.uk
Modern European | £24

Thomas Hetherwick's eyecatching design has won plaudits and many awards. Sitting on the beach it looks like a gigantic accumulation of driftwood, with full-length windows and an interior concept that's like eating beneath a towering iceberg. David Whiteside cooks an all-week lunch menu (with breakfasts too at weekends), and references many of today's buzzwords. Salt-and-pepper chilli squid, ham hock and Puy lentil salad dressed in honey and mustard, saffron-scented fish chowder, braised shoulder of lamb with mash – it's all here. Kids will love the place, and they'll appreciate having their own menu, while puddings such as East Beach ice cream sundae will bring out the inner kid in all of us. An admirably concise wine selection just about covers most bases. Prices open at £12.95, or £3.95 a glass.

Chef/s: David Whiteside. **Open:** Mon to Sat L 12 to 3, Sun L 12 to 3.30, all week D (June to Aug) 6.30 to 8.30, Thurs to Sat D (Sept to June) 6.30 to 8.00. **Closed:** 23 to 26 Dec. **Meals:** alc (main courses £9 to £17). **Service:** 10% optional for groups of 7 or more people. **Details:** Cards accepted. 65 seats. 80 seats outside. Wheelchair access. Music. Children allowed. Car parking.

Ginger Fox

Convivial country pub star
Henfield Road, Albourne, BN6 9EA
Tel no: (01273) 857888
www.gingermanrestaurants.com
Modern British | £25

Ben McKellar's country venture is a fully-grown pub success story. Whether you are taking advantage of the garden and admiring the thatched roof topped with a fox stalking a pheasant, or sitting inside amid open fires, wood and stone floors, colourful armchairs and leather banquettes, all is busy, convivial and unreservedly good-natured. Visitors have been delighted with the 'seasonal food, the robust flavours, the game selection, the well-cooked fish'. While the kitchen works in tandem with regional producers, inspiration comes from near and far: homespun English diehards (braised oxtail with parsnip mash) sit happily beside classic European ideas (crispy plaice, squid and chickpea salad to start, say, then local cod fillet with white bean, wild mushroom and Toulouse sausage). Desserts like 'an incredibly light' steamed maple and walnut pudding or brioche bread-and-butter pudding close proceedings. House wine £13.50.

Chef/s: David Keates, Ben McKellar. **Open:** all week L 12 to 2 (12 to 4 Sat, 12.30 to 4 Sun), all week D 6 to 10 (6.30 to 10 Sat and Sun). **Meals:** alc (main courses £9 to £18). Set L £10 (2 courses). **Service:** not inc. **Details:** Cards accepted. 50 seats. 90 seats outside. Separate bar. Wheelchair access. Music. Children allowed. Car parking.

ISLE OF WIGHT

Robert Thompson at the Hambrough

Cooking with a touch of genius
Hambrough Road, Ventnor, Isle of Wight, PO38 1SQ
Tel no: (01983) 856333
www.thehambrough.com
Modern French | £45

The quirky resort town of Ventnor is enjoying a renaissance, and Robert Thompson's arrival at the Hambrough last summer heralded a sea change in the kitchen at this welcoming boutique hotel, set on an elegant street of Victorian town-houses perched

above the esplanade. The light, airy and comfortable dining room, now firmly established as the island's premier foodie destination, boasts commanding views over the harbour and out to sea. Thompson turns out beautifully executed, labour-intensive dishes that draw inspiration from their surroundings, showcasing local produce alongside a host of fine ingredients from further afield. The signature starter, a terrine of lightly smoked eel with foie gras, pork belly and Granny Smith apple, is a skilfully concocted study in rich, earthy flavours and mouth-pleasing textures. The stand-out dish at inspection was an exquisite lasagne of local scallops, pungent truffles and silky Jerusalem artichoke purée, sealed and baked in a large scallop shell. Prised open at the table, it filled the room with an attention-grabbing aroma. Main courses maintain the wow factor, with dishes that charm rather than challenge, as in a beautifully composed presentation of succulent black leg chicken with stuffed morels, crisp tips of asparagus and an intensely flavoured forcemeat boudin. A thick slab of brill was poached to pillowy perfection, topped with a glossy slick of tangy sauce matelote and served on layers of lovage-scented mash sautéed chanterelle mushrooms and braised salsify. Pre-eminent among the puddings was an inspired combination of unctuous blackberry soufflé and Ventnor stout ice cream. The Hambrough's hefty wine list presents a near-comprehensive choice of terroirs and varietals, with some interesting options in the £20-£30 range and ample temptation for big spenders, too. A commendable 16 wines are sold by the glass, from £5 to £9, including a lip-smacking pink Champagne, a crisp Slovenian Pinot Grigio, a supple Pinot Noir and a mouth-filling Margaux.

Chef/s: Robert Thompson. **Open:** Tue to Sat L 12 to 1.30, D 7 to 9.30. **Closed:** Sun, Mon, 2 weeks Jan, 2 weeks Nov, 2 weeks April. **Meals:** Set L £20 (2 courses) to £24. Set D £38 (2 courses) to £45. Tasting menu £59. **Service:** not inc. **Details:** Cards accepted. 30 seats. 20 seats outside. Air-con. Separate bar. No mobile phones. Music. Children allowed.

Content brought to you by **The Good Food Guide 2010**. Please see pages 20-21 for further details.

Tourist Information Centres

When you arrive at your destination, visit an Official Partner Tourist Information Centre for quality assured help with accommodation and information about local attractions and events, or email your request before you go. To search for attractions and Tourist Information Centres on the move just text INFO to 62233, and a web link will be sent to your mobile phone. To find a Tourist Information Centre by region visit enjoyEngland.com/find-tic.

AYLESBURY	The Kings Head	01296 330559	tic@aylesburyvaledc.gov.uk
BANBURY	Spiceball Park Road	01295 259855	banbury.tic@cherwell-dc.gov.uk
BICESTER	Bicester Visitor Centre	01869 369055	bicester.vc@cherwell-dc.gov.uk
BRIGHTON	Royal Pavilion Shop	0906 711 2255	brighton-tourism@brighton-hove.gov.uk
BURFORD	The Brewery	01993 823558	burford.vic@westoxon.gov.uk
CANTERBURY	12/13 Sun Street	01227 378100	canterburyinformation@canterbury.gov.uk
CHICHESTER	29a South Street	01243 775888	chitic@chichester.gov.uk
COWES	9 The Arcade	01983 813818	info@islandbreaks.co.uk
CROYDON	Croydon Clocktower	020 8253 1009	tic@croydon.gov.uk
DOVER	The Old Town Gaol	01304 205108	tic@doveruk.com
GRAVESEND	Towncentric	01474 337600	info@towncentric.co.uk
HASTINGS	Queens Square	01424 781111	hic@hastings.gov.uk
LEWES	187 High Street	01273 483448	lewes.tic@lewes.gov.uk
MAIDSTONE	Town Hall, Middle Row	01622 602169	tourism@maidstone.gov.uk
MARGATE	12-13 The Parade	0870 2646111	margate.tic@visitor-centre.net
MARLOW	31 High Street	01628 483597	tourism_enquiries@wycombe.gov.uk
NEWBURY	The Wharf	01635 30267	tourism@westberks.gov.uk
NEWPORT	The Guildhall	01983 813818	info@islandbreaks.co.uk
OXFORD	Oxford Information Centre	01865 726871	tic@oxford.gov.uk
PORTSMOUTH	Clarence Esplanade	023 9282 6722	vis@portsmouthcc.gov.uk
PORTSMOUTH	The Hard	023 9282 6722	vis@portsmouthcc.gov.uk
RAMSGATE	17 Albert Court	0870 2646111	ramsgate.tic@visitor-centre.net
RICHMOND	Old Town Hall	020 8940 9125	info@visitrichmond.co.uk

ROCHESTER	95 High Street	01634 843666	visitor.centre@medway.gov.uk
ROMSEY	Heritage & Visitor Centre	01794 512987	romseytic@testvalley.gov.uk
ROYAL TUNBRIDGE WELLS	The Old Fish Market	01892 515675	touristinformationcentre@tunbridgewells.gov.uk
RYDE	81-83 Union Street	01983 813818	info@islandbreaks.co.uk
RYE	The Heritage Centre	01797 226696	ryetic@rother.gov.uk
SANDOWN	8 High Street	01983 813818	info@islandbreaks.co.uk
SHANKLIN	67 High Street	01983 813818	info@islandbreaks.co.uk
SOUTHAMPTON	9 Civic Centre Road	023 8083 3333	tourist.information@southampton.gov.uk
SWANLEY	Swanley Library	01322 614660	touristinfo@swanley.org.uk
WINCHESTER	Guildhall	01962 840500	tourism@winchester.gov.uk
WINDSOR	Royal Windsor Shopping Centre	01753 743900	windsor.tic@rbwm.gov.uk
WITNEY	26A Market Square	01993 775802	witney.vic@westoxon.gov.uk
WOODSTOCK	Oxfordshire Museum	01993 813276	woodstock.vic@westoxon.gov.uk
WORTHING	Marine Parade	01903 221066	tic@worthing.gov.uk
YARMOUTH	The Quay	01983 813818	info@islandbreaks.co.uk

Regional Contacts and Information

For more information on accommodation, attractions, activities, events and holidays in South East England, contact the regional or local tourism organisations. Their websites have a wealth of information and many produce free publications to help you get the most out of your visit.

The following publications are available from Tourism South East by logging on to www.visitsoutheastengland.com or by calling (023) 8062 5400

E-Brochures
Family Fun
Time for Us

South East England – We know just the place...

Quality
visitor attractions

VisitBritain operates a Visitor Attraction Quality Assurance Service.

Participating attractions are visited annually by trained, impartial assessors who look at all aspects of the visit, from initial telephone enquiries to departure, customer service to catering, as well as all facilities and activities.

Only those attractions which have been assessed by Enjoy England and meet the standard receive the quality marque, your sign of a Quality Assured Visitor Attraction.

Look out for the quality marque and visit with confidence.

Where to Stay

Entries appear alphabetically by town name in each county. A key to symbols appears on page 6. Maps start on page 394. A listing of all Enjoy England assessed accommodation appears at the end of the region.

HURLEY, Berkshire Map ref 2C2
SAT NAV SL6 5NE

Hurley Riverside Park
Hurley, Maidenhead SL6 5NE
t (01628) 824493 **f** (01628) 825533 **e** info@hurleyriversidepark.co.uk
w hurleyriversidepark.co.uk ONLINE MAP GUEST REVIEWS ONLINE BOOKING LAST MINUTE OFFERS

⊟ (138)	£12.00–£23.00
⊟ (138)	£12.00–£23.00
⅄ (62)	£10.00–£20.00
⊞ (10)	£280.00–£460.00
200 touring pitches	

SPECIAL PROMOTIONS
Check our website for short
breaks and late deals

Family-run Park situated alongside the River Thames. Ideal for visiting LEGOLAND® Windsor and Oxford. Access to the Thames Path. Gold David Bellamy Conservation Award. We welcome Tourers, Tents & Motorhomes. Electric, Multi-service & Hardstanding pitches available. Caravan Holiday Home and ReadyTent Hire. Free showers and disabled facilities. Shop.

open March to October
payment credit/debit cards, cash, cheques

directions M4 J8/9 or M40 J4, onto A404(M),
third exit to Henley (A4130). Past Hurley Village
turn right into Shepherds Lane.

General ⊟ ⓦ ⛤ ⛐ ⌂ ⚲ ☼ ⊡ ◖ ▷ ♀ ⓦ Leisure ▶ ⌁ ⚏

Looking for something else?

You can also buy a copy of our popular guide 'B&B' including guest accommodation, B&B's, guest houses, farmhouses, inns, and campus and hostel accommodation in England 2010.
Now available in good bookshops and online at **enjoyenglanddirect.com**

£11.99

READING, Berkshire Map ref 2C2   SAT NAV RG7 1SP

TOURING & CAMPING PARK

57 touring pitches

Wellington Country Park - Caravan & Campsite
Odiham Road, Riseley, Nr Reading RG7 1SP
t (0118) 932 6444 f (0118) 932 6445 e info@wellington-country-park.co.uk
w **wellington-country-park.co.uk** ONLINE MAP ONLINE BOOKING

Set within beautiful woodlands and parklands, fees includes FREE entry to the Park with nature trails, children's play areas, miniature railway, sand pits, crazy golf. Special events all year. **directions** Hampshire/Berkshire border between Reading and Basingstoke. • M4 junction 11 A33 towards Basingstoke. • M3 junction 5 B3349 Reading. Sat Nav enter B3349 or Odiham Road, Riseley. **open** February to November **payment** credit/debit cards, cash, cheques

General 🗐 🐕 🛒 🛉 🅿 ☼ 🔌 🏪 🚰 ✕   Leisure ∪ ⚲ ⚠

FORDINGBRIDGE, Hampshire Map ref 2B3   SAT NAV SP6 2JY

HOLIDAY PARK · ROSE AWARD CARAVAN HOLIDAY PARK

🚐 (233)	£10.00–£40.00
🚛 (233)	£10.00–£40.00
⛺ (233)	£10.00–£40.00
🏠 (131)	£199–£995
🚏 (131)	£125.00–£795.00

233 touring pitches

Sandy Balls Holiday Centre
Godshill, Fordingbridge SP6 2JY
t (01425) 653042 f (01425) 653067 e post@sandy-balls.co.uk
w **sandy-balls.co.uk** ONLINE BOOKING LAST MINUTE OFFERS

Nestled in 120 acres of woods and parkland, guests can enjoy dinner at The Bistro, woodland walks, swimming pools, relax at Tempus health & beauty or get active at the Cycle Centre! **directions** Sandy Balls is situated at the western end of Godshill village, a little more than a mile from Fordingbridge on the B3078. **open** All year **payment** credit/debit cards, cash, cheques

General ⚲ 🗐 🍴 🐕 🛒 🛉 🅿 ☼ 🔌 🚰 🏪 📶 ✕   Leisure ∪ ⚲ ♪ 🎣 🏹 ⚑ ⚠

GOSPORT, Hampshire Map ref 2C3   SAT NAV PO13 9BG

HOLIDAY, TOURING & CAMPING PARK

🚐 (120)	£17.00–£22.00
🚛 (120)	£17.00–£22.00
⛺ (120)	£12.00–£19.00
🚏 (30)	£225.00–£470.00

120 touring pitches

Kingfisher Caravan Park
Browndown Road, Stokes Road, Gosport, Lee-On-The-Solent PO13 9BG
t (023) 9250 2611 f (023) 9258 3583 e info@kingfisher-caravan-park.co.uk
w **kingfisher-caravan-park.co.uk**

Family-run park, very close to the sea, with views across the Solent to the Isle of Wight. Clubhouse, Restaurant, Shop, Launderette, Children's Room. Caravans for hire and for sale. **directions** M27 Junction 11, A32 towards Gosport. **open** All year **payment** credit/debit cards, cash, cheques

General ⚲ 🗐 🐕 🛒 🛉 🅿 ☼ 🔌 🚰 🏪 📶 ✕   Leisure ♪ ⚑ 🎵 🏹

HAMBLE, Hampshire Map ref 2C3   SAT NAV SO31 4HR

HOLIDAY, TOURING & CAMPING PARK

🚐 (77)	£15.00–£32.00
🚛 (77)	£15.00–£32.00
⛺	£13.00–£27.00
🏠 (8)	£355–£851
🚏 (14)	£274.00–£881.00

77 touring pitches

Riverside Holidays
Satchell Lane, Hamble, Southampton SO31 4HR
t (023) 8045 3220 f (023) 8045 3611 e enquiries@riversideholidays.co.uk
w **riversideholidays.co.uk** ONLINE MAP LAST MINUTE OFFERS

Quiet park overlooking marina and River Hamble, on edge of picturesque sailing village with many pubs and restaurants. Caravan holiday homes and pine lodges for hire, plus camping and touring facilities. **directions** Leave M27 at junction 8, follow signs for Hamble. Pass Tesco, continue over two mini roundabouts. Through traffic lights and take immediate left into Satchell Lane. **open** All year **payment** credit/debit cards, cash, cheques

General 🗐 🐕 🛉 🅿 ☼ 🚲 🔌 🚰 🏪   Leisure ⚓ ∪ ⚲ ♪

NEW MILTON, Hampshire Map ref 2B3   SAT NAV BH25 5NH

Glen Orchard Holiday Park
Walkford Lane, New Milton BH25 5NH
t (01425) 616463 **f** (01425) 638655 **e** enquiries@glenorchard.co.uk
w glenorchard.co.uk

🚎 (19)   £170.00–£580.00

Small family park in secluded, landscaped setting close to beaches, forest, riding, golf and fishing. Convenient for Bournemouth, Christchurch, Lymington, Southampton and Isle of Wight. **directions** A35 Lyndhurst to Bournemouth approximately 8 miles, at Hinton turn left into Ringwood Road after 0.75 mile Walkford Road, after 0.75 mile turn left into Walkford Lane. **open** March to October **payment** credit/debit cards, cash, cheques

General ▣ ♟ ☼ Leisure ▶ ∪ ♿ ✦ ◉ ⚠

RINGWOOD, Hampshire Map ref 2B3   SAT NAV BH24 2SB

Shamba Holidays
230 Ringwood Road, St Leonards, Ringwood BH24 2SB
t (01202) 873302 **f** (01202) 873392 **e** enquiries@shambaholidays.co.uk
w shambaholidays.co.uk ONLINE MAP LAST MINUTE OFFERS

🚐 (150)   £18.00–£28.00
🚎 (150)   £18.00–£28.00
⛺ (150)   £18.00–£28.00
150 touring pitches

Great for exploring Hampshire and Dorset. Family-run touring and camping park close to New Forest and Bournemouth. Modern toilet/shower facilities, heated indoor/outdoor pool, licensed clubhouse, games room, play area, takeaway, shop. **directions** Located off the main A31 Wimborne to Ringwood road, turn left at signboard into East Moors Lane. Approximately 1 mile on right-hand side. **open** March to October **payment** credit/debit cards, cash, cheques

General ▣ ♟ ⚞ ⓟ ♟ ☼ 🅿 ⌨ ⓒ ☎ 🅿 ✕ Leisure ▶ ∪ ♩ ⚞ ⚲ ❦ ♟ ✦ ⚠

ROMSEY, Hampshire Map ref 2C3   SAT NAV SO51 6FH

Hill Farm Caravan Park
Branches Lane, Sherfield English, Romsey SO51 6FH
t (01794) 340402 **f** (01794) 342358 **e** gjb@hillfarmpark.com

🚐 (70)   £14.00–£28.00
🚎 (70)   £14.00–£28.00
⛺ (40)   £14.00–£28.00
🚎 (6)   £280.00–£500.00
70 touring pitches

Set in 11 acres of beautiful countryside on the edge of the New Forest, our family-run site provides an ideal base from which to visit the area. Touring pitches from March to October, holiday homes from February to January. **directions** Directions given at time of booking. **open** Touring & Camping March to October, Statics February to December **payment** cash, cheques

General ⚘ ▣ ♕ ♟ ⚞ ♟ ☼ 🖥 🅿 ⓒ ☎ 🅿 Leisure ▶ ∪ ♩ ⚠

WINCHESTER, Hampshire Map ref 2C3   SAT NAV SO21 1HL

Morn Hill Caravan Club Site
Alresford Road, Winchester SO21 1HL
t (01962) 869877
w caravanclub.co.uk

THE
CARAVAN
CLUB

🚐 (120)   £10.60–£23.20
🚎 (120)   £10.60–£23.20
120 touring pitches

An ideal base from which to explore the area – Winchester is an old cathedral city of considerable charm for it has retained many of its ancient buildings. Oxford, Windsor, The New Forest and Stonehenge all within an hour's drive. **directions** From M3 jct 10 A31 (signposted Alton). Left at roundabout (Percy Hobbs sign), signposted Easton. Immediate turn in front of pub, top of lane for Caravan Club. **open** April to November **payment** credit/debit cards, cash, cheques

General ▣ ♟ ⓟ ♟ ☼ 🖥 🅿 ⓒ ☎ 🅿 Leisure ▶ ♩ ⚠

ARRETON, Isle of Wight Map ref 2C3 — SAT NAV PO30 3DL

Perreton Farm

East Lane, Arreton, Newport PO30 3DL
t (01983) 865218 e roger@turboweb.org
w **islandbreaks.co.uk**

🚐 (10)	£9.00–£10.00
🚏 (10)	£9.00–£10.00
⛺ (10)	£8.00–£10.00

10 touring pitches

Farm with countryside views, quiet location. Ideal for walkers and cyclists with plenty of footpaths. Cycle track nearby with hire facilities on farm. Dogs welcome. Good pubs in village. **directions** Please contact us for directions **open** April to October **payment** cash, cheques

General 🐕 🔥 ☀ ▣ 🚿 🔌 ♿   Leisure ► ∪ ⚲ ⌁

BEMBRIDGE, Isle of Wight Map ref 2C3 — SAT NAV PO35 5PL

Whitecliff Bay Holiday Park

Hillway Road, Bembridge PO35 5PL
t (01983) 872671 f (01983) 872941 e holiday@whitecliff-bay.com
w **whitecliff-bay.com** ONLINE MAP ONLINE BOOKING LAST MINUTE OFFERS

🚐 (400)	£4.00–£45.00
🚏 (400)	£4.00–£45.00
⛺ (400)	£4.00–£35.00
🏠 (130)	£82–£821
🏚 (100)	£112.00–£966.00

400 touring pitches

SPECIAL PROMOTIONS
Special offers are available from time to time. Please visit our website for full details.

Situated in an area of outstanding natural beauty, the park offers great-value family holidays. There are facilities on site for all ages. Pets welcome in low season.

open March to end of October
payment credit/debit cards, cash, cheques, euros

directions From A3055 turn onto B3395 at Brading and follow signposts.

General ▣ 🐕 ⚡ 🚻 🔥 ☀ ▣ 🚿 🔌 ⏱ ♿ 🔌 ✕   Leisure ► ⌁ ⚓ ↖ ♟ 🎵 🎣 ⛰

FRESHWATER, Isle of Wight Map ref 2C3 — SAT NAV PO40 9SH

Heathfield Farm Camping

Heathfield Road, Freshwater PO40 9SH
t (01983) 407822 e web@heathfieldcamping.co.uk
w **heathfieldcamping.co.uk** GUEST REVIEWS

🚏 (50)	£10.50–£16.00
⛺ (60)	£4.25–£5.25

60 touring pitches

Family camping in a quiet, rural area with magnificent sea and downland views. Located on the outskirts of Freshwater village, 2 miles from Yarmouth ferry port and the Needles. **directions** Please contact us for directions **payment** credit/debit cards, cash

General ⚡ ▣ 🚰 🐕 🚻 🔥 ☀ ▣ 🔌 ⏱ ♿ 🔌   Leisure ∪ ⚲ ⛰

RYDE, Isle of Wight Map ref 2C3

Roebeck Camping and Caravan Park

Gatehouse Road, Upton Cross, Ryde PO33 4BS
t (01983) 611475 e andrew.cross@roebeck-farm.co.uk
w **roebeck-farm.co.uk** ONLINE MAP ONLINE BOOKING

(6)	£4.50
(6)	£4.50
(20)	£4.50
32 touring pitches	

A small campsite set in 10 acres of farmland on the outskirts of Ryde, with toilet, shower and laundry facilities. Also tipi hire available. **directions** Please contact us for directions **open** May to October **payment** credit/debit cards, cash, cheques, euros

General   Leisure

RYDE, Isle of Wight Map ref 2C3

Whitefield Forest Touring Park

Brading Road, Ryde PO33 1QL
t (01983) 617069 e pat&louise@whitefieldforest.co.uk
w **whitefieldforest.co.uk**

(50)	£11.50–£17.50
(50)	£11.50–£17.50
(50)	£11.50–£17.50
100 touring pitches	

New family-run touring park located in the tranquil setting of Whitefield Forest. All pitches are level and spacious, with new amenities block including baby, family and disabled facilities. **directions** Just off A3055 follow to Brading, at Tescoes roundabout straight accross, site approx half mile on left hand side. **open** 30 March to 5 October **payment** credit/debit cards, cash, cheques

General   Leisure

SANDOWN, Isle of Wight Map ref 2C3

Cheverton Copse Holiday Park Ltd

Scotchells Brook Lane, Sandown, Isle of Wight PO36 0JP
t (01983) 403161 f (01983) 408942 e holidays@chevertoncopse.com
w **chevertoncopse.com** ONLINE MAP GUEST REVIEWS LAST MINUTE OFFERS

(1)	£484–£807
(57)	£259.00–£709.00

SPECIAL PROMOTIONS
Many special offers available, please see website for current offers.

Set in 4 acres of safe and attractive wooded parkland, only 1.75 miles from Sandown Bay. Quietly resting among the trees, Cheverton Copse is within easy reach of the many amenities and attractions of Sandown and Shanklin.

open Open 21st March to 7th November 2009
payment credit/debit cards, cheques

directions Please contact us for directions

General
Leisure

SHANKLIN, Isle of Wight Map ref 2C3   SAT NAV PO37 7PJ

Landguard Holidays
Landguard Manor Road, Shanklin PO37 7PJ
t (01983) 863100 **f** (01983) 867896 **e** enquiries@landguardholidays.co.uk
w landguardholidays.co.uk ONLINE MAP ONLINE BOOKING

🚐	£6.00–£34.00
⛺	£354–£1379
🏠	£204.00–£919.00

Landguard Holidays enjoys a beautiful woodland setting on the edge of Shanklin, close to the town centre and the picturesque olde worlde village of Shanklin. **directions** From Ryde take A3055. Turn right onto the A3056 then take the fourth turning on the left and continue along this road until you reach the Park. **open** March to October **payment** credit/debit cards, cheques

General 🔲 🐕 🎿 🏕 🏍 🍴 👕 ✕   Leisure 🎣 🏹 ⚲ 🍷 🎵 🎢

SHANKLIN, Isle of Wight Map ref 2C3   SAT NAV PO37 7LL

Lower Hyde Holiday Park
Landguard Road, Shanklin PO37 7LL
t 0871 664 9752 **f** (01983) 862532 **e** holidaysales.lowerhyde@park-resorts.com
w park-resorts.com ONLINE MAP ONLINE BOOKING

🚐	£6.00–£27.00
⛺	£5.00–£24.00
🏠	£433–£1544
🏠	£217–£774
🏠	£233.00–£1084.00

The seaside resort of Shanklin is a popular family location with sandy beaches, gift shops, fun amusements and an old village packed full of character. **directions** Take the A3055 towards Shanklin. Turn right onto A3056, take the fourth turning on the left and continue along the road. The Park entrance on your right. **open** March to October **payment** credit/debit cards, cheques

General 🔲 🐕 🎿 🏍 🎮 🍴 👕 ✕   Leisure ⚲ 🎣 🏹 🍷 🎵

ST HELENS, Isle of Wight Map ref 2C3   SAT NAV PO33 1YL

Carpenters Farm Campsite
Carpenters Road, St Helens PO33 1YL
t (01983) 874557 **e** info@carpentersfarms.co.uk
w carpentersfarm.co.uk LAST MINUTE OFFERS

🚐	(70)	£10.00–£15.00
🚐	(70)	£10.00–£15.00
⛺	(70)	£10.00–£15.00
	70 touring pitches	

Farm campsite with beautiful views in picturesque rural setting, adjacent to RSPB Reserve and SSSI. Close to beaches and attractions. Relaxed atmosphere on site. Family groups and pets very welcome. **directions** Please contact us for directions **open** All year **payment** cash, cheques

General 🔲 🐕 🎿 🏍 ☀ 🎮 👕   Leisure ∪ 🏌 🎢

ST HELENS, Isle of Wight Map ref 2C3   SAT NAV PO33 1YA

Nodes Point Holiday Park
Nodes Road, St Helens PO33 1YA
t 0871 664 9758 **f** (01983) 874696 **e** holidaysales.nodespoint@park-resorts.com
w park-resorts.com ONLINE MAP ONLINE BOOKING

🚐	£6.00–£30.00
⛺	£5.00–£27.00
🏠	£396–£1319
🏠	£216–£769
🏠	£216.00–£1059.00

Enjoy spectacular coastal views from 65 acres of parkland running down to the beach. The golden sands of Ryde, and Sandown's fun pier are just a short drive away. **directions** From A3055, go straight ahead onto the B3330 towards St Helens. After 2 miles as the road curves to the right, turn left into the Park. **open** March to October **payment** credit/debit cards, cheques

General 🔲 🐕 🎿 🏕 🏍 🎮 👕 ✕   Leisure ▶ ∪ 🎣 🍷 🎵 🔍

THORNESS BAY, Isle of Wight Map ref 2C3

SAT NAV PO31 8NJ

Thorness Bay Holiday Park

Thorness Lane, Nr Cowes, Thorness PO31 8NJ
t 0871 664 9779 **f** (01983) 822213 **e** holidaysales.thornessbay@park-resorts.com
w **park-resorts.com** ONLINE MAP ONLINE BOOKING

🚐	£6.00–£30.00
🚐	£6.00–£30.00
▲	£5.00–£22.00
♠	£382–£1344
🛏	£196–£1344
🏕	£202.00–£1014.00

With stunning views from the Park, a stroll through leafy woodland brings you to the sea. **directions** Take the A3054 towards Newport. After Shalfleet, turn left at the garage and follow the road. After 2 miles turn left towards the entrance to the park. **open** March to October **payment** credit/debit cards, cheques

General 🔌 🐕 🛒 💷 📻 🍴 ⛱ 👕 ✕ **Leisure** ∪ 🎣 🗲 ⚡ 🎵 🎯

YARMOUTH, Isle of Wight Map ref 2C3

SAT NAV PO41 0TS

The Orchards Holiday Caravan & Camping Park

Main Road, Newbridge PO41 0TS
t (01983) 531331 **f** (01983) 531666 **e** info@orchards-holiday-park.co.uk
w **orchards-holiday-park.co.uk** GUEST REVIEWS LAST MINUTE OFFERS

🚐	£15.00–£26.00
🚐	£15.00–£26.00
▲	£15.00–£26.00
🏕	£230.00–£895.00
175 touring pitches	

Situated in beautiful countryside. 65 luxury holiday caravans and 175 touring pitches. 2 pools, shop, takeaway, dog-walking area and more. Excellent for walking and cycling. New facilities centre 09. See website for offers. **directions** From Yarmouth, take A3054 to Newport. 3 miles turn right at Horse and Groom Inn. Follow signs to Newbridge. Entrance opposite post-office. **open** 7th February 2009 to 2nd January 2010 **payment** cash, cheques

General 🔌 🐕 🛒 💷 📻 ☼ 📺 🍴 👕 ⛱ **Leisure** ⛶ ∪ 🎣 🗲 🎯 ⛰

ASHFORD, Kent Map ref 3B4

SAT NAV TN26 1NQ

Broadhembury Holiday Park (C & C)

Steeds Lane, Kingsnorth, Kent TN26 1NQ
t (01233) 620859 **f** (01233) 620918 **e** holidaypark@broadhembury.co.uk
w **broadhembury.co.uk** ONLINE MAP GUEST REVIEWS ONLINE BOOKING LAST MINUTE OFFERS

🚐 (60)	£18.00–£22.00
🚐 (60)	£18.00–£22.00
▲ (50)	£16.00–£20.00
🏕 (5)	£245.00–£435.00
60 touring pitches	

For walking, cycling, visiting castles and gardens or just relaxing, Broadhembury is a park for all seasons. Convenient for Channel crossings and Canterbury. Excellent facilities for families, disabled people and couples. **directions** Junction 10 off M20 - take A2070 for approx. 2 miles - turn left at 2nd roundabout following signs for Kingsnorth. Park signposted from hereon. **open** All year **payment** credit/debit cards, cash, cheques

General ♿ 🔲 📶 🐕 🛒 💷 📻 ☼ 📺 🚲 💷 👕 ⛱ 🔰 **Leisure** ⛶ ∪ 🗲 🎯 ⛰

BIRCHINGTON, Kent Map ref 3C3

SAT NAV CT7 0HD

Two Chimneys Caravan Park

Shottendane Road, Birchington CT7 0HD
t (01843) 843157 **f** (01843) 848099 **e** info@twochimneys.co.uk
w **twochimneys.co.uk**

🚐 (100)	£18.00–£29.00
🚐 (50)	£18.00–£29.00
▲ (100)	£16.50–£26.50
🏕 (10)	£325.00–£665.00
250 touring pitches	

A friendly, family-run country site near sandy beaches. Spacious, level pitches. Modern wc/shower and laundry facilities including disabled. Children's play and ball-games areas. Holiday Hire Available. Caravan Storage. **directions** A2 then A28 to Birchington. Turn right into Park Lane, bear left into Manston Road, left at crossroads (B2049), site on right. **open** Easter to October **payment** credit/debit cards, cash, cheques

General 🔲 🛒 💷 📻 ☼ 📺 🍴 👕 ⛱ 🔰 **Leisure** ∪ 🏌 🛝 🗲 🎣 🎯 🎯 ⛰

CANTERBURY, Kent Map ref 3B3

Yew Tree Park

Stone Street, Canterbury CT4 5PL
t (01227) 700306 f (01227) 700306 e info@yewtreepark.com
w **yewtreepark.com** ONLINE MAP LAST MINUTE OFFERS

🚐 (20)	£13.20–£18.50
🚐 (5)	£13.20–£18.50
🛖 (20)	£13.20–£18.50
🏠 (8)	£195.00–£450.00

45 touring pitches

Picturesque country park close to Canterbury, centrally located for exploring Kent. Naturally landscaped touring and camping facilitie Holiday Apartments, Lodge and static units. Outdoor heated pool. **directions** On B2068, 4 miles south of Canterbury, 9 miles north o M20, jct 11, then turn by Chequers Inn. Park entrance on left han side. **open** March to October **payment** credit/debit cards, cash, cheques

General 🗄 ⓦ 🛒 ⌂ ☼ 🔌 🅿 🐕 Leisure 🎣 ⛰

FOLKESTONE, Kent Map ref 3B4

Black Horse Farm Caravan Club Site

385 Canterbury Road, Densole, Folkestone CT18 7BG
t (01303) 892665
w **caravanclub.co.uk**

🚐 (140)	£12.20–£25.30
🚐 (140)	£12.20–£25.30

140 touring pitches

SPECIAL PROMOTIONS
Special member rates mean you can save your membership subscription in less than a week. Visit our website to find out more.

Set in the heart of farming country in the Kentish village of Densole on the Downs. This i a quiet and relaxed country site, ideally suited for families wishing to visit the many interestin local attractions including the historic city of Canterbury. For nature lovers there are many walks.

open All year
payment credit/debit cards, cash, cheques

directions From M20 jct 13 on A260 to Canterbury, 2 miles from junction with A20, sit on left 200 yds past Black Horse inn.

General 🗄 ⓦ 🐕 🛒 ⌂ ☼ 🔌 🔌 🅿 🐕 🆆
Leisure ▶ 🎿 ⛰

KINGSDOWN, Kent Map ref 3C4

Kingsdown Park Holiday Village

Upper Street, Kingsdown, Deal CT14 8EU
t (01304) 361205 f (01304) 380125 e info@kingsdownpark.co.uk
w **kingsdownpark.net** ONLINE MAP ONLINE BOOKING LAST MINUTE OFFERS

🏠 (50) £219–£677

This picturesque park provides the perfect base for exploring Kent Comfortable lodges and excellent leisure facilities ensure you are not disappointed. **directions** Please contact us for directions **open** March to October and 20 December to 3 January **payment** credit/ debit cards, cash, cheques

General ♿ 🗄 ⓦ 🛒 ☼ ✕ Leisure ▶ ⛳ 🚲 🎿 ☂ 🍸 🎯 ⛰

MAIDSTONE, Kent Map ref 3B3

SAT NAV ME17 1XH

Bearsted Caravan Club Site
Ashford Road, Hollingbourne ME17 1XH
t 01622 730018 f 01622 734498

£12.20–£25.30
£12.20–£25.30
69 touring pitches

SPECIAL PROMOTIONS
Special member rates mean you can save your membership subscription in less than a week. Visit our website to find out more.

The site gently slopes towards the open perimeter grounds of Leeds Castle. Surrounded by fields this site offers an ideal peaceful stop off point en route to the ferry ports. For longer stays its ideally located for exploring the beautiful countryside of Kent and its various tourist attractions.

open All year

directions Leave M20 at junction 8, at roundabout turn into road signposted Bearsted, Maidstone. Site on left in 1/2 mile.

General 🔲 🐦 🐾 🔲 🔲 🖑
Leisure 🅰

MARDEN, Kent Map ref 3B4

SAT NAV TN12 9ND

Tanner Farm Park
Tanner Farm, Goudhurst Road, Marden TN12 9ND
t (01622) 832399 f (01622) 832472 e enquiries@tannerfarmpark.co.uk
w **tannerfarmpark.co.uk**

(100)   £13.00–£19.00
(33)   £13.00–£19.00
(20)   £13.00–£19.00
100 touring pitches

Secluded park on beautiful family farm. Ideal touring base for the area. Gold David Bellamy Conservation Award. Bed and breakfast also available. Green Tourism Business Scheme silver. [Caravan Club AS.] **directions** From A21 or A229 onto B2079; midway between Marden and Goudhurst. **open** All year **payment** credit/debit cards, cash, cheques

General 🔲🔲👋🐦🏋🛏🐾☀🔲🔲🖑🏕🔲 Leisure ✏🔍🅰

BURFORD, Oxfordshire Map ref 2B1

SAT NAV OX18 4JJ

Burford Caravan Club Site
Bradwell Grove, Burford OX18 4JJ
t (01993) 823080 f (01993) 824632
w **caravanclub.co.uk**

(119)   £14.00–£26.90
(119)   £14.00–£26.90
119 touring pitches

Attractive, spacious site opposite Cotswold Wildlife Park. Burford has superb Tudor houses, a museum and historic inns. A great base from which to explore the Cotswolds. **directions** From roundabout at A40/A361 junction in Burford, take A361 signposted Lechlade. Site on right after 2.5 miles. Site signposted from roundabout. **open** July to November **payment** credit/debit cards, cash, cheques

General 🔲🏋🐾☀🔲🔲🖑🏕🔲 Leisure 🅰

STANDLAKE, Oxfordshire Map ref 2C1

SAT NAV OX29 7PZ

Hardwick Parks

The Downs, Standlake, Witney OX29 7PZ
t (01865) 300501 **f** (01865) 300037 **e** info@hardwickparks.co.uk
w hardwickparks.co.uk ONLINE MAP

🚐 (214)	£17.50–£19.50
🚃 (214)	£17.50–£19.50
⛺ (214)	£14.50–£16.50
🏠	£226.00–£499.00
214 touring pitches	

Rural park near Witney with lakes and river on site. Licensed air conditioned clubhouse and air conditioned shower block. Tents, caravans and motorhomes welcome. Holiday caravans for hire and sale. **directions** Four and a half miles from Witney, signposted from the A415. **open** April to October **payment** credit/debit cards, cash, cheques

General 🔲 🕎 🐾 🛁 🔥 🌡☼ 🔲 🚲 🔌 🔒 🏧 ✕ Leisure 🎣 🍷

REDHILL, Surrey Map ref 2D2

SAT NAV RH1 3AH

Alderstead Heath Caravan Club Site

Dean Lane, Merstham, Redhill RH1 3AH
t (01737) 644629
w caravanclub.co.uk

THE
CARAVAN
CLUB

🚐 (150)	£12.20–£25.10
🚃 (150)	£12.20–£25.10
150 touring pitches	

Quiet site with views over rolling, wooded North Downs. Denbies Wine Estate nearby. For day trips, try Chessington and Thorpe Park and the lively city of Brighton. Non-members welcome. **directions** M25 jct 8, A217 towards Reigate, fork left after 300 yds towards Merstham. 2.5 miles, left at T-junction onto A23. 0.5 miles, turn right into Shepherds Hill (B2031). 1 mile, left into Dean Lane. **open** All year **payment** credit/debit cards, cash, cheques

General 🔲 🕎 🔲 🌡☼ 🔲 🔌 🔒 🏧 Leisure 🏔

BATTLE, Sussex Map ref 3B4

SAT NAV TN33 0SL

Crowhurst Park

Telham Lane, Battle, East Sussex TN33 0SL
t (01424) 773344 **f** (01424) 775727 **e** enquires@crowhurstpark.co.uk
w crowhurstpark.co.uk ONLINE BOOKING

🏠	£275–£1020

Development of pine lodges within the grounds of a 17thC country estate. Facilities include leisure club with indoor swimming pool, bar, restaurant and children's playground. David Bellamy Gold Conservation Award. **directions** Two miles south of Battle on A2100. **open** 1st March to 8th January **payment** credit/debit cards, cash, cheques

General 🔲 🕎 🛁 🔲 ☼ ✕ Leisure 🏊 🎣 🍷 🍴 🎵 🎯 🏔

BATTLE, Sussex Map ref 3B4 — SAT NAV TN33 9LR

Normanhurst Court Caravan Club Site

Stevens Crouch, Battle TN33 9LR
t (01424) 773808 f (01424) 775196
w **caravanclub.co.uk**

THE CARAVAN CLUB

🚐 (149) £12.20–£25.10
🚚 (149) £12.20–£25.10
149 touring pitches

SPECIAL PROMOTIONS
Special member rates mean you can save your membership subscription in less than a week. Visit our website to find out more.

Situated in a former garden with magnificent specimen trees – the rhododendrons are a riot of colour in the Spring. Located close to the 1066 Trail, great for walkers, nature lovers and families. The seaside towns of Eastbourne and Hastings are just a short drive away.

open March to November
payment credit/debit cards, cash, cheques

directions From Battle, turn left onto A271. Site is 3 miles on left.

General ▢ 🐕 ⊞ 🌧 ⏰ 🔌 🌀 🚻 📶
Leisure ⚠

BEXHILL-ON-SEA, Sussex Map ref 3B4 — SAT NAV TN39 5JA

Cobbs Hill Farm

Cobbs Hill Farm Caravan & Camping Park, Watermill Lane, Bexhill-on-Sea TN39 5JA
t (01424) 213460 f (01424) 221358 e cobbshillfarmuk@hotmail.com
w **cobbshillfarm.co.uk**

🚐 (55) £10.00–£12.00
🚚 (55) £10.00–£12.00
⛺ (55) £11.00–£13.00
🏠 (2) £140.00–£350.00
55 touring pitches

Quiet, family-run park in the Sussex country. A network of footpaths providing country walks with a small selection of farm animals. No club house. Play area and space to play games. Touring and hire vans, level pitches, tent and rally fields. Near Hastings, Battle and Eastbourne.

open April to Oct
payment credit/debit cards, cash, cheques

directions The park is signed posted off the A269 to the north of Bexhill, 1 mile down Watermill Lane on the left.

General ▢ 🐕 ⚡ ⊞ 🌧 ☀ ⏰ 🔌 🌀 🚻 **Leisure** ⚠

BOGNOR REGIS, Sussex Map ref 2C3

SAT NAV PO22 9RP

Rowan Park Caravan Club Site

Rowan Way, Bognor Regis PO22 9RP
t (01243) 828515 f (01243) 869189
w **caravanclub.co.uk**

CARAVAN
CLUB

(94)   £12.20–£25.10
(94)   £12.20–£25.10
94 touring pitches

SPECIAL PROMOTIONS
Special member rates mean
you can save your
membership subscription in
less than a week. Visit our
website to find out more.

Conveniently situated alongside the A29 and
about 2 miles from the beach. The town of
Bognor Regis is a traditional seaside resort with
many entertainments. For the theatre goer - yo
are not far from the Chichester Festival Theatre
and Arundel, which has a music and drama
festival at the end of August.

open April to November
payment credit/debit cards, cash, cheques

directions From roundabout on A29, 1 mile
north of Bognor, turn left into Rowan Way, site
100 yds on right, opposite Halfords superstore.

General
Leisure

BRIGHTON & HOVE, Sussex Map ref 2D3

SAT NAV BN2 5TS

Sheepcote Valley Caravan Club Site

East Brighton Park, Brighton BN2 5TS
t (01273) 626546 f (01273) 682600
w **caravanclub.co.uk**

CARAVAN
CLUB

(169)   £14.90–£28.90
(169)   £14.90–£28.90
169 touring pitches

SPECIAL PROMOTIONS
Special member rates mean
you can save your
membership subscription in
less than a week. Visit our
website to find out more.

Located on the South Downs, just 2 miles from
Brighton. Visit the Marina, with its shops, pubs,
restaurants and cinema, and take a tour of the
exotic Royal Pavilion. Brighton is a lively town
with all the usual attractions of a seaside holida
resort.

open All year
payment credit/debit cards, cash, cheques

directions M23/A23, join A27 (Lewes). B2123
(Falmer/Rottingdean). Right, onto B2123
(Woodingdean). In 2 miles, at traffic lights, right
(Warren Road). In 1 mile, left (Wilson Avenue).

General
Leisure

CHICHESTER, Sussex Map ref 2C3

HOLIDAY & CAMPING PARK

Wicks Farm Camping Park

Redlands Lane, West Wittering, Chichester PO20 8QE
t (01243) 513116 f (01243) 511296 e wicks.farm@virgin.net
w **wicksfarm.co.uk**

⊞ (40)	£14.00–£28.00
⚑ (40)	£14.00–£28.00

A small rural site, ideal for families with young children. **directions** From A27 at Chichester follow the signs for Witterings A286/B2179 straight on to West Wittering. Wicks Farm is 2nd on right past Lamb pub, 6 miles from Chichester. **open** March to October **payment** credit/debit cards, cash, cheques

General ▣ ♈ ⚏ ⋔ ☼ ⊕ ℃ ♨ ⊞ **Leisure** ⚲ ⋂

CHICHESTER 5 MILES, Sussex Map ref 2C3

HOLIDAY, TOURING & CAMPING PARK

Bell Caravan Park

Bell Lane, Birdham, Chichester PO20 7HY
t (01243) 512264

⚑ (15)	£14.00
⚑ (15)	£14.00

Quiet, sheltered park convenient for Chichester and the coast. At village of Birdham, turn left into Bell Lane. Park is a few hundred yards on the left. **directions** Take the A286 from Chichester for approx 5 miles. At Birdham village turn left into Bell Lane. Park is a few hundred yards on left. **open** March to October **payment** cash, cheques

General ♈ ⚏ ⋔ ☼ ♨ ⊕ ℃ ♨ **Leisure** ► ∪ ⚲ ♩

EASTBOURNE, Sussex Map ref 3B4

TOURING & CAMPING PARK

Fairfields Farm Caravan & Camping Park

Eastbourne Road, Westham, Pevensey BN24 5NG
t (01323) 763165 f (01323) 469175 e enquiries@fairfieldsfarm.com
w **fairfieldsfarm.com** GUEST REVIEWS

⚑ (60)	£12.50–£17.50
⊞ (60)	£12.50–£17.50
⚑ (60)	£12.50–£17.50
60 touring pitches	

SPECIAL PROMOTIONS
Special low season midweek offer: 3 nights for the price of 2. Contact us for more details.

A quiet country touring site on a working farm. Clean facilities, lakeside walk with farm pets and free fishing for campers. Close to the beautiful seaside resort of Eastbourne, and a good base from which to explore the diverse scenery and attractions of south east England.

open April to October
payment credit/debit cards, cash, cheques

directions From A27 Pevensey roundabout, travel through Pevensey towards castle, then through Westham. Turn left (B2191) towards Eastbourne. Over level crossing and we are on left.

General ▣ ♈ ⚏ ⋔ ☼ ♨ ⊕ ℃ ♨
Leisure ♩

HORAM, Sussex Map ref 2D3 — SAT NAV TN21 0YD

Horam Manor Touring Park
Horam, Heathfield TN21 0YD
t (01435) 813662 e camp@horam-manor.co.uk
w **horam-manor.co.uk** ONLINE MAP ONLINE BOOKING

(40) £15.50–£19.35
(10) £15.50–£19.35
(40) £15.50–£19.35
90 touring pitches

An established park with modern facilities including free hot water and showers. A tranquil setting in an Area of Outstanding Natural Beauty. On the A267, 10 miles north of Eastbourne. Open March to October. **directions** Situated on the A267, the main road from Heathfield to Eastbourne. **payment** cash, cheques

General 🔲📶🐕📵🏧☀️♿🔌🚻 **Leisure** ►∪⚲🚴⚓♨️

HORSHAM, Sussex Map ref 2D2 — SAT NAV RH13 8NX

Honeybridge Park
Honeybridge Lane, Dial Post, Horsham RH13 8NX
t (01403) 710923 f (01403) 710923 e enquiries@honeybridgepark.co.uk
w **honeybridgepark.co.uk**

(160) £14.00–£23.00
(100) £14.00–£23.00
(80) £14.00–£23.00
200 touring pitches

Delightfully situated within an Area of outstanding natural beauty. Large hardstanding and grass pitches, heated facilities, licensed shop. Ideal located between London and coast. Storage available. Holiday homes for sale. **directions** On A24 travelling south, turn left 1 mile past Dial Post turning. At Old Barn Nurseries continue for 300 yds and site is on the right. **open** All year **payment** credit, debit cards, cash, cheques, euros

General 🔲🐕🛒📵☀️🔌♿🚻🚿 **Leisure** ►🚴⚓🔦♨️

LITTLEHAMPTON, Sussex Map ref 3A4 — SAT NAV BN17 7PH

Littlehampton Caravan Club Site
Mill Lane, Wick, Littlehampton BN17 7PH
t 01903 716176
w **caravanclub.co.uk**

THE CARAVAN CLUB

£12.20–£25.30
£12.20–£25.30
115 touring pitches

SPECIAL PROMOTIONS
Special member rates mean you can save your membership subscription in less than a week. Visit our website to find out more.

Nearby Arundel Castle

Set on the outskirts of this delightful seaside resort within walking distance of the town centre and its beach. Littlehampton has a beautiful natural harbour at the mouth of the River Arun, along which a scenic riverside walkway runs. There's plenty to do - waterside restaurants, golf course, museum and the Look and Sea Visitor Centre.

open April 2010 to January 2011

directions Leave A27 onto A284 signposted Littlehampton. Site on left of Mill Lane.

General 🔲🐕📵🏧🔌🔌🚻🚿
Leisure ♨️

PEVENSEY BAY, Sussex Map ref 3B4

Bay View Park Ltd

Old Martello Road, Pevensey Bay, Pevensey BN24 6DX
t (01323) 768688 f (01323) 769637 e holidays@bay-view.co.uk
w **bay-view.co.uk**

(40)	£14.50–£21.00
(4)	£14.50–£21.00
(50)	£14.50–£21.00
(9)	£194.00–£595.00

94 touring pitches

Family site on a private road next to the beach. Play area. New showers and laundry. Small, well-stocked shop. On site, par 3, 9 hole golf and refreshments. **directions** On A259 coast road between Pevensey Bay and Eastbourne. **open** March to October **payment** credit/debit cards, cash, cheques

General ▢ ⚘ ⊁ ⚞ ⫙ ⟐ ☼ ⚏ ⊙ ⚲ ⊞ Leisure ▶ ↗ ⚠

SELSEY, Sussex Map ref 2C3

Green Lawns Holiday Park

Paddock Lane, Selsey, Chichester, West Sussex PO20 9EJ
t (01243) 606080 f (01243) 606068 e holidays@bunnleisure.co.uk
w **bunnleisure.co.uk** ONLINE MAP LAST MINUTE OFFERS

(1)	£690–£1650
(20)	£171.00–£875.00

Offers leafy lanes, duck ponds and open green spaces for privacy, peace and quiet but with access to all Bunn Leisure's facilities with a free Bus service. The Viking Music and Dance Club hosts world class entertainment and the tennis courts can be found here.

open March to October
payment credit/debit cards, cash, cheques

directions From A27 Chichester by-pass take B2145 to Selsey. Green Lawns is clearly signed on right once you are in town.

General ▢ ⚘ ⊁ ⚞ ⫙ ⟐ ☼ ✕
Leisure ▶ ∪ ⚲ ⚞ ↗ ⚘ ⚲ ⚲ ♫ ☝ ⚠

SELSEY, Sussex Map ref 2C3

SAT NAV PO20 9EL

Warner Farm Camping & Touring Park

Warner Lane, Selsey, Chichester, West Sussex PO20 9EL
t (01243) 604499 f (01243) 604499 e touring@bunnleisure.co.uk
w **warnerfarm.co.uk** ONLINE MAP LAST MINUTE OFFERS

(80)   £19.50–£33.50
(50)   £27.50–£43.50
(120)   £17.50–£31.50
250 touring pitches

Great value, top quality, fun filled family camping and touring holidays. Well maintained Standard, Electric and Full Service pitches, excellent NEW facilities. Separate washing up areas and purpose built barbecues positioned in the adjoining playing field. Stay here and make use of all the great facilities and famous entertainment.

open March to October
payment credit/debit cards, cash, cheques

directions From A27 Chichester by-pass take B2145 to Selsey. West Sands is clearly signed on right once you are in town.

General 🔲 👤 🐕 🏊 📺 📷 ☼ 🍴 🎮 ☕ 🛒 🚐 ✕
Leisure ▶ ∪ ♋ ⚒ 🎣 ⚓ 🎿 🏆 🎵 🎯 ⛰

SELSEY, Sussex Map ref 2C3

SAT NAV PO20 9BH

West Sands Holiday Park

Mill Lane, Selsey, Chichester, West Sussex PO20 9BH
t (01243) 606080 f (01243) 606068 e holidays@bunnleisure.co.uk
w **bunnleisure.co.uk** ONLINE MAP LAST MINUTE OFFERS

(5)   £440–£1600
(37)   £171.00–£875.00

The liveliest of our parks on the South Coast offering family fun in fantastic seaside location. Famous for the best entertainment with top acts and live performances. Kid's entertainment daily include character visits and clubs for 0-17 year olds. Enjoy the tropical pools and health suite located here.

open March to October
payment credit/debit cards, cash, cheques

directions From A27 Chichester by-pass take B2145 to Selsey. West Sands is clearly signed on right once you are in the town.

General 🔲 👤 🐕 🏊 📺 📷 ☼ ✕
Leisure ▶ ∪ ♋ ⚒ 🎣 ⚓ 🎿 🏆 🎵 🎯 ⛰

SELSEY, Sussex Map ref 2C3

White Horse Holiday Park

Paddock Lane, Selsey, Chichester, West Sussex PO20 9EJ
t (01243) 606080 f (01243) 606068 e holidays@bunnleisure.co.uk
w **bunnleisure.co.uk** ONLINE MAP LAST MINUTE OFFERS

(20)   £171.00–£875.00

With its coveted award for its traditional atmosphere it is perfect for families. Offering a relaxed holiday, though never far from the fun and entertainment with open air swimming pool, all weather multi-sports area, kids club, shop and gaming arcade and a full size football pitch and playground.

open March to October
payment credit/debit cards, cash, cheques

directions From A27 Chichester by-pass take B2145 to Selsey. White Horse is clearly signed on the right once you are in town.

General 🔲 ⚙ 🐕 🔋 🏥 🌞 ✕
Leisure ⌐ ∪ ⚭ 🚲 ♪ ᚴ ♟ ♫ 🔊 ⚱

WASHINGTON, Sussex Map ref 2D3

Washington Caravan & Camping Park

London Road, Washington, West Sussex RH20 4AJ
t (01903) 892869 f (01903) 893252 e washcamp@amserve.com
w **washcamp.com**

(21)   £19.00
(5)   £19.00
(80)   £19.00
21 touring pitches

The park is set in beautifully landscaped grounds beneath the South Downs affording the right atmosphere for an enjoyable stay. Well situated for visiting places of interest. **directions** Please contact us for directions **payment** credit/debit cards, cash, cheques

General 🔲 🐕 🔋 🏥 🔊 🚻 Leisure ∪

OFFICIAL TOURIST BOARD GUIDE
Hotels
2010
England's quality-assessed hotels
enjoyEngland.com

Looking for something else?

You can also buy a copy of our popular guide 'Hotels' including country house and town house hotels, metro and budget hotels, serviced apartments, restaurants with rooms and Spas in England 2010.

Now available in good bookshops and online at
enjoyenglanddirect.com

£10.99

All Assessed Accommodation

Berkshire

DORNEY REACH

Amerden Caravan & Camping Park ★★★★
Touring & Camping Park
Old marsh Lane, Dorney Reach,
Maidenhead
SL6 0EE
t (01628) 627461
e beverly@amerdencaravanpark.co.
uk

HURLEY

Hurleyford Farm Ltd ★★★★
Holiday Park
Mill Lane, Hurley, Maidenhead
SL6 5ND
t (01628) 829009

Hurley Riverside Park ★★★★
Holiday Park
Hurley, Maidenhead
SL6 5NE
t (01628) 824493
e info@hurleyriversidepark.co.uk
w hurleyriversidepark.co.uk

READING

Wellington Country Park - Caravan & Campsite ★★★
Touring & Camping Park
Odiham Road, Riseley, Nr Reading
RG7 1SP
t (0118) 932 6444
e info@wellington-country-park.co.
uk
w wellington-country-park.co.uk

Buckinghamshire

BEACONSFIELD

Highclere Farm Camp Site ★★★★
Touring & Camping Park
Highclere Farm Camp Site, Newbarn Lane, Beaconsfield
HP9 2QZ
t (01494) 874505
e enquiries@highclerefarmpark.co.
uk
w highclerefarmpark.co.uk

OLNEY

Emberton Country Park ★★
Touring & Camping Park
Emberton, Olney
MK46 5FJ
t (01234) 711575
e embertonpark@milton-keynes.
gov.uk
w mkweb.co.uk/embertonpark

Hampshire

ANDOVER

Wyke Down Touring Caravan & Camping Park ★★★
Touring & Camping Park
Picket Piece, Andover
SP11 6LX
t (01264) 352048
e p.read@wykedown.co.uk
w wykedown.co.uk

ASHURST

Forestry Commission Ashurst Caravan & Camping Site ★★★
Touring & Camping Park
Lyndhurst Road, Ashurst,
Southampton
SO40 7AR
t (0131) 314 6505
e fe.holidays@forestry.gov.uk
w forestholidays.co.uk

BROCKENHURST

Black Knowl (New Forest) ★★
Touring & Camping Park
Aldridge Hill, Brockenhurst
SO42 7QD
t (01590) 623600
w caravanclub.co.uk

Forestry Commission Hollands Wood Caravan & Camping Site ★★★ *Touring & Camping Park*
Lyndhurst Road, Brockenhurst
SO42 7QH
t (0131) 314 6505
e fe.holidays@forestry.gov.uk
w forestholidays.co.uk

Forestry Commission Roundhill Caravan & Camping Site ★★★
Touring & Camping Park
Beaulieu Road, Brockenhurst
SO42 7QL
t (0131) 314 6505
e fe.holidays@forestry.gov.uk
w forestholidays.co.uk

FORDINGBRIDGE

Sandy Balls Holiday Centre ★★★★★ *Holiday Park*
ROSE AWARD
Godshill, Fordingbridge
SP6 2JY
t (01425) 653042
e post@sandy-balls.co.uk
w sandy-balls.co.uk

FRITHAM

Forestry Commission Ocknell/ Longbeech Caravan & Camping Site ★★ *Touring & Camping Park*
Fritham, Lyndhurst
SO43 7HH
t (0131) 314 6505
e fe.holidays@forestry.gov.uk
w forestholidays.co.uk

GOSPORT

Kingfisher Caravan Park ★★★
Holiday, Touring & Camping Park
Browndown Road, Stokes Road,
Gosport, Lee-On-The-Solent
PO13 9BG
t (023) 9250 2611
e info@kingfisher-caravan-park.co.
uk
w kingfisher-caravan-park.co.uk

HAMBLE

Riverside Holidays ★★★
Holiday, Touring & Camping Park
Satchell Lane, Hamble,
Southampton
SO31 4HR
t (023) 8045 3220
e enquiries@riversideholidays.co.uk
w riversideholidays.co.uk

HAYLING ISLAND

Fishery Creek Caravan & Camping Park ★★★★
Touring & Camping Park
Fishery Lane, Hayling Island
PO11 9NR
t (023) 9246 2164
e camping@fisherycreek.fsnet.co.uk
w keyparks.co.uk

Hayling Island Holiday Park ★★★★ *Holiday Park* **ROSE AWARD**
Manor Road, Hayling Island
PO11 0QS
t 0870 777 6754
e hayling@weststarholidays.co.uk
w weststarholidays.co.uk
🖼

HOLMSLEY

Holmsley Caravan and Camping Site ★★★ *Touring & Camping Park*
Forest Road, Holmsley, Christchurch
BH23 7EQ
t (01425) 674502
e holmsley.site@forestholidays.co.
uk
w forestholidays.co.uk

LYNDHURST

Denny and Matley Wood Caravan and Camping Site ★★
Touring & Camping Park
Beaulieu Road, Lyndhurst
SO43 7FZ
t (023) 8029 3144
e dennywood@hotmail.co.uk
w forestholidays.co.uk

MILFORD ON SEA

Carrington Park ★★★★★
Holiday Park
New Lane, Milford-on-Sea,
Lymington
SO41 0UQ
t (01590) 642654
e office@carringtonpark.co.uk
w ukparks.co.uk/carrington

Downton Holiday Park Ltd ★★★★ *Holiday Park* **ROSE AWARD**
Shorefield Road, Milford-on-Sea,
Lymington
SO41 0LH
t (01425) 476131
e info@downtonholidaypark.co.uk
w downtonholidaypark.co.uk

Lytton Lawn Touring Park ★★★★
Touring & Camping Park
Lymore Lane, Milford-on-Sea,
Lymington
SO410TX
t (01590) 648331
e holidays@shorefield.co.uk
w shorefield.co.uk

Shorefield Country Park ★★★★★
Holiday Park **ROSE AWARD**
Shorefield Road, Milford-on-Sea,
Lymington
SO41 0LH
t (01590) 648331

NEW MILTON

Glen Orchard Holiday Park ★★★★ *Holiday Park*
Walkford Lane, New Milton
BH25 5NH
t (01425) 616463
e enquiries@glenorchard.co.uk
w glenorchard.co.uk

Hoburne Bashley ★★★★
Holiday Park
Sway Road, New Milton
BH25 5QR
t (01425) 612340
e enquiries@hoburne.com
w hoburne.com

Hoburne Naish ★★★★★
Holiday Park **ROSE AWARD**
Christchurch Road, New Milton
BH25 7RE
t (01425) 273586
e enquiries@hoburne.com
w hoburne.com

Setthorns Caravan and Camping Site ★★★ *Touring & Camping Park*
Wotton, New Milton
BH25 5WA
t (01590) 681020
w forestholidays.co.uk

OWER

Green Pastures Caravan Park ★★★ *Touring Park*
Green Pastures Farm, Whitemoor Lane, Romsey
SO51 6AJ
t (023) 8081 4444
e enquiries@greenpasturesfarm.
com
w greenpasturesfarm.com/

LYNDHURST

Shamba Holidays ★★★★
Touring & Camping Park
230 Ringwood Road, St Leonards,
Ringwood
BH24 2SB
t (01202) 873302
e enquiries@shambaholidays.co.uk
w shambaholidays.co.uk

ROMSEY

Hill Farm Caravan Park ★★★★
Holiday, Touring & Camping Park
Branches Lane, Sherfield English,
Romsey
SO51 6FH
t (01794) 340402
e gjb@hillfarmpark.com

WARSASH

Dibles Park Company Ltd ★★★★
Touring Park
Dibles Park, Dibles Road, Warsash,
Southampton
SO31 9SA
t (01489) 575232
e dibles.park@btconnect.com
w diblespark.co.uk

Solent Breezes Holiday Park ★★
Holiday Park
Hook Lane, Warsash, Southampton
SO31 9HG
t (01489) 572084

WINCHESTER

Morn Hill Caravan Club Site ★★
Touring & Camping Park
Alresford Road, Winchester
SO21 1HL
t (01962) 869877
w caravanclub.co.uk

Isle of Wight

APSE HEATH

Old Barn Touring Park ★★★★
Touring & Camping Park
Cheverton Farm, Newport Road,
Apse Heath
PO36 9PJ
t (01983) 866414
e oldbarn@weltinet.com
w oldbarntouring.co.uk

Village Way Caravan & Camping Site ★★★
Holiday, Touring & Camping Park
Newport Road, Apse Heath
PO36 9PJ
t (01983) 863279
e info@islandbreaks.co.uk

ARRETON

Perreton Farm ★★
Touring & Camping Park
East Lane, Arreton, Newport
PO30 3DL
t (01983) 865218
e roger@turboweb.org
w islandbreaks.co.uk

ATHERFIELD BAY

Chine Farm Camping Site ★★★
Touring & Camping Park
Military Road, Atherfield Bay,
Ventnor
PO38 2JH
t (01983) 740901
e jill@chine-farm.co.uk
w chine-farm.co.uk

BEMBRIDGE

Sandhills Holiday Park ★★★
Holiday Park
Whitecliff Bay, Bembridge
PO35 5QB
t (01983) 872277
e enquiries@sandhillsholidaypark.
com
w sandhillsholidaypark.com

Whitecliff Bay Holiday Park ★★★
Holiday Park
Hillway Road, Bembridge
PO35 5PL
t (01983) 872671
e holiday@whitecliff-bay.com
w whitecliff-bay.com

BRIGHSTONE

Grange Farm Brighstone Bay
★★ *Holiday & Touring Park*
Grange Chine, Military Road,
Brighstone
PO30 4DA
t (01983) 740296
e grangefarm@brighstonebay.fsnet.
co.uk
w brighstonebay.fsnet.co.uk

BROOK

Compton Farm ★★ *Holiday Park*
Brook, Newport
PO30 4HF
t (01983) 740215
e info@islandbreaks.co.uk

COLWELL BAY

Colwell Bay Caravan Park ★★★★
Holiday Park
Madeira Lane, Colwell, Freshwater
PO40 9SR
t (01983) 752403
e james.bishop1@tinyworld.co.uk
w isleofwight-colwellbay.co.uk

COWES

Sunnycott Caravan Park ★★★★
Holiday Park
Rew Street, Gurnard
PO31 8NN
t (01983) 292859
e info@sunnycottcaravanpark.co.uk
w sunnycottcaravanpark.co.uk

EAST COWES

Waverley Park Holiday Centre
★★★
Holiday, Touring & Camping Park
1 Old Road, East Cowes
PO32 6AW
t (01983) 293452
e holidays@waverley-park.co.uk
w waverley-park.co.uk

FRESHWATER

Heathfield Farm Camping ★★★★
Touring & Camping Park
Heathfield Road, Freshwater
PO40 9SH
t (01983) 407822
e web@heathfieldcamping.co.uk
w heathfieldcamping.co.uk

NITON

Meadow View Caravan Site ★
Holiday Park
Newport Road, Ventnor
PO38 2NS
t (01983) 730015

NORTON

**Warners Norton Grange Classic
Resort** ★★★ *Holiday Village*
Warners Holiday Centre, Norton
Grange, Norton, Yarmouth
PO41 0SD
t (01983) 760323
e melanie.cox@bourne-leisure.co.uk
w nortongrange.co.uk

ROOKLEY

Rookley Country Park ★★★★
Holiday, Touring & Camping Park
Rookley Country Park, Main Road,
Rookley
PO38 3LU
t (01983) 721606
e info@islandviewhols.co.uk
w islandviewhols.co.uk

RYDE

Beaper Farm ★★★
Touring & Camping Park
Brading Road, Ryde
PO33 1QJ
t (01983) 615210
e beaper@btinternet.com
w beaperfarm.com

**Isle of Wight Self Catering -
Pondwell Bungalows** ★★★
Holiday, Touring & Camping Park
Salterns Road, Seaview
PO34 5AQ
t (01983) 612330
e info@isleofwightselfcatering.co.uk
w isleofwightselfcatering.co.uk

**Roebeck Camping and Caravan
Park** ★★★ *Touring & Camping Park*
Gatehouse Road, Upton Cross, Ryde
PO33 4BS
t (01983) 611475
e andrew.cross@roebeck-farm.co.uk
w roebeck-farm.co.uk

Whitefield Forest Touring Park
★★★★ *Touring & Camping Park*
Brading Road, Ryde
PO33 1QL
t (01983) 617069
e pat&louise@whitefieldforest.co.uk
w whitefieldforest.co.uk

SANDOWN

**Adgestone Camping and
Caravanning Club Site** ★★★★
Touring & Camping Park
Lower Adgestone Road, Adgestone,
Isle of Wight
PO36 0HL
t (01983) 403432
w campingandcaravanningclub.co.
uk/adgestone

**Cheverton Copse Holiday Park
Ltd** ★★★★ *Holiday Park*
ROSE AWARD
Scotchells Brook Lane, Sandown,
Isle of Wight
PO36 0JP
t (01983) 403161
e holidays@chevertoncopse.com
w chevertoncopse.com

Fairway Holiday Park ★★★
Holiday Park
The Fairway, Sandown
PO36 9PS
t (01983) 403462
e enquiries@fairwayholidaypark.co.
uk
w fairwayholidaypark.co.uk

Fort Holiday Park ★★★
Holiday Park
Avenue Road, Sandown, Isle of
Wight
PO36 8BD
t (01983) 402858
e bookings@fortholidaypark.co.uk
w fortholidaypark.co.uk

Fort Spinney Holiday Chalets
★★★★★ *Holiday Park*
Yaverland Road, Sandown
PO36 8QB
t (01983) 402360
e fortspinney@iowight.com
w iowight.com/spinney

Sandown Holiday Chalets ★★★
Holiday Park
Avenue Road, Sandown
PO36 9AP
t (01983) 404025
e chalets@iowight.com
w iowight.com/chalets

SEAVIEW

**Isle of Wight Self Catering -
Salterns** ★★★ *Holiday Park*
Salterns Road, Seaview
PO34 5AQ
t (01983) 612330
e info@isleofwightselfcatering.co.uk
w isleofwightselfcatering.co.uk

**Isle of Wight Self Catering -
Tollgate** ★★★ *Holiday Park*
Salterns Road, Seaview
PO34 5AQ
t (01983) 612330
e info@isleofwightselfcatering.co.uk
w isleofwightselfcatering.co.uk

SHANKLIN

Landguard Holidays ★★★★
Holiday, Touring & Camping Park
Landguard Manor Road, Shanklin
PO37 7PJ
t (01983) 863100
e enquiries@landguardholidays.co.
uk
w landguardholidays.co.uk

Lower Hyde Holiday Park ★★★★
Holiday, Touring & Camping Park
ROSE AWARD
Landguard Road, Shanklin
PO37 7LL
t 0871 664 9752
e holidaysales.lowerhyde@park-
resorts.com
w park-resorts.com

Ninham Country Holidays
Holiday & Touring Park
Ninham, Shanklin, Isle of Wight
PO37 7PL

ST HELENS

Carpenters Farm Campsite ★★★
Touring & Camping Park
Carpenters Road, St Helens
PO33 1YL
t (01983) 874557
e info@carpentersfarms.co.uk
w carpentersfarm.co.uk

Field Lane Holiday Park ★★★★★
Holiday Park
Field Lane, St Helens
PO33 1UX
t (01983) 872779
e info@hillgroveandfieldlane.co.uk
w fieldlane.co.uk

Nodes Point Holiday Park ★★★★
Holiday, Touring & Camping Park
Nodes Road, St Helens
PO33 1YA
t 0871 664 9758
e holidaysales.nodespoint@park-
resorts.com
w park-resorts.com

Old Mill Holiday Park ★★★★★
Holiday Park **ROSE AWARD**
Mill Road, Nr Ryde, St Helens
PO33 1UE
t (01983) 872507
e web@oldmill.co.uk
w oldmill.co.uk

ST LAWRENCE

The Undercliff Glen Caravan Park
★★★★★ *Holiday Park*
Undercliff Drive, St Lawrence
PO38 1XY
t (01983) 730261
e info@undercliffglencaravanpark.
co.uk
w undercliffglencaravanpark.co.uk

THORNESS BAY

Thorness Bay Holiday Park
★★★★
Holiday, Touring & Camping Park
ROSE AWARD
Thorness Lane, Nr Cowes, Thorness
PO31 8NJ
t 0871 664 9779
e holidaysales.thornessbay@park-
resorts.com
w park-resorts.com

WROXALL

**Appuldurcombe Gardens Holiday
Park** ★★★★
Holiday, Touring & Camping Park
ROSE AWARD
Appuldurcombe Road, Wroxall
PO38 3EP
t (01983) 852597
e info@appuldurcombegardens.co.
uk
w appuldurcombegardens.co.uk

YARMOUTH

**The Orchards Holiday Caravan &
Camping Park** ★★★★★
Holiday & Touring Park
ROSE AWARD
Main Road, Newbridge
PO41 0TS
t (01983) 531331
e info@orchards-holiday-park.co.uk
w orchards-holiday-park.co.uk

Silver Glades Caravan Park
★★★★ *Holiday Park*
Solent Road, Cranmore
PO41 0XZ
t (01983) 760172
e holiday@silvergladesiow.co.uk
w silvergladesiow.co.uk

Kent

ASHFORD

**Broadhembury Holiday Park (C &
C)** ★★★★★
Holiday, Touring & Camping Park
Steeds Lane, Kingsnorth, Kent
TN26 1NQ
t (01233) 620859
e holidaypark@broadhembury.co.
uk
w broadhembury.co.uk

BIRCHINGTON

Quex Caravan Park ★★★★★
Holiday & Touring Park
Park Road, Birchington
CT7 0BL
t (01843) 841273
e info@keatfarm.co.uk
w keatfarm.co.uk

Two Chimneys Caravan Park
★★★★★
Holiday, Touring & Camping Park
Shottendane Road, Birchington
CT7 0HD
t (01843) 843157
e info@twochimneys.co.uk
w twochimneys.co.uk

CANTERBURY

**Canterbury Camping and
Caravanning Club Site** ★★★★
Touring & Camping Park
Bekesbourne Lane, Canterbury,
Canterbury
CT3 4AB
t (01227) 463216
w campingandcaravanningclub.co.
uk/canterbury

Yew Tree Park ★★★★
Holiday, Touring & Camping Park
Stone Street, Canterbury
CT4 5PL
t (01227) 700306
e info@yewtreepark.com
w yewtreepark.com

CAPEL LE FERNE

Little Satmar Holiday Park
★★★★★
Holiday, Touring & Camping Park
Winehouse Lane, Capel-le-Ferne,
Folkestone
CT18 7JF
t (01303) 251188
w katefarm.co.uk

Varne Ridge Holiday Park
★★★★★ *Holiday & Touring Park*
145 Old Dover Road, Capel-le-Ferne,
Folkestone
CT18 7HX
t (01303) 251765
e info@varne-ridge.co.uk
w varne-ridge.co.uk

DYMCHURCH

Dymchurch Caravan Park ★★★★
Holiday Park
St Marys Road, Dymchurch, Romney
Marsh
TN29 0PW
t (01303) 872303

E & J Piper Caravan Park ★★★★
Holiday Park
St Marys Road, Dymchurch, Romney
Marsh
TN29 0PN
t (01303) 872103

New Beach Holiday Park ★★★★
Holiday, Touring & Camping Park
ROSE AWARD
Hythe Road, Dymchurch, Kent
TN29 0JX
t (01303) 872233
e newbeachholiday@aol.com

EASTCHURCH

Ashcroft Coast Holiday Park
★★★★ *Holiday Park*
Plough Road, Eastchurch, Sheerness
ME12 4JH
t 0871 664 9701
e holidaysales.ashcroftcoast@park-resorts.com
w park-resorts.com

Shurland Dale Holiday Park
★★★★★ *Holiday Park*
Warden Road, Eastchurch,
Sheerness, Sheerness
ME12 4EN
t 0871 664 9769
e holidaysales.shurland@park-resorts.com
w park-resorts.com

Warden Springs Holiday Park
★★★★
Holiday, Touring & Camping Park
Thorn Hill Road, Eastchurch,
Sheerness, Sheerness
ME12 4HF
t 0871 664 9790
e holidayparks.wardensprings@park-resorts.com
w park-resorts.com

FOLKESTONE

Black Horse Farm Caravan Club
Site ★★★★★
Touring & Camping Park
385 Canterbury Road, Densole,
Folkestone
CT18 7BG
t (01303) 892665
w caravanclub.co.uk

Folkestone Camping and
Caravanning Club Site ★★★★★
Touring & Camping Park
The Warren, Folkestone, Folkestone
CT19 6NQ
t (01303) 255093
w campingandcaravanningclub.co.uk/flokestone

KINGSDOWN

Kingsdown Park Holiday Village
★★★★★ *Holiday Park*
Upper Street, Kingsdown, Deal
CT14 8EU
t (01304) 361205
e info@kingsdownpark.co.uk
w kingsdownpark.net

LEYSDOWN ON SEA

Harts Holiday Park ★★
Holiday, Touring & Camping Park
Leysdown Road, Leysdown-on-Sea,
Sheerness
ME12 4RG
t (01795) 510225

MAIDSTONE

Bearsted Caravan Club Site
★★★★★ *Touring & Camping Park*
Ashford Road, Hollingbourne
ME17 1XH
t 01622 730018

Pine Lodge Touring Park
★★★★★ *Touring & Camping Park*
A20 Ashford Road, Hollingbourne,
Maidstone
ME17 1XH
t (01622) 730018
w caravanclub.co.uk

MARDEN

Tanner Farm Park ★★★★★
Touring & Camping Park
Tanner Farm, Goudhurst Road,
Marden
TN12 9ND
t (01622) 832399
e enquiries@tannerfarmpark.co.uk
w tannerfarmpark.co.uk

MARTIN MILL

Hawthorn Farm Caravan &
Camping Park ★★★★
Holiday, Touring & Camping Park
Station Road, Martin Mill, Dover
CT15 5LA
t (01304) 852658
e info@keatfarm.co.uk
w keatfarm.co.uk/

MINSTER-IN-THANET

Wayside Caravan Park ★★★★★
Holiday Park
Way Hill, Minster, Ramsgate
CT12 4HW
t (01843) 821272
e lydia@scott9330.freeserve.co.uk
w waysidecaravanpark.co.uk

MONKTON

The Foxhunter Park ★★★★★
Holiday Park ROSE AWARD
Monkton Street, Monkton, Ramsgate
CT12 4JG
t (01843) 821311
e foxhunter@aol.com
w thefoxhunterpark.co.uk

NEW ROMNEY

Marlie Farm Holiday Park ★★★
Holiday, Touring & Camping Park
Dymchurch Road, New Romney,
New Romney
TN28 8UE
t (01797) 363060

Romney Sands Holiday Park
★★★★ *Holiday Park*
The Parade, Greatstone, New
Romney
TN28 8RN
t 0871 664 9760
e holidaysales.romneysands@park-resorts.com
w park-resorts.com

RAMSGATE

Manston Caravan & Camping
Park ★★★★
Holiday, Touring & Camping Park
Manston Court Road, Manston,
Ramsgate
CT12 5AU
t (01843) 823442

Nethercourt Touring Park ★★★
Touring & Camping Park
Nethercourt Hill, Ramsgate
CT11 0RX
t (01843) 595485

ROCHESTER

Allhallows Leisure Park ★★★★
Holiday Park
Allhallows Leisure Park, Allhallows,
Rochester
ME3 9QD
t 0870 405 0152
e trina.davis@bourneleisure.co.uk
w havenholidays.com/allhallows

SANDWICH

Sandwich Leisure Park ★★★★★
Holiday, Touring & Camping Park
Woodnesborough Road, Sandwich
CT13 0AA
t (01304) 612681
e info@coastandcountryleisure.com
w coastandcountryleisure.com

SEAL

Oldbury Hill Camping and
Caravanning Club Site ★★★★
Touring & Camping Park
Seal, Seal, Sevenoaks
TN15 0ET
t (01732) 762728
w campingandcaravanningclub.co.uk/oldburyhill

SEASALTER

Alberta Holiday Park ★★★
Holiday, Touring & Camping Park
Faversham Road, Seasalter,
Whitstable
CT5 4BJ
t (01227) 274485

Homing Park ★★★★
Holiday, Touring & Camping Park
Church Lane, Seasalter, Whitstable
CT5 4BU
t (01227) 771777
e info@homingpark.co.uk
w homingpark.co.uk

SHEERNESS

Sheerness Holiday Park ★★
Holiday, Touring & Camping Park
Halfway Road, Milford-on-Sea,
Sheerness
ME12 3AA
t (01795) 662638
w cinqueportleisure.com

ST-MARGARETS-AT-CLIFFE

St Margarets Holiday Park
★★★★★ *Holiday Park*
ROSE AWARD
Reach Road, St Margarets-at-Cliffe,
Dover
CT15 6AE
t 0871 664 9772
e holidaysales.stmargaretsbay@park-resorts.com
w park-resorts.com

ST NICHOLAS AT WADE

St Nicholas Camping Site ★★
Touring & Camping Park
Streete Farm House, Court Road, St
Nicholas At Wade, Birchington
CT7 0NH
t (01843) 847245

THURNHAM

Cold Blow 3 *Bunkhouse*
Cold Blow Farm, Cold Blow Lane,
Maidstone
ME14 3LR
t (01622) 735038

Coldblow Farm Bunkbarns
Bunkhouse
Cold Blow Lane, Thurnham,
Maidstone
ME14 3LR
t (01622) 735038
e campingbarns@yha.org.uk
w coldblow-camping.co.uk

Coldblow Farm Camping Barn
Camping Barn
Cold Blow Lane, Thurnham,
Maidstone
ME14 3LR
t (01622) 735038
e campingbarns@yha.org.uk
w coldblow-camping.co.uk

WHITSTABLE

Seaview Holiday Park ★★★
Holiday Park
St Johns Road, Whitstable,
Whitstable
CT5 2RY
t (01227) 792246

WROTHAM HEATH

Gate House Wood Touring Park
★★★★ *Touring Park*
Ford Road, Wrotham Heath,
Sevenoaks
TN15 7SD
t (01732) 843062
e gatehousewood@btinternet.com

Oxfordshire

BANBURY

Bo Peep Caravan Park ★★★★
Holiday & Touring Park
Aynho Road, Adderbury, Banbury
OX17 3NP
t (01295) 810605
e warden@bo-peep.co.uk
w bo-peep.co.uk

BURFORD

Burford Caravan Club Site ★★★★
Touring Park
Bradwell Grove, Burford
OX18 4JJ
t (01993) 823080
w caravanclub.co.uk

CHADLINGTON

Chipping Norton Camping and
Caravanning Club Site ★★★★
Touring & Camping Park
Chipping Norton Road, Chadlington,
Chipping Norton
OX7 3PE
t (01608) 641993
w campingandcaravanningclub.co.uk/chippingnorton

KINGHAM

Bluewood Park ★★★★★
Holiday Park ROSE AWARD
Churchill Heath, Chipping Norton
OX7 6UJ
t (01608) 659946
e info@bluewoodpark.com
w bluewoodpark.com

MOLLINGTON

Anita's Touring Caravan Park
★★★★ *Touring & Camping Park*
The Yews, Church Farm, Mollington
OX17 1AZ
t (01295) 750731
e anitapoll@btopenworld.com
w caravancampsites.co.uk

OXFORD

The Camping & Caravanning Club
Site ★★ *Touring & Camping Park*
426 Abingdon Road, Oxford
OX1 4XN

STANDLAKE

Hardwick Parks ★★★
Holiday, Touring & Camping Park
The Downs, Standlake, Witney
OX29 7PZ
t (01865) 300501
e info@hardwickparks.co.uk
w hardwickparks.co.uk

incoln Farm Park ★★★★★
ouring & Camping Park
ligh Street, Standlake, Witney
X29 7RH
  (01865) 300239
  info@lincolnfarm.touristnet.uk.
  com
  lincolnfarmpark.co.uk

Surrey

ALBURY

dgeley Holiday Park ★★★★
oliday Park
arley Green, Albury, Guildford
U5 9DW
  (01483) 202129
  edgeley@haulfryn.co.uk

CHERTSEY

**hertsey Camping and
aravanning Club Site ★★★★**
ouring & Camping Park
ridge Road, Chertsey, Chertsey
T16 8JX
  (01932) 562405
  campingandcaravanningclub.
  uk/chertsey

EAST HORSLEY

**lorsley Camping and
aravanning Club Site ★★★★**
ouring & Camping Park
ckham Road North, West Horsley,
eatherhead
T24 6PE
  (01483) 283273
  campingandcaravanningclub.co.
  uk/horsley

ELSTEAD

uttenham Camping Barn
amping Barn
loolford Lane, Elstead, Godalming
U8 6LL

REDHILL

**lderstead Heath Caravan Club
ite ★★★★**
ouring & Camping Park
ean Lane, Merstham, Redhill
H1 3AH
  (01737) 644629
  caravanclub.co.uk

WALTON-ON-THAMES

**Valton on Thames Camping and
aravanning Club Site ★★★**
amping Park
ield Common Lane, Walton-on-
hames
T12 3QG
  (01932) 220392
  campingandcaravanningclub.co.
  uk/waltononthames

Sussex

BATTLE

rowhurst Park ★★★★★
loliday Park **ROSE AWARD**
elham Lane, Battle, East Sussex
N33 0SL
  (01424) 773344
  enquires@crowhurstpark.co.uk
  crowhurstpark.co.uk

**lormanhurst Court Caravan Club
ite ★★★★★** *Touring Park*
stevens Crouch, Battle
N33 9LR
  (01424) 773808
  caravanclub.co.uk

BEXHILL-ON-SEA

obbs Hill Farm ★★★★
oliday, Touring & Camping Park
obbs Hill Farm Caravan &
amping Park, Watermill Lane,
exhill-on-Sea
N39 5JA
  (01424) 213460
  cobbshillfarmuk@hotmail.com
  cobbshillfarm.co.uk

BOGNOR REGIS

**Butlins Bognor Regis Resort
★★★★** *Holiday Village*
Upper Bognor Road, Bognor Regis,
Bognor Regis
PO21 1JJ
t   0845 070 4754
w butlins.com

Copthorne Caravans ★★★★
Holiday Park **ROSE AWARD**
Rose Green Road, Bognor Regis
PO21 3ER
t   (01243) 262408
e   copthornecaravans@dsl.pipex.
    com

**Riverside Caravan Centre
(Bognor) Ltd ★★★★★**
Holiday Park
Shripney Road, Bognor Regis
PO22 9NE
t   (01243) 865823
e   info@rivcentre.co.uk
w rivcentre.co.uk

**Rowan Park Caravan Club Site
★★★★★** *Touring & Camping Park*
Rowan Way, Bognor Regis
PO22 9RP
t   (01243) 828515
w caravanclub.co.uk

BRACKLESHAM BAY

South Downs ★★ *Holiday Village*
South Downs Holiday Village,
Bracklesham Lane, Bracklesham Bay,
Chichester
PO20 8JE
t   (01243) 673683

BRIGHTON & HOVE

**Sheepcote Valley Caravan Club
Site ★★★★★**
Touring & Camping Park
East Brighton Park, Brighton
BN2 5TS
t   (01273) 626546
w caravanclub.co.uk

CAMBER

**Camber Sands Holiday Park
★★★★** *Holiday Park*
New Lydd Road, Camber, Rye
TN31 7RT
t   0871 664 9718
e   holidaysales.cambersands@park-
    resorts.com
w park-resorts.com

CHICHESTER

**Wicks Farm Camping Park
★★★★★** *Holiday & Camping Park*
Redlands Lane, West Wittering,
Chichester
PO20 8QE
t   (01243) 513116
e   wicks.farm@virgin.net
w wicksfarm.co.uk

CHICHESTER 5 MILES

Bell Caravan Park ★★
Holiday, Touring & Camping Park
Bell Lane, Birdham, Chichester
PO20 7HY
t   (01243) 512264

CROWBOROUGH

**Crowborough Camping and
Caravanning Club Site ★★★★**
Touring & Camping Park
Eridge Road, Crowborough,
Crowborough
TN6 2TN
t   (01892) 664827
w campingandcaravanningclub.co.
    uk/crowborough

EASTBOURNE

**Fairfields Farm Caravan &
Camping Park ★★★**
Touring & Camping Park
Eastbourne Road, Westham,
Pevensey
BN24 5NG
t   (01323) 763165
e   enquiries@fairfieldsfarm.com
w fairfieldsfarm.com

GRAFFHAM

**Graffham Camping and
Caravanning Club Site ★★★★**
Touring & Camping Park
Graffham, Graffham, Petworth
GU28 0QJ
t   (01798) 867476
w campingandcaravanningclub.
    uk/graffham

HAILSHAM

**Peel House Farm Caravan Park
(Touring) ★★★**
Holiday, Touring & Camping Park
Sayerland Lane, Polegate, Hailsham
BN26 6QX
t   (01323) 845629
e   peelhousefarmcp@btinternet.com

HASTINGS

Coghurst Hall Holiday Park ★★★
Holiday, Touring & Camping Park
Ivyhouse Lane, Hastings, Hastings
TN35 4NP
t   (01424) 757955

**Combe Haven Holiday Park
★★★★** *Holiday Park*
Harley Shute Road, St Leonards-on-
Sea
TN38 8BZ
t   (01424) 427891

Rocklands Holiday Park ★★★★
Holiday Park
Rocklands Lane, East Hill, Hastings
TN35 5DY
t   (01424) 423097

**Stalkhurst Camping & Caravan
Park ★★★**
Holiday, Touring & Camping Park
Ivyhouse Lane, Hastings
TN35 4NN
t   (01424) 439015
e   stalkhurstpark@btinternet.com

HORAM

**Horam Manor Touring Park
★★★★** *Touring & Camping Park*
Horam, Heathfield
TN21 0YD
t   (01435) 813662
e   camp@horam-manor.co.uk
w horam-manor.co.uk

HORSHAM

Honeybridge Park ★★★★
Holiday Park
Honeybridge Lane, Dial Post,
Horsham
RH13 8NX
t   (01403) 710923
e   enquiries@honeybridgepark.co.uk
w honeybridgepark.co.uk

**Sumners Ponds Fishery &
Campsite** *Touring Park*
Chapel Lane, Barns Green, Horsham
RH13 0PR

LITTLEHAMPTON

Littlehampton Caravan Club Site
Camping and Caravan Park
Mill Lane, Wick, Littlehampton
BN17 7PH
t   01903 716176
w caravanclub.co.uk

LYMINSTER

Brookside Caravan Park ★★★
Holiday Park
Lyminster Road, Lyminster,
Littlehampton
BN17 7QE
t   (01903) 713292
e   mark@brooksideuk.com
w brooksideuk.com

PAGHAM

**Church Farm Holiday Village
★★★★★** *Holiday Park*
Church Road, Bognor Regis
PO21 4NR
t   0870 405 0151
e   churchfarm@bourne-leisure.co.uk
w churchfarm-park.co.uk

PEVENSEY

**Norman's Bay Camping and
Caravanning Club Site ★★★★**
Touring & Camping Park
Normans Bay, Pevensey
BN24 6PR
t   (01323) 761190
w campingandcaravanningclub.co.
    uk/normansbay

PEVENSEY BAY

Bay View Park Ltd ★★★
Holiday, Touring & Camping Park
Old Martello Road, Pevensey Bay,
Pevensey
BN24 6DX
t   (01323) 768688
e   holidays@bay-view.co.uk
w bay-view.co.uk

RUNCTON

**Chichester Lakeside Holiday Park
★★★**
Holiday, Touring & Camping Park
Vinnetrow Road, Runcton,
Chichester
PO20 1QH
t   (01243) 787715
e   lakeside@parkholidaysuk.com
w parkholidaysuk.com/caravansales/
    parks/sussex/chichester_lakeside

RYE HARBOUR

**Frenchman's Beach Holiday Park
★★★**
Holiday, Touring & Camping Park
Rye Harbour Road, Rye Harbour,
Rye
TN31 7TX
t   (01797) 223011

SELSEY

**Green Lawns Holiday Park
★★★★★** *Holiday Park*
ROSE AWARD
Paddock Lane, Selsey, Chichester,
West Sussex
PO20 9EJ
t   (01243) 606080
e   holidays@bunnleisure.co.uk
w bunnleisure.co.uk

**Warner Farm Camping & Touring
Park ★★★★★** *Touring Park*
Warner Lane, Selsey, Chichester,
West Sussex
PO20 9EL
t   (01243) 604499
e   touring@bunnleisure.co.uk
w warnerfarm.co.uk

West Sands Holiday Park ★★★★
Holiday Park **ROSE AWARD**
Mill Lane, Selsey, Chichester, West
Sussex
PO20 9BH
t   (01243) 606080
e   holidays@bunnleisure.co.uk
w bunnleisure.co.uk

White Horse Holiday Park ★★★★
Holiday Park **ROSE AWARD**
Paddock Lane, Selsey, Chichester,
West Sussex
PO20 9EJ
t (01243) 606080
e holidays@bunnleisure.co.uk
w bunnleisure.co.uk

**Slindon Camping and
Caravanning Club Site** ★★
Touring Park
Slindon Park, Slindon, Arundel
BN18 0RG
t (01243) 814387
w campingandcaravanningclub.co.uk/slindon

Southdown Caravan Park ★★★
Holiday & Touring Park
Henfield Road, Small Dole, Henfield
BN5 9XH
t (01903) 814323

**Chichester Camping and
Caravanning Club Site** ★★★
Touring & Camping Park
Main Road, Emsworth, Emsworth
PO10 8JH
t (01243) 373202
w campingandcaravanningclub.co.uk/chinchester

Beauport Holiday Park ★★★
Holiday Park
The Ridge West, St Leonards-on-Sea
TN37 7PP
t (01424) 851246

**Honeys Green Touring Caravan
Park** ★★★
Holiday, Touring & Camping Park
Oak Lodge, Hartfield Road, Uckfield
TN8 5NF
t (01732) 860205

**Washington Caravan & Camping
Park** ★★★★
Touring & Camping Park
London Road, Washington, West
Sussex
RH20 4AJ
t (01903) 892869
e washcamp@amserve.com
w washcamp.com

Winchelsea Sands Holiday Park
★★★ *Holiday Park*
Winchelsea Sands Holiday Park,
Winchelsea Beach, Winchelsea
TN36 4NB
t (01797) 226442

**Northbrook Farm Caravan Club
Site** ★★★★ *Touring Park*
Titnore Way, Worthing
BN13 3RT
t (01903) 502962
w caravanclub.co.uk

Onslow Caravan Park ★★★
Holiday Park
Onslow Drive, Ferring, Worthing
BN12 5RX
t (01903) 243170
e islandmeadow@fsmail-net.uk
w islandmeadow.co.uk

Walkers and cyclists welcome

Look out for quality-assessed accommodation displaying the Walkers Welcome and Cyclists Welcome signs.

Participants in these schemes actively encourage and support walking and cycling. In addition to special meal arrangements and helpful information, they'll provide a water supply to wash off the mud, an area for drying wet clothing and footwear, maps and books to look up cycling and walking routes and even an emergency puncture-repair kit! Bikes can also be locked up securely undercover.

The standards for these schemes have been developed in partnership with the tourist boards in Northern Ireland, Scotland and Wales, so wherever you're travelling in the UK you'll receive the same welcome.

Tower Bridge, London, England.

London

London

There is nowhere in the world quite like London. The capital of England and Britain, and the biggest city in the EU, London is a vibrant, multi-cultural, 24-hour city.

Culture and Heritage

There is a stimulating blend of old and new, the buzz of the city and the tranquility of its many open spaces which make London unique for both tourists and locals alike. Over 300 languages are spoken in London, contributing to the city's own fascinating culture, making it a fantastic place to visit and experience cultures from all over the world.

There is always something new to see or do in London. At the same time, the city retains its fantastic historical features, such as the Royal Botanic Gardens, Tower of London, Westminster Palace, Westminster Abbey & St Margaret's Church and, to the south east, Maritime Greenwich – all are UNESCO World Heritage Sites.

Attractions

London has the greatest concentration of major attractions in Britain. There are 238 attractions which are free to enter, and there is nowhere else in the world where you can see so much for so little. If modern art is your thing then the world's most visited modern art gallery, Tate Modern (which is free except for major exhibitions) is a must. If you don't mind paying, the London Eye with its fabulous views of the city, is an experience you cannot afford to miss.

Shopping

If its shopping you want, you will never get bored in London with over 30,000 shops to choose from and a burgeoning reputation in the fashion world. Oxford Street is Europe's biggest shopping area, Bond Street is designer label paradise, and the street markets of Camden, Portobello Road and Brick Lane are perfect for vintage hunters.

Sport

Football is the most popular sport in London and is home to several of England's leading football clubs. London boasts 13 professional teams – more than any other city in the world. London also has four rugby union teams and is home to two test cricket grounds (Lords and The Oval) as well as Wimbledon, home to the only Grand Slam tennis event still played on grass. London has been chosen to host the 2012 Olympic Games, making it the first city in the world to host the Summer Olympics 3 times.

Food and Drink

London is a world-class destination for food-lovers. With its smart restaurants, informal gastropubs, superb delis and buzzing cafes, there really is

something to suit all tastes. And the choice is staggering – you'll find cuisine from over 70 countries and over 6,000 restaurants from which to choose: 45 of which are Michelin-starred (2009)

Music and Nightlife

London's music scene and heritage is truly spectacular. There are 400 live music venues catering for everything from opera and jazz to rock and hip hop. All over the city you will find famous musical landmarks and reminders of some of the capital's biggest music stars. Summer is a great time for live music in London – you can enjoy everything from pop and rock festivals to the world's largest classical musical festival – the Proms.

It may have been 1777 when Samuel Johnson famously declared 'When a man is tired of London, he is tired of life; for there is in London all that life can afford.' But it is still true today.

Where to Go

 Attractions with this sign participate in the **Visitor Attraction Quality Assurance Scheme** (see page 6) which recognises high standards in all aspects of the visitor experience.

ENTERTAINMENT & CULTURE

Apsley House
Westminster, W1J 7NT
(020) 7499 5676
www.english-heritage.org.uk
Apsley House is the former residence of the first Duke of Wellington. This great 18th-century town house pays homage to the Duke's dazzling military career, which culminated in his victory at Waterloo in 1815.

British Museum
Camden, WC1B 3DG
(020) 7323 8299
www.thebritishmuseum.ac.uk
Permanent display and special exhibitions of works of man from prehistory to the present day. Permanent displays of antiquities from around the world.

Chelsea Football Club Stadium Tours
Hammersmith and Fulham, SW6 1HS
0871 984 1955
www.chelseafc.com/tours
The Chelsea FC Stadium Tour remains one of the most popular football tours in the world. This behind-the-scenes look at the stadium is a fun, exciting, informative and interactive experience, tailored for football fans of all ages.

Discover
Newham, E15 4BG
(020) 8536 5555
www.discover.org.uk
A magical place where children up to 11 years, and their carers can create stories through play.

Estorick Collection of Modern Italian Art
Islington, N1 2AN
(020) 7704 9522
www.estorickcollection.com
World-famous collection of Italian Futurists, Modigliani, Morandi and others in a beautiful Georgian house. Also temporary exhibitions, events, library and shop.

Geffrye Museum
Hackney, E2 8EA
(020) 7739 9893
www.geffrye-museum.org.uk
Period rooms depict the style of English middle class living rooms, 1600 to the present.

Greenwich Heritage Centre
Greenwich, SE18 4DX
(020) 8854 2452
www.greenwich.gov.uk
Delve into local history, archaeology, geology and natural history. Also temporary exhibitions and Saturday Club.

Imperial War Museum
Southwark, SE1 6HZ
(020) 7416 5320
www.iwm.org.uk
Thousands of exhibits illuminate the story of conflicts involving Britain and the Commonwealth since 1914.

London's Transport Museum
Westminster, WC2E 7BB
(020) 7379 6344
www.ltmuseum.co.uk
The history of transport – spectacular vehicles, special exhibitions, guided tours, film shows, children's craft workshops.

Lord's Tour (MCC)
Westminster, NW8 8QN
(020) 7616 8595
lords.org/history/tours-of-lords
Guided tour of Lord's Cricket Ground including the Long Room, MCC Museum, Real Tennis Court, Mound Stand and Indoor School.

Museum of London
City of London, EC2Y 5HN
0870 444 3852
www.museumoflondon.org.uk
The Museum of London is the world's largest urban history museum, the permanent galleries tell the story of London from pre-historic times to the present.

Museum of the Order
of St John
Islington, EC1M 4DA
(020) 7324 4070
www.sja.org.uk/museum
A 16thC gatehouse with a 12thC crypt
containing treasures of the Knights
of St John and the social history
collections of St John Ambulance.

National Gallery
Westminster, WC2N 5DN
(020) 7747 2888
www.nationalgallery.org.uk
The National Gallery has one of the
greatest collections of European
paintings in the world. A permanent
collection spans the period 1250–1900
and consists of over 2,300 Western
European paintings by many of the
world's famous artists.

National Maritime
Museum
Greenwich, SE10 9NF
(020) 8858 4422
www.nmm.ac.uk
Trace Britain's rich seafaring history,
including exploration, Nelson, trade
and empire, plus environmental issues.

National Portrait Gallery
Westminster, WC2H 0HE
(020) 7306 0055
www.npg.org.uk
With the world's largest collection of
portraits, the National Portrait Gallery
is the essential guide to 400 years of
Britain's greatest movers and shakers.

Royal Air Force
Museum Hendon
Barnet, NW9 5LL
(020) 8205 2266
www.rafmuseum.org
Discover aviation history. Exciting
display of suspended aircraft, touch
screen technology, simulator rides and
film shows.

Royal London Hospital
Archives and Museum
Tower Hamlets, E1 2AA
(020) 7377 7608
www.brlcf.org.uk
Archives and museum housed in the
crypt of a fine 19thC Gothic church
where the story of the Royal London
Hospital (founded 1740) is told.

Southbank Centre
Lambeth, SE1 8XX
0871 663 2501
www.southbankcentre.co.uk
Wide-ranging programmes include
classical and world music, rock, pop,
jazz, dance, literature and visual arts.

Tate Britain
Westminster, SW1P 4RG
(020) 7887 8888
www.tate.org.uk
Tate Britain presents the world's
greatest collection of British art in a
dynamic series of new displays and
exhibitions.

Tate Modern
Southwark, SE1 9TG
(020) 7887 8888
www.tate.org.uk/modern
The UK's largest modern art gallery.
Masterpieces by Dali, Picasso, Warhol
and Matisse. Excellent exhibitions.

The Original London
Sightseeing Tour
Westminster, SW18 1TB
(020) 8877 1722
www.theoriginaltour.com
London's 'The Original Tour' offers
guests a hop-on, hop-off tour
including live and digitally recorded
commentaries, a free river cruise and a
unique Kid's Club.

Tower Bridge Exhibition
Southwark, SE1 2UP
(020) 7403 3761
www.towerbridge.org.uk
Enjoy breathtaking views from
walkways 140 ft above the Thames.
Also Victorian engine rooms.

Victoria and Albert
Museum
Kensington and Chelsea,
SW7 2RL
(020) 7942 2000
www.vam.ac.uk
Where can you see ceramics, furniture,
fashion, glass, jewellery, metalwork,
photographs, sculpture, textiles and
paintings? Where else but the V&A, the
greatest museum of art and design,
and home to 3,000 years' worth of
amazing art ...

Wimbledon Lawn
Tennis Museum
Merton, SW19 5AE
(020) 8944 1066
www.wimbledon.org
A fantastic collection of memorabilia
dating from 1555, including
Championship Trophies. Art Gallery,
220-degree cinema and special
exhibitions, reflecting the game and
championships of today.

FAMILY FUN

Chessington World
of Adventures
Kingston upon Thames, KT9 2NE
0870 444 7777
www.chessington.com
Explore Chessington - it's a whole world
of adventures! Soar on the Vampire
rollercoaster or discover the mystery of
Tomb Blaster. Take a walk on the wild
side in the Trails of the Kings or visit the
park's own SEA LIFE Centre.

Royal Observatory
Greenwich
Greenwich, SE10 9NF
(020) 8858 4422
www.nmm.ac.uk
Explore time, space and astronomy
in the galleries. Stand on the Prime
Meridian, longitude zero.

The London Eye
Lambeth, SE1 7PB
0870 500 0600
www.londoneye.com/
Enjoy panoramic views up to 25
miles on clear days from this 443 ft
observation wheel.

HERITAGE

BBC Television
Centre Tours
Hammersmith and Fulham,
W12 7RJ
0870 603 0304
www.bbc.co.uk/tours
The general tour is of the BBC Television
Centre. Areas visited (depending on
availability) include studios, news
centre, dressing rooms, interactive
studio and the Blue Peter Garden. The
CBBC Tour is suitable for 7–12 year olds.

Chiswick House
Hounslow, W4 2RP
(020) 8995 0508
www.english-heritage.org.uk
The celebrated villa of Lord Burlington
with impressive grounds featuring
Italianate garden with statues, temples,
obelisks and urns.

Churchill Museum and
Cabinet War Rooms
Westminster, SW1A 2AQ
(020) 7930 6961
www.iwm.org.uk
Learn more about the man who
inspired Britain's finest hour at the
highly interactive and innovative
Churchill Museum, the world's first
major museum dedicated to life of the
'greatest Briton'. Step back in time and
discover the secret ...

Eltham Palace
Greenwich, SE9 5QE
(020) 8294 2548
elthampalace.org.uk/
Spectacular fusion of 1930s Art Deco villa and magnificent 15thC Great Hall. Period gardens.

Hampton Court Palace
Richmond upon Thames, KT8 9AU
0870 752 7777
www.hrp.org.uk
Tour Henry VIII's state apartments, the royal gardens and maze. Hear costumed guides recreate history.

HMS Belfast
Southwark, SE1 2JH
(020) 7940 6300
www.iwm.org.uk
Launched in 1938, HMS Belfast served throughout WWII, playing a leading part in the Normandy Landings.

Kenwood House
Camden, NW3 7JR
(020) 8348 1286
www.english-heritage.org.uk
See panoramic views of London from this beautifully appointed 18thC villa remodelled by Adams.

Old Royal Naval College
Greenwich, SE10 9LW
(020) 8269 4791
www.greenwichfoundation.org.uk
Admire Sir Christopher Wren's baroque masterpiece in landscaped grounds beside the Thames. Glorious Painted Hall and visitor centre.

Somerset House
Westminster, WC2R 1LA
(020) 7845 4670
www.somerset-house.org.uk
Somerset House is a place for enjoyment, refreshment, arts and learning. This magnificent 18thC building houses the celebrated collections of the Courtauld Institute of Art Gallery, Gilbert Collection and Hermitage Rooms.

Southwark Cathedral
Southwark, SE1 9DA
(020) 7367 6700
www.southwark.anglican.org/cathedral
Oldest Gothic church in London (c1220) with interesting memorials connected with the Elizabethan theatres of Bankside.

Tower of London
Tower Hamlets, EC3N 4AB
0870 756 6060
www.hrp.org.uk
The Tower of London spans over 900 years of British history. Fortress, palace, prison, arsenal and garrison, it is one of the most famous fortified buildings in the world, and houses the Crown Jewels, armouries, Yeoman Warders and ravens.

NATURE & WILDLIFE

London Wetland Centre
Richmond upon Thames, SW13 9WT
(020) 8409 4400
www.wwt.org.uk
Europe's best urban site for watching wildlife. Bird Airport viewing observatory and interactive discovery centre.

Events 2010

Chelsea Flower Show
London
www.rhs.org.uk
May

Daily Mail Ideal Home Show
London
www.idealhomeshow.co.uk/
20 March–05 April

East London Mela
London
www.eastlondon-mela.com
August

Get Loaded in the Park
London
www.getloadedinthepark.com
29th August

Hampton Court Palace Beer and Jazz Festival
London
www.pwrevents.com/hcbandj
August

London Marathon
London
www.virginlondonmarathon.com/
April

London Open House Weekend
London
www.londonopenhouse.org/public/london/event.html
September

London to Brighton Veteran Car Run
London
www.lbvcr.com
October

Mayor's Thames Festival
London
www.thamesfestival.org/
September

Notting Hill Carnival
London
www.thenottinghillcarnival.com/
28th–29th August

State Opening of Parliament
London
www.parliament.uk
November-December

The BBC Proms
London
www.bbc.co.uk/proms/
July–September

The Lord Mayor's Show
London
www.lordmayorsshow.org/
November

The Tower Festival
London
www.towerfestival.com
September

University Boat Race
London
www.theboatrace.org
April

Wimbledon Tennis Championships
London
www.wimbledon.org
21st June–4th July

Where to Eat

London has great places to eat. The restaurant reviews on these pages are just a small selection from the highly respected *The Good Food Guide 2010*. Please see pages 20–21 for further information on the guide and details of a Special Offer for our readers.

EAST SHEEN

The Victoria
upmarket gastropub with appealing menus
West Temple, East Sheen, SW14 7RT
Tel no: (020) 8876 4238
www.thevictoria.net
Modern British | £28

Bought by TV chef Paul Merrett in the summer of 2008, this upmarket gastropub-with-rooms is set in a quiet, leafy residential road near Sheen Common. It draws appreciative families for well-priced Saturday brunch and Sunday lunch offerings, but there's a more grown-up ambience in the evening. The appealing modern menus combine classics (crispy chicken Caesar salad with poached egg; boiled collar of bacon with spinach dumplings and parsley sauce) with more avant-garde offerings (salmon sashimi with a shallot and chilli crunch and cucumber pickle to start, or a main course of butternut and chickpea tagine with medjool dates, coriander yoghurt and flatbread). There are good chocolate brownies for dessert. The fashionable wine list fits the bill, with house wine at £14.

Chef/s: Paul Merrett. **Open:** all week L 12 to 2.30 (Sat 8.30 to 3, Sun 12 to 8), D 6 to 10 (Sat 6 to 10.30, Sun 6 to 8). **Meals:** alc (main courses £11 to £18). **Service:** 12.5% (optional). **Details:** Cards accepted. 45 seats. 60 seats outside. Air-con. Separate bar. Wheelchair access. Music. Children allowed. Car parking.

ISLINGTON

The Albion
Smart Georgian local
10 Thornhill Road, Islington, N1 1HW
Tel no: (020) 7607 7450
www.the-albion.co.uk
Anglo-Irish | £28

Surrounded by upmarket Georgian houses, this recent venture from Richard Turner has a suitably 18th century feel, with candles and chandeliers casting a dim glow over an uncluttered and tasteful interior of soft blue and stripped wood. Equally smart are dishes like salted mallard with cranberry sauce; pork belly and caper terrine and Arbroath fishcakes with bacon, duck egg and sweet pea sauce. But dig a little deeper, into Irish stew and roast beef marrow with caper gravy, and you'll find the same rustic Anglo-Irish cooking that helped chef Liam Kirwan put previous venture the Sand's End on the culinary map. Locals love summers in the garden and for a party of 10 you can go the whole hog and order a roast suckling pig, complete with trimmings. House wine from £14 a bottle.

Chef/s: Liam Kirwan. **Open:** all week L12 to 3 (10 to 4 Sat, Sun), D 6 to 10. **Meals:** alc (main courses £11 to £18). Set L £12.50 (2 courses) to £15. **Service:** 10% (optional). **Details:** Cards accepted. 94 seats. 108 seats outside. Wheelchair access. Music. Children allowed.

The Capital
Finely-tuned French gem
22 Basil Street, Knightsbridge, SW3 1AT
Tel no: (020) 7589 5171
www.capitalhotel.co.uk
French | £70

Reporters love the 'small size, intimacy and charming French ambience' of this hotel dining room, still a 'little-known gem'. The timeless interior combines classic elegance with retro charm via pale wood panelling and 1970s-style chandeliers. The result is intimate, relaxed and highly personal. Eric Chavot's cooking is solidly French, gently modern and at times surprisingly simple. Rump of venison might come with sweet pickled cabbage, velvety blackcurrant jus and an artful sprinkling of nuts and berries – a forest theme, but from the yielding meat to the toasty crunch of hazelnut, each ingredient is given space to shine. The same passion for quality runs through every aspect of the meal – olive oil that adds a fragrant, peppery warmth to a salt-crusted focaccia is second-to-none, while an amuse of sea bass tartare comes 'with a perfect chorizo cromesqui'. Similarly, a crab lasagne arrives with a seared scallop and a 'gloriously intense, silky' langoustine cappuccino that calls for 'more crusty, oven-fresh bread to mop up every trace'. Further delights are to be had in a burgeoning cheese trolley and exemplary petits fours. This is cooking that rarely misses a beat. At inspection a dessert that combined creamy vanilla tapioca pearls, roasted banana, crunchy popcorn, tart mango sorbet and boozy rum pannacotta was the only instance of flavour overload. The wine list may have you digging deep. French regions are covered in detail (look out for wines from the hotel's own vineyard, the Levin winery in the Loire Valley), but the rest of the world gets more than a passing glance. There are some excellent wines by the glass – just as well as bottles start from £31.
Chef/s: Eric Chavot. **Open:** all week L 12 to 2.30, D 7 to 11 (10.30 Sun). **Meals:** Set L £27.50 (2 courses) to £33. Set D £55 (2 courses) to £63. **Service:** 12.5% (optional). **Details:** Cards accepted. 32 seats. Air-con. Separate bar. No music. Wheelchair access. Children allowed. Car parking.

Princi
135 Wardour Street, Soho, W1F 0UT
Tel no: (020) 7478 8888
www.princi.co.uk
Italian

Restaurateur Alan Yau and Milanese baker Rocco Princi's nifty Italian bakery-cum-café bears all the hallmarks of a slick, professional operation. There's a busy buzz to the glossy, good-looking room where cheerful staff dispense food and drink with a can-do charm. Select

your choice from counter displays of breads, pastries, quiches, pizza slices, salads (beetroot, walnut and gorgonzola, £4.50) or generous hot dishes (spinach and ricotta cannelloni, £6). It's all well-made and well priced. House wine £16. Open all week.

Tierra Brindisa
A true taste of Spain
46 Broadwick Street, Soho, W1F 7AF
Tel no: (020) 7534 1690
www.tierrabrindisa.com
Spanish | £22

When Spanish produce supplier Brindisa opened Tapas Brindisa, it earned a reputation for running one of the most authentic Spanish venues in town. This Soho offshoot is no different. There's a stab at interior design with a 'garish' green-and-white tiled dining room (with rather cramped tables) and a lovely light bar area next to the open kitchen. On the food front things kick off simply, with a plate of Joselito ham before going on to other staples of the tapas repertoire such as lamb cutlets served with a good romesco sauce. More unusual is lentil stew with soft Tiétar goats' curd or quails in escabèche. Iberian cheeses make a fine alternative to desserts such as pears in Rioja. House Spanish from £14.50.
Chef/s: Jose Pizarro. **Open:** Mon to Sat L 12 to 5, D 5 to 11. **Closed:** 25 and 26 Dec, 2 weeks Aug, bank hols, Sun. **Meals:** alc (main courses £4 to £16). Set menus £25 to £35. **Service:** 12.5% (optional). **Details:** Cards accepted. 50 seats. 4 seats outside. Air-con. Wheelchair access. Music. Children allowed.

Content brought to you by **The Good Food Guide 2010**. Please see pages 20–21 for further details.

Tourist Information Centres

When you arrive at your destination, visit an Official Partner Tourist Information Centre for quality assured help with accommodation and information about local attractions and events, or email your request before you go. To search for attractions and Tourist Information Centres on the move just text INFO to 62233, and a web link will be sent to your mobile phone. To find a Tourist Information Centre by region visit enjoyEngland.com/find-tic.

BRITAIN & LONDON VISITOR CENTRE	1 Regent Street	0870 1566366	@responseuk.co.uk
CITY OF LONDON	St Paul's Churchyard		greig.oldbury@cityoflondon.gov.uk
GREENWICH	46 Greenwich Church Street	0870 608 2000	tic@greenwich.gov.uk
LEWISHAM	Lewisham Library	020 8297 8317	tic@lewisham.gov.uk

Regional Contacts and Information

For more information on accommodation, attractions, activities, events and holidays in London, contact Visit London. When you arrive at your destination, visit an Official Partner Tourist Information Centre for quality assured help, or email your request before you go. To search for attractions and Tourist Information Centres on the move just text INFO to 62233, and a web link will be sent to your mobile phone.

The publications listed are available from the following organisations:

Go to **visitlondon.com** for all you need to know about London. Look for inspirational itineraries with great ideas for weekends and short breaks.

Or call 0870 1 LONDON (0870 1 566 366) for:

• **A London visitor information pack**

• **Visitor information on London**
Speak to an expert for information and advice on museums, galleries, attractions, riverboat trips, sightseeing tours, theatre, shopping, eating out and much more! Or simply go to visitlondon.com.

• **Accommodation reservations**

Where to Stay

A key to symbols appears on page 6. Maps start on page 394. A listing of all Enjoy England assessed accommodation appears at the end of the region.

Looking for something else?

You can also buy a copy of our popular guide 'Hotels' including country house and town house hotels, metro and budget hotels, serviced apartments, restaurants with rooms and Spas in England 2010. Now available in good bookshops and online at **enjoyenglanddirect.com**

£10.99

LONDON E4, Inner London

Lee Valley Campsite

Sewardstone Road, Chingford, Epping E4 7RA
t (020) 8529 5689 f (020) 8559 4070 e scs@leevalleypark.org.uk
w **leevalleypark.org.uk** ONLINE MAP GUEST REVIEWS

🚐 (200)	£11.70–£15.20
🚐 (200)	£11.70–£15.20
⛺ (200)	£11.70–£15.20
🏠	£81.90–£106.40
200 touring pitches	

An ideal holiday venue that lets you mix the pleasure of the countryside with the excitement of central London. With excellent facilities including an on-site shop and children's play area. **directions** M25 jct 6, follow signs to Chingford. Turn left at the roundabout and the campsite is 2 miles on the right. **payment** credit/debit cards, cash, cheques

General 🔲🐾🔣🔟🔅🎱🚲🐕🎯📶 Leisure ∪ 🏌 ⛰

LONDON SE2, Inner London

Abbey Wood Caravan Club Site

Federation Road, London SE2 0LS
t (020) 8311 7708 f (020) 8311 1465
w **caravanclub.co.uk**

THE
CARAVAN
CLUB

🚐 (202)	£14.90–£28.90
🚐 (202)	£14.90–£28.90
202 touring pitches	

SPECIAL PROMOTIONS
Special member rates mean you can save your membership subscription in less than a week. Visit our website to find out more.

It feels positively rural when you reach this verdant, gently sloping, secure site with its mature tree screening and spacious grounds. This site is the ideal base for exploring the captial or as an alternative, nearby Greenwich, offers its own blend of fascinating attractions.

open All year
payment credit/debit cards, cash, cheques

directions On M2 turn off at A221. Then turn right into McLeod Road, right into Knee Hill and the site is the 2nd turning on the right.

General 🔲📶🔟🔅🎱🐕🎯📶
Leisure ⛰

LONDON SE19, Inner London

Crystal Palace Caravan Club Site

Crystal Palace Parade, London SE19 1UF
t (020) 8778 7155 f (020) 8676 0980
w **caravanclub.co.uk**

(126)   £14.90–£28.90
(126)   £14.90–£28.90
126 touring pitches

SPECIAL PROMOTIONS
Special member rates mean
you can save your
membership subscription in
less than a week. Visit our
website to find out more.

A busy but friendly site on the edge of a
pleasant park with many attractions for children.
Popular with European families in the summer.
In close proximity to all of London's attractions
Tower Bridge, Imperial War Museum, London
Eye and Lords Tour to name but a few.

open All year
payment credit/debit cards, cash, cheques

directions Turn off the A205, South Circular
road at West Dulwich into Croxted Road. The
site is adjacent to the BBC television mast.

General
Leisure

All Assessed Accommodation

Inner London

LONDON E4

Lee Valley Campsite ★★★★
Touring & Camping Park
Sewardstone Road, Chingford,
Epping
E4 7RA
t   (020) 8529 5689
e   scs@leevalleypark.org.uk
w leevalleypark.org.uk

LONDON SE2

Abbey Wood Caravan Club Site
★★★★★ *Touring & Camping Park*
Federation Road, London
SE2 0LS
t   (020) 8311 7708
w caravanclub.co.uk

LONDON SE19

Crystal Palace Caravan Club Site
★★★★★ *Touring & Camping Park*
Crystal Palace Parade, London
SE19 1UF
t   (020) 8778 7155
w caravanclub.co.uk

Help before you go

 When it comes to your next break, the first stage of your journey could be closer than you think.

You've probably got a Tourist Information Centre nearby which is there to serve the local community – as well as visitors. Knowledgeable staff will be happy to help you, wherever you're heading.

Many Tourist Information Centres can provide you with maps and guides, and it's often possible to book accommodation and travel tickets too.

You'll find the address of your nearest centre in your local phone book, or look in the regional sections in this guide for a list of Tourist Information Centres.

Holkham Beach in Norfolk, Holkham Hall Estate, Norfolk, England.

East of England

Bedfordshire, Cambridgeshire, Essex,
Hertfordshire, Norfolk, Suffolk

East of England

Based around the ancient kingdom of East Anglia, the East of England is a region where tradition is a way of life, eccentric customs are commonplace and people take the time to offer the warmest of welcomes.

Beautiful timber-framed villages, traditional market towns, gently rolling countryside and unspoilt coastline – this is England as you always thought it should be – right on London's doorstep.

The region covers 7,380 square miles stretching approximately 109 miles from north to south; and 108 miles east to west. Perfect for touring.

The Broads are Britain's largest nationally protected wetland, stretching out from The Wash. The Fens are noted for their dramatic skies and sweeping vistas. To the west of the region, the rolling Dunstable Downs offer chalk life flora and fauna. All offer fantastic wildlife-spotting, the region is one of the UK's best places for birdwatching.

The coastline comprises unspoilt sandy beaches, tiny fishing villages, crumbling cliffs, estuaries, shingle spits and Britain's best mudflats and salt marshes. Here smugglers inns nestle close to the waters where Lord Nelson learnt to sail. Enjoy the fun-packed family resorts of Great Yarmouth and Southend contrasted by the quieter idyllic coastal towns such as Southwold and Cromer.

Inland, explore the inspirational landscapes of artists, authors and films – such as Constable Country, where Britain's greatest landscape painter, John Constable, was born and worked. Whilst picturesque Lavenham in Suffolk is England's best preserved medieval town, from 14th to16th Century it was a major wool and cloth making centre.

Cycling is a great way to get around and explore quiet rural lanes, country pubs and a superb collection of churches. Look out as well for scrumptious culinary delights. The area is the 'Food Basket of Britain' – delicious hams, fine ales and wine, prize-winning jams, seafood treats and fresh fruit and vegetables.

Discover the spectacular colours and delicate fragrances of some of Britain's finest gardens, and magnificent treasure houses such as Woburn Abbey, Hatfield House, Blickling Hall and Royal Sandringham - alongside ancient castles, steam trains, intriguing museums and a rich aviation and maritime heritage.

Bedfordshire

Explore the ancient county town of Bedford, with its riverside gardens and connections to John Bunyan. To the north are pretty limestone villages with warm and welcoming inns and pubs, many of which were used by airmen, including Glenn Miller, based at the WW2 airbases during the War.

Ampthill

The picturesque, narrow streets are lined with fine Georgian buildings and quaint antique shops. Ampthill Park was once home to a 15th-century castle, where Henry VIII stayed. It was also here that his wife, Katherine of Aragon, was kept during their divorce proceedings. A stone cross now marks the spot. Market day is Thursday and there is a Farmers' Market on the last Saturday in each month.

Dunstable

The Dunstable Downs are the highest point in the East of England at 244 m (801 feet), providing superb views over Bedfordshire and the Vale of Aylesbury. Part of the Chiltern Hills, they were formed by chalk deposited on the seabed when the area was still underwater about 70 million years ago. This is a great place for a picnic and kite flying - you can buy them from the countryside centre, which also has a Downs exhibition.

Grand Union Canal

The canal runs through the Dacorum area, passing through Hemel Hempstead, Berkhamsted and Tring. Francis Egerton, The Duke of Bridgewater, known as The 'Father of Inland Navigation', who inspired the canal system had his home at Ashridge. The Grand Union Canal is for all, whether fishing, boating or just having fun. Enjoy the atmosphere, take in the 'roses and castles' narrowboats and original mileposts; see the many working examples of canal life such as pump houses, keeper's cottages and ancient locks.

Leighton Buzzard

The town's ancient street market is held on Tuesdays and Saturdays in the market square and high street, and the highly popular farmers market is held on the third Saturday and first Tuesday of each month. A network of streets and quaint shopping mews are great for exploring and lead to the market square with its pentagonal market cross adorned with statues.

Woburn

The Normans had a great impact in 1145 when Hugh de Bolebec founded the Abbey which has remained a major influence ever since. Following the dissolution of the monasteries, the land passed in to the hands of the Russell family, who later became the Dukes of Bedford. The Abbey today is an 18th-century palatial mansion open to visitors. The treasures on view are acknowledged as one of the finest private collections in England. Also part of the estate is the award-winning Woburn Safari Park with its game reserve and Sea Lion Cove, a golf course and antiques centre.

Cambridgeshire

The world famous University City of Cambridge is noted for its historic colleges, magnificent King's College Chapel, punting on the river and bookshops. There are many renowned restaurants, great shopping and hidden treasures of University College Gardens - Clare, Emmanuel and Newnham are particularly spectacular and a great place to unwind.

Ely

The city of Ely is rich in history, charm and beauty and is the jewel in the crown of the Fens. Dominating the skyline it is one of the England's most beautiful and largest cathedrals. Known locally as the 'Ship of the Fens', the cathedral is also home to the only national museum dedicated to stained glass. Ely's most famous resident and former MP, Oliver Cromwell, lived in Ely for many years before becoming Lord Protector of England. His home is open to the public throughout the year and visitors can learn more about him in specially restored rooms and exhibits about 17th-century life. The city has a splendid array of historic buildings with a beautiful waterside area where you can enjoy a boat trip, riverside walk or explore the many cafes and antiques shops.

The Fens

Nearly a million acres of beautiful black soil and wildlife rich water, perfect for birdwatching, boating and fishing. Over the centuries the land has been drained by man to create some of the most fertile soil in Britain; growing flowers, fruit and vegetables. Criss-crossed by waterways they offer stunning skyscapes and unforgettable sunsets, plus some of Britain's most important nature reserves. Because it is so flat, it's ideal walking or cycling country.

Huntingdon

The market town of Huntingdon stands proudly on the north bank of the River Great Ouse, at the junction of the A1 and A14, often referred to as the Crossroads of Eastern England. The centre of Huntingdon is now mainly traffic-free, making it a pleasant environment for the pedestrian to wander through, admiring some of the 150 properties listed as being of Special Architectural or Historic Interest. Huntingdon's most famous son, Oliver Cromwell, 'Lord Protector of the Commonwealth' from 1653 until his death in 1658, was born in Huntingdon. Riverside Park, with its many beautiful trees, provides picturesque scenery. There is an attractive riverside terrace, complete with seating and mooring facilities, from where there are impressive views of Westside Common, the former mill and the fine old bridge. Built in 1332, it has six arches and is considered to be one of the finest medieval bridges still left in England today.

Peterborough

3,000 years of heritage and an extensive choice of leisure and activity pursuits provide a dynamic experience that will exceed the expectations of leisure and business visitors alike. A magnificent Norman cathedral sits amid peaceful precincts just a few metres from the city's exciting shopping and leisure facilities.

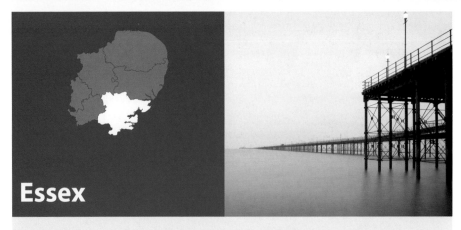

Essex

Chelmsford, County Town of Essex since 1250, offers first class shopping and over 100 places to eat and drink. Places to visit include Chelmsford Museum, Essex County Cricket Club, Riverside Ice and Leisure and Chelmsford Cathedral. Special events, including the Cathedral Festival, add vibrancy to the town centre.

Brightlingsea

Sitting at the mouth of the River Colne, with superb walks alongside the creek, it is a major yachting centre with one of the best stretches of sailing on the East Coast. The town is also home to one of England's oldest timber-framed buildings, the 13th-century Jacobs Hall.

Burnham on Crouch

Known as the 'Cowes of the East Coast', the attractive quayside is lined with colour-washed houses, boat-building yards and sailing clubs. The famous clock tower dates from 1877. The town is also noted for its annual regatta, oysters, smuggling tales and long walks along the sea walls.

Clacton on Sea

Clacton is a popular seaside town with tree-lined streets, sand/shingle beaches and beautiful clifftop gardens. The fun-packed 19th-century pier offers fairground rides and sea fishing. Try out a range of watersports, or take a pleasure flight from the Clacton Aero Club. Enjoy an evening out at the Princes and West Cliff Theatres - venues for spectacular shows, attracting a host of top showbiz names.

Colchester

Britain's oldest recorded town, is home to a superb Norman castle keep, Roman remains and great shopping. To the north is pretty Constable Country (Dedham) and Manningtree, home of the 17th-century, Witchfinder General, Matthew Hopkins.

Frinton-on-Sea

Often called 'the seaside town that time forgot' Frinton has a Victorian charm. Tree-lined residential avenues sweep down to the elegant Esplanade and cliff-top greensward. The long stretch of sand beach is quiet and secluded while the main shopping street (Connaught Avenue) has been dubbed the "Bond Street" of East Anglia.

Saffron Walden

The picturesque medieval town of Saffron Walden is situated in the heart of some of the finest rolling countryside of Essex. It is a small country market town with early origins, the name Walden meaning "Valley of Britons". The town was designated a Conservation Area in 1968 and there are some 400 buildings in the town of special architectural or historic interest and much care has been taken to conserve the historic character of the town centre which has retained the original medieval layout.

Southend on Sea

Bright, vibrant and exciting – Southend offers a glorious seven mile stretch of coastline. Award-winning beaches, beautiful parks and gardens, family fun attractions, museums, art galleries and exhilarating watersports. Take a walk along the world's longest pleasure pier (stretching 1.33 miles in the Thames estuary) or ride the little train to the end.

Hertfordshire

Hertford is an historic county town, set at confluence of four rivers and a royal borough for more than 1,000 years. The castle stands in delightful gardens, whilst the town is largely a conservation area. There are many Georgian shop-fronts, delightful old pubs, and antique shops, especially along St. Andrew Street.

Berkhamsted

A thriving town steeped in history where William the Conqueror received the crown of England at the castle in 1066. Berkhamsted enjoys a beautiful setting on the banks of the River Bulbourne and the Grand Union Canal, making it an ideal base to explore the glorious Chiltern Hills and West Hertfordshire Downs either by foot or aboard a brightly painted narrowboat. Discover the literary links with Geoffrey Chaucer, Graham Greene and J.M Barrie. The characterful 16th-century architecture is not lost on the large number of unique retailers and restaurateurs who provide the thriving picturesque town with a fashionable buzz. Designer clothes, antiques and gift shops nestle alongside award winning eateries and a Saturday market.

Bishop's Stortford

The ancient market town of Bishop's Stortford is superbly situated in rural Hertfordshire. It is a modern lively town with a long and varied history. There is much to see in the town - a rich collection of 16th and 17th-century buildings in the centre, including several of the old inns made famous when the town was an important staging post on the route between London and both Newmarket and Cambridge. The River Stort, running through

the town centre, provides leisurely activities and is popular with walkers, anglers and visiting narrow-boats.

Sawbridgeworth

Described as 'one of the best small towns in the county', Sawbridgeworth prospered from the malting industry and is dominated by a 13th century church spire. The riverside maltings have been converted into an antiques centre whilst the town centre is a conservation area with picturesque streets and Georgian/Victorian buildings.

St Albans

Take time to enjoy St Albans, a city with a wealth of remarkable heritage from over 2000 years. Discover the city's magnificent cathedral and museums. Explore the old historic streets packed with specialist shops, markets, pubs, cafés and restaurants or relax in the green oasis of Verulamium Park. St Albans has something to offer everyone.

Tring

Tring is an historic market town, nestling in the foothills of the Chilterns. The town really prospered under the watchful eye of the Rothschild family whose legacy was predominantly one of the architecture they influenced. Sir Walter Rothschild founded the Zoological Museum. Other interesting places are Tring Parkand, the church with its connections with the family of George Washington and, of course, the Chiltern Hills. Friday is market day and a selection of food and assorted goods and produce is available. A Farmers Market is held fortnightly.

Norfolk

Norwich boasts some of the finest medieval architecture in Britain with its enchanting cathedral and castle. In contrast the city's newest centerpiece, The Forum, represents contemporary architecture at its best. Eat in quality restaurants, and shop in modern malls and individual shops in the numerous Lanes. Norwich truly is a fine city that offers a warm welcome.

The Broads

The Broads is an enchanted land: waterways; wet, tangled woodlands; mysterious fens, and immense grazing marshes stretching as far as the eye can see. The Broads is also home to exceptional plants and animals, like the swallowtail butterfly, which is found nowhere else in Britain.

The Norfolk and Suffolk Broads area covers 303 sq km, including over 125 miles (200 km) of navigable waterways. There are six rivers - the Bure, Ant, Thurne, Yare, Chet, and Waveney, and 43 Broads (or shallow lakes). The Broads were formed in medieval times (9th-13th centuries), when peat was dug out to use as fuel. Over the centuries water levels rose and the peat diggings flooded, forming the Broads. Today the Broads has the status of a national park - a place protected for its outstanding landscape and wildlife for everyone to enjoy.

Great Yarmouth

Great Yarmouth with 15 miles of glorious sandy beaches is one of the UK's most popular seaside

resorts, with an enviable mix of sandy beaches, attractions, entertainment and heritage with quality accommodation. Behind the glitter and bright lights, lies a charming town that is steeped in history. Discover one of the most complete medieval town walls in England, the historic South Quay and Nelson's 'other' column.

Holt

The quaint lanes and yards that house the bookshops, galleries, antique and bric-a-brac shops create a bustling example of the ideal town. At Christmas all the shops and buildings are draped with lights, which create a magical festive atmosphere. On the edge of town lies Holt Country Park, with car parking, a picnic area, nature trails and an adventure playground, it's a perfect spot for a family outing. A mile west is Letheringsett with an early 19th-century watermill which still stone-grinds corn. The idyllic countryside around Holt and the Glaven valley is perfect for exploring on foot or by bicycle.

King's Lynn

King's Lynn is more than just a medieval port. The town is now a treasure trove for history lovers with narrow streets and handsome merchant houses in the old town. See the only surviving Hanseatic warehouse in the country and plenty of fascinating visitor attractions to help bring the 'olden days' alive. Down by the river, you can take a ferry over to the west bank and take in the outstanding view of King's Lynn's townscape. There is a vibrant mix of theatres, cinemas, arts festivals, exhibitions, museums, pubs, stylish café bars and restaurants.

Suffolk

The county town of Ipswich is England's oldest continuously settled Anglo-Saxon town - with medieval streets and architectural gems - from the decorative plasterwork of the 'Ancient House' (c.1670), to Sir Norman Foster's award-winning Willis Corroon building. Twelve medieval churches stand testimony to the importance of the town as it developed in the Middle Ages.

Aldeburgh

A charming, traditional seaside town that harks back to an earlier age. There is a traditional boating lake for model yachts, a local museum, and historic 16th-century Moot Hall. The fishermen still draw their boats up on to the shore and sell fish from the beach. Aldeburgh was one of the leading ports on the East Coast and its shipbuilding was renowned. Sir Francis Drake's ships "Pelican" and "Greyhound" were built locally. The industry declined as the river Alde silted up.

Bury St Edmunds

Bury St Edmunds grew up around the powerful medieval Abbey of St Edmund. Although the abbey was dissolved by Henry VIII and fell into ruin, the town has continued to prosper. The streets still follow the grid pattern devised by the abbots, and many other reminders of the abbey remain. Some of the abbey ruins have been sympathetically converted into houses and the Great Court is a prize-winning public garden. The history is part of everyday life and it is what endows Bury St Edmunds with special character. Authors and

visitors from Daniel Defoe to Charles Dickens have admired the town – one 19th-century writer, William Cobbett, dubbed it 'the nicest little town in the world'.

Lowestoft

The town of Lowestoft is situated on the most easterly point in Great Britain. Famous for its wonderful stretches of award winning beaches and rich maritime heritage, the town is a perfect holiday location for the young and young at heart. It has a successful combination of wide stretches of beach to the one side and wooded broadland to the other, giving the resort an eclectic appeal. Visit the recently renovated Yacht Marina and nearby docks. Enjoy the traditional amusements at both South Pier and Claremont Pier or refuel at the eateries and bars. One of the regions largest attractions, New Pleasurewood Hills Theme Park, is located nearby.

Newmarket

Newmarket is internationally recognised as the 'Home of Horseracing'. There are training yards accommodating over 2400 horses, horse walks, an equine swimming pool, and Tattersalls Thoroughbred Auctioneers, where horses exchange hands for vast sums of money. Arrive early in the morning to witness the horses out exercising on the gallops. For a unique experience combine this with a visit to the National Horseracing Museum, the National Stud, or an afternoon at the races at either of the two courses, both within close proximity to the town. A market is held on Tuesday and Saturday.

Where to Go

 Attractions with this sign participate in the **Visitor Attraction Quality Assurance Scheme** (see page 6) which recognises high standards in all aspects of the vistor experience.

ENTERTAINMENT & CULTURE

Bedford Museum
Bedford, Bedfordshire MK40 3XD
(01234) 353323
www.bedfordmuseum.org
Journey through the human and natural history of north Bedfordshire, glimpse wonders from distant lands.

Christchurch Mansion
Ipswich, Suffolk IP4 2BE
(01473) 433554
www.ipswich.gov.uk/museums
Fine Tudor mansion in superb landscaped gardens. Works by Constable and Gainsborough.

Imperial War Museum Duxford
Cambridge, Cambridgeshire CB22 4QR
(01223) 835000
www.iwm.org.uk/duxford
Superb collection of aircraft, tanks, military vehicles and naval exhibits.

Mid-Norfolk Railway
Dereham, Norfolk NR20 5LE
(01362) 690633
www.mnr.org.uk
WW2 themed station, tea rooms and museum. Picnic area, orchard and footpaths. Open Sundays and Bank Holidays, Easter to September.

Shuttleworth Collection
Biggleswade, Bedfordshire SG18 9EP,
(01767) 627970
www.shuttleworth.org
See a unique collection of aircraft spanning 100 years of flight, plus historic vehicles.

Verulamium Museum
St. Albans, Hertfordshire AL3 4SW
(01727) 751810
The award-winning museum of everyday life in Roman Britain. See Roman soldiers demonstrate their tactics.

FAMILY FUN

Adventure Island
Southend-on-Sea, Essex SS1 1EE
(01702) 443400
www.adventureisland.co.uk
Plenty of great rides at one of the best value theme parks in the South East.

BeWILDerwood
Norwich, Norfolk NR12 8JW
(01603) 783900
www.bewilderwood.co.uk
Treehouses, zip wires, jungle bridges, boat trips, marsh walks and great organic food!

Go Ape! High Wire Forest Adventure - Thetford
Brandon, Suffolk IP27 0AF
0845 643 9215
www.goape.co.uk
Go Ape! and tackle a high wire forest adventure, featuring rope bridges, swings and slides.

Pleasurewood Hills Leisure Park
Lowestoft, Suffolk NR32 5DZ
(01502) 586000
www.pleasurewoodhills.com
Thrills, family rides and great entertainment. Try Wizzy Dizzy, Thunderstruck or Wipeout extreme rollercoaster.

Sea-Life Adventure
Southend-on-Sea, Essex SS1 2ER
(01702) 442200
www.sealifeadventure.co.uk
Explore over 40 displays featuring sea life from all over the world. Cafe, play centre.

HERITAGE

Audley End House
Saffron Walden, Essex CB11 4JF
(01799) 522399
www.english-heritage.org.uk/server/show/nav.12088
Experience the sumptuous splendour and artistic treasures of one of England's grandest stately homes.

Cathedral and Abbey Church of St. Alban
St. Albans, Hertfordshire AL1 1BY
(01727) 860780
This Norman abbey church, on the site of St Alban's martyrdom, features England's longest nave.

Ely Cathedral
Ely, Cambridgeshire CB7 4DL
(01353) 667735
www.cathedral.ely.anglican.org
One of England's finest cathedrals. Guided tours include the Octagon, West Tower and monastic precincts.

Framlingham Castle
Woodbridge, Suffolk IP13 9BP
(01223) 582700
www.english-heritage.org.uk/framlingham
Visit the magnificent castle home of Mary Tudor featuring 12thC curtain walls and thirteen towers.

Grimes Graves
Thetford, Norfolk IP26 5DE
(01223) 582700
www.english-heritage.org.uk
Remarkable Neolithic flint mines. Over
400 pits and shafts – one open to the
public.

Hatfield House
Hatfield, Hertfordshire AL9 5NQ
(01707) 287010
www.hatfield-house.co.uk
The Marquess of Salisbury's
magnificent Jacobean house.
Childhood home of Queen Elizabeth I.
Exquisite gardens.

Holkham Hall
Wells-next-the-Sea, Norfolk
NR23 1AB
(01328) 710227
www.holkham.co.uk
Classic 18thC Palladian hall, rich in
artistic and architectural history, on a
working agricultural estate.

**Ickworth House, Park
and Gardens**
Bury St Edmunds, Suffolk
IP29 5QE
(01284) 735270
www.nationaltrust.org.uk/main/w-
ckworthhouseparkandgarden
Discover this extraordinary oval house
containing important collections and
set in stunning parkland landscaped by
Capability Brown.

Kings College Chapel
Cambridge, Cambridgeshire
CB2 1ST
(01223) 331212
www.kings.cam.ac.uk
Breathtaking Gothic architecture,
priceless art treasures and home to the
world famous choir.

**North Norfolk Railway
(The Poppy Line)**
Sheringham, Norfolk NR26 8RA
(01263) 820800
www.nnrailway.co.uk
Five-mile heritage railway with stations
at Sheringham, Weybourne and Holt.
Steam trains daily in summer.

Norwich Cathedral
Norwich, Norfolk NR1 4EH
(01603) 218321
www.cathedral.org.uk
Majestic Norman cathedral with
exceptional 14thC roof bosses
depicting bible scenes. Cloisters and
cathedral close.

Oliver Cromwell's House
Ely, Cambridgeshire CB7 4HF
(01353) 662062
www.eastcambs.gov.uk/tourism
Cromwell's family home. Period rooms,
exhibitions on 17thC life and Civil War.

Sandringham
King's Lynn, Norfolk PE35 6EN
(01553) 612908
www.sandringhamestate.co.uk
Country retreat of HM The Queen.
A delightful house with 60 acres of
magnificent gardens.

Woburn Abbey
Woburn, Bedfordshire
MK17 9WA
(01525) 290333
www.discoverwoburn.co.uk
Palladian mansion set in a beautiful
3,000-acre deer park. Superb furniture
and art collections.

NATURE AND WILDLIFE

Banham Zoo
Norwich, Norfolk NR16 2HE
(01953) 887771
www.banhamzoo.co.uk
Wildlife spectacular featuring some
of the world's most exotic, rare and
endangered animals.

Colchester Zoo
Colchester, Essex CO3 0SL
(01206) 331292
www.colchester-zoo.co.uk
Get close to one of the best cat and
primate collections in the country.

National Stud
Newmarket, Cambridgeshire
CB8 0XE
(01638) 663464
www.nationalstud.co.uk
See thoroughbred stallions, mares and
foals, and observe the running of a
modern stud farm.

RHS Garden Hyde Hall
Chelmsford, Essex CM3 8ET
(01245) 400256
www.rhs.org.uk/hydehall
This 28 acre hilltop garden has low
rainfall and features a dedicated dry
garden. Year round interest.

**RSPB Minsmere
Nature Reserve**
Saxmundham, Suffolk IP17 3BY
(01728) 648281
www.rspb.org.uk/minsmere
One of the RSPB's finest reserves.
Birdwatching hides and trails, events,
guided walks, visitor centre.

**RSPB The Lodge
Nature Reserve**
Sandy, Bedfordshire SG19 2DL
(01767) 680551
www.rspb.org.uk/thelodge
Explore woodland and heath, spot
varied birds and wildlife. Also formal
organic gardens.

The Raptor Foundation
Huntingdon, Cambridgeshire
PE28 3BT
(01487) 741140
www.raptorfoundation.org.uk
Get close to nature's most stunning
creatures: owls, hawks, falcons and
eagles. Flying displays.

Willows Farm Village
St. Albans, Hertfordshire
AL4 0PF
0870 129 9718
Discover your animal instincts.
Meet farmyard favourites including
newborns, plus adventure activities
and children's shows.

Woburn Safari Park
Woburn, Bedfordshire
MK17 9QN
(01525) 290407
www.woburn-hospitality.co.uk/
woburn_safari_lodge
Drive through a spectacular park
with lions, tigers and elephants just a
windscreen's width away.

**Woodside Animal Farm
and Leisure Park**
Luton, Bedfordshire LU1 4DG
(01582) 841044
www.woodsidefarm.co.uk
Seven acre park. Rare breeds, wildlife,
farm animals, hands on sessions, farm
shop, adventure play.

Wrest Park
Bedford, Bedfordshire
MK45 4HS
(01223) 582700
www.english-heritage.org.uk
Magnificent formal gardens laid out
over 150 years including Chinese
pavilion, wooded walks and orangery.

**WWT Welney
Wetland Centre**
Wisbech, Norfolk PE14 9TN
(01353) 860711
www.wwt.org.uk
Track wild swans at this wetland nature
reserve, featuring an amazing new eco-
friendly visitor centre.

OUTDOOR ACTIVITIES

Broads Tours
The Broads, Norfolk NR12 8RX
(01603) 782207
www.broads.co.uk
Cruise the Broads in comfort on a
luxury double-decker or traditional
river bus.

Events 2010

Aldeburgh Festival of Music and the Arts
Saxmundham
www.aldeburgh.co.uk
June

Bedford International Kite Festival
Bedford
www.bedford.gov.uk
May

Cambridge Folk Festival
Cherry Hinton
www.cambridgefolkfestival.co.uk
July/August

Clacton Airshow
Clacton-on-Sea
www.tendringdc.gov.uk
August

Eel Day
Ely
www.eastcambs.gov.uk
May

Essex Country Show, Barleylands
Billericay
www.essexcountryshow.co.uk/
September

Great Annual Re-creation of Tudor Life
Sudbury
www.kentwell.co.uk
June/July

Great Yarmouth Maritime Festival
Great Yarmouth
www.maritime-festival.co.uk
September

Harpenden Highland Gathering
www.harpenden-lions.co.uk
July

Hatfield House Country Show
Hatfield
www.hatfield-house.co.uk
August

Latitude Festival
Beccles
www.latitudefestival.co.uk
July

Lowestoft Seafront Air Festival
Lowestoft
www.lowestoftairfestival.co.uk/
July

Luton International Carnival
Luton
www.luton.gov.uk
May

Norfolk and Norwich Festival
Norwich
www.nnfestival.org.uk
7th-22nd May

Norwich Food Festival
Norwich
www.visitnorwich.co.uk
September-October

Rhythms of the World, Hitchin
Hitchin
www.rotw.org.uk
July

Royal Norfolk Show
Norwich
www.royalnorfolkshow.co.uk
July

Southend Airshow
Southend-on-Sea
www.southendairshow.com
23rd-24th May

St. Albans Festival
St. Albans
www.stalbans.gov.uk
June-July

St. George's Day Festival
Bedford
www.english-heritage.org.uk
April

Stilton Cheese Rolling Contest
Peterborough
www.stilton.org
3rd May

Suffolk Show
Ipswich
www.suffolkshow.co.uk
May

Tring Canal Festival
Tring
www.tringcanalfestival.org.uk
May

Twinwood Festival
Bedford
www.twinwoodevents.com
28th-30th August

V Festival
Chelmsford
www.vfestival.com/
21st-22nd August

Woburn Oyster Festival
Milton Keynes
www.woburnoysterfestival.co.uk
September

World Snail Racing Championships
Congham
www.snailracing.net
July

Help before you go

When it comes to your next break, the first stage of your journey could be closer than you think.

You've probably got a Tourist Information Centre nearby which is there to serve the local community – as well as visitors. Knowledgeable staff will be happy to help you, wherever you're heading.

Many Tourist Information Centres can provide you with maps and guides, and it's often possible to book accommodation and travel tickets too.

You'll find the address of your nearest centre in your local phone book, or look in the regional sections in this guide for a list of Tourist Information Centres.

Where to Eat

The East of England region has great places to eat. The restaurant reviews on these pages are just a small selection from the highly respected *The Good Food Guide 2010*. Please see pages 20–21 for further information on the guide and details of a Special Offer for our readers.

BEDFORDSHIRE

The Plough at Bolnhurst

Big-flavour food shines out
Kimbolton Road, Bolnhurst, MK44 2EX
Tel no: (01234) 376274
www.bolnhurst.com
Modern British | £30

In a county not richly endowed with good eating, the Plough shines out like a beacon. It's a whitewashed Tudor inn, with tiny windows (and not many of them) contributing to a most singular feel. Low beamed ceilings frame the candlelit scene, and the kitchen is open to view from both bar and restaurant, which proves a powerful lure. Satisfied customers write that 'this is top-quality local produce cooked to produce big, wonderful flavours, with no daft eclectic combinations'. They had enjoyed the house black pudding as a starter (which may come with Montgomery Cheddar hash, pancetta and red wine sauce), braised beef and a side of red cabbage followed by apple tart – unimpeachable winter comfort food.

Other good ideas have been Portland crab served in a raviolo in crab and coriander bisque, roast turbot with confit garlic and cavolo nero, and an Indian-influenced veggie main course of lentil dhal with cauliflower, spinach, raita and an onion bhaji. Bread-and butter pudding and a range of homemade ice creams are among the sweet options. It all takes place in an atmosphere of great conviviality. An exemplary wine list, arranged by style, is crammed with pedigree bottles, enthusiastically annotated and ordered at fair prices. Choice by the glass (from £3.25) is handsome enough in itself.
Chef/s: Martin Lee. **Open:** Tue to Sun L 12 to 2, Tue to Sat D 6.30 to 9.30. **Closed:** Mon, 26 Dec to 14 Jan.
Meals: alc (main courses £12 to £25). Set L £13 (2 courses) to £17. **Service:** not inc. **Details:** Cards accepted. 80 seats. 30 seats outside. No music. Wheelchair access. Children allowed. Car parking.

CAMBRIDGESHIRE

The Crown Inn

Relaxed gastropub with seasonal offerings
Bridge Road, Broughton, PE28 3AY
Tel no: (01487) 824428
www.thecrowninnrestaurant.co.uk
Gastropub | £24

The Crown commands a prime position opposite the church on the road that runs through this hamlet north of Huntingdon. It's a heart-warming country pub with small paned windows, stone floors, a rustic bar and separate dining room leading onto the garden. The kitchen, now headed by chef/patron David Anderson, delivers an eclectic menu that features a number of Mediterranean influences (potato gnocchi with rabbit sauce) to complement modern British dishes of, say, am hock terrine with piccalilli or roast lamb teamed with mash and thyme and red wine sauce. For dessert, there may be syrup sponge pudding with egg custard. Wines from £13.

Chef/s: David Anderson. **Open:** Wed to Sun L 12 to 2.30, Wed to Sat D 7 to 10. **Closed:** Mon and Tue. **Meals:** alc main courses £10 to £16). Set L £11.50 (2 courses) to £14. **Service:** not inc. **Details:** Cards accepted. 60 seats. 12 seats outside. Separate bar. Wheelchair access. Music. Children allowed. Car parking.

The Hole in the Wall
ccomplished seasonal cooking
High Street, Little Wilbraham, CB21 5JY
el no: (01223) 812282
www.the-holeinthewall.com
Modern British | £28

Midway between Cambridge and Newmarket, this heavily timbered sixteenth century inn makes a highly appealing showcase for Christopher and Jennifer Leeton's friendly approach. Its name comes from the opening where local farm workers once collected their beer after a day's hard graft. In partnership with experienced restaurateur Stephen Bull, a carefully sourced menu has been put together, and the cooking shows real flair. Start, perhaps, with a homemade game sausage, grilled and teamed with pickled red cabbage, apple purée and redcurrant jus, before considering a simple fish dish such as lemon sole served with purple sprouting broccoli, crushed new potatoes and a brown shrimp hollandaise, or the local lamb that is braised for eight hours and accompanied by turnips, lemon thyme mash, creamed carrots and mint jelly. Rhubarb fool with orange and ginger and a passion fruit sorbet is typical of the vibrantly flavoured desserts. Southern French varietals, a Colombard and a Cabernet at £14.50 head up a concise, usefully annotated wine list.

Chef/s: Christopher Leeton. **Open:** Tue to Sun L 12 to , Tue to Sat D 7 to 9. **Closed:** 2 weeks Jan, 2 weeks Oct. **Meals:** alc (main courses £11 to £17). Set Sun L £17.50 (2 courses) to £21. **Service:** not inc. **Details:** Cards accepted. 0 seats. 20 seats outside. Wheelchair access. Children allowed. Car parking.

Cricketers
Clavering, CB11 4QT
Tel no: (01799) 550442
www.thecricketers.co.uk
Gastropub

Simple hearty cooking with an Italian twist is as much a draw at this atmospheric English hostelry as the fact that it's run by Jamie Oliver's parents. The regularly changing menu is ordered à la carte in the bar at lunch and dinner, but for dinner in the restaurant it is set at £23.50/£29.50 for 2/3 courses. Expect rabbit with

gnocchi and wild mushrooms, venison with poached pear and bitter chocolate sauce or free-range chicken with citrus salsa verde. Wines from £12.80. Open all week. Accommodation.

The Pier at Harwich
Fresh seafood and harbour views
The Quay, Harwich, CO12 3HH
Tel no: (01255) 241212
www.milsomhotels.com
Seafood | £30

There are no prizes for guessing the location or the long-lasting appeal of this amenable hotel slap-bang on Harwich quayside. Seafood is the lure, and the kitchen scoops up the pick of the catch for menus that please the old guard and fashion-conscious foodies alike. Diners in the first-floor restaurant can admire the views before partaking of home-smoked salmon, moules marinière or something trendy such as fillet of halibut with passion fruit vinaigrette. Meat-eaters could try venison, wild mushroom and port pie, while crowd-pleasing desserts might include white chocolate and pistachio torte. House wine is £14. Simpler food is also available in the ground-floor Ha'penny Pier bistro.

Chef/s: Chris Oakley. **Open:** all week L 12 to 2, D 6 to 9.30. **Meals:** alc (main courses £14 to £32). Set L £18.50 (2 courses) to £24. Set Sun L £25.50. **Service:** 10%. **Details:** Cards accepted. 60 seats. 20 seats outside. Air-con. Separate bar. No mobile phones. Music. Children allowed. Car parking.

St James
Contemporary neighbourhood restaurant
30 High Street, Bushey, WD2 3DN
Tel no: (020) 8950 2480
www.stjamesrestaurant.co.uk
Modern British | £40

This bright, contemporary restaurant stands opposite St James church in the heart of Bushey, and eager reporters testify to the ongoing popularity. The name of the game is to combine good-quality ingredients with uncomplicated cooking to produce a menu with broad appeal. There might be smoked duck with woodland salad and orange vinaigrette, mains of roast saddle of venison with homemade sausage and butternut squash purée or a simple grilled lemon sole. Desserts could take in Toblerone cheesecake. House wine is £13.50.

Chef/s: Calvin Hill. **Open:** Mon to Sat L 12.30 to 2.30, D 6.30 to 10. **Closed:** bank hols. **Meals:** alc (main courses £13 to £21). Set L £14.95 (2 courses). Set D £16.95 (2 courses). **Service:** 12.5% (optional). **Details:** Cards accepted. 100 seats. 20 seats outside. Air-con. Separate bar. No mobile phones. Wheelchair access. Music. Children allowed. Car parking.

The Tilbury
Fervent local food crusader
1 Watton Road, Datchworth, SG3 6TB
Tel no: (01438) 815550
www.thetilbury.co.uk
Modern British | £28

TV chef Paul Bloxham is a fervent supporter of 'seasonal and regional British foods', and his latest venture – a sympathetically refurbished village pub not far from Knebworth – flies the flag with pride and gusto. In a bid to keep food miles to a minimum, most of the kitchen's culinary building blocks come from named suppliers in Hertfordshire and neighbouring counties – anything from Farmer Sharp's steak tartare with potato biscuits to hefty plates of Great Dunmow free-range pig. Daily market menus and specials also tap into the wider network for the likes of Shetland scallops with smoked black pudding, apple sauce and pea purée, Cornish red mullet with octopus bourride and parsley aïoli, or slow-cooked Herdwick mutton shank with couscous and green sauce. Desserts conjure up a mix of nursery flavours (apple and blackberry crumble) and contemporary hits (honey and ginger pannacotta with poached forced rhubarb). Carafes of house wine (from £9.95) head the intelligently assembled global wine list.
Chef/s: Paul Bloxham and Ben Crick. **Open:** all week L 12 to 3 (12 to 6 Sun), Mon to Sat D 6 to 11. **Meals:** alc (main courses £10 to £23). Set L £13.95 (2 courses) to £17.95. Set D £17.95 (2 courses) to £21.50. Sun L £16.95. **Service:** not inc. **Details:** Cards accepted. 70 seats. 40 seats outside. Separate bar. No mobile phones. Wheelchair access. Music. Children allowed. Car parking.

NORFOLK

Cley Windmill
Cley-next-the-sea, NR25 7RP
Tel no: (01263) 740209
www.cleywindmill.co.uk
British

Standing proud above the North Norfolk salt marshes, Cley Windmill is a photogenic heritage hotspot and an oddball hideaway – if you fancy bed and board in a tower. It also offers intimate evening meals to guests and visitors alike. The sum of £25 buys you a daily changing three-course dinner – perhaps pigeon salad with baby beetroot and seared pancetta, fillet of salmon on a herbed potato cake, and homemade meringue with poached berries and cream. House wine is £12.75. Open all week D only.

Morston Hall
A class act by the coast
The Street, Morston, NR25 7AA
Tel no: (01263) 741041
www.morstonhall.com
Modern British | £55

'A perfect gem of North Norfolk!', exclaimed one reporter after sampling the pleasures of the Blackistons' secluded brick-and-flint mansion opposite Morston Quay. It may put on a grand face, with its high walls, Jacobean exterior and trim gardens, but the mood is as intimate and personable as can be and everyone has a good word to say about the 'terrific' service from keen young staff. After drinks in the conservatory, dinner revolves around a daily four-course menu (no choice) brimming with local flavours. At its most acutely seasonal, the kitchen might thrill with a risotto of local summer vegetables and beetroot foam, before Morston crab salad with Stiffkey samphire (picked a few miles away). Roast fillet of beef or lightly curried saddle of lamb are also true to the region – the lamb served with coriander mash, celeriac and white wine jus. For dessert, blueberry soufflé has been singled out, although the finale might involve passion fruit tart with nectarine sorbet or artisan British cheeses. The impeccably chosen global wine list is organised by grape variety, and there is particularly fine drinking to be had from the French regions (note the Trimbach Alsace Rieslings) and the Antipodes. Prices start at £18 (£4 a glass).
Chef/s: Galton Blackiston and Richard Bainbridge. **Open:** Sun L 12.30 for 1 (1 sitting), all week D 7.30 for 8 (1 sitting). **Closed:** 25 and 26 Dec, Jan. **Meals:** Set Sun L £34, Set D £55 (4 courses). **Service:** not inc. **Details:** Cards accepted. 50 seats. No music. No mobile phones. Wheelchair access. Children allowed. Car parking.

SUFFOLK

The Trinity, Crown and Castle
Welcoming mix of old and new
Orford, IP12 2LJ
Tel no: (01394) 450205
www.crownandcastle.co.uk
Modern British | £35

A traditional nineteenth-century hotel this might appear on the outside, but its inner self harks back to the sixteenth century, albeit as a light, bright contemporary space with beamed ceilings, bare boards and polished tables in adjoining dining rooms. Menus, too, follow modern lines. Own-smoked trout combines with beetroot and new potato salad and horseradish cream, and pork belly lardons come with spiced pear, watercress salad and medlar jelly. More traditionally, Aberdeen Angus sirloin has been well-timed, enriched with Café de Paris glaze and served with good hand-cut chips, while pub-style lunches offer moules marinière, eggs Benedict and Suffolk

steak and ale shortcrust pie. Warm loganberry jam and frangipane tart is a properly indulgent dessert. With plenty by the glass, the chatty, style-organised wine list suits the welcoming, unpretentious setting created by TV presenter Ruth Watson (Channel 4's Country House Rescue) and her husband David. Italian house white and Chilean red are £14.50.
Chef/s: Ruth Watson. **Open:** all week L 12.15 to 2.15, D 6.45 to 9.15. **Closed:** 4 to 7 Jan. **Meals:** alc (main courses £14 to £20). Set L £20 (2 courses) to £25. Set Sun L £17.95 (2 courses) to £23.95. Set D £25 (2 courses) to £35. **Service:** not inc. **Details:** Cards accepted. 50 seats. Separate bar. No music. No mobile phones. Wheelchair access. Children allowed. Car parking.

Riverside Restaurant
Quayside, Woodbridge, IP12 1BH
Tel no: (01394) 382587
www.theriverside.co.uk
Modern British

Sitting next to the river Deben is the gastroarts complex of the Riverside, where a combined film and dinner deal (£30) should sort an evening out very comprehensively. Otherwise, look to the carte for rollmops in sour-cream and chives (£6), with maybe sage and lemon-crusted rump of Ketley Farm lamb (£17) or Loch Duart salmon with spring onion mash and garlic and chilli butter (£16) to follow. A range of inspired desserts (£6) includes caramelised pineapple with lemongrass granita. Wines from £14. Open all week. Closed Sun D.

Tourist Information Centres

When you arrive at your destination, visit an Official Partner Tourist Information Centre for quality assured help with accommodation and information about local attractions and events, or email your request before you go. To search for attractions and Tourist Information Centres on the move just text INFO to 62233, and a web link will be sent to your mobile phone. To find a Tourist Information Centre by region visit enjoyEngland.com/find-tic.

ALDEBURGH	152 High Street	01728 453637	atic@suffolkcoastal.gov.uk
BEDFORD	St Pauls Square	01234 221712	TouristInfo@bedford.gov.uk
BISHOP'S STORTFORD	The Old Monastery	01279 655831	tic@bishopsstortford.org
BRAINTREE	Town Hall Centre	01376 550066	tic@braintree.gov.uk
BURY ST EDMUNDS	6 Angel Hill	01284 764667	tic@stedsbc.gov.uk
CAMBRIDGE	Wheeler Street	0871 226 8006	tourism@cambridge.gov.uk
COLCHESTER	Tymperleys Clock Museum	01206 282920	vic@colchester.gov.uk
DISS	Meres Mouth	01379 650523	dtic@s-norfolk.gov.uk
ELY	Oliver Cromwell's House	01353 662062	tic@eastcambs.gov.uk
FELIXSTOWE	91 Undercliff Road West	01394 276770	ftic@suffolkcoastal.gov.uk
FLATFORD	Flatford Lane	01206 299460	flatfordvic@babergh.gov.uk
HARWICH	Iconfield Park	01255 506139	harwichtic@btconnect.com
HEREFORD	1 King Street	01432 268430	tic-hereford@herefordshire.gov.uk
HUNSTANTON	Town Hall	01485 532610	hunstanton.tic@west-norfolk.gov.uk
IPSWICH	St Stephens Church	01473 258070	tourist@ipswich.gov.uk
KING'S LYNN	The Custom House	01553 763044	kings-lynn.tic@west-norfolk.gov.uk
LAVENHAM	Lady Street	01787 248207	lavenhamtic@babergh.gov.uk
LETCHWORTH GARDEN CITY	33-35 Station Road	01462 487868	tic@letchworth.com
LOWESTOFT	East Point Pavilion	01502 533600	touristinfo@waveney.gov.uk
MALDON	Coach Lane	01621 856503	tic@maldon.gov.uk

NEWMARKET	Palace House	01638 667200	tic.newmarket@forest-heath.gov.uk
NORWICH	The Forum	01603 727927	tourism@norwich.gov.uk
PETERBOROUGH	3-5 Minster Precincts	01733 452336	tic@peterborough.gov.uk
ROSS-ON-WYE	Swan House	01989 562768	tic-ross@herefordshire.gov.uk
SAFFRON WALDEN	1 The Market Place	01799 510444	tourism@uttleford.gov.uk
SOUTHEND-ON-SEA	Pier Entrance	01702 215620	vic@southend.gov.uk
SOUTHWOLD	69 High Street	01502 724729	southwold.tic@waveney.gov.uk
ST ALBANS	Town Hall	01727 864511	tic@stalbans.gov.uk
STOWMARKET	The Museum of East Anglian Life	01449 676800	tic@midsuffolk.gov.uk
SUDBURY	Town Hall	01787 881320	sudburytic@babergh.gov.uk
WITHAM	61 Newland Street	01376 502674	ticwitham@braintree.gov.uk
WOODBRIDGE	Station Buildings	01394 382240	wtic@suffolkcoastal.gov.uk

Regional Contacts and Information

For more information on accommodation, attractions, activities, events and holidays in Eastern England, contact the regional or local tourism organisations. Their websites have a wealth of information and many produce free publications to help you get the most out of your visit.

East of England Tourism

Tel: (01284) 727470
Email: info@eet.org.uk
Web: www.visiteastofengland.com

The comprehensive website is updated daily. Online brochures and information sheets can be downloaded including Whats's New; Major Events; Lights, Camera, Action! (film and television locations); Stars and Stripes (connections with the USA) and a range of Discovery Tours around the region.

Where to Stay

Entries appear alphabetically by town name in each county. A key to symbols appears on page 6. Maps start on page 394. A listing of all Enjoy England assessed accommodation appears at the end of the region.

CAMBRIDGE, Cambridgeshire Map ref 2D1

SAT NAV CB1 8NQ

TOURING & CAMPING PARK

Cherry Hinton Caravan Club Site

Lime Kiln Road, Cherry Hinton CB1 8NQ
t (01223) 244088 **f** (01223) 412546
w caravanclub.co.uk

THE CARAVAN CLUB

🚐 (60)   £12.20–£25.10
🚐 (60)   £12.20–£25.10
60 touring pitches

SPECIAL PROMOTIONS
Special member rates mean you can save your membership subscription in less than a week. Visit our website to find out more.

Imaginatively landscaped site set in old quarry workings and within a site of special scientific interest, bordered by a nature trail. It's just a 10 minute bus journey from site into city centre. Take a guided walk or punt along the backs or the River Cam.

open All year
payment credit/debit cards, cash, cheques

directions M11 jct 9 onto A11. After 7 miles sli road signposted Fulbourn and Tevisham. In Fulbourn continue to roundabout signposted Cambridge. At traffic lights turn left. Left again into Lime Kiln Road.

General 🖥 🛢 📷 ☼ 🔌 ⏚ 🖙 🐾 WP

Where is my pet welcome?

Some properties welcome well-behaved pets. Look for the 🐕 in the accommodation listings. You can also buy a copy of our popular guide 'Pets Come Too!' Now available in good bookshops and online at **enjoyenglanddirect.com**

£9.99

CAMBRIDGE, Cambridgeshire Map ref 2D1

Highfield Farm Touring Park

Long Road, Comberton, Cambridge CB23 7DG
t (01223) 262308 f (01223) 262308

🚐 (60)   £12.50–£16.00
🚍 (60)   £12.50–£16.00
⛺ (60)   £10.00–£15.00
120 touring pitches

SPECIAL PROMOTIONS
Low-season rate for Senior
Citizens - 10% discount for
stay of 3 nights or longer.

A popular, family-run park with excellent facilities close to the university city of Cambridge and Imperial War Museum, Duxford. Ideally situated for touring East Anglia within easy access of the Cambridge park and rides. Please view our website for further information.

open April to October
payment cash, cheques, euros

directions From Cambridge, A428 to Bedford. After 3 miles, left at roundabout, follow sign to Comberton. From M11 jct 12, A603 to Sandy (0.5 miles). Then B1046 to Comberton.

General 🔲 🕮 🐕 🛍 📷 ☼ 🛒 ♿ 📳 🎯 🚻 🆚
Leisure ▸ ∪ ⚓ ⚑

HEMINGFORD ABBOTS, Cambridgeshire Map ref 3A2

Quiet Waters Caravan Park

Hemingford Abbots, Huntingdon PE28 9AJ
t (01480) 463405 f (01480) 463405 e quietwaters.park@btopenworld.com
w **quietwaterscaravanpark.co.uk**

🚐 (20)   £13.50–£17.00
🚍 (20)   £13.50–£17.00
⛺ (20)   £13.50–£17.00
🏠 (9)   £265.00–£390.00
20 touring pitches

A quiet riverside park situated in centre of picturesque village. Many local walks and cycle routes. Ideal for fishing from own banks. Family run. **directions** Junction 25 off the A14. 13 miles from Cambridge, 5 miles from Huntingdon. Nearest town St Ives 2 miles. **open** April to October **payment** credit/debit cards, cash, cheques

General 🔲 ⚄ 🐕 🛍 📷 ☼ 🎯 📳 🚻   Leisure ∪ ⚓

HUNTINGDON, Cambridgeshire Map ref 3A2 SAT NAV PE28 0BB

Grafham Water Caravan Club Site

Church Road, Grafham, Huntingdon PE28 0BB
t (01480) 810264
w **caravanclub.co.uk**

🚐 (76)   £14.00–£26.90
🚃 (76)   £14.00–£26.90
76 touring pitches

SPECIAL PROMOTIONS
Special member rates mean
you can save your
membership subscription in
less than a week. Visit our
website to find out more.

This is an attractive site situated half a mile west of picturesque Grafham village and a similar distance north of Grafham Water. Remarkably peaceful, surrounded by arable land and a narrow tree belt. Heated outdoor swimming pool and children's play area. Activities nearby include cycling, horse riding, tennis and golf.

payment credit/debit cards, cash, cheques

directions Turn left off A1 at roundabout in Buckden onto B661; turn right and follow caravan signs.

General 🔲 🐕 🚿 ♨ 😊 🛢 🚻 📶
Leisure ∪ ⚲ 🏊 🎣 🏔

HUNTINGDON, Cambridgeshire Map ref 3A2 SAT NAV PE28 2AZ

Houghton Mill Caravan Club Site

Mill Street, Houghton, Huntingdon PE28 2AZ
t (01480) 466716
w **caravanclub.co.uk**

🚐   £14.00–£26.90
🚃   £14.00–£26.90
65 touring pitches

SPECIAL PROMOTIONS
Special member rates mean
you can save your
membership subscription in
less than a week. Visit our
website to find out more.

Situated on the banks of the Great Ouse with spectacular views across the river to the National Trust's Houghton Mill, the last working watermill on this river. Milling demonstrations are held every Sunday during the season and visitors can purchase the flour. There's an abundance of footpaths and bridleways to walkers, horse riders and cyclists.

open April to November

directions From Houghton village continue straight through market square into Mill Street, pass church on right. Site entrance on left before last house.

General 🔲 🐕 🚿 😊 🛢 🚻 📶

PETERBOROUGH, Cambridgeshire Map ref 3A1

SAT NAV PE2 5UU

★★★★★
TOURING PARK

🚐 (252) £14.00–£26.90
🚍 (252) £14.00–£26.90
252 touring pitches

SPECIAL PROMOTIONS
Special member rates mean you can save your membership subscription in less than a week. Visit our website to find out more.

Ferry Meadows Caravan Club Site

Ham Lane, Peterborough PE2 5UU
t (01733) 233526 f (01733) 239880
w **caravanclub.co.uk**

THE CARAVAN CLUB

Probably the perfect family holiday site, ideally located in a country park with steam trains, lake, cycle and walking trails and every kind of sporting facility laid on. Enjoy sailing, windsurfing and course fishing or head to Peterborough for ice or roller skating, bowling, shopping and theatre.

open All year
payment credit/debit cards, cash, cheques

directions From any direction, on approaching Peterborough, follow the brown signs to Nene Park and Ferry Meadows.

General 🔲 📶 🐕 📁 ☀ 🔄 🔌 🚮 🛗 ⛲ WP
Leisure ⛺

WYTON, Cambridgeshire Map ref 3A2

SAT NAV PE28 2AA

★★★★
HOLIDAY PARK

🚐 (40)   £16.00
🚍 (10)   £16.00
⛺ (10)   £12.00
40 touring pitches

Wyton Lakes Holiday Park

Banks End, Wyton, Huntingdon PE28 2AA
t (01480) 412715 f (01480) 412715 e loupeter@supanet.com
w **wytonlakes.com** ONLINE MAP

Adults-only park. Some pitches beside the on-site carp and coarse-fishing lakes. River frontage. Close to local amenities. **directions** Exit 23 off A14. Follow signs A141 March. Go past 4 roundabouts. At 4th roundabout take A1123 to St Ives. Park approx 1 mile on right. **open** April to October **payment** cash, cheques

General 📶 🐕 📁 ☀ 🚮 🛗 ⛲ Leisure 🎣

CLACTON-ON-SEA, Essex Map ref 3B3

SAT NAV CO16 9QY

★★★★
HOLIDAY PARK

🚍 £159.00–£769.00

Highfield Grange Holiday Park

London Road, Clacton-on-Sea CO16 9QY
t 0871 664 9746 f (01255) 689805 e holidaysales.highfieldgrange@park-resorts.com
w **park-resorts.com** ONLINE MAP ONLINE BOOKING

One of the largest parks in Clacton, famous for its golden beaches, Victorian Pier, amusements and some good seaside shopping! **directions** Follow the A12 Colchester, take the A120 leading to the A133 Clacton-on-Sea. Highfield is on the B1441 clearly signposted on the left. **open** March to October **payment** credit/debit cards, cheques

General 🔲 🐕 🚲 📁 ☀ 🚮 🛗 ⛲ ✕ Leisure 🏊 🎣 🍴 ♪ ⛺

MERSEA ISLAND, Essex Map ref 3B3
SAT NAV CO5 8SE

Waldegraves Holiday Park
Waldegraves Lane, West Mersea, Colchester CO5 8SE
t (01206) 382898 f (01206) 385359 e holidays@waldegraves.co.uk
w **waldegraves.co.uk** ONLINE MAP ONLINE BOOKING LAST MINUTE OFFERS

🚐 (60)   £12.00–£25.00
🚏 (60)   £12.00–£25.00
⛺ (60)   £12.00–£25.00
🏠 (25)   £220.00–£380.00
60 touring pitches

Ideal family park, grassland sheltered with trees and four fishing lakes, undercover golf driving range, pitch and putt, heated swimming pool, private beach, two play areas. Licensed bar and restaurant. **directions** Junction 26 off A12 join B1025 to Mersea Island cross the Strood take left fork to East Mersea. 2nd right. **open** March to November **payment** credit/debit cards, cash, cheques

General 🔲 📶 🐾 🚾 🏢 🔥 ☀️ 🔌 🔄 🛒 🍴 ✕ Leisure ▶ ⚓ ⚘ 🍷 🎵 🎣 ⛰

WALTON-ON-THE-NAZE, Essex Map ref 3C2
SAT NAV CO14 8HL

Naze Marine Holiday Park
Hall Lane, Walton-on-the-Naze CO14 8HL
t 0871 664 9755 f (01255) 682427 e holidaysales.nazemarine@park-resorts.com
w **park-resorts.com** ONLINE MAP ONLINE BOOKING

🚐   £7.00–£25.00
🏠   £157.00–£864.00

A lively park with plenty to see and do and off the park and a traditional seaside town and beach nearby. **directions** Follow A12 to Colchester. Take A120 as far as the A133. Take A133 to Weeley and the B1033 to Walton seafront. The park is on the left. **open** March to October **payment** credit/debit cards, cheques

General 🔲 🐾 🚾 🔥 🔄 🛒 ✕ Leisure 🎣 🍷 ⛰

BAWBURGH, Norfolk Map ref 3B1
SAT NAV NR9 3LX

Norfolk Showground Caravan Club Site
Long Lane, Bawburgh, Norwich NR9 3LX
t (01603) 742708 f (01603) 741906
w **caravanclub.co.uk**

THE
CARAVAN
CLUB

🚐 (60)   £10.60–£23.20
🚏 (60)   £10.60–£23.20
60 touring pitches

A charming and secluded site set adjacent to the Norfolk Showground, this is an ideal escape. Golf course and well-stocked fishing lakes nearby. **directions** Turn off A47 Norwich southern bypass at Longwater intersection (Bawburgh). Follow signpost Bawburgh, site entrance on right 0.25 miles. **open** April to November **payment** credit/debit cards, cash, cheques

General 🔲 🐾 🏢 🔥 ☀️ 🔌 🔄 🔄 🛒 🇼🇵 Leisure ▶ ⚓

CROMER, Norfolk Map ref 3C1

Seacroft Caravan Club Site

Runton Road, Cromer NR27 9NH
t (01263) 514938 **f** (01263) 511512
w **caravanclub.co.uk**

enjoyEngland.com ★★★★★ TOURING & CAMPING PARK

(130) £14.90–£30.70
(130) £14.90–£30.70
130 touring pitches

SPECIAL PROMOTIONS
Special member rates mean you can save your membership subscription in less than a week. Visit our website to find out more.

Ideal site for a family holiday ... bonus of a leisure complex inclu... restaurant and outdoor heated sw... An entertainment programme runs ... season. The surrounding area offers p... attract all ages, including golf, sea and ... water fishing and birdwatching.

open April 2010 to January 2011
payment credit/debit cards, cash, cheques

directions Turn left off A149 (Cromer-Sheringham). Site entrance on left in 1 mile.

General
Leisure

FAKENHAM, Norfolk Map ref 3B1 — SAT NAV NR21 7NY

Fakenham Racecourse

The Racecourse, Fakenham NR21 7NY
t (01328) 862388 **f** (01328) 855908 **e** caravan@fakenhamracecourse.co.uk
w **fakenhamracecourse.co.uk** ONLINE MAP ONLINE BOOKING

enjoyEngland.com ★★★ TOURING PARK

(120) £12.00–£25.00
(30) £12.00–£25.00
(30) £7.00–£25.00
120 touring pitches

SPECIAL PROMOTIONS
Open to all but with discounts for Caravan Club members. Special rates for rally groups. Check website for events.

Fakenham Racecourse is the ideal base for caravanning and camping holidays in Norfolk. Just 10 miles from a magnificent coastline and on the edge of the market town of Fakenham, the site is set in beautiful countryside and sheltered by conifers. The grounds and modern facilities are excellently maintained.

open All year
payment credit/debit cards, cash, cheques

directions On all major approach routes to Fakenham follow brown signs stating 'Racecourse' and showing 'caravan and tent' symbols. Site entrance on Hempton Road.

General
Leisure

key to symbols see page 6

YARMOUTH, Norfolk Map ref 3C1

SAT NAV NR31 9PY

enjoyEngland.com

★★★★
HOLIDAY, TOURING
& CAMPING PARK

Breydon Water Holiday Park (Bure Village)
Butt Lane, Burgh Castle, Great Yarmouth NR31 9PY
t 0871 664 9710 **f** (01493) 781627 **e** holidaysales.breydonwater@park-resorts.com
w park-resorts.com ONLINE MAP ONLINE BOOKING

(150)	£6.00–£34.00
(150)	£5.00–£34.00
(20)	£157.00–£864.00
150 touring pitches	

This lively park is split into two halves just a short walk apart. Choose Yare Village for family fun and Bure Village for a more relaxing break. **directions** Once you get close to the park you will find Bure Village is on the right, Yare Village is on the left a furthe along. **open** March to October **payment** credit/debit cards, chequ

General 🔲 ⊁ ⌂ ☀ 📞 🛒 🚻 ✕ Leisure ⚲ 🍷 ♫ ⛰

GREAT YARMOUTH, Norfolk Map ref 3C1

SAT NAV NR29 3QG

enjoyEngland.com

★★★★
TOURING PARK

The Grange Touring Park
Yarmouth Road, Ormesby St Margaret NR29 3QG
t (01493) 730306 **f** (01493) 730188 **e** info@grangetouring.co.uk
w grangetouring.co.uk GUEST REVIEWS LAST MINUTE OFFERS

🚐	£9.50–£15.50
🚐 (13)	£9.50–£15.50
▲	£9.50–£15.50
47 touring pitches	

Level grassy park with lighting, made-up roadways and first-class facilities. 3 miles north of Great Yarmouth, at the junction of A149 and B1159. 1 mile from the Broads. **directions** Situated on the B1159, 3 miles north of Great Yarmouth by roundabout at north end of Caister bypass. **open** End of March to October **payment** credit/debit cards, cash, cheques, euros

General ⚡ 🔲 ♨ ⊁ 🏠 ⌂ ☀ 📞 🛒 🚻 Leisure ⚑ ∪ 🚴 ♪ ♫ ⛰

GREAT YARMOUTH, Norfolk Map ref 3C1

SAT NAV NR30 4AU

enjoyEngland.com

★★★★★
HOLIDAY PARK

Great Yarmouth Caravan Club Site
Great Yarmouth Racecourse, Jellicoe Road, Great Yarmouth NR30 4AU
t (01493) 855223 **f** (01493) 854709
w caravanclub.co.uk

THE
CARAVAN
CLUB

🚐 (115)	£12.20–£25.30
🚐 (115)	£12.20–£25.30
115 touring pitches	

Spacious, level site in a very popular family resort offering wide, sandy beaches, countless seaside attractions and fishing, golf, sailboarding, ballroom dancing and bowls. **directions** Travel north on A149, left at lights (within 1 mile past 40 mph sign on southe outskirts of Caister) into Jellicoe Road. Within 0.25 miles, left into racecourse entrance. **open** April to November **payment** credit/del cards, cash, cheques

General 🔲 ⊁ ⌂ ☀ 📞 🛒 🚻 🚰 Leisure ⚑ ♫ ⛰

GREAT YARMOUTH, Norfolk Map ref 3C1

SAT NAV NR29 3NW

enjoyEngland.com

★★★★
HOLIDAY PARK

Summerfields Holiday Village
Beach Road, Scratby, Great Yarmouth NR29 3NW
t 01692 582277 **f** (01493) 730292
w richardsonsgroup.net LAST MINUTE OFFERS

🏚	£125–£550
🏘	£250.00–£550.00

Featuring an indoor heated pool with sauna, spa bath and solarium. Amusements and entertainment for children and adults. Chalet and caravan accommodation. Eight hundred yards from the beach. **directions** Please contact us for directions **payment** credit, debit cards, cheques

General ⊁ 🏠 ⌂ ☀ ✕ Leisure ⚲ 🍷 ♫ ♦ ⛰

HANWORTH, Norfolk Map ref 3B1

SAT NAV NR11 7HN

Deer's Glade Caravan and Camping Park

Whitepost Road, Hanworth, Norwich NR11 7HN
t (01263) 768633 f (01263) 768633 e info@deersglade.co.uk
w **deersglade.co.uk** ONLINE MAP ONLINE BOOKING

(100)	£10.50–£15.50
(100)	£10.50–£15.50
(125)	£10.50–£15.50
125 touring pitches	

A quiet, rural, family-run park in a lovely woodland clearing, in north Norfolk. Ideal for walking, fishing, cycling, spotting wildlife and visiting the north Norfolk coast and Norfolk Broads. **directions** Halfway between Aylsham and Cromer, turn off A140 towards Suffield Green. The park is half a mile on the right. **open** All year **payment** credit/debit cards, cash, cheques

General Leisure

HEMSBY, Norfolk Map ref 3C1

SAT NAV NR29 4HT

Hemsby Beach Holiday Village

Beach Road, Hemsby, Great Yarmouth NR29 4HT
t (01692) 582277
w **richardsonsgroup.net** ONLINE BOOKING LAST MINUTE OFFERS

(200)	£135–£550

Family holiday village with great on-site facilities, children's club & daily entertainment. Just minutes from the sandy beach, arcades & diners on Beach Road. **directions** Please contact us for directions **open** April to October **payment** credit/debit cards, cash, cheques

General Leisure

HEMSBY, Norfolk Map ref 3C1

SAT NAV NR29 4AR

Seacroft

Beach Road, Hemsby-on-Sea NR29 4AR
t (01493) 733610
w **richardsonsgroup.net** LAST MINUTE OFFERS

(250)	£250–£350

Adult only catered site with on-site entertainment. Themed breaks include 60s, 70s, cabaret & comedy. Suitable for the modern 50 year old & the more mature holidaymaker. **directions** Please contact us for directions **open** Except January **payment** credit/debit cards, cash, cheques

General Leisure

key to symbols see page 6

HUNSTANTON, Norfolk Map ref 3B1　　　SAT NAV PE36 5BB

Searles Leisure Resort

South Beach Road, Hunstanton PE36 5BB
t (01485) 534211 f (01485) 533815 e bookings@searles.co.uk
w **searles.co.uk** ONLINE MAP ONLINE BOOKING LAST MINUTE OFFERS

🚐 (157)	£16.00–£44.00
🚙 (50)	£16.00–£44.00
⛺ (125)	£17.00–£39.00
🚍 (156)	£250.00–£1350.00

332 touring pitches

SPECIAL PROMOTIONS
Superb themed breaks every autumn. Beauty breaks, music weekends, Turkey and Tinsel breaks. Please check website for more details.

The quality family holiday resort. Family-run, established for fifty years, Searles has somethi for everyone: excellent pitches and hook-ups, superb accommodation, bars, restaurants, entertainment, swimming pools, nine-hole gol course, fishing lake and more - all 200 yds fro a sandy beach. The ideal base for exploring th Norfolk coast.

open 14th February to 30th November
payment credit/debit cards, cash, cheques

directions From King's Lynn take the A149 to Hunstanton. Upon entering Hunstanton follow B1161 to South Beach.

General 🔧🖥️🛜🐕🛗💷📶☀️🔌🚿🛝👕📞🛜
Leisure ▶🎣🏊⚓🎿🏑🎯🍺🎵🎯⛰️

MUNDESLEY, Norfolk Map ref 3C1　　　SAT NAV NR11 8BT

Mundesley

Paston Road, Norwich NR11 8BT
t (01263) 721553

🏠 (180)	£225–£450

Adult only catered holiday village, providing a programme of entertainment & activities. Just a few minutes walk from Mundesl Beach & close to the seaside villages of Cromer & Sheringham. **directions** Please contact us for directions **open** All year **paymen** credit/debit cards, cash, cheques

General 🍴✕ Leisure 🛜🍺🎵🎯

MUNDESLEY, Norfolk Map ref 3C1

Sandy Gulls Caravan Park

Cromer Road, Mundesley NR11 8DF
t (01263) 720513

(40)	£12.00–£23.00
(40)	£12.00–£23.00
(2)	£250.00–£445.00

40 touring pitches

SPECIAL PROMOTIONS
New holiday caravans for
sale and hire.

The area's only cliff-top touring park. Located just south of Cromer. All pitches have panoramic sea views, electric/TV hook-ups. Free access to superb shower facilities. Miles of clean, sandy beaches and rural footpaths. Managed by the owning family for forty years. Gold David Bellamy Conservation Award. Adults only.

payment cash, cheques, euros

directions From Cromer drive south along coast road for 5 miles.

General
Leisure

SANDRINGHAM, Norfolk Map ref 3B1

The Sandringham Estate Caravan Club Site

Glucksburgh Woods, Sandringham PE35 6EZ
t (01553) 631614 f (01553) 631719
w **caravanclub.co.uk**

(136)	£14.90–£28.90
(136)	£14.90–£28.90

136 touring pitches

SPECIAL PROMOTIONS
Special member rates mean
you can save your
membership subscription in
less than a week. Visit
caravanclub.co.uk to find out
more.

Set in the heart of the Royal Estate this is one of The Club's most prestigious sites. Take a walk to Sandringham House, the famous residence of the Royal Family and enjoy the Country Fair – kids will love the nature trails, land train ride and adventure playground.

open All year
payment credit/debit cards, cash, cheques

directions Take A149 from King's Lynn (signposted Hunstanton). After approx 2 miles turn right onto B1439 (signposted West Newton). Site on left after 0.5 miles. For details on other routes visit caravanclub.co.uk.

General
Leisure

STANHOE, Norfolk Map ref 3B1　　　　SAT NAV PE31 8PU

The Rickels Caravan and Camping Park
Bircham Road, Stanhoe, King's Lynn PE31 8PU
t (01485) 518671

🚐	£10.00–£13.00
🚏	£10.00–£13.00
⛺	£10.00–£13.00

30 touring pitches

The Rickels is a quiet, friendly, high-quality family-run park in 3 acres of grassland with a peaceful, relaxed atmosphere where you can enjoy a pleasant and restful holiday. Adults only. **directions** Please contact us for directions **open** April to October **payment** cash, cheques

General 🔲 🐕 ⛱ ☀ ♨ 🔌 🚽 🚻 📶　　Leisure 🚲 ✏

SWAFFHAM, Norfolk Map ref 3B1　　　　SAT NAV IP26 5BZ

The Covert Caravan Club Site
High Ash, Hilborough, Thetford IP26 5BZ
t (01842) 878356
w **caravanclub.co.uk**

THE
CARAVAN
CLUB

🚐	(103)	£8.10–£18.80
🚏	(103)	£8.10–£18.80

103 touring pitches

Secluded site in beautiful wooded countryside owned by the Forestry Commission. Ideal for the wildlife observer and good for walkers. Own sanitation required. **directions** Site entrance from A1065, 2 miles north of Mundford and 2.7 miles south of Hilborough. **open** April to November **payment** credit/debit cards, cash, cheques

General 🐕 🔌 🚽 📶

BUNGAY, Suffolk Map ref 3C1　　　　SAT NAV NR35 1HG

Outney Meadow Caravan Park
Outney Meadow, Bungay NR35 1HG
t (01986) 892338 f (01986) 896627
w **outneymeadow.co.uk**

🚐	(45)	£12.00–£16.00
🚏	(45)	£12.00–£16.00
⛺	(45)	£12.00–£16.00

45 touring pitches

Easy walking distance to Bungay market town. Situated between the River Waveney (canoe trail) and golf course, ideal base for exploring the beautiful countryside. Fishing, bikes and canoes available. **directions** Please contact us for directions **open** March – October **payment** cash, cheques

General 🔲 🐕 ⛱ ☀ 🔲 ♨ 🔌 🚽 🚻 📶　　Leisure ⛳ 🚲 ✏

DUNWICH, Suffolk Map ref 3C2　　　　SAT NAV IP17 3DQ

Cliff House Holiday Park
Minsmere Road, Dunwich, Saxmundham IP17 3DQ
t (01728) 648282 f (01728) 648996 e info@cliffhouseholidays.co.uk
w **cliffhouseholidays.co.uk** ONLINE MAP

🚐	(60)	£16.00–£27.00
🚏	(20)	£16.00–£27.00
⛺	(50)	£16.00–£27.00

110 touring pitches

Secluded woodland park offering privacy with access to the beach. 06 and 07 winner of East of England Holiday Park of the Year. Got David Bellamy Conservation Award. **directions** From Ipswich head north on A12 through Yoxford. At Westleton turn left through village turn right to Dulwich heath. 2nd turn right at sign. **open** 1 march to 31st Oct **payment** credit/debit cards, cash, cheques, euro

General 🔲 🐕 🔲 ⛱ ☀ 🔲 ♨ 🔌 🚽 🚻 📶 ✖　　Leisure ⛳ ⛳ 🚲 ✏ 🎾 ♪ 🎣 🏛

KESSINGLAND, Suffolk Map ref 3C2

SAT NAV NR33 7PJ

Heathland Beach Caravan Park
London Road, Kessingland NR33 7PJ
t (01502) 740337 f (01502) 742355 e heathlandbeach@btinternet.com
w **heathlandbeach.co.uk** ONLINE MAP GUEST REVIEWS ONLINE BOOKING

🚐	£18.00–£28.00
🚐	£18.00–£28.00
⛺	£10.00–£28.00
🏠 (6)	£285.00–£560.00
63 touring pitches	

Heathland Beach is a spacious, award-winning, family-owned holiday park situated on a picturesque cliff overlooking the secluded beach at Kessingland. Heathland Beach abounds with excellent facilities. **directions** Off A12 onto B1437 between Kessingland and Lowestoft. **open** Easter to end of October **payment** credit/debit cards, cash, cheques

General Leisure

All Assessed Accommodation

Cambridgeshire
CAMBRIDGE
Appleacre Park ★★ *Touring Park*
...don Road, Fowlmere, Royston
...8 7RU
(01763) 208354
ajbearpark@aol.com
appleacrepark.co.uk

Cherry Hinton Caravan Club Site
★★★★ *Touring & Camping Park*
...e Kiln Road, Cherry Hinton
...8NQ
(01223) 244088
caravanclub.co.uk/cambridge

Highfield Farm Touring Park
★★★★ *Touring & Camping Park*
...ng Road, Comberton, Cambridge
...23 7DG
(01223) 262308

GREAT SHELFORD
Cambridge Camping and Caravanning Club Site ★★★★
...uring Park
Cabbage Moor, Great Shelford,
...mbridge
...2 5NB
(01223) 841185
campingandcaravanningclub.co.uk/cambridge

HEMINGFORD ABBOTS
Quiet Waters Caravan Park
★★★
...liday, Touring & Camping Park
...mingford Abbots, Huntingdon
...28 9AJ
(01480) 463405
quietwaters.park@btopenworld.com
quietwaterscaravanpark.co.uk

HUNTINGDON
Grafham Water Caravan Club Site
★★★★★ *Holiday & Touring Park*
Church Road, Grafham, Huntingdon
PE28 0BB
t (01480) 810264
w caravanclub.co.uk

Houghton Mill Caravan Club Site
★★★★ *Touring Park*
Mill Street, Houghton, Huntingdon
PE28 2AZ
t (01480) 466716
w caravanclub.co.uk

MARCH
Fields End Water ★★★★
Touring & Camping Park
2 Fields End Bungalow, Benwick
Road, Doddington, March,
Cambridgeshire
PE15 0TY

PETERBOROUGH
Ferry Meadows Caravan Club Site
★★★★★ *Touring Park*
Ham Lane, Peterborough
PE2 5UU
t (01733) 233526
w caravanclub.co.uk

ST NEOTS
St Neots Camping and Caravanning Club Site ★★★★
Touring Park
Hardwick Road, Eynesbury, St Neots
PE19 2PR
t (01480) 474404
w campingandcaravanningclub.co.uk/stneots

WISBECH
Virginia Lake Caravan Park
★★★★ *Holiday Park*
Smeeth Road, St Johns Fen End,
Wisbech
PE14 8JF
t (01945) 430167
e louise@virginialake.co.uk
w virginialake.co.uk

WYTON
Wyton Lakes Holiday Park ★★★★
Holiday Park
Banks End, Wyton, Huntingdon
PE28 2AA
t (01480) 412715
e loupeter@supanet.com
w wytonlakes.com

Essex
BRENTWOOD
Kelvedon Hatch Camping and Caravanning Club Site ★★★★
Touring & Camping Park
Warren Lane, Doddinghurst,
Brentwood
CM15 0JG
t (01277) 372773
w campingandcaravanningclub.co.uk/kelvedonhatch

CLACTON-ON-SEA
Highfield Grange Holiday Park
★★★★ *Holiday Park*
London Road, Clacton-on-Sea
CO16 9QY
t 0871 664 9746
e holidaysales.highfieldgrange@park-resorts.com
w park-resorts.com

Valley Farm Holiday Park ★★★★
Holiday Park
Valley Road, Clacton-on-Sea
CO15 6LY
t 0871 664 9788
e holidaysales.valleyfarm@park-resorts.com
w park-resorts.com

EAST MERSEA
Coopers Beach Holiday Park
★★★★ *Holiday Park*
East Mersea, Colchester
CO5 8TN
t (01206) 383236

Cosway Holiday Home Park
★★★★★ *Holiday Park*
Fen Lane, East Mersea, Colchester
CO5 8UA
t (01206) 383252

Fen Farm Camping and Caravan Site ★★★★ *Holiday Park*
Moore Lane, East Mersea, Colchester
CO5 8UA
t (01206) 383275
w mersea-island.com/fenfarm

GOLDHANGER
Osea Leisure Park ★★★★
Holiday Park
Goldhanger Road, Heybridge
CM9 4SA
t (01621) 854695
w osealeisure.com

key to symbols see page 6

JAYWICK

Martello Beach Holiday Park
★★★★
Holiday, Touring & Camping Park
Belsize Avenue, Jaywick, Clacton-on-Sea
CO15 2LF
t 0871 664 9782
e holidaysales.martellobeach@park-resorts.com
w park-resorts.com

LOUGHTON

Debden House Camp Site ★★
Touring & Camping Park
Debden Green, Loughton
IG10 2NZ
t (020) 8508 3008
e debdenhouse@newham.govt.uk
w debdenhouse.com

MERSEA ISLAND

Waldegraves Holiday Park ★★★★
Holiday, Touring & Camping Park
Waldegraves Lane, West Mersea, Colchester
CO5 8SE
t (01206) 382898
e holidays@waldegraves.co.uk
w waldegraves.co.uk

SOUTHMINSTER

Eastland Meadows Country Park
★★★ *Holiday Park*
East End Road, Bradwell-on-Sea, Southminster
CM0 7PP
t (01621) 776577
e enquiries@eastlamdmeadows.co.uk
w eastlandmeadows.co.uk

St Lawrence Holiday Park ★★
Holiday Park
10 Main Road, St Lawrence Bay, Southminster
CM0 7LY
t (01621) 779434
e office@slcaravans.co.uk
w slcaravans.co.uk

Waterside Holiday Park ★★★
Holiday & Touring Park
Main Road, St Lawrence Bay, Southminster
CM0 7LY
t 0871 664 9794
e holidaysales.waterside@park-resorts.com
w park-resorts.com

STEEPLE

Corfe Castle Camping and Caravanning Club Site ★★★
Holiday, Touring & Camping Park
Steeple Manor, Steeple, Wareham
BH20 5PA
t (01929) 480280
w campingandcaravanningclub.co.uk/corfecastle

Steeple Bay Holiday Park ★★
Holiday, Touring & Camping Park
Canney Road, Steeple, Southminster
CM0 7RS
t (01621) 773991

ST OSYTH

Oaklands Holiday Park ★★★
Holiday Park
Colchester Road, Clacton-on-Sea
CO16 8HW
t (01255) 820432

The Orchards Holiday Village
★★★ *Holiday Park*
Point Clear, Clacton-on-Sea
CO16 8LJ
t (01442) 230300
w haven.com

Seawick Holiday Park ★★★
Holiday, Touring & Camping Park
Beach Road, St Osyth
CO16 8SG
t (01255) 820416

St Osyth Beach Holiday Park
★★★
Holiday, Touring & Camping Park
Beach Road, Clacton-on-Sea
CO16 8SG
t 0845 815 9795

WALTON-ON-THE-NAZE

Naze Marine Holiday Park ★★★
Holiday Park
Hall Lane, Walton-on-the-Naze
CO14 8HL
t 0871 664 9755
e holidaysales.nazemarine@park-resorts.com
w park-resorts.com

WEELEY

Homestead Lake Park ★★★★
Holiday, Touring & Camping Park
Thorpe Road, Weeley, Clacton-on-Sea
CO16 9JN
t (01255) 833492

Weeley Bridge Holiday Park
★★★★ *Holiday Park*
Clacton Road, Weeley, Clacton-on-Sea
CO16 9DH
t 0871 664 9797
e holidaysales.weeleybridge@park-resorts.com
w park-resorts.com

Hertfordshire

HERTFORD

Hertford Camping and Caravanning Club Site ★★★★
Touring & Camping Park
The Camping & Caravan Site, Mangrove Road, Hertford, Hertford
SG13 8AJ
t (01992) 586696
w campingandcaravanningclub.co.uk/hertford

WALTHAM CROSS

Theobalds Park Camping and Caravanning Club Site ★★★
Touring & Camping Park
Bulls Cross Ride, Waltham Cross
EN7 5HS
t (01992) 620604
w campingandcaravanningclub.co.uk/theobaldspark

Norfolk

BACTON

Castaways Holiday Park ★★★
Holiday Park
Paston Road, Bacton, Norwich
NR12 0JB
t (01692) 650436
e castaways.bacton@hotmail.co.uk
w castawaysholidaypark.co.uk

The Red House Chalet and Caravan Park ★★★★ *Holiday Park*
Paston Road, Norwich
NR12 0JB
t (01692) 650815

BACTON-ON-SEA

Cable Gap Holiday Park ★★★★★
Holiday Park **ROSE AWARD**
Coast Road, Bacton
NR12 0EW
t (01692) 650667
e holiday@cablegap.co.uk
w cablegap.co.uk

BANHAM

Applewood Caravan and Camping Park ★★★★ *Touring Park*
Banham Zoo, Norfolk, Norwich
NR16 2HE
t (01953) 715318
e info@banhamzoo.co.uk
w banhamzoo.co.uk

BAWBURGH

Norfolk Showground Caravan Club Site ★★★★ *Touring Park*
Long Lane, Bawburgh, Norwich
NR9 3LX
t (01603) 742708
w caravanclub.co.uk

BEESTON REGIS

Beeston Regis Caravan Park ★★★
Holiday, Touring & Camping Park
Cromer Road, West Runton, Cromer
NR27 9QZ
t (01263) 823614
e info@beestonregis.co.uk
w beestonregis.co.uk

BELTON

Wild Duck Holiday Park ★★★★
Holiday Park
Howards Common, Belton, Great Yarmouth
NR31 9NE
t (01493) 780268
e austin.james@bourne-leisure.co.uk
w havenholidayhomes.co.uk

BURGH CASTLE

Breydon Water Holiday Park (Yare) ★★★★
Holiday, Touring & Camping Park
Butt Lane, Burgh Castle, Great Yarmouth
NR31 9PY
t (01442) 830135
w park-resorts.com

Burgh Castle Marina and Caravan Park ★★★
Holiday, Touring & Camping Park
Butt Lane, Burgh Castle, Great Yarmouth
NR31 9PZ
t (01493) 780331
e info@burghcastlemarina.co.uk
w burghcastlemarina.co.uk

BURGH ST PETER

Waveney River Centre ★★★★
Holiday Park
Staithe Road, Burgh St Peter
NR34 0BT
t (01502) 677343
e info@waveneyrivercentre.co.uk
w waveneyrivercentre.co.uk

BURNHAM DEEPDALE

Deepdale Camping ★★★★
Camping Park
Deepdale Farm, Main Road, King's Lynn
PE31 8DD
t (01485) 210256
e info@deepdalefarm.co.uk
w deepdalefarm.co.uk

CAISTER-ON-SEA

Caister Holiday Park ★★★
Holiday Park
Ormesby Road, Caister-on-Sea, Great Yarmouth
NR30 5NQ
t (01493) 728931
w havenholidays.com

Eastern Beach Caravan Park
★★★★ *Holiday Park*
Manor Road, Caister-on-Sea, Great Yarmouth
NR30 5HH
t (01493) 720367
w easternbeachcaravanpark.co.uk

Elm Beach Caravan Park Ltd
★★★★ *Holiday Park*
Manor Road, Caister-on-Sea, Great Yarmouth
NR30 5HG
t (01493) 721630
e enquiries@elmbeachcaravanpark.com
w elmbeachcaravanpark.com

Wentworth Holidays ★★★
Holiday Park
9 Bultitudes Loke, Caister-on-Sea
NR30 5DH
t (01493) 720382

CALIFORNIA

Beachside Holidays (Norfolk)
★★★★ *Holiday Park*
Wakefield Court, California, Scratby, Great Yarmouth
NR29 3QT
t (01493) 730279
e holidays@theseaside.org
w beachside-holidays.co.uk

CLIPPESBY

Clippesby Hall ★★★★★
Holiday Park
Hall Lane, Clippesby, The Broads
NR29 3BL
t (01493) 367800
e holidays@clippesby.com
w clippesby.com

CROMER

Forest Park Caravan Site ★★★
Touring & Camping Park
Northrepps Road, Northrepps, Cromer
NR27 0JR
t (01263) 513290

Seacroft Caravan Club Site
★★★★★ *Touring & Camping Park*
Runton Road, Cromer
NR27 9NH
t (01263) 514938
w caravanclub.co.uk

EAST HARLING

The Dower House Touring Park
★★★★ *Touring & Camping Park*
Thetford Forest, East Harling, Norwich
NR16 2SE
t (01953) 717314

EAST RUNTON

Woodhill Park ★★★★
Holiday, Touring & Camping Park
ROSE AWARD
Cromer Road, East Runton, Cromer
NR27 9PX
t (01263) 512242
e info@woodhill-park.com
w woodhill-park.com

FAKENHAM

Fakenham Racecourse ★★★
Touring Park
The Racecourse, Fakenham
NR21 7NY
t (01328) 862388
e caravan@fakenhamracecourse.uk
w fakenhamracecourse.co.uk

The Old Brick Kilns ★★★★★
Touring & Camping Park
Little Barney Lane, Barney, Fakenham
NR21 0NL
t (01328) 878305
e enquiries@old-brick-kilns.co.uk
w old-brick-kilns.co.uk

GREAT HOCKHAM

Thetford Forest Camping and Caravan Club Site ★★★★
Holiday, Touring & Camping Park
Wretham Road, Great Hockham, Thetford
IP24 1PA
t (01953) 498455
w campingandcaravanningclub.co.uk/thetford

GREAT YARMOUTH

**eydon Water Holiday Park
ure Village) ★★★★**
liday, Touring & Camping Park
t Lane, Burgh Castle, Great
rmouth
31 9PY
0871 664 9710
holidaysales.breydonwater@park-
resorts.com
park-resorts.com

erry Tree Holiday Park ★★★★
liday Park ROSE AWARD
l Road, Great Yarmouth
31 9QR
0871 641 0191
parkdeanholidays.co.uk/cherry-
tree-holiday-park.htm

e Grange Touring Park ★★★★
uring Park
rmouth Road, Ormesby St
argaret
29 3QG
(01493) 730306
info@grangetouring.co.uk
grangetouring.co.uk

asmere Caravan Park (T.B.)
★★ *Touring Park*
ltitudes Loke, Yarmouth Road,
ister-on-Sea
30 5DH
(01493) 720382

**eat Yarmouth Caravan Club
e ★★★★★** *Holiday Park*
eat Yarmouth Racecourse, Jellicoe
ad, Great Yarmouth
30 4AU
(01493) 855223
caravanclub.co.uk

pton Holiday Village ★★★★
liday Park
arren Lane, Hopton, Great
rmouth
31 9BW
(01502) 730214

tters Leisure Resort ★★★★★
liday Village
ast Road, Hopton-on-Sea, Great
rmouth
31 9BX
(01502) 730345
potters@pottersholidays.com
pottersholidays.com

ashore Holiday Park ★★★
liday Park
orth Denes, Great Yarmouth
30 4HG
(01493) 851131

ummerfields Holiday Village
★★★ *Holiday Park*
ach Road, Scratby, Great
rmouth
R29 3NW
01692 582277
richardsonsgroup.net

auxhall Holiday Park ★★★★★
liday & Touring Park
cle New Road, Great Yarmouth
30 1TB
(01493) 857231

HANWORTH

**eer's Glade Caravan and
amping Park ★★★★★**
ouring & Camping Park
hitepost Road, Hanworth, Norwich
R11 7HN
(01263) 768633
info@deersglade.co.uk
deersglade.co.uk

HEACHAM

eacham Beach Holiday Park
★★★ *Holiday Park*
outh Beach Road, Heacham, King's
ynn
E31 7BD
0871 664 9743
holidaysales.heachambeach@
park-resorts.com
park-resorts.com

Meadows Caravan Park ★★★★
Holiday Park
Meadows Caravan Park, Lamsey
Lane, King's Lynn
PE31 7LA
t (01553) 636243
e mcdonnellcaravans@fsmail.net
w mcdonnellcaravans.co.uk

HEMSBY

Hemsby Beach Holiday Village
★★ *Holiday Park*
Beach Road, Hemsby, Great
Yarmouth
NR29 4HT
t (01692) 582277
w richardsonsgroup.net

**Newport Caravan Park (Norfolk)
Ltd ★★★★**
Holiday, Touring & Camping Park
Newport Road, Hemsby, Great
Yarmouth
NR29 4NW
t (01493) 730405
e enquiries@newportcaravanpark.
co.uk
w newportcaravanpark.co.uk

Seacroft ★ *Holiday Village*
Beach Road, Hemsby-on-Sea
NR29 4AR
t (01493) 733610
w richardsonsgroup.net

HUNSTANTON

Manor Park Holiday Village
★★★★ *Holiday & Touring Park*
Manor Road, Hunstanton
PE36 5AZ
t (01485) 532300
e info@manor-park.co.uk
w manor-park.co.uk

Searles Leisure Resort ★★★★★
Holiday, Touring & Camping Park
South Beach Road, Hunstanton
PE36 5BB
t (01485) 534211
e bookings@searles.co.uk
w searles.co.uk

MUNDESLEY

Mundesley ★★ *Holiday Village*
Paston Road, Norwich
NR11 8BT
t (01263) 721553

Sandy Gulls Caravan Park ★★★
Holiday & Touring Park
Cromer Road, Mundesley
NR11 8DF
t (01263) 720513

NORTH RUNCTON

**Kings Lynn Caravan & Camping
Park ★★★** *Touring Park*
New Road, North Runcton, King's
Lynn
PE33 0RA
t (01553) 840004

NORTH WALSHAM

Two Mills Touring Park ★★★★★
Touring Park
Scarborough Hill, Yarmouth Road,
North Walsham
NR28 9NA
t (01692) 405829
e enquiries@twomills.co.uk
w twomills.co.uk

NORWICH

**Norwich Camping and
Caravanning Club Site ★★★**
Holiday Park
Martineau Lane, Norwich
NR1 2HX
t (01603) 620060
w campingandcaravanningclub.co.
uk/norwich

**Reedham Ferry Touring and
Camping Park ★★★★**
Holiday, Touring & Camping Park
Ferry Road, Reedham, Norwich
NR13 3HA
t (01493) 700999
e reedham.ferry@aol.com
w archerstouringpark.co.uk

OVERSTRAND

Ivy Farm Holiday Park ★★★★
Holiday, Touring & Camping Park
1 High Street, Overstrand, Cromer
NR27 0AB
t (01263) 579239
e enquiries@ivy-farm.co.uk
w ivy-farm.co.uk

PENTNEY

Pentney Park Caravan Site
★★★★ *Touring & Camping Park*
Main Road, Pentney, King's Lynn
PE32 1HU
t (01760) 337479
e holidays@pentney.demon.co.uk
w pentney-park.co.uk

SAHAM HILLS

Lowe Caravan Park ★★★★
Touring & Camping Park
Ashdale, Hills Road, Saham Hills,
Thetford
IP25 7EZ
t (01953) 881051
w lowecaravanpark.co.uk

SANDRINGHAM

**Sandringham Camping and
Caravanning Club Site ★★★★★**
Touring Park
The Sandringham Estate, Double
Lodges, Sandringham
PE35 6EA
t (01485) 542555
w campingandcaravanningclub.co.
uk/sandringham

**The Sandringham Estate Caravan
Club Site ★★★★★** *Touring Park*
Glucksburgh Woods, Sandringham
PE35 6EZ
t (01553) 631614
w caravanclub.co.uk

SCRATBY

California Cliffs Holiday Park
★★★★ *Holiday Park*
Rottenstone Lane, Scratby, Great
Yarmouth
NR29 3QU
t 0871 664 9716
e holidaysales.californiacliffs@park-
resorts.com
w park-resorts.com

Green Farm Caravan Park
★★★★★ *Holiday & Touring Park*
Beach Road, Scratby
NR29 3NW
t (01493) 730440
e contact@greenfarmcaravanpark.
com
w greenfarmcaravanpark.com

Scratby Hall Caravan Park ★★★★
Touring & Camping Park
Thoroughfare Lane, Scratby, Great
Yarmouth
NR29 3PH
t (01493) 730283

SHADWELL

**Thorpe Woodland Caravan &
Camping Site ★★**
Touring & Camping Park
Shadwell, Thetford
IP24 2RX
t (01283) 228607
e lizzie.leatherbarrow@fores
tholidays.co.uk
w forestholidays.co.uk

SNETTISHAM

**Diglea Caravan and Camping
Park ★★★**
Holiday, Touring & Camping Park
Beach Road, Snettisham, King's
Lynn
PE31 7RA
t (01485) 541367

STANHOE

**The Rickels Caravan and Camping
Park ★★★★** *Touring Park*
Bircham Road, Stanhoe, King's Lynn
PE31 8PU
t (01485) 518671

SWAFFHAM

The Covert Caravan Club Site
★★★★ *Touring Park*
High Ash, Hilborough, Thetford
IP26 5BZ
t (01842) 878356
w caravanclub.co.uk

THORNHAM

The Haven Caravan Park ★★★★
Holiday Park
Church Street, Thornham,
Hunstanton
PE36 6NJ
t (01553) 636243
e mcdonnellcaravans@fsmail.net
w mcdonnellcaravans.co.uk

UPPER SHERINGHAM

Woodlands Caravan Park ★★★★
Holiday & Touring Park
Holt Road, Upper Sheringham,
Sheringham
NR26 8TU
t (01263) 823802
e info@woodlandscaravanpark.co.
uk
w woodlandscaravanpark.co.uk

WELLS-NEXT-THE-SEA

Pinewoods Holiday Park ★★★★
Holiday Park
Beach Road, Wells-next-the-Sea
NR23 1DR
t (01328) 713200
e pinewoods@lineone.net

WEST RUNTON

**West Runton Camping and
Caravanning Club Site ★★★★★**
Touring & Camping Park
Holgate Lane, West Runton, Cromer
NR27 9NW
t (01263) 837544
w campingandcaravanningclub.co.
uk/westrunton

WEYBOURNE

Kelling Heath Holiday Park
★★★★★
Holiday, Touring & Camping Park
ROSE AWARD
Sandy Hill Lane, Weybourne,
Sheringham
NR25 7HW
t (01263) 588181
e info@kellingheath.co.uk
w kellingheath.co.uk

Weybourne Holiday Homes
★★★★ *Holiday Park*
Weybourne Holiday Park,
Weybourne, Sheringham
NR25 7EX
t (01263) 588440
e weyholhom@aol.com
w weybourne.org.uk

WORTWELL

**Little Lakeland Touring and
Holiday Caravan Park ★★★★**
Holiday & Touring Park
Wortwell, Harleston
IP20 0EL
t (01986) 788646
e information@littlelakeland.co.uk
w littlelakeland.co.uk

Suffolk

BENHALL

Whitearch (Touring Caravan) Park
★★★ *Holiday Park*
Main Road, Benhall
IP17 1NA
t (01728) 604646

BRANTHAM

Stour Valley Bunkhouse
Bunkhouse
Brantham Hall, Brantham,
Manningtree
CO11 1PT
t (01473) 327090
e stourvalley@yha.org.uk
w yha.org.uk

BUCKLESHAM

Westwood Caravan Park ★★★★
Holiday, Touring & Camping Park
Old Felixstowe Road, Bucklesham,
Ipswich
IP10 0BW
t (01473) 659637
e info@westwoodcaravanpark.co.uk
w westwoodcaravanpark.co.uk

BUNGAY

Outney Meadow Caravan Park
★★★ *Touring & Camping Park*
Outney Meadow, Bungay
NR35 1HG
t (01986) 892338
w outneymeadow.co.uk

CORTON

Broadland Sands Holiday Park
★★★★ *Holiday Park* **ROSE AWARD**
Coast Road, Corton, Lowestoft
NR32 5LG
t (01502) 730939
e admin@broadlandsands.co.uk
w broadlandsands.co.uk

DUNWICH

Cliff House Holiday Park ★★★★
Holiday Park
Minsmere Road, Dunwich,
Saxmundham
IP17 3DQ
t (01728) 648282
e info@cliffhouseholidays.co.uk
w cliffhouseholidays.co.uk

ELVEDEN

Center Parcs Elveden Forest
★★★★★ *Forest Holiday Village*
Brandon
IP27 0YZ
t 0870 067 3030
w centerparcs.co.uk/villages/
elveden/index.jsp

FELIXSTOWE

Felixstowe Beach Holiday Park
★★★ *Holiday Park*
Walton Avenue, Felixstowe
IP11 2HA
t (01394) 283393
e christinajones@parkholidayuk.
com
w parkholidaysuk.com

Peewit Caravan Park ★★★★
Touring & Camping Park
Walton Avenue, Felixstowe
IP11 2HB
t (01394) 284511
e peewitpark@aol.com
w peewitcaravanpark.co.uk

Suffolk Sands Holiday Park ★★
Holiday Park
Carr Road, Felixstowe
IP11 2TS
t (01394) 273434

KESSINGLAND

Alandale Park ★★ *Holiday Park*
Bethel Drive, Kessingland
NR33 7SD
t (01502) 740610

Heathland Beach Caravan Park
★★★★★
Holiday, Touring & Camping Park
ROSE AWARD
London Road, Kessingland
NR33 7PJ
t (01502) 740337
e heathlandbeach@btinternet.com
w heathlandbeach.co.uk

Kessingland Beach Holiday Park
★★★
Holiday, Touring & Camping Park
Beach Road, Kessingland
NR33 7RW
t 0871 664 9749

**Kessingland Camping and
Caravanning Club Site** ★★★★
Touring & Camping Park
Whites Lane, Kessingland, Lowestoft
NR33 7TF
t (01502) 742040
w campingandcaravanningclub.co.
uk/kessingland

LOWESTOFT

**Beach Farm Residential and
Holiday Park Limited** ★★★★
Holiday Park
Arbor Lane, Pakefield
NR33 7BD
t (01502) 572794
e beachfarmpark@aol.com
w beachfarmpark.co.uk

Warner Holidays ★★★★
Holiday Village
Gunton Hall Classic Resort, Gunton
Avenue, Lowestoft, Lowestoft
NR32 5DF
t (01502) 730288
w tiscover.co.uk/gb/guide/5gb,en/
objectid,acc16143gb/home.html

OULTON BROAD

Broadland Holiday Village
★★★★★ *Holiday Park*
ROSE AWARD
Marsh Road, Oulton Broad,
Lowestoft
NR33 9JY
t (01502) 573033
e info@broadlandvillage.co.uk
w broadlandvillage.co.uk

PAKEFIELD

Pakefield Caravan Park ★★★★
Holiday Park
Arbor Lane, Pakefield
NR33 7BQ
t (01502) 561136

POLSTEAD

**Camping Caravanning Club
Polestead Site**
Holiday, Touring & Camping Park
Holt Road, Bower House Tye,
Polstead, Suffolk
CO6 5BZ

WEST ROW

The Willows ★★★
Touring & Camping Park
Hurdle Drove, West Row, Bury St
Edmunds
IP28 8RB
t (01638) 715963
e tedandsue@hotmail.co.uk
w thewillowscampsite.co.uk

WOODBRIDGE

Forest Camping ★★★
Touring & Camping Park
Tangham Campsite, Rendlesham
Forest Centre, Woodbridge
IP12 3NF
t (01394) 450707
e admin@forestcamping.co.uk
w forestcamping.co.uk

Country ways

The Countryside Rights of Way Act gives people new rights to walk on areas of open countryside and registered commonland.

To find out where you can go and what you can do, as well as information about taking your dog to the countryside, go online at countrysideaccess.gov.uk.

And when you're out and about...

Always follow the Country Code

- Be safe – plan ahead and follow any signs
- Leave gates and property as you find them
- Protect plants and animals, and take your litter home
- Keep dogs under close control
- Consider other people

Viaduct, Monsal Dale, Derbyshire, England.

East Midlands

Derbyshire, Leicestershire & Rutland, Lincolnshire,
Northamptonshire, Nottinghamshire

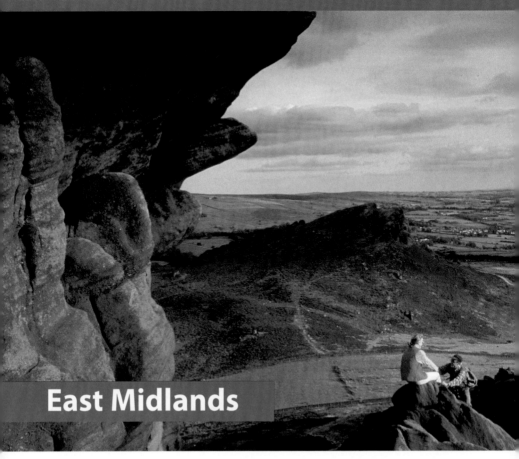

East Midlands

The East Midlands area offers the great outdoors in abundance: with the dramatic landscape of the country's first national park, the Peak District; covering hundreds of square miles of spectacular moorlands, hills, lush valleys, forests and reservoirs. The Peak District can offer every outdoor pastime from walking and climbing to the gentler activities of painting and photography or just taking it easy and watching the world go by.

One of the country's least wooded regions is being dramatically transformed by The National Forest across Leicestershire and Derbyshire (also Staffordshire in the Heart of England). Already 700 miles of Forest paths can be explored in over 400 ancient and new woodlands – perfect for walking and wildlife

watching, cycling and horse-riding. For even more outdoors, escape to the rolling hills of the Lincolnshire Wolds.

For heritage lovers, the region offers a fabulous choice of majestic castles, grand stately homes and magnificent gardens; Chatsworth in Derbyshire is one of the most visited stately homes in England with lots to see and do. The mysterious art of Well Dressing is practiced in Derbyshire towns and villages during the months of May through to September. Marvel at the beautiful and intricate pictures that are created using only growing things such as flowers, berries and leaves.

For sea and sand lovers, head to Lincolnshire where the region's coastline extends from The Wash in the south to the Humber Estuary in the north. There is a good choice of family resorts; Skegness, Mablethorpe and Ingoldmells are popular for their clean, award-winning beaches. Prefer to live it up? Then head for Derby, Lincoln, Nottingham and Leicester, cosmopolitan cities offering culture, good shopping and lively night life.

Excitement seekers can see the thrilling Red Arrows 'loop the loop' in their Lincolnshire homeland skies or enjoy exhilarating racing at Silverstone or Donnington. The East Midlands has something for everyone!

Derbyshire

Derby's compact city centre makes exploring easy. Three free museums, Derby Cathedral, which boasts the second highest church tower in England, Royal Crown Derby, famed the world over for lavishly decorated china, and Pride Park Football Stadium which offers behind the scene tours of the magnificent grounds. A city with something for everyone!

Bakewell

Bakewell is a picturesque market town that crosses the River Wye and lies right in the heart of the Peak District National Park. The town dates back to Saxon times and is home to the famous Bakewell pudding. Bakewell earns a mention in the Domesday Book, calling the town 'Badequella', meaning Bath-Well, referring to the warm springs of the area.

Bolsover

A visit to Bolsover District can be rewarding in so many ways, not only to appreciate Bolsover Castle, a 17th-century house containing richly painted rooms, Indoor Riding House and Venus Garden, but to see how man has lived and worked down through the ages. The Caves at Creswell Crags, set into a limestone gorge, show how our Ice Age ancestors lived and hunted, leaving behind the bones of reindeer, mammoth and wild horse together with primitive tools which can be seen in the Visitor Centre.

Buxton

Buxton is the Bath of the north. Its warm springs were appreciated by the Romans who called the place Aquae Arnmetiae. Much later Elizabethan courtiers made the hazardous journey to bathe in and drink the local water.

Buxton today is one of Derbyshire's main holiday resorts and an ideal centre for exploring and enjoying the countryside, including over 500 square miles of National Park which surround it. Buxton has an annual festival in July which mainly includes music and is internationally renowned. In addition to the festival there is also the Well Dressing Festival which is usually held during the second week of July.

Chesterfield

The town famous for the 'Crooked Spire' of its Parish Church, standing on the skyline like a question mark, is also home to one of the largest open-air markets in the country. More than 200 stalls pack the town centre every Monday, Friday and Saturday throughout the year. On Thursdays there's a flea market, and a farmers' market takes place on the second Thursday of each month.

Peak District

The Peak District has something for everyone. In the north you can roam on wild open moorland with magnificent views overlooking sites such as the Derwent Dams. Further south, stroll alongside sparkling rivers in wildlife-rich valleys far from the hustle and bustle of town. The Peak Park Rangers lead regular guided walks – from a long hike along the Pennine Way or other long distant trails, to a ghost walk or tour around a village or town. Visit grand houses such as Chatsworth with its farmyard and adventure playground, or the caverns at Castleton featuring unique Blue John stone, stalactites and stalagmites and even a boat ride underground.

Leicestershire & Rutland

Vibrant, cosmopolitan and cultured, historic but futuristic, buzzing yet relaxed. Unusual shops, fine restaurants, a vibrant nightlife and a strong cultural diversity have all contributed to Leicester's recent style revolution. Travel to infinity and beyond at the National Space Centre and experience live music at De Montfort Hall.

Market Harborough

Lying halfway between Leicester and Northampton is the town of Market Harborough. Located at a crossing point of the River Welland, the town was created in the mid-12th century as a planned market town and, as such, it could be described as a 'medieval new town'. In 1645 Charles I made Market Harborough his headquarters and held a hurried Council of War before the decisive Battle of Naseby. Afterwards Cromwell occupied the town and from here wrote to Parliament, while the church was turned into a temporary prisoner-of-war camp.

Melton Mowbray

The market town of Melton Mowbray has a long established association with foxhunting, pork pies and Stilton cheese, it is a popular and lively place to visit, especially on market days and has

a rich and varied heritage. Melton's history is still evident today, the cathedral-sized St Mary's Church dates from 1170. Known as the stateliest and most impressive of all Leicestershire churches, its 100-foot tower dominates the town. Relax in the gentle rolling countryside, ancient villages and hunting traditions in the east. The historic Charnwood Forest offers rocky outcrops and Iron Age settlements.

Rutland

Tiny Rutland, just 20 miles across, may be the smallest county in England but it's packed with a host of things for you to do during your stay. With its two bustling market towns, Oakham and Uppingham, and more than forty picturesque villages of thatched, stone-built cottages, there's so much to see in Rutland it's hard to know where to start. You'll find plenty of opportunities to enjoy an active break in Rutland. Watersports enthusiasts should head for Rutland Water where you can hire a canoe or rowing boat to paddle around the sheltered creek and harbour at Whitwell. If you're feeling a little more energetic, you could even launch a sailboard or boat and strike out further across the reservoir. Cycle hire is also available and for the really energetic there is a 25 mile cycling and walking circuit around the water. For the keen angler Rutland Water is a must, stocked with around 130,000 trout each year; some of the best trout fishing in Europe is available here. Whatever you choose to do, you'll find that Rutland is England's best kept secret, set amidst part of the English countryside that's largely undiscovered and unspoilt.

Lincolnshire

Lincoln is a vivacious city with magnificent heritage, centred on its world famous Cathedral and Castle. The historic Cathedral Quarter is close to some of the major attractions and offers unique shopping experience and a lively arts and events programme.

Brigg

Brigg grew up as a crossing point on the River Ancholme. Today it is a thriving market town with a colourful history of fairs and markets. The Ancholme offers some of the most prolific fishing waters in eastern England, and its valley is ideal for walkers and ramblers. Paths run along the riverbank north to the Humber at South Ferriby, passing picturesque bridges such as Horkstow Bridge, designed by Sir John Rennie.

Cleethorpes

In 2007, Cleethorpes was awarded the prestigious Quality Coast Award for its high quality beaches and resort facilities. Offering the calm and tranquil lakeside and boating lake or the hustle and bustle of the seafront, promenade and the new meridian development; with many great attractions for all the family to enjoy… Cleethorpes really is a spectacular resort to visit!

Grimsby

Grimsby, once the largest fishing port in the world, is steeped in the richest of maritime and heritage experiences. Gain an insight into life at sea at the award-winning National Fishing Heritage Centre. From April to October you can experience the harsh

reality of life aboard a deep-sea trawler. Despite the decline in the fishing industry, a visit to Grimsby is not complete without a trip to the bustling dock area where you can still buy a variety of fish for sale.

Mablethorpe

Mablethorpe is a charming resort situated to the north of Lincolnshire's coastline. It is a wonderful centre for families and senior citizens who return again and again. Mablethorpe has a wealth of things for the visitor to do; the Seal Sanctuary and Nature Centre, play centres, funfairs and a super range of charming shops to pick up that special memento.

Skegness

Skegness has a beautiful, award-winning sandy beach that stretches for miles - the perfect haven for all the family. There is so much to do that it's difficult to know where to start. The Seal Sanctuary and Animal Centre, museums, kids' adventure centres, crazy golf, ten-pin bowling, Laser Quest, funfairs, and shopping; the nightlife is fantastic too. The illuminations begin in July and continue well into November lighting up the whole of the resort.

Spalding

Spalding, in the peaceful South Lincolnshire Fens, is a town that has to be seen to be believed! Georgian terraces front the tree-lined River Welland which runs through the centre of the town. Overlooking the river stands Ayscoughfee Hall and Gardens, which were given to the people of Spalding. The beautiful late-medieval Hall once belonged to a wool merchant. Today it houses a museum depicting life in the area over the centuries.

Northamptonshire

Northampton, the largest town in England, is a vibrant energetic place by day and by night. Once famous around the world as `shoe town`, it is now beginning to be known as `motor city` with Silverstone Circuit, Santa Pod and Rockingham speedways close-by. Althorp, the ancestral home of the Spencer family and the final resting place of Diana, Princess of Wales is nearby.

Earls Barton

There are records that a village has been on the site of Earls Barton since before 600 AD when the economy was based on growing barley, rye and wheat. Today Earl's Barton is a thriving village just seven miles east of Northampton. All Saints Church has a famous Saxon tower dating from 970 AD. In the grounds of Barkers shoe factory there is an exhibition of footwear manufacture and early photographs. There is also a shoe workers cottage to see how they lived in times long gone.

Fotheringhay Village

Situated on the River Nene, Fotheringhay is steeped in history. Fotheringhay Castle was built in 1100 and it was here that Mary Queen of Scots was held prisoner before her execution in February 1587. Whilst little remains of the castle it is worth a climb for the magnificent views. The church of St Mary and All Saints dates back to the 15th century and Edward of York founded a college there in 1415.

Oundle

Situated beside a meander in the River Nene the ancient market town of Oundle is edged by water meadows, popular with anglers, walkers and artists it also provides a wonderful spot for wildlife spotting. Oundle is also famous for its public school with many buildings of outstanding architectural and historical interest in the town.

Speedsters

Why not have a go at Kart racing at Whilton Mill? Car and bike track events at Rockingham in Corby, or enjoy the fun of Santa Pod's dragsters. If your passion is Formula One, then Silverstone is at hand (although the 2010 Grand Prix has moved to Donnington Park in Derbyshire). And if cars are not enough, you can test drive a tank at 'Tanks A Lot' in Helmdon, or for extreme water sports visit the Nene White Water Rafting centre.

Nottinghamshire

The city of Nottingham is famous for its lace industry and the legend of the infamous outlaw Robin Hood. Under the city is a unique labyrinth of caves cut by hand in early medieval times. The city is now becoming a sophisticated urban environment with more café-bars and elegant restaurants than any comparable city, and an enviable reputation for clubs, theatres, cinemas and galleries.

Eastwood

The birthplace of D.H. Lawrence who changed English literature for ever with his novel 'Lady Chatterley's Lover'. In the 20th century, when Lawrence was growing up, the area was dominated by the coal mining industry. The house is a tiny terrace but is a glimpse into the author's early life and works. A short walk is Durban House which offers a look into the past of the Barber Walker Mining Company.

Mansfield

The largest town in the county, lying on the River Maun, from which the town name comes. A 700-year-old market is the hub of this bustling town but there are plenty of other shopping opportunities from the usual high street stores and shopping centres to individual boutiques and specialist stores. Mansfield Museum and Art Gallery is full of local heritage. Water Meadows is the ultimate in swimming fun and a super day out for all the family.

Newark

Newark is a picturesque town situated on the banks of the River Trent. The Georgian Town Hall overlooks the market place but the town is famous for six annual antique fairs held at Newark County Showground. Thousands of international antique hunters descend on the thousands of stalls in search of a bargain! The town is home to Newark Air Museum with 65 aircraft. But for relaxation nearby North Clifton is home to a meditation centre and Japanese garden.

Newstead Abbey

Originally an Augustinian priory, Newstead became the Byron family seat in 1540. The Abbey's most famous owner, Lord Byron, sold the property in 1818. Newstead Abbey house, owned by Nottingham City Council, is open to the public to explore the private apartments used by the romantic poet. There are splendid Victorian room settings, interesting furniture and paintings throughout the house which is set in extensive formal gardens and parkland of 300 acres.

Southwell

Famous for the Minster church which boasts some of the best medieval stone carving in England Southwell is a prosperous small town with many elegant Regency houses. Southwell Minster is thought by many to be the 'best kept secret' among all English cathedrals. Outside the town is the best-preserved workhouse in England, owned by The National Trust it offers a chance to explore the workshops and dormitories of an early 'welfare' institution. There are interactive displays charting poverty through the ages.

Where to Go

 Attractions with this sign participate in the **Visitor Attraction Quality Assurance Scheme** (see page 6) which recognises high standards in all aspects of the visitor experience.

ENTERTAINMENT & CULTURE

Conkers Discovery Centre
Moira, Leicestershire, DE12 6GA
(01283) 216633
www.visitconkers.com
Interactive journey of adventure in the National Forest. Trails, lakes, assault course and play areas.

Crich Tramway Village
Matlock, Derbyshire, DE4 5DP
(01773) 854321
www.tramway.co.uk
Take the controls of a vintage tram in this lovingly restored period village.

Newark Castle and Conflict
Newark, Nottinghamshire, NG24 1BG
(01636) 655765
www.newark-sherwood.gov.uk
Discover the castle's important role in Newark's past and the town's Civil War history.

Rockingham Motor Speedway
Corby, Northamptonshire, NN17 5AF
(01536) 500500
www.rockingham.co.uk
Rockingham is the ultimate entertainment venue. Home to the SCSA racing series and host to a variety of driving experiences.

Silverstone Circuit
Silverstone, Northamptonshire, NN12 8TN
0870 458 8200
www.silverstone.co.uk
The home of British motor racing. Race meetings, driving experiences and shop.

The Curve
Leicester, Leicestershire, LE1 1TQ
(0116) 2423560
www.curveonline.co.uk
This exceptional new theatre features two exciting auditoria and state of the art technology.

FAMILY FUN

Foxton Locks
Foxton, Leicestershire, LE16 7RA
(01908) 302500
www.foxtonlocks.com
Fascinating ten lock 'staircase' climbing a 75 ft hill. The museum explores Britain's canal development.

National Space Centre
Leicester, Leicestershire, LE4 5NS
0870 607 7223
www.spacecentre.co.uk
Test your abilities as an astronaut and complete your training at Lunar Base 2025.

Twin Lakes Park
Melton Mowbray, Leicestershire, LE14 4SB
(01664) 567777
www.twinlakespark.co.uk
All-weather family fun. Superb rides and ten themed playzones, set in a beautiful country park.

HERITAGE

78 Derngate
Northampton, Northamptonshire, NN1 1UH
(01604) 603407
www.78derngate.org.uk
Charles Rennie MacKintosh's last major commission, a striking transformed terraced house.

Althorp
Northampton, Northamptonshire, NN7 4HQ
(01604) 770107
www.althorp.com
Experience 500 years of history at the Spencer family home. Diana exhibition and magnificent treasures.

Alford Manor House
Alford, Lincolnshire, LN13 9HT
(01507) 463073
www.alfordmanorhouse.co.uk
Reputedly the largest thatched manor house in the country, Alford Manor House was built to a traditional H plan in 1611.

Belton House
South Kesteven, Lincolnshire, NG32 2LS
(01476) 566116
www.nationaltrust.org.uk
The crowning achievement of Restoration country house architecture, built 1685–1688. Formal gardens, orangery and landscaped park.

Belvoir Castle
Melton Mowbray, Leicestershire, NG32 1PE
(01476) 871002
www.belvoircastle.com
The fourth castle on this site since Norman times. Superb furniture, paintings and porcelain.

Bolsover Castle
Bolsover, Derbyshire, S44 6PR
(01246) 822844
www.english-heritage.org.uk/bolsover
A 17thC house on the site of a Norman fortress, enchanting and romantic.

Bosworth Battlefield Heritage Centre
Market Bosworth, Leicestershire,
CV13 0AD
(01455) 290429
www.bosworthbattlefield.com
Relive the famous battle and follow a journey from 15thC England to the present day.

Carsington Water
Ashbourne, Derbyshire,
DE6 1ST
(01629) 540696
www.stwater.co.uk
Find out the story of Carsington in the visitor centre. Trails, watersports, cycle hire and fishery.

Chatsworth
Bakewell, Derbyshire, DE45 1PP
(01246) 582204
www.chatsworth.org
Enjoy over 30 richly decorated rooms, a garden with fountains, maze, farmyard and playground.

Creswell Crags
Bolsover, Derbyshire, S80 3LH
(01909) 720378
www.creswell-crags.org.uk
Dramatic limestone gorge containing caves occupied by the most northerly of Ice Age hunters.

Doddington Hall
Lincoln, Lincolnshire, LN6 4RU
(01522) 694308
www.doddingtonhall.com
This superb Elizabethan mansion boasts walled courtyards, turrets, gatehouse and six acres of romantic gardens.

Gainsborough Old Hall
Gainsborough, Lincolnshire,
DN21 2NB
(01427) 612669
www.Lincolnshire.gov.uk/gainsborougholdhall
Superb medieval manor house with original kitchens, great hall, tower. Connections with the Mayflower Pilgrims.

Great Central Railway
Leicester, Leicestershire,
LE11 1RW
(01509) 230726
www.gcrailway.co.uk
Britain's only double-track, main line steam railway, crossing eight miles of scenic Leicestershire countryside.

Grimsthorpe Castle, Park and Gardens
Grimsthorpe, Lincolnshire,
PE10 0LY
(01778) 591205
www.grimsthorpe.co.uk
Unravel over 800 years of history, wander state-rooms full of paintings, tapestries and objets d'art. Tearoom.

Haddon Hall
Bakewell, Derbyshire, DE45 1LA
(01629) 812855
www.haddonhall.co.uk
This magnificent medieval and Tudor manor house is virtually untouched by time. Wonderful terraced gardens.

Hardwick Hall
Chesterfield, Derbyshire,
S44 5QJ
(01246) 850430
www.nationaltrust.org.uk/hardwick
Elizabethan country house, gardens and park. Outstanding collections of furniture, tapestry and needlework.

Lincoln Castle
Lincoln, Lincolnshire, LN1 3AA
(01522) 511068
www.lincolnshire.gov.uk/lincolncastle
Share marvellous city views from the Norman castle and inspect an original Magna Carta.

Lincoln Cathedral
Lincoln, Lincolnshire, LN2 1PX
(01522) 561600
www.lincolncathedral.com
Visit the majestic medieval cathedral used in The Da Vinci Code film. Stunning hilltop setting.

Lyveden New Bield
Peterborough,
Northamptonshire, PE8 5AT
(01832) 205358
www.nationaltrust.org.uk/lyveden
Unfinished yet fascinating Elizabethan lodge, begun 1595. Designed to represent Sir Thomas Tresham's Catholic faith.

Newstead Abbey
Nottingham, Nottingham,
NG15 8NA
(01623) 455900
www.nottinghamcity.gov.uk/newsteadabbey
Romantic country house, formerly an Augustinian priory. The ancestral home of Lord Byron.

Oakham Castle
Oakham, Rutland, LE15 6HW
(01572) 758441
www.rutland.gov.uk/castle
See one of the finest examples of late 12thC architecture and sculptures in the Great Hall.

Peveril Castle
Hope Valley, Derbyshire,
S33 8WQ
(01433) 620613
www.english-heritage.org.uk
Inspirational views from this 11thC hilltop ruin above Castleton. Impressive curtain wall and keep.

Rockingham Castle
Market Harborough,
Northamptonshire, LE16 8TH
(01536) 770240
www.rockinghamcastle.com
An Elizabethan house within the walls of a Norman castle. Splendid artworks, extensive views and gardens.

Rufford Abbey Country Park
Newark, Nottinghamshire,
NG22 9DF
(01623) 821338
www.nottinghamshire.gov.uk/ruffordcp
Picturesque remains of a 12thC Cistercian monastery and later country house. Exhibition in the undercroft.

St Botolph's Church (Boston Stump)
Boston, Lincolnshire, PE21 6NP
(01205) 362864
www.parishofboston.org
*Boston Stump 700 yrs – April to December 2009
Her Royal Highness the Princess Royal visited Boston Stump on the 2nd December 2008 to launch the celebrations of the 700th Anniversary Programme.*

Sulgrave Manor
Sulgrave, Northamptonshire,
OX17 2SD
(01295) 760205
www.sulgravemanor.org.uk
Visit the small manor house of George Washington's ancestors. Washington souvenirs and Shakespeare period furniture.

attershall Castle
attershall, Lincolnshire,
N4 4LR
(1526) 342543
ww.nationaltrust.org.uk
ramatic 15thC red brick tower, built
r Ralph Cromwell, powerful Lord
easurer of England 1433–43.

NATURE & WILDLIFE

he Workhouse
outhwell, Nottinghamshire,
G25 0PT
1636) 817250
emarkable surviving example of a
orkhouse. An audio guide brings
0thC inhabitants back to life.

radgate Country Park
eicester, Leicestershire,
E6 0HE
116) 236 2713
ww.goLeicestershire.com/
utdoors/thedms
radgate park is a 340 hectare ancient
er park which was the home of Lady
ane Grey, 9 day Queen of England
553).

Castle Ashby Gardens
Castle Ashby,
Northamptonshire, NN7 1LQ
(01604) 695200
www.castleashbygardens.co.uk
Elizabethan mansion, arboretum and
Capability Brown gardens. Renowned
for native wild flowers and flowering
bulbs.

**National Water
Sports Centre**
Nottingham, Nottinghamshire,
NG12 2LU
(0115) 982 1212
www.nwscnotts.com
An Olympic-standard water sports
course of 2000m with rowing,
canoeing, artificial canoe slalom
course, water ski lagoon and a country
park for picnic and walks.

**Rutland Water
Nature Reserve**
Oakham, Rutland, LE15 8PX
(01572) 770651
www.rutlandwater.u-net.com
The nature reserve consists of a narrow
strip of land stretching for 7 miles
covering an area of 350 acres.

**Salcey Forest Tree
Top Walk**
Hartwell, Northamptonshire,
NN17 3BB
(01780) 444920
www.forestry.gov.uk/salceyforest
Salcey Forest; get a birds eye view
of this wonderful woodland on the
tremendous Tree Top Way.

**Sherwood Forest National
Nature Reserve**
Mansfield, Nottinghamshire,
NG21 9HN
(01623) 823202
www.nottinghamshire.gov.uk/
sherwoodforestcp
See the mighty Major Oak and follow a
nature trail. Visitor centre and events.

Twycross Zoo
Hinckley, Leicestershire,
CV9 3PX
(01827) 880250
www.twycrosszoo.com
Meet Twyford's famous gorillas, orangutans and chimpanzees plus many
other mammals, birds and reptiles.

Events 2010

Althorp Literary Festival
Northampton
www.althorp.com
June

**British Superbike
Championship**
Louth
www.britishsuperbike.com/
September

Buxton Festival
Buxton
www.buxtonfestival.co.uk/
July

Chatsworth Country Fair
Bakewell
www.countryfairoffice.co.uk
September

Crick Boat Show
Crick
www.crickmarina.com/
boatshow.htm
May

DH Lawrence Festival
Eastwood
www.broxtowe.gov.uk
August–September

Goose Fair
Nottingham
www.nottinghamgoosefair.
co.uk/
October

International Byron Festival
Nottingham
July

Jousting
Rockingham
www.rockinghamcastle.com
June

**Lincolnshire Wolds Walking
Festival**
www.woldswalkingfestival.
co.uk
22nd May–6th June

**Peak District Walking
Festival**
Derby
www.visitpeakdistrict.com
April–May

Robin Hood Festival
Nottingham
www.nottinghamshire.gov.uk/
robinhoodfestival/
July–August

Silverstone Classic
Silverstone
www.silverstoneclassic.com/
July

**Spalding Flower Parade
and Festival**
Spalding
www.flowerparade.org
May

Waddington Air Show
Waddington
www.waddingtonairshow.
co.uk
July

Wirksworth Festival
Wirksworth
www.wirksworthfestival.co.uk
September

Where to Eat

The East Midlands region has great places to eat. The restaurant reviews on these pages are just a small selection from the highly respected *The Good Food Guide 2010*. Please see pages 20–21 for further information on the guide and details of a Special Offer for our readers.

DERBYSHIRE

Darleys
Modern food in a terrific setting
Darley Abbey Mills, Haslams Lane,
Darley Abbey, DE22 1DZ
Tel no: (01332) 364987
www.darleys.com
Modern British | £35

Darley's was refurbished at the outset of 2009, but it is still brimful of charm, as many regular reporters continue to confirm. It's in the former canteen of an old cotton mill, and has wonderful views (try to bag a table next to the windows, where one diner remembers seeing the Derwent 'in mesmerising spate over the weir'). Jonathan Hobson cooks in modern British style, with plaudits coming in this year for 'very tasty' wild mushroom and Taleggio ravioli with rosemary and truffle foam, a duo of beef (fillet and shin) with puréed carrot and bay leaf sauce, and venison 'cooked to a lovely pink' and served with spinach mousse, parsnip rösti and a sauce of Marsala. If you're in the market for fish, consider spiced monkfish with a smoked haddock beignet and butternut squash purée. Populist desserts such as warm Black Forest gâteau with cherry jelly and white chocolate ice cream will send you away happy. The single-sheet wine list offers a good international spread from £14.50, or £3.50 a glass.

Chef/s: Jonathan Hobson. **Open:** all week L 12 to 2 (2.30 Sun), Mon to Sat D 7 to 9 (9.30 Sat). **Closed:** bank hols, 2 weeks after 25 Dec. **Meals:** alc (main courses £17 to £22). Set L £15.95 (2 courses) to £17.95. Set Sun L £17.95 (2 courses) to £20. **Service:** not inc. **Details:** Cards accepted. 60 seats. 16 seats outside. Air-con. Separate bar. Wheelchair access. Music. Children allowed. Car parking.

George Hotel
Simple, fresh food
Main Road, Hathersage, S32 1BB
Tel no: (01433) 650436
www.george-hotel.net
Modern British | £35

This rather handsome old coaching inn with its small paned windows, oak beams and open fires once accommodated Charlotte Brontë and provided inspiration for her novel Jane Eyre. Today, it is a comfortably appointed hotel with a restaurant at its heart, where Helen Heywood cooks an accomplished modern British menu that attracts a loyal band of regulars. Breast of wood pigeon makes a robust starter, and comes with honey roasted pumpkin salad, while mains run from a thick steak of red pepper-crusted cod (served with warm chorizo and chickpea salad and basil dressing), to sirloin of beef, which comes with a cannelloni of 12-hour braised shin, fondant potato, red wine sauce and roasted garlic foam. Dessert could offer mandarin jelly with warm chocolate ravioli. Freshly baked breads and petits fours excel too, and tasting notes make choosing wine easier. Bottle prices start at £15.95.

Chef/s: Helen Heywood. **Open:** all week L 12 to 2.30, D 6.30 to 10. **Meals:** Set L £28 (2 courses) to £35. Sun L £19.95 (2 courses) to £39.50 (4 courses). Set D £28 (2 courses) to £35. **Service:** not inc. **Details:** Cards accepted 45 seats. Separate bar. No mobile phones. Wheelchair access. Music. Children allowed. Car parking.

and relaxed charm. In the kitchen Andrew Gilbert likes to keep things simple, using pinpoint accuracy of timing, careful balance and pretty much faultless composition to make an impact. And make an impact he does. Expect a bedrock of modern British ideas with additions from France, Italy and beyond in starters such as saddle of rabbit stuffed with apple and sage, wrapped in Serrano ham and served on artichoke purée. For main course, loin of Lincolnshire lamb might arrive with Lancashire hotpot or a fine piece of roast turbot may be voguishly paired with savoury Savoy cabbage, lobster mashed potato, broad beans and vanilla dressing. Desserts bring on vibrant assemblies such as a technically perfect hot pineapple tarte Tatin with coconut ice cream and candied chilli. Immense effort and care have gone into the wine list, which picks fine names from France and beyond and has a fair spread of prices. Some 17 house recommendations begin with Corney & Barrow French at £14.75.

Chef/s: Andrew Gilbert. **Open:** Wed to Fri and Sun L 12 to 2.30, Wed to Sun D 7 to 9. **Closed:** Mon, Tue, 27 to 30 Dec, bank hols. **Meals:** Set L £21 (2 courses) to £25. Set D £38. **Service:** not inc. **Details:** Cards accepted. 34 seats. 6 seats outside. Air-con. Separate bar. No mobile phones. Wheelchair access. Music. Children allowed.

LEICESTERSHIRE & RUTLAND

Olive Branch
Welcoming village pub
Main Street, Clipsham, LE15 7SH
Tel no: (01780) 410355
www.theolivebranchpub.com
Gastropub | £28

The Olive Branch appears rustic and unassuming – an impression reinforced by its beams, exposed stone walls, log fires and bare tables. It all has the air of a true country local, albeit one with menus running from wild mushroom risotto to turbot with crab ravioli and crab bisque. The kitchen concentrates on excellent raw materials, much of it locally sourced and details are not overlooked: praise is heaped on bread, local cheeses and homemade ice creams and sorbets. Pub staples such as Lincolnshire sausages with mustard mash and onion gravy are done very well and classic puddings include egg custard or treacle tarts. The modern wine list is just right for the job, unfussy, imaginative and great value. Prices start at £14.

Chef/s: Sean Hope. **Open:** all week L 12 to 2 (Sat 5, Sun 3), D 7 to 9.30 (Sun 9). **Closed:** 25 and 26 Dec, 1 Jan. **Meals:** alc (main courses £14 to £25). Set L £16.50 (2 courses) to £19.50. Sun L £24.50. Set D £20 (2 courses) to £25. **Service:** not inc. **Details:** Cards accepted. 48 seats. 24 seats outside. Separate bar. Wheelchair access. Music. Children allowed. Car parking.

LINCOLNSHIRE

Elio's
11 Market Place, Barton-upon-Humber, DN18 5DA
Tel no: (01652) 635147
Italian

Opened in 1983, Elio Grossi's engaging Italian trattoria-with-rooms is an ever-popular fixture of the Humberside scene, noted for its conservatory/courtyard and the kitchen's fondness for fish. The day's specials could run from Scottish scallops with crispy bacon and leek sauce (£8.95) and Genovese style red bream with olives, sun-dried tomatoes, pesto and pine kernels to osso buco in gremolata sauce (£15.95) or calf's liver veneziana. Pizzas, pasta, steaks and creamy desserts (£5.75) complete the package. Italian regional wines from £12.95 a litre. Open Mon to Sat D only.

Magpies
A personally run Wolds favourite
71-75 East Street, Horncastle, LN9 6AA
Tel no: (01507) 527004
www.dineatthemagpies.co.uk
Modern British | £38

Magpies is a quietly confident, personally run restaurant set in a row of black and white cottages. Inside, Caroline Gilbert is in charge of the mellow dining room, providing a welcome blend of discreet sophistication

NOTTINGHAMSHIRE

French Living
A patriotic foodie package
27 King Street, Nottingham, NG1 2AY
Tel no: (0115) 9585885
www.frenchliving.co.uk
French | £17

Stéphane and Louise Luiggi's self-styled 'capsule of Frenchness' is a generous celebration of all things Gallic. Out front is a deli/café dealing in all sorts of provisions, while the cellar is given over to a rustic, redbricked bistro-style restaurant. The kitchen responds to its surroundings by dishing out bowls of bouillabaisse and cassoulet, as well as dipping into the bourgeois world of mouclade Rochelaise, medallions of pork with chopped gherkins and – of course – crème brûlée. French cheeses and wines (from £9.50) complete the patriotic package.

Chef/s: Jeremy Tourne. **Open:** Tue to Sat L 12 to 2 (2.30 Sat), D 6 to 10. **Closed:** Sun, Mon, 24 Dec to 2 Jan. **Meals:** alc (main courses £11 to £18). Set L £8.50 (2 courses) to £10.50. Set D £12.50 to £21.50 (3 courses). **Service:** 10% (optional). **Details:** Cards accepted. 43 seats. Air-con. Music. Children allowed.

Content brought to you by **The Good Food Guide 2010.** Please see pages 20–21 for further details.

Tourist Information Centres

When you arrive at your destination, visit an Official Partner Tourist Information Centre for quality assured help with accommodation and information about local attractions and events, or email your request before you go. To search for attractions and Tourist Information Centres on the move just text INFO to 62233, and a web link will be sent to your mobile phone. To find a Tourist Information Centre by region visit enjoyEngland.com/find-tic.

ASHBOURNE	13 Market Place	01335 343666	ashbourneinfo@derbyshiredales.gov.uk
ASHBY-DE-LA-ZOUCH	North Street	01530 411767	ashby.tic@nwleicestershire.gov.uk
BAKEWELL	Old Market Hall	01629 813227	bakewell@peakdistrict-npa.gov.uk
BRACKLEY	2 Bridge Street	01280 700111	tic@southnorthants.gov.uk
BRIGG	The Buttercross	01652 657053	brigg.tic@northlincs.gov.uk
BUXTON	The Crescent	01298 25106	tourism@highpeak.gov.uk
CASTLETON	Buxton Road	01433 620679	castleton@peakdistrict-npa.gov.uk
CHESTERFIELD	Rykneld Square	01246 345777	tourism@chesterfield.gov.uk
CLEETHORPES	42-43 Alexandra Road	01472 323111	cleetic@nelincs.gov.uk
DERBY	Assembly Rooms	01332 255802	tourism@derby.gov.uk
HORNSEA	120 Newbegin	01964 536404	hornsea.tic@eastriding.gov.uk
LEICESTER	7/9 Every Street	0906 294 1113	info@goleicestershire.com
LINCOLN	9 Castle Hill	01522 873213	tourism@lincoln.gov.uk
MATLOCK	Crown Square	01629 583388	matlockinfo@derbyshiredales.gov.uk
NORTHAMPTON	Northampton Visitor Centre	01604 838800	northampton.tic@northamptonshireenterprise.ltd.uk
NOTTINGHAM CITY	1-4 Smithy Row	08444 775 678	tourist.information@nottinghamcity.gov.uk
OLLERTON	Tourist Information Centre	01623 824545	sherwoodheath@nsdc.info
OUNDLE	14 West Street	01832 274333	oundletic@east-northamptonshire.gov.uk
RIPLEY	Town Hall	01773 841488	touristinformation@ambervalley.gov.uk
SLEAFORD	Advice Centre, Money's Yard,	01529 414294	tic@n-kesteven.gov.uk
SWADLINCOTE	Sharpe's Pottery Museum	01283 222848	Jo@sharpespotterymuseum.org.uk

Regional Contacts and Information

The publications listed are available from the following organisations:

East Midlands Tourism
Web: www.discovereastmidlands.com
Discover East Midlands

Experience Nottinghamshire
Tel: 0844 477 5678
Web: www.visitnotts.com
Nottinghamshire Essential Guide, Where to Stay
Guide, Stay Somewhere Different, City Breaks,
Family Days Out
Robin Hood Breaks
Pilgrim Fathers

Peak District and Derbyshire
Web: www.visitpeakdistrict.com
Peak District and Derbyshire Visitor
Guide
Well Dressing
Camping and Caravanning Guide
Peak District and Derbyshire Outdoor Activities

Lincolnshire
Tel: (01522) 873800
Web: www.visitlincolnshire.com
Visit Lincolnshire – Destination Guide, Great
Days Out, Gardens & Nurseries, Aviation
Heritage,
Good Taste
Keep up with the flow

Explore Northamptonshire
Tel: (01604) 609393
Web: www.explorenorthamptonshire.
co.uk
Explore Northamptonshire Visitor Guide,
Country Map

Leicestershire
Tel: 0844 888 5181
Web: www.goleicestershire.co.uk
Inspiring short breaks and holidays in
Leicestershire
Stay, Play, Explore
Great Days Out in Leicestershire

Discover Rutland
Tel: (01572) 653026
Web: www.discover-rutland.co.uk
Discover Rutland

Where to Stay

Entries appear alphabetically by town name in each county. A key to symbols appears on page 6. Maps start on page 394. A listing of all Enjoy England assessed accommodation appears at the end of the region.

ALSOP-EN-LE-DALE, Derbyshire Map ref 4B2 SAT NAV DE6 1QU

Rivendale Caravan & Leisure Park

Rivendale Caravan & Leisure Park, Buxton Road, Ashbourne DE6 1QU
t (01335) 310311 f (01335) 842311 e enquiries@rivendalecaravanpark.co.uk
w **rivendalecaravanpark.co.uk** LAST MINUTE OFFERS

▄🚐 (81)	£12.90–£21.70
🚐 (81)	£12.90–£21.70
⚊ (30)	£10.00–£21.70
▭	£260.00–£395.00

111 touring pitches

SPECIAL PROMOTIONS
Receive £15 discount for every 7-night stay (includes multiples of 7-night stays).

Surrounded by spectacular Peak District scenery, convenient for Alton Towers, Chatsworth, Dove Dale and Carsington Water. Ideal for cyclists and ramblers with a network of footpaths and trails accessible directly from site. Choice of all-grass, hardstanding or 50/50 pitches. Closed 7 January to 1 February.

payment credit/debit cards, cash, cheques

directions From A515, Rivendale is situated 6.5 miles north of Ashbourne, directly off the A515 Buxton road on the right-hand side, travelling north.

General 🔥 🖥 ⊕ 🐓 🛠 🛖 🏠 ☼ 🖭 🛏 🛒 🛉 📱 ✕ Leisure ∪ 🚲 🜲 🍷 🎣 ⋒

Looking for something else?

You can also buy a copy of our popular guide 'Hotels' including country house and town house hotels, metro and budget hotels, serviced apartments, restaurants with rooms and Spas in England 2010. Now available in good bookshops and online at **enjoyenglanddirect.com**

£10.99

AMBERGATE, Derbyshire Map ref 4B2

SAT NAV DE56 2JH

The Firs Caravan Club Site

Crich Lane, Belper DE56 2JH
t (01773) 852913
w **caravanclub.co.uk**

CARAVAN CLUB

🚐 (82)   £14.00–£26.90
🚍 (82)   £14.00–£26.90
82 touring pitches

SPECIAL PROMOTIONS
Special member rates mean
you can save your
membership subscription in
less than a week. Visit our
website to find out more.

The Firs is set within a special landscape area
situated on a hilltop in the heart of the
Derbyshire countryside. Peaceful and well
presented, there are breathtaking views to the
west over the edge of the Derwent Valley Mills
World Heritage Site. It is a popular touring base
for the Peak District and Derbyshire Dales.

open April to November
payment credit/debit cards, cash, cheques

directions M1 jct 28, A38 (Ripley). 5.75 miles
A610 (Ambergate). 3 miles A6 (Belper). 0.5 miles
A609, B6013. Continue into Crich Lane. Site on
left in 1.25 miles.

General 🖥 🐕 🛎 🝰 ☀ 🔌 🖸 🍴
Leisure ▶ 🏊

ASHBOURNE, Derbyshire Map ref 4B2

SAT NAV DE6 3JL

Blackwall Plantation Caravan Club Site

Kirk Ireton, Ashbourne DE6 3JL
t (01335) 370903 f (01335) 372152
w **caravanclub.co.uk**

CARAVAN CLUB

🚐 (130)   £12.20–£25.10
🚍 (130)   £12.20–£25.10
130 touring pitches

Set in a pine plantation, on rising ground, beautifully landscaped.
Within walking distance of Carsington Reservoir. Good walking and
cycling area. Explore the Peak District National Park. Alton Towers
15miles. **directions** Take A517 from Ashbourne. In 4.5miles, turn
left at signpost to Carsington Water/Atlow/Hognaston. At
crossroads, turn right signposted to Carsington Water. On the right
after 1mile. **open** March to November **payment** credit/debit cards,
cash, cheques

General 🖥 🐕 🝰 ☀ 🔌 🖸 🍴 🏧   Leisure ⛰

BAKEWELL, Derbyshire Map ref 4B2

SAT NAV DE45 1PN

★★★★★
TOURING PARK

🚐 (120) £15.30–£30.00
🚃 (120) £15.30–£30.00
120 touring pitches

SPECIAL PROMOTIONS
Special member rates mean
you can save your
membership subscription in
less than a week. Visit our
website to find out more.

Chatsworth Park Caravan Club Site
Chatsworth, Bakewell DE45 1PN
t (01246) 582226 f (01246) 583762

THE
CARAVAN
CLUB

Breathtaking setting in walled garden on the
Estate, with views of the sheep - cropped rolling
countryside to the west. Children will love the
farmyard and adventure playground. Visit the
house with its beautifully proportioned rooms,
paintings and formal gardens.

payment credit/debit cards, cash, cheques

directions From Bakewell on A619. In 3.75 miles
on the outskirts of Baslow turn right at
roundabout (signposted Sheffield). Site entrance
on right in 150 yds.

General 🖩 📶 🐕 📠 🌣 📢 🕀 💧 🗑️
Leisure 🏔

BUXTON, Derbyshire Map ref 4B2

SAT NAV SK17 9TQ

★★★
TOURING &
CAMPING PARK

🚐 (30) £12.00–£15.00
🚃 (30) £12.00–£15.00
⛺ (30) £8.50–£12.00
30 touring pitches

Cottage Farm Caravan Park
Beech Croft, Blackwell in the Peak, Buxton SK17 9TQ
t (01298) 85330 e mail@cottagefarmsite.co.uk
w **cottagefarmsite.co.uk**

We are a family-run site, southerly facing with easy access from the
A6. We can boast a beautiful walk along the River Wye at nearby
Cheedale. Limited facilities Nov-Mar. **directions** 6 miles from Buxton
& Bakewell signposted on the A6. **open** Limited opening during
winter months **payment** credit/debit cards, cash, cheques

General 🐕 ⚲ 📠 🌣 🚿 📢 🕀 💧

BUXTON, Derbyshire Map ref 4B2

SAT NAV SK17 0DT

★★★
HOLIDAY, TOURING
& CAMPING PARK

🚐 (95) £11.25–£15.50
🚃 (14) £11.25–£15.50
⛺ (30) £11.25–£15.50
125 touring pitches

Newhaven Caravan and Camping Park
Newhaven, Buxton SK17 0DT
t (01298) 84300 f (01332) 726027 e bobmacara@ntlworld.com
w **newhavencaravanpark.co.uk**

Halfway between Ashbourne and Buxton in the Peak District
National Park. Well-established park with modern facilities, close to
the Tissington and High Peak trails, historic houses and Derbyshire
Dales. **directions** Half way between Ashbourne and Buxton on the
A515 at junction with A5012. **open** March to October **payment**
credit/debit cards, cash, cheques

General 🖩 🐕 ⚲ 📠 🌣 📧 📢 🕀 💧 Leisure 🎣 🏔

BUXTON, Derbyshire Map ref 4B2

SAT NAV SK17 6UJ

★★★★★
TOURING & CAMPING PARK

Grin Low Caravan Club Site

Grin Low Road, Ladmanlow, Buxton SK17 6UJ
t (01298) 77735 f (01298) 70684
w **caravanclub.co.uk**

THE
CARAVAN
CLUB

🚐 (117) £12.20–£25.10
🚃 (117) £12.20–£25.10
117 touring pitches

SPECIAL PROMOTIONS
Special member rates mean
you can save your
membership subscription in
less than a week. Visit our
website to find out more.

A site conveniently placed for just about
everything going on in and around the Peak
District. Buxton, with its colourful Pavilion
Gardens and Opera House offering a wide range
of events make a great day or evening out.
You'll be surrounded by the Peak District
National Park – ideal for walkers and cyclists.

open March to November
payment credit/debit cards, cash, cheques

directions From Buxton left off A53 Buxton to
Leek road. Within 1.5 miles at Grin Low signpost,
in 300 yds turn left into site approach road; site
entrance 0.25 miles.

General ▫ ◌ ▥ ◠ ☼ ▱ ◷ ☎ 🆆🅿
Leisure ⚠

DERBY, Derbyshire Map ref 4B2

SAT NAV DE72 3EP

★★★
TOURING PARK

Elvaston Castle Caravan Club Site

Borrowash Road, Elvaston, Derby DE72 3EP
t (01332) 571342
w **caravanclub.co.uk**

THE
CARAVAN
CLUB

🚐 (44) £9.30–£20.70
🚃 (44) £9.30–£20.70
44 touring pitches

Site attractively laid out within 280-acre country park where
squirrels and rabbits roam freely and colourful azaleas and
rhododendrons abound in season. Many walks to choose from or
take a trip into nearby Derby. **directions** Leave A50, turn right onto
B5010. Continue left on B5010, in about 1 mile turn left into
country park. Site on left. **open** April to November **payment** credit/
debit cards, cash, cheques

General 🐕 ▥ ◠ ▱ ◷ Leisure ▶ 🎣

RIPLEY, Derbyshire Map ref 4B2

SAT NAV DE55 4ES

★★★★
TOURING & CAMPING PARK

Golden Valley Caravan & Camping

Golden Valley, Coach Road, Alfreton DE55 4ES
t (01773) 513881 e enquiries@goldenvalleycaravanpark.co.uk
w **goldenvalleycaravanpark.co.uk** ONLINE MAP GUEST REVIEWS

🚐 (45) £20.00–£25.00
🚃 (10) £20.00–£25.00
⚕ (100) £15.00–£25.00
🏠 (1) £500–£750

Secluded woodland hideaway. All-weather children's play facilities.
caravan and tent pitches. Jacuzzi, gymnasium, pool table, bar, cafe
and takeaway. Fishing. Nr Butterley Railway. Fort Adventure facility.
Gold Conservation Award. **directions** M1 jct 26 onto A610. Follow
signs to Alfreton. Turn right at lights at Codnor. Then right onto
Alfreton Road. Follow for 1 mile. **open** All year **payment** credit/
debit cards, cash, cheques

General ⚘ ▫ 🐕 ▤ ▥ ◠ ☼ ▱ ▱ ◷ ☎ 🆆🅿 ✕ Leisure ▶ ∪ ♿ 🎣 ⚽ 🎵 ✎ ⚠

STAVELEY, Derbyshire Map ref 4B2

SAT NAV S43 3LS

Poolsbrook Country Park Caravan Club Site

Staveley, Chesterfield S43 3LS
t (01246) 470659
w **caravanclub.co.uk**

(86) £14.00–£26.60
(86) £14.00–£26.60
86 touring pitches

SPECIAL PROMOTIONS
Special member rates mean
you can save your
membership subscription in
less than a week. Visit our
website to find out more.

This site incorporates a number of sustainable resource and energy features and is set within the 165-acre Pools Brook Country Park. Once th site of a colliery, the land has been transforme into this tremendous country park with amenities including visitor centre, cafe and children's adventure play area. With lakes for fishing, extensive trails for cyclists and walkers explore, an added bonus is that the country park also adjoins the Trans-Pennine Trail.

open April to November
payment credit/debit cards, cash, cheques

directions M1 jct 30 onto A616, then A619 (Chesterfield). 2.5 miles left into Fan Road (Poolsbrook Country Park). Follow signs to Poolsbrook Country Park Only. Site entrance or right.

General ▢ ⚲ ⚲ ⟨ ⟨ ☀ ⚲ ⟨ ⚲
Leisure ⟋

SWADLINCOTE, Derbyshire Map ref 4B3

SAT NAV DE12 8HZ

Beehive Farm Woodland Lakes

Rosliston, Swadlincote DE12 8HZ
t (01283) 763981 e info@beehivefarm-woodlandlakes.co.uk
w **beehivefarm-woodlandlakes.co.uk** ONLINE MAP

(25) £16.00–£19.00
(5) £16.00–£19.00
(60) £10.00–£20.00
30 touring pitches

In the heart of the National Forest and within easy reach of the Derbyshire Dales and many great local attractions, Beehive Farm Woodland Lakes is a great place to stay. **directions** Please contact us for directions **open** All year except Xmas and New Year **payment** credit/debit cards, cash, cheques

General ⟨ ⚲ ⟨ ☀ ▢ ⚲ ⚲ ⚲ Leisure ▸ ⟋ ⟨

BOSTON, Lincolnshire Map ref 3A1

SAT NAV PE20 3QU

Orchard Park

Frampton Lane, Hubberts Bridge, Boston PE20 3QU
t (01205) 290368 f (01205) 290247 e info@orchardpark.co.uk
w **orchardpark.co.uk** ONLINE MAP

£15.00
£15.00
£7.50–£15.00
(4) £230.00–£250.00
87 touring pitches

Just a five-minute riverside walk takes you to the village, station and pub serving meals all day. Coarse fishing available on site. Situated between the Forty Foot River and the B1192. No children. **directions** On B1192 between A52 (Boston-Grantham) and A1121 (Boston-Sleaford). **open** All year **payment** cash, cheques

General ⚲ ▢ ⚲ ⟨ ⚲ ⟨ ⟨ ☀ ▢ ⚲ ⟨ ⚲ ✕ Leisure ▸ ⟲ ⟋ ⧠ ♫ ⚲ ⟨

BURGH-LE-MARSH, Lincolnshire Map ref 4D2   SAT NAV PE24 5LN

Sycamore Lakes

Skegness Road, Burgh le Marsh PE24 5LN
t (01754) 811411 **f** (01754) 811411
w **sycamorelakes.co.uk** ONLINE MAP

(54)	£15.00–£17.00	
(54)	£15.00–£17.00	
(54)	£15.00–£17.00	
(4)	£375–£455	
(5)	£345–£375	
54 touring pitches		

Set in 30 acres of landscaped grounds with four fishing lakes (well stocked with carp, tench, rudd, roach and perch). Spacious, level pitches (hard standing and grass) with hook-ups. Superb amenity block. Lakeside cafeteria, Sunday lunch, carvery/steak evenings. Tackle shop, dog walk and footpaths. Also self-catering lakeside cottages and cabins. Sycamore lakes premier static caravan park, sales.

open March to November
payment cash, cheques

directions Situated on the A158 between Burgh-le-Marsh and Skegness at Sycamore Lakes roundabout.

General ▫ ⊦ ⚇ ⏅ ☼ ▦ ⛽ ◉ ♟ ▨ ✕   Leisure ▸ ∪ ⤴ ◭

HORNCASTLE, Lincolnshire Map ref 4D2   SAT NAV LN9 5PP

Ashby Park

Ashby Park, West Ashby LN9 5PP
t (01507) 527966 **f** (01507) 524539 **e** ashbypark@btconnect.com
w **ukparks.co.uk/ashby**

(90)	£13.00–£24.00	
(10)	£13.00–£24.00	
(10)	£13.00–£17.00	
110 touring pitches		

David Bellamy Gold Conservation Award park offering a friendly atmosphere, good walks, seven fishing lakes. Set in 70 acres of unspoilt countryside. Luxury holiday homes for sale also touring pitches. **directions** 1.5 miles north of Horncastle between the A153 and the A158. **open** 1 March to 6 January **payment** credit/debit cards, cash, cheques

General ▫ ⊦ ▥ ⏅ ☼ ▦ ⛽ ◖ ♟ ▨   Leisure ▸ ∪ ⤴

LINCOLN, Lincolnshire Map ref 4C2   SAT NAV LN6 0EY

Hartsholme Country Park

Skellingthorpe Road, Lincoln LN6 0EY
t (01522) 873578 **f** (01522) 873577 **e** hartsholmecp@lincoln.gov.uk
w **lincoln.gov.uk** ONLINE MAP

	£13.20–£18.20	
	£13.20–£18.20	
(10)	£7.00–£18.20	
26 touring pitches		

Our 3 star English Tourism rated site offers flat, level grassy pitches set in mature wooded parkland. Easy access to city centre and local attractions. Open for weekends throughout November. **directions** Main entrance is on the B1378 (Skellingthorpe Road). It is signposted from the A46 (Lincoln Bypass) and from the B1003 (Tritton Road). **open** March to October **payment** credit/debit cards, cash, cheques

General ⊦ ⚇ ⏅ ☼ ⛽ ♟ ✕   Leisure ⤴ ◭

NORTH SCARLE, Lincolnshire Map ref 4C2　　　SAT NAV LN6 9EN

Lowfields Country Holiday Fishing Retreat

Eagle Road, North Scarle, Lincoln LN6 9EN
t (01522) 778717 **e** lowretreat@aol.com
w **lowfields-retreat.co.uk** ONLINE MAP GUEST REVIEWS ONLINE BOOKING LAST MINUTE OFFERS

🏠 (1)　£372–£691
🚐 (2)　£391–£725
⛺ (120)　£207.00–£536.00

Beautiful setting with 300-year-old mature woodland lakes, Bellamy Gold Award, Wildlife everywhere! Holiday caravans for sale/hire. Cottages/cabin for hire. Pets welcome. Great friendly atmosphere. Lincolnshire. **directions** From A46 take A1133 towards Gainsborough. Continue through Collingham and look out for our large Brown Tourist signs just after Besthorpe. **open** All year **payment** credit/debit cards, cash, cheques

General 🔲 🐕 🏠 ☼　Leisure ► ∪ ⏋ ⚲

SCUNTHORPE, Lincolnshire Map ref 4C1　　　SAT NAV DN15 9DH

Brookside Caravan Park

Stather Road, Burton-upon-Stather, Scunthorpe DN15 9DH
t (01724) 721369 **e** brooksidecp@aol.com
w **brooksidecaravanpark.co.uk** ONLINE MAP GUEST REVIEWS

🚐 (15)　£16.00
🚐 (15)　£16.00–£13.00
⛺ (5)　£16.00
35 touring pitches

Quiet, family-run park that will meet all your requirements, with views over the River Trent and woodland. **directions** Leave M181 and follow signs for Normanby Hall Country Park (A1077). Left on B1430 Burton Stather. Left at Sheffield Arms. Down hill. Entrance 250 yds on right. **open** All year **payment** cash, cheques

General 🔧 🔲 💧 🐕 🏠 🏠 ☼ 🅿 🚐 🔳 🍴 📶　Leisure ► ∪ ⏋ ⚲

SKEGNESS, Lincolnshire Map ref 4D2　　　SAT NAV PE25 3TQ

Richmond Holiday Centre

T/A Richmond Holiday Centre, Richmond Drive, Skegness, Skegness PE25 3TQ
t (01754) 762097 **f** (01754) 765631 **e** sales@richmondholidays.com
w **richmondholidays.com**

🚐 (67)　£15.00–£22.00
🚐 (67)　£15.00–£22.00
⛺ (120)　£190.00–£520.00
67 touring pitches

The ideal holiday base, a gentle stroll from the bustling resort of Skegness with its funfairs, sandy beaches and donkey rides. Nightly entertainment during the peak weeks. **directions** Head for the coach park/Tesco's on Richmond Drive, we are approx half-a-mile past the Tesco's traffic lights on the right hand side. **open** March to November **payment** credit/debit cards, cash, cheques

General 🔲 💧 🐕 🔳 🏠 🏠 ☼ 🅿 🚐 🍴 ✕　Leisure ⚲ 🎣 🍴 🎵 ⚘ ⚲

SKEGNESS, Lincolnshire Map ref 4D2　　　SAT NAV PE25 1JF

Skegness Water Leisure Park

Walls Lane, Skegness PE25 1JF
t (01754) 899400 **f** (01754) 897867 **e** enquiries@skegnesswaterleisurepark.co.uk
w **skegnesswaterleisurepark.co.uk**

🚐　£14.00
🚐　£18.00
⛺　£14.00
250 touring pitches

Family-orientated caravan and camping site 'where the coast meets the countryside'. Ten-minute walk to award-winning beaches with scenic, rural views. **directions** A52 north from Skegness 2.5 miles. Turn left at Cheers pub into Walls Lane. Site is last but one on left side of road. **open** March to November **payment** credit/debit cards, cash, cheques

General 🔲 🐕 🔳 🏠 🏠 ☼ 🚐 🔳 🍴 ✕　Leisure ∪ ⏋ 🍴 🎵

SPANBY, Lincolnshire Map ref 3A1

Highfields Country Holiday Fishing Retreat

Mareham Lane, Spanby, Sleaford NG34 0AT
t (01529) 241185 e info@highretreat.co.uk
w **highfields-retreat.co.uk** ONLINE MAP GUEST REVIEWS ONLINE BOOKING LAST MINUTE OFFERS

  (2)   £343–£725
(20)   £326.00–£536.00

Beautiful setting, three attractive fishing lakes, mature woodland, holiday caravans for sale, log cabins for sale/hire. Personal service. Pets Welcome. Acres and acres in which to roam free! **directions** Follow the Brown Tourist signs from the A52 near Threekingham. We are 0.5 mile off the A52. **open** All year **payment** credit/debit cards, cash, cheques

General 🐕 ☼ Leisure ▶ ∪ ⚓

FINESHADE, Northamptonshire Map ref 3A1

Top Lodge Caravan Club Site

Fineshade, Duddington, Corby, Corby NN17 3BB
t (01780) 444617
w **caravanclub.co.uk**

THE
CARAVAN
CLUB

(83)   £9.30–£20.70
(83)   £9.30–£20.70
83 touring pitches

SPECIAL PROMOTIONS
Special member rates mean you can save your membership subscription in less than a week. Visit our website to find out more.

Tranquil, open meadowland site surrounded by woodland where you can walk freely, watch birds and deer and enjoy a profusion of wild flowers. A visit to Brarnsdale Gardens at Oakham, Geoff Hamilton's horticultural legacy, is a must. Own sanitation required.

open March to November
payment credit/debit cards, cash, cheques

directions Turn right off A43 at junction A47 Corby (signposted Fineshade). Top Lodge within 0.5 mile.

General 🐕 🔌 🚻 🚰 ⬜
Leisure ⚓

NOTTINGHAM, Nottinghamshire Map ref 4C2   SAT NAV NG12 2LU

★★
TOURING &
CAMPING PARK

🚐 (52)   £10.00–£13.00
🚐 (52)   £13.00–£15.00
🅰 (360)   £7.00–£13.00
52 touring pitches

SPECIAL PROMOTIONS
Special Promotions Available
Upon Request. Electric hook-
up available for £4.00.

National Water Sports Centre Caravan & Camping Park

Adbolton Lane, Holme Pierrepont, Nottingham NG12 2LU
t 01159 824 721 e nwsccampsite@nottscc.gov.uk
w **nwscnotts.com** ONLINE MAP GUEST REVIEWS LAST MINUTE OFFERS

Set in a 270-acre country park the National Water Sports Centre is just 3 miles from Nottingham
City Centre with local bus and train services. At the main centre, activities available include white
water rafting, water skiing, windsurfing and canoeing along with great walks and good cycling
too.

open All year
payment credit/debit cards, cash, cheques

directions 3 Miles From City Centre on A52.
(Please See Website)

General 🔥🗺🐕🎿🏕🔌☀♨🔄🍴🚐✕ Leisure ▶⛳🏌🍺🎿⛰

WORKSOP, Nottinghamshire Map ref 4C2   SAT NAV S80 3AE

★★★★★
TOURING PARK

🚐 (183)   £14.90–£28.90
🚐 (183)   £14.90–£28.90
183 touring pitches

SPECIAL PROMOTIONS
Mid-week discount: pitch fee
for standard pitches for
stays on any Tue, Wed or
Thu night outside peak
season dates will be
reduced by 50%.

Clumber Park Caravan Club Site

Limetree Avenue, Clumber Park, Worksop S80 3AE
t (01909) 484758 f (01909) 479611
w **caravanclub.co.uk**

THE
CARAVAN
CLUB

There's a great feeling of spaciousness here, for
the site is on 20 acres within 4,000 acres of
parkland. Set in the heart of Sherwood Forest
and redeveloped to a high standard in 2002.
Visit Nottingham Castle and the watersports
centre at Holme Pierrepont.

open All year
payment credit/debit cards, cash, cheques

directions From the junction of the A1 and A5
take the A614 signposted to Nottingham for 0.5
miles. Turn right into Clumber Park site. The club
is signposted thereafter.

General 🗺📶🏕🔌☀🔄🚐🍴🚐
Leisure ⛰

All Assessed Accommodation

Derbyshire

ALSOP-EN-LE-DALE

...vendale Caravan & Leisure Park
★★★
...liday, Touring & Camping Park
...endale Caravan & Leisure Park,
...xton Road, Ashbourne
...6 1QU
(01335) 310311
enquiries@rivendalecaravanpark.
co.uk
rivendalecaravanpark.co.uk

AMBERGATE

...e Firs Caravan Club Site
★★★★ *Touring & Camping Park*
...ch Lane, Belper
...56 2JH
(01773) 852913
caravanclub.co.uk

ASHBOURNE

...hbourne Camping Caravanning
...ub ★★★★
...uring & Camping Park
...glers Coach House, Belper Road,
...hbourne, Derbyshire
...6 3EN

...hbourne Heights Park
...liday, Touring & Camping Park
...nny Bentley, Ashbourne,
...rbyshire
...6 1LE
01335 350228
northdales.co.uk/asbourne

...ackwall Plantation Caravan
...ub ★★★★ *Touring & Camping Park*
...k Ireton, Ashbourne
...6 3JL
(01335) 370903
caravanclub.co.uk

...llow Top Holiday Park ★★★★
...liday, Touring & Camping Park
...xton Road, Sandybrook,
...hbourne
...6 2AQ
(01335) 344020
enquiries@callowtop.co.uk
callowtop.co.uk

BAKEWELL

...atsworth Park Caravan Club
...te ★★★★★ *Touring Park*
...atsworth, Bakewell
...45 1PN
(01246) 582226

BELPER

...oadholme Lane Caravan Park
★★★ *Touring Park*
...oadholme Lane, Belper
...E56 2JF
(01773) 823517
broadholme-caravanpark.co.uk

BIRCHOVER

...rchover *Camping Barn*
...rn Farm, Birchover, Matlock
...E4 2BL
(01629) 650245

BUXTON

...ottage Farm Caravan Park ★★★
...ouring & Camping Park
...eech Croft, Blackwell in the Peak,
...uxton
...K17 9TQ
(01298) 85330
mail@cottagefarmsite.co.uk
cottagefarmsite.co.uk

...rin Low Caravan Club Site
★★★★ *Touring & Camping Park*
...rin Low Road, Ladmanlow, Buxton
...K17 6UJ
(01298) 77735
caravanclub.co.uk

Lime Tree Park ★★★★
Holiday, Touring & Camping Park
ROSE AWARD
Dukes Drive, Buxton
SK17 9RP
t (01298) 22988

Newhaven Caravan and Camping
Park ★★★
Holiday, Touring & Camping Park
Newhaven, Buxton
SK17 0DT
t (01298) 84300
e bobmacara@ntlworld.com
w newhavencaravanpark.co.uk

DERBY

Elvaston Castle Caravan Club Site
★★★ *Touring Park*
Borrowash Road, Elvaston, Derby
DE72 3EP
t (01332) 571342
w caravanclub.co.uk

EDALE

Edale *Camping Barn*
Cotefield Farm, Ollerbrook, Hope
Valley
S33 7ZG
t (01433) 670273

EYAM

YHA Bretton *Bunkhouse*
Bretton, Eyam, Hope Valley
S32 5QD
t 0870 770 5720
w yha.org.uk

FLAGG

Knotlow Farm ★★
Touring & Camping Park
Flagg, Buxton
SK17 9QP
t (01298) 85313

Pomeroy Caravan and Camping
Park ★★ *Touring & Camping Park*
Street House Farm, Pomeroy,
Buxton
SK17 9QG
t (01298) 83259

HADFIELD

Crowden Camping and
Caravanning Club Site ★★
Touring & Camping Park
Crowden, Glossop
SK13 1HZ
t (01457) 866057
w campingandcaravanningclub.co.
uk/crowden

HATHERSAGE

Abney Camping Barn
Camping Barn
Abney, Hathersage, Hope Valley
S32 1AH
t (01433) 650481
w independenthostelguide.co.uk

HAYFIELD

Hayfield Camping and
Caravanning Club Site ★★★
Camping Park
Kinder Road, Hayfield, High Peak
SK22 2LE
t (01663) 745394
w campingandcaravanningclub.co.
uk/hayfield

MIDDLETON

Castle Farm Camping Barn
Camping Barn
Middleton-by-Youlgreave, Bakewell
DE45 1LS
t (01629) 636746

RIPLEY

Golden Valley Caravan &
Camping ★★★★
Touring & Camping Park
Golden Valley, Coach Road, Alfreton
DE55 4ES
t (01773) 513881
e enquiries@goldenvalleycar
avanpark.co.uk
w goldenvalleycaravanpark.co.uk

STAVELEY

Poolsbrook Country Park Caravan
Club Site ★★★★★ *Touring Park*
Staveley, Chesterfield
S43 3LS
t (01246) 470659
w caravanclub.co.uk

SWADLINCOTE

Beehive Farm Woodland Lakes
★★★ *Touring & Camping Park*
Rosliston, Swadlincote
DE12 8HZ
t (01283) 763981
e info@beehivefarm-woodl
andlakes.co.uk
w beehivefarm-woodlandlakes.co.uk

TADDINGTON

Taddington Camping Barn
Camping Barn
The Woodlands, Taddington, Buxton
SK17 9UD
t (01298) 85730

TANSLEY

Lickpenny Caravan Park ★★★★
Touring Park
Lickpenny Lane, Tansley, Matlock
DE4 5GF
t (01629) 583040
e lickpenny@btinternet.com
w lickpennycaravanpark.co.uk

Packhorse Farm Bungalow C&C
★★★ *Touring Park*
Packhorse Farm, Foxholes Lane,
Matlock
DE4 5LF
t (01629) 580950

WHATSTANDWELL

Birchwood Farm Caravan Park
★★
Holiday, Touring & Camping Park
Wirksworth Road, Whatstandwell,
Matlock
DE4 5HS
t (01629) 822280
e carol@birchwoodfcp.co.uk
w birchwoodfcp.co.uk

YOULGREAVE

Bakewell Camping and
Caravaning Club Site ★★★★
Touring & Camping Park
Hopping Farm, Youlgreave,
Bakewell
DE45 1NA
t (01629) 636555
w campingandcaravanningclub.co.
uk/bakewell

Leicestershire & Rutland

MARKET BOSWORTH

Bosworth Water Trust ★★★
Touring & Camping Park
Wellesborough Road, Market
Bosworth
CV13 6PD
t (01455) 291876
e info@bosworthwatertrust.co.uk
w bosworthwatertrust.co.uk

MARKET HARBOROUGH

Brook Meadow ★★
Holiday & Camping Park
Welford Road, Sibbertoft, Market
Harborough
LE16 9UJ
t (01858) 880886
e brookmeadow@farmline.com
w brookmeadow.co.uk

MOIRA

Conkers Camping and
Caravanning Club Site ★★★★
Touring Park
Enterprise Glade, Bath Lane, Moira,
Swadlincote
DE12 6BD
t (01283) 224925
e customerservices@yha.org.uk
w campingandcaravanningclub.co.
uk/conkers

WHISSENDINE

Greendale Farm Caravan &
Camping Park ★★★★
Touring & Camping Park
Pickwell Lane, Whissendine,
Oakham
LE15 7LB
t (01664) 474516
e enq@rutlandgreendale.co.uk
w rutlandgreendale.co.uk

Lincolnshire

ANDERBY CREEK

Anderby Springs Caravan Estate
★★★ *Holiday Park*
The White House, Anderby Creek,
Skegness, Skegness
PE24 5XW
t (01754) 872265
w ukparks.co.uk/anderby/

BARTON-UPON-HUMBER

Silver Birches Tourist Park ★★★
Touring & Camping Park
Waterside Road, Barton-upon-
Humber
DN18 5BA
t (01652) 632509
e info@silverbirchescaravanpark.co.
uk

BOSTON

Orchard Park ★★★
Holiday, Touring & Camping Park
Frampton Lane, Hubberts Bridge,
Boston
PE20 3QU
t (01205) 290368
e info@orchardpark.co.uk
w orchardpark.co.uk

Pilgrims Way Caravan and
Camping Park
Holiday, Touring & Camping Park
Church Green Road, Fishtoft,
Boston, Lincs
PE21 0QY

BURGH-LE-MARSH

Sycamore Farm ★★★
Holiday, Touring & Camping Park
Chalk Lane, Burgh le Marsh,
Skegness, Skegness
PE24 5HN
t (01754) 810833
e lloyd@sycamorefarm.co.uk
w sycamorefarm.net

Sycamore Lakes ★★★★
Touring & Camping Park
Skegness Road, Burgh le Marsh
PE24 5LN
t (01754) 811411
w sycamorelakes.co.uk

CHAPEL ST LEONARDS

Tomlinsons Leisure Park ★★★★
Holiday Park **ROSE AWARD**
South Road, Chapel St Leonards,
Skegness
PE24 5TL
t (01754) 872241
w tomlinsons-leisure.co.uk

CROFT

Pine Trees Caravan Park ★★★
Touring Park
Croft Bank, Skegness, Skegness
PE24 4RE
t (01754) 762949
e pinetreesholidays@yahoo.co.uk
w pinetreesholidays.co.uk

EAST FIRSBY

**Manor Farm Caravan and
Camping Park ★★★**
Touring & Camping Park
Manor Farm, East Firsby, Market
Rasen
LN8 2DB
t (01673) 878258
e info@lincolnshire-lanes.com
w lincolnshire-lanes.com

FLEET HARGATE

Delph Bank Caravan Park ★★★★
Touring & Camping Park
Old Main Road, Fleet Hargate, Fleet
Hargate
PE12 8LL
t (01406) 422910
e enquiries@delphbank.co.uk
w delphbank.co.uk

FOLKINGHAM

Low Farm Touring Park ★★★
Touring Park
Spring Lane, Folkingham,
Folkingham
NG34 0SJ
t (01529) 497322

HORNCASTLE

Ashby Park ★★★★
Holiday, Touring & Camping Park
Ashby Park, West Ashby
LN9 5PP
t (01507) 527966
e ashbypark@btconnect.com
w ukparks.co.uk/ashby

**Elmhirst Lakes Caravan Park
★★★★** *Holiday Park*
Elmhirst Road, Horncastle,
Horncastle
LN9 5LU
t (01507) 527533
e info@elmhirstlakes.co.uk
w elmhirstlakes.co.uk

HUMBERSTON

**Thorpe Park Holiday Centre
★★★★** *Holiday Park*
Thorpe Park Holiday Centre,
Grimsby
DN35 0PW
t (01442) 868325
e theresa.ludlow@bourne-leisure.
co.uk
w british-holidays.co.uk

INGOLDMELLS

Coastfield Caravan Park ★★★
Holiday Park
Vickers Point, Roman Bank,
Ingoldmells, Skegness
PE25 1JU
t (01754) 872592

Country Meadows ★★★★
Holiday & Touring Park
Anchor Lane, Ingoldmells,
Ingoldmells
PE25 1LZ
t (01754) 874455
e brochure@countrymeadows.co.uk
w countrymeadows.co.uk

Kingfisher Park ★★★ *Holiday Park*
Sea Lane, Ingoldmells, Ingoldmells
PE25 1PG
t (01754) 872465
e kingfisherpark@e-lindsey.gov.uk

KIRKBY-ON-BAIN

**Woodhall Spa Camping and
Caravanning Club Site ★★★★**
Touring & Camping Park
Wellsyke Lane, Kirkby-on-Bain,
Woodhall Spa
LN10 6YU
t (01526) 352911
w campingandcaravanningclub.co.
uk/woodhallspa

LINCOLN

Hartsholme Country Park ★★★
Touring Park
Skellingthorpe Road, Lincoln
LN6 0EY
t (01522) 873578
e hartsholmecp@lincoln.gov.uk
w lincoln.gov.uk

MABLETHORPE

Golden Sands Holiday Park ★★★
Holiday & Touring Park
Quebec Road, Mablethorpe
LN12 1QJ
t (01507) 477871
w goldensands-park.co.uk

Grange Leisure Park ★★
Holiday & Touring Park
Alford Road, Mablethorpe,
Mablethorpe
LN12 1NE
t (01507) 472814
e pulse@lincolnshiretourism.com
w grangeleisurepark.co.uk

Holivans Ltd ★★★ *Touring Park*
Dept G, Quebec Road, Mablethorpe,
Mablethorpe
LN12 1QH
t (01507) 473327
e holivans@enterprise.net
w holivans.co.uk

**Mablethorpe Camping and
Caravanning Club Site ★★★★**
Touring & Camping Park
Highfields, 120 Church Lane,
Mablethorpe, Mablethorpe
LN12 2NU
t (01507) 472374
w campingandcaravanningclub.co.
uk/mablethorpe

**Trusthorpe Springs Leisure Park
★★** *Holiday & Touring Park*
Mile Lane, Trusthorpe, Mablethorpe
LN12 2QQ
t (01507) 441384
e d.brailsford@ukonline.co.uk

MUMBY

Inglenook Caravan Park ★★★
Touring Park
Hogsthorpe Road, Mumby, Alford,
Alford
LN13 9SE
t (01507) 490365
e pulse@lincolnshiretourism.com

NORMANBY

**Normanby Hall Country Park
Accommodation ★★★**
Touring Park
Normanby, Scunthorpe, Scunthorpe
DN15 9HU
t (01724) 720588
e normanby.hall@northlincs.gov.uk
w northlincs.gov.uk/normanby

NORTH SCARLE

**Lowfields Country Holiday Fishing
Retreat ★★★★** *Holiday Park*
ROSE AWARD
Eagle Road, North Scarle, Lincoln
LN6 9EN
t (01522) 778717
e lowretreat@aol.com
w lowfields-retreat.co.uk

OLD LEAKE

Long Acres ★★★★
Touring & Camping Park
Station Road, Old Leake, Boston
PE22 9RF
t (01205) 871555
e lacp@btconnect.com
w longacres-caravanpark.co.uk

SALTFLEET

Sunnydale Holiday Park ★★★★★
Holiday & Touring Park
ROSE AWARD
Sea Lane, Saltfleet, Louth
LN11 7RP
t (01507) 338100
w gbholidayparks.co.uk

SCUNTHORPE

Brookside Caravan Park ★★★★★
Touring Park
Stather Road, Burton-upon-Stather,
Scunthorpe
DN15 9DH
t (01724) 721369
e brooksidecp@aol.com
w brooksidecaravanpark.co.uk

SKEGNESS

**Bryanston Kenmore Southview
Ltd ★★★★** *Holiday & Touring Park*
Burgh Road, Skegness, Skegness
PE25 2LA
t (01754) 896000
e holidays@southview-leisure.com
w southview-leisure.com

**Butlins at Skegness Butlins
Limited ★★★★** *Holiday Village*
Roman Bank, Skegness
PE25 1NJ
t (01754) 762311

Butlins Skegness Caravans ★★★
Holiday & Touring Park
Butlins Skyline Caravan Park,
Ingoldmells, Skegness
PE25 1NJ
t (01754) 614444
e skegnesscaravanbookings@
bourne-leisure.co.uk
w butlins.com/skegness

Manor Farm Caravan Park ★★
Touring & Camping Park
Sea Road, Anderby
PE24 5YB
t (01507) 490372
e skegnessinfo@e-lindsey.gov.uk

Richmond Holiday Centre ★★★
Holiday & Touring Park
T/A Richmond Holiday Centre,
Richmond Drive, Skegness, Skegness
PE25 3TQ
t (01754) 762097
e sales@richmondholidays.com
w richmondholidays.com

**Skegness Sands Touring Site
★★★★** *Holiday & Touring Park*
Skegness Sands, Winthorpe Avenue,
Skegness, Skegness
PE25 1QZ
t (01754) 761484
e info@skegnesssands.co.uk
w skegnesssands.co.uk

**Skegness Water Leisure Park
★★★**
Holiday, Touring & Camping Park
Walls Lane, Skegness
PE25 1JF
t (01754) 899400
e enquiries@skegnesswaterle
isurepark.co.uk
w skegnesswaterleisurepark.co.uk

Walsh's Holiday Park ★★★★
Holiday Park
Roman Bank, Skegness
PE25 1QP
t (01754) 764485

SPANBY

**Highfields Country Holiday
Fishing Retreat ★★★★**
Holiday Park **ROSE AWARD**
Mareham Lane, Spanby, Sleaford
NG34 0AT
t (01529) 241185
e info@highretreat.co.uk
w highfields-retreat.co.uk

SUTTON-ON-SEA

Cherry Tree Site ★★★★★
Touring Park
Huttoft Road, Sutton-on-Sea
LN12 2RU
t (01507) 441626
e info@cherrytreesite.co.uk
w cherrytreesite.co.uk

SUTTON ST EDMUND

**Orchard View Caravan & Camping
Park ★★★**
Holiday, Touring & Camping Park
102 Broadgate, Sutton St Edmund
Spalding
PE12 0LT
t (01945) 700482
e raymariaorchardview@btinterne
com

TRUSTHORPE

**Seacroft Holiday Estate Ltd
★★★★** *Holiday & Touring Park*
ROSE AWARD
Sutton Road, Trusthorpe,
Mablethorpe
LN12 2PN
t (01507) 472421
e info@seacroftcaravanpark.co.uk
w seacroftcaravanpark.co.uk

**Sutton Springs Holiday Estate
★★★** *Holiday Park*
Sutton Road, Trusthorpe,
Mablethorpe
LN12 2PZ
t (01507) 441333
e d.brailsford@ukonline.co.uk

WOODHALL SPA

Bainland Country Park ★★★★★
Holiday, Touring & Camping Park
ROSE AWARD
Horncastle Road, Woodhall Spa,
Woodhall Spa
LN10 6UX
t (01526) 352903
e bookings@bainland.co.uk
w bainland.co.uk

Northamptonshire

FINESHADE

**Top Lodge Caravan Club Site
★★★★** *Touring Park*
Fineshade, Duddington, Corby,
Corby
NN17 3BB
t (01780) 444617
w caravanclub.co.uk

Nottinghamshire

NEWARK

lestone Caravan Park ★★★★★
uring Park
eat North Road, Cromwell,
wark, Newark
623 6JE
 (01636) 821244
 enquiries@experiencenottingham
 shire.com

NOTTINGHAM

National Water Sports Centre Caravan & Camping Park ★★
Touring & Camping Park
Adbolton Lane, Holme Pierrepont,
Nottingham
NG12 2LU
t 01159 824 721
e nwsccampsite@nottscc.gov.uk
w nwscnotts.com

RUFFORD

Center Parcs Sherwood Forest
★★★★★ *Forest Holiday Village*
Rufford, Newark
NG22 9DN
w centerparcs.co.uk/villages/
 sherwood/index.jsp

SOUTH MUSKHAM

Smeaton's Lakes Caravan and Fishing Park ★★★
Touring & Camping Park
Great North Road, Newark, Newark
NG23 6ED
t (01636) 605088
e lesley@smeatonslakes.co.uk
w smeatonslakes.co.uk

SUTTON IN ASHFIELD

Teversal Camping and Caravanning Club Site ★★★★★
Touring & Camping Park
Silverhill Lane, Teversal, Sutton-in-
Ashfield
NG17 3JJ
t (01623) 551838
e stay@shardaroba.co.uk
w campingandcaravanningclub.co.
 uk/teversal

WORKSOP

Clumber Park Caravan Club Site
★★★★★ *Touring Park*
Limetree Avenue, Clumber Park,
Worksop
S80 3AE
t (01909) 484758
w caravanclub.co.uk

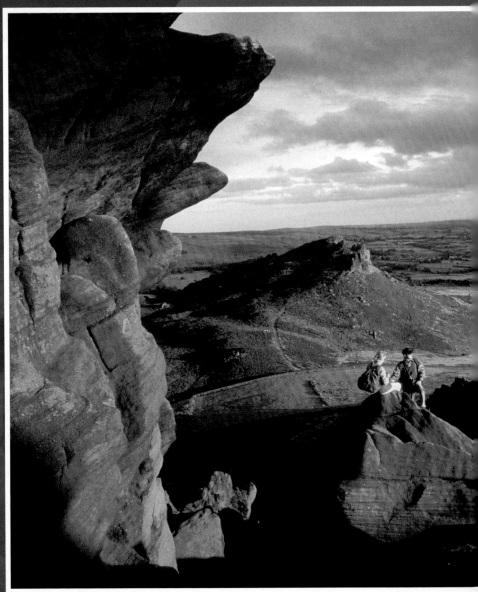

The Roaches, Peak District, Staffordshire, England.

Heart of England

Herefordshire, Shropshire, Staffordshire, Warwickshire, West Midlands, Worcestershire

Heart of England

Like the rest of England, the Heart of England is charmingly individual, but the bonus is that the Heart of England is at the hub of Britain's road network, so exploring every last bit of it is made very easy!

You can even fly direct into the international airport at Birmingham right in the centre of the region. Birmingham is also now able to offer a world-class cultural scene, superb shopping, top attractions, fantastic restaurants, music and nightlife, major international events and exhibitions.

Take some time to visit the Cotswolds, taking in the many honey-coloured villages. The potteries of Staffordshire to the north of the region are close to Shakespeare's Stratford-on-Avon and the nearby lesser-known parts of Warwickshire. Close by lies the Black Country, and a visit here will reveal a rich seam of art, crafts, tradition and culture with modern architectural design sitting alongside villages from the Victorian era.

Explore the counties of Herefordshire and Shropshire along the beautiful borderlands of England and Wales, sampling the myriad of excellent restaurants and locally produced food. In Worcestershire you can find fine churches, historic buildings and a thriving arts scene with internationally acclaimed festivals and events.

This is just a taster of what's on offer in the Heart of England, visit and discover the rest!

Herefordshire

An ancient city on the banks of the River Wye, Hereford is the commercial and artistic heart of the county. Don't be surprised to find historic buildings housing modern shops and modern buildings holding historic treasures. The Left Bank Village grace the banks of the beautiful River Wye.

Eastnor

Mainly known for Eastnor Castle, Eastnor is in the centre of the county, between the Cotswolds and the Welsh Marches. In the dramatic setting of the Malvern Hills and surrounded by a beautiful deer park, arboretum and lake, the fairy-tale castle is the home of the Hervey-Bathurst family. Eastnor has undergone a triumphant renaissance in recent years and many of the castle's treasures are now displayed for the first time in richly decorated splendour.

Leominster

Located in the heart of the beautiful border countryside, where England and Wales nudge each other back and forth along Offa's Dyke, lies Leominster, an historic market town. Leominster (pronounced 'Lemster') dates back to the 7th century and is named after Earl Leofric, the husband of Lady Godiva who famously rode naked through the streets of Coventry on horseback. The town possesses some fine examples of architecture throughout the ages. See medieval

overhangs in Drapers Lane and School Lane, and Georgian splendour on Broad Street. The town centre has recently become semi-pedestrianised, recreating the bustling atmosphere of a market town. A market is still held each Friday in Corn Square.

Ross-on-Wye

Perched on a sandstone cliff high above a broad loop of the magnificent River Wye, the dramatic setting of Ross-on-Wye belies the friendliness of a town that has restored the spirits of world-weary travellers for centuries. A striking 17th-century market hall dominates the town centre and while the upper storey is now a fascinating heritage centre, the lower level still shelters twice-weekly markets. There is also an excellent range of shops from antiques and craft specialists to some of the more familiar high street names.

Symonds Yat

The river has carved a dramatic gorge through towering limestone cliffs that are home to a myriad of birds including the rare peregrine falcon. The two settlements nestling in the depths of the gorge, offer a variety of attractions and are connected, during the day and when conditions allow, by an unusual man-powered rope ferry. The rope ferry offers a tranquil way to cross from Symonds Yat East to Symonds Yat West. The watery thoroughfare of the River Wye provides endless opportunities for leisure and relaxation. Renowned the world over for the quality of its salmon, the river is loved by fishermen. Walkers enjoy the rich wildlife along the banks and canoeists can paddle for miles through magnificent scenery.

Shropshire

The county town of Shrewsbury is a stunning historic town with over 660 listed buildings and some very strange street names. Part of the town's medieval street plan still exists as a unique maze of narrow alleys, which criss-cross the town centre. You will find great shopping and a colourful indoor market.

Bridgnorth

Bridgnorth is actually two towns: the High Town (good views down) and the Low Town (good views up). The Low Town was once a thriving port along the banks of the River Severn; while others preferred to live around the castle and the churches, high on the cliffs above. Many of the 16th and 17th-century houses still remain. High and Low are connected by England's oldest (and steepest) inland funicular railway, The Bridgnorth Cliff Railway. At 201 feet long and rising 110 feet, it is easier than walking. The more energetic can amble up one of the seven sets of steps of the steep cartway, where goods were once hauled to the market above. The carts are gone but the markets remain. Antiques and local produce are particular specialities. By the time you reach the top, you'll probably need a sit down – and where better than the Castle Gardens. What's left of the Castle leans at an alarming angle, even greater than the Tower of Pisa.

Ironbridge

It was at Ironbridge that the large-scale production of cast iron was first developed using a process pioneered by Abraham Darby. Items made in Ironbridge were shipped all over the world. Here in 1779 the world's first cast iron bridge was built spanning the River Severn – beautifully constructed, totally innovative – today the Ironbridge stands as a permanent reminder of an industrial past. Ironbridge is regarded as the birthplace of the Industrial Revolution and is a UNESCO World Heritage Site. The nine Ironbridge Gorge Museums tell this momentous story and offer a chance to step back to a time when the pounding of steam hammers and clatter of horses'

hooves on cobbles were commonplace. You can also visit The Maws Craft Centre, the Open Air Museum of Steel Sculpture, a Victorian Police Station and Old Court House. There are leisure boat trips on the River, walks and cycle ways and you can even turn your hand to making a Coracle with the Green Wood Trust.

Telford

Telford is named after Thomas Telford the renowned civil engineer. Gleaming buildings and hi-tech businesses mark it out as a town for the future. One of the UK's fastest growing and most successful new towns, it contrasts with its neighbour, Ironbridge the birthplace of the Industrial Revolution. The Wrekin is a curious, legendary hill which is 1,335 feet tall and perhaps Shropshire's best known landmark. From the top you can see 15 counties and it dominates the view of Telford and Ironbridge.

Staffordshire

Stafford, regionally renowned as a bed of floral splendour, attracts visitors from all over the British Isles. Stunning annual displays from May to October draw visitors back time and again. Stafford Castle and its visitor centre, glorious parks, tranquil walks and busy shopping thoroughfares are waiting to be discovered. Do as little or as much as you want.

Alton

For sheer breathtaking exhilaration there is Britain's number one attraction, Alton Towers. Nestling in beautiful countryside, it has more than 125 rides and attractions for all the family, beautifully landscaped into magnificent gardens. For more horticultural delights, visit the Dorothy Clive Garden, Bridgemere Garden World or Byrkley Park – or seek out the Victorian gardens of Biddulph Grange, a truly unique national treasure.

Lichfield

Just north of Birmingham is Lichfield, surrounded by Staffordshire countryside, it has a long and rich history. Famous for its magnificent, three spired, cathedral, Lichfield has been home to some of Britain's much loved and respected dignitaries such as the writer and wit, Samuel Johnson, actor and playwright David Garrick and Erasmus Darwin, inventor, scientist and grandfather of Charles Darwin. The Lichfield Garrick is an exciting venue

in the Midlands for art, theatre and conferences. Unusual and interesting shopping, plus a wide range of restaurants with dishes from around the world, help create an experience not to be missed.

Stoke-on-Trent

The UK's capital of china and known all over the world as The Potteries, with its unique combination of factory shops, visitor centres, ceramic museums and factory tours. Award-winning museums tell the full story of 'The Potteries', including outstanding ceramic collections and the opportunity to throw your own pot. The city boasts internationally acclaimed visitor centres at Royal Doulton, Spode and Wedgwood all offering craft demonstrations, factory tours, stunning museum collections and exciting shopping opportunities. Pick up a bargain at one of the 40 or so pottery factory shops, selling everything from dinner services to figurines, tiles to jewellery.

The Peak District

Explore the Peak District, ideal for leisure and activity holidays. From the spectacular crags and dales of the Staffordshire Moorlands to the sweeping panoramas of the White Peak, you'll find ample opportunity for walking, hiking and cycling, or the more daring challenges of rock climbing, caving and hang gliding. Leek is the principal town of the Staffordshire Moorlands and the most important centre on the south western edge of the Peak District. Locally it is called 'The Queen of the Moorlands' and stands on a hill in a large bend in the River Churnet.

Warwickshire

The historic town of Warwick is best known for its magnificent castle, home to generations of the all-powerful Earls of Warwick. A magnificent fortress towering over the banks of the River Avon, Warwick Castle is one of the finest medieval castles in England. There is much to explore in Warwick itself plus a wealth of antique and gift shops.

Kenilworth

Discover the ruined glory of Elizabethan England amid the red sandstone ruins of Kenilworth Castle. Hear of lovers' trysts, bloody battles and water pageants. Visit Leicester's Gatehouse, reopened following a £2.5m restoration project. The gatehouse includes a major exhibition exploring the connections between Kenilworth and Elizabeth I. From the castle, stroll through Abbey Fields with its lake, remains of an historic abbey, swimming pool (both indoors and outdoors) and children's play area. See the cottages of 'Little Virginia' where Sir Walter Raleigh planted England's first potatoes.

Royal Leamington Spa

Royal Leamington Spa is a fashionable and elegant regency town in the heart of South Warwickshire. With Georgian and Victorian architecture, tree-lined avenues and squares, stunning parks and gardens, it offers a unique shopping, dining and cultural experience. The magnificent Royal Pump Rooms house the elegant Assembly Rooms, a traditional café and the town's art gallery and museum. See displays on the historic use of the Pump Rooms and spa treatments. You can even sample the spa water! Opposite the Royal Pump Rooms lie the Jephson Gardens, perfect for a gentle stroll. These Grade II listed gardens of horticultural excellence have undergone a £4.3 million restoration project and include a sensory garden, temperate glasshouse, refurbished boathouse and children's play area.

Rugby

Home to the game of Rugby Football, where the sport began in 1823. Rugby School, where the game originated is still used for matches to this day. Enthusiasts from all over the world visit to see the statue of William Webb Ellis and read the famous words on the commemoration plaque at Rugby School Close. Rugby School itself dominates much of the centre and south of the town. It was the subject of the famous Thomas Hughes novel *'Tom Brown's School Days'*.

Stratford-upon-Avon

Discover the town in which Shakespeare was born and grew up, where he gained inspiration for his work and even where he used to poach deer! Beautifully situated on the River Avon, Stratford has a number of attractions linked to its famous son. A stroll along the River Avon will lead you to Holy Trinity Church – Shakespeare's final resting place. Stratford has many other attractions including Guide Friday, The Butterfly Farm and Cox's Yard. For the visitor, the area offers the best of town and country – not one but two world renowned motor museums, Britain's national organic garden and a living Roman fort, canals and country churches, great houses and battlefields. The surrounding countryside has six fascinating and historical National Trust houses and gardens, including Hidcote Manor and Charlecote Park, with their recent restoration work and exciting new discoveries.

West Midlands

Birmingham is a city where yesterday and today combine to give you a city full of surprises. With its fascinating history and world-class cultural scene, combined with superb shopping, major international events and exhibitions, great nightlife and award-winning restaurants, Birmingham has a unique quality that brings with it an exciting and dynamic spirit.

Coventry

Coventry, city of myth and legend, famous for Lady Godiva and St George the dragon-slayer, is the ideal visitor destination with its great shopping facilities, range of bars, restaurants and historical buildings. Discover the city that is re-inventing itself. Coventry possesses a whole host of historic buildings and beautiful parks right in the centre of the city. From the Mediaeval St Mary's Guildhall and the alms houses of Fords and Bonds Hospitals to the new modern Priory Gardens and Garden of International Friendship.

The Black Country

Tour the Black Country and you travel a trail through time, from a primeval shallow sea, to the birth of the Industrial Revolution, to the modern day. A visit to The Black Country reveals a rich seam of art, crafts, tradition and culture set amidst historic towns and inviting green countryside. Just 30 minutes by bus or train from Birmingham International Airport you can watch Black Country artisans in authentic 18th- and 19th-century workshops busy at their crafts. Well worth a visit are the leatherworks at Walsall, the Red House Cone and Broadfield House glass-making museums at Dudley and the enamelling workshops at Bilston. Alternatively, visit the Black Country Living Museum at Dudley, where you will see the painstakingly reconstructed original buildings and cross the portal into Victorian times, magically recreated for you. Prepare to be amazed by the colourful flotillas of narrowboats and myriad of canals that twine through the towns and countryside. Perhaps you prefer to walk along quiet nature trails or through peaceful green countryside where you can see historic castles and stately homes. Or spend time at Sandwell Valley Country Park, home to rare, native farm breeds like the Tamworth pig.

Wolverhampton

The city has a vibrant and multi-cultural offering for the tourist ranging from a visit to Wightwick Manor to view William Morris originals to a day out at the races at Wolverhampton's all weather race course, Dunstall Park. Then end your day with an evening at the Grand Theatre or one of the many concerts at the Civic Halls. Other award-winning attractions such as Bantock House and Park, Moseley Old Hall, Wolverhampton Art Gallery, Bilston Craft Gallery & Museum only enhance the city further.

Worcestershire

Situated on the banks of the River Severn, the city of Worcester has a rich and varied heritage to explore from the 11th-century cathedral to Royal Worcester porcelain factory with its museum and visitor centre. Apart from historical interests, there are a variety of other attractions including riverside walks, boat trips and excellent high street and speciality shopping.

Broadway

Broadway is reputed to be one of the most beautiful villages in the country; the honey-coloured stone of the houses have attracted visitors for centuries. The village stands at the foot of the Cotswold Hills immediately adjacent to the base of the 1,026 ft high Fish Hill which is the highest point of the northern end of the hills. The superb skyline is dominated by Broadway Tower, a folly built by the sixth Earl of Coventry in the 18th century. It is situated in a 30-acre country park and from the top of its 65 ft tower spectacular views can be enjoyed over 12 counties.

Droitwich

Unique among the spa towns of Britain, Droitwich achieved fame and recognition as a Brine Spa. The natural brine contains 2.5 lbs of salt per gallon – 10 times stronger than sea water and only rivalled by the Dead Sea. Visitors do not drink the waters at Droitwich, but experience the therapeutic and remedial benefits by floating weightless in the warm brine of the bathing pool. Surrounded by beautiful Worcestershire countryside, Droitwich is

a town of great charm and character, offering its visitors plenty to see and enjoy.

Evesham

The town witnessed the Battle of Evesham in 1265 when Simon de Montfort, known as the father of the English Parliament, was brutally killed. His remains were brought by the monks from the battlefield, (Greenhill at the north of the town) and solemnly buried in front of the High Altar in the Abbey Church. A modest stone memorial in the park marks the spot where the burial took place.

The Malverns

The Malverns are the centre piece of a wonderful region stretching from lowland, riverside Upton upon Severn to Malvern itself, and up the River Teme's winding course through northwest Worcestershire's hills to delightful Tenbury Wells. The pure water of the Malvern Hills springs made Malvern a 19th-century spa with the elegance to become a place of culture, attracting people like Sir Edward Elgar and George Bernard Shaw. From the hills you will see some of England's grandest views, eastwards towards the Cotswolds, northwards to Shropshire and westward to the misty mountains of Wales.

Upton upon Severn

Located in the south of Worcestershire, the pretty town of Upton upon Severn is a haven for boat enthusiasts. It was an important coaching stop and the many Georgian Inns are a testament to this, notably the White Lion, which is said to be the model for parts of Henry Fielding's 'Tom Jones'.

Where to Go

 Attractions with this sign participate in the **Visitor Attraction Quality Assurance Scheme** (see page 6) which recognises high standards in all aspects of the visitor experience.

ENTERTAINMENT & CULTURE

Avoncroft Museum of Historic Buildings
Bromsgrove, Worcestershire,
B60 4JR
(01527) 831363
www.avoncroft.org.uk
Wander re-erected historic buildings:
a working windmill, furnished houses
and more.

Black Country Living Museum
Dudley, West Midlands, DY1 4SQ
(0121) 557 9643
www.bclm.co.uk
Wander through original shops and
houses, ride fairground attractions,
view the underground coalmine.
Friendly open-air museum.

Blists Hill Victorian Town
Telford, Shropshire, TF7 5DU
(01952) 884391
www.ironbridge.org.uk
Travel back in time to a superbly
recreated Victorian town and meet the
costumed locals.

Cadbury World
Birmingham, West Midlands,
B30 2LU
0845 450 3599
www.cadburyworld.co.uk
Unwrap the story of Cadbury's
chocolate, with chocolate-making
demonstrations and free samples.
Shop, restaurant, free parking.

Compton Verney
Stratford-upon-Avon,
Warwickshire, CV35 9HZ
(01926) 645500
www.comptonverney.org.uk
Art gallery featuring six permanent
collections, including British folk art,
Chinese bronzes and Neapolitan
masterpieces.

Heritage Motor Centre
Stratford-upon-Avon,
Warwickshire, CV35 0BJ
(01926) 641188
www.heritage-motor-centre.co.uk
See the world's largest collection of
British cars. Interactive exhibitions,
rallies, events and shows.

Ironbridge Gorge Museums
Telford, Shropshire, TF8 7DQ
(01952) 884391
www.ironbridge.org.uk
World Heritage Site featuring ten
brilliant museums, from a Victorian
town to Coalport China.

Jackfield Tile Museum
Telford, Shropshire, TF8 7LJ
(01952) 884391
www.ironbridge.org.uk
At the Jackfield Tile Museum there are
tiles everywhere! The Victorians were
on a mission to not only make them,
but also to use them.

Museum of The Gorge
Telford, Shropshire, TF8 7NH
(01952) 884391
www.ironbridge.org.uk
At the Museum of the Gorge you can
view a 12 metre scale model of the
Gorge as it was in 1796.

Royal Air Force Museum Cosford
Telford, Shropshire, TF11 8UP
(01902) 376200
www.rafmuseum.org
Experience our Fun 'n' Flight
interactives and the flight simulator.
Browse warplanes, missiles and aero-
engine collections. Gallery, gifts and
restaurant.

The Courtyard Theatre
Stratford-upon-Avon,
Warwickshire, CV37 6BH
0844 800 1110
www.rsc.org.uk
Catch performances of Shakespeare
and other leading writers. Great all-
year programme.

The Elgar Birthplace Museum
Worcester, Worcestershire,
WR2 6RH
(01905) 333224
www.elgarmuseum.org
The great composer's country cottage
birthplace. The new Elgar Centre
explores his life, music and inspirations.

Thinktank-Birmingham Science Museum
Birmingham, West Midlands, B4 7XG
(0121) 202 2222
www.thinktank.ac
Investigate everything from locomotives and aircraft to taste buds and intestines.

FAMILY FUN

Alton Towers
Alton Towers area, Staffordshire, ST10 4DB
0870 520 4060
www.altontowers.com
High-adrenalin adventure on rides like Oblivion, Nemesis and Congo River Rapids. Children's attractions include Tweenies show.

Enginuity
Telford, Shropshire, TF8 7DG
(01952) 884391
www.ironbridge.org.uk
Put your ingenuity to the test at this interactive design and technology centre.

Go Ape! Highwire Forest Adventure - Cannock Forest
Rugeley, WS15 2UQ, Staffordshire
0845 643 9215
www.goape.co.uk
Take to the trees and experience an exhilarating course of rope bridges, tarzan swings and zip slides...all set high above the forest floor.

HERITAGE

Eastnor Castle
Ledbury, Herefordshire, HR8 1RL
(01531) 633160
www.eastnorcastle.com
Explore a fairytale Georgian castle that's a treasure trove of armour, pictures, tapestries and Italian furniture.

Ragley Hall
Stratford-upon-Avon, Warwickshire, B49 5NJ
(01789) 762090
www.ragleyhall.com
Delightful Palladian family home of the Marquess and Marchioness of Hertford. Formal gardens, beautiful parkland.

Red House Glass Cone
Stourbridge, West Midlands, DY8 4AZ
(01384) 812750
www.redhousecone.co.uk
Watch live glassmaking at this rare 18thC glass cone. Audio tour around the tunnels and furnace.

Severn Valley Railway
Bewdley, Worcestershire, DY12 1BG
(01299) 403816
www.svr.co.uk
Journey from Kidderminster to Bewdley via Bridgnorth and Highley by steam railway. Collection of locomotives and passenger coaches.

Shakespeare's Birthplace
Stratford-upon-Avon, Warwickshire, CV37 6QW
(01789) 204016
www.shakespeare.org.uk
The house where Shakespeare was born in 1564. See the acclaimed exhibition of his life.

Shugborough Estate
Stafford, Staffordshire, ST17 0XB
(01889) 881388
www.shugborough.org.uk
Rare, surviving, working estate featuring magnificent mansion house, servants' quarters, model farm and walled garden.

Warwick Castle
Warwick, Warwickshire, CV34 4QU
0870 442 2000
www.warwick-castle.co.uk
Tour the state rooms, armoury, dungeon, torture chamber, 'Kingmaker' and more at this enthralling medieval castle.

Wedgwood Visitor Centre
Stoke-on-Trent, Staffordshire, ST12 9FA
(01782) 282986
www.thewedgwoodvisitorcentre.com
Displays and factory tours provide a fascinating living memorial to the great English potter.

Weston Park
Stafford, Staffordshire, TF11 8LE
(01952) 852100
www.weston-park.com
The grounds combine 1,000 acres of natural beauty with three centuries of garden design.

NATURE & WILDLIFE

Birmingham Botanical Gardens and Glasshouses
Birmingham, West Midlands, B15 3TR
(0121) 454 1860
www.birminghambotanicalgardens.org.uk
Journey from tropical rainforest to desert conditions through four glasshouses. Landscaped, themed gardens and adventure playground.

Dudley Zoological Gardens
Dudley, West Midlands, DY1 4QB
(01384) 215313
www.dudleyzoo.org.uk
Lions and tigers, snakes and spiders. Rare and exotic animals, fair rides and land train.

Garden Organic Ryton
Coventry, Warwickshire, CV8 3LG
(024) 7630 3517
www.gardenorganic.org.uk
UK's national centre for organic gardening – 10 acres of glorious gardens and the Vegetable Kingdom.

Hatton Farm Village at Hatton Country World
Warwick, Warwickshire, CV35 8XA
(01926) 843411
www.hattonworld.com
Animals and children's fun in the Farm Village, crafts and gifts in the Shopping Village.

National Sea Life Centre
Birmingham, West Midlands,
B1 2HL
(0121) 643 6777
www.sealifeeurope.com
Marvel at over 3,000 sea creatures.
Experience the world's first 360-degree
transparent, tubular underwater walk-
through tunnel.

The Trentham Estate
Stoke-on-Trent, Staffordshire,
ST4 8AX
(01782) 646646
www.trenthamleisure.co.uk
England's largest garden restoration
project, 750 acres of park, woodland,
boat trips and retail village.

Hergest Croft Gardens
Kington, Herefordshire,
HR5 3EG
(01544) 230160
www.hergest.co.uk
Enjoy all-year interest: spring bulbs,
rhododendrons, azaleas, roses and
spectacular autumn colour.

Hoo Farm Animal
Kingdom
Telford, Shropshire, TF6 6DJ
(01952) 677917
www.hoofarm.com
Bottle feed lambs, ride ponies and
bikes, or watch the sheep steeplechase.

West Midland Safari
& Leisure Park
Bewdley, Worcestershire,
DY12 1LF
(01299) 402114
www.wmsp.co.uk
Drive-through safari, reptile house,
sea-lion theatre, hippo lakes, animal
encounters, amusements – all in 200
acres.

Events 2010

Crafts at the Castle
Warwick
www.warwick-castle.com
November

Flavours of Herefordshire
Food Festival
Holmer
www.visitherefordshire.co.uk/
October

Godiva Festival
Coventry
www.godivafestival.com
July

Herefordshire Walking
Festival
Unknown
www.visitherefordshire.co.uk
June

Large Model Aircraft Rally
Shifnal
www.rafmuseum.org
July

Lichfield Festival
Lichfield
www.lichfieldfestival.org
July

Ludlow Food & Drink
Festival
Ludlow
www.foodfestival.co.uk
September

Mini Fortnight - Events,
Exhibitions and Displays
Stratford-upon-Avon
www.minifestival.co.uk
August

RAF Cosford Air Show
Shifnal
www.cosfordairshow.co.uk
June

Shrewsbury Flower Show
Shrewsbury
www.shrewsburyflowershow.
org.uk
August

Spring Gardening Show
www.threecounties.co.uk/
springgardening
6th-9th May

Stratford-upon-Avon
Festival of Food
Stratford-upon-Avon
www.stratfordtcm.co.uk/
festivals-foodfest.php
September

The Royal Show
Coventry
www.royalshow.org.uk
July

University of the
Great Outdoors
www.visitherefordshire.co.uk/
May

V Festival
Stafford
www.vfestival.com
21–22 August

Warwick Castle
Summer Concerts
Warwick
www.warwick-castle.com
July

Warwick Folk Festival
Warwick
www.warwickfolkfestival.co.uk
July

Wenlock Olympian Games
Much Wenlock
www.wenlock-olympian-
society.org.uk
July

Worcester Festival
Worcester
www.worcesterfestival.co.uk
August

Where to Eat

The Heart of England region has great places to eat. The restaurant reviews on these pages are just a small selection from the highly respected *The Good Food Guide 2010*. Please see pages 20–21 for further information on the guide and details of a Special Offer for our readers.

HEREFORDSHIRE

The Malthouse Restaurant
Inspired and intricate food
Church Lane, Ledbury, HR8 1DW
Tel no: (01531) 634443
www.malthouse-ledbury.co.uk
Modern British | £27

Make your way up a cobbled lane just off Ledbury's market square to find this atmospheric restaurant spread over two floors of a converted barn, with a delightful walled courtyard out front. Exposed beams, pictures and mirrors provide the backdrop to Ken Wilson's food, which is 'both inspired and inspiring', according to one reporter. Intricacy is his culinary hallmark, and there's always a great deal happening on the plate, whether it's Japanese crispy pork belly with smoked eel, mushrooms, pea shoots and soy broth or Madgetts Farm duck breast with duck hash, sweet potatoes, turnips and orange pepper sauce. Menus are short, but specials widen the choice – spiced

baked cod with couscous, chickpeas and baby tomato stew, say. To finish, consider iced tiramisu parfait with marzipan ice cream and chocolate syrup. House wines are £13.

Chef/s: Ken Wilson. **Open:** Sat L 12 to 1.30, Tue to Sat D 7 to 9 (9.30 Fri, Sat). **Closed:** 25 Dec, 1 to 5 Jan, 1 week Nov. **Meals:** alc (main courses £15 to £17). **Service:** 10% parties of 8 plus. **Details:** Cards accepted. 30 seats. 16 seats outside. No mobile phones. Wheelchair access. Music. Children allowed.

The Stagg Inn
Herefordshire pub star
Titley, HR5 3RL
Tel no: (01544) 230221
www.thestagg.co.uk
Modern British | £30

Steve and Nicola Reynolds have done Herefordshire proud during their 10 years in residence at this handsome country inn, which stands at the junction of several ancient drovers' roads. They have retained the feel of the place as a genuine hostelry, while serving top-drawer food. Precise, uncluttered cooking is the deal, and it comes with bright ideas, assured style and honest endeavour in abundance. As you might expect, Steve taps into Herefordshire's rich larder, although he looks to Cornwall for fish specials (perhaps seared scallops on celeriac and cumin purée). Domestic enterprise also shows up across the board, from home-baked breads to home-cured chorizo (perhaps served in a pasta dish with squid, tomato and chilli). Herefordshire beef is given full rein (rump steak with red wine sauce and chips), and other big local names also figure prominently: Madgett's Farm duck breast is pointed up with a complex, sweet and spicy sauce of ginger, mustard and Sauternes. To finish, crème rûlée is subjected to all sorts of twists; otherwise, the **i**tchen might send out lemon tart with Cassis sorbet. **T**he cracking cheeseboard features a prodigious array **f**rom England and Wales, while the 100-bin wine list **o**ffers an intelligent choice, with a broad sweep of **g**rape varieties and regions, keen prices and plentiful **h**alf-bottles; it even finds room for a local representative **f**rom Broadfield Court. House selections start at £13.50 **(**£2.35 a glass).

Chef/s: Steve Reynolds. **Open:** Tue to Sun L 12 to 2, Tue to **S**at D 6.30 to 9. **Closed:** 2 weeks Nov, 1 week Jan. **Meals:** alc (main courses £15 to £18). **Service:** not inc. **Details:** Cards accepted. 70 seats. 16 seats outside. **S**eparate bar. No music. No mobile phones. Children **a**llowed. Car parking.

SHROPSHIRE

The Clive
Bromfield, Ludlow, SY8 2JR
Tel no: (01584) 856565
www.theclive.co.uk
Modern British

Just north of Ludlow on the A49, this 18th century **f**armhouse is now a contemporary restaurant-with-**r**ooms (with an adjoining bar and courtyard). Local **p**roduce drives the menu and dishes work best when **k**ept simple. Lunch on terrine of pork and local game **o**r home-cooked Shropshire ham with poached eggs **(**£9.95) or dine on saddle of venison with dauphinoise **p**otatoes, braised red cabbage and Cassis sauce **(**£18.95). Local cheeses (from £5.95) are an alternative **t**o sticky toffee pudding. House wine is £13.30. Open **a**ll week.

Waterdine
Seasonal cooking delivers the goods
Llanfair Waterdine, LD7 1TU
Tel no: (01547) 528214
www.waterdine.com
Modern British | £33

On the Shropshire-Welsh border, the 16th-century **d**rover's inn still has some country pub trappings, although the focus is now on its intimate dining rooms. **K**en Adams can clearly deliver the goods. His timing is **a**ssured, and the kitchen scores heavily with the quality **o**f its raw materials, some of it home-grown: spiced **b**lack pudding on crushed apples with Hereford cider **s**auce is a spot-on modern starter, while flavourful leg **o**f organic Welsh mountain lamb is roasted in Lebanese **s**pices and served with a fine vegetable and anchellini **(**pasta) ragoût. Elsewhere, local game such as Mortimer **F**orest deer might appear with pheasant, braised **b**eetroot, celeriac and a good red wine sauce, or fresh **C**ornish hake teamed with crab risotto. Desserts can **a**stonish: try black rice pudding with pineapple and **c**oconut cream or mulberry mousse with elderflower

cream. Booking is essential. The concise but impeccably chosen wine list opens at £17.50.

Chef/s: Ken Adams. **Open:** Thu to Sun L 12 to 1.30, Tue to Sat D 7 to 8.30. **Closed:** Mon, 1 week June and Sept. **Meals:** Set L £26.50 (2 courses) to £32.50. Set Sun L £22.50. Set D £32.50. **Service:** not inc. **Details:** Cards accepted. 24 seats. Separate bar. No music. No mobile phones. Wheelchair access. Children allowed. Car parking.

STAFFORDSHIRE

The Holly Bush Inn
Fuss-free pub grub and fine ales
Salt, ST18 0BX
Tel no: (01889) 508234
www.hollybushinn.co.uk
Gastropub | £17

Born sometime in the 12th century, this trimly thatched inn lays claim to being the 'second oldest licensed pub in the country', and it certainly looks the part with its carved beams, plank ceiling and knick-knacks. Real ale drinkers get full satisfaction from a splendid line-up of brews, and the food is a fuss-free assortment of honest pub grub with some neat local touches (braised lamb with apples and Packington free-range pork chops with a honey-mustard glaze) slipped in between the steaks and battered cod. 'Order the food at the bar and grab a table – quick' as no bookings are taken and the place fills up quickly. House wine is £10.95.

Chef/s: Paul Hillman. **Open:** Mon to Sat 12 to 9.30, Sun 12 to 9. **Closed:** 25 and 26 Dec. **Meals:** alc (main courses £5 to £16). **Service:** not inc. **Details:** Cards accepted. 64 seats. 80 seats outside. No music. Wheelchair access. Children allowed. Car parking.

WARWICKSHIRE

Restaurant Bosquet
Ever-popular Gallic charmer
97A Warwick Road, Kenilworth, CV8 1HP
Tel no: (01926) 852463
www.restaurantbosquet.co.uk
French | £32

Since setting out their stall in 1981, Bernard and Jane Lignier have gained a reputation as an endearing double act – thanks to their infectious Gallic charm and the mood of chatty domesticity that permeates their affable little restaurant. The rich, bold flavours of Bernard's native southwest France define much of his food, which is why he is generous with the foie gras and cooks his chips in goose fat. Devotees of this overtly earthy style revel in the delights of herb-crusted saddle of lamb with butter-bean stew, breast of pheasant stuffed with apricots on a port and chestnut sauce, and saddle of venison with truffle oil, chocolate and Cassis sauce. Fish dishes vary with the market, and the roll-call of desserts might range from blueberry and almond tart to raspberries and strawberries with a Muscat sabayon. Jurançon, Madiran, Cahors and other names from the southwest dominate the patriotically French wine list. Prices start at £15.50.

Chef/s: Bernard Lignier. **Open:** Tue to Fri L 12 to 1.15, Tue to Sat D 7 to 9.15. **Closed:** Sun, Mon and 1 week Christmas, 2 weeks Aug. **Meals:** alc (main courses £20 to £22). Set L and D £31.50. **Service:** not inc. **Details:** Cards accepted. 26 seats. No music. No mobile phones. Wheelchair access. Children allowed.

WEST MIDLANDS

Opus Restaurant
Excellent ingredients and inspiring dishes
54 Cornwall Street, Birmingham, B3 2DE
Tel no: (0121) 2002323
www.opusrestaurant.co.uk
Modern British | £30

Opus looks thoroughly urban, but it has been just as careful as many a country village eaterie in sourcing from pedigree suppliers – from Carlingford oysters to free-range meats. A chef's table in the kitchen allows up to eight diners a backstage view of proceedings through five inventive courses. There's plenty going on out front too, in the form of quail with pumpkin risotto and bacon, Dover sole on the bone with lemon thyme butter, or slow-braised collar of pork with creamed potatoes and winter veg. Desserts ramp up the indulgence factor with Valrhona chocolate tart and salted peanut ice cream. An inspired international wine list starts at £14.50.

Chef/s: David Colcombe. **Open:** Mon to Fri L 12 to 2.15, Mon to Sat D 6 to 9.30 (7 to 10 Sat). **Closed:** Sun, bank hols, 25 Dec to 1 Jan. **Meals:** alc (main courses £13 to £35). Set L and D £15.50 (2 courses) to £18.50. **Service:** 10% (optional). **Details:** Cards accepted. 85 seats. Air-con. Separate bar. No music. Wheelchair access. Children allowed.

WORCESTERSHIRE

Brockencote Hall
A country hotel of some class
Chaddesley Corbett, DY10 4PY
Tel no: (01562) 777876
www.brockencotehall.com
French | £38

The interior of this lovingly maintained Victorian mansion reflects the owners' individual taste: easy pastels, floral drapes, comfortable upholstered seating and fine white table linen in the dining room. With 25 years and more in the business, Alison and Joseph Petitjean have perfected the personable approach that has delighted a generation of visitors, evident in everything from the good housekeeping to the welcoming staff. Prize draw, though, must be Didier Philipot's accomplished modern French cooking.

Quality produce shines through, whether in a luxurious starter of dodine of Perigord duck foie gras with Armagnac and salt flower, truffle salad and toasted brioche mousseline, or in a main course which sees venison noisettes accompanied by etuvée of Savoy cabbage and smoked bacon, parsnip mousseline, green Chartreuse and bitter chocolate jus. Honey and spice roast pears with toffee mousse, pear soup and gingerbread ice cream holds up the style through to the finish. The wine list offers house wines from £16 a bottle.

Chef/s: Didier Philipot. **Open:** all week L 12 to 1.30, D 7 to 9.30. **Meals:** alc (main courses £18 to £28). Set L £15 (2 courses) to £19. Set Sun L £27.50. Set D £26.30 (2 courses) to £34.30. **Service:** not inc. **Details:** Cards accepted. 75 seats. Separate bar. No mobile phones. Wheelchair access. Music. Children allowed. Car parking.

The Talbot
Teme Valley cuisine
Knightwick, WR6 5PH
Tel no: (01886) 821235
www.the-talbot.co.uk
Gastropub | £32

The Clift family have clocked up 25 years at their 15th-century coaching inn overlooking the River Teme. It's very much a pub with a restaurant, rather than the other way around, matched by a well-executed cooking style that is rustic rather than refined. An industrious kitchen makes the best of local and seasonal supplies – rabbit casserole, cold raised pork and game pies, pot-roasted shoulder of mutton – and produces its own bread and preserves; even beer is brewed on the premises. House wine is £12.25.

Chef/s: Kate Parffrey. **Open:** all week, L 12 to 2, D 6.30 to 9 (Sun 7). **Meals:** alc (main courses £10 to £22). Set L Sun £27. Set D £27. Details: Cards accepted. 30 seats. 30 seats outside. No music. No mobile phones. Wheelchair access. Children allowed. Car parking.

Content brought to you by **The Good Food Guide 2010**. Please see pages 20–21 for further details.

Tourist Information Centres

When you arrive at your destination, visit an Official Partner Tourist Information Centre for quality assured help with accommodation and information about local attractions and events, or email your request before you go. To search for attractions and Tourist Information Centres on the move just text INFO to 62233, and a web link will be sent to your mobile phone. To find a Tourist Information Centre by region visit enjoyEngland.com/find-tic.

BEWDLEY	Load Street	01299 404740	bewdleytic@wyreforestdc.gov.uk
BIRMINGHAM	Tourism Centre & Ticketshop	0844 888 3883	callcentre@marketingbirmingham.com
BRIDGNORTH	The Library	01746 763257	bridgnorth.tourism@shropshire.gov.uk
CHURCH STRETTON	Church Street	01694 723133	churchstretton.scf@shropshire.gov.uk
COVENTRY CATHEDRAL	Coventry Cathedral	024 7622 5616	tic@cvone.co.uk
COVENTRY RICOH	Phoenix Way	0844 873 6397	richoh@cvone.co.uk
COVENTRY TRANSPORT MUSEUM	Millenium Place	024 7622 5616	tic@cvone.co.uk
IRONBRIDGE	Ironbridge Gorge Museum Trust	01952 884391	tic@ironbridge.org.uk
LEAMINGTON SPA	The Royal Pump Rooms	01926 742762	leamington@shakespeare-country.co.uk
LEEK	Stockwell Street	01538 483741	tourism.services@staffsmoorlands.gov.uk
LICHFIELD	Lichfield Garrick	01543 412112	info@visitlichfield.com
LUDLOW	Castle Street	01584 875053	ludlow.tourism@shropshire.gov.uk
MALVERN	21 Church Street	01684 892289	malvern.tic@malvernhills.gov.uk
OSWESTRY	Mile End	01691 662488	tic@oswestry-bc.gov.uk
RUGBY	Rugby Visitor Centre	01788 533217	visitor.centre@rugby.gov.uk
SHREWSBURY	The Music Hall	01743 281200	visitorinfo@shrewsbury.gov.uk
SOLIHULL	Central Library	0121 704 6130	artscomplex@solihull.gov.uk
STAFFORD	Gatehouse Theatre	01785 619619	tic@staffordbc.gov.uk
STOKE-ON-TRENT	Victoria Hall, Bagnall Street	01782 236000	stoke.tic@stoke.gov.uk
STRATFORD-UPON-AVON	Bridgefoot	0870 160 7930	stratfordtic@shakespeare-country.co.uk
TAMWORTH	Tamworth Information Centre	01827 709581	tic@tamworth.gov.uk
WARWICK	The Court House	01926 492212	touristinfo@warwick-uk.co.uk
WORCESTER	The Guildhall	01905 728787	touristinfo@cityofworcester.gov.uk

Regional Contacts and Information

Marketing Birmingham
Tel: (0121) 202 5115
Web: www.visitbirmingham.com

Shropshire Tourism
Tel: (01743) 462462
Web: www.shropshiretourism.co.uk

Visit Coventy & Warwickshire
Tel: (024) 7622 7264
Web: www.visitcoventryandwarwickshire.co.uk

Destination Staffordshire
Tel: 0870 500 4444
Web: www.enjoystaffordshire.com

Visit Herefordshire
Tel: (01432) 260621
Web: www.visitherefordshire.co.uk

Stoke-on-Trent
Tel: (01782) 236000
Web: www.visitstoke.co.uk

Shakespeare Country
Tel: 0870 160 7930
Web: www.shakespeare-country.co.uk

Destination Worcestershire
Tel: (01905) 728787
Web: www.visitworcestershire.org

If you have
access needs...

Guests with hearing, visual or mobility needs can feel confident about booking accommodation that participates in the National Accessible Scheme (NAS).

Look out for the NAS symbols which are included throughout the accommodation directory. Using the NAS could help make the difference between a good holiday and a perfect one!

You can also search for NAS rated accommodation at enjoyengland.com/stay or buy a copy of the new OpenBritain guide, available from Tourism for All - tel 0845 124 9971

Where to Stay

Entries appear alphabetically by town name in each county. A key to symbols appears on page 6. Maps start on page 394. A listing of all Enjoy England assessed accommodation appears at the end of the region.

BROMYARD, Herefordshire Map ref 2B1

SAT NAV WR6 5TE

Bromyard Downs Caravan Club Site
Brockhampton, Bringsty, Bromyard WR6 5TE
t (01885) 482607
w **caravanclub.co.uk**

CARAVAN CLUB

🚐 (40)　£8.00–£15.00
🚎 (40)　£8.00–£15.00
40 touring pitches

Secluded woodland site set in beautiful countryside between the cathedral cities of Hereford and Worcester, with many lovely walks nearby. Perfect for exploring historic houses, museums and steam railways. **directions** Site on left of A44 (Worcester-Bromyard) about 0.25 miles past Brockhampton (National Trust) entrance. **open** Apr to October **payment** credit/debit cards, cash, cheques

General 🐕 ⊕ ☺

EARDISLAND, Herefordshire Map ref 2A1

SAT NAV HR6 9BG

Arrow Bank Holiday Park
Nun House Farm, Eardisland, Leominster HR6 9BG
t (01544) 388312 f (01544) 388312 e enquiries@arrowbankholidaypark.co.uk
w **arrowbankholidaypark.co.uk**

🚐 (36)　£13.00–£19.00
🚎 (2)　£13.00–£19.00
⛺ (14)　£13.00–£19.00
🏠 (3)　£300.00–£425.00
50 touring pitches

Parkland setting with hard-standing and grass pitches. Heated amenity block with disabled facilities and laundry chem-loo, water and waste water points. Wi-Fi access and fishing on site. **direction** From Leominster, follow A44 West, after Morrisons bear right to Eardisland. Park entrance on right just after village sign. **payment** credit/debit cards, cash, cheques

General 🗄 ♿ 🐕 🏔 ☼ 🛲 ⊕ ☺ ☏ 🖵　Leisure ✈

Looking for something else?

You can also buy a copy of our popular guide 'B&B' including guest accommodation, B&B's, guest houses, farmhouses, inns, and campus and hostel accommodation in England 2010.
Now available in good bookshops and online at **enjoyenglanddirect.com**

£11.99

ROSS-ON-WYE, Herefordshire Map ref 2A1

SAT NAV

150 touring pitches

Broadmeadow Caravan Park

Broadmeadows, Ross-on-Wye HR9 7BW
t (01989) 768076 f (01989) 566030 e broadm4811@aol.com
w **broadmeadow.info** ONLINE MAP

150 pitches available with luxurious facilities, on the edge of Ross-on-Wye. **directions** Please contact us for directions **open** April to September **payment** credit/debit cards, cash

General ⬚ 🐕 🛒 📶 ☼ ⊟ 🚲 📞 🚻 ☕ Leisure ▶ 🏊

SYMONDS YAT WEST, Herefordshire Map ref 2A1

SAT NAV HR9 6BY

🚐 (8)	£10.00–£14.00	
🚙 (8)	£10.00–£14.00	
⛺ (8)	£10.00–£20.00	
🏠 (3)	£195.00–£330.00	

8 touring pitches

Sterrett's Caravan Park

Symonds Yat West, Ross-on-Wye, Symonds Yat HR9 6BY
t (01594) 832888 / (01594) 833162
w **ukparks.co.uk/sterretts**

Grass or hard standing pitches for touring vans, tents welcome. luxury caravans for hire close to river Wye and ideal for touring the Wye Valley and Forest of Dean. **directions** Mid way A40 Ross on Wye to Monmouth. Follow signs to Symonds Yat West. **open** 1st Feb to 30th Nov **payment** cash, cheques

General ⬚ 🐕 🛒 📶 ☼ 📞 🚻 ☕ Leisure ▶ 🚴 🏊 ⛰

ELLESMERE, Shropshire Map ref 4A2

SAT NAV SY12 0QF

🚐	£19.00–£24.00	
🚙	£19.00–£24.00	
🏠 (1)	£305.00–£445.00	

60 touring pitches

Fernwood Caravan Park

Lyneal, Ellesmere SY12 0QF
t (01948) 710221 f (01948) 710324 e enquiries@fernwoodpark.co.uk
w **fernwoodpark.co.uk**

Picturesque, 25-acre country park for static holiday homes, tourers and motor homes. 40-acre adjacent woodland and lake for coarse fishing. Shop and launderette. Pets welcome. **directions** From A495 in Welshampton take B5063 1 mile over canal bridge 1st turning on right. **open** 1st March to 30th Nov **payment** credit/debit cards, cash, cheques

General ⬚ 🐕 🛞 📶 ☼ ⊟ 📞 🚻 ☕ Leisure ▶ 🏊 ⛰

PRESTHOPE, Shropshire Map ref 4A3   SAT NAV TF13 6DQ

TOURING PARK

🚐 (71)   £8.00–£15.00
🚕 (71)   £8.00–£15.00
71 touring pitches

SPECIAL PROMOTIONS
Special member rates mean
you can save your
membership subscription in
less than a week. Visit our
website to find out more.

Presthope Caravan Club Site
Stretton Road, Much Wenlock TF13 6DQ
t (01746) 785234 e enquiries@caravanclub.co.uk
w **caravanclub.co.uk**

THE
CARAVAN
CLUB

An interesting site for the naturalist with
abundant wildlife on site, beautiful countryside
surrounds and it's a real find for the walker.
Explore the Long Mynd and Cardingmill Valley.
There are a number of National Trust properties
in the area and the towns of Shrewsbury, Telford
and Bridgnorth are all well worth visiting.

open April to September
payment credit/debit cards, cash, cheques

directions From A458 (signposted Shrewsbury)
in 0.25 miles turn left onto B4371. Site on left.

General 🐕 🔌 🛏 🆚
Leisure 🎵

BLACKSHAW MOOR, Staffordshire Map ref 4B2   SAT NAV ST13 8TW

TOURING PARK

🚐 (89)   £12.20–£25.10
🚕 (89)   £12.20–£25.10
89 touring pitches

Blackshaw Moor Caravan Club Site
Blackshaw Moor Caravan Club Site, Blackshaw Moor, Leek ST13 8TW
t (01538) 300203
w **caravanclub.co.uk**

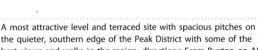

THE
CARAVAN
CLUB

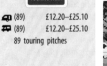

A most attractive level and terraced site with spacious pitches on
the quieter, southern edge of the Peak District with some of the
best views and walks in the region. **directions** From Buxton on A5
site on left 200 yards past Blackshaw Mooor Sign. From Leek on
A53 site on right within 3 miles. **open** March 2010 to January 2011
payment credit/debit cards, cash, cheques

General 📺 🔌 🐕 🚿 🛁 🔌 🛏 🆚   Leisure 🎵

RUGELEY, Staffordshire Map ref 4B3   SAT NAV WS15 2TX

HOLIDAY PARK

ROSE
AWARD
CARAVAN
HOLIDAY
PARK

🏠 (9)   £249.00–£499.00

Silver Trees Holiday Park - Static Vans
Stafford Brook Road, Penkridge Bank, Rugeley, Cannock Chase, Staffordshire WS15 2TX
t (01889) 582185 f (01889) 582373 e info@silvertreesholidaypark.co.uk
w **silvertreesholidaypark.co.uk** ONLINE MAP GUEST REVIEWS

Rose Award holiday homes on quiet woodland park, suitable for
couples and families enjoying wildlife, walks, cycling on Cannock
Chase. Area of Outstanding Natural Beauty. View deer from your
caravan! **directions** From A51 or A34 follow brown tourist signs for
Silver Trees Holiday Park, the park is located between Rugeley and
Penkridge on Cannock Chase. **open** March to January **payment**
credit/debit cards, cash, cheques

General 📺 🛏 🛁 ☼   Leisure U 🏊 🚴 🎣

STOKE-ON-TRENT, Staffordshire Map ref 4B2   SAT NAV ST10 3DW

The Star Caravan & Camping Park

Star Road, Cotton, Alton Towers area ST10 3DW
t (01538) 702219 **f** (01538) 703704
w starcaravanpark.co.uk ONLINE MAP GUEST REVIEWS

(60)	£15.00–£18.00
(10)	£10.00–£20.00
(50)	£10.00–£22.00
(8)	£295.00–£495.00

120 touring pitches

SPECIAL PROMOTIONS
Early-season discounts on caravan holiday homes. Free 2nd-day admission to Alton Towers for 2 persons (ring for information).

The closest touring park to Alton Towers. Strict 11pm-all-quiet rule on site. No single-sex groups allowed. Families and mixed couples always welcomed. Set in stunning countryside surrounded by mature trees and hedgerows. 10 miles from 4 market towns, and only 4 miles from the Peak District National Park.

open March to November
payment credit/debit cards, cash, cheques

directions From Alton Towers, 1 mile to crossroads at Cotton, turn right up the hill, entrance 300m on the right.

General ▢ ⊕ ✿ ⊞ ☎ ⊙ ☀ 🎣 Leisure ∪ 🚲 🏊 ⚑

STRATFORD-UPON-AVON, Warwickshire Map ref 2B1   SAT NAV CV37 9SR

Dodwell Park

Evesham Road (B439), Dodwell, Stratford-upon-Avon CV37 9SR
t (01789) 204957 **e** enquiries@dodwellpark.co.uk
w dodwellpark.co.uk ONLINE MAP

(50)	£15.50–£16.50
(50)	£15.50–£16.50
(50)	£14.50–£15.50

50 touring pitches

Small, family-run touring park 2 miles SW of Stratford-upon-Avon on B439. Country walks to River Avon and Luddington village. Ideal for visiting Warwick Castle, Shakespeare's birthplace and Cotswolds. Brochure on request. **directions** Leaving Stratford-Upon-Avon take the B439 signposted 'B349 Bidford' (also signposted Racecourse) for 2 miles, we are on left (after going over a large hill) **open** All year **payment** credit/debit cards, cash, cheques

General ✿ ⊞ ☎ ⊙ ☀ 🎣 Leisure 🚲 🏊

WARWICK, Warwickshire Map ref 4B3   SAT NAV CV34 6HN

Warwick Racecourse Caravan Club Site

Hampton Street, Warwick CV34 6HN
t (01926) 495448 **e** enquiries@caravanclub.co.uk
w caravanclub.co.uk

THE
CARAVAN
CLUB

(55)	£12.20–£25.10
(55)	£12.20–£25.10

55 touring pitches

Set on grass and tarmac in the racecourse enclosure. 6 minutes from the centre of Warwick. **directions** Please contact us for directions **payment** credit/debit cards, cash

General ▢ ☀ 🎣 ⊙

BIRMINGHAM, West Midlands Map ref 4B3

SAT NAV B47 6JX

(108) £14.00–£26.90
(108) £14.00–£26.90
108 touring pitches

SPECIAL PROMOTIONS
Special member rates mean
you can save your
membership subscription in
less than a week. Visit our
website to find out more.

Chapel Lane Caravan Park
Chapel Lane, Wythall, Birmingham B47 6JX
t (01564) 826483 f (01564) 829346
w **caravanclub.co.uk**

THE
CARAVAN
CLUB

Wythall is a quiet, rural area yet convenient for
Birmingham (nine miles) and the NEC (13 miles)
Visit Cadbury's World or explore the surrounding
countryside and local canals. It's great for those
with an intrest in our industrial heritage for
there are stacks of fascinating museums.

open All year
payment credit/debit cards, cash, cheques

directions From M1 jct 23a, jct 3 off M42 then
A435 to Birmingham. After 1 mile at roundabout
take 1st exit, Middle Lane. Turn right at church
then immediately right into site.

General 🗗 📶 📱 🌣 🔌 💬 🚻 🚾
Leisure ⛰

EVESHAM, Worcestershire Map ref 2B1

SAT NAV WR11 7PR

(100) £21.00–£27.00
(20) £21.00–£27.00
(4) £300.00–£440.00
120 touring pitches

Ranch Caravan Park
Honeybourne, Evesham WR11 7PR
t (01386) 830744 f (01386) 833503 e enquiries@ranch.co.uk
w **ranch.co.uk** ONLINE MAP

An established family-run holiday park located in Honeybourne, 6
miles from Evesham. Level pitches in a landscaped setting. Well
situated for visiting the Cotswolds and Shakespeare Country.
directions From A46 Evesham bypass take B4035 to Badsey and
Bretforton. Caravan park signposted from Bretforton. **open** March to
November **payment** credit/debit cards, cash, cheques

General 🗗 🐾 🚶 📱 🌣 🔌 🚲 💬 🚻 🚾 ✕ Leisure 🎣 🍴 🎵 🌸 ⛰

All Assessed Accommodation

Herefordshire

BROMYARD

omyard Downs Caravan Club
e ★★★★ *Touring Park*
ockhampton, Bringsty, Bromyard
6 5TE
(01885) 482607
caravanclub.co.uk

EARDISLAND

row Bank Holiday Park
★★★
liday, Touring & Camping Park
SE AWARD
n House Farm, Eardisland,
ominster
6 9BG
(01544) 388312
enquiries@arrowbankholidaypark.
co.uk
arrowbankholidaypark.co.uk

HEREFORD

cksall Caravan and Camping
rk ★★★★★
liday & Touring Park
ordiford, Hereford
1 4LP
(01432) 870213
karen@lucksallpark.co.uk
lucksallpark.co.uk

LEOMINSTER

irview Holiday Park ★★★★
liday Park
e Willows, Hatfield, Leominster
6 0SD
(01568) 760428
info@fairviewholidaypark.co.uk
fairviewholidaypark.co.uk

LITTLE TARRINGTON

ereford Camping and
aravanning Club Site ★★★★★
uring & Camping Park
tle Tarrington, Hereford
1 4JA
(01432) 890243
enquiries@millpond.co.uk
campingandcaravanningclub.co.
uk/hereford

PEMBRIDGE

wnsend Touring Park ★★★★★
uring & Camping Park
e Granary, Townsend Farm,
embridge, Leominster
6 9HB
(01544) 388527
info@townsendfarm.co.uk
townsendfarm.co.uk

PETERCHURCH

oston Mill Park C & C ★★★★★
liday & Touring Park
eterchurch, Golden Valley
2 0SF
(01981) 550225
info@poston-mill.co.uk
bestparks.co.uk

ROSS-ON-WYE

roadmeadow Caravan Park
★★★★ *Touring & Camping Park*
oadmeadows, Ross-on-Wye
9 7BW
(01989) 768076
broadm4811@aol.com
broadmeadow.info

SHOBDON

earl Lake Leisure Park ★★★★★
oliday Park
obdon, Leominster
6 9NQ
(01568) 708326
info@pearllake.co.uk
bestparks.co.uk

SYMONDS YAT WEST

Sterrett's Caravan Park ★★★★
Holiday & Touring Park
Symonds Yat West, Ross-on-Wye,
Symonds Yat
HR9 6BY
t (01594) 832888 / (01594) 833162
e enquiries@caravanclub.co.uk
w ukparks.co.uk/sterretts

Shropshire

ALL STRETTON

All Stretton Bunk House
Bunkhouse
Batch Valley, All Stretton
SY6 6JW
t (01694) 722593
e frankiegoode@zoom.uk

BRIDGNORTH

Park Grange Holidays ★★★★
Holiday Park
Morville, Bridgnorth
WV16 4RN
t (01746) 714285
e info@parkgrangeholidays.co.uk
w parkgrangeholidays.co.uk

Stanmore Hall Touring Park
★★★★ *Touring Park*
Stourbridge Road, Bridgnorth
WV15 6DT
t (01746) 761761
e stanmore@morris-leisure.co.uk
w morris-leisure.co.uk

ELLESMERE

Fernwood Caravan Park ★★★★★
Holiday & Touring Park
Lyneal, Ellesmere
SY12 0QF
t (01948) 710221
e enquiries@fernwoodpark.co.uk
w fernwoodpark.co.uk

HAUGHTON

Ebury Hill Camping &
Caravanning Club Site ★★★★
Touring & Camping Park
Ebury Hill, Haughton, Telford
TF6 6BU
t (01743) 709334
w stmem.com/eburyhill/

HOPTON HEATH

Ashlea Pools Country Park-Log
Cabins ★★★★★ *Holiday Park*
ROSE AWARD
Hopton Heath, Craven Arms
SY7 0QD
t (01547) 530430
e ashleapools@surfbay.dircon.co.uk
w ashleapools.co.uk

KINNERLEY

Oswestry Camping and
Caravanning Club Site ★★★★★
Touring Park
Kinnerley, Oswestry
SY10 8DY
t (01743) 741118
e oswestry.site@campingandcarav
anningclub.co.uk
w campingandcaravanningclub.co.
uk/oswestry

LUDLOW

Orleton Rise Holiday Home Park
★★★★★ *Holiday & Touring Park*
Green Lane, Orleton, Ludlow
SY8 4JE
t (01584) 831617

MUCH WENLOCK

Stokes Cottage *Bunkhouse*
Newtown House Farm, Much
Wenlock, Shropshire
TF13 6DB

PRESTHOPE

Presthope Caravan Club Site
★★★ *Touring Park*
Stretton Road, Much Wenlock
TF13 6DQ
t (01746) 785234
e enquiries@caravanclub.co.uk
w caravanclub.co.uk

SHREWSBURY

Beaconsfield Farm Caravan Park
★★★★★ *Holiday & Touring Park*
ROSE AWARD
Upper Battlefield, Shrewsbury,
Shrewsbury
SY4 4AA
t (01939) 210370
e mail@beaconsfield-farm.co.uk
w beaconsfield-farm.co.uk

Oxon Hall Touring Park ★★★★★
Holiday & Touring Park
Welshpool Road, Oxon, Shrewsbury
SY3 5FB
t (01743) 340868
e oxon@morris-leisure.co.uk
w morrisleisure.com

Staffordshire

ALREWAS

Kingfisher Holiday Park ★★★★★
Holiday & Touring Park **ROSE AWARD**
Fradley Junction, Alrewas, Lichfield
DE13 7DN
t (01283) 790407
e mail@kingfisherholidaypark.com
w kingfisherholidaypark.com

ALSTONEFIELD

Gateham Cottage & the Coach
House *Camping Barn*
Gateham Grange, Alstonefield,
Ashbourne
DE6 2FT
t (01335) 310349
e gateham.grange@btinternet.com
w cressbrook.co.uk/hartingt/
gateham/

BLACKSHAW MOOR

Blackshaw Moor Caravan Club
Site ★★★★★ *Touring Park*
Blackshaw Moor Caravan Club Site,
Blackshaw Moor, Leek
ST13 8TW
t (01538) 300203
w caravanclub.co.uk

BREWOOD

Homestead Caravan Park ★★★★
Holiday Park
Shutt Green, Brewood,
Wolverhampton
ST19 9LX
t (01902) 851302
e info@caravanparkstaffordshire.co.
uk
w caravanparkstaffordshire.co.uk

BUTTERTON

Butterton B *Camping Barn*
Fenns Farm, Wetton Road, Leek
ST13 7ST
t (01538) 304185

Butterton Camping Barns
Camping Barn
Fenns House, Wetton Road, Leek
ST13 7ST
t (01538) 304185

CHEDDLETON

Glencote Caravan Park ★★★★★
Holiday, Touring & Camping Park
Station Road, Cheddleton, Leek
ST13 7EE
t (01538) 360745
e canistay@glencote.co.uk
w glencote.co.uk

LEEK

Leek Camping and Caravanning
Club Site ★★★★
Touring & Camping Park
Blackshaw Grange, Blackshaw Moor,
Leek
ST13 8TL
t (01538) 300285
w campingandcaravanningclub.co.
uk/leek

LONGNOR

Nab End Camping Barn
Camping Barn
Nab End Farm, Hollinsclough,
Buxton
SK17 0RJ
t (01298) 83225
e david@nabendfarm.co.uk
w nabendfarm.co.uk

OVERSEAL

Swainswood Leisure Park
★★★★★ *Holiday Park*
ROSE AWARD
159 Moira Road, Overseal,
Swadlincote
DE12 6JD

RUGELEY

Cannock Chase Camping &
Caravanning Club ★★★★
Touring & Camping Park
Old Youth Hostel, Wandon, Rugeley
WS15 1QW
t (01889) 582166
w campingandcaravanningclub.co.
uk

Silver Trees Holiday Park - Static
Vans ★★★★ *Holiday Park*
ROSE AWARD
Stafford Brook Road, Penkridge
Bank, Rugeley, Cannock Chase,
Staffordshire
WS15 2TX
t (01889) 582185
e info@silvertreesholidaypark.co.uk
w silvertreesholidaypark.co.uk

SHEEN

Sheen Bunkhouse *Bunkhouse*
Peak Stones, Buxton
SK17 0ES
t (01298) 84501
e grahambelfield@fsmail.net

STOKE-ON-TRENT

The Star Caravan & Camping Park
★★★★★
Holiday, Touring & Camping Park
ROSE AWARD
Star Road, Cotton, Alton Towers
area
ST10 3DW
t (01538) 702219
w starcaravanpark.co.uk

UTTOXETER

Uttoxeter Racecourse Caravan
Club Site ★★ *Touring Park*
Uttoxeter Racecourse, Wood Lane,
Uttoxeter
ST14 8BD
t (01889) 564172
w caravanclub.co.uk

Warwickshire

ASTON CANTLOW

Island Meadow Caravan Park
★★★
Holiday, Touring & Camping Park
The Mill House, Aston Cantlow,
Stratford-upon-Avon
B95 6JP
t (01789) 488273
e holiday@islandmeadowcar
avanpark.co.uk
w islandmeadowcaravanpark.co.uk

STRATFORD-UPON-AVON

Dodwell Park ★★★
Touring & Camping Park
Evesham Road (B439), Dodwell,
Stratford-upon-Avon
CV37 9SR
t   (01789) 204957
e   enquiries@dodwellpark.co.uk
w   dodwellpark.co.uk

WARWICK

**Warwick Racecourse Caravan Club
Site ★★★** *Touring Park*
Hampton Street, Warwick
CV34 6HN
t   (01926) 495448
e   enquiries@caravanclub.co.uk
w   caravanclub.co.uk

West Midlands

BIRMINGHAM

Chapel Lane Caravan Park
★★★★★ *Touring Park*
Chapel Lane, Wythall, Birmingham
B47 6JX
t   (01564) 826483
w   caravanclub.co.uk

BODYMOOR HEATH

**Kingsbury Water Park Camping
and Caravanning Club Site**
★★★★★ *Touring & Camping Park*
Bodymoor Heath Lane, Bodymoor
Heath, Sutton Coldfield
B76 0DY
t   (01827) 874101
w   campingandcaravanningclub.co.
    uk/kingsbury

MERIDEN

Somers Wood Caravan Park
★★★★★ *Touring Park*
Somers Road, Meriden, Coventry
CV7 7PL
t   (01676) 522978
e   enquiries@somerswood.co.uk
w   somerswood.co.uk

Worcestershire

EVESHAM

Ranch Caravan Park ★★★★★
Holiday & Touring Park
Honeybourne, Evesham
WR11 7PR
t   (01386) 830744
e   enquiries@ranch.co.uk
w   ranch.co.uk

HANLEY SWAN

**Blackmore Camping and
Caravanning Club Site ★★★★★**
Touring & Camping Park
Blackmore End, Hanley Swan,
Worcester
WR8 0EE
t   (01684) 310280
w   campingandcaravanningclub.co.
    uk/blackmore

ROMSLEY

**Clent Hills Camping and
Caravanning Club Site ★★★★**
Touring Park
Fieldhouse Lane, Romsley,
Halesowen
B62 0NH
t   (01562) 710015
w   campingandcaravanningclub.co.
    uk/clenthills

STOURPORT-ON-SEVERN

Lickhill Manor Caravan Park
★★★★★ *Holiday Park*
Stourport-on-Severn
DY13 8RL
t   (01299) 871041
e   excellent@lickhillmanor.co.uk
w   lickhillmanor.co.uk

WOLVERLEY

**Wolverley Camping and
Caravanning Club Site ★★★★**
Touring & Camping Park
Brown Westhead Park, Wolverley,
Kidderminster
DY10 3PX
t   (01562) 850909
w   campingandcaravanningclub.ce
    uk/wolverley

WYRE PIDDLE

Rivermead Holiday Home Park
★★★★★ *Holiday Park*
Church Street, Wyre Piddle,
Pershore
WR10 2JF
t   (01386) 561250
e   enquiries@rivermeadcaravanpa
    co.uk
w   rivermeadcaravanpark.co.uk

Bank holiday
dates for your diary

Holiday	2010	2011
New Year's Day	1st Jan	3rd Jan
Good Friday	2nd Apr	22nd Apr
Easter Monday	5th Apr	25th Apr
Early May Bank Holiday	3rd May	2nd May
Liberation Day (Channel Islands)	9th May	9th May
Spring Bank Holiday	31st May	30th May
Summer Bank Holiday	30th Aug	29th Aug
Christmas Bank Holiday	27th Dec	27th Dec
Boxing Day Holiday	28th Dec	26th Dec

Finding great family days out and short breaks

7 MINUTES

There are 112 Saturdays, Sundays and Bank Holidays each year. So why not make the most of them by getting out and about and enjoying England. For hundreds of money saving offers and ideas visit **enjoyEngland.com/value**

ENJOY EVERY MINUTE, enjoy**England**.com

North York Moors, North Yorkshire, England.

Yorkshire

Yorkshire

Yorkshire is full of so many different experiences. It's big and boundless, a mix of magnetic landscapes, seductive seascapes and vibrant cities that change by the minute and the mile.

Yorkshire Coast

Explore North Yorkshire's beautiful Heritage Coast with its towering cliffs, sandy beaches and traditional seaside resorts. Enjoy fishing festivals, regattas and sea sports galore or take a walk along the Cleveland Way National Trail (North Sea Trail) which hugs the coastline.

Scarborough has been a seaside destination for over 100 years while the historic charm of Whitby is world famous. The elegant town of Filey boasts five miles of golden sand and is always a family favourite. Lying between these three famous towns are some of the Yorkshire Coast's best-kept secrets – sweeping golden bays and tiny fishing villages. Sheltered in narrow ravines and located in the North York Moors National Park, the villages of Robin Hood's Bay, Runswick Bay and Staithes all owe their existence to the fishing industry. It is easy to imagine the smugglers that once frequented this area.

Yorkshire Dales

The Yorkshire Dales offers some of the finest scenery in the world. This distinctive network of dry stonewalls ushers in twisty country lanes through rugged high fells, heather-clad moors, ancient, broadleaf woodland and sleepy meadows. A rich pageant of rare species populate the varied

habitats of the Dales, from delicate wild flowers to numerous birds and other species. This wealth of natural beauty has earned the Dales the status of National Park and Area of Outstanding Natural Beauty – official recognition and protection of its environmental importance.

Pennine Yorkshire

Easily accessible from Manchester and Leeds, and bordered by the Peak District National park to the south; Pennine Yorkshire is an area perfect for touring and exploring. Superb scenery and landscapes, walking and cycling opportunities abound. Rise to the challenge of the hills, meander around the wooded valleys or stroll along the towpaths of the canals and rivers.

Yorkshire Wolds

The Yorkshire Wolds are a series of gently undulating hills and valleys, south of the North York Moors and stretching in an arc from the city of Hull and the market town of Beverley to the coastal resorts of Filey and Bridlington on the Yorkshire coast. The countryside is spectacular. Open roads lead to the charming and ancient market towns of Howden, Hedon, Pocklington, Driffield and the historic town of Beverley, appealing not only for

its glorious Gothic Minster but also for its lovingly preserved old streets and buildings.

South Yorkshire

For something faster paced, try Leeds. A shopaholic's dream – from the exquisite Victorian arcades to the contemporary complex The Light and the vibrant Kirkgate Market. Also renowned as an international hub of leading arts, culture and world-class sporting venues… just some of the many things that make Leeds such a great place.

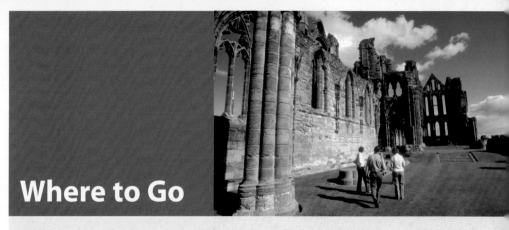

Where to Go

 Attractions with this sign participate in the **Visitor Attraction Quality Assurance Scheme** (see page 6) which recognises high standards in all aspects of the vistor experience.

ENTERTAINMENT & CULTURE

Bronte Parsonage Museum
Haworth, West Yorkshire, BD22 8DR
(01535) 642323
www.bronte.org.uk
The home of Charlotte, Emily and Anne Brontë, set in moorland that inspired their writing.

Clifton Park Museum
Rotherham, South Yorkshire, S65 2AA
(01709) 336633
www.visitrotherham.org
Local pottery, antiquities, natural and social history. Restored period kitchen. Temporary exhibitions.

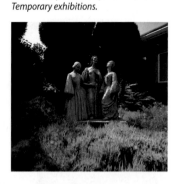

Dinostar – The Dinosaur Experience
Hull, East Riding of Yorkshire, HU1 1TH
(01482) 320424
www.dinostar.co.uk
Hear a raptor roar and touch triceratops bones at this exciting interactive exhibition of dinosaurs.

East Riding Rural Life Museum
Beverley, East Riding of Yorkshire, HU16 5TF
(01482) 392777
www.eastriding.gov.uk
Complete working windmill with museum relating to rural life in the East Riding.

Ferens Art Gallery
Hull, East Riding of Yorkshire, HU1 3RA
(01482) 613902
www.hullcc.gov.uk/museums
Browse Old Masters, marine paintings, 20thC and contemporary works. Exhibitions, workshops, live art, shop and cafe.

National Coal Mining Museum for England
Wakefield, West Yorkshire, WF4 4RH
(01924) 848806
Discover the hidden world of mining through the centuries. Unique buildings, displays and activities.

National Media Museum
Bradford, West Yorkshire, BD1 1NQ
0870 701 0200
www.nationalmediamuseum.org.uk
Seven floors devoted to film, photography, television, radio and the web, plus a giant screen IMAX.

National Railway Museum
York, North Yorkshire, YO26 4XJ
0844 815 3139
www.nrm.org.uk
Awesome trains, interactive fun – and the world's largest railway museum is free.

Streetlife Museum
Hull, East Riding of Yorkshire, HU1 1PS
(01482) 613902
www.hullcc.gov.uk/museums
Displays cover 200 years of transport: railways, cycles, cars, trams, plus simulated mail coach ride.

Thackray Museum
Leeds, West Yorkshire, LS9 7LN
(0113) 244 4343
www.thackraymuseum.org
Fascinating story of medicine. Experience Victorian Leeds slums, or explore the human body.

Waterways Museum
Goole, East Riding of Yorkshire, DN14 5TB
(01405) 768730
Story of Goole's development as a canal terminus and North Sea port connection.

Weston Park Museum
Sheffield, South Yorkshire, S10 2TP
(0114) 278 2612
www.sheffieldgalleries.org.uk
Vast historical, archaeological and decorative arts collection. Fascinating temporary exhibitions.

ithernsea Lighthouse useum
ithernsea, East Riding of orkshire, HU19 2DY
1964) 614834
agnificent view of Withernsea from p of the 127ft-high lighthouse. Local story museum and the Kay Kendall emorial Museum. HM Coastguard nd RNLI collection.

orld of James Herriot
hirsk,North Yorkshire, YO7 1PL
1845) 524234
ww.worldofjamesherriot.org
e 1940s home and surgery of the mous vet, featuring TV studios and teractive children's gallery.

scape Castleford
astleford, West Yorkshire, F10 4TA
371 200 3221
ww.xscape.co.uk
timate family fun: 170 metre indoor al snow slope, 14 screen cinema mplex, 20 lane bowling alley, shops d refreshments.

rk Castle Museum
ork, North Yorkshire, YO1 9RY
1904) 687687
ww.yorkcastlemuseum.org.uk
xperience everyday life through e centuries with period rooms and constructed streets, including the ew-look Victorian Street.

orkshire Air Museum
ork, North Yorkshire, YO41 4AU
1904) 608595
ww.yorkshireairmuseum.co.uk
he Yorkshire Air Museum is based n a unique WWII Bomber Command tation with fascinating exhibits and ttractive Memorial Gardens that have on 3 consecutive Yorkshire in Bloom wards. The exhibits cover a wide range f aviation history.

FAMILY FUN

Magna Science Adventure Centre
Rotherham, South Yorkshire, S60 1DX
(01709) 720002
www.visitmagna.co.uk
Embark on an unforgettable, interactive science adventure. Explore earth, air, fire and water.

HERITAGE

Beverley Guildhall
Beverley, East Riding of Yorkshire, HU17 9XX
(01482) 392783
www.eastriding.gov.uk
Medieval building with later remodelling. Home to the borough's ancient charters and civic treasures.

Brodsworth Hall and Gardens
Doncaster, South Yorkshire, DN5 7XJ
(01302) 722598
www.english-heritage.org.uk
An 1860s Italianate country house that reveals a Victorian family's changing fortunes. Marvellous labyrinthine gardens.

Castle Howard
Malton, North Yorkshire, YO60 7DA
(01653) 648444
www.castlehoward.co.uk
Magnificent 18thC house, stunning parkland, outdoor guided tours, adventure playground, shops, cafes. A superb day out.

Fountains Abbey
Ripon, North Yorkshire, HG4 3DY
(01765) 608888
www.fountainsabbey.org.uk
Britain's largest monastic ruin, founded by Cistercian monks in 1132, with a captivating 18thC landscaped garden.

Harewood House
Leeds, West Yorkshire, LS17 9LG
(0113) 218 1010
www.harewood.org
A treasure trove of stunning architecture, exquisite Adam interiors, Chippendale furniture, fine porcelain and art collections.

JORVIK Viking Centre
York, North Yorkshire, YO1 9WT
(01904) 615505
www.jorvik-viking-centre.co.uk
Journey back 1,000 years into York's thrilling Viking past along reconstructed streets. Meet a Viking face-to-face!

Keighley and Worth Valley Railway
Haworth, West Yorkshire, BD22 8NJ
(01535) 645214
www.kwvr.co.uk
Fully operational, preserved railway with award winning stations. Popular film and television location.

North York Moors National Park Centre
Danby, North Yorkshire, YO21 2NB
(01439) 772737
www.visitthemoors.co.uk
North York Moors National Park Centre on the banks of the River Esk. Newly refurbished with interactive exhbitions, av presentation, Inspired by... Gallery, children's climbing wall, indoor and outdoor play areas.

Sewerby Hall and Gardens
Bridlington, East Riding of Yorkshire, YO15 1EA
(01262) 673769
www.bridlington.net/sewerby
Fine country house overlooking Bridlington Bay, featuring 50 acres of lovingly maintained gardens and grounds.

Temple Newsam House and Farm
Leeds, West Yorkshire, LS15 0AD
(0113) 247 8391
Tudor-Jacobean mansion with rich art collections. Europe's largest working rare breeds farm – over 400 animals.

Whitby Abbey
Whitby, North Yorkshire, YO22 4JT
(01947) 603568
www.english-heritage.org.uk/whitbyabbey
Be enchanted by an abbey that has inspired religious devotion and literary works across the centuries.

York Minster
York,North Yorkshire, YO1 7HH
(01904) 557216
www.yorkminster.org
The largest medieval Gothic cathedral in northern Europe and a treasure house of amazing stained glass.

NATURE & WILDLIFE

Brockholes Farm Visitor Centre
Doncaster, South Yorkshire, DN3 3NH
(01302) 535450
Meet farm animals including pedigree Limousin cattle, plus smaller furry friends. Woodland walk, exotic birds.

Ponderosa Rural Therapeutic Centre
Heckmondwike, West Yorkshire, WF16 0PL
(01924) 235276
Activities for disadvantaged and disabled children, based around rare breeds, greenhouses, reptile house and lakes.

RSPB Bempton Cliffs Reserve
Bridlington, East Riding of Yorkshire, YO15 1JF
(01262) 851179
www.rspb.org.uk
Observe vast numbers of sea birds around spectacular cliffs. Star species include gannets, kittiwakes and puffins.

RSPB Old Moor Nature Reserve
Barnsley, South Yorkshire, S73 0YF
(01226) 751593
www.rspb.org.uk
RSPB nature reserve covering 250 acres. All-year birdwatching interest. Visitor centre with hands-on displays.

Sheffield Botanical Gardens
Sheffield, South Yorkshire, S10 2LN
(0114) 267 1115
www.sbg.org.uk
Listed 19thC gardens, featuring over 5,500 plant species from across the globe, set in 19 acres.

The Deep
Hull, East Riding of Yorkshire, HU1 4DP
(01482) 381000
www.thedeep.co.uk
Explore the history of the world's oceans at one of the most spectacular aquariums.

Wentworth Castle Gardens
Barnsley, South Yorkshire, S75 3ET
(01226) 776040
www.wentworthcastle.org
Recently rediscovered 18thC gardens. National Collections, 500 acre parkland, walks, follies, viewing platform.

Events 2010

Art in the Gardens
Sheffield
www.artinthegardens.org.uk/
September

Bradford Mela
Bradford
www.bradfordmela.org.uk
12th-13th June

Ebor Festival
York
www.ebor-festival.co.uk
August

English Mystery Plays
Barnsley
www.englishmysteryplays.com
June-July

FuseLeeds 2010
Leeds
www.fuseleeds.org.uk
April-May

Grassington Dickensian Festival
Grassington
www.grassington.uk.com
December

Great Yorkshire Show
Harrogate
www.greatyorkshireshow.co.uk
July

Harrogate Autumn Flower Show
Harrogate
www.flowershow.org.uk/
September

Harrogate International Festival
Leeds
www.harrogate-festival.org.uk/
July

Haworth 1940's Weekend
Haworth
www.haworth1940s.co.uk/
15th-16th May

Ilkley Summer Festival
Ilkley
www.ilkley.org/summerfestival/
August

JORVIK Viking Festival
York
www.jorvik-viking-centre.co.uk
15th-20th February

Kettlewell Scarecrow Festival
Kettlewell
www.kettlewell.info/scarecrow.cfm
August

Kite Festival
Leeds
www.harewood.org
May

Leeds Festival
Wetherby
www.leedsfestival.com
27th-29th August

Ryedale Folk Weekend
Pickering
www.festivalonthemoor.co.uk
May

Scarborough Jazz Festival
Scarborough
www.scarboroughjazzfestival.co.uk
September

Seafest Festival
Scarborough
www.seafest.org.uk
July

Spring Flower Show, Harrogate
Harrogate
www.flowershow.org.uk
22nd-25th April

Steam Gala Weekend
Haworth
www.kwvr.co.uk
June

The Queen's Golden Jubilee International Joust
Leeds
www.royalarmouries.org
August

The St Ledger Festival
Doncaster
www.doncaster-racecourse.co.uk/
September

York Festival of Food and Drink
York
www.yorkfestivaloffoodanddrink.com/
September

York Literature Festival
York
www.yorkfestivals.com
February-March

York Roman Festival
York
www.yorkfestivals.com
May

Yorkshire Comedy Festival
York
www.yorkshirecomedyfestival.org/
July

Where to Eat

Yorkshire has great places to eat. The restaurant reviews on this page are just a small selection from the highly respected *The Good Food Guide 2010*. Please see pages 20-21 for further information on the guide and details of a Special Offer for our readers.

BURNSALL

Devonshire Fell
Modern brasserie in stunning Dales location
Burnsall, BD23 6BT
Tel no: (01756) 729000
www.devonshirehotels.co.uk
Modern European | £29

The sturdy stone Fell had become the weaker link in the Devonshire trio of Wharfedale eateries, but with new chef Dan Birk it's taken a sharp upward turn. He comes with an impressive CV and brings technique, timing and elegant presentation that applies as well to the bar menu of sausage and mash and steak and ale pie as to the à la carte. Choose starters of sea bass fillet and miniature ratatouille or tender slices of wood pigeon breast on Bury black pudding with a silky celeriac purée. Follow with Dales lamb, sea bream or an outstanding dish of tender venison on sautéed Savoy cabbage, caramelised root vegetables and a deep grand-veneur sauce, sweetened with redcurrant and a hint of bitter chocolate. Desserts of parfaits, brûlées, tarts and pannacottas all stay on the money. Factor in fabulous Wharfedale views, a smart set of bedrooms and this is once again a cherishable Dales asset.
Chef/s: Daniel Birk. **Open:** all week L 12 to 3, D 6.30 to 9.30 (Fri and Sat to 10, Sun to 9). **Meals:** alc (main courses £16 to £18). Set L and D £23 (2 courses) to £29. Sun L £11.95. **Service:** 12.5% (optional). **Details:** Cards accepted. 40 seats. Separate bar. Wheelchair access. Music. Children allowed. Car parking.

> Content brought to you by **The Good Food Guide 2010**. Please see pages 20–21 for further details.

YORK

J. Baker's Bistro Moderne
Affordable fine dining and fun
7 Fossgate, York, YO1 9TA
Tel no: (01904) 622688
www.jbakers.co.uk
Modern British | £28

A high roller right in York's gastro-epicentre, Jeff Baker's self-styled 'bistro moderne' is pitched squarely as a populist venue for our times. Rather than desperately seeking accolades, it aims to deliver good food for all at prices that won't crash the system. The ground-floor restaurant lives and breathes laid-back cosmopolitan style, with subdued colours, a few pictures and flower arrangements providing the backdrop, while upstairs is a seductive chocolate room dedicated to toothsome delights. At lunchtime, a flexible grazing menu rules: order and eat at your own pace from a snappy assortment of little dishes including snail and chestnut 'ragoo' or black pudding pasties with hazelnut pease pudding. Evening meals raise the bar with forthright, fancy-free offerings such as crunchy lamb belly with smoked eel, eggplant and pimento or slowcooked pork cheeks with Thai ketchup, seared squid and buttered noodles. Jeff Baker may be serious about food, but he has a sense of fun and isn't averse to playing a few mischievous tricks on the taste buds. A starter dubbed 'pot of tea and bacon buttie' involves pheasant, pancetta and prunes, roast Yorkshire mallard is served with 'leftover Xmas pudding' and desserts include the deliciously tongue-in-cheek peanut butter and jelly sandwich with sarsaparilla. House wines from £13.95 head the praiseworthy, price-conscious list.
Chef/s: Jeff Baker. **Open:** Tue to Sat L 12 to 2.30, D 6 to 10. **Closed:** Sun and Mon, first week Jan. **Meals:** Set menu £24 (2 courses) to £28 (3 courses) to £38 (7 courses). **Service:** 10% (optional). **Details:** Cards accepted. 56 seats. Separate bar. Wheelchair access. Music. Children allowed.

Tourist Information Centres

When you arrive at your destination, visit an Official Partner Tourist Information Centre for quality assured help with accommodation and information about local attractions and events, or email your request before you go. To search for attractions and Tourist Information Centres on the move just text INFO to 62233, and a web link will be sent to your mobile phone. To find a Tourist Information Centre by region visit enjoyEngland.com/find-tic.

AYSGARTH FALLS	Aysgarth Falls NP Centre	01969 662910	aysgarth@ytbtic.co.uk
BEVERLEY	34 Butcher Row	01482 391672	beverley.tic@eastriding .gov.uk
BRADFORD	City Hall	01274 433678	tourist.information@bradford.gov.uk
BRIDLINGTON	25 Prince Street	01262 673474	bridlington.tic@eastriding.gov.uk
DANBY	The Moors Centre, Danby Lodge	01439 772737	moorscentre@northyorkmoors-npa.gov.uk
DONCASTER	Blue Building	01302 734309	tourist.information@doncaster.gov.uk
FILEY	Filey TIC	01723 383637	fileytic@scarborough.gov.uk
GRASSINGTON	National Park Centre	01756 751690	grassington@ytbtic.co.uk
GUISBOROUGH	Priory Grounds	01287 633801	guisborough_tic@redcar-cleveland.gov.uk
HALIFAX	Piece Hall	01422 368725	halifax@ytbtic.co.uk
HARROGATE	Royal Baths	01423 537300	tic@harrogate.gov.uk
HAWES	Dales Countryside Museum	01969 666210	hawes@ytbtic.co.uk
HAWORTH	2/4 West Lane	01535 642329	haworth@ytbtic.co.uk
HEBDEN BRIDGE	Visitor and Canal Centre	01422 843831	hebdenbridge@ytbtic.co.uk
HELMSLEY	Helmsley Castle	01439 770173	helmsley@ytbtic.co.uk
HOLMFIRTH	49-51 Huddersfield Road	01484 222444	holmfirth.tic@kirklees.gov.uk
HUDDERSFIELD	3 Albion Street	01484 223200	huddersfield.tic@kirklees.gov.uk
HULL	1 Paragon Street	01482 223559	tourist.information@hullcc.gov.uk
HUMBER BRIDGE	North Bank Viewing Area	01482 640852	humberbridge.tic@eastriding.gov.uk
ILKLEY	Town Hall	01943 602319	ilkley@ytbtic.co.uk
KNARESBOROUGH	9 Castle Courtyard	0845 389 0177	kntic@harrogate.gov.uk
LEEDS	Gateway Yorkshire	0113 242 5242	tourinfo@leeds.gov.uk
LEEMING BAR	The Yorkshire Maid	01677 424262	leeming@ytbtic.co.uk
LEYBURN	4 Central Chambers	01748 828747	leyburn@ytbtic.co.uk

MALHAM	National Park Centre	01969 652380	malham@ytbtic.co.uk
MALTON	58 Market Place	01653 600048	maltontic@btconnect.com
OTLEY	Otley Library & Tourist Information	01943 462485	otleytic@leedslearning.net
PATELEY BRIDGE	18 High Street	0845 389 0177	pbtic@harrogate.gov.uk
PICKERING	Ropery House	01751 473791	pickering@ytbtic.co.uk
REETH	Hudson House, The Green	01748 884059	reeth@ytbtic.co.uk
RICHMOND	Friary Gardens	01748 828742	richmond@ytbtic.co.uk
RIPON	Minster Road	01765 604625	ripontic@harrogate.gov.uk
ROTHERHAM	40 Bridgegate	01709 835904	tic@rotherham.gov.uk
SCARBOROUGH	Brunswick Shopping Centre	01723 383636	tourismbureau@scarborough.gov.uk
SCARBOROUGH	Harbourside TIC	01723 383636	harboursidetic@scarborough.gov.uk
SETTLE	Town Hall	01729 825192	settle@ytbtic.co.uk
SHEFFIELD	Visitor Information Point	0114 2211900	visitor@yorkshiresouth.com
SKIPTON	35 Coach Street	01756 792809	skipton@ytbtic.co.uk
SUTTON BANK	Sutton Bank Visitor Centre	01845 597426	suttonbank@ytbtic.co.uk
THIRSK	Thirsk Tourist Information Centre	01845 522755	thirsktic@hambleton.gov.uk
TODMORDEN	15 Burnley Road	01706 818181	todmorden@ytbtic.co.uk
WAKEFIELD	9 The Bull Ring	0845 601 8353	tic@wakefield.gov.uk
WETHERBY	Library & Tourist Info. Centre	01937 582151	wetherbytic@leedslearning.net
WHITBY	Langborne Road	01723 383637	whitbytic@scarborough.gov.uk
WITHERNSEA	131 Queen Street	01964 615683	withernsea.tic@eastriding.gov.uk
YORK	The De Grey Rooms	01904 550099	info@visityork.org
YORK	Outer Concourse, Railway Station	01904 550099	info@visityork.org

Regional Contacts and Information

For more information on accommodation, attractions, activities, events and holidays in Yorkshire, contact the regional tourism organisation. Their website has a wealth of information and produces many free publications to help you get the most out of your visit.

The following publications are available from the Yorkshire Tourist Board by logging on to www.yorkshire.com or calling 0844 888 5123

Yorkshire Accommodation Guide 2010

Information on Yorkshire, including hotels, self catering, camping and caravan parks

Make Yorkshire Yours Magazine

This entertaining magazine is full of articles and features about what's happening in Yorkshire, including where to go and what to do.

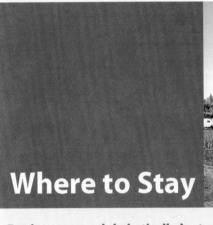

Where to Stay

Entries appear alphabetically by town name in each county. A key to symbols appears on page 6. Maps start on page 394. A listing of all Enjoy England assessed accommodation appears at the end of the region.

ALLERSTON, Yorkshire Map ref 5D3 — SAT NAV YO18 7PQ

Vale of Pickering Caravan Park

Vale of Pickering Caravan Park, Allerston, Pickering YO18 7PQ
t (01723) 859280 f (01723) 850060 e tony@valeofpickering.co.uk
w **valeofpickering.co.uk**

⬛	£14.00–£22.00
⬛	£14.00–£22.00
⬛	£11.00–£20.00

120 touring pitches

Family-owned park in Allerston. High standard of service and superb facilities. Peacefully located in open countryside offering panoramic views. A well-stocked licenced shop. Closed 3 January to 5 March. **directions** Helmsley to Scarborough A170. Turn right down village of Allerston on the B1415 to Malton. Continue out of Village for approx 700 yds. **payment** credit/debit cards, cash, cheques

General ⬛🐕🛝⬛⬛☀⬛⬛⬛⬛⬛ Leisure ⌐∪✎⛰

BARDSEY, Yorkshire Map ref 4B1 — SAT NAV LS17 9DY

Haighfield Caravan Park

5 Blackmoor Lane, Bardsey, Leeds LS17 9DY
t (01937) 574658 e haighfieldcp@aol.com
w **haighfieldcaravanpark.co.uk**

⬛	£10.00–£14.00
⬛	£10.00–£14.00
⬛ (3)	£220.00–£450.00

4 touring pitches

Award-winning pristine countryside park. Excellent location 20 minutes from leeds Wetherby and Harrogate. Perfect for touring Yorkshire. Rose award static holiday homes to hire. Very tranquil setting open all year. **directions** Situated off A58 (Leeds Wetherby road) turn into Bardsey at Church lane past Bardsy church and Bingley Arms. Park top of hill on left. **open** All year **payment** credit/debit cards, cash, cheques

General ⬛⬛⬛⬛⬛☀⬛ Leisure ⌐∪✎

Looking for something else?

You can also buy a copy of our popular guide 'Self Catering' including self-catering holiday homes, approved caravan holiday homes, boat accommodation and holiday cottage agencies in England 2010. Now available in good bookshops and online at **enjoyenglanddirect.com**

£11.99

BEDALE, Yorkshire Map ref 5C3

SAT NAV DL7 9BW

RATING
APPLIED FOR

Pembroke Caravan Park
19 Low Street, Leeming Bar, Bedale DL7 9BW
t (01677) 422608 e craggs9bw@btinternet.com

🚐 (25) £10.00–£14.00
🚐 (25) £10.00–£14.00
⛺ (25) £8.00–£14.00
🚐 (3) £140.00–£180.00
25 touring pitches

Small, sheltered site catering for touring vans, including motor caravans and tents. Excellent A1 night halt. **directions** Come off A1 at Leeming services - turn right into Leeming Bar - at mini roundabout straight over - park entrance on right 800 yds. **open** March to October **payment** cash, cheques

General 🛒 🐕 🏪 🏕 ☼ 🎮 🛏 📞 🚻 ♿   Leisure ▶ ∪ ♪

BOLTON ABBEY, Yorkshire Map ref 4B1

SAT NAV BD23 6AN

★★★★★
TOURING PARK

Strid Wood Caravan Club Site
Bolton Abbey, Skipton BD23 6AN
t (01756) 710433 f (01342) 410258
w caravanclub.co.uk

THE
CARAVAN
CLUB

🚐 (57) £14.00–£26.90
🚐 (57) £14.00–£26.90
57 touring pitches

One of the prettiest sites on our network and part of the Bolton Abbey Estate in open glades surrounded by woodland and the glorious Yorkshire Dales. **directions** Turn off A59 onto B6160, after 3miles turn right into Strid car park. Please note that approach from north on B6160 is unsuitable for caravans. **open** March 2010 to January 2011 **payment** credit/debit cards, cash, cheques

General 🛏 🐕 🏪 🏕 🎮 📞 🚻 ♿ 🅿

BRANDESBURTON, Yorkshire Map ref 4C1

SAT NAV YO25 8SB

★★★
TOURING &
CAMPING PARK

Fosse Hill Caravan Park
Catwick Lane, Brandesburton, Hornsea YO25 8SB
t (01964) 542608 f (01964) 543010 e tony@fossehill.co.uk
w fossehill.co.uk

🚐 £20.00–£30.00
🚐 £20.00–£30.00
⛺ (30) £15.00–£25.00
90 touring pitches

Fosse Hill Caravan Park is a family freindly touring caravan site located in Brandesburton. Conveniently situated for Hull, Beverley, Bridlington and Yorkshire Wolds. **directions** Please contact us for directions **open** March 1st to November 1st **payment** credit/debit cards, cash, cheques

General 🛒 🛥 🏪 🏕 ☼ 📞 🚻 ♿ 🅿 ✕   Leisure ▶ ♪ 🍴 ♫ ⛰

CLAXTON, Yorkshire Map ref 4C1

SAT NAV YO60 7RX

★★★★
HOLIDAY, TOURING
& CAMPING PARK

Foxhill Park
Claxton to Harton Lodge Road, Claxton, York, North Yorkshire YO60 7RX
t (01904) 468355 f (01904) 468560 e enquiries@foxhillpark.com
w foxhillpark.com

🚐 (36) £13.00–£15.00
🚐 £13.00–£15.00
⛺ (20) £10.00–£12.00
56 touring pitches

Foxhill is located on the outskirts of the pretty village of Claxton, with excellent access from the A64 York to Scarborough road, good bus service. Castle Howard nearby. Family run. **directions** Located off the A64 between York and Malton, 8 miles east of York. Take exit sign-posted Claxton and Stamford Bridge. Foxhill is on your left. **open** 1st March to 31st October **payment** cash, cheques

General 🛏 ♫ 🛒 🛥 🏪 ☼ 🎮 🛏 📞 🚻 🅿   Leisure ▶ ♪

FILEY, Yorkshire Map ref 5D3   SAT NAV YO14 0PU

★★★★★
HOLIDAY PARK

🚐 £12.00–£20.00
🚙 £12.00–£20.00
🅰 (25) £12.00–£20.00
60 touring pitches

Orchard Farm Holiday Village
Stonegate, Hunmanby, Filey YO14 0PU
t (01723) 891582   f (01723) 891582   e info@orchardfarmholidayvillage.co.uk
w **orchardfarmholidayvillage.co.uk**

Family park in edge-of-village location with easy access to resorts of Filey, Scarborough and Bridlington. Amenities include children's play area, fishing lake and entertainment during peak season. **directions** From A165 from Scarborough take 1st right to Hunmanby under railway bridge 1st right. **open** March to October **payment** cash, cheques

General 🖳 🐕 🏕 🖿 🅿 ☼ 🚿 🛝 🚻   Leisure ► ∪ ⌕ ↯ ⚑ ♬ ✦ ⁄⊓

FOLLIFOOT, Yorkshire Map ref 4B1   SAT NAV HG3 1TZ

★★★★
TOURING PARK

🚐 (71) £9.30–£20.70
🚙 (71) £9.30–£20.70
71 touring pitches

Great Yorkshire Showground Caravan Club
Railway Road, Off Wetherby Road, Harrogate HG3 1TZ
t (01423) 560470   f (01342) 410258
w **caravanclub.co.uk**

THE
CARAVAN
CLUB

A flat, pleasantly open site, convenient for visits to Harrogate, the floral capital of Yorkshire. Not only does the town have splendid examples of municipal gardens, but it also hosts two major flower shows. **directions** Turn left off A661 (Wetherby-Harrogate). Site on right in 400 yds. **open** March to September **payment** credit/debit cards, cash, cheques

General 🖳 🐕 🛝 🚻   Leisure ►

GILLING WEST, Yorkshire Map ref 5C3   SAT NAV DL10 5LJ

★★★★
TOURING PARK

🚐 (66) £10.60–£23.20
🚙 (66) £10.60–£23.20
66 touring pitches

SPECIAL PROMOTIONS
Special member rates mean you can save your membership subscription in less than a week. Visit caravanclub.co.uk to find out more.

Hargill House Caravan Club Site
Gilling West, Richmond DL10 5LJ
t (017488) 822734   f (01342) 410258
w **caravanclub.co.uk**

THE
CARAVAN
CLUB

This is an intimate, gently sloping site in the old town of Richmond. Breathtaking views over the Yorkshire Dales National Park. It's Heriot country and you'll find many of the locations used in the famous series. It's also the area where our greatest landscape artist, J M W Turner, travelled and painted and found the subjects for some of his most famous watercolours.

open March to November
payment credit/debit cards, cash, cheques

directions Leave the A1 at Scotch Corner and go onto the A66. After 1.5 miles turn left at the crossroads. Site entrance is a further 100 yds on left. For details on other routes visit caravanclub.co.uk.

General 🖳 🐕 🛝 🖿 ☼ 🚿 🛝 🚻 🚾
Leisure ► ⌕

GUISBOROUGH, Yorkshire Map ref 5C3

SAT NAV TS14 6QA

RATING APPLIED FOR

Tocketts Mill Leisure Park
Tocketts Mill Caravan Park, Skelton Road, Guisborough, North Yorkshire TS14 6QA
t 01278 610182 e enquiries@tockettsmill.co.uk

(108)   £50.00–£65.00
(108)   £400.00–£600.00

Set in a valley with 35 acres of woodland with steam and the 17th century working watermill.

open 1st March to 4th January
payment cash

directions Take the A171 Whitby to Guisborough road then the A173 to Skelton, over the first roundabout then next left.

General
Leisure

HARMBY, Yorkshire Map ref 5C3

SAT NAV DL8 5NU

TOURING & CAMPING PARK

Lower Wensleydale Caravan Club Site
Harmby, Leyburn DL8 5NU
t (01969) 623366
w caravanclub.co.uk

THE CARAVAN CLUB

£10.60–£23.20
£10.60–£23.20
92 touring pitches

Set within the hollow of a disused quarry, now overrun with wild flowers and mosses. This site offers charming pitching areas. Many interesting attractions nearby and wonderful walking country.
directions From east on A684, turn right 0.75 miles past railway bridge; turn immediately left and follow signs to site entrance.
open April to November **payment** credit/debit cards, cash, cheques

General   Leisure

HARROGATE, Yorkshire Map ref 4B1

SAT NAV HG3 2LT

HOLIDAY & TOURING PARK

High Moor Farm Park
Skipton Road, Felliscliffe, Pateley Bridge HG3 2LT
t (01423) 563637 f (01423) 529449 e highmoorfarmpark@btconnect.com

(200)   £19.00–£21.00
(57)   £19.00
200 touring pitches

Secluded site surrounded by trees on the edge of the Yorkshire Dales. **directions** On A59 4 miles west of Harrogate. **open** April to October **payment** credit/debit cards, cash, cheques

General   Leisure

HARROGATE, Yorkshire Map ref 4B1 — SAT NAV HG3 1JH

Rudding Holiday Park

Follifoot, Harrogate HG3 1JH
t 01423 870439 f (01423) 870859 e holiday-park@ruddingpark.com
w **ruddingpark.co.uk** ONLINE MAP LAST MINUTE OFFERS

£16.50–£33.00
£16.50–£33.00
£16.50–£33.00
141 touring pitches

SPECIAL PROMOTIONS
Peak season: 7 nights for the price of 6. Off-peak season: 4 nights for the price of 3.

Award-winning campsite just 3 miles south of Harrogate, in peaceful setting, offering Deer House pub, swimming pool, golf course, six-hole short course, driving range and shop. Closed February. Self-catering timber lodges also available.

payment credit/debit cards, cash, cheques, euros

directions Situated only 3 miles south of Harrogate, Rudding Park lies just off the A658 linking the A61 from Leeds to the A59 York Road.

General Leisure

HAWORTH, Yorkshire Map ref 4B1 — SAT NAV BD22 9SS

Upwood Holiday Park

Black Moor Road, Oxenhope, Haworth BD22 9SS
t (01535) 644242 e info@upwoodpark.co.uk
w **upwoodpark.co.uk** ONLINE MAP GUEST REVIEWS LAST MINUTE OFFERS

£9.50–£24.50
(2) £9.50
(15) £9.50
(2) £150.00–£345.00
60 touring pitches

SPECIAL PROMOTIONS
Tent Pods available 2009

A family-owned park pleasantly situated close to the Yorkshire Dales National Park - an ideal base from which to explore the area by car or on foot. Large, modern toilet facilities, comfortable lounge bar serving snacks, games room with pool and arcade games, small shop for essential items.

open 1st March to 4th January
payment credit/debit cards, cash, cheques, euros

directions Please contact us for directions

General Leisure

HEBDEN BRIDGE, Yorkshire Map ref 4B1 SAT NAV HX7 5RU

enjoyEngland.com ★★★★★ TOURING PARK

(45) £9.30–£20.20
(45) £9.30–£20.20
45 touring pitches

Lower Clough Foot Caravan Club Site

Cragg Vale, Hebden Bridge HX7 5RU
t (01422) 882531 **f** (01342) 410258 **e** enquiries@caravanclub.co.uk
w caravanclub.co.uk

Pretty site, set in a grassy enclave, well screened by mature trees and bordered by a stream. Good for walkers. Enjoy Victorian style shops in nearby Hebden Bridge. **directions** Turn off A646 onto B6138. Site on right in 1 mile. **open** April to November **payment** credit/debit cards, cash, cheques

General Leisure

HOLMFIRTH, Yorkshire Map ref 4B1 SAT NAV HD9 7TD

enjoyEngland.com ★★★★ TOURING & CAMPING PARK

(62) £15.00–£17.00
(62) £13.50–£15.50
(62) £6.00–£19.00
62 touring pitches

Holme Valley Camping and Caravan Park

Thongsbridge, Holmfirth HD9 7TD
t (01484) 665819 **f** (01484) 663870 **e** enquiries@homevalleycamping.com
w holmevalleycamping.com

Picturesque, setting in 'Summer Wine' country. Grass, concrete, gravel pitches. 16-amp hook-ups. Well-stocked food shop. Off-licence. Fishing in small lake and river. Kiddie's play area. Five minutes' walk from village. **directions** The entrance to our lane is 1 mile north of Holmfirth, off A6024. Passing bottle banks, continue to valley bottom. (No vehicular access from A616.) **open** All year **payment** credit/debit cards, cash, cheques, euros

General Leisure

KNARESBOROUGH, Yorkshire Map ref 4B1 SAT NAV HG5 9HH

enjoyEngland.com ★★★★★ TOURING PARK

(74) £14.00–£26.90
(74) £14.00–£26.90
74 touring pitches

SPECIAL PROMOTIONS
Special member rates mean you can save your membership subscription in less than a week. Visit our website to find out more.

Knaresborough Caravan Club Site

New Road, Scotton, Knaresborough HG5 9HH
t (01423) 860196 **f** (01342) 410258
w caravanclub.co.uk

Set in Lower Nidderdale, the site offers a gateway to the Yorkshire Dales and the many attractions of the North of England. Knaresborough is an historic market town with a town crier, ancient walkways and castle ruins, in summer enjoy the annual Bed Race and Knaresborough Festival.

open March 2010 to January 2011
payment credit/debit cards, cash, cheques

directions Turn right off A59 onto B6165. After approximately 1.5 miles turn right immediately after petrol station into New Road. Site is on right-hand side after 50 yds.

General
Leisure

LITTLE WEIGHTON, Yorkshire Map ref 4C1   SAT NAV HU20 3XJ

Croft Park
55 Rowley Road, Little Weighton, Beverley HU20 3XJ
t (01482) 840600 **f** (01482) 840600 **e** info@croftpark.com
w **croftpark.com** ONLINE MAP GUEST REVIEWS LAST MINUTE OFFERS

🚐	£24.00
🚏	£24.00
🏠 (1)	£395–£695
12 touring pitches	

Croft Park Caravan Site is a small and select, family-run site near Beverley in East Yorkshire situated just 4 miles from the South Cave Junction of the A63. **directions** Directions available on website. **open** 1st March to 31st October **payment** credit/debit cards, cash, cheques

General   Leisure

MARKINGTON, Yorkshire Map ref 5C3   SAT NAV HG3 3NR

Yorkshire Hussar Inn Caravan Park
High Street, Markington, Nr Harrogate HG3 3NR
t (01765) 677327 **e** enquiry@yorkshire-hussar-inn.co.uk
w **yorkshire-hussar-inn.co.uk** ONLINE MAP

🚐 (12)	£16.00–£20.00
🚏 (2)	£16.00–£20.00
⛺ (6)	£16.00–£20.00
🏠	£280.00–£375.00
12 touring pitches	

Yorkshire Hussar Inn Holiday Caravan Park is a secluded family park behind a village pub, with luxury holiday caravans for hire Tourers and tents. Close to Fountains Abbey and Dales. **directions** Please contact us for directions **open** Easter to October **payment** cash, cheques

General   Leisure

PICKERING, Yorkshire Map ref 5D3   SAT NAV YO18 8PG

Wayside Caravan Park
Wrelton, Pickering YO18 8PG
t (01751) 472608 **f** (01723) 512373 **e** waysideparks@freenet.co.uk
w **waysideparks.co.uk**

🚐 (40)	£17.00
🚏 (10)	£16.00
50 touring pitches	

Sheltered, quiet, south-facing holiday home, touring park, delightfully located with lovely country views. A walker's paradise. Steam railway. Castle Howard nearby. Whitby, Scarborough and York within a 45-minute drive. Holiday homes for sale. **directions** Two and a half miles west of Pickering at Wrelton off A170 - Follow signs. **open** 31 March to 31 October **payment** credit/debit cards, cash, cheques

General   Leisure

ROOS, Yorkshire Map ref 4D1   SAT NAV HU12 0JQ

Sand-le-Mere Caravan & Leisure Park
Seaside Lane, Tunstall HU12 0JQ
t (01964) 670403 **f** (01964) 671099 **e** info@sand-le-mere.co.uk
w **sand-le-mere.co.uk**

🚐 (16)	£10.00–£17.00
🚏 (2)	£10.00–£17.00
🏠 (26)	£149.00–£436.00
25 touring pitches	

A great place to visit, an even better place to stay, with its superb coastal setting, natural park and mere, plus first-class facilities. **directions** From Hull to Hedon take the B1362 at Withernsea, B1242 to Roos. Look for brown signs marked SLM. **open** 1 February to 1 January **payment** credit/debit cards, cash, cheques, euros

General   Leisure

SCARBOROUGH, Yorkshire Map ref 5D3 — SAT NAV YO11 3NN

Cayton Village Caravan Park Ltd

Mill Lane, Cayton Bay, Scarborough YO11 3NN
t (01723) 583171 e info@caytontouring.co.uk
w **caytontouring.co.uk**

🚐	£11.50–£26.00
🚎	£11.50–£26.00
⛺	£9.00–£20.00

200 touring pitches

The very best of coast and country. Luxurious facilities, adventure playground and site shop. Beach 1.5 mile, Scarborough 3 miles, Filey 4 miles. Adjoining village with fish shop, bus sevice and pubs. **directions** From A64 take B1261 to Filey. In Cayton turn left into Mill Lane. From A165 turn inland at Cayton Bay Roundabout onto Mill Lane. **open** 1st March to 31st October. **payment** credit/debit cards, cash, cheques

General 🔲 🐕 🦮 💷 📶 ☼ 🚮 🚗 📞 🕙 ☎ **Leisure** ⛳ ⛵ 🚣 ⛰

SCARBOROUGH, Yorkshire Map ref 5D3 — SAT NAV YO14 9PS

Crows Nest Caravan Park

Crows Nest Caravan Park, Gristhorpe, Filey YO14 9PS
t (01723) 582206 f (01723) 582206 e enquiries@crowsnestcaravanpark.com
w **crowsnestcaravanpark.com** ONLINE MAP ONLINE BOOKING LAST MINUTE OFFERS

🚐	(50)	£15.00–£25.00
🚎	(50)	£15.00–£25.00
⛺	(100)	£15.00–£22.00
🏠	(40)	£200.00–£510.00

150 touring pitches

Situated on the glorious Yorkshire coast between Scarborough and Filey. This family owned, Rose Award winning park is a perfect base. The facilities are of a very high standard, including heated - indoor swimming pool, children's play area and supermarket. Holidays and short breaks for families and couples. Tents and tourers welcome.

open March to October
payment credit/debit cards, cash, cheques

directions Just off A165 between Scarborough (5 miles) and Filey (2 miles). Turn off at roundabout with Esso petrol station. Well signposted.

General 🔲 🐕 🦮 💷 📶 ☼ 🚗 📞 🕙 ☎
Leisure 🚣 ⛳ 🍽 🎵 🏊 ⛰

SCARBOROUGH, Yorkshire Map ref 5D3 — SAT NAV YO11 3NU

Flower of May Holiday Parks Ltd

Flower of May Holiday Parks Ltd, Lebberston, Scarborough YO11 3NU
t (01723) 584311 f (01723) 581361 e info@flowerofmay.com
w **flowerofmay.com**

THE CARAVAN CLUB

🚐	(220)	£18.00–£25.00
🚎	(30)	£18.00–£25.00
⛺	(50)	£14.00–£25.00
🏠	(20)	£350.00–£600.00

300 touring pitches

Excellent family-run park. Luxury indoor pool, adventure playground and golf course. Ideal for coast and country. Prices per pitch, per night, four people with car. Luxury hire caravans. Seasonal serviced pitches. **directions** From A64 take the A165 Scarborough/Filey coast road. Well signposted at Lebberston. **open** Easter to October **payment** credit/debit cards, cash

General 🔲 🐕 🦮 💷 📶 ☼ 🚗 🚗 📞 🕙 ☎ **Leisure** ⛳ ⛵ 🚣 ⛳ 🍽 🎵 🏊 ⛰

SCARBOROUGH, Yorkshire Map ref 5D3 — SAT NAV YO13 9BE

Jasmine Park

Cross Lane, Snainton, Scarborough YO13 9BE
t 01723 859240 f (01723) 859240 e enquiries@jasminepark.co.uk
w **jasminepark.co.uk** ONLINE MAP ONLINE BOOKING LAST MINUTE OFFERS

(74)	£17.00–£25.00
(74)	£17.00–£25.00
A (20)	£17.00–£25.00
(1)	£200.00–£400.00
94 touring pitches	

Family-owned, tranquil park in picturesque countryside setting between Scarborough (8 miles) and Pickering. Superbly maintained facilities. Yorkshire Caravan Park of the Year 200C to 2004. National Silver Award 2005. Tents and tourers welcome. Seasonal pitches and storage available. Luxury caravan for hire.

open March to October
payment credit/debit cards, cash, cheques

directions Turn south off the A170 in Snainton opposite the junior school at traffic lights. Signposted.

YORKSHIRE
Moors&Coast
Tourism Awards
WINNER

General 🔲 🐕 🔧 🚿 🔥 ☼ 🚲 🔌 🗑 📞 ♿
Leisure ► ∪ 🎣 ♪

SCARBOROUGH, Yorkshire Map ref 5D3 — SAT NAV YO11 3PE

Lebberston Touring Park

Lebberston, Scarborough YO11 3PE
t (01723) 585723 e info@lebberstontouring.co.uk
w **lebberstontouring.co.uk** ONLINE MAP GUEST REVIEWS

	£14.50–£22.00
	£14.50–£22.00
125 touring pitches	

Quiet country location. Well-spaced pitches. Extensive south-facing views. Ideal park for a peaceful, relaxing break. Fully modernised amenity blocks. Dogs on lead. Finalist in both the White Rose Awards 2008 and the Moors and Coast Awards 2008. David Bellamy Gold Conservation Award. **directions** Please contact us for directions **open** 1st March to 31st October **payment** credit/debit cards, cash, cheques

General 🔲 📶 🐕 🔧 🚿 🔥 ☼ 🔌 🚲 🔌 🗑 📞 ♿

SCARBOROUGH, Yorkshire Map ref 5D3

SAT NAV YO12 5TG

Pinewood Holiday Park

Racecourse Road (A170), Scarborough, North Yorkshire YO12 5TG
t 01723 367278 07787378111 **e** info@pinewood-holiday-park.co.uk
w **pinewood-holiday-park.co.uk** LAST MINUTE OFFERS

🚐	£12.00
🚐 (5)	£12.00
⛺ (20)	£12.00
🏠 (16)	£30–£80

5 touring pitches

SPECIAL PROMOTIONS
2 nights minimum stay. 3 nights minimum stay over bank holidays. 4 nights at Easter Christmas, and New Year. Birthday and Anniverary packages.

A quiet family-run site set in 7 acres with stunning country side views. Perfectly situated within walking distance of Scarborough town, and a great base for exploring North Yorkshire. 10 adult only caravan pitches, tenting field and a Tipi camp, with both traditional authentic American Indian Tipis and modern Tipis.

open All year
payment credit/debit cards, cash, cheques

directions See website for directions.

General 🐕 ⛺ ☼ 📞 🎱 🚐
Leisure 🌙

SKIPSEA, Yorkshire Map ref 4D1

SAT NAV YO25 8TZ

Skipsea Sands Holiday Village

Mill Lane, Skipsea, Hornsea YO25 8TZ
t (01262) 468210 **f** (01262) 468454 **e** info@skipseasands.co.uk
w **hoseasons.co.uk** ONLINE MAP ONLINE BOOKING

🚐	£15.00–£32.00
🏠	£162.00–£779.00

An all action park just perfect for fun family holidays! **directions** Take the B1242 into Skipsea, once you enter the village you will see Skipsea Sands signposted to the left just after a sharp left hand bend. **open** March to October **payment** credit/debit cards, cheques

General 🗐 🐕 🖥 🅿 📞 🎱 ✕ Leisure ► ∪ ♿ 🍸 🎵 ✎ ⚙

SLINGSBY, Yorkshire Map ref 5C3

SAT NAV YO62 4AP

Robin Hood Caravan Park

Slingsby, York YO62 4AP
t (01653) 628391 **f** (01653) 628392 **e** info@robinhoodcaravanpark.co.uk
w **robinhoodcaravanpark.co.uk** ONLINE MAP ONLINE BOOKING LAST MINUTE OFFERS

🚐 (38)	£16.00–£27.00
🚐 (38)	£16.00–£27.00
⛺ (38)	£15.00–£20.00
🏠 (16)	£165.00–£480.00

38 touring pitches

A privately owned park set in the heart of picturesque Ryedale. Peaceful and tranquil, but within easy reach of York, North Yorkshire Moors, Flamingo Land and the coast. **directions** Situated on the edge of Slingsby with access off the B1257 Malton to Helmsley road. **open** March to October **payment** credit/debit cards, cash, cheques

General 🗐 🐕 🖥 🏠 🅿 ☼ 🚐 🎱 📞 🅿 🎱 Leisure ∪ 🌙 ✎

SNEATON, Yorkshire Map ref 5D3

SAT NAV YO22 5JE

★★★★
TOURING PARK

🚐 (93)   £9.30–£20.70
🚎 (93)   £9.30–£20.70
93 touring pitches

SPECIAL PROMOTIONS
Special member rates mean
you can save your
membership subscription in
less than a week. Visit our
website to find out more.

Low Moor Caravan Club Site

Sneaton, Whitby YO22 5JE
t (01947) 810505 f (01342) 410258 e natalie.tiller@caravanclub.co.uk
w **caravanclub.co.uk**

THE
CARAVAN
CLUB

Relax on this tranquil site set in the North
Yorkshire Moors National Park and very much in
Heartbeat Country. An ideal site for dog owners
and the moors are a paradise for walkers. For
the less energetic there are scenic drives
through forests and across moors.

open April to November
payment credit/debit cards, cash, cheques

directions Turn left off A171 (Scarborough-
Whitby). In 13.5 miles turn onto B1416. In 1.75
miles turn left through red gates. Site on right.

General 🐕 ⊕ 🅥

STIRTON, Yorkshire Map ref 4B1

SAT NAV BD23 3LQ

★★★
HOLIDAY, TOURING
& CAMPING PARK

🚐   £15.00–£20.00
🚎   £15.00–£20.00
20 touring pitches

Tarn House Caravan Park

Stirton, Nr Skipton, Yorkshire BD23 3LQ
t (01756) 795309 e reception@tarnhouse.net
w **partingtons.com** ONLINE MAP ONLINE BOOKING

Family-run caravan park situated in a rural
location in the beautiful Yorkshire Dales. Bar on
park, fantastic views.

open 1 March to 15 November
payment credit/debit cards, cash, cheques

directions 1.25 miles north west of Skipton.

General 🅥 ✕
Leisure ♪

THIRSK, Yorkshire Map ref 5C3

Thirsk Racecourse Caravan Club Site
Thirsk YO7 1QL
t (01845) 525266
w **caravanclub.co.uk**

🚐 (60)   £9.30–£20.70
🚐 (60)   £9.30–£20.70
60 touring pitches

Pitches are within sight of the racecourse main stand, looking over the famous turf, surrounded by Herriot Country and the Dales. **directions** Site on left of A61 (Thirsk-South Kilvington). **open** April to October **payment** credit/debit cards, cash, cheques

General 🗍 🐕 🛢 ⌂ 🔌 🕒 Leisure ►

THORNE, Yorkshire Map ref 4C1

Elder House Touring Park
Sandtoft Road, Crow Tree Bank, Thorne Levels, Doncaster DN8 5TD
t (01405) 813173

🚐 (10)   £11.00
🚐   £11.00
⛺   £11.00
10 touring pitches

Elder House Touring Park offers landscaped gardens in lovely surroundings and ample space for exercising your dog. Modern toilet block with showers and shaving points, also a disabled toilet and shower. **directions** M18 J5 M180 leave for A18 towards Scunthorpe at the Black Bull turn right into Crow Tree Bank 500 yds turn left down farm drive to end. **open** All year except Xmas and New Year **payment** cash, cheques

General 🐕 ⌂ 🛢 🔌 🏆 📺 Leisure ► ✈

WHITBY, Yorkshire Map ref 5D3

Flask Inn Holiday Home Park
Robin Hoods Bay, Fylingdales, Whitby YO22 4QH
t (01947) 880592 f (01947) 880592 e info@flaskinn.com
w **flaskinn.com** ONLINE MAP GUEST REVIEWS

🏠 (10)   £260.00–£480.00

Small, family-run site between Whitby and Scarborough, in the North York Moors. All super-luxury caravans have central heating and double glazing. Also Freeview TV, DVD, fridge/freezer and microwave. Outside decking and seating. **directions** Situated on the A171, 7 miles to Whitby, 12 miles to Scarborough and 4 miles to Robin Hood's Bay. **open** From Easter to October. **payment** credit/debit cards, cash, cheques

General 🗍 🛒 🛢 ☼ 🕒 ✕ Leisure ∪ ✈ 🏆 🎢

WHITBY, Yorkshire Map ref 5D3

Ladycross Plantation Touring Caravan Park
Egton, Whitby YO21 1UA
t (01947) 895502 e enquiries@ladycrossplantation.co.uk
w **ladycrossplantation.co.uk**

🚐 (94)   £15.30–£18.35
🚐 (6)   £15.30–£18.35
100 touring pitches

Peaceful woodland site within NYM National Park. Ideal for exploring Whitby, north east coast, Heartbeat Country, NYM Steam Railway and beautiful local villages. David Bellamy Gold Conservation Award. Welcome Host. **directions** A171 Whitby - Teesside road, approx 5 miles from Whitby take turning signposted Ladycross Plantation, Egton, Glaisdale, Grosmont, NYM Railway. Avoid roads signposted Egton from A169. **open** March to October **payment** credit/debit cards, cash, cheques

General 🗍 🐕 🛒 🛢 ⌂ ☼ 🔌 🚲 🔌 🕒 🏆 📺

WHITBY, Yorkshire Map ref 5D3

SAT NAV YO22 4UF

Middlewood Farm Holiday Park

Middlewood Lane, Fylingthorpe, Whitby YO22 4UF
t (01947) 880414 f (01947) 880871 e info@middlewoodfarm.com
w middlewoodfarm.com ONLINE MAP GUEST REVIEWS LAST MINUTE OFFERS

🚐 (20)	£13.00–£22.00
🚍 (20)	£13.00–£22.00
▲ (80)	£8.00–£19.00
🚏 (30)	£165.00–£620.00

100 touring pitches

SPECIAL PROMOTIONS
3 night short breaks in our
Luxury HIRE caravans....early
and late season only, from
£120.

Peaceful, 5 star award-winning family park. A walker's paradise with magnificent, panoramic coastal and moorland views! Level, sheltered, hardstandings, luxury Heated facilities, private wash-cubicles, Bath, children's Play Area. 10 minutes walk to pub/shops/beach and Robin Hood's Bay. Superb caravans for hire. A friendly welcome awaits!

open All year
payment credit/debit cards, cash, cheques

directions Follow A171 Scarborough/Whitby road, signposted from Fylingthorpe/Robin Hood's Bay junction. In Fylingthorpe turn onto Middlewood Lane. Park is 500 yds. Follow brown tourist signs.

General 🔲 🐕 🛗 📶 🍴 ⬆ 🚿 🏪
Leisure ∪ 🚴 🎣 ⛰

WOMBLETON, Yorkshire Map ref 5C3

SAT NAV YO62 7RY

Wombleton Caravan Park

Moorfield Lane, Wombleton, Helmsley YO62 7RY
t (01751) 431684 e info@wombletoncaravanpark.co.uk
w wombletoncaravanpark.co.uk ONLINE MAP GUEST REVIEWS ONLINE BOOKING

🚐 (100)	£15.00–£19.00
🚍 (8)	£15.00–£19.00
▲ (10)	£8.00–£17.00

118 touring pitches

Halfway between Helmsley and Kirkbymoorside, a flat level site with electric hook-ups, modern shower block/disabled facilities. A small shop for general enquiries, touring and seasonal pitches, tents welcome. directions Please contact us for directions open March to October payment credit/debit cards, cash, cheques

General 🔲 🐕 🛗 📶 ☀ 🚐 🍴 ⬆ 🚿 🏪 Leisure ▶ ∪

YORK, Yorkshire Map ref 4C1

SAT NAV YO61 1RY

Alders Caravan Park

Home Farm, Monk Green, Alne nr Easingwold, York YO61 1RY
t (01347) 838722 f (01347) 838722 e enquiries@homefarmalne.co.uk
w alderscaravanpark.co.uk ONLINE MAP

🚐	£16.00–£17.50
🚍	£16.00
▲	£16.00–£17.50

87 touring pitches

A working farm in historic parkland where visitors may enjoy peace and tranquillity. York (on bus route), moors, dales and coast nearby. Tastefully landscaped, adjoins village cricket ground. Woodland walk. directions From A19 exit at Alne sign, in 1.5 miles turn left a T-junction, 0.5 miles park on left in village centre. open March to October payment credit/debit cards, cash, cheques

General 🔲 🐕 🛗 📶 ☀ 🚐 🍴 ⬆ 🚿 Leisure ▶ ∪ 🎣 ▾

YORK, Yorkshire Map ref 4C1   SAT NAV HG5 0SE

Allerton Park Caravan Park

Allerton Mauleverer, Knaresborough HG5 0SE
t (01423) 330569 f (01759) 371377 e christine.hind@tiscali.co.uk
w **yorkshireholidayparks.co.uk**

(20)	£12.00–£14.00
(20)	£12.00–£14.00
(20)	£12.00–£14.00
(3)	£320–£640
(2)	£210.00–£410.00
20 touring pitches	

A peaceful camping and caravan park 0.5 miles east of the A1 leading from the A59 York to Harrogate road. An ideal touring base for the York area. **directions** Please contact us for directions **open** 1 February to 3 January **payment** credit/debit cards, cash, cheques

General 🐕 🏠 ⛱ ☀ 🅿 🚻   **Leisure** ∪ ⚠

YORK, Yorkshire Map ref 4C1   SAT NAV YO32 9TH

Beechwood Grange Caravan Club Site

Malton Road, York YO32 9TH
t (01904) 424637 f (01342) 410258
w **caravanclub.co.uk**

CARAVAN CLUB

(115)	£14.00–£26.90
(115)	£14.00–£26.90
115 touring pitches	

SPECIAL PROMOTIONS
Special member rates mean you can save your membership subscription in less than a week. Visit our website to find out more.

Situated in open countryside outside York this is an ideal base from which to explore this fascinating city or discovering Yorkshires varied attractions. An ideal site for families with plenty of space for children to play. There's plenty to do nearby - York with its Minster, National Railway Museum and Jorvik Viking Centre.

open March 2010 to January 2011
payment credit/debit cards, cash, cheques

directions From A64 on junction of A1237 York ring road and A1036 leading to A64, north of York. 3rd roundabout turn right onto road signed local traffic only. Site at end of drive.

General 🐕 🏠 ⛱ ☀ 🅿 🚻   **Leisure** ▶ ♪ ⚠

YORK, Yorkshire Map ref 4C1   SAT NAV YO23 1JQ

Rowntree Park Caravan Club Site

Terry Avenue, York YO23 1JQ
t (01904) 658997 f (01342) 410258
w **caravanclub.co.uk**

CARAVAN CLUB

(102)	£14.90–£28.90
(102)	£14.90–£28.90
102 touring pitches	

On the banks of the river Ouse in the heart of York, this popular site is just a few minutes' walk from the city centre. York is a feast, there's so much to see and do. **directions** A64 onto A19 signposted York centre. After 2 miles join one-way system. Keep left over bridge. Left at International Caravan Club site. Right onto Terry Avenue. Site on right in 0.25 miles. **open** All year **payment** credit/debit cards, cash, cheques

General 🐕 🏠 ⛱ ☀ 🅿 🚻   **Leisure** ▶ ♪

YORK, Yorkshire Map ref 4C1 — SAT NAV YO61 1ET

Goosewood Holiday Park

Sutton on the Forest, York, Easingwold YO61 1ET
t (01347) 810829 f (01347) 811498 e enquiries@goosewood.co.uk
w **flowerofmay.com**

(90)	£20.00–£25.00
(10)	£20.00–£25.00
(24)	£236–£845

100 touring pitches

SPECIAL PROMOTIONS
Three night weekends, ring
for details.

A quiet peaceful park with fishing lake, childre
adventure play area and health suite. A perfec
place to relax and amble through wooded wa
Ideal for visiting historic City of York and
surrounding beauty spots of Yorkshire. A warn
welcome!

open 1st February to end December
payment credit/debit cards, cash

directions Please contact us for directions

General
Leisure

YORK, Yorkshire Map ref 4C1 — SAT NAV YO41 1AN

Weir Caravan Park

Buttercrambe Road, Stamford Bridge, York YO41 1AN
t (01759) 371377 f (01759) 371377 e enquiries@yorkshireholidayparks.co.uk
w **yorkshireholidayparks.co.uk**

(20)	£12.00–£14.00
(20)	£12.00–£14.00
(10)	£12.00–£14.00
(6)	£245.00–£430.00

20 touring pitches

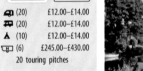

On level grassland 7 miles east of York on the A166. Near the rive
where fishing is available. Village, pubs, restaurants etc, are within
five-minute walk. **directions** Please contact us for directions **open**
March to October **payment** credit/debit cards, cash, cheques

General   Leisure

YORK, Yorkshire Map ref 4C1 — SAT NAV YO32 9ST

York Touring Caravan Site

Towthorpe Lane, Towthorpe, York YO32 9ST
t (01904) 499275 f (01904) 499271 e info@yorkcaravansite.co.uk
w **yorkcaravansite.co.uk** ONLINE MAP GUEST REVIEWS

(20)	£15.00–£21.00
(20)	£15.00–£21.00
(10)	£15.00–£21.00

40 touring pitches

Small family-run secluded park in countryside setting, 5 miles from
York centre. Spacious pitches, luxury free showers and toilets. On-
site driving range and 9-hole golf course. **directions** Travelling on
the A64 towards Scarborough/Malton take the turn-off to the left
signposted Strensall/Haxby. We are 1 mile down that road on the
left. **open** All year **payment** credit/debit cards, cash, cheques

General   Leisure

All Assessed Accommodation

Yorkshire

ACASTER MALBIS

or End Farm ★★★★
...day, Touring & Camping Park
...r End, Acaster Malbis, York
...3 2UQ
...(01904) 706727
...moorendfarm@acaster99.fsnet.co.
...uk
...moor-end-farm.co.uk

ALLERSTON

**e of Pickering Caravan Park
★★★** *Touring & Camping Park*
...e of Pickering Caravan Park,
...rston, Pickering
...8 7PQ
...(01723) 859280
...tony@valeofpickering.co.uk
...valeofpickering.co.uk

BARDSEY

ghfield Caravan Park ★★★★★
...day Park ROSE AWARD
...lackmoor Lane, Bardsey, Leeds
...7 9DY
...(01937) 574658
...haighfieldcp@aol.com
...haighfieldcaravanpark.co.uk

BARMSTON

rmston Beach Holiday Park
...★★ Holiday Park ROSE AWARD
...ds Lane, Barmston, Hornsea
...25 8PJ
...(01442) 830185
...angie.pyle@park-resorts.com
...park-resorts.com

BEDALE

mbroke Caravan Park
...mping and Caravan Park
...Low Street, Leeming Bar, Bedale
...7 9BW
...(01677) 422608
...craggs9bw@btinternet.com

BEVERLEY

rmston Farm Holiday Park
★★★★ Holiday Park
...rmston Farm, Barmston Lane,
...verley
...17 0TP
...(01482) 863566
...enquiry@barmstonfarm.co.uk
...barmstonfarm.co.uk

BOLTON ABBEY

rid Wood Caravan Club Site
★★★★ Touring & Camping Park
...lton Abbey, Skipton
...23 6AN
...(01756) 710433
...caravanclub.co.uk

BRANDESBURTON

acre Lakeside Park ★★★★
...liday & Touring Park
...ven Road, Brandesburton,
...ornsea
...025 8RT
...0800 180 4556
...chalets@dacrepark.co.uk
...dacrepark.co.uk

osse Hill Caravan Park ★★★
...uring & Camping Park
...atwick Lane, Brandesburton,
...ornsea
...025 8SB
...(01964) 542608
...tony@fossehill.co.uk
...fossehill.co.uk

BRIDLINGTON

orth Bay Leisure Limited ★★★★
...liday Park ROSE AWARD
...ne Kiln Lane, Bridlington
...016 6TG
...(01262) 673733
...enquiries@northbayleisure.co.uk
...northbayleisure.co.uk

The Poplars Touring Park ★★★★
Touring & Camping Park
45 Jewison Lane, Sewerby,
Bridlington
YO15 1DX
t   (01262) 677251
w thepoplars.co.uk

South Cliff Caravan Park ★★★★
Holiday, Touring & Camping Park
Wilsthorpe, Bridlington
YO15 3QN
t   (01262) 671051
e   southcliff@eastriding.gov.uk
w southcliff.co.uk

BURTON-IN-LONSDALE

**Gallaber Farm Caravan Park
★★★★**
Holiday, Touring & Camping Park
Gallaber Farm, Burton-in-Lonsdale,
Lancaster
LA6 3LU
t   (01524) 261361
e   gallaber@btopenworld.com
w gallaber.btinternet.co.uk

CAYTON BAY

Cayton Bay Holiday Park ★★★★
Holiday Park
Mill Lane, Cayton Bay, Scarborough
YO11 3NJ
t   (01723) 583111
e   holidaysales.caytonbay@park-
resorts.com
w park-resorts.com

Cliff Farm Caravan Park ★★★★★
Holiday Park
Mill Lane, Cayton Bay, Scarborough
YO11 3NN
t   (01723) 582239

CLAXTON

Foxhill Park ★★★★
Holiday, Touring & Camping Park
Claxton to Harton Lodge Road,
Claxton, York, North Yorkshire
YO60 7RX
t   (01904) 468355
e   enquiries@foxhillpark.com
w foxhillpark.com

CONSTABLE BURTON

**Constable Burton Hall Caravan
Park ★★★★** *Touring Park*
Constable Burton, Leyburn
DL8 5LJ
t   (01677) 450428

CROPTON

**Spiers House Caravan and
Camping Site ★★★★**
Touring & Camping Park
Forestry Commission, Cropton,
Pickering
YO18 8ES
t   (0131) 314 6453
e   fe.holidays@forestry.gov.uk
w forestholidays.co.uk

DUNNINGTON

Ashfield Caravan Park ★★★★
Touring & Camping Park
Hagg Lane, Dunnington, York
YO19 5PE
t   (01904) 489147
w ashfieldtouringcaravanpark.co.uk

ESCRICK

The Hollicarrs ★★★★★
Holiday Park
Riccall Road, Escrick, York
YO19 6EA
t   0800 980 8070
e   sales@thehollicarrs.com
w thehollicarrs.com

FARNHAM

**Kingfisher Caravan and Camping
Park ★★★★**
Holiday, Touring & Camping Park
Low Moor Lane, Scotton,
Knaresborough
HG5 9JB
t   (01423) 869411

FILEY

**Filey Brigg Caravan and Camping
Park ★★★★**
Touring & Camping Park
Church Cliff Drive, North Cliff,
Arndale, Filey
YO14 9ET
t   (01723) 513852
e   fileybrigg@scarborough.gov.uk

**Orchard Farm Holiday Village
★★★★** *Holiday Park*
Stonegate, Hunmanby, Filey
YO14 0PU
t   (01723) 891582
e   info@orchardfarmholidayvillage.
co.uk
w orchardfarmholidayvillage.co.uk

Primrose Valley Holiday Park
★★★★★ Holiday & Touring Park
Primrose Valley, Filey
YO14 9RF
t   (01723) 513771
w primrosevalley-park.co.uk

FLAMBOROUGH

**Thornwick & Sea Farm Holiday
Centre ★★★★**
ROSE AWARD
North Marine Road, Bridlington
YO15 1AU
t   (01262) 851550
e   enquiries@thornwickbay.com
w thornwickbay.co.uk

FOLLIFOOT

**Great Yorkshire Showground
Caravan Club ★★★★** *Touring Park*
Railway Road, Off Wetherby Road,
Harrogate
HG3 1TZ
t   (01423) 560470
w caravanclub.co.uk

GILLING WEST

**Hargill House Caravan Club Site
★★★★** *Touring Park*
Gilling West, Richmond
DL10 5LJ
t   (017488) 822734
w caravanclub.co.uk

GRISTHORPE BAY

**Blue Dolphin Holiday Park
★★★★**
Holiday, Touring & Camping Park
Blue Dolphin Holiday Park,
Gristhorpe Bay, Filey
YO14 9PU
t   (01723) 513771
w bluedolphin-park.co.uk

GUISBOROUGH

Tocketts Mill Leisure Park
Holiday, Touring & Camping Park
Tocketts Mill Caravan Park, Skelton
Road, Guisborough, North Yorkshire
TS14 6QA
t   01278 610182
e   enquiries@tockettsmill.co.uk

HARMBY

**Lower Wensleydale Caravan Club
Site ★★★** *Touring & Camping Park*
Harmby, Leyburn
DL8 5NU
t   (01969) 623366
w caravanclub.co.uk

HARROGATE

High Moor Farm Park ★★★★★
Holiday & Touring Park
Skipton Road, Felliscliffe, Pateley
Bridge
HG3 2LT
t   (01423) 563637
e   highmoorfarmpark@btconnect.
com

Reynard Crag Park ★★★★★
Holiday Park
Reynard Crag Lane, Burstwith,
Harrogate
HG3 2JQ
t   07793 049567
e   reynardcrag@btconnect.com
w reynardcragpark.co.uk

Ripley Caravan Park ★★★★★
Holiday, Touring & Camping Park
Knaresborough Road, Ripley, Ripley
(Yorks)
HG3 3AU
t   (01423) 770050
w ripleycaravanpark@talk21.com

Rudding Holiday Park ★★★★★
Holiday, Touring & Camping Park
ROSE AWARD
Follifoot, Harrogate
HG3 1JH
t   01423 870439
e   holiday-park@ruddingpark.com
w ruddingpark.co.uk

Warren Forest Caravan Park
★★★★★ Holiday Park
Warsill, Harrogate
HG3 3LH
t   (01765) 620683
e   enquiries@warrenforestpark.co.uk
w warrenforestpark.co.uk

HAWES

**Bainbridge Ings Caravan and
Camping Site ★★★**
Holiday, Touring & Camping Park
Bainbridge Ings Caravan and
Camping Site, Hawes
DL8 3NU
t   (01969) 667354
e   janet@bainbridge-ings.co.uk
w bainbridge-ings.co.uk

Honeycott Caravan Park ★★★★
Holiday Park
Ingleton Road, Hawes
DL8 3LH
t   (01772) 632246
e   info@lamaleachparkestates.co.uk
w honeycott.co.uk

HAWORTH

Upwood Holiday Park ★★★★
Holiday, Touring & Camping Park
Black Moor Road, Oxenhope,
Haworth
BD22 9SS
t   (01535) 644242
e   info@upwoodpark.co.uk
w upwoodpark.co.uk

HEBDEN BRIDGE

**Lower Clough Foot Caravan Club
Site ★★★★★** *Touring Park*
Cragg Vale, Hebden Bridge
HX7 5RU
t   (01422) 882531
e   enquiries@caravanclub.co.uk
w caravanclub.co.uk

HELMSLEY

**Golden Square Caravan and
Camping Park ★★★★★**
Touring & Camping Park
Oswaldkirk, Helmsley
YO62 5YQ
t   (01439) 788269
e   barbara@goldensquarecar
avanpark.freeserve.co.uk
w goldensquarecaravanpark.com

HIGH BENTHAM

Riverside Caravan Park ★★★★★
Holiday, Touring & Camping Park
Wenning Avenue, Bentham,
Lancaster
LA2 7LW
t (01524) 261272
e info@riversidecaravanpark.co.uk
w riversidecaravanpark.co.uk

HINDERWELL

**Serenity Touring Caravan &
Camping Park ★★★★**
Touring & Camping Park
Saltburn-by-the-Sea
TS13 5JH
t (01947) 841122

HOLMFIRTH

**Holme Valley Camping and
Caravan Park ★★★★**
Touring & Camping Park
Thongsbridge, Holmfirth
HD9 7TD
t (01484) 665819
e enquiries@homevalleycamping.
com
w holmevalleycamping.com

HORNSEA

Longbeach Leisure Park ★★★★
Holiday Park
South Cliff, Hornsea
HU18 1TL
t (01964) 532506
w longbeach-leisure.co.uk

HUTTON-LE-HOLE

**Hutton le Hole Caravan Park
★★★★** *Touring & Camping Park*
Westfield Lodge, Hutton-le-Hole,
Kirkbymoorside
YO62 6UG
t (01751) 417261
e rwstrickland@farmersweekly.net
w westfieldlodge.co.uk

INGLETON

Parkfoot Holiday Homes ★★★★★
Holiday Park
Bentham Road, Ingleton, Carnforth
LA6 3HR
t (01524) 261833
e parkfoot.ingleton@virgin.net
w parkfoot.co.uk

KEARBY WITH NETHERBY

Maustin Park Ltd ★★★★★
Holiday, Touring & Camping Park
ROSE AWARD
Wharfe Lane, Kearby, Wetherby
LS22 4DA
t (0113) 288 6234
e info@maustin.co.uk
w maustin.co.uk

KILDALE

Kildale Camping Barn
Camping Barn
Park Farm, Kildale, Stokesley
YO21 2RN
t (01642) 722847
e parkfarm_2000@yahoo.co.uk
w kildalebarn.co.uk

KIRKBYMOORSIDE

Farndale *Camping Barn*
Oak House, High Farndale, York
YO62 7LH
t (01751) 433053
e pipmead@aol.com
w yha.org.uk

KNARESBOROUGH

**Knaresborough Caravan Club Site
★★★★★** *Touring Park*
New Road, Scotton, Knaresborough
HG5 9HH
t (01423) 860196
w caravanclub.co.uk

LANGTHORPE

Old Hall Holiday Park ★★★★
Holiday & Touring Park
Skelton Road, Langthorpe,
Boroughbridge, Harrogate
YO51 9BZ
t (01423) 323190
e phil.brierley@which.net
w yhcparks.info

LEEDS

St Helena's Caravan Site ★★★★
Holiday, Touring & Camping Park
Otley Old Road, Horsforth, Leeds
LS18 5HZ
t (0113) 284 1142

LITTLE WEIGHTON

Croft Park ★★★★★
Touring & Camping Park
55 Rowley Road, Little Weighton,
Beverley
HU20 3XJ
t (01482) 840600
e info@croftpark.com
w croftpark.com

LOFTHOUSE

**Studfold Farm Caravan and
Camping Park ★★★★**
Touring & Camping Park
Studfold Farm, Lofthouse, Pateley
Bridge
HG3 5SG
t (01423) 755210
e ianwalker@studfold.fsnet.co.uk
w studfoldfarm.co.uk

LONG PRESTON

Gallaber Park ★★★★
Holiday & Touring Park
Long Preston, Settle
BD23 4QF
t (01729) 851397
e info@gallaberpark.com
w gallaberpark.com

LOW ROW

**Low Row Camping Barn/
Bunkhouse** *Bunkhouse*
Low Whita Farm, Low Row,
Richmond
DL11 6NT
t (01748) 884601
e rwcclarkson@aol.com

MALTON

**Wolds Way Caravan and Camping
★★★★** *Touring & Camping Park*
West Farm, West Knapton, Malton
YO17 8JE
t (01944) 728463
e knapton.wold.farms@farming.co.
uk
w ryedalesbest.co.uk

MARKINGTON

**Yorkshire Hussar Inn Caravan
Park ★★★★**
Holiday, Touring & Camping Park
High Street, Markington, Nr
Harrogate
HG3 3NR
t (01765) 677327
e enquiry@yorkshire-hussar-inn.co.
uk
w yorkshire-hussar-inn.co.uk

MARSDEN

**Standedge Caravan and Campsite
★★★** *Touring & Camping Park*
The Carriage House, Manchester
Road, Marsden
HD7 6NL
t (01484) 844419
e info@carriage-house.co.uk
w carriage-house.co.uk

MASHAM

Black Swan Holiday Park ★★★★
Holiday, Touring & Camping Park
Masham
HG4 4NF
t (01765) 689477
e info@blackswanholiday.co.uk
w blackswanholiday.co.uk

NAWTON

**Wrens of Ryedale Caravan and
Camp Site ★★★★**
Touring & Camping Park
Gale Lane, Nawton, Kirkbymoorside
YO62 7SD
t (01439) 771260
e maria@wrensofryedale.co.uk
w wrensofryedale.co.uk

NEWTON-LE-WILLOWS

**Lindale Holiday Park - Dell
Lodges ★★★★** *Holiday Park*
ROSE AWARD
Lindale Holiday Park Luxury Pine
Lodge, Newton-le-Willows, Bedale
DL8 1TA
t (01677) 450842
e info@lindalepark.co.uk
w lindalepark.co.uk

NORTHALLERTON

**Cote Ghyll Caravan & Camping
Park ★★★★★**
Holiday, Touring & Camping Park
ROSE AWARD
Osmotherley, Northallerton
DL6 3AH
t (01609) 883425
e hills@coteghyll.com
w coteghyll.com

Lovesome Hill Farm *Bunkhouse*
Lovesome Hill, Northallerton
DL6 2PB
t (01609) 772311

NOSTELL

**Nostell Priory Holiday Home Park
★★★★★**
Holiday, Touring & Camping Park
Nostell Priory Estate, Wakefield
WF4 1QE
t (01924) 863938
e park@nostellprioryholidaypark.co.
uk
w nostellprioryholidaypark.co.uk

PATRINGTON

**Patrington Haven Leisure Park
Ltd ★★★★★** *Holiday Park*
Patrington Haven, Patrington, Hull
HU12 0PT
t (01964) 630071
e guy@phlp.co.uk
w phlp.co.uk

PICKERING

Wayside Caravan Park ★★★★
Holiday, Touring & Camping Park
Wrelton, Pickering
YO18 8PG
t (01751) 472608
e waysideparks@freenet.co.uk
w waysideparks.co.uk

POCKLINGTON

South Lea Caravan Park ★★★★
Touring & Camping Park
The Balk, Pocklington, York
YO42 2NX
t (01759) 303467
e southlea@fsmail.net
w south-lea.co.uk

RAYWELL

**Raywell Hall Country Lodges
★★★★** *Holiday Park*
Raywell Cottages, Cottingham
HU16 5YL
w raywellhall.co.uk

REIGHTON GAP

**Reighton Sands Holiday Park
★★★**
Holiday, Touring & Camping Park
Reighton Gap, Filey
YO14 9SJ
t (01723) 513771
w reightonsands-park.co.uk

RICHMOND

Richmond Camping Barn
Camping Barn
East Applegarth Farm, Westfields,
Richmond
DL10 4SD
t (01748) 822940

RIPON

**Sleningford Watermill Caravan
Camping ★★★★★**
Touring & Camping Park
North Stainley, Ripon
HG4 3HQ
t (01765) 635201
e sleningford@hotmail.co.uk
w sleningfordwatermill.co.uk

**Woodhouse Farm Caravan &
Camping Park ★★★★**
Holiday, Touring & Camping Park
Winksley, Ripon
HG4 3PG
t (01765) 658309
e woodhouse.farm@talk21.com
w woodhousewinksley.com

RISEBOROUGH

Cliff Farm *Camping Barn*
Cliff Farm Holidays, Camping Barn
Kirkbymoorside
YO62 6SS
t (01751) 473792
w clifffarmholidays.com

ROECLIFFE

**Boroughbridge Camping and
Caravanning Club Site ★★★★★**
Touring & Camping Park
Bar Lane, Roecliffe, York
YO51 9LS
t (01423) 322683
w campingandcaravanningclub.co
uk/boroughbridge

ROOS

**Sand-le-Mere Caravan & Leisure
Park ★★★★** *Holiday & Touring Pk*
ROSE AWARD
Seaside Lane, Tunstall
HU12 0JQ
t (01964) 670403
e info@sand-le-mere.co.uk
w sand-le-mere.co.uk

RUDSTON

**Thorpe Hall Caravan and
Camping Site ★★★★**
Touring & Camping Park
Thorpe Hall, Rudston, Driffield
YO25 4JE
t (01262) 420393
e caravansite@thorpehall.co.uk
w thorpehall.co.uk

SALTWICK BAY

**Whitby Holiday Park - Touring
Park ★★★★** *Holiday & Touring Pk*
Whitby Holiday Park, Saltwick Bay,
Whitby
YO22 4JX
t (01947) 602664
e info@whitbyholidaypark.co.uk
w whitbypark.co.uk

SCARBOROUGH

Browns Caravan Park ★★★★★
Holiday & Touring Park
Mill Lane, Cayton Bay, Scarborough
YO11 3NN
t (01723) 582303
e info@brownscaravan.co.uk
w brownscaravanpark.co.uk

...ton Village Caravan Park Ltd
★★★ Touring & Camping Park
... Lane, Cayton Bay, Scarborough
...1 3NN
... (01723) 583171
...nfo@caytontouring.co.uk
...caytontouring.co.uk

...ws Nest Caravan Park ★★★★
...day Park ROSE AWARD
...ws Nest Caravan Park,
...thorpe, Filey
...4 9PS
...01723) 582206
...enquiries@crowsnestcaravanpark.
...com
...crowsnestcaravanpark.com

...wer of May Holiday Parks Ltd
...★★★
...iday, Touring & Camping Park
...wer of May Holiday Parks Ltd,
...berston, Scarborough
...1 3NU
...(01723) 584311
...nfo@flowerofmay.com
...flowerofmay.com

...mine Park ★★★★★
...iday, Touring & Camping Park
...ss Lane, Snainton, Scarborough
...3 9BE
...01723) 859240
...nfo@jasminepark.co.uk
...jasminepark.co.uk

...berston Touring Park
★★★★ Touring Park
...berston, Scarborough
...1 3PE
...(01723) 585723
...info@lebberstontouring.co.uk
...lebberstontouring.co.uk

...ewood Holiday Park ★★★
...iday, Touring & Camping Park
...ecourse Road (A170),
...rborough, North Yorkshire
...2 5TG
...01723 367278 07787378111
...info@pinewood-holiday-park.co.
...uk
...pinewood-holiday-park.co.uk

...alby Close Park ★★★★
...iday, Touring & Camping Park
...SE AWARD
...niston Road, Scarborough
...3 0DA
...(01723) 365908
...info@scalbyclosepark.co.uk
...scalbyclosepark.co.uk

...arborough Camping and
...ravanning Club Site ★★★★★
...uring Park
...ld Lane, Burniston Road,
...arborough
...13 0DA
...(01723) 366212
...campingandcaravanningclub.co.
...uk/scarborough

SETTLE

...ngcliffe Park ★★★★
...liday, Touring & Camping Park
...ttle
...24 9LX
...(01729) 822387
...info@langcliffe.com
...langcliffe.com

SHERIFF HUTTON

...eriff Camping and Caravanning
...ub Site ★★★★
...uring & Camping Park
...acken Hill, Sheriff Hutton, York
...060 6QG
...(01347) 878660
...info@campingandcaravannin
...gclub.co.uk
...campingandcaravanningclub.co.
...uk/sheriff

SKIPSEA

Far Grange Park Ltd ★★★★★
Holiday Park
Hornsea Road, Skipsea, Driffield
YO25 8SY
t (01262) 468010
e andy.such@bourne-leisure.co.uk
w fargrangepark.co.uk

Skipsea Sands Holiday Village
★★★★
Holiday, Touring & Camping Park
ROSE AWARD
Mill Lane, Skipsea, Hornsea
YO25 8TZ
t (01262) 468210
e info@skipseasands.co.uk
w hoseasons.co.uk

Skirlington Leisure Park ★★★★★
Holiday, Touring & Camping Park
ROSE AWARD
Hornsea Road, Skipsea, Hornsea
YO25 8SY
t (01262) 468213
e enquiries@skirlington.com
w skirlington.com

SKIRLAUGH

Burton Constable Holiday Park &
Arboretum ★★★★★
Holiday, Touring & Camping Park
The Old Lodges, Sproatley, Hornsea
HU11 4LN
t (01964) 562508
e info@burtonconstable.co.uk
w burtonconstable.co.uk

SLINGSBY

Robin Hood Caravan Park
★★★★★
Holiday, Touring & Camping Park
ROSE AWARD
Slingsby, York
YO62 4AP
t (01653) 628391
e info@robinhoodcaravanpark.co.uk
w robinhoodcaravanpark.co.uk

Slingsby Camping and
Caravanning Club Site ★★★★★
Touring & Camping Park
The Green, Slingsby, York
YO62 4AA
t (01653) 628335
w campingandcaravanningclub.co.
uk/slingsby

SNEATON

Low Moor Caravan Club Site
★★★★ Touring Park
Sneaton, Whitby
YO22 5JE
t (01947) 810505
e natalie.tiller@caravanclub.co.uk
w caravanclub.co.uk

SOUTH OTTERINGTON

Otterington Touring Caravan and
Camping ★★★★
Holiday, Touring & Camping Park
Station Lane, South Otterington,
Northallerton
DL7 9JB
t (01609) 780263

STAINFORTH

Knight Stainforth Hall Caravan
and Campi ★★★★
Holiday, Touring & Camping Park
Little Stainforth, Settle
BD24 0DP
t (01729) 822200
e info@knightstainforth.co.uk
w knightstainforth.co.uk

STIRTON

Tarn House Caravan Park ★★★
Holiday, Touring & Camping Park
Stirton, Nr Skipton, Yorkshire
BD23 3LQ
t (01756) 795309
e reception@tarnhouse.net
w partingtons.com

STRENSALL

Moorside Caravan Park ★★★★
Touring Park
Lords Moor Lane, Strensall
YO32 5XJ
t (01904) 491208
w moorsidecaravanpark.co.uk

THIRSK

Thirsk Racecourse Caravan Club
Site ★★ Touring & Camping Park
Thirsk
YO7 1QL
t (01845) 525266
w caravanclub.co.uk

York House Caravan Park
★★★★★ Holiday & Touring Park
Balk, Thirsk
YO7 2AQ
t (01423) 323190
e phil.brierley@which.net
w yhcparks.info

THORALBY

Bishopdale Bunkhouse
The Old School Bunkhouse,
Thoralby, Leyburn
DL8 3TB
t (01629) 592633

THORNE

Elder House Touring Park ★★★★
Touring Park
Sandtoft Road, Crow Tree Bank,
Thorne Levels, Doncaster
DN8 5TD
t (01405) 813173

THORNTON DALE

Overbrook Caravan Park ★★★★
Touring Park
Maltongate, Pickering
YO18 7SE
t (01751) 474417
w overbrookcaravanpark.co.uk

THRESHFIELD

Long Ashes Park ★★★★
Holiday Park
Threshfield, Skipton
BD23 5PN
t (01756) 752261
e info@longashespark.co.uk
w longashespark.co.uk

Wood Nook Caravan Park ★★★★
Holiday, Touring & Camping Park
Skirethorns, Threshfield, Skipton
BD23 5NU
t (01756) 752412
e enquiries@woodnook.net
w woodnook.net

THRYBERGH

Thrybergh Country Park Camping
& Caravan ★★★
Holiday, Touring & Camping Park
Doncaster Road, Rotherham
S65 4NU
t (01709) 850353
w rotherham.gov.uk/tourism/count
ryparks

WESTERDALE

Westerdale Bunkhouse
Broadgate Farm, Westerdale, Whitby
YO21 2DE
t (01287) 660259

WHITBY

Flask Inn Holiday Home Park
★★★★ Holiday Park ROSE AWARD
Robin Hoods Bay, Fylingdales,
Whitby
YO22 4QH
t (01947) 880592
e info@flaskinn.com
w flaskinn.com

High Straggleton Farm Caravan
Site ★★ Holiday & Camping Park
High Straggleton Farm, Sandsend
Road, Whitby
YO21 3SR
t (01947) 602373
e derekatkinson@farmersweekly.net
w highstraggleton.co.uk

Ladycross Plantation Touring
Caravan Park ★★★★★
Touring & Camping Park
Egton, Whitby
YO21 1UA
t (01947) 895502
e enquiries@ladycrossplantation.co.
uk
w ladycrossplantation.co.uk

Middlewood Farm Holiday Park
★★★★★
Holiday, Touring & Camping Park
ROSE AWARD
Middlewood Lane, Fylingthorpe,
Whitby
YO22 4UF
t (01947) 880414
e info@middlewoodfarm.com
w middlewoodfarm.com

Northcliffe & Seaview Holiday
Parks ★★★★★
Holiday & Touring Park
Bottoms Lane, High Hawsker,
Whitby
YO22 4LL
t (01947) 880477
e enquiries@northcliffe-seaview.
com
w northcliffe-seaview.com

Partridge Nest Farm Holiday
Caravans ★★★ Holiday Park
Eskdaleside, Sleights, Whitby
YO22 5ES
t (01947) 810450
e barbara@partridgenestfarm.com
w partridgenestfarm.com

Sandfield House Farm Caravan
Park ★★★★★ Touring Park
Sandsend Road, Whitby
YO21 3SR
t (01947) 602660
e info@sandfieldhousefarm.co.uk
w sandfieldhousefarm.co.uk

WILSTHORPE

The White House Caravan Park
★★★★★ Holiday Park
Wilsthorpe, Bridlington
YO15 3QN
t (01262) 673894

WITHERNSEA

Willows Holiday Park ★★★★
Holiday, Touring & Camping Park
Highfield Caravans, Queen Street,
Withernsea
HU19 2PN
t (01964) 612233
e info@highfield.caravans.co.uk
w highfield-caravans.co.uk

Withernsea Sands Holiday Village
★★★★ Holiday Park
North Road, Withernsea
HU19 2BS
t 0871 644 9704
e angie.pyle@park-resorts.com
w park-resorts.com

WOMBLETON

Wombleton Caravan Park
★★★★★ Touring & Camping Park
Moorfield Lane, Wombleton,
Helmsley
YO62 7RY
t (01751) 431684
e info@wombletoncaravanpark.co.
uk
w wombletoncaravanpark.co.uk

YORK

Alders Caravan Park ★★★★★
Touring & Camping Park
Home Farm, Monk Green, Alne nr
Easingwold, York
YO61 1RY
t (01347) 838722
e enquiries@homefarmalne.co.uk
w alderscaravanpark.co.uk

**Allerton Park Caravan Park
★★★★**
Holiday, Touring & Camping Park
ROSE AWARD
Allerton Mauleverer, Knaresborough
HG5 0SE
t (01423) 330569
e christine.hind@tiscali.co.uk
w yorkshireholidayparks.co.uk

**Beechwood Grange Caravan Club
Site ★★★★★** *Touring Park*
Malton Road, York
YO32 9TH
t (01904) 424637
w caravanclub.co.uk

**Castle Howard Lakeside Holiday
Park ★★★★**
Holiday, Touring & Camping Park
Coneysthorpe, Malton
YO60 7DD
t (01653) 648316
e lakeside@castlehoward.co.uk
w castlehoward.co.uk

Goosewood Holiday Park ★★★★
Holiday & Touring Park
Sutton on the Forest, York,
Easingwold
YO61 1ET
t (01347) 810829
e enquiries@goosewood.co.uk
w flowerofmay.com

**Rowntree Park Caravan Club Site
★★★★★** *Touring & Camping Park*
Terry Avenue, York
YO23 1JQ
t (01904) 658997
w caravanclub.co.uk

Weir Caravan Park ★★★★
Holiday & Touring Park
ROSE AWARD
Buttercrambe Road, Stamford
Bridge, York
YO41 1AN
t (01759) 371377
e enquiries@yorkshireholidaypa
co.uk
w yorkshireholidayparks.co.uk

**YCP York Caravan Park and
Storage ★★★★★** *Touring Park*
Stockton Lane, York
YO32 9UB
t (01904) 424222
e mail@yorkcaravanpark.com
w yorkcaravanpark.com

York Touring Caravan Site ★★
Touring & Camping Park
Towthorpe Lane, Towthorpe, Yor
YO32 9ST
t (01904) 499275
e info@yorkcaravansite.co.uk
w yorkcaravansite.co.uk

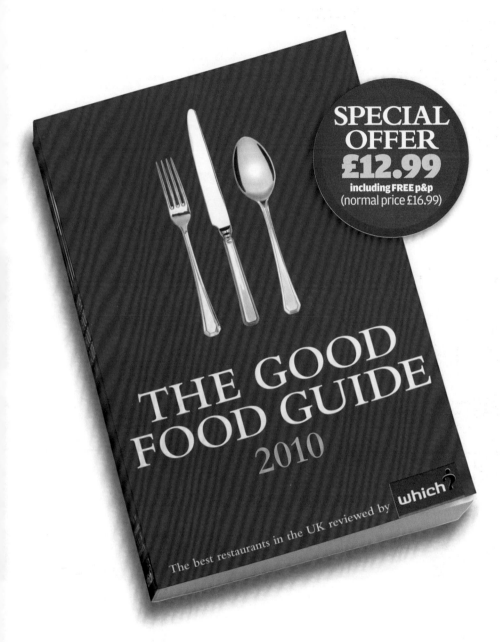

Blackpool Pleasure Beach, Blackpool, England.

North West England

Cheshire, Cumbria, Lancashire,
Manchester, Merseyside

North West England

This is the region for city breaks, exploring famously fashionable haunts, historic streets and buildings. It's a region to walk, cycle and discover the landscapes and wildlife of unspoilt villages. The Lake District, England's largest national park covering 880 square miles, offers calmness and solitude even though 12 million visitors enjoy the area every year. The dramatic scenery with soaring mountains, waterfalls and lakes really do offer a get-away-from-it-all break.

The 300-square mile Forest of Bowland, an Area of Outstanding Natural Beauty, full of wild flora and fauna, heather moorland and rare birds, offers superb walking and nature spotting opportunities. For water lovers the North West has over 1,000 kilometres of magnificent coastline and is home to Blackpool, Britain's favourite seaside resort.

England's North West is bursting with cultural confidence from outstanding national museums and art galleries to magical sculptures and blockbuster theatre events. The region is also steeped in sporting heritage – the professional football game was born here, and as well as being home to two of the biggest and most glamorous football clubs in the world, the region can lay claim to five additional premiership football teams. There are golf courses aplenty but if its speed on four legs you want, then a day out at one of the region's five stunning race courses is in order. Of course the most famous steeplechase in the world, the Grand National, is run annually at Aintree.

If you are looking for somewhere for your holidays, the North West is brimming with places to stay, attractions to visit, good food and a reputation for quality produce. In fact everything you need, all brought to you with renowned warmth and friendliness.

Cheshire

Situated on the River Dee, glorious Chester is one of the British Heritage Cities. The surviving Roman streets, surrounded by walkable walls, are so compact that you can easily sightsee on foot. Step back in time amid Georgian and Victorian architecture, shop in the unique medieval two-tier galleries called the Rows and enjoy the city's classy café culture.

Alderley Edge

Alderley Edge is a picturesque town, which takes its name from the wooded escarpment towering above the Cheshire plain, with fine views and walks. The town of Alderley Edge has excellent shops, restaurants and bars and entertains many premiership footballers and members of the 'Cheshire Set'. There are many historic buildings including Chorley Old Hall - the oldest surviving manor house in Cheshire.

Bollington

Bollington nestles in the western most foothills of the Pennine range of hills above the Cheshire plain, adjacent to the Peak District National Park. Bollington provides an easy base for those interested in walking or boating on the canal, or riding the converted railway track known as the Middlewood Way.

Bunbury

Bunbury is a charming village with many old cottages and narrow winding lanes. Home to Bunbury Watermill, a restored 19th-century watermill and working museum, it is an ideal starting point to discover Cheshire's canals. A mile to the north you negotiate the two wide-beamed staircase locks, well known in canal cruising circles. As part of the Four Counties Ring this is a wonderful way to see Cheshire and its surrounds from a different view.

Knutsford

Knutsford is said to derive its name from the Danish King Canute who supposedly 'forded' the River Lily in 1016. Elizabeth Gaskell, the famous novelist, spent most of her life in Knutsford. Her novel '*Cranford*' is set in Victorian Knutsford and the house where she grew up is situated on what is now Gaskell Avenue. Popular in July for the glorious RHS Flower Show at Tatton Park which spans 2,000 acres, with 1,000 acres of deer park and 50 acres of gardens.

Macclesfield

Macclesfield became the centre of Britain's silk industry during the Industrial Revolution. There are many attractive Georgian mills, houses, inns, churches and chapels. Cobbled streets and quaint old buildings stand side-by-side with modern shops and three markets. The town is the western gateway to the Peak District, with many beautiful walks on its doorstep and stunning views of the surrounding countryside.

Malpas

Malpas is one of the oldest towns in Cheshire with good timber-framed, old brick buildings. Set in the quiet winding lanes of South Cheshire, there are good opportunities for gentle country walks and cycle rides. Nearby Cholmondeley Castle overlooks 800 acres of parkland and water gardens. Particularly attractive is the Temple Garden with its rockery, lake and islands.

Cumbria

Carlisle is a city of strategic importance, the castle is testament to the years of feuding over the English-Scottish border. Explore its imposing dungeons and labyrinths, find the Licking Stones and prisoners' carvings, and discover how Bonnie Prince Charlie captured the castle in 1745. Be sure also to visit the nearby citadel, built by Henry VIII.

Ambleside

Ambleside, one of the jewels of the Lakes, is set in the centre of the Lake District at the head of Lake Windermere. Blessed with beautiful scenery, this bustling market town provides everything a visitor could want – from the numerous shops offering wares for walkers and climbers to the many eating and drinking places.

Bowness-on-Windermere

The views from Bowness out across the lake and up to the mountains are some of the finest in the Lake District. Many kinds of lake excursions can be made; hire a row boat or take a trip on the 'steamer' out across England's longest lake (almost 11 miles). The town is an ideal base for a walking or climbing holiday, exploring the rugged beauty of the Duddon Valley and the quieter Lake District fells.

Grange-over-Sands

Genteel Grange-over-Sands is an excellent example of a prosperous, Edwardian seaside resort. Steeped in elegance and charm, this is the perfect place to indulge in a very English pastime – a leisurely stroll along the fine promenade, a walk in the Ornamental Gardens and afternoon tea in one of the many fine cafes.

Grizedale

Grizedale Forest Park offers superb views of Coniston Water, Windermere and Grizedale Valley itself. Take a walk up to the highest point at Carron Crag (317 m) and enjoy a panorama of the central Lake District fells.

Grasmere

Grasmere is perhaps best known as the home of William Wordsworth, a place he once described as "The most loveliest spot that man hath found". Set alongside Grasmere Lake, Grasmere is shrouded by a panorama of fells and mountains that provide the atmosphere so beloved of Wordsworth and the Romantic poets.

Keswick

Famous as a centre for walking since the reign of Queen Victoria, Keswick is right in the heart of magnificent fell country. Mighty Skiddaw can be attempted direct from the town while a host of famous fell tops in nearby Borrowdale and the spectacular Newlands valley are just a few minutes away by bus.

Ullswater

The lake is set against a breathtaking backdrop of mountain scenery; a truly dramatic picture, as you see a shoreline of green fields, woodlands and sheer rock faces rise from the lake's mirrored surface. It is not surprising that Ullswater inspired William Wordsworth, who wrote his most famous poem after he discovered multitudes of wild daffodils along the lakeshore.

Lancashire

Lancaster gave its name to the great county of Lancashire as well as to the Royal House of Lancaster. Lancaster Castle is still owned by her Majesty the Queen and is still a working building, housing two crown courts and a prison. Guided tours throughout the year offer you a glimpse behind its high walls.

Blackpool

It's a town full of firsts: taller, faster roller coasters, bigger clubs, even the biggest mirror ball in the world plus world-class shows, cosmopolitan restaurants, vibrant nightlife, an active sports scene and breathtakingly beautiful scenery on its doorstep. Blackpool is the UK's most visited seaside resort, with its magnificent tower and the Pleasure Beach providing 40 acres of fun with breathtaking attractions and great entertainment – it really does have something for everyone.

Colne Valley

The Colne Valley has much to explore including the Huddersfield Narrow Canal and Standedge Tunnel, the longest, deepest and highest canal tunnel in Britain. Wander along the canal and visit a number of interesting small villages.

Forest of Bowland

The Forest of Bowland is an Area of Outstanding Natural Beauty (AONB). This protected landscape offers stunning scenery, diverse natural habitats and a real feeling of remoteness and tranquility. The area remains unspoilt and even the well-trodden network of paths that criss-cross it remain an unobtrusive part of the ever changing habitats for many of Britain's rare species of birds and wildlife. Even at the height of the season you can wander along through the countryside and farmland without meeting a soul.

Lytham

A traditional coastal village steeped in heritage, largely through the famous landmark windmill on the green, the town's 'signature building'. The town's bygone age and colourful past is clearly illustrated, constantly reminding us of its Victorian values and unforgettable charm.

Morecambe

Famous for fabulous sunsets and stunning views across the bay to the Lake District; Morecambe has all the attractions of a traditional seaside town. Five miles of flat promenade are ideal for a walk along the sea front to take in those views.

Ribble Valley

The pretty village of Dunsop Bridge in the Ribble Valley has officially been declared the very centre of the British Isles. 'The Journey Through the Centre of the Kingdom' a 46-mile way marked walk is certainly the most adventurous route to take. Idyllic country life continues as it always has done throughout the area in the treasure trove of well-preserved villages.

Manchester & Merseyside

Visitors who have not been to Manchester for a while may no longer recognise the city which is now considered one of Britain's 'coolest' cities. In the last decade huge construction projects have transformed the landscape of the world's first industrial city and Manchester is now a truly contemporary metropolis.

Manchester

Developments include museums such as the Imperial War Museum North and Urbis, the Lowry Centre, a thriving art and culture scene, and the architecturally stunning Bridgewater Hall, a state-of-the-art international concert venue. Other major projects include the City of Manchester Stadium, built to host the 2002 Commonwealth games; this is now the permanent home of Manchester City Football club.

It is not hard to spot Manchester's past. Central Library, inspired by the Pantheon in Rome, is the largest municipal library in the world; and the magnificent Royal Exchange Theatre, formerly the Cotton Exchange, now houses the world's largest theatre-in-the-round.

Manchester's diverse culture mix means there's a great range of places to eat and drink and Manchester is a shopping destination in its own right, thought by many to rival London.

Merseyside

Merseyside is most famous as a port town and the birthplace of The Beatles, the region has many claims to fame, so many in fact, it actually appears in the Guinness Book of World Records as the place with the most records.

Liverpool is more than just a city with a big reputation, it is the centre of an area of beauty, culture and entertainment with much to explore. The European Capital of Culture in 2008 showcased Liverpool as a city of creative thinking and wonderful cultural attractions. The architecture is world-class, with more listed

buildings than any other city outside London. Liverpool boasts two cathedrals - The Anglican Cathedral and the Metropolitan Cathedral. Well worth a visit is the refurbished World Museum Liverpool and Walker Art Gallery. Tate Liverpool and Merseyside Maritime Museum are housed on the UNESCO-listed waterfront at the Albert Dock, whilst there don't forget to retrace the steps of the Fab Four at the Beatles Story.

Liverpool has several theatres which offer a range of contemporary, classic and touring productions. When you are tired of the superb shopping and the buzz of the city, head out the beaches and dunes in Sefton and Wirral Peninsula for some relaxation.

Merseyside offers plenty of sporting choices, football at Liverpool or Everton, horseracing at Haydock or Aintree. Take in some golf at some of Europe's best courses in Wirral or Southport. Or top-class rugby league at St. Helens. Merseyside genuinely does have something for everyone.

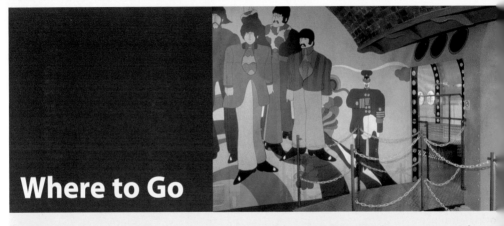

Where to Go

 Attractions with this sign participate in the **Visitor Attraction Quality Assurance Scheme** (see page 6) which recognises high standards in all aspects of the visitor experience.

ENTERTAINMENT & CULTURE

Beatles Story
Liverpool, Merseyside, L3 4AD
(0151) 709 1963
www.beatlesstory.com
Take an enlightening and atmospheric journey through the life, times, culture and music of The Beatles.

FACT (Foundation for Art & Creative Technology)
Liverpool, Merseyside, L1 4DQ
(0151) 707 4405
www.fact.co.uk
FACT is the UK's leading organisation for commissioning and exhibiting film, video, and new media art, with galleries, cinemas, a shop, bar and café, plus FREE exhibitions and Wi-Fi.

Harris Museum and Art Gallery
Preston, Lancashire, PR1 2PP
(01772) 258248
www.harrismuseum.org.uk
Share the best of Preston's heritage. Collections of paintings, sculpture, textiles, costume, glass and ceramics.

Imperial War Museum North
Manchester, Greater Manchester, M17 1TZ
(0161) 836 4000
www.iwm.org.uk/north/
Dynamic displays reflect how war shapes people's lives. Award-winning waterside museum with viewing platform.

John Rylands Library
Manchester, Greater Manchester, M3 3EH
(0161) 306 0555
www.library.manchester.ac.uk/
Over four million printed items and vast electronic resources, housed in an outstanding Neo-Gothic building.

Lady Lever Art Gallery
Wirral, Merseyside, CH62 5EQ
(0151) 478 4136
www.ladyleverartgallery.org.uk
The first Lord Leverhulme's collection of British paintings 1750–1900, furniture, Wedgwood pottery, oriental porcelain.

Liverpool Empire Theatre
Liverpool, Merseyside, L1 1JE
(0151) 708 3204
www.liverpoolempire.org.uk
Experience the best in large-scale entertainment at the regions premier live entertainment venue.

Manchester Art Gallery
Manchester, Greater Manchester, M2 3JL
(0161) 235 8888
www.manchestergalleries.org
Six centuries of great art, craft, design and costume. Interactives plus exciting exhibitions and events.

National Football Museum
Preston, Lancashire, PR1 6RU
(01772) 908442
www.nationalfootballmuseum.com
Journey through football history, see the FIFA World Cup collection and check out the interactives gallery.

National Waterways Museum
Ellesmere Port, Cheshire, CH65 4FW
(0151) 355 5017
www.nwm.org.uk
The UK's largest collection of inland waterway craft. Working forge, Power Hall, industrial heritage exhibitions.

Tate Liverpool
Liverpool, Merseyside, L3 4BB
(0151) 702 7400
www.tate.org.uk/liverpool
Be inspired by the National Collection of Modern Art in the North. Free daily talks, shop and cafe.

The Museum of Science and Industry (MOSI)
Manchester, Greater Manchester, M3 4FP
(0161) 832 2244
www.mosi.org.uk
Five historic buildings packed with fascinating displays, hands-on galleries, working machinery and special exhibitions.

The World of Beatrix Potter
Windermere, Cumbria, LA23 3BX
(01539) 488444
www.hop-skip-jump.com
Discover the real Miss Potter, journey with Peter Rabbit, visit all your favourite characters. Unforgettable magic!

**ullie House Museum
nd Art Gallery**
rlisle, Cumbria, CA3 8TP
228) 618718
ww.tulliehouse.co.uk
mething for everyone: Jacobean
use, herb garden, history, Pre-
phaelite art, local minerals and
eractive fun.

alker Art Gallery
verpool, Merseyside, L3 8EL
51) 478 4613
ww.walkerartgallery.org.uk
e of Europe's finest galleries:
tstanding Old Masters, Victorian and
e-Raphaelite pictures, plus modern
tish works.

orld Museum Liverpool
verpool, Merseyside, L3 8EN
151) 478 4613
ww.worldmuseumliverpool.org.uk
vard-winning, Natural History Centre,
anetarium and collections: from the
nazonian rain forest to outer space.

FAMILY FUN

ackpool Tower & Circus
ackpool, Lancashire, FY1 4BJ
1253) 622242
ww.theblackpooltower.co.uk
tertainment for all, night and day.
mous Ballroom and Tower Circus.
ngle Jim's Adventure Playground.

amelot Theme Park
horley, Lancashire, PR7 5LP
371 663 6400
ww.camelotthemepark.co.uk
ep in to the magical world of
amelot and be transported back to
time where dragons roam free, King
rthur rules and knights do battle on
orseback.

**ullivers World
heme Park**
Varrington, Cheshire, WA5 9YZ
1925) 444888
ww.gulliversfun.co.uk
ll day family magic featuring 30 rides
nd attractions. Suits children aged
–13.

leasure Beach
ackpool, Lancashire, FY4 1EZ
371 222 1234
ww.pleasurebeachblackpool.com
reat family adventure: thrill rides
cluding new Infusion, plus fabulous
hows like Hot Ice.

andcastle Waterpark
ackpool, Lancashire, FY4 1BB
1253) 343602
ww.sandcastle-waterpark.co.uk
subtropical paradise, including
yphoon Lagoon wave pool, fun pool
nd 300-ft Gentle Giant waterslide.

HERITAGE

Beeston Castle
Tarporley, Cheshire, CW6 9TX
(01829) 260464
www.visitCheshire.com/site/beeston
Ruined 13thC castle on top of the
Peckforton Hills. Splendid views over
eight counties. Exhibitions.

Birdoswald Roman Fort
Brampton, Cumbria, CA8 7DD
(01697) 747602
www.english-heritage.org.uk
A Roman fort, turret and milecastle
displaying the best-preserved defences
of any fort on Hadrian's Wall.

Blue Planet Aquarium
Knutsford, Cheshire, WA16 6QN
(01625) 374400
www.tattonpark.org.uk
Explore the neoclassical mansion, vast
gardens, Tudor Old Hall and working
historical farm. Glorious deer park.

**Brantwood, Home
of John Ruskin**
Coniston, Cumbria, LA21 8AD
(01539) 441396
www.brantwood.org.uk
Explore the former home and estate
of John Ruskin. Outstanding Lakeland
views.

Chester Cathedral
Chester, Cheshire, CH1 2HU
(01244) 324756
www.chestercathedral.com
A 14th–15thC cathedral. Spectacular
carved choir stalls, wonderful stained
glass and 12thC monastic building.
Audio tour.

**Dove Cottage, Wordsworth
Museum & Art Gallery**
Grasmere, Cumbria, LA22 9SH
(01539) 435544
www.wordsworth.org.uk
Wordsworth's home during his most
creative period. Guided tours and
award-winning museum displaying
manuscripts and memorabilia.

Hoghton Tower
Preston, Lancashire, PR5 0SH
(01254) 852986
www.hoghtontower.co.uk
Handsome English Renaissance
architecture, magnificent state
apartments, banqueting hall,
dungeons, unusual dolls' house
collection.

**Jodrell Bank Visitor
Centre & 3D Theatre**
Holmes Chapel, Cheshire,
SK11 9DL
(01477) 571339
www.jb.man.ac.uk
See the world famous Lovell Telescope
along the Observational Pathway. Also
3D theatre, exhibition, arboretum.

Muncaster Experience
Ravenglass, Cumbria, CA18 1RQ
(01229) 717614
www.muncaster.co.uk
Haunted castle with glorious gardens
and vistas. Also World Owl Trust
headquarters. Daily bird show.

**Speke Hall, Gardens &
Estate**
Liverpool, Merseyside, L24 1XD
(0151) 427 7231
www.nationaltrust.org.uk
Enjoy a wonderful, rambling Tudor
mansion with rich Victorian interiors.
Landscaped gardens and countryside
walks.

Tatton Park
Northwich, Cheshire, CW9 6NA
(01565) 777353
www.arleyhallandgardens.com
Impressive Victorian Jacobean
Hall with award-winning gardens.
Plant nursery, restaurant, shop and
woodland trails.

NATURE & WILDLIFE

Blackpool Zoo
Blackpool, Lancashire, FY3 8PP
(01253) 830830
www.blackpoolzoo.org.uk
See over 1,500 of the world's rare and
exotic animals. Play area, miniature
railway, shops.

Bowland Wild Boar Park
Chipping, Lancashire,
PR3 2QT
(01995) 61554
www.wildboarpark.co.uk
View wild boar, cattle, llama, wallabies, red squirrels and pet lambs. Ideal for young families.

Chester Zoo
Chester, Cheshire,
CH2 1LH
(01244) 380280
www.chesterzoo.org
Meet more than 7,000 animals and 500 species, from elephants to miniature monkeys, including the rare and endangered.

WWT Martin Mere Wetland Centre
Ormskirk, Lancashire,
L40 0TA
(01704) 895181
www.wwt.org.uk
Observe over 1,600 ducks, geese, flamingos, cranes, swans, and now beavers. Events, visitor centre and shop.

OUTDOOR ACTIVITIES

Anderton Boat Lift - Lift Trips
Northwich, Cheshire, CW9 6FW
(01606) 786777
www.andertonboatlift.co.uk
Ride on the world's first boat lift and visit the modern operations centre. Canalside walks.

Ullswater Steamers
Ullswater, Cumbria, CA11 0US
(01768) 482229
www.ullswater-steamers.co.uk
One and two hour cruises from Ullswater's Howtown pier, Glenridding pier house and Pooley Bridge pier house.

Windermere Lake Cruises, Waterhead
Ambleside, Cumbria, LA22 0EY
(01539) 443360
www.windermere-lakecruises.co.uk
Windermere Lake Cruises offer more than just a ferry service. We hold private charters, lunch cruises, buffet cruises, corporate hospitality, public sailings, group travel. Steamers and launches sail daily throughout the year from Waterhead.

Events 2010

Africa Oye
Liverpool
www.africaoye.com/
June

Arley Horse Trials and Country Fair 2010
Northwich
www.arleyhallandgardens.com
May

Blackpool Illuminations Switch On
Blackpool
www.visitblackpool.com/illuminations
September

Burnley Balloon Festival
Burnley
www.visitlancashire.com
July–August

CEV European Championship Tour Beach Volleyball
Blackpool
www.volleyblackpool.com
September

Chester Food and Drink Festival 2010
Chester
www.chesterfoodanddrink.com/
April

Chester Literature Festival
Chester
www.chesterfestivals.co.uk/site/literature-festival
October

Chester Summer Music Festival
Chester
www.chesterfestivals.co.uk/
July

Cholmondeley Pageant of Power 2010
Malpas
www.pageantofpower.com
July

Colour Chart: Reinventing Colour, 1950 to Today
Liverpool
www.tate.org.uk/liverpool
All Year

Creamfields
Runcorn
www.creamfields.com
28th–29th August

Great British Rhythm and Blues Festival
Colne
www.bluesfestival.co.uk
27th–30th August

Mathew Street Music Festival 2010
Liverpool
www.visitliverpool.com
28th–29th August

Nantwich Food and Drink Festival
Nantwich
www.nantwichfoodfestival.co.uk/
September

Out2Dance
Blackpool
www.out2dance.co.uk
28th–31st May

Pendle Walking Festival
www.pendle.gov.uk/walking
August–September

Pennine Lancashire Festival of Food and Culture
Blackburn
www.penninelancashirefestivals.com
August–September

RHS Flower Show 2010 at Tatton Park
Knutsford
www.rhs.org.uk/whatson/events/
July

Showzam
Blackpool
www.showzam.co.uk
12th–21st February

Tractor Pulling
Great Eccleston
www.nwtpc.co.uk
28th–29th August

World Fireworks Championships
Blackpool
www.visitblackpool.com/
September–October

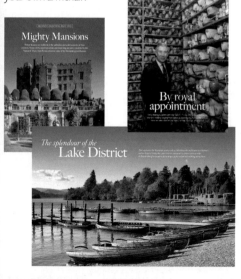

Where to Eat

The North West England region has great places to eat. The restaurant reviews on these pages are just a small selection from the highly respected **The Good Food Guide 2010**. Please see pages 20–21 for further information on the guide and details of a Special Offer for our readers.

CHESHIRE

Simon Radley at The Chester Grosvenor

Formal but fun, with great details
Eastgate, Chester, CH1 1LT
Tel no: (01244) 324024
www.chestergrosvenor.com
Modern European | £65

In the newly refurbished dining room that now bears his name, Simon Radley is at his inventive and playful best. The revamped room is still suitably formal, and eating here is still an occasion – but thanks to new, sinkably soft chairs, it's a far more comfortable one. Readers rate the details that bookend a meal: well-loved bread and cheese trolleys, 'fab' canapes such as crispy fried whitebait with fennel mayonnaise, and 'fine' petits fours. What goes between isn't bad, either. Listed with typical brevity as 'spices', one starter might be cod with old-fashioned, creamy curry sauce, mussels, and a perfect poached egg raviolo. To follow, roe deer with

an onion 'study' of crisp shallot rings and an onion Tati might share a plate with Iberico pork belly and apple sauce. Desserts are a chance to play with more humble but well-loved flavour combinations. A 'compression' of banana is alongside an accurately Snickers-like iced salty peanut parfait. Readers say 'wow'. Service ranges from slickly professional to surprisingly gauche, but the skilled wine team is a great advantage to anyone lost in a bewilderingly extensive list. Bottles are from £25. However, being in the presence of (mainly French) greatness is justification for the unleashing of a bigger budget.

Chef/s: Simon Radley. **Open:** Tue to Sat D 7 to 9.30 (Fri, Sat from 6). **Closed:** Sun and Mon, 25 and 26 Dec, 1 week Jan. **Meals:** Set D £65 (3 courses) to £75 (8 courses). **Service:** 12.5% (optional). **Details:** Cards accepted. 45 seats. Air-con. Separate bar. No music. No mobile phones. Wheelchair access. Car parking.

The Wizard

A magic place
Macclesfield Road, Nether Alderley, SK10 4UB
Tel no: (01625) 584000
www.ainscoughs.co.uk
Modern British | £26

A 16th century, whitewashed inn not far from Alderley Edge is home to one of Martin Ainscough's rapidly growing empire of northern restaurants. The dining room has beamed ceilings and bare wood tables, and the emphasis is on brasserie dishes cooked with style and precision. Beer-battered haddock, gammon with pineapple chutney, and Cumberland sausages with mash and onion gravy will please traditionalists, but there are also more contemporary dishes such as salmon on crushed new potatoes with goats' cheese and basil oil. Crispy duck spring rolls

ight kick things off, and chocolate brownie with
hocolate ice cream bring down the curtain. Wine
ices start at £11.50.

hef/s: Paul Beattie. **Open:** Tue to Sun L 12 to 2, Tue to
t D 7 to 9.30. **Closed:** 26 Dec to 3 Jan. **Meals:** Set L and
£10 (2 courses). **Service:** 10% (optional). **Details:** Cards
ccepted. 80 seats. 20 seats outside. Wheelchair access.
usic. Children allowed. Car parking.

CUMBRIA

Underscar Manor

tricate dishes in an Italianate villa
plethwaite, Keswick, CA12 4PH
l no: (01768) 775000
ww.keswickrestaurant.co.uk
odern British | £45

et high above Keswick, looking out towards
erwentwater and Borrowdale, Underscar Manor is
very inch the perfectly positioned Lakeland retreat.
uilt as an Italianate villa, complete with a campanile,
is surrounded by lush gardens bursting with blooms,
hile the interior flaunts its English pedigree. The
hole place is a tribute to serious nurturing. Meals
the conservatory-style dining room comprise a
uccession of exceedingly intricate dishes drawn from
e modern European repertoire, although Lakeland
gredients always figure in the mix. The signature
heese soufflé ('served in different styles') is about as
rosaic as it gets, with other starters moving quickly
to the elaborate world of, say, white crab and
callop ravioli with a seared scallop, lemongrass and
ry vermouth sauce. Elsewhere, it's accomplished
artnerships all the way: a dinky steak and mushroom
udding beside fillet of Cumbrian Fell beef, a gamey
agoût to accompany loin of local venison, and an
range puff pastry tart to set off crispy roast Barbary
uck breast and Grand Marnier sauce. Desserts come
ull circle with a hot, sweet soufflé ; otherwise, try
omething relatively simple such as warm apple tart
vith prune and Armagnac ice cream. France puts down
substantial marker on the reputable wine list; house
elections are £24.

hef/s: Robert Thornton. **Open:** all week L 12 to 1, D 7 to
.30. **Closed:** 2 to 3 days beginning of Jan. **Meals:** Set L
25 (2 courses) to £28. Set D £38 (5 courses). **Service:** not
nc. **Details:** Cards accepted. 55 seats. 12 seats outside. No
music. No mobile phones. Car parking.

Swinside Lodge

Grange Road, Newlands, Keswick, CA12 5UE
Tel no: (017687) 72948
www.swinsidelodge.com
Modern British

Standing alone in beautiful open countryside, this
handsome Georgian residence is just a stroll from lovely
Derwentwater. Four-course dinners (£40) are pointed

up with local flavours: cream of celeriac and Blengdale
Blue cheese soup with white truffle oil might precede
fillet of Cumbrian beef in traditional partnership with
Savoy cabbage, pickled walnuts and red wine jus.
To conclude, choose a slate of Cumbrian cheeses or
a dessert such as banana, date and pecan sponge
pudding with white chocolate custard. Wines from
£16.50. Open all week D only.

LANCASHIRE

The Clog and Billycock

Never-fail, über-local gastro grub
Billinge End Road, Pleasington, Blackburn, BB2 6QB
Tel no: (01254) 201163
www.theclogandbillycock.com
Gastropub | £24

The newest gastro-horse in the Ribble Valley Inns
stable works along comfortingly familiar lines. Take a
seat somewhere in the spacious interior, probably near
one of the trademark photos of local suppliers. Flap
the huge menu like a wobble board, order at a pay
point, and prepare for extraordinarily large portions.
It's hard to go wrong, but über-local choices include a
crumpet with fresh Lancashire curd cheese, cress and
beetroot or a shared wooden platter of seafood with
perky pickled accompaniments. Devilled Goosnargh
chicken or Fleetwood fish pie are among never-fail
main courses and specials include plenty of seasonal
game. An obsession with nursery puddings could lead
to an encounter with tapioca, though the 'length of
Lancashire' cheeseboard is difficult to pass by. Chilean
house wines are £13.50.

Chef/s: Ian Rudge. **Open:** all week L 12 to 2 (noon to
8.30pm Sun), D 6 to 9 (from 5.30 Sat, noon to 8.30pm
Sun). **Closed:** 25 Dec. **Meals:** alc (main courses £10 to
£18). **Service:** not inc. **Details:** Cards accepted. 130 seats.
50 seats outside. No music. Wheelchair access. Children
allowed. Car parking.

The Highwayman

Super-boozer that celebrates local produce
Burrow, LA6 2RJ
Tel no: (01524) 273338
www.highwaymaninn.co.uk
British | £23

'Is it a gastropub,' muses a reader, 'or just a pub that
does really good food?' It's certainly no ordinary local,
being one of a mini-chain of super-boozers under the
Ribble Valley Inns umbrella. More atmospheric than its
East Lancs siblings (Three Fishes, Clog and Billycock),
one could pop in for a half of Thwaites Lancaster
Bomber or Double Century, but many diners journey
cross-county just for the food. The menu 'celebrates
local produce', for example Flookburgh shrimps with
blade mace butter, Herdwick mutton pudding and
Lancashire curd tart, which the kitchen 'cooks well'.

Hamfisted presentation and unbalanced dishes are, however, sometimes evident. The wine list is definitely more gastropub than local, with representation from big names and regions, starting at £13.50.

Chef/s: Michael Ward. **Open:** all week L 12 to 2 (12 to 8 Sun), D 6 to 9 (5.30 to 9 Sat, 12 to 8 Sun). **Meals:** alc (main courses £9 to £20). **Service:** not inc. **Details:** Cards accepted. 120 seats. 60 seats outside. Separate bar. No music. Wheelchair access. Children allowed. Car parking.

MANCHESTER

EastzEast

Princess Street, Manchester, M1 7DL
Tel no: (0161) 2445353
www.eastzeast.com
Indian

The EastzEast mini-chain recently extended to Preston, but the original, at the base of a hotel on the outskirts of town, is perhaps still the best. The restaurant is reliably busy. Readers are attracted by its relatively 'upmarket' air and Punjabi dishes, which might include a Lahore lamb chop handi (£9.95) or karahi chicken masala desi (£8.45), cooked on the bone with tomatoes galore. They've also noted the cheek-by-jowl approach to seating, which can be hair-raising when there's hot food on the move. House wine is £12.50. Dinner only.

The Modern
Cool cocktails and creative cooking
Urbis, Cathedral Gardens, Manchester, M4 3GB
Tel no: (0161) 6058282
www.themodernmcr.co.uk
Modern British | £27

At the top of Manchester's museum of urban life, The Modern offers verve, cocktails and cooking with intent. Drinks in the upstairs bar are some of the finest in the city, and a menu dedicated, though not feverishly, to good local produce has serious appeal. Potted this and terrine of that feature heavily. Start, perhaps, with potted smoked mackerel and ribbons of cucumber pickled with dill. Braised Ribble Valley pork hock comes with a hearty but surprisingly effective double-hander of smooth champ and Puy lentils: be assured that lighter alternatives are available. Dessert could be a Valrhona tart with addictive ice cream studded with caramelised hazelnuts. It's all served competently in a long room accented with sage green and muddy brown, streamlined but not unfriendly. House bottles a £15.30 kick off a compact but colourfully described list.

Chef/s: Paul Faulker. **Open:** Mon to Sun L 12 to 3 (4.45 Sun), Mon to Sat D 5 to 9.45, all week bar food midday to 11. **Closed:** 25 and 26 Dec. **Meals:** alc (main courses £10 to £23). Set L and D £15 (2 courses) to £18. **Service:** not inc. **Details:** Cards accepted. 64 seats. Air-con. Separate bar. Wheelchair access. Music. Children allowed.

MERSEYSIDE

raiche

avour-filled, mind-expanding menus

Rose Mount, Oxton, CH43 5SG
el no: (0151) 6522914
ww.restaurantfraiche.com

odern French | £40

one too shabby' report readers of Merseyside's most
rious restaurant, with a little understatement. Chef-
atron Marc Wilkinson is, notoriously, a one-man band,
poking alone for his 20-cover restaurant in a leafy
onservation village not far from deepest Liverpool.
e's also responsible for commissioning the caramel-
oloured glass artworks that set a calm tone in the
nall room, and training a front of house team that has
ained confidence and professionalism apace. Food,
oo, moves on; a spring inspection found less reliance
n powders and piles, and impressive technical ability
oplied even-handedly, in the pursuit of flavour rather
nan showing off. Set menus come in three guises,
scending in price and complexity from the three-
ourse Elements, through the six-course Signature to
ne surprise Bespoke option, which showcases the
ost daring of Wilkinson's dishes. That's not to say
gnature doesn't expand the mind – who knew that
ny, crunchy passion fruit seeds provide just the right
uity acidity to offset sweet Menai mussels and rich
auliflower velouté? The menu might continue with
oft, slow-cooked pork belly with intense raisin purée
nd an architecturally curved take on crackling, and the
erfect piece of lemon sole with bright, citrus-soused
uinoa. Earthy parsley root, and just a sprinkling of
arsley sherbert, might work impressively with a loin
f Cumbrian lamb, and several services of different
ouse-made breads are on hand to gather either the
st lick of a fine, light sauce or the final smear of salty
rench seaweed butter. To finish, choose either from
ne well-kept – and firmly Gallic – cheese trolley, or the
ay's dessert, perhaps an artful rhubarb 'crumble' with a

pleasingly miniature ball of coconut ice cream. Though
comprehensive, with plenty of halves, the wine list isn't
designed solely for those with deep pockets. House
bottles are around £19 (£4.50 a glass).
Chef/s: Marc Wilkinson. **Open:** Fri and Sat L 12 to 1.30,
Wed to Sun D 7 to 9 (6 to 8 Sun). **Closed:** Mon, Tue,
25 Dec, first 2 weeks Jan. **Meals:** Set L £20 (2 courses)
to £25. Set D £40. Bespoke menu £55. **Service:** not inc.
Details: Cards accepted. 20 seats. 8 seats outside. Separate
bar. No mobile phones. Wheelchair access. Music.

The Side Door

Good-value ticket for culture vultures
29a Hope Street, Liverpool, L1 9BQ
Tel no: (0151) 7077888
www.thesidedoor.co.uk
Modern European | £25
Just round the corner from the Philharmonic Hall and
Liverpool's theatreland hot spots, this unpretentious
two-floored bistro is a handy ticket for culture vultures
and foodies alike. Rustic bare floors and deep red
walls set the tone for a menu that does some eclectic
conjuring tricks with North Country ingredients. Expect
to find confit duck with creamed lentils alongside chilli-
fried squid with king prawn and wild mushroom risotto
or whole sea bass and caponata in competition with
roast Goosnargh duck breast and sweet sherry shallots.
Light lunches are brilliant value, and puddings play
it straight, with the likes of Seville orange tart. Global
wines start at £13.
Chef/s: Sean Millar. **Open:** Mon to Sat L 12 to 2.30, D 5
to 10. **Closed:** Sun, 25 Dec, bank hols. **Meals:** alc (main
courses £11 to £16). Set D £15.95 to £27.95. **Service:** 10%
parties over 6. **Details:** Cards accepted. 50 seats. Air-con.
Wheelchair access. Music. Children allowed.

Tourist Information Centres

When you arrive at your destination, visit an Official Partner Tourist Information Centre for quality assured help with accommodation and information about local attractions and events, or email your request before you go. To search for attractions and Tourist Information Centres on the move just text INFO to 62233, and a web link will be sent to your mobile phone. To find a Tourist Information Centre by region visit enjoyEngland.com/find-tic.

ACCRINGTON	Town Hall	01254 380293	tourism@hyndburnbc.gov.uk
ASHTON-UNDER-LYNE	Council Offices	0161 343 4343	tourist.information@tameside.gov.uk
BARNOLDSWICK	The Council Shop	01282 666704	tourist.info@pendle.gov.uk
BARROW-IN-FURNESS	Forum 28	01229 876505	touristinfo@barrowbc.gov.uk
BLACKBURN	50-54 Church Street	01254 53277	visit@blackburn.gov.uk
BLACKPOOL	1 Clifton Street	01253 478222	tic@blackpool.gov.uk
BOLTON	Central Library Foyer	01204 334321	tourist.info@bolton.gov.uk
BOWNESS	Glebe Road	015394 42895	bownesstic@lake-district.gov.uk
BURNLEY	Burnley Bus Station	01282 664421	tic@burnley.gov.uk
BURY	The Met Arts Centre	0161 253 5111	touristinformation@bury.gov.uk
CARLISLE	Old Town Hall	01228 625600	tourism@carlisle-city.gov.uk
CLEVELEYS	Victoria Square	01253 853378	cleveleystic@wyrebc.gov.uk
CLITHEROE	12-14 Market Place	01200 425566	tourism@ribblevalley.gov.uk
CONISTON	Ruskin Avenue	015394 41533	mail@conistontic.org
DISCOVER PENDLE CENTRE	Boundary Mill Sores	01282 856186	discoverpendle@pendle.gov.uk
FLEETWOOD	Old Ferry Office	01253 773953	fleetwoodtic@wyrebc.gov.uk
GARSTANG	Council Offices	01995 602125	garstangtic@wyrebc.gov.uk
KENDAL	Town Hall	01539 725758	kendaltic@southlakeland.gov.uk
KESWICK	Moot Hall	017687 72645	keswicktic@lake-district.gov.uk
LANCASTER	29 Castle Hill	01524 32878	lancastervic@lancaster.gov.uk

LIVERPOOL 08 PLACE	Whitechapel	0151 233 2459	contact@liverpool08.com
LIVERPOOL ALBERT DOCK	Anchor Courtyard	0151 2332008	08place@liverpool.com
LIVERPOOL JOHN LENNON AIRPORT	Arrivals Hall, South Terminal	0906 680 6886	info@visitliverpool.com
LYTHAM ST ANNES	Visitor & Travel Information Centre	01253 725610	touristinformation@fylde.gov.uk
MANCHESTER	Manchester Visitor Centre	0871 222 8223	touristinformation@marketing-manchester.co.uk
MORECAMBE	Old Station Buildings	01524 582808	morecambetic@lancaster.gov.uk
OLDHAM	12 Albion Street	0161 627 1024	ecs.tourist@oldham.gov.uk
PENDLE HERITAGE CENTRE	Park Hill	01282 661701	heritage.centre@pendle.gov.uk
PENRITH	Middlegate	01768 867466	pen.tic@eden.gov.uk
PRESTON	The Guildhall	01772 253731	tourism@preston.gov.uk
ROCHDALE	Touchstones	01706 924928	tic@link4life.org
SALFORD	The Lowry, Pier 8	0161 848 8601	tic@salford.gov.uk
SOUTHPORT	112 Lord Street	01704 533333	info@visitsouthport.com
ST HELENS	The World of Glass	01744 755150	info@sthelenstic.com
STOCKPORT	Staircase House	0161 474 4444	tourist.information@stockport.gov.uk
WHITEHAVEN	Market Hall	01946 598914	tic@copelandbc.gov.uk
WIGAN	62 Wallgate	01942 825677	tic@wlct.org
WINDERMERE	Victoria Street	015394 46499	windermeretic@southlakeland.gov.uk

Regional Contacts and Information

There are various publications and guides about England's North West available from the following Tourist Boards or by logging on to www.visitenglandsnorthwest.com or calling 0845 600 6040:

Visit Chester and Cheshire

Chester Railway Station, 1st Floor, West Wing Offices,
Station Road, Chester, CH1 3NT
Tel: (01244) 405600
Tel: 0845 073 1324 (accommodation booking)
Email: info@visitchesterandcheshire.co.uk
Web: www.visitchester.com or www.visitcheshire.com

Cumbria Tourism

Windermere Road, Staveley, Kendal, LA8 9PL
Tel: (015398) 22222
Email: info@cumbriatourism.org
Web: www.golakes.co.uk

The Lancashire and Blackpool Tourist Board

St. George's House, St. George's Street,
Chorley, PR7 2AA
Tel: (01257) 226600 (Brochure request)
Email: info@visitlancashire.com
Web: www.visitlancashire.com

Visit Manchester – The Tourist Board For Greater Manchester

Town Hall Extension
Lloyd Street
Manchester
M60 2LA
Tel: 0871 222 8223
Email: touristinformation@visitmanchester.com
Web: www.visitmanchester.com

The Mersey Partnership – The Tourist Board for Liverpool City Region

12 Princes Parade, Liverpool, L3 1BG
Tel: (0151) 233 2008 (information enquiries)
Tel: 0844 870 0123 (accommodation booking)
Email: info@visitliverpool.com
(accommodation enquiries)
Email: 08place@liverpool.gov.uk
(information enquiries)
Web: www.visitliverpool.com

Where to Stay

Entries appear alphabetically by town name in each county. A key to symbols appears on page 6. Maps start on page 394. A listing of all Enjoy England assessed accommodation appears at the end of the region.

CHESTER, Cheshire Map ref 4A2

SAT NAV CH2 4HS

Chester Fairoaks Caravan Club Site

Rake Lane, Little Stanney, Chester CH2 4HS
t (0151) 355 1600 e firtrees@chester-holidays.co.uk
w **caravanclub.co.uk**

🚐 (100)   £14.90–£28.90
🚏 (100)   £14.90–£28.90
100 touring pitches

SPECIAL PROMOTIONS
Special member rates mean
you can save your
membership subscription in
less than a week. Visit our
website to find out more.

A tranquil site only six miles from the walled ci
of Chester with its famous zoo, historic sites,
top-class entertainment and excellent shopping
Take an open-top bus or walk around the walls
to absorb the colourful atmosphere.

open All year
payment credit/debit cards, cash, cheques

directions From M53 take jct 10 and join A511
Travel towards Queensferry, follow brown signs.
Turn left in Little Stanney at signpost Chorlton.
Site 0.25 miles on left.

General 🗔 🎺 📺 ⏲ ☀ 🔌 🍴 ⏏ 🚽 ⚓
Leisure ⚠

Where is my pet welcome?

Some properties welcome well-behaved pets. Look for the 🐕 in the accommodation listings. You can also buy a copy of our popular guide 'Pets Come Too!' Now available in good bookshops and online at **enjoyenglanddirect.com**

£9.99

APPLEBY-IN-WESTMORLAND, Cumbria Map ref 5B3

SAT NAV CA16 6EJ

Wild Rose Park
Ormside, Appleby-in-Westmorland CA16 6EJ
t (01768) 351077 f (01768) 352551 e reception@wildrose.co.uk
w **wildrose.co.uk** ONLINE MAP LAST MINUTE OFFERS

⊟ (226)	£17.00–£31.50
⊞ (157)	£17.00–£31.50
▲ (65)	£17.00–£31.50

226 touring pitches

Friendly, family park in the lovely, unspoilt Eden Valley with mountain views. Within easy reach of the Lakes and the Dales. Spotless, super loos and private wash cubicles. **directions** Please contact us for directions **open** All year **payment** credit/debit cards, cash, cheques

General ⊟ ⊼ ⊻ ⊑ ⌂ ☼ ⊡ ⊙ ☎ ⊡ ✕ Leisure ♪ ⊀ ● ⋔

ARMATHWAITE, Cumbria Map ref 5B2

SAT NAV CA4 9SY

Englethwaite Hall Caravan Club Site
Armathwaite, Carlisle CA4 9SY
t (01228) 560202 e enquiries@caravanclub.co.uk
w **caravanclub.co.uk**

THE CARAVAN CLUB

⊟ (63)	£9.30–£21.00
⊞ (63)	£9.30–£21.00

63 touring pitches

SPECIAL PROMOTIONS
Special member rates mean you can save your membership subscription in less than a week. Visit our website to find out more.

A tranquil site, scattered with rhododendrons from the garden of the former old hall. Walkers will love this beautiful area - the Eden Valley riverside walk is special with views to the Lakeland Fells from the footpaths and wild flower scattered country lanes.

payment credit/debit cards, cash, cheques

directions Exit M6/A6 onto B6263, in 1.75 miles turn right. Site on right in about 2.75 miles.

General ⊼ ⊡ ⊙ ⊡
Leisure ♪

BOUTH, Cumbria Map ref 5A3 SAT NAV LA12 8JN

Black Beck Caravan Park

Bouth, Nr Ulverston, Cumbria LA12 8JN
t (01229) 861274 f (01229) 861041 e reception@blackbeck.net
w **blackbeck.com** ONLINE MAP ONLINE BOOKING

🚐 (25)	£14.00–£19.50
🚐 (4)	£14.00–£19.50
🏠 (1)	£215–£555
🏕 (3)	£215.00–£555.00

39 touring pitches

SPECIAL PROMOTIONS
10% off 7 day tourer
booking. Rebook within 28
days of holiday and receive
15% discount.

Black Beck is situated within the Lake District National Park, nestled in the beautiful Rusland Valley between the southern tips of Lake Windermere and Coniston. Surrounded by spectacular woodland scenery. Jacuzzi and sauna.

open 1 March to 15 November
payment credit/debit cards, cash, cheques

directions M6 jct 36. A590 towards Barrow, Newby Bridge. Pass steam railway, Next right to Bouth. Left at T-junction, 0.5 miles right after hump-backed bridge.

General 🔥 🖥 🐾 🛒 🚿 ☀ 📺 🛢 📞 🚐
Leisure ∪ 🚲 🎣 ⛰

CONISTON, Cumbria Map ref 5A3 SAT NAV LA12 8DL

Crake Valley Holiday Park

Water Yeat, Blawith, Ulverston LA12 8DL
t (01229) 885203 f (01229) 885203 e crakevalley@coniston1.fslife.co.uk
w **crakevalley.co.uk**

🛖 (6)	£17.00
🏕 (15)	£210.00–£590.00

Small, top-graded holiday park. Caravans and lodges for hire in secluded setting opposite Coniston Water. Ideal base for touring the Lakes. **directions** Please contact us for directions **open** March to October **payment** cash, cheques

General 🖥 🐾 🛒 ☀

CONISTON, Cumbria Map ref 5A3

Park Coppice Caravan Club Site

Coniston LA21 8LA
t (01539) 441555 f (01342) 410258 e enquiries@caravanclub.co.uk
w **caravanclub.co.uk**

THE CARAVAN CLUB

🚐 (280)   £12.20–£25.10
🚏 (280)   £12.20–£25.10
280 touring pitches

SPECIAL PROMOTIONS
Special member rates mean you can save your membership subscription in less than a week. Visit our website to find out more.

Set in 63 acres of National Trust woodland with pitches grouped in open glades. Access from the bottom of the site across fields to Coniston Water. Take a steamboat ride on the Coniston Gondola or hire a boat. Needless to say the walking is matchless and birdwatchers will have their binoculars in constant use.

open March to November
payment credit/debit cards, cash, cheques

directions Follow A593, 1.5 miles south of Coniston village. Final approach from the north or south is narrow in places.

General 🔲 🔭 📱 🎣 ☼ ⬛ 🎮 🛒 🚻 🚐
Leisure 🏊 ⛰

GRANGE-OVER-SANDS, Cumbria Map ref 5A3

ROSE AWARD CARAVAN HOLIDAY PARK

Greaves Farm Caravan Park

Field Broughton, Grange-over-Sands LA11 6HU
t (01539) 536329

🚐 (10)   £15.00–£17.00
🚏   £15.00–£17.00
▲ (10)   £14.00–£18.00
🏠 (2)   £290.00–£425.00
10 touring pitches

Small, quiet site two miles north of Cartmel. A convenient base for Lake District touring, and under personal supervision of the owner. Directions given with booking confirmation. **directions** Please contact us for directions **open** March to October **payment** cash, cheques

General 🔭 📱 🎣 ☼ 🎮 🛒 🚻

GRANGE-OVER-SANDS, Cumbria Map ref 5A3

SAT NAV LA11 6RB

Meathop Fell Caravan Club Site

Meathop, Grange-over-Sands LA11 6RB
t (01539) 532912 f (01342) 410258 e enquiries@caravanclub.co.uk
w **caravanclub.co.uk**

(131)   £14.00–£26.90
(131)   £14.00–£26.90
131 touring pitches

SPECIAL PROMOTIONS
Special member rates mean you can save your membership subscription in less than a week. Visit our website to find out more.

This gentle and peaceful site is an ideal base from which to explore North Lancashire and th southern Lake District. You'll find literary associations everywhere, from Wordsworth at Dove cottage, Grasmere to Beatrix Potter at Sawrey Gallery at Hawkshead. Windermere and Coniston are great for water-based activities.

open All year
payment credit/debit cards, cash, cheques

directions M6 jct 36, A590 to Barrow. After about 3.25 miles take slip road and follow A59 to Barrow. At 1st roundabout follow International Camping signs. Steep approach.

General ⬚ 🕪 🛋 🅟 ☼ 🔲 🐕 🛅 🚿 🅦🅟
Leisure ⛺

KENDAL, Cumbria Map ref 5B3

SAT NAV LA8 0JZ

Low Park Wood Caravan Club Site

Sedgwick, Kendal LA8 0JZ
t (01539) 560186 f (01342) 410258 e enquiries@caravanclub.co.uk
w **caravanclub.co.uk**

(141)   £14.00–£26.90
(141)   £14.00–£26.90
141 touring pitches

SPECIAL PROMOTIONS
Special member rates mean you can save your membership subscription in less than a week. Visit our website to find out more.

Set in National Trust woodland, on the site of a 19th C gunpowder mill this peaceful country sit is a haven for birdwatchers, freshwater fisherman and wildflower enthusiasts. A dog-friendly site with extensive woodland to walk them in. Kendal, a small market town famous fe its mint cake, isn't far for shopping.

open March to November
payment credit/debit cards, cash, cheques

directions Leave M6 at jct 36 and go onto A59 signed South Lakes. After approximately 3.25 miles leave via slip road (signed Milnthorpe, Barrow) at roundabout and follow caravan signs

General ⬚ 🐕 🛋 🅟 ☼ 🔲 🐕 🚿 🅦🅟
Leisure 🎣 ⛺

KENDAL, Cumbria Map ref 5B3   SAT NAV LA7 7NN

Waters Edge Caravan Park
Crooklands, Kendal LA7 7NN
t (01539) 567708 e info@watersedgecaravanpark.co.uk
w **watersedgecaravanpark.co.uk**

🚐 (26)	£13.50–£23.00
🚲 (26)	£13.50–£23.00
▲ (5)	£10.00–£23.00

26 touring pitches

Friendly site in open countryside. Lake District, Morecambe, Yorkshire Dales nearby. All hardstanding pitches. Lounge, bar, pool room, patio area. Shower block with laundry. Local pub/restaurant within 300yds. **directions** Leave M6 at jct 36, take A65 to Kirkby Lonsdale, then A65 to Crooklands. Site approx 0.75 miles on the right. **open** 1 March to 14 November **payment** credit/debit cards, cash, cheques

General 🗑 🐕 🔌 📷 ☼ 🎱 🍴 💷 🕐 ☎   Leisure ∪ 🎣 🍷 ✈

KESWICK, Cumbria Map ref 5A3   SAT NAV CA12 4TE

Castlerigg Farm Camping & Caravan Site
Castlerigg, Keswick CA12 4TE
t (01768) 772479 f (01768) 774718 e info@castleriggfarm.com
w **castleriggfarm.com** ONLINE MAP GUEST REVIEWS ONLINE BOOKING LAST MINUTE OFFERS

🚐	£15.00–£17.00
🚲	£15.00–£17.00
▲ (80)	£10.20–£12.60

18 touring pitches

A quiet, family-run site with exceptional panoramic views. Ideal base for walking. Approximately 25 minutes' walk to Keswick. Site located on left of lane. **directions** A66 Penrith follow Keswick signs - don't enter town - A591 signposted Windermere, 1 mile almost top of hill, turn right up lane Castlerigg Farm Camp site on left. **open** March to November **payment** credit/debit cards, cash, cheques

General 🔌 🗑 🐕 🔌 📷 💷 🕐 ☎ 🚙 ✗   Leisure ▶ ∪ 🚴 🎣

KESWICK, Cumbria Map ref 5A3   SAT NAV CA12 4TE

Castlerigg Hall Caravan & Camping Park
Castlerigg Hall, Keswick CA12 4TE
t (01768) 774499 e info@castlerigg.co.uk
w **castlerigg.co.uk** ONLINE MAP LAST MINUTE OFFERS

🚐 (58)	£19.50–£24.00
🚲 (58)	£19.50–£24.00
▲ (120)	£15.00–£18.50
🏠 (7)	£240.00–£490.00

Our elevated position commands wonderful panoramic views of the surrounding fells. Formerly a Lakeland hill farm, Castlerigg Hall has been sympathetically developed into a quality touring park. **directions** Head out of Keswick on the A591 direction Windermere. At the top of the hill turn right at the brown tourist sign indicating Castlerigg Hall. **open** 12 March to 9 November **payment** credit/debit cards, cash, cheques

General 🗑 🐕 🔌 📷 ☼ 💷 🕐 ☎ 🚙 ✗   Leisure ∪ 🚴 🎣

KIRKBY LONSDALE, Cumbria Map ref 5B3   SAT NAV LA6 2SE

Woodclose Caravan Park
Chapel House Lane, Casterton, Kirkby Lonsdale LA6 2SE
t (015242) 71597 f (01524) 272301 e info@woodclosepark.co.uk
w **woodclosepark.com** ONLINE MAP LAST MINUTE OFFERS

🚐 (17)	£11.00–£21.50
🚲 (17)	£11.00–£21.50
▲ (18)	£11.00–£15.50

17 touring pitches

An exclusive site situated between the Lakes and the Dales. Camping field with Wigwams, which sleep up to 5 people price TBC. Children's play area and shop. David Bellamy Gold Conservation Award. **directions** M6 jct 36, follow A65 for approx 6 miles. The park entrance can be found just past Kirkby Lonsdale on the left-hand side, up the hill. **open** March to November (1st January for holiday home owners) **payment** credit/debit cards, cash, cheques

General 🔌 🗑 🐕 🔌 📷 ☼ 🚙 💷 🕐 ☎   Leisure ▶ ∪ 🚴 🎣 ⛰

KIRKBY STEPHEN, Cumbria Map ref 5B3   SAT NAV CA17 4SZ

Pennine View Caravan Park

Station Road, Kirkby Stephen CA17 4SZ
t (01768) 371717

Family-run caravan park on edge of small market town of Kirkby Stephen, just off A685. Easy reach of Lake District and Yorkshire Dales. **directions** M6 Junction 38 onto A685 signposted Kirkby Stephen 11 miles. A66 at Brough onto A685 for Kirkby Stephen 5 miles. **open** March to October **payment** credit/debit cards, cash, cheques

🚐 (48)	£17.20–£19.00
🚏	£17.20–£19.00
⛺ (10)	£17.20–£19.00

58 touring pitches

General 🔲 🐕 🛒 📞 🕒 🚽   **Leisure** 🚴 ⛰

LAMPLUGH, Cumbria Map ref 5A3   SAT NAV CA14 4SH

Dockray Meadow Caravan Club Site

Lamplugh CA14 4SH
t (01946) 861357
w **caravanclub.co.uk**

THE
CARAVAN
CLUB

🚐 (53)	£9.30–£20.70
🚏 (53)	£9.30–£20.70

53 touring pitches

SPECIAL PROMOTIONS
Special member rates mean you can save your membership subscription in less than a week. Visit our website to find out more.

Site close to lesser-known lake beauties including Cogra Moss, Ennerdale, Loweswater and Buttermere. Within easy reach of popular Keswick and Derwentwater. Watch the red squirrels around the site and revel in the glorious fell scenery during your stay. For the energetic there are plenty of walks from and around the site.

open April to November
payment credit/debit cards, cash, cheques

directions From A66 turn onto A5086. In 6.5 miles turn left at signpost for Lamplugh Green. Turn right at signpost for Croasdale. Site on left.

General 🐕 📞 🕒 🚐   **Leisure** 🎣

NEWBY BRIDGE, Cumbria Map ref 5A3   SAT NAV LA12 8NF

Newby Bridge Country Caravan Park

Canny Hill, Newby Bridge LA12 8NF
t (01539) 531030 f (01539) 530105 e info@cumbriancaravans.co.uk
w **cumbriancaravans.co.uk**

Situated in a delightfully secluded setting on the outskirts of Newby Bridge within easy walking distance of Lake Windermere. One- and two-bedroom luxury caravans for hire - weekly or short breaks. **directions** Please contact us for directions **open** Open 1 March to 31 October. **payment** credit/debit cards, cash, cheques, euros

🏠 (1)	£300–£535
🚐 (7)	£200.00–£495.00

General 🔲 🐕 🏪 🛒 📞 ☼ 🔲 📞 🕒 🚽 ✕   **Leisure** ∪ 🎣

NEWLANDS, Cumbria Map ref 5A3

SAT NAV CA12 5UG

£10.60–£23.20
£10.60–£23.20
60 touring pitches

Low Manesty Caravan Club Site

Manesty, Keswick CA12 5UG
t (01768) 777275 e enquiries@caravanclub.co.uk
w **caravanclub.co.uk**

THE
CARAVAN
CLUB

Set in National Trust woodland, close to Derwentwater. There are numerous walks you can take direct from walks - the choice is huge. If the Lakes themselves are the main attraction, Derwentwater is busy with boats and a marina.

directions From B5289 turn right over bridge (1/2 mile past Borrowdale Hotel). Site on right in 1 mile.

General ⚓ 🐕 ⬦ 🚐
Leisure 🚣

PENRITH, Cumbria Map ref 5B2

SAT NAV CA11 0JB

(50)   £19.50–£22.00
(10)   £19.50–£22.00
60 touring pitches

Flusco Wood Caravan Park

Flusco, Penrith CA11 0JB
t (01768) 480020

A very high-standard and quiet woodland touring caravan park with fully serviced pitches and centrally heated amenity building. Short drive to many attractions and places of interest in the Lake District. **directions** M6 jct 40, travel west on A66 towards Keswick. After about 4 miles turn right (signposted Flusco). Entrance along lane on the left. **open** Easter to November **payment** credit/debit cards, cash, cheques

General 🖥 🐕 ♿ 🏕 🔥 ☼ 📶 🍴 🚐 ⬦ 🍴   Leisure ∪ 🚴 🚣 🏔

POOLEY BRIDGE, Cumbria Map ref 5A3

SAT NAV CA10 2NA

(20)   £12.00–£22.00
(90)   £12.00–£22.00

Waterside House Campsite

Waterside House, Howtown, Ullswater CA10 2NA
t (01768) 486332 f (01768) 486332 e enquire@watersidefarm-campsite.co.uk
w **watersidefarm-campsite.co.uk** ONLINE MAP GUEST REVIEWS

Beautiful lakeside location on working farm with excellent toilet, shower and laundry facilities. Mountain bike, Canadian canoe and boat hire. Boat storage available. **directions** M6 jct 40, A66 to Keswick (1 mile), then A592 (Ullswater and Pooley Bridge). Right at church, right again along Howtown Road (1 mile). 2nd site on right. **open** March to October **payment** credit/debit cards, cash, cheques

General 🖥 🐕 ♿ 🏕 🔥 ☼ 🚐 ⬦ 🍴   Leisure ∪ 🚴 🚣 🏔

SILLOTH, Cumbria Map ref 5A2   SAT NAV CA7 4PE

Tanglewood Caravan Park

Causewayhead, Silloth CA7 4PE
t (01697) 331253 e tanglewoodcaravanpark@hotmail.com
w **tanglewoodcaravanpark.co.uk** ONLINE MAP

🚐	£18.00
🚐	£18.00
⛺ (10)	£18.00
🚐	£250.00–£410.00

21 touring pitches

Tanglewood is a friendly, family-run park on the edge of the beautiful, relaxing Lake District National Park. We pride ourselves on our quality of service. Pet-friendly. **directions** Please contact us for directions **open** All year except February **payment** credit/debit cards, cash, cheques

General 🔲 🐕 🏥 ☀ ♨ 🖭 🕒 🚽 💧   Leisure ▸ ⌐ 🏌 🎣 ⛰

TROUTBECK, Cumbria Map ref 5A3   SAT NAV

Troutbeck Head Caravan Club Site

Troutbeck, Penrith CA11 0SS
t (01768) 483521
w **caravanclub.co.uk**

🚐	£14.90–£28.30
🚐	£14.90–£28.30

151 touring pitches

SPECIAL PROMOTIONS
Special member rates mean you can save your membership subscripton in less than a week . Visit our website to find out more .

Set in classical north Lakeland countryside, near Ullswater and surrounded by the great outdoor. Fabulous for nature lovers and walkers alike, th site nestles in a valley alongside a babblling brook. A lake cruise on Ullswater is a must with option of a scenic walk between Howtown and Glenridding.

open March 2010 to January 2011

directions Leave M6 at junction 40 onto A66. Turn left onto A5091. Site on right in about 1.2: mile.

General 🔲 🐕 🍴 🏥 🖭 🖭 🕒 💧
Leisure 🎣 ⛰

ULLSWATER, Cumbria Map ref 5A3   SAT NAV CA11 0JF

Waterfoot Caravan Park

Pooley Bridge, Penrith, Ullswater CA11 0JF
t (017684) 86302 f (01768) 486728 e enquiries@waterfootpark.co.uk
w **waterfootpark.co.uk** ONLINE MAP

🚐	£17.00–£25.00
🚐 (34)	£17.00–£25.00

34 touring pitches

Set in the grounds of a Georgian mansion overlooking Ullswater. Excellent facilities including reception, shop, licensed bar and games room. Children's play area. David Bellamy Conservation Gold Award. **directions** M6 jct 40, follow signs marked Ullswater Steamers. West on A66 1 mile. Left at roundabout onto A592 (Ullswater). Waterfoot located on right. Not sat nav compatible **open** 1 March to 14 November **payment** credit/debit cards, cash, cheques

General 🔲 🐕 🎿 🍴 🏥 ☀ ♨ 🖭 🕒 💧   Leisure ∪ ⌐ 🏌 🎣 ⛰

WINDERMERE, Cumbria Map ref 5A3

SAT NAV LA23 3HB

Braithwaite Fold Caravan Club Site

Glebe Road, Bowness-on-Windermere, Windermere LA23 3HB
t (01539) 442177 **e** enquiries@caravanclub.co.uk
w caravanclub.co.uk

CARAVAN
CLUB

(66)   £14.00–£26.90
(66)   £14.00–£26.90
66 touring pitches

An attractively laid out site, close to the shores of Windermere and within easy walking distance of the town. Windermere has an excellent sailing centre from which you can enjoy sailing, windsurfing and canoeing. **directions** From A592 follow signs for Bowness Bay, in 300 yds turn right into Glebe Road. Site on right. **open** March to November **payment** credit/debit cards, cash, cheques

General 🐕 Leisure

WINDERMERE, Cumbria Map ref 5A3

SAT NAV LA23 3DL

Fallbarrow Park

Rayrigg Road, Bowness-on-Windermere, Windermere LA23 3DL
t 01539 569835 **f** (01524) 782243 **e** enquiries@southlakelandparks.co.uk
w slholidays.co.uk ONLINE MAP ONLINE BOOKING LAST MINUTE OFFERS

£18.50–£27.00
£18.50–£27.00
(15)   £303–£1136
(22)   £305.00–£719.00
38 touring pitches

Fallbarrow is set amongst 27 acres of wooded parkland, which extends to the shores of the lake Windermere boasting an unrivalled setting. A stroll to the village of Bowness on Windemere. **directions** Please contact us for directions **open** 1 March to 14 January **payment** credit/debit cards, cash, cheques

General Leisure

WINDERMERE, Cumbria Map ref 5A3

SAT NAV LA12 8NR

Hill of Oaks Park

Tower Wood, Windermere LA12 8NR
t (015395) 31578 **f** (01539) 530431 **e** enquires@hillofoaks.co.uk
w hillofoaks.co.uk ONLINE MAP GUEST REVIEWS LAST MINUTE OFFERS

(43)   £11.00–£29.00
(43)   £11.00–£29.00
43 touring pitches

Award-winning Park located on the shores of Windermere. The park has a play area and nature walks through the woodland. Five jetties, boat launching and access to watersport activities. **directions** M6 jct 36, head west on A590 towards Barrow and Newby Bridge. At roundabout turn right, onto A592. Park is approx 3 miles on the left-hand side. **open** March to November **payment** credit/debit cards, cash, cheques

General Leisure

WINDERMERE, Cumbria Map ref 5A3

SAT NAV LA23 1PA

Limefitt Park

Patterdale Road, Windermere LA23 1PA
t 01539 569835 **f** (01524) 782243 **e** enquiries@southlakelandparks.co.uk
w slholidays.co.uk ONLINE MAP GUEST REVIEWS ONLINE BOOKING LAST MINUTE OFFERS

(12)   £16.50–£23.00
(12)   £18.50–£27.00
(10)   £428–£931
(5)   £305.00–£647.00

Limefitt is in one of Lakelands most beautiful valleys, capturing the very essence of the Lake District National Park, in the centre of the Troutbeck Valley between Ullswater and Windermere. **directions** Please contact us for directions **open** 1 March to 14 January **payment** credit/debit cards, cash, cheques

General Leisure

WINDERMERE, Cumbria Map ref 5A3   SAT NAV LA23 3PG

Park Cliffe Camping & Caravan Estate

Birks Road, Windermere, Cumbria LA23 3PG
t 015395 31344   f (01539) 531971   e info@parkcliffe.co.uk
w **parkcliffe.co.uk**

(70)	£24.50–£27.50
(70)	£24.50–£27.50
(100)	£19.75–£32.50
(2)	£160.00–£595.00
70 touring pitches	

Park Cliffe offers pitches for tents, tourers, motorhomes and caravans for hire in the Lake District. 2009 Awards, Silver Winner Enjoy England Excellence, AA Northwest Campsite of the Year. **directions** Exit M6 jct 36, follow A590 towards Barrow. At Newby Bridge take A592 towards Windermere. After 3.6 miles turn right into Birks Road. **open** 1 March to 14 November **payment** credit/debit cards, cash, cheques

General 🔲👤🐕🚲🏪🌂☀️🍴🛒☕🚐✕   Leisure ▶∪🎣🍷🎣

WINDERMERE, Cumbria Map ref 5A3   SAT NAV LA23 1LF

White Cross Bay Holiday Park and Marina

Ambleside Road, Troutbeck Bridge, Windermere LA23 1LF
t 01539 569835   f (01524) 782243   e enquiries@southlakelandparks.co.uk
w **slholidays.co.uk** ONLINE MAP GUEST REVIEWS ONLINE BOOKING LAST MINUTE OFFERS

(23)	£16.50–£23.00
(8)	£16.50–£23.00
(75)	£364–£1143
(58)	£237.00–£748.00
18 touring pitches	

White Cross Bay nestles on the shores of lake Windermere south of Ambleside in the very heart of the Lake District. **directions** Please contact us for directions **open** 1 March to 14 Jan **payment** credit/debit cards, cash, cheques

General 🔧🔲👤🐕🚲🏪🌂☀️🍴🛒☕🚐✕   Leisure ▶∪🏊🚲🎣🎱🍷🎵🎣⛰

BLACKPOOL, Lancashire Map ref 4A1   SAT NAV FY4 4XN

Marton Mere Holiday Village

Mythop Road, Blackpool FY4 4XN
t (01253) 767544   e andy.cressey@bourne-leisure.co.uk
w **martonmere-park.co.uk**

A beautiful country park next to a nature reserve, only a few miles from the Bright Lights of Blackpool. Fantastic leisure facilities and an exceptionally lively programme of entertainment. **directions** Please contact us for directions

General 🔲🐕🚲🏪🌂🍴🛒☕✕   Leisure ▶🏊🚲🎱🍷🎵🎣

BLACKPOOL, Lancashire Map ref 4A1   SAT NAV FY3 0AX

Newton Hall Holiday Park
Staining Road, Staining, Blackpool, Lancashire FY3 0AX
t (01253) 882512 f (01253) 893101 e reception@newtonhall.net
w **newtonhall.net** ONLINE MAP ONLINE BOOKING

(23)   £180.00–£555.00

SPECIAL PROMOTIONS
Rebook within 28 days to
receive 15% discount, 3
nights minimum stay.

Family park ideally situated in open countryside,
2.5 miles from Blackpool tower. Caravans and
flats for hire. New club with regular live
entertainment. Indoor swimming pool. Fishing
pond. Indoor bowling.

open 1 March to 15 November
payment credit/debit cards, cash, cheques

directions M55 junction 4,3rd exit. Right at 4th
traffic lights past zoo. 3rd exit at roundabout.1
mile on right Staining Rd. Park on right.

General 🖥 ⌖ 🛒 🕮 ☼ ✕
Leisure ∪ ⌕ 🎣 🍺 ♪ 🔍 ⛰

BLACKPOOL, Lancashire Map ref 4A1   SAT NAV FY6 8NB

Windy Harbour Holiday Park
Windy Harbour Road, Singleton, Poulton Le Fylde FY6 8NB
t (01253) 883064 e info@windyharbour.net
w **windyharbour.net** ONLINE MAP ONLINE BOOKING

£15.00–£23.00
£15.00–£23.00
(11)   £165.00–£565.00
130 touring pitches

SPECIAL PROMOTIONS
10% discount on 7 day
touring holidays, rebook
holiday within 28 days to
receive 15% discount.

Situated on banks of River Wyre in the beautiful
Fylde countryside. Family-run park with many
facilities including club with family room, newly
refurbished swimming pool, extensive outdoor
play area, amusement arcade and shop. Very
easy access from M55 motorway.

open 1 March to 15 November
payment credit/debit cards, cash, cheques

directions From M6 onto M55 take jct 3
signposted Fleetwood (A585). At traffic lights go
straight ahead onto Windy Harbour Road. The
park is straight ahead.

General 🖥 ⌖ 🛒 🕮 ☼ 🎁 ♨ 🚗 ☕ 🐕 🖨 ✕
Leisure ∪ ⌕ 🎣 🍺 ♪ 🔍 ⛰

FLEETWOOD, Lancashire Map ref 4A1

SAT NAV FY7 8JX

ⓦ (9)   £180.00–£460.00

Broadwater Caravan Park

Fleetwood Road, Fleetwood FY7 8JX
t (01253) 872796 f (01253) 877133 e reception@broad-water.co.uk
w **partingtons.com**

Family run caravan park, ideally situated for Cleveleys, Blackpool and Fleetwood. Licensed club, childrens room, pool, spa, sauna, playground, arcade. We do not have any pitch for tents, touring or motor caravans as we sole deal with static caravans.

directions Please contact us for directions

open March-November
payment credit/debit cards, cash, cheques

General 🔥 ⑭
Leisure ⚞

GISBURN, Lancashire Map ref 4B1

SAT NAV BB7 4JJ

🛏 (3)   £469–£825
ⓦ (3)   £156.00–£348.00

Todber Park

Burnley Road, Gisburn, Clitheroe BB7 4JJ
t (01539) 569835 e enquiries@southlakelandparks.co.uk
w **slholidays.co.uk** ONLINE MAP GUEST REVIEWS ONLINE BOOKING LAST MINUTE OFFERS

Todber is an ideal country retreat set amongst stunning scenery in the Ribble Valley. Todber overlooks Pendle Hill and enjoys panoramic views over the stunning Ribble valley. **directions** Please contact us for directions **open** 1st March-14 November **payment** credit/debit cards, cash, cheques

General 🖾 🐕 🎿 🍴☼ ✕ Leisure ▶ ∪ 🚲 🥊 🍷 🎣 ⚲ ⛰

HEYSHAM, Lancashire Map ref 5A3

SAT NAV LA3 2XA

🔌   £15.00–£19.00
ⓦ (32)   £378.00–£497.00
87 touring pitches

Ocean Edge Leisure Park, Heysham

Moneyclose Lane, Heysham, Morecambe LA3 2XA
t 01539 569835 f (01524) 855884 e enquiries@southlakelandparks.co.uk
w **slholidays.co.uk** ONLINE MAP ONLINE BOOKING LAST MINUTE OFFERS

Ocean Edge is close to the historic village of Heysham on the southern shores of Morecombe Bay. Set on the shore edge in an elevated location overlooking the Irish Sea. **directions** Please contact us for directions **open** 1 March to 15 November **payment** credit/debit cards, cash, cheques

General 🔥🖾⑭🐕🎿🍴🌣☼🖾🚐🔌🍷🚐✕ Leisure ▶∪🚲🥊🎣🍷🎵⚲⛰

KIRKHAM, Lancashire Map ref 4A1   SAT NAV PR4 3HA

⊡ (3)   £279.00–£395.00

Mowbreck Holiday and Residential Park

Mowbreck Lane, Wesham, Preston PR4 3HA
t (01772) 682494   f (01772) 672986   e info@mowbreckpark.co.uk
w **mowbreckpark.co.uk** ONLINE MAP

No noisy amusement arcades. Relax in this picturesque setting. Family run to the highest standards. Ideal location to enjoy the Fylde coast. Just one hour from Manchester and North Yorkshire. **directions** Exit M55 Jct 3 - Follow signs Kirkham & Wesham - Take first left at St Josephs Church into Mowbreck Lane - Follow lane approx 1/2 mile. **open** Open 1st March to 16th January **payment** credit/debit cards, cash, cheques

General ⊡ ✦ ⬚ ☼   Leisure ▶ ∪ ♪

LANCASTER, Lancashire Map ref 5A3   SAT NAV LA2 9HH

🚐 (36)   £12.50–£15.50
🚙 (4)   £12.50–£15.50
▲ (5)   £9.50–£12.50
45 touring pitches

New Parkside Farm Caravan Park, Lancaster

Denny Beck, Caton Road, Lancaster LA2 9HH
t (01524) 770723

Peaceful, friendly park on a working farm with extensive views of the Lune Valley and Ingleborough. Excellent base for exploring the unspoilt coast and countryside of North Lancashire. **directions** Leave M6 at junction 34, A683 east towards Caton/Kirkby Lonsdale, caravan park entrance 1 mile from motorway junction on the right (signposted). **open** March to October **payment** cash, cheques

General ✦ ⬚ ☼ 🚘 ⊡ ⎈ ⚑   Leisure ♪

LYTHAM, Lancashire Map ref 4A1   SAT NAV PR4 3HN

🚐   £17.50
▲ (5)   £14.50
45 touring pitches

Little Orchard Caravan Park

Shorrocks Barn, Back Lane, Weeton, Kirkham, Preston PR4 3HN
t 01253 836658
w **littleorchardcaravanpark.com** GUEST REVIEWS

Quiet family run setting overlooks woods, open fields and fruit orchard. Close to two coarse fisheries and trout lake. 45 hardstanding all weather pitches. Ideal for mature people and quiet families. **directions** M55 junction 3 turn north Fleetwood A55 left Greenhalgh Lane T junction turn right caravan park on first left. **open** 14th Feb to 1st Jan **payment** cash, cheques

General ✦ ⬚ ☼ 🚘 ⊡ ⚑ ⊞   Leisure ▶ ∪ ♪

MORECAMBE, Lancashire Map ref 5A3   SAT NAV LA3 3DF

🏠 (18)   £410.00–£571.00

Regent Leisure Park

Westgate, Morecambe LA3 3DF
t 01539 569835   f (01524) 832247   e enquiries@southlakelandparks.co.uk
w **slholidays.co.uk** ONLINE MAP ONLINE BOOKING LAST MINUTE OFFERS

Regent's excellent facilities include family cabaret lounge, indoor children's play area, an indoor leisure centre with heated pool and an all weather sports pitch. Caravans fully equipped two/three bedrooms. **directions** Please contact us for directions **open** 1 March to 15 January **payment** credit/debit cards, cash, cheques

General ⟲ ⊡ ⚘ ✦ 🍴 ⬚ ⚑ ☼ ⊡ ⎈ ✕   Leisure ▶ 🚲 ♪ ☂ ♟ ♫ ● ⛰

MORECAMBE, Lancashire Map ref 5A3

SAT NAV LA4 4TQ

(56)	£18.00
(56)	£18.00
	£15.00
(15)	£195.00–£405.00
56 touring pitches	

Venture Caravan Park

Langridge Way, Westgate, Morecambe LA4 4TQ
t (01524) 412986 f (01524) 422029 e mark@venturecaravanpark.co.uk
w **venturecaravanpark.co.uk**

Family-run park, 0.75 miles from the sea. Local amenities and restaurants just a walk away. Easy access to the Lake District, Yorkshire Dales and Blackpool. **directions** Please contact us for directions **open** All year **payment** credit/debit cards, cash, cheque

General 🖬 🐾 🎱 💢 🏠 ☼ 🍴 🐕 🚻 🚾 ✕   Leisure ▶ 🏊 🎣 🎾 🍺 🎵 🔍 🎢

WEST BRADFORD, Lancashire Map ref 4A1

SAT NAV BB7 3JG

(80)	£19.00–£23.00
	£19.00–£23.00
(20)	£15.00–£43.00
	£204.00–£453.00
100 touring pitches	

Three Rivers Woodland Park

Eaves Hall Lane, West Bradford, Clitheroe BB7 3JG
t (01200) 423523 f (01200) 442383 e enquiries@threeriverspark.co.uk
w **threeriverspark.co.uk**

A family park set in 45 acres. An ideal base for visiting the Trough of Bowland and Yorkshire Dales, yet only two miles from Clitheroe. Luxury holiday hire caravans with central heating and double-glazing. **directions** Please contact us for directions **payment** cred debit cards, cash, cheques

General 🖬 🕎 🐾 🎱 💢 🏠 🔲 🐕 🚼 🚻   Leisure 🏊 🎾 🍺 🎢

BURY, Greater Manchester Map ref 4B1

SAT NAV BL8 1DA

(85)	£14.00–£26.90
(85)	£14.00–£26.90
85 touring pitches	

SPECIAL PROMOTIONS
Special member rates mean you can save your membership subscription in less than a week. Visit our website to find out more.

Burrs Country Park Caravan Club Site

THE
CARAVAN
CLUB

Woodhill Road, Bury BL8 1BN
t (0161) 761 0489 e enquiries@caravanclub.co.uk

On a historic mill site, Burrs has much to offer, including relaxing river and countryside walks, the East Lancashire Steam Railway passing by a well as easy access into Manchester. There are many opportunities for outdoor pursuits in the country park, such as climbing, abseiling and canoeing.

open All year
payment credit/debit cards, cash, cheques

directions From A676 (signposted Ramsbottom follow signs for Burrs Country Park.

General 🖬 🕎 🐾 🏠 🔲 🐕 🚼 🚾

ROCHDALE, Greater Manchester Map ref 4B1

SAT NAV OL11 5UP

Gelder Wood Country Park

Oak Leigh Cottage, Ashworth Road, Rochdale OL11 5UP
t (01706) 364858 f (01706) 364858 e gelderwood@aol.com

🚐	£16.00
🚐 (16)	£16.00
🛖 (4)	£16.00
24 touring pitches	

The country park comprises 10 acres of well-maintained grounds and 15 acres of mature woodland. Within walking distance of several restaurants to suit all tastes. AA 3*. **directions** Please contact us for directions **open** All year **payment** cash, cheques

General 🐕 📷 ☼ ♨ 🔌 📞 🚻 **Leisure** ▸ ∪ 🎵

ROCHDALE, Greater Manchester Map ref 4B1

SAT NAV OL15 0AT

Hollingworth Lake Caravan Park

Roundhouse Farm, Hollingworth Lake, Littleborough OL15 0AT
t (01706) 378661

🚐 (30)	£10.00–£16.00
🚐 (10)	£10.00–£16.00
🛖 (10)	£8.00–£16.00
50 touring pitches	

A popular, five-acre park adjacent to Hollingworth Lake, at the foot of the Pennines, within easy reach of many local attractions. Backpackers walking the Pennine Way are welcome at this family-run park. Hardstanding and grass area. Excellent train service into Manchester Victoria. 20 minutes from Littleborough/Smithybridge.

open All year
payment cash, cheques

directions From M62. Jct 21 Milnrow. Follow Hollingworth Lake Country Park signs to the Fishermans Inn/The Wine Press. Take Rakewood Road then 2nd on right.

General 🔲 ⚡ 📷 ☼ 🔌 📞 🚻 🚐
Leisure ∪ 🎵

THURSTASTON, Merseyside Map ref 4A2

SAT NAV CH61 0HN

Wirral Country Park Caravan Club Site

Station Road, Thurstaston, Wirral CH61 0HN
t (0151) 648 5228 f (0151) 648 9107
w **caravanclub.co.uk**

🚐 (92) £12.50–£25.10
🚏 (92) £12.50–£25.10
92 touring pitches

SPECIAL PROMOTIONS
Special member rates mean
you can save your
membership subscription in
less than a week. Visit
www.caravanclub.co.uk
to find out more.

The Wirral is a peninsula of great beauty with
unspoilt green space and wonderful sea views.
The site has several flat grassy pitching areas
separated by trees. Wirral is an ideal place for
the sportsman, cycling, young families and for
those with less energetic interests.

open March to November

directions On the A540 in the village of
Thurstaston, heading north from Heswall, turn
left into Station Road at the sign stating Wirral
Country Park Centre.

General 🖥 🐕 📶 ⛺ 🔌 🚻 📶 💧
Leisure ⛲

All Assessed Accommodation

Cheshire

CHESTER

**Chester Fairoaks Caravan Club
Site ★★★★★**
Touring & Camping Park
Rake Lane, Little Stanney, Chester
CH2 4HS
t (0151) 355 1600
e firtrees@chester-holidays.co.uk
w caravanclub.co.uk

**Manor Wood Caravan Park
★★★★★**
Holiday, Touring & Camping Park
Coddington, Chester
CH3 9EN
t (01829) 782990
e info@manorwoodcaravans.co.uk
w cheshire-caravan-sites.co.uk

DELAMERE

**Delamere Forest Camping and
Caravanning Club Site ★★★★★**
Touring & Camping Park
Station Road, Delamere, Northwich
CW8 2HZ
t (01606) 889231
w campingandcaravanningclub.co.
    uk/delamereforest

FRODSHAM

Ridgeway Country Holiday Park
★★★★ *Holiday Park*
Alvanley, Frodsham
WA6 6XQ
t (01928) 734981
e enquiries@ridgewaypark.com
w ridgewaypark.com
🏕

WHITEGATE

Lamb Cottage Caravan Park
★★★★★ *Holiday & Touring Park*
Dalefords Lane, Whitegate,
Northwich
CW8 2BN
t (01606) 882302
w lambcottage.co.uk

WILDBOARCLOUGH

Underbank Camping Barn
Camping Barn
Wildboarclough, Macclesfield
SK11 0BL
t 0870 770 6113

WINSFORD

Elm Cottage Caravan Park ★★★★
Touring & Camping Park
Chester Lane, Little Budworth,
Winsford
CW7 2QJ
t (01829) 760544
e chris@elmcottagecp.co.uk
w elmcottagecp.co.uk

Lakeside Caravan Park ★★★★
Holiday Park ROSE AWARD
Stocks Hill, Winsford
CW7 4EF
t (01606) 861043
e enquiries@thornleyleisure.co.uk

Cumbria

ALLONBY

Manor House Caravan Park
★★★★
Holiday, Touring & Camping Park
ROSE AWARD
Edderside Road, Allonby, Maryport
CA15 6RA
t (01900) 881236
e holidays@manorhousepark.co.uk
w manorhousepark.co.uk

Spring Lea Caravan Park ★★★★
Holiday, Touring & Camping Park
Main Road, Allonby, Maryport
CA15 6QF
t (01900) 881331

AMBLESIDE

Skelwith Fold Caravan Park
★★★★★ *Holiday & Touring Park*
Ambleside, Ambleside
LA22 0HX
t (01539) 432277
e info@skelwith.com
w skelwithfold.co.uk

APPLEBY-IN-WESTMORLAND

Wild Rose Park ★★★★★
Holiday, Touring & Camping Park
Ormside, Appleby-in-Westmorland
CA16 6EJ
t (01768) 351077
e reception@wildrose.co.uk
w wildrose.co.uk

ARMATHWAITE

**Englethwaite Hall Caravan Club
Site ★★★★** *Touring Park*
Armathwaite, Carlisle
CA4 9SY
t (01228) 560202
e enquiries@caravanclub.co.uk
w caravanclub.co.uk

BASSENTHWAITE

Bassenthwaite Lakeside Lodges
★★★★★ *Holiday Park*
ROSE AWARD
Scarness, Keswick, Keswick
CA12 4QZ
t (01768) 776641
e enquiries@bll.ac
w bll.ac

Skiddaw House *Bunkhouse*
Skiddaw Forrest, Bassenthwaite
CA12 4QX
t 07747 174293
e skiddawhouse@yahoo.co.uk
w skiddawhouse.co.uk
📷🏕

BOOT

**Eskdale Camping and
Caravanning Club Site ★★★★★**
Camping Park
Holmrook, Boot, Holmrook
CA19 1TH
t (01946) 723253
w campingandcaravanningclub.co.
    uk/eskdale

...dale Camping & Caravanning ...b Site - Camping Barn
...nping Barn
...t, Holmrook
...9 1TH
t (01946) 723253
e ...alison.bollons@campingandcarav
...anningclub.co.uk
w ...hollinsfarmcampsite.co.uk

BORROWDALE

...nah Hoggus *Camping Barn*
...orneythwaite Farm, Borrowdale
...2 5XQ
t (01946) 758198
e info@lakelandcampingbarns.co.uk
w lakelandcampingbarns.co.uk

BOTHEL

...iddaw View at Stay Lakeland
★★★ *Holiday Park* **ROSE AWARD**
...thel, Nr Bassenthwaite, Keswick
...3 9QW
t 0845 468 0936
e info@staylakeland.co.uk
w skiddawview.co.uk

BOUTH

...ack Beck Caravan Park
★★★★ *Holiday & Touring Park*
...SE AWARD
...uth, Nr Ulverston, Cumbria
...8 JN
t (01229) 861274
e reception@blackbeck.net
w blackbeck.co.uk

BRAYSTONES

...rnside Caravan Park ★★★
...liday, Touring & Camping Park
...aystones, Beckermet, Egremont
...21 2YL
t (01946) 822777
e tom@seacote.com
w tarnside.co.uk

BROUGHTON IN FURNESS

...ll End *Camping Barn*
...ll End Barn, Thornthwaite,
...oodland Hall, Woodland,
...oughton-in-Furness
...20 6DF
t (01229) 716340

BURGH-BY-SANDS

...llside Farm *Camping Barn*
...mping-Bunk Barn, Boustead Hill,
...rgh-by-Sands
...5 6AA

BUTTERMERE

...agg Barn *Camping Barn*
...agg Farm, Cockermouth
...13 9XA
t (01768) 770204

CARLISLE

...andy Dinmont Caravan and ...amping Site ★★★★
...ouring & Camping Park
...ackford, Carlisle
...6 4EA
t (01228) 674611
e dandydinmont@btopenworld.
com
w caravan-camping-carlisle.itgo.com

COCKERMOUTH

...iolet Bank Holiday Home Park
★★★★ *Holiday Park* **ROSE AWARD**
...imonscales Lane, Cockermouth
...A13 9TG
t (01900) 822169
e john@justsearching.co.uk
w violetbank.co.uk

CONISTON

...rake Valley Holiday Park
★★★★ *Holiday Park*
...OSE AWARD
...ater Yeat, Blawith, Ulverston
...A12 8DL
t (01229) 885203
e crakevalley@coniston1.fslife.co.uk
w crakevalley.co.uk

Park Coppice Caravan Club Site
★★★★ *Touring & Camping Park*
Coniston
LA21 8LA
t (01539) 441555
e enquiries@caravanclub.co.uk
w caravanclub.co.uk

CROSBY-ON-EDEN

Bluebell Camping Barn *Bunkhouse*
Crosby House, Crosby-on-Eden,
Carlisle
CA6 4QZ
t (01228) 573600
e joanneharper1@aol.com

EGREMONT

Horse & Groom Court *Bunkhouse*
Market Place, Egremont
CA22 2AE
t (01946) 758198
e info@horseandgroomcourt.co.uk
w horseandgroomcourt.co.uk

ENNERDALE

High Gillerthwaite *Camping Barn*
Ennerdale, Cleator
CA23 3AX
t (01768) 772645

FLOOKBURGH

Lakeland Leisure Park ★★★★
Holiday, Touring & Camping Park
Moor Lane, Flookburgh, Grange-
over-Sands
LA11 7LT
t (01539) 558556
e sioned.richards@bourne-leisure.
co.uk
w haven.com/lakeland

GILCRUX

The Beeches Caravan Park
★★★★★ *Holiday Park*
ROSE AWARD
Gilcrux, Wigton, Cockermouth
CA7 2QX
t (01697) 321555
e holiday@thebeechescaravanpark.
com
w thebeechescaravanpark.com

GLENRIDDING

Swirral *Camping Barn*
Greenside, Glenridding, Ullswater
CA11 0PL
t (01946) 758198
e info@lakelandcampingbarns.co.uk
w lakelandcampingbarns.co.uk

GRANGE-OVER-SANDS

Greaves Farm Caravan Park
★★★★ *Holiday & Touring Park*
ROSE AWARD
Field Broughton, Grange-over-Sands
LA11 6HU
t (01539) 536329

Meathop Fell Caravan Club Site
★★★★★ *Touring Park*
Meathop, Grange-over-Sands
LA11 6RB
t (01539) 532912
e enquiries@caravanclub.co.uk
w caravanclub.co.uk

GREAT LANGDALE

Greenhowe Caravan Park ★★★★
Holiday Park **ROSE AWARD**
Great Langdale, Ambleside
LA22 9JU

GREYSTOKE

Thanet Well
Holiday, Touring & Camping Park
Greystoke, Nr Penrith, Cumbria
CA11 0XX

HAWKSHEAD

The Croft Caravan and Camp Site
★★★★
Holiday, Touring & Camping Park
North Lonsdale Road, Hawkshead
LA22 0NX
t (01539) 436374
w hawkshead-croft.co.uk

HESKET NEWMARKET

Hudscales Camping Barn
Camping Barn
Hudscales Farm, Hesket Newmarket,
Caldbeck
CA7 8JZ
t (01768) 772645
e info@lakelandcampingbarns.co.uk
w lakelandcampingbarns.co.uk

HOLME

Sunnymead Holiday Park ★★★★
Holiday Park **ROSE AWARD**
2 Kirkgate, Holme-next-the-Sea,
Hunstanton
PE36 6LH
t (01485) 525381
e sunnymeadholpark@aol.com
w heacham-on-line.co.uk/sunny
meadcorner

HOLMROOK

Seven Acres Caravan Park ★★★★
Holiday, Touring & Camping Park
ROSE AWARD
Holmrook, Ravenglass
CA19 1YD
t (01946) 822777
e reception@seacote.com
w sevenacrespark.co.uk

KENDAL

Kendal Camping and Caravanning Club ★★★★ *Touring Park*
Shap Road, Kendal, Kendal
LA9 6NY
t (01539) 741363
w campingandcaravanningclub.co.
uk/kendal

Low Park Wood Caravan Club Site ★★★★ *Touring Park*
Sedgwick, Kendal
LA8 0JZ
t (01539) 560186
e enquiries@caravanclub.co.uk
w caravanclub.co.uk

Waters Edge Caravan Park
★★★★
Holiday, Touring & Camping Park
Crooklands, Kendal
LA7 7NN
t (01539) 567708
e info@watersedgecaravanpark.co.
uk
w watersedgecaravanpark.co.uk

KESWICK

Castlerigg Farm Camping & Caravan Site ★★★★
Touring & Camping Park
Castlerigg, Keswick
CA12 4TE
t (01768) 772479
e info@castleriggfarm.com
w castleriggfarm.com

Castlerigg Hall Caravan & Camping Park ★★★★
Holiday, Touring & Camping Park
Castlerigg Hall, Keswick
CA12 4TE
t (01768) 774499
e info@castlerigg.co.uk
w castlerigg.co.uk

Derwentwater Camping and Caravanning Club Site ★★★
Touring & Camping Park
Keswick, Keswick
CA12 5EN
t (01768) 772579
w campingandcaravanningclub.co.
uk/derwentwater

Keswick Camping and Caravanning Club Site ★★★★
Touring & Camping Park
Keswick, Keswick
CA12 5EP
t (01768) 772392
w campingandcaravanningclub.co.
uk/keswick

Low Briery Holiday Village
★★★★ *Holiday Park* **ROSE AWARD**
Penrith Road, Keswick
CA12 4RN
t (01768) 772044
e lowbriery@wyrenet.co.uk
w keswick.uk.com

Scotgate Holiday Park ★★★★
Holiday, Touring & Camping Park
Braithwaite, Keswick
CA12 5TF
t (01768) 778343
e info@scotgateholidaypark.co.uk
w scotgateholidaypark.co.uk

KIRKBY LONSDALE

Woodclose Caravan Park
★★★★★
Holiday, Touring & Camping Park
Chapel House Lane, Casterton,
Kirkby Lonsdale
LA6 2SE
t (015242) 71597
e info@woodclosepark.co.uk
w woodclosepark.com

KIRKBY STEPHEN

Pennine View Caravan Park
★★★★★ *Touring & Camping Park*
Station Road, Kirkby Stephen
CA17 4SZ
t (01768) 371717

LAMBRIGG

Wythmoor Camping Barn
Camping Barn
Wythmoor Farm, Lambrigg, Kendal
LA8 0DH
t (01946) 758198
e info@lakelandcampingbarns.co.uk
w lakelandcampingbarns.co.uk

LAMPLUGH

Dockray Meadow Caravan Club Site ★★★★ *Touring Park*
Lamplugh
CA14 4SH
t (01946) 861357
w caravanclub.co.uk

LOUGHRIGG

Neaum Crag ★★★★★ *Holiday Park*
Loughrigg, Ambleside
LA22 9HG
t (01539) 433221
e neaumcrag@ktdbroadband.com
w neaumcrag.co.uk

LOWESWATER

Swallow *Camping Barn*
Waterend Farm, Loweswater,
Cockermouth
CA13 0SU
t (01946) 758198
e info@lakelandcampingbarns.co.uk
w lakecampingbarns.co.uk

MILNTHORPE

Fell End Caravan Park ★★★★★
Holiday, Touring & Camping Park
Slack Head Road, Hale, Milnthorpe
LA7 7BS
t (01524) 781918
e enquiries@pureleisuregroup.com
w fellendcaravanpark.co.uk

NEWBIGGIN-ON-LUNE

Bents Camping Barn *Camping Barn*
Bents Farm, Newbiggin-on-Lune,
Kirkby Stephen
CA17 4NX
t (01946) 758198
e info@lakelandcampingbarns.co.uk
w lakelandcampingbarns.co.uk

NEWBY BRIDGE

Newby Bridge Country Caravan Park ★★★★★ *Holiday Park*
ROSE AWARD
Canny Hill, Newby Bridge
LA12 8NF
t (01539) 531030
e info@cumbriancaravans.co.uk
w cumbriancaravans.co.uk

NEW HUTTON

Ashes Exclusively Adult Caravan Park ★★★★★ *Touring Park*
New Hutton, Kendal
LA8 0AS
t (01539) 731833
e info@ashescaravanpark.co.uk
w ashescaravanpark.co.uk

NEWLANDS

Catbells *Camping Barn*
Low Skelgill, Newlands, Keswick
CA12 5UE
t (01946) 758198
e info@lakelandcampingbarns.co.uk
w lakelandcampingbarns.co.uk

Low Manesty Caravan Club Site ★★★★ *Touring Park*
Manesty, Keswick
CA12 5UG
t (01768) 777275
e enquiries@caravanclub.co.uk
w caravanclub.co.uk

ORTON

Westmorland Touring & Caravan Park ★★★★ *Holiday & Touring Park*
Orton, Penrith
CA10 3SB
t (01539) 711322
e caravans@westmorland.com
w westmorland.com

PENRITH

Flusco Wood Caravan Park ★★★★★ *Holiday & Touring Park*
Flusco, Penrith
CA11 0JB
t (01768) 480020

Lowther Holiday Park ★★★★★
Holiday, Touring & Camping Park
Eamont Bridge, Penrith
CA10 2JB
t (01768) 863631
e info@lowther-holidaypark.co.uk
w lowther-holidaypark.co.uk

PLANTATION BRIDGE

Windermere Camping and Caravanning Club Site ★★★★★
Holiday, Touring & Camping Park
Ashes Lane, Plantation Bridge, Kendal
LA8 9JS
t (01539) 821119
w campingandcaravanningclub.co.uk/windermere

POOLEY BRIDGE

Waterside House Campsite ★★★★ *Camping Park*
Waterside House, Howtown, Ullswater
CA10 2NA
t (01768) 486332
e enquire@watersidefarm-campsite.co.uk
w watersidefarm-campsite.co.uk

RAVENGLASS

Ravenglass Camping and Caravanning Club Site ★★★★
Touring & Camping Park
The Camping & Caravanning Club Site, Ravenglass, Ravenglass
CA18 1SR
t (01229) 717250
w campingandcaravanningclub.co.uk/ravenglass

SANDWITH

Tarn Flatt Barn *Camping Barn*
Sandwith, Whitehaven, St Bees
CA28 9UX
t (01946) 758198
e stay@tarnflattfarm.co.uk
w lakelandcampingbarns.co.uk

SILLOTH

Seacote Caravan Park ★★★★
Holiday & Touring Park
Skinburness Road, Silloth
CA7 4QJ
t (01697) 331121
e seacote@bfcltd.co.uk
w seacotecaravanpark.co.uk

Solway Holiday Village ★★★
Holiday, Touring & Camping Park
Skinburness Drive, Silloth
CA7 4QQ
t (01697) 331236
e solway@hagansleisure.co.uk
w hagansleisure.co.uk

Stanwix Park Holiday Centre ★★★★★
ROSE AWARD
Holiday, Touring & Camping Park
Greenrow, Silloth
CA7 4HH
t (01697) 332666
e enquiries@stanwix.com
w stanwix.com

Tanglewood Caravan Park ★★★
Holiday, Touring & Camping Park
Causewayhead, Silloth
CA7 4PE
t (01697) 331253
e tanglewoodcaravanpark@hotmail.com
w tanglewoodcaravanpark.co.uk

ST BEES

Seacote Park ★★★★
Holiday, Touring & Camping Park
ROSE AWARD
The Beach, St Bees
CA27 0ET
t (01946) 822777
e reception@seacote.com
w seacote.com

ST JOHNS-IN-THE-VALE

St John's in the Vale
Camping Barn
Low Bridge End Farm, St Johns-in-the-Vale, Keswick
CA12 4TS
t (01946) 758198
e info@campingbarn.com
w campingbarn.com

TROUTBECK

Camping & Caravanning Site - Troutbeck ★★★★
Holiday, Touring & Camping Park
Hutton Moor End, Troutbeck, Penrith
CA11 0SX
t (01768) 779149
e troutbeck@campingandcaravanningclub.co.uk
w campingandcaravanningclub.co.uk

Troutbeck Head Caravan Club Site ★★★★★
Holiday, Touring & Camping Park
Troutbeck, Penrith
CA11 0SS
t (01768) 483521
w caravanclub.co.uk

ULLSWATER

Quiet Site Caravan Park ★★★★★
Holiday, Touring & Camping Park
Ullswater, Penrith
CA11 0LS
t 07768 727016
e info@thequietsite.fsnet.co.uk
w thequietsite.co.uk

Waterfoot Caravan Park ★★★★★

Holiday & Touring Park
Pooley Bridge, Penrith, Ullswater
CA11 0JF
t (017684) 86302
e enquiries@waterfootpark.co.uk
w waterfootpark.co.uk

ULVERSTON

Bardsea Leisure Park ★★★★
Holiday & Touring Park
Priory Road, Ulverston
LA12 9QE
t (01229) 584712

WALTON

Sandysike Bunkhouse *Bunkhouse*
Sandysike, Walton, Brampton
CA8 2DU
t (01697) 72330
e sandysike@talk21.com
w nationaltrail.co.uk/hadrianswall/accommodation.asp

WASDALE

Murt *Camping Barn*
Nether Wasdale, Wasdale
CA20 1ET
t (01946) 758198
e info@lakelandcampingbarns.co.uk
w lakelandcampingbarns.co.uk

WHINFELL

Center Parcs Whinfell Forest ★★★★★ *Forest Holiday Village*
Whinfell, Penrith
CA10 2DW
t 0870 067 3030
w centerparcs.co.uk/villages/whinfell/index.jsp

WINDERMERE

Braithwaite Fold Caravan Club Site ★★★★ *Touring Park*
Glebe Road, Bowness-on-Windermere, Windermere
LA23 3HB
t (01539) 442177
e enquiries@caravanclub.co.uk
w caravanclub.co.uk

Fallbarrow Park ★★★★★
Holiday & Touring Park
ROSE AWARD
Rayrigg Road, Bowness-on-Windermere, Windermere
LA23 3DL
t 01539 569835
e enquiries@southlakelandparks.co.uk
w slholidays.co.uk

Hill of Oaks Park ★★★★★
Holiday & Touring Park
Tower Wood, Windermere
LA12 8NR
t (015395) 31578
e enquires@hillofoaks.co.uk
w hillofoaks.co.uk

Limefitt Park ★★★★★
Holiday, Touring & Camping Park
ROSE AWARD
Patterdale Road, Windermere
LA23 1PA
t 01539 569835
e enquiries@southlakelandparks.co.uk
w slholidays.co.uk

Park Cliffe Camping & Caravan Estate ★★★★★
Holiday, Touring & Camping Park
ROSE AWARD
Birks Road, Windermere, Cumbria
LA23 3PG
t 015395 31344
e info@parkcliffe.co.uk
w parkcliffe.co.uk

White Cross Bay Holiday Park & Marina ★★★★

Holiday & Touring Park
Ambleside Road, Troutbeck Bridge, Windermere
LA23 1LF
t 01539 569835
e enquiries@southlakelandparks.uk
w slholidays.co.uk

BANKS

Riverside Holiday Park ★★★
Holiday, Touring & Camping Park
Southport New Road, Banks, Nr Southport
PR9 8DF
t (01704) 228886
e reception@riversideleisurecentre.co.uk
w riversideleisurecentre.co.uk

BLACKPOOL

Marton Mere Holiday Village ★★★★ *Holiday, Touring & Camping Park*
Mythop Road, Blackpool
FY4 4XN
t (01253) 767544
e andy.cressey@bourne-leisure.co.uk
w martonmere-park.co.uk

Newton Hall Holiday Park ★★★
Holiday Park
Staining Road, Staining, Blackpool, Lancashire
FY3 0AX
t (01253) 882512
e reception@newtonhall.net
w newtonhall.net

Sunset Park ★★★★★ *Holiday Park*
Sower Carr Lane, Hambleton, Poulton Le Fylde
FY6 9EQ
t (01253) 700222
e sales@sunsetpark.co.uk
w sunsetpark.co.uk

Windy Harbour Holiday Park ★★★★
Holiday, Touring & Camping Park
Windy Harbour Road, Singleton, Poulton Le Fylde
FY6 8NB
t (01253) 883064
e info@windyharbour.net
w windyharbour.net

CABUS

Claylands Caravan Park ★★★★
Holiday, Touring & Camping Park
Weavers Lane, Garstang, Preston
PR3 1AJ
t (01524) 791242
e alan@claylandscaravanpark.co.uk
w claylandscaravanpark.co.uk

CAPERNWRAY

Old Hall Caravan Park ★★★★★
Holiday & Touring Park
Capernwray, Carnforth
LA6 1AD
t (01524) 733276
e oldhall.uk.com/

CARNFORTH

Netherbeck Holiday Home Park ★★★★ *Holiday Park*
North Road, Carnforth
LA5 9NG
t (01524) 735101
e info@netherbeck.co.uk
w netherbeck.co.uk

CHIPPING

Chipping Camping Barn
Camping Barn
Forest of Bowland, Chipping, Preston
PR3 2GQ
t (01995) 61209
w yha.org.uk

CLITHEROE

**heroe Camping and
avanning Club Site** ★★★★
ring & Camping Park
sford Road, Clitheroe, Clitheroe
 3LA
(01200) 425294
campingandcaravanningclub.co.
uk/clitheroe

COCKERHAM

ss Wood Caravan Park
★★★ *Holiday & Touring Park*
nbles Lane, Cockerham,
ıcaster
 OES
(01524) 791041
mosswood.co.uk

CROSTON

yal Umpire Caravan Park
★★★
iday, Touring & Camping Park
uthport Road, Croston, Leyland
26 9JB
(01772) 600257
royalumpire.co.uk

DOWNHAM

A New Hey *Camping Barn*
st Lane Farmhouse, Downham,
:heroe
7 4DS
0870 770 8868
yha.org.uk

FLEETWOOD

oadwater Caravan Park ★★★
liday, Touring & Camping Park
etwood Road, Fleetwood
7 8JX
(01253) 872796
reception@broad-water.co.uk
partingtons.com

la Gran ★★★★ *Holiday Park*
etwood Road, Fleetwood
7 8JY
(01253) 872555
enquiries@british-holidays.co.uk
calagran-park.co.uk

GISBURN

odber Park ★★★
oliday, Touring & Camping Park
ırnley Road, Gisburn, Clitheroe
7 4JJ
(01539 569835
enquiries@southlakelandparks.co.
uk
slholidays.co.uk

HEYSHAM

**:ean Edge Leisure Park,
eysham** ★★★
oliday, Touring & Camping Park
oneyclose Lane, Heysham,
orecambe
\3 2XA
01539 569835
enquiries@southlakelandparks.co.
uk
slholidays.co.uk

KIRKHAM

**owbreck Holiday and
esidential Park** ★★★★★
oliday Park
owbreck Lane, Wesham, Preston
R4 3HA
(01772) 682494
info@mowbreckpark.co.uk
mowbreckpark.co.uk

LANCASTER

**New Parkside Farm Caravan Park,
Lancaster** ★★★
Touring & Camping Park
Denny Beck, Caton Road, Lancaster
LA2 9HH
t (01524) 770723

Wyreside Lakes Fishery ★★★
Touring & Camping Park
Sunnyside Farmhouse, Gleaves Hill
Road, Lancaster
LA2 9DG
t (01524) 792093
e wyreside2003@yahoo.co.uk
w wyresidelakes.co.uk

LYTHAM

Little Orchard Caravan Park ★★★
Touring & Camping Park
Shorrocks Barn, Back Lane, Weeton,
Kirkham, Preston
PR4 3HN
t 01253 836658
w littleorchardcaravanpark.com

LYTHAM ST ANNES

Blackpool Holiday Centre ★★
Holiday Village
Clifton Drive North, Lytham St
Annes
FY8 2SX
t 0870 601 0472
w pontins-blackpool.com

Eastham Hall Caravan Park
★★★★ *Holiday & Touring Park*
Saltcotes Road, Lytham St Annes
FY8 4LS
t (01253) 737907
e ehcplytham@aol.com
w ukparks.co.uk/easthamhall

MORECAMBE

Regent Leisure Park, Morecambe
★★★★ *Holiday Park*
Westgate, Morecambe
LA3 3DF
t 01539 569835
e enquiries@southlakeparks.co.
uk
w slholidays.co.uk

**Venture Caravan Park,
Morecambe** ★★★★
Holiday, Touring & Camping Park
Langridge Way, Westgate,
Morecambe
LA4 4TQ
t (01524) 412986
e mark@venturecaravanpark.co.uk
w venturecaravanpark.co.uk

**Westgate Caravan Park,
Morecambe** ★★★★
Holiday & Touring Park
Westgate, Morecambe
LA3 3DE
t (01524) 411448
w westgatecaravanpark.co.uk/

NETHER KELLET

The Hawthorns Caravan Park
★★★★★ *Holiday Village*
Nether Kellet, Carnforth
LA6 1EA
t (01524) 732079
w hawthornscaravanpark.co.uk/

PAYTHORNE

Twynghyll Leisure Park ★★★★★
Holiday Park
Paythorne, Clitheroe
BB7 4JD
t (01200) 445465
e bpalmer@genie.co.uk
w twynghyll.co.uk/

PILLING

**Fold House Holiday Home and
Lodge Park** ★★★★★ *Holiday Park*
Head Dyke Lane (A588), Pilling,
Preston
PR3 6SJ
t (01253) 790267
e fhcp@foldhouse.co.uk
w foldhouse.co.uk

POULTON-LE-FYLDE

Poulton Plaiz Holiday Park ★★★
Holiday, Touring & Camping Park
Garstang Road West, Poulton Le
Fylde
FY6 8AR
t (01253) 888930
e info@poultonplaiz.co.uk
w poultonplaiz.co.uk

RIMINGTON

Rimington Caravan Park ★★★★★
Holiday & Touring Park
Hardacre Lane, Gisburn, Nr Clitheroe
BB7 4EE
t (01200) 445355
e rimingtoncaravanpark@btint
ernet.com
w rimingtoncaravanpark.co.uk

SCARISBRICK

**Hurlston Hall Country Caravan
Park** ★★★★ *Holiday & Touring Park*
Hurlston Lane, Scarisbrick, Ormskirk
L40 8HB
t (01704) 841064

SILVERDALE

Far Arnside Caravan Park
★★★★★ *Holiday Park*
Holgates Caravan Parks Ltd,
Middlebarrow Plain, Carnforth,
Carnforth
LA5 0SH
t (01524) 701508
e caravan@holgates.co.uk
w holgates.co.uk

Holgates Caravan Park ★★★★★
Holiday, Touring & Camping Park
ROSE AWARD
Cove Road, Silverdale, Carnforth
LA5 0SH
t (01524) 701508
e caravan@holgates.co.uk
w holgates.co.uk

ST MICHAEL'S ON WYRE

Wyreside Farm Park ★★★
Holiday, Touring & Camping Park
Allotment Lane, St Michael's-on-
Wyre
PR3 0TZ
t (01995) 679797
e penny.wyresidefarm@freenet.co.
uk
w riverparks.co.uk

TOSSIDE

Crowtrees Park ★★★★
Holiday Park **ROSE AWARD**
Tosside, Nr Settle, Skipton, North
Yorkshire
BD23 4SD
t (01729) 840278
e hol@crowtreespark.co.uk
w crowtreespark.co.uk

TRAWDEN

Trawden Camping Barn
Camping Barn
Middle Beardshaw Head Farm,
Burnley Road, Colne
BB8 8PP
t (01282) 865257

WEST BRADFORD

Three Rivers Woodland Park
★★★
Holiday, Touring & Camping Park
Eaves Hall Lane, West Bradford,
Clitheroe
BB7 3JG
t (01200) 423523
e enquiries@threeriverspark.co.uk
w threeriverspark.co.uk

WREA GREEN

Ribby Hall Village - Cottages
★★★★★ *Holiday Village*
Ribby Road, Wrea Green, Near
Blackpool
PR4 2PR
t 0800 085 1717
e enquiries@ribbyhall.co.uk
w ribbyhall.co.uk

Greater Manchester

BURY

**Burrs Country Park Caravan Club
Site** ★★★★★ *Touring Park*
Woodhill Road, Bury
BL8 1BN
t (0161) 761 0489
e enquiries@caravanclub.co.uk

ROCHDALE

Gelder Wood Country Park
★★★★★ *Touring & Camping Park*
Oak Leigh Cottage, Ashworth Road,
Rochdale
OL11 5UP
t (01706) 364858
e gelderwood@aol.com

Hollingworth Lake Caravan Park
★★★
Holiday, Touring & Camping Park
Roundhouse Farm, Hollingworth
Lake, Littleborough
OL15 0AT
t (01706) 378661

Merseyside

AINSDALE

**Willowbank Holiday Home and
Touring Park** ★★★★★
Holiday & Touring Park
Willowbank Caravan Park, Coastal
Road, Ainsdale, Southport
PR8 3ST
t (01704) 571566
e info@willowbankcp.co.uk
w willowbankcp.co.uk

THURSTASTON

**Wirral Country Park Caravan Club
Site** ★★★★ *Touring Park*
Station Road, Thurstaston, Wirral
CH61 0HN
t (0151) 648 5228
w caravanclub.co.uk

Hadrian's Wall, near Housesteads, Northumberland, England.

North East England

County Durham, Northumberland,
Tyne & Wear

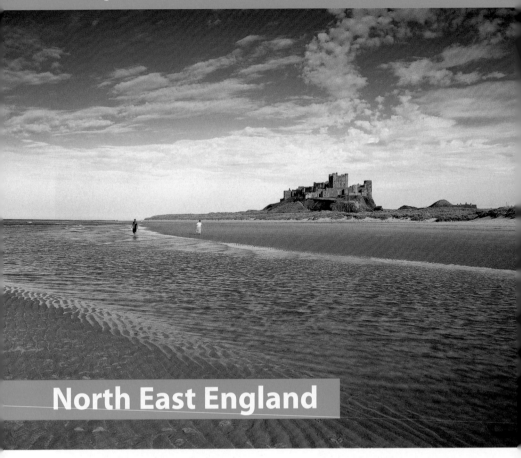

North East England

North East England is a place of contrast. To the east is coast whilst to the west you will find heathery hills and moody mountains with the famous World Heritage Site Hadrian's Wall running right through the middle. The result? There's lots to do, both indoors and out.

Sparkling cities like Newcastle, Gateshead and Durham are thriving with lots of shopping and plenty of nightlife. Bustling market towns and pretty villages are scattered around the region.

North East England can lay claim to being The Cradle of English Christianity – St Aidan came to Holy Island in AD635 and English history was first written by Bede, at Jarrow. There's also Durham, with 'the finest Norman Cathedral in the world'.

It has been home to pioneers across the centuries. The world's first public railway steamed into life here, and the award-winning Gateshead Millennium Bridge is one of the world's most celebrated pieces of architecture.

Characters! The North East is filled with them! Naturally friendly, people will make time to tell you about the place that fills them with pride.

Enjoy a taste of British life here and you can be guaranteed of a truly passionate experience.

County Durham

Durham's history and heritage is truly rich in all senses. Durham Cathedral, as the final resting place for St Cuthbert, became the most important centre for Medieval pilgrimages in North England. Together with the adjacent Castle, it has been a World Heritage Site since 1987.

Durham City

Durham is a compact but thriving city. A wide range of shops and restaurants co-exist happily with the Victorian Market. Much of the shopping area is closed to traffic, which makes for a more relaxed atmosphere and allows visitors to watch the street entertainment in the cobbled Market Place, particularly during July and August. The monthly Farmer's Market is a welcome addition to the City's events and there are fresh local specialities to take home. In the Spring and Summer, stunning floral displays adorn the City for which Durham regularly wins prizes.

It is however possible to escape the bustle by following one of the many paths that lead to the river. Take the 'Prince Bishop' river cruiser for a gentle trip taking in the many stunning views. The stretch of river by the Racecourse is well known for the annual Durham Regatta which is held in June. The regatta was founded in its present form in 1834, making it the second oldest in the county, even older than Henley. The Regatta attracts over 600 crews from all over the world. The adjacent Walkergate development provides a range of cafes, bars and restaurants.

Outside the City

Whether you're a walker, cyclist, adrenalin junkie, or simply want fresh air – County Durham has it all. Heralded for its superb natural landscape, breathtaking scenery, magnificent waterways and miles of coastline it is no wonder the county is so popular with visitors who enjoy the great outdoors.

Experience the natural wonders that will take your breath away such as the mighty High Force waterfall, the stunning unspoilt scenery of the Durham Dales and North Pennines Area of Outstanding Natural Beauty.

Northumberland

For all its current peaceful nature, Northumberland has a turbulent past evidenced by its flush of castles; more are found here than anywhere else in Britain. A testament to Roman construction is Hadrian's wall, a World Heritage Site. Bamburgh is the historic capital while today Alnwick and Morpeth contest which is the county town.

Alnwick

A medieval market town in the heart of the county; the recently refurbished Market Place is the centre for local events including the Alnwick Fair, Music Festival and the Farmers' Market held on the last Friday of every month. Take a visit to Alnwick Castle and nearby Alnwick Garden; a wonderful day out for all the family. Alnwick has long sandy beaches, quiet friendly villages, the Simonside and Cheviot hills. There are Areas of Outstanding Natural Beauty at the North Pennines and Northumberland Coast including a 40-mile stretch of Heritage Coast between Berwick and Amble.

Bamburgh

Famous for its castle which stands on a rocky outcrop overlooking miles of beautiful sandy beach, Bamburgh Castle dominates the Northumbrian landscape and has been described as the 'finest castle in England'.

Chillingham Castle

Reputedly the most haunted castle in Britain, the castle occupied a strategic position during the county's bloody feuds with the Border Reivers. Enjoy a visit to the castle with surrounding lawns, formal gardens and scenic woodland walk.

Holy Island and Lindisfarne

Originally founded by an Irish Monk, St Aidan, and home of the 7th-century Lindisfarne Gospels, Lindisfarne remains a holy Christian site and place of pilgrimage for many visitors. As well as Lindisfarne Castle and Priory, enjoy its shops, busy harbour, bird watching, fishing and golf – just some of the activities to be found. Visit Holy Island and explore the Castle, Priory and Heritage Centre, where you can 'turn the pages' (via a computer screen) of the brilliantly illuminated 7th-century Lindisfarne Gospels, which has been described as the most beautiful illuminated manuscript in the world. Don't forget to visit Inner Farne island particularly in summer for a close encounter with thousands of nesting seabirds, including puffin, shag and four types of tern.

Morpeth

Situated mid County, Morpeth fans out into rolling pasture lands, wood valleys and winding country road. Morpeth stands on the River Wansbeck and offers great shopping, and the charming Carlise Park, home to the William Turner Gardens. The historic clock tower overlooks an attractive market place which hosts the regular farmer's markets.

Tyne & Wear

The City of Newcastle-upon-Tyne (also the county town) has much to offer; from historic stately homes and ancient castles to beautiful gardens and exciting theme parks. The people of Tyne & Wear have a justified reputation for being some of the friendliest people in the country.

Newcastle-upon-Tyne and Gateshead

Newcastle-upon-Tyne and Gateshead offer a mix of the modern and historic and are renowned for excellent shopping, nightlife and a programme of festivals and events. Explore the beautiful architecture, including the ancient city walls and castle; enjoy the stunning quayside with its waterfront bars and galleries. Don't miss the public art, such as the Angel of the North. Hadrian's Wall, is quite a spectacular sight, the wall, built on the

orders of the Roman Emperor Hadrian around AD 122, stretched from the East to West coast of Britain and has been designated a World Heritage Site since 1987. The river Tyne and the river Wear are the two main rivers that flow through the county, which is where the name 'Tyne and Wear' derives from.

North Tyneside

This popular visitor destination, just 8 miles east of Newcastle and Gateshead, features Whitley Bay, Tynemouth, Cullercoats, North Shields and Wallsend. Fantastic family attractions include Blue Flag beaches, markets, the Fish Quay, outlet shopping, an aquarium, a railway museum, a world heritage site and vibrant nightlife.

South Tyneside

Sandy beaches, dramatic cliffs, colourful amusements, seafront parks and a year round entertainment programme. This stunning resort close to Newcastle, Gateshead and Sunderland offers historically significant attractions, cycling and walking trails, a vibrant art scene, compact shopping facilities and lively nightlife. The twin Anglo-Saxon monastery of Wearmouth-Jarrow is the nomination for World Heritage Status 2009.

Sunderland

Sunderland is a city by the sea which balances a relaxing green environment, stunning coastal scenery, outstanding heritage, cultural and sporting attractions and an exciting programme of events. Look out for the National Glass Centre, Sunderland Museum & Winter Gardens, Washington Old Hall and Sunderland Empire.

Where to Go

 Attractions with this sign participate in the **Visitor Attraction Quality Assurance Scheme** (see page 6) which recognises high standards in all aspects of the visitor experience.

ENTERTAINMENT & CULTURE

Arbeia Roman Fort and Museum
South Shields, Tyne & Wear, NE33 2BB
(01914) 561369
www.twmuseums.org.uk/arbeia
Step back in time! Fort remains, museum, reconstructions of fort gateway, barrack and officer's house.

BALTIC Centre for Contemporary Art
Gateshead, Tyne & Wear, NE8 3BA
(01914) 781810
www.balticmill.com
Catch the dynamic programme of contemporary visual art in Gateshead's landmark industrial building on the Tyne

Beamish Museum
Beamish, County Durham, DH9 0RG
(01913) 704000
www.beamish.org.uk
Revisit the early 1800s and 1900s around the town, colliery village, farm, 1825 railway and Pockerley Manor.

Captain Cook Birthplace Museum
Middlesbrough, Tees Valley, TS7 8AT
(01642) 311211
www.captcook-ne.co.uk
Exciting insights into the world's most famous navigator and explorer – plus 18thC life below decks.

Discovery Museum
Newcastle-upon-Tyne, Tyne & Wear, NE1 4JA
(01912) 326789
www.twmuseums.org.uk/discovery
Discover Newcastle Story, Live Wires, Science Maze and Fashion Works. Experiences for the whole family.

Hartlepool Art Gallery
Hartlepool, Tees Valley, TS24 7EQ
(01429) 869706
www.destinationhartlepool.com
The art gallery has a varied programme of art and craft exhibitions. Former church building also includes the TIC and a bell tower viewing platform looking over Hartlepool.

Hartlepool's Maritime Experience
Hartlepool, Tees Valley, TS24 0XZ
(01429) 860077
www.hartlepoolsmaritimeexperience.com
Relive a remarkable maritime era at this authentic reconstruction of an 18thC seaport.

Hexham Old Gaol
Hexham, Northumberland, NE46 3NH
(01434) 652349
www.tynedaleheritage.org
Tour the 14thC Old Gaol and dungeon. Meet the gaoler, see a Reiver raid, and dress up.

Killhope, The North of England Lead Mining Museum
Bishop Auckland, County Durham, DL13 1AR
(01388) 537505
www.killhope.org.uk
Britain's most complete lead mining site, with Northern England's largest working water wheel. Award-winning attraction.

Locomotion: The National Railway Museum at Shildon
Shildon, County Durham,
DL4 1PQ
(01388) 777999
www.locomotion.uk.com
View 60 vehicles, plus historic buildings with lively interactive displays. Play/picnic areas, gift shop, cafe.

mima (Middlesbrough Institute of Modern Art)
Middlesbrough, Tees Valley,
TS1 2AZ
(01642) 726720
www.visitmima.com
Inspiring modern and contemporary art in central Middlesbrough. Free admission. Changing fine art and craft exhibitions.

Segedunum Roman Fort, Baths and Museum
Wallsend, Tyne & Wear,
NE28 6HR
(0191) 369347
www.twmuseums.org.uk/segedunum
Step back 1,800 years amid buildings and remains of Hadrian's Wall. Exciting computer interactives enhance interpretation.

Sunderland Museum and Winter Gardens
Sunderland, Tyne & Wear,
SR1 1PP
(0191) 532323
www.twmuseums.org.uk/sunderland
Eleven imaginative galleries, from textiles to Lost Worlds, plus gardens bursting with exotic plants and trees.

The Bowes Museum
Barnard Castle, County Durham,
DL12 8NP
(01833) 690606
www.thebowesmuseum.org.uk
Outstanding European fine and decorative arts, acclaimed exhibitions programme, special events and great children's activities.

FAMILY FUN

Nature's World
Middlesbrough, Tees Valley,
TS5 7YN
(01642) 594895
www.naturesworld.org.uk
Be fascinated by the futuristic Hydroponicum and Eco Centre, demonstration gardens and wildlife. Great family attraction.

HERITAGE

Alnwick Castle
Alnwick, Northumberland,
NE66 1NQ
(01665) 510777
www.alnwickcastle.com
A dazzling medieval castle with glorious state rooms, art and architecture, plus unique interactive Knights Quest.

Bamburgh Castle
Bamburgh, Northumberland,
NE69 7DF
(01668) 214515
www.bamburghcastle.com
Once home to Northumbria kings, a treasure house of arms, armour, paintings. Stunning coastal views.

Belsay Hall Castle and Gardens
Belsay, Northumberland,
NE20 0DX
(01661) 881636
www.english-heritage.org.uk/belsay
Explore the 14thC castle, neoclassical hall and outstanding landscaped gardens, including the renowned quarry garden.

Durham Castle
Durham, County Durham,
DH1 3RW
(0191) 343800
www.durhamcastle.com
A superb Norman castle and chapel, medieval kitchens and great hall – all just awaiting your discovery.

Durham Cathedral
Durham, County Durham,
DH1 3EH
(0191) 386 4266
www.durhamcathedral.co.uk
Admire Europe's finest Romanesque architecture, see the ancient tombs of St Cuthbert and The Venerable Bede.

Head of Steam Darlington Railway Museum
Darlington, Tees Valley, DL3 6ST
(01325) 460532
www.drcm.org.uk
See, touch, feel and smell living railway heritage in one of the world's oldest railway stations.

Kielder Castle Forest Park Centre
Kielder, Northumberland,
NE48 1ER
(01434) 250209
www.forestry.gov.uk/northeastengland
Visitor centre for Kielder Forest. Includes exhibitions about forestry and conservation. Shop, information centre, tearoom.

National Glass Centre
Sunderland, Tyne and Wear,
SR6 0GL
(0191) 155555
www.nationalglasscentre.com
Discover the colourful local industry of glass, watch glassmaking and try it yourself. Spectacular gift shop.

Raby Castle
Staindrop, County Durham,
DL2 3AH
(01833) 660202
www.rabycastle.com
The medieval ancestral home of Lord Barnard, with large deer park, walled gardens and carriage collection.

Saltburn Miniature Railway
Saltburn-by-the-Sea, Tees Valley,
TS10 1SF
(01642) 502863
A 15" gauge miniature railway running from the seafront to the Valley Gardens and Woodland Centre. First established in 1947 and operated solely by volunteers.

Saltburn Smugglers Heritage Centre
Saltburn-by-the-Sea, Tees Valley,
TS12 1HF
(01287) 625252
www.redcar-cleveland.gov.uk/museums
Meet costumed characters in ancient fishermen's cottages and unravel tales of the King of the Smugglers!

Seven Stories, the Centre for Children's Books
Newcastle-upon-Tyne, Tyne & Wear, NE1 2PQ
0845 271 0777
www.sevenstories.org.uk
Britain's first centre dedicated to children's literature. Enjoy best loved books, exhibitions and creative activities.

Summerhill Visitor Centre
Hartlepool, Tees Valley, TS25 4LL
(01429) 284584
www.sunnysummerhill.com
Summerhill is a 100-acre Country Park on the western edge of Hartlepool that has been transformed for conservation and outdoor sports.

Tynemouth Priory
Tynemouth, Tyne & Wear, NE30 4BZ
(01912) 571090
www.english-heritage.org.uk/tynemouth
Wander the soaring ruins of this dramatic 13thC priory church, set on a steep headland between the River Tyne and the North Sea.

Wallington House, Walled Garden and Grounds
Cambo, Northumberland, NE61 4AR
(01670) 773600
www.nationaltrust.org.uk
A 17thC mansion noted for its Pre-Raphaelite paintings, dolls' houses collection, lovely parkland and walled garden.

Warkworth Castle
Warkworth, Northumberland, NE65 0UJ
(01665) 711423
www.english-heritage.org.uk/warkworth
The magnificent keep of Warkworth dominates one of the most impressive fortresses in northern England, dating back to the 12th century.

Weardale Railway
Stanhope, County Durham, DL13 2YS
(01388) 526203
www.weardale-railway.org.uk
All aboard the steam railway for a picturesque eight-mile adventure from Wolsingham to Stanhope. (Check availability.)

NATURE & WILDLIFE

Hall Hill Farm
Durham, County Durham, DH7 0TA
(01388) 731333
www.hallhillfarm.co.uk
Stroke the animals, take a farm trailer ride. Gift shop, tearoom, picnic and play area. Great family fun.

Hamsterley Forest
Bishop Auckland, County Durham, DL13 3NL
(01388) 488312
www.forestry.gov.uk/northeastengland
Enjoy fresh air, woodland walks, cycle routes, a forest drive and picnic areas across 5,000 acres.

High Force Waterfall
Middleton-in-Teesdale, County Durham, DL12 0QG
(01833) 640209
www.rabycastle.com/high_force.htm
Walk through woodlands and see England's largest waterfall cascading into its plunge-pool. Gift shop, picnic/parking areas.

WWT Washington Wetland Centre
Washington, Tyne and Wear, NE38 8LE
(01914) 165454
www.wwt.org.uk/visit/washington
A conservation site covering 100 acres of wetland and woodland with diverse wildfowl, insects and flora.

OUTDOOR ACTIVITIES

Hadrian's Wall Path National Trail
Hexham, Northumberland
(01912) 691600
www.nationaltrail.co.uk/hadrianswall
This 84-mile path, providing access to Hadrian's Wall opened to the public on May 23 2003.

Events 2010

BRASS - Durham International Festival
Durham
www.brassfestival.co.uk
July

Durham Regatta
Durham
www.durham-regatta.org.uk
June

Gateshead Summer Flower Show
Gateshead
www.gateshead.gov.uk
July-August

Great North Bike Ride
Seahouses
www.greatnorthbikeride.com
August

Great North Run
www.greatrun.org
June

Newcastle Science Festival
Newcastle upon Tyne
www.newcastlesciencefest.com
March

Northumberland County Show
Corbridge
www.northcountyshow.co.uk
24th May

Sunderland International Air Show
Sunderland
www.sunderland-airshow.com
July

Tall Ships Race 2010
Hartlepool
www.hartlepooltallships2010.com
7th-10th August

Where to Eat

The North East England region has great places to eat. The restaurant reviews on these pages are just a small selection from the highly respected *The Good Food Guide 2010*. Please see pages 20–21 for further information on the guide and details of a Special Offer for our readers.

COUNTY DURHAM

Seaham Hall, The White Room
Well-judged food that's very pleasing
Lord Byron's Walk, Seaham, SR7 7AG
Tel no: (0191) 5161400
www.seaham-hall.com
Modern British | £50

Chef Kenny Atkinson has come home to the North East, and menus packed with local produce, give or take the odd shimeji mushroom, suggest he's glad to be back. His new playground is the White Room, really two pale dining rooms in the hotel where Lord Byron made his ill-advised wedding vows. Neutral apart from pieces of Sunderland glass, the White Room demands that the food be the main feature. Atkinson's response is measured but effective, a series of well-judged dishes whose cumulative effect is very pleasing indeed. The little shimeji, pickled, are an effective counterpoint to a terrine of confit duck and foie gras, and curry-roasted cod with chestnuts and parsnip velouté plays with various earthy notes. To follow, loin of Northumberland pork with confit belly and braised cheek showcases the animal with finesse, and a Valrhona chocolate pavé is elevated by the presence of fabulous coffee ice cream. Atkinson's arrival isn't the only innovation: though some aesthetic details still beg for attention, the hotel is in the hands of new owners and service is discernibly sharper than it has been. The wine list retains its pleasing scope, with Francophiles well catered for and China-lovers not overlooked. Dr Loosen Riesling (£5.50) does a great job at entry level by the glass; bottles are from £20.
Chef/s: Kenny Atkinson. **Open:** Wed to Sun L 12 to 2, all week D 7 to 10. **Meals:** Set L £17.50 (2 courses) to £23.50. Set D £50 (3 courses) to £65 (7 courses). Sun L £25. **Service:** not inc. **Details:** Cards accepted. 50 seats. Air-con. Separate bar. No mobile phones. Wheelchair access. Music. Children allowed. Car parking.

The Rose and Crown
Lovingly tended, showpiece village inn
Romaldkirk, DL12 9EB
Tel no: (01833) 650213
www.rose-and-crown.co.uk
British | £30

It's 20 years since Christopher and Alison Davy put their names above the door of this showpiece inn overlooking Romaldkirk village green. During their stewardship they have cared lovingly for the place – and it shows in every detail, from the crackling logs in the old stone fireplace to the relentlessly ticking grandfather clock. The bar is just the spot for a lunch or supper of salmon fishcakes or pork sausage and black pudding with mustard mash. By contrast, dinner in the elegant candlelit restaurant is a more sedate affair, with a four-course menu promising precise dishes such as roast Lunesdale duck breast with fruit compote and ort jus or chargrilled calf's liver with sweet onion onfit and green peppercorn sauce. North Country heeses, and desserts including sticky toffee pudding lose proceedings. House wine is £15.50.

Chef/s: Christopher Davy and Andrew Lee. **Open:** Sun L 2 to 1.30, all week D 7.30 to 8.45. **Closed:** 23 to 26 Dec. **Meals:** Set D £30 (4 courses). Set Sun L £17.75. **Service:** not inc. **Details:** Cards accepted. 24 seats. 24 eats outside. Separate bar. No music. No mobile phones. Wheelchair access. Children allowed. Car parking.

NORTHUMBERLAND

afé Lowrey

Brasserie favourites with panache

3-35 The Broadway, Darras Hall, Ponteland, NE20 9PW
Tel no: (01661) 820357
www.cafelowrey.co.uk

Modern British | £25

Ian Lowrey's bright, modern eatery is just a little way over the border into Northumberland. Properly dressed, well-spaced tables add class to the essentially informal approach, and the food is all about brasserie favourites presented with a perhaps unexpected level of panache. Grilled black pudding with mash, crispy onions and mustard cream is a loin-girding, cold-weather starter. Those of lighter tastes might open with a soufflé of Cheddar and spinach. Then it's on to fish, either simply grilled and served with mushy peas and chips, or in the shape of sea bass with crayfish and basil cream sauce. Meaty crowd-pleasers include the likes of sirloin steak or duck leg confit. Less familiar preparations might prove even more tempting, as in the venison loin that comes with goats' cheese mash, red cabbage and griottine cherries. Chocolate tart or crème brûlée round things off in style. Wines are an inspired international jumble, with prices from £13.50.

Chef/s: Ian Lowrey. **Open:** Sat L 12 to 2, Sun L 12 to 3, Tue to Sat D 5.30 to 10. **Closed:** bank hols. **Meals:** alc (main courses £11 to £23). Set D £13.50 (2 courses) to £15.50. Set Sun L £13.95. **Service:** not inc. **Details:** Cards accepted. 70 seats. Air-con. Wheelchair access. Music. Children allowed. Car parking.

TYNE & WEAR

Eslington Villa

Victorian retreat, modern food

8 Station Road, Low Fell, Gateshead, NE9 6DR
Tel no: (0191) 4876017
www.eslingtonvilla.co.uk

Modern British | £25

The villa is an imposing Victorian mansion built around 1880 for a prominent local businessman, who clearly wanted a rural refuge away from the revolutionary industrial heat of the north east. There are two acres of leafy landscaped grounds and the place is blessed

with eminently pleasing views. Those who come to eat as well as retreat can expect a menu of international standbys enlivened with a few creative flourishes: smoked haddock fishcakes and slow-cooked lamb shank with parsley mash are joined by Mediterranean bedfellows (wild mushroom risotto) and visitors from faraway lands (marinated prawns with crispy won tons, tandoori-spiced monkfish). To finish, consider praline crêpe with orange salad or vanilla cheesecake with roasted plums. House wines from £13.50 kick of the 60-bin list.

Chef/s: Andrew Moore. **Open:** Mon to Fri L 12 to 2, Sun L 12 to 3. Mon to Sat D 7 to 10. **Closed:** 25 and 26 Dec, bank hols. **Meals:** Set L £17 (2 courses) to £19. Set Sun L £18. Set D £19 (2 courses) to £23. **Service:** not inc. **Details:** Cards accepted. 80 seats. 12 seats outside. Separate bar. Wheelchair access. Music. Children allowed. Car parking.

Tourist Information Centres

When you arrive at your destination, visit an Official Partner Tourist Information Centre for quality assured help with accommodation and information about local attractions and events, or email your request before you go. To search for attractions and Tourist Information Centres on the move just text INFO to 62233, and a web link will be sent to your mobile phone. To find a Tourist Information Centre by region visit enjoyEngland.com/find-tic.

MIDDLESBROUGH	PO Box 69	01642 729700	middlesbrough_tic@middlesbrough.gov.uk
ALNWICK	2 The Shambles	01665 511333	alnwicktic@alnwick.gov.uk
ALTRINCHAM	20 Stamford New Road	0161 912 5931	tourist.information@trafford.gov.uk
AMBLE	Queen Street Car Park	01665 712313	ambletic@alnwick.gov.uk
BARNARD CASTLE	Woodleigh	01833 690909	tourism@teesdale.gov.uk
BELLINGHAM	Fountain Cottage, Main Street	01434 220616	bellinghamtic@btconnect.com
BERWICK-UPON-TWEED	106 Marygate	01289 330733	tourism@berwick-upon-tweed.gov.uk
BISHOP AUCKLAND	Town Hall Ground Floor	01388 604922	bishopauckland.touristinfo@durham.gov.uk
CHESTER	Town Hall	01244 402111	tis@chester.gov.uk
CONGLETON	Town Hall	01260 271095	tourism@congleton.gov.uk
CORBRIDGE	Hill Street	01434 632815	corbridgetic@btconnect.com
CRASTER	Craster Car Park	01665 576007	crastertic@alnwick.gov.uk
DARLINGTON	13 Horsemarket	01325 388666	tic@darlington.gov.uk
DURHAM	2 Millennium Place	0191 384 3720	touristinfo@durhamcity.gov.uk
ELLESMERE PORT	Unit 22b	0151 356 7879	cheshireoaks.cc@visitor-centre.net
GATESHEAD	Central Library	0191 433 8420	tic@gateshead.gov.uk
GATESHEAD	The Sage Gateshead	0191 478 4222	tourism@gateshead.gov.uk
HALTWHISTLE	Railway Station	01434 322002	haltwhistletic@btconnect.com
HARTLEPOOL	Hartlepool Art Gallery	01429 869706	hpooltic@hartlepool.gov.uk

HEXHAM	Wentworth Car Park	01434 652220	hexham.tic@tynedale.gov.uk
KNUTSFORD	Council Offices	01565 632611	ktic@macclesfield.gov.uk
MACCLESFIELD	Macclesfield	01625 504114	informationcentre@macclesfield.gov.uk
MORPETH	The Chantry	01670 500700	morpeth.tic@northumberland.gov.uk
NANTWICH	Civic Hall	01270 537359	touristi@crewe-nantwich.gov.uk
NEWCASTLE AIRPORT	Tourist Information Desk	0191 214 4422	niatic@hotmail.com
NEWCASTLE-UPON-TYNE	Newcastle Information Centre	0191 277 8000	tourist.info@newcastle.gov.uk
NORTH SHIELDS	Unit 18	0191 2005895	ticns@northtyneside.gov.uk
NORTHWICH	Information Centre	01606 353534	tourism@valeroyal.gov.uk
ONCE BREWED	Northumberland NP Centre	01434 344396	tic.oncebrewed@nnpa.org.uk
PETERLEE	4 Upper Yoden Way	0191 586 4450	touristinfo@peterlee.gov.uk
REDCAR	West Terrace	01642 471921	redcar_tic@redcar-cleveland.gov.uk
ROTHBURY	Northumberland NP Centre	01669 620887	tic.rothbury@nnpa.org.uk
SALTBURN by sea	3 Station Buildings	01287 622422	saltburn_tic@redcar-cleveland.gov.uk
SEAHOUSES	Seafield Car Park	01665 720884	seahousesTIC@berwick-upon-tweed.gov.uk
SOUTH SHIELDS	South Shields Museum & Gallery	0191 454 6612	museum.tic@s-tyneside-mbc.gov.uk
SOUTH SHIELDS	Sea Road	0191 455 7411	foreshore.tic@s-tyneside-mbc.gov.uk
STANHOPE	Durham Dales Centre	01388 527650	durham.dales.centre@durham.gov.uk
STOCKTON-ON-TEES	Stockton Central Library	01642 528130	touristinformation@stockton.gov.uk
SUNDERLAND	50 Fawcett Street	0191 553 2000	tourist.info@sunderland.gov.uk
WARRINGTON	The Market Hall	01925 428585	informationcentre@warrington.gov.uk
WHITLEY BAY	Park Road	0191 2008535	ticwb@northtyneside.gov.uk
WILMSLOW	The Information Centre	01625 522275	i.hillaby@macclesfield.gov.uk
WOOLER	Wooler TIC, The Cheviot Centre	01668 282123	woolerTIC@berwick-upon-tweed.gov.uk

Regional Contacts and Information

Log on to the North East England website at **www.visitnortheastengland.com** for further information on accommodation, attractions, events and special offers throughout the region. A range of free guides are available for you to order online or by calling 0844 2495090

Holiday and Short Breaks Guide

Information on North East England, including hotels, bed and breakfast, self catering, caravan and camping parks and accessible accommodation as well as events and attractions throughout the region.

Walking Guide

Circular trails and long distance routes through breathtaking countryside.

Where to Stay

Entries appear alphabetically by town name in each county. A key to symbols appears on page 6. Maps start on page 394. A listing of all Enjoy England assessed accommodation appears at the end of the region.

DALTON PIERCY, Co Durham Map ref 5C2   SAT NAV TS27 3HY

Ashfield Caravan Park
Dalton Piercy, Hartlepool TS27 3HY
t (01429) 269969 e info@ashfield-caravanpark.co.uk
w **ashfield-caravanpark.co.uk** ONLINE MAP GUEST REVIEWS ONLINE BOOKING LAST MINUTE OFFERS

🚐 (68)	£17.00–£19.00
🚐 (20)	£17.00–£19.00
⛺ (40)	£10.00–£44.00

Open 2008, family-run site with clubhouse shop, laundry, games room, washing up area and modern shower block. Five minutes from Hartlepool. No pets allowed. More information on website. **directions** Please contact us for directions **open** 1st April to 31st January **payment** cash

General 🔲 ⓦ 🔧 🅿 ☀ 🔌 🕒 🚿 🏧   Leisure ► ∪ ⤴ 🍷 🎵 🎣

DURHAM, Co Durham Map ref 5C2   SAT NAV DH6 4QA

Strawberry Hill Farm Camping & Caravanning Park
Running Waters, Old Cassop, Durham DH6 4QA
t (01913) 723457 f (01913) 722512 e info@strawberryhf.co.uk
w **strawberry-hill-farm.co.uk** ONLINE MAP GUEST REVIEWS

🚐 (35)	£14.50–£17.50
🚐 (6)	£14.50–£17.50
⛺ (10)	£14.50–£17.50
🏠 (3)	£220.00–£350.00
41 touring pitches	

Situated in open countryside with magnificent, panoramic views. Ideally situated to explore the World Heritage site of the castle and cathedral. For further details please see website. **directions** Exit junction 61 A1(M). Take A177 (Bowburn). Travel to 2nd set of traffic lights. Turn right, park 4 miles on left. Shorter route available on website. **open** March to December **payment** credit/debit cards, cash, euros

General 🔲 🐕 🔧 🏠 🅿 ☀ 🔌 🚲 🔌 🕒 🚿 🏧   Leisure ∪ ⤴

Looking for something else?

You can also buy a copy of our popular guide 'Hotels' including country house and town house hotels, metro and budget hotels, serviced apartments, restaurants with rooms and Spas in England 2010. Now available in good bookshops and online at **enjoyenglanddirect.com**
£10.99

DURHAM, Co Durham Map ref 5C2

SAT NAV DH1 1TL

Grange Caravan Club Site

Meadow Lane, Carrville, Durham DH1 1TL
t (01913) 844778 f (01913) 839161
w **caravanclub.co.uk**

🚐 (76)   £14.00–£26.90
🚍 (76)   £14.00–£26.90
76 touring pitches

SPECIAL PROMOTIONS
Special member rates mean
you can save your
membership subscription in
less than a week. Visit our
website to find out more.

An open, level site within easy reach of the City
Durham with walks from the site into the city.
Durham is steeped in history and the panoramic
views from every vantage point make it one of
the most picturesque cities in the UK. A visit to
Durham Catherdal and Castle is a must.

open All year
payment credit/debit cards, cash, cheques

directions A1(M) jct 62, A690 towards Durham.
Turn right after 50 miles. Signposted Maureen
Terrace and brown caravan sign.

General 🖥 ♿ 🐕 🚿 ☀ 🚗 🛒 🎁
Leisure ⛰

STOCKTON-ON-TEES, Co Durham Map ref 5C3

SAT NAV TS18 2QW

White Water Caravan Club Park

Tees Barrage, Stockton-on-Tees TS18 2QW
t (01642) 634880
w **caravanclub.co.uk**

🚐 (115)   £10.60–£23.20
🚍 (115)   £10.60–£23.20
115 touring pitches

SPECIAL PROMOTIONS
Special member rates mean
you can save your
membership subscription in
less than a week. Visit our
website to find out more.

Pleasantly landscaped site, part of the largest
white-water canoeing and rafting course built to
an international standard in Britain. Nearby
Teesside Park for shopping, restaurants, cinema
and bowling. Birdwatchers, wildlife enthusiasts
and walkers will be spoilt for choice with over
30 miles of coastline a short drive away.

open All year
payment credit/debit cards, cash, cheques

directions Come off the A66 Teesside Park.
Follow Teesdale sign, go over Tees Barrage
Bridge, turn right. Site 200 yds on the left.

General 🖥 🐕 🚿 ☀ 🚗 🛒 🎁
Leisure ▶ 🚣 🎣 ⛰

BAMBURGH, Northumberland Map ref 5C1

HOLIDAY &
TOURING PARK
★★★

🚐 (34) £18.00–£20.00
🚏 (34) £18.00–£20.00
34 touring pitches

Glororum Caravan Park

Glororum Caravan Park, Glororum, Bamburgh NE69 7AW
t (01668) 214457 **f** (01668) 214622 **e** info@glororum-caravanpark.co.uk
w **glororum-caravanpark.co.uk**

Situated 1 mile from Bamburgh in peaceful surroundings within easy reach of many historic castles including Alnwick with its magnificent gardens. Endless walks on award-winning beaches only a mile away. No tents. **directions** Please contact us for directions **open** 1st March to end November **payment** credit/debit cards, cash, cheques

General 🛁🔥🐕🔌📶🏠☼🚮🚐🅿🇬🇧☎ Leisure ▶∪☍🚴♒⚓

BAMBURGH, Northumberland Map ref 5C1

HOLIDAY, TOURING
& CAMPING PARK
★★★

🚐 (80) £20.00–£25.00
🚏 (80) £20.00–£25.00
🏕 (20) £250.00–£450.00
80 touring pitches

Kaims Country Park

Bradford House, Bamburgh NE70 7JT
t (01668) 213432 **f** (01668) 213891 **e** info@kaimscountrypark.com
w **kaimscountrypark.com**

Beautiful walking country. Close to Bamburgh, Seahouses, Wooler and Cheviot Hills. Pre-booking advised during school holidays. Open March to November. Kaims Country Park is signposted from the B1341. **directions** Please contact us for directions **open** All year **payment** credit/debit cards, cash, cheques

General 🛁🔦🐕🔥🏠☼🚮🅿☎✕ Leisure ♒⚓

BAMBURGH, Northumberland Map ref 5C1

HOLIDAY, TOURING
& CAMPING PARK
★★★★

ROSE
AWARD
CARAVAN
HOLIDAY
PARK

🚐 (150) £13.00–£23.00
🚏 (150) £13.00–£23.00
🏕 (30) £9.50–£23.00
🏕 (27) £295.00–£595.00
150 touring pitches

SPECIAL PROMOTIONS
Please see website for special offers and details of our wigwams too!

Waren Caravan and Camping Park

Waren Mill, Bamburgh, Northumberland NE70 7EE
t 01668 214366 **f** (01668) 214224 **e** waren@meadowhead.co.uk
w **meadowhead.co.uk** ONLINE MAP GUEST REVIEWS LAST MINUTE OFFERS

Nestled in coastal countryside with spectacular views to Holy Island and Bamburgh Castle. Waren offers restaurant-bar, splash-pool and play facilities. Our happy environment is great if you wish to stay on-site but we also make a great base from which to explore Northumberland's coast and castles.

open 13 March to 30 October
payment credit/debit cards, cash, cheques, euros

directions Follow B1342 from A1 to Waren Mill towards Bamburgh. By Budle turn right, follow Meadowhead's Waren Caravan and Camping Park signs.

General ⚡🛁🔦🐕🔥🏠☼🚮🅿☎🚮✕
Leisure ♒⚓🎿🍴♒⚓

ERWICK-UPON-TWEED, Northumberland Map ref 5B1   SAT NAV TD15 1QU

Seaview Caravan Club Site

Billendean Road, Berwick-upon-Tweed TD15 1QU
t (01289) 305198
w **caravanclub.co.uk**

THE **CARAVAN CLUB**

🚐 (98)   £12.20–£25.30
🚐 (98)   £12.20–£25.30
98 touring pitches

SPECIAL PROMOTIONS
special member rates mean
you can save your
membership subscription in
less than a week. Visit
www.caravanclub.co.uk
to find out more.

Our northernmost site in England combines the spectacular scenery of Northumberland with visits across the border to Scotland. Overlooking the river estuary and with wonderful views of Holy Island from certain pitches. A 30-minute walk into Berwick and you'll find Elizabethan ramparts, shops and many places of interest.

open March 2010 to January 2011.

directions From A1(M) from north avoiding the town centre stay on the A1 Berwick bypass for about 4.5 miles. Turn left onto the A1167 signposted Tweedmouth, Spittal. In about 1.5 miles at the roundabout into Billendean Terrace, site on the right.

General 🔲 🐕 💷 📱 🔌 🕿 📶

HAYDON BRIDGE, Northumberland Map ref 5B2   SAT NAV NE47 6BY

Poplars Riverside Caravan Park

East Lands End, Hexham NE47 6BY
t (01434) 684427

🚐 (8)   £15.00
🚐 (8)   £15.00
⛺ (3)   £9.00–£15.00

A secluded riverside site situated on the banks of the river Tyne with fishing near to village and convenient for Hadrians Wall. **directions** A69. Newcastle-Carlisle Road. Look for caravan signs near bridge in village. **open** March to October **payment** cash, cheques

General 🔲 🐕 💷 📱 🔌 🕿 Leisure ∪ 🎣

HEXHAM, Northumberland Map ref 5B2   SAT NAV NE46 4RP

Fallowfield Dene Caravan and Camping Park

Fallowfield Dene Caravan and Camping Park, Acomb, Hexham NE46 4RP
t (01434) 603553 e info@fallowfielddene.co.uk
w **fallowfielddene.co.uk** ONLINE MAP

🚐 (26)   £16.00–£17.00
🚐 (6)   £16.00–£17.00
⛺ (5)   £9.50–£12.00
32 touring pitches

In unspoilt countryside, 3.75 miles from the village of Acomb, 2 miles from Hexham. The site is within easy reach of Hadrian's Wall and many places of interest. **directions** Please contact us for directions **open** March to November **payment** credit/debit cards, cash, cheques

General 🔲 🐕 💷 ☀ 📱 🔌 🕿 📶 Leisure ∪

POWBURN, Northumberland Map ref 5B1
SAT NAV NE66 4H

River Breamish Caravan Club Site
River Breamish Caravan Club Site, Alnwick NE66 4HY
t (01665) 578320
w **caravanclub.co.uk**

(76) £12.20–£25.10
(76) £12.20–£25.10
76 touring pitches

SPECIAL PROMOTIONS
Special member rates mean
you can save your
membership subscription in
less than a week. Visit our
website to find out more.

This site is set amid the Cheviot Hills, with excellent walking and cycling in the immediate area. A footbridge in Branton takes you over the river to the delightful Breamish Valley. At the National Park Centre at Ingram, staff will help plan your stay, and the Centre sells maps and guidebooks as well as free leaflets.

open March to November
payment credit/debit cards, cash, cheques

directions Turn off A1 onto A697; in about 20 miles (0.25 miles past Powburn) turn left immediately past service station on right. Site right.

General ▯ ⚲ 🛏 🏠 ☼ 🔲 🔲 🛒 🚻 🚐
Leisure ⛰

ROTHBURY, Northumberland Map ref 5B1
SAT NAV NE61 4PZ

Nunnykirk Caravan Club Site
Nunnykirk, Morpeth NE61 4PZ
t (01669) 620762
w **caravanclub.co.uk**

(84) £8.10–£18.80
(84) £8.10–£18.80
84 touring pitches

The peace and tranquillity of this site makes it a haven for wildlife. Space, fresh air and open countryside abound. Hill-walkers will enjoy the splendour of the nearby Simonside Hills. **directions** From B6342, cross bridge at foot of 1:8 hill and turn right into private road. Site on right in 0.25 miles. **open** April to October **payment** credit/debit cards, cash, cheques

General ⚲ 🔲 🚻 Leisure ♪

SEAHOUSES, Northumberland Map ref 5C1
SAT NAV NE68 7SP

Seafield Caravan Park
Seafield Road, Seahouses NE68 7SP
t (01665) 720628 f (01665) 720088 e info@seafieldpark.co.uk
w **seafieldpark.co.uk** ONLINE MAP LAST MINUTE OFFERS

(18) £24.00–£45.00
(18) £24.00–£45.00
(28) £245.00–£695.00
18 touring pitches

Luxurious holiday homes for hire on Northumberland's premier park. Superior, fully serviced touring pitches. Prices include full use of Ocean Club facilities. Gold Award Winner Enjoy England Awards for Excellence 2006. **directions** Take the B1340 from Alnwick for 14 miles. East to coast. **open** 9th Feb to 9th Jan **payment** credit/debit cards, cash, cheques

General ⚙ ▯ ⚇ ⚲ 🏠 ☼ 🔲 🔲 🚻 Leisure ▶ ∪ 🚲 ♪ 🎣 ⛰

EAHOUSES, Northumberland Map ref 5C1   SAT NAV NE68 7UR

Springhill Farm Caravan & Camping Site
Springhill Farm, Seahouses, Northumberland NE68 7UR
t (01665) 721820 **e** enquiries@springhill-farm.co.uk
w springhill-farm.co.uk ONLINE MAP GUEST REVIEWS

A quiet family-run site with 25 caravan and camping pitches. Located on the Northumberland Coast line with fantastic views of Bamburgh Castle and the Farne Islands. **directions** 1 mile from Seahouses, 3.25 miles from Bamburgh, 15 miles from Alnwick, 20 miles from Berwick. **open** Easter to October **payment** credit/debit cards, cash, cheques

🚐	£10.00–£28.00
🚐 (15)	£10.00–£28.00
⛺ (10)	£12.00–£30.00
15 touring pitches	

General 🅿 🐕 🚻 🌧 ☼ 🚿 🎮 👕   **Leisure** ► ∪ ♿ 🎣 ⚲

All Assessed Accommodation

Co Durham

BARNARD CASTLE

t Lendings ★★★
day, Touring & Camping Park
rtforth, Barnard Castle, Co
ham
2 9TJ

BEAMISH

oby Shafto Caravan Park
★★
day, Touring & Camping Park
nberry Plantation, Stanley
9 0RY
(01913) 701776
info@bobbyshaftocaravanpark.co.
uk
bobbyshaftocaravanpark.co.uk

BISHOP AUCKLAND

omer House Camping Barn
nkhouse
Front Street, Frosterley, Bishop
ckland, Co Durham
13 2QS
🐕 🎣

BLACKHALL COLLIERY

imdon Dene Holiday Park
★★★ *Holiday & Touring Park*
ast Road, Blackhall Colliery
27 4BN
0871 664 9737
holidaysales.crimdondene@park-
resorts.com
park-resorts.com

COTHERSTONE

ae Park Caravan Site ★★★★
uring Park
therstone
.12 9UQ
(01833) 650302

DALTON PIERCY

shfield Caravan Park ★★★★
uring & Camping Park
alton Piercy, Hartlepool
.27 3HY
(01429) 269969
info@ashfield-caravanpark.co.uk
ashfield-caravanpark.co.uk

DARLINGTON

ewbus Grange Country Park
★★★
oliday, Touring & Camping Park
urworth Road, Neasham,
arlington
L2 1PE
(01325) 720973
newbusgrangecp@btconnect.
com
newbusgrangecountrypark.co.uk

DURHAM

Finchale Abbey Caravan Park
★★★★ *Touring Park*
Finchale Abbey Farm, Durham
DH1 5SH
t (01913) 866528
e godricawatson@hotmail.com
w finchaleabbey.co.uk

Grange Caravan Club Site
★★★★★ *Touring & Camping Park*
Meadow Lane, Carrville, Durham
DH1 1TL
t (01913) 844778
w caravanclub.co.uk

Strawberry Hill Farm Camping & Caravaning Park ★★★★
ROSE AWARD
Holiday, Touring & Camping Park
Running Waters, Old Cassop, Durham
DH6 4QA
t (01913) 723457
e info@strawberryhf.co.uk
w strawberry-hill-farm.co.uk

EBCHESTER

Byreside Caravan Site ★★★★
Touring & Camping Park
Hamsterley Colliery
NE17 7RT
t (01207) 560280
e byresidecaravansite@hotmail.co.uk
w byresidecaravansite.co.uk

FROSTERLEY

Heatherview Leisure Park
★★★★★ *Holiday Park*
Park Leisure 2000 LTD, Stanhope
DL13 2PS
t (01388) 528728
e heatherview@parkleisure.co.uk
w heatherview.co.uk

Kingfisher Country Park ★★★★★
Holiday Park
Landieu, Frosterley
DL13 2SJ
t (01388) 527230
e kingfisher@parkleisure.co.uk
w kingfisherpark.co.uk

LARTINGTON

Barnard Castle Camping and Caravanning Club Site ★★★★★
Touring & Camping Park
Lartington, Lartington, Barnard Castle
DL12 9DG
t (01833) 630228
w campingandcaravanningclub.co.uk/barnardcastle

MIDDLETON-IN-TEESDALE

Holwick *Camping Barn*
Middleton-in-Teesdale
DL12 0NJ
t (01833) 640506

RAMSHAW

Craggwood Caravan Park ★★★
Holiday & Touring Park
Gordon Lane, Ramshaw, Evenwood
DL14 0NS
t (01388) 835866
e billy6482@btopenworld.com
w craggwoodcaravanpark.co.uk

STOCKTON-ON-TEES

White Water Caravan Club Park
★★★★★ *Touring & Camping Park*
Tees Barrage, Stockton-on-Tees
TS18 2QW
t (01642) 634880
w caravanclub.co.uk

WINSTON

Winston Caravan Park ★★★
Holiday & Touring Park
Front Street, Winston
DL2 3RH
t (01325) 730228
e m.willetts@ic24.net
w touristnetuk.com/ne/winston

Northumberland

AMBLE

Amble Links Holiday Park
★★★★★ *Holiday Park*
Links Road, Amble
NE65 0SD
t (01665) 710530
e amble@parkleisure.co.uk
w amblelinksholidaypark.co.uk

ASHINGTON

Wansbeck Riverside Park Caravan and Camping Site ★★
Touring & Camping Park
Wansbeck Riverside Park, Ashington
NE63 8TX
t (01670) 812323
e wansbeckcaravan@aol.com
w wansbeck.gov.uk

BAMBURGH

Glororum Caravan Park ★★★
Holiday & Touring Park
Glororum Caravan Park, Glororum, Bamburgh
NE69 7AW
t (01668) 214457
e info@glororum-caravanpark.co.uk
w glororum-caravanpark.co.uk

Kaims Country Park ★★★
Holiday, Touring & Camping Park
Bradford House, Bamburgh
NE70 7JT
t (01668) 213432
e info@kaimscountrypark.co.uk
w kaimscountrypark.co.uk

Waren Caravan and Camping Park ★★★★
Holiday, Touring & Camping Park
ROSE AWARD
Waren Mill, Bamburgh, Northumberland
NE70 7EE
t 01668 214366
e waren@meadowhead.co.uk
w meadowhead.co.uk
♿

BARRASFORD

Barrasford Arms Camping Barn
Camping Barn
Barrasford
NE48 4AA
t (01434) 681237
e barrasfordarmshotel@yahoo.co.uk
w barrasfordarms.com
🐕 🎣

BEADNELL

Beadnell Bay Camping and Caravanning Club Site ★★
Touring & Camping Park
Beadnell, Chathill
NE67 5BX
t (01665) 720586
w campingandcaravanningclub.co.uk/beadnellbay

BEAL

Haggerston Castle Holiday Park
★★★★★
Holiday, Touring & Camping Park
ROSE AWARD
Haggerston Castle, Beal, Berwick-upon-Tweed
TD15 2PA
t (01289) 381333
e enquiries@british-holidays.co.uk
w haggerstoncastle-park.co.uk
🐕 🎣 ♿

BELLINGHAM

Bellingham Camping and Caravanning Club Site ★★★★
Touring & Camping Park
The Croft, Bellingham, Hexham
NE48 2JY
t (01434) 220175
w campingandcaravanningclub.co.uk/bellingham

Demesne Farm Campsite & Bunkhouse ★★★
Touring & Camping Park
Demesne Farm, Bellingham
NE48 2BS
t (01434) 220258
e stay@demesnefarmcampsite.co.uk
w demesnefarmcampsite.co.uk

YHA Bellingham Bunkhouse
Bunkhouse
Demesne Farm, Bellingham
NE48 2BS
t (01434) 220258
e stay@demesnefarmcampsite.co.
uk

BERWICK-UPON-TWEED

Beachcomber Campsite ★★
Touring & Camping Park
Goswick, Berwick-upon-Tweed
TD15 2RW
t (01289) 381217
e johngregson@micro-plus-web.net
w lindisfarne.org.uk/beachcomber

Berwick Holiday Park ★★★★
Holiday Park **ROSE AWARD**
Magdalene Fields, Berwick-upon-
Tweed
TD15 1NE
t (01289) 307113
e berwick@bourne-leisure.co.uk
w british-holidays.co.uk

Seaview Caravan Club Site
★★★★ *Touring & Camping Park*
Billendean Road, Berwick-upon-
Tweed
TD15 1QU
t (01289) 305198
w caravanclub.co.uk

CORBRIDGE

Well House Farm - Corbridge
★★★ *Touring & Camping Park*
Well House Farm, Newton,
Stocksfield
NE43 7UY
t (01661) 842193
e info@wellhousefarm.co.uk
w wellhousefarm.co.uk

CRASTER

Proctors Stead Caravan Site ★★★
Holiday, Touring & Camping Park
Dunstan Village, Craster
NE66 3TF
t (01665) 576613

CRESSWELL

Cresswell Towers Holiday Park
★★★★ *Holiday Park*
Cresswell
NE61 5JT
t 0871 664 9734
e holidaysales.cresswelltowers@
park-resorts.com
w park-resorts.com

Golden Sands Holiday Park
★★★★★ *Holiday Park*
ROSE AWARD
Beach Road, Cresswell
NE61 5LF
t (01670) 860256
e enquiries@northumbrianleisure.
co.uk
w northumbrianleisure.co.uk

DUNSTAN

**Dunstan Hill Camping and
Caravan Club Site ★★★★**
Touring & Camping Park
Dunstan Hill, Dunstan, Alnwick
NE66 3TQ
t (01665) 576310
w campingandcaravanningclub.co.
uk/dunstanhill

EAST ORD

Ord House Country Park ★★★★★
Holiday, Touring & Camping Park
East Ord, Berwick-upon-Tweed
TD15 2NS
t (01289) 305288
e enquiries@ordhouse.co.uk
w ordhouse.co.uk

GREENHEAD

Roam-n-Rest Caravan Park ★★★
Touring & Camping Park
Raylton House, Greenhead
CA8 7HA
t (01697) 747213

HALTWHISTLE

**Haltwhistle Camping and
Caravanning Club Site ★★★★**
Touring & Camping Park
Haltwhistle, Haltwhistle
NE49 0JP
t (01434) 320106
w campingandcaravanningclub.co.
uk/haltwhistle

HAYDON BRIDGE

**Poplars Riverside Caravan Park
★★★★**
Holiday, Touring & Camping Park
East Lands End, Hexham
NE47 6BY
t (01434) 684427

HEXHAM

**Fallowfield Dene Caravan and
Camping Park ★★★★**
Touring & Camping Park
Fallowfield Dene Caravan and
Camping Park, Acomb, Hexham
NE46 4RP
t (01434) 603553
e info@fallowfielddene.co.uk
w fallowfielddene.co.uk

Heathergate Country Park
★★★★★ *Holiday Park*
Lowgate, Hexham
NE46 2NN
t (01434) 609030
e info@heathergate.co.uk
w heathergate.co.uk

Hexham Racecourse Caravan Site
★★★ *Touring & Camping Park*
High Yarridge, Yarridge Road,
Hexham
NE46 2JP
t (01434) 606847
e hexrace@aol.com
w hexham-racecourse.co.uk

Kielder Caravan & Camping Site
Holiday, Touring & Camping Park
Kielder Campsite, Kielder, Hexham
NE48 1EJ

LONGHORSLEY

**Forget-Me-Not Holiday Park
★★★★**
Holiday, Touring & Camping Park
Croftside, Longhorsley
NE65 8QY
t (01670) 788364
e info@forget-me-notholidaypark.
co.uk
w forget-me-notholidaypark.co.uk

MELKRIDGE

**Hadrian's Wall Caravan and
Camping Site ★★★★**
Touring & Camping Park
Melkridge Tilery, Haltwhistle
NE49 9PG
t (01434) 320495
e info@romanwallcamping.co.uk
w romanwallcamping.co.uk

NEWBIGGIN-BY-THE-SEA

**Church Point Holiday Park
★★★★** *Holiday Park*
High Street, Newbiggin-by-the-Sea
NE64 6DP
t (01670) 817443
e holidaysales.churchpoint@park-
resorts.com
w park-resorts.com

NORTH SEATON

Sandy Bay Holiday Park ★★★★
Holiday & Touring Park
North Seaton
NE63 9YD
t 0871 664 9764
e holidaysales.sandybay@park-
resorts.com
w park-resorts.com

OTTERBURN

Border Forest Caravan Park ★★★
Holiday, Touring & Camping Park
Cottonshopeburnfoot, Otterburn
NE19 1TF
t (01830) 520259
e borderforest@btinternet.com
w borderforest.com

OVINGHAM

The High Hermitage Caravan Park
★★★
Holiday, Touring & Camping Park
The Hermitage, Main Road, Prudhoe
NE42 6HH
t (01661) 832250
e highhermitage@onetel.com
w highhermitagecaravanpark.co.uk

POWBURN

River Breamish Caravan Club Site
★★★★★ *Touring & Camping Park*
River Breamish Caravan Club Site,
Alnwick
NE66 4HY
t (01665) 578320
w caravanclub.co.uk

ROTHBURY

Coquetdale Caravan Park ★★★★
Holiday Park
Whitton, Rothbury
NE65 7RU
t (01669) 620549
e enquiry@coquetdalecaravanpark.
co.uk
w coquetdalecaravanpark.co.uk

Nunnykirk Caravan Club Site
★★★★ *Touring Park*
Nunnykirk, Morpeth
NE61 4PZ
t (01669) 620762
w caravanclub.co.uk

SCREMERSTON

Northumbrian Wigwam Village
Camping Barn
Borewell Farm, Scremerston
TD15 2RJ
t (01289) 307107
e info@northumbrianwigwams.
w northumbrianwigwams.com

SEAHOUSES

Seafield Caravan Park ★★★★★
Holiday & Touring Park
ROSE AWARD
Seafield Road, Seahouses
NE68 7SP
t (01665) 720628
e info@seafieldpark.co.uk
w seafieldpark.co.uk

**Springhill Farm Caravan &
Camping Site ★★★**
Touring & Camping Park
Springhill Farm, Seahouses,
Northumberland
NE68 7UR
t (01665) 721820
e enquiries@springhill-farm.co.u
w springhill-farm.co.uk

SLALEY

Springhouse Country Park ★★
Holiday, Touring & Camping Park
Bluesky Resorts Ltd, Slaley
NE47 0AW
t (01434) 673241
e andyb@bluesky-resorts.co.uk
w springhousecaravanpark.co.uk

STONEHAUGH

Stonehaugh Campsite ★★
Touring & Camping Park
The Old Farmhouse, Stonehaugh
Shields, Stonehaugh
NE48 3BU
t (01434) 230798
e carole.townsend@btconnect.co
w stonehaugh.fsbusiness.co.uk

WOOLER

Mounthooly *Bunkhouse*
College Valley, Kirknewton
NE71 6DX
t (01668) 216358
e pauline@college-valley.co.uk
w college-valley.co.uk

Riverside Country Park
Holiday, Touring & Camping Park
Wooler, Northumberland
NE71 6NJ

Tyne and Wear
WHITLEY BAY

Whitley Bay Holiday Park ★★★
Holiday Park
The Links, Whitley Bay
NE16 4BR
t 0871 664 9800
e holidaysales.whitleybay@park-
resorts.com
w park-resorts.com

Edinburgh Military Tattoo, City of Edinburgh, Scotland.

Scotland

Scotland

Scotland is a diverse and extraordinary country, with a rich and fascinating history. The country has nearly 800 islands, only 300 of which are inhabited, and is home to some of the most beautiful landscapes in the world. A land of contrasts, Scotland boasts vibrant and exciting cities, breathtaking lochs, mountains and coastlines. Scotland is bordered by England to the south, the Atlantic Ocean to the west and the North Sea to the east.

Aberdeen

Aberdeen is a lively, cosmopolitan city. The sparkling granite buildings make up the "Granite Mile" along Union Street – gateway to numerous shops, restaurants and bars. Nearby, the Aberdeen Art Gallery exhibits the work of young contemporary Scottish and English painters, as well as a selection of modern textiles and jewellery. Further north of the centre between the distinctive spires of King's College Chapel and St Machar's Cathedral, lie the cobbled streets of Old Aberdeen. Most fascinating is the city's maritime heritage, positioned on the north east coast, you can visit the impressive Maritime Museum which depicts the history of early fishing to hi-tech oil exploration.

Dundee

Dundee has in recent years become a magnet to visitors because of its diverse and fascinating heritage sights. The city proudly remembers its industrial and maritime heritage, visit Captain Scott's famous polar exploration ship RRS Discovery, berthed at Discovery Point. There are many fascinating and historic attractions to visit in the nearby towns and villages too. The area is also Scotland's ancient and historic heartland, whose roots begin from the early Scottish Kings and the Declaration of Independence in 1320 to the ancestral home of the late Queen Mother at Glamis Castle, which is open to visitors.

Edinburgh

Scotland's capital city and one of Britain's most exciting tourist destinations. There are two sides to Edinburgh – the historic Old Town with the medieval Edinburgh Castle and cobblestone alleys, and the elegant but classic Georgian New Town. Old and New Towns have been awarded UNESCO World Heritage Status twice over. The city is home to 4,500 listed buildings – the highest

concentration in the world. The combination of such varied architecture, vibrant events such as the Military Tattoo, Edinburgh Festival Fringe, and celebrations such as Hogmanay in December, give Edinburgh its unique character. Together, they create a dynamic and fascinating city which truly captures the magical spirit of Scotland.

Glasgow

Scotland's largest city, Glasgow is famous for its culture, architecture and design. Situated on the River Clyde on the country's west coast, it's known as Scotland's style capital – a title reflected in its art deco brass, stylish shops, cultural centres, more than 30 art galleries and museums and an annual programme of performing arts and festivals. Spectacular Scottish countryside and coastal views are within easy reach and the city is only a short trip of 42 miles from Scotland's capital city of Edinburgh.

Isle of Lewis

Lewis forms part of the Outer Hebrides (Western Isles) a chain of islands with the most spectacular silver beaches, culture and wildlife – a haven for outdoor activities and a wonderful place to unwind. Freshwater and sea lochs provide a great resource for fishing and bird life. This is where you can take boat trips to spot whales, dolphins, seals and

puffins, or a guided walk to see otters, buzzards and deer.

Inverness

Inverness prides itself as being the main cultural centre of the north of Scotland. The city is host to a lively programme of music, concert and dance events and stages the Highland Games in June each year. The annual award winning Scottish Showtime has been running for 30 years– a fast moving and colourful spectacle of Highland ceilidhs, traditional song, dance and music. The city is set in beautiful surroundings amongst parks and gardens, and is a regular winner of Britain in Bloom.

Orkney

Orkney, off the northern tip of mainland Scotland, is a group of over 70 islands, only 17 of which are inhabited. Most of Orkney's locals live in the main towns of Kirkwall and Stromness, where you'll find great tourist attractions and activities to suit every interest. The quiet sandy beaches, stunning scenery, abundance of wildlife, fresh quality cuisine and warm welcoming hospitality make these islands an ideal place for a relaxing visit or an action-packed holiday. For such a small place, there's a lot to see and do in Orkney. Kirkwall, the islands' capital is dominated by the magnificent St Magnus Cathedral, which tells the tale of Viking invasions.

Where to Go

 Attractions with this sign participate in the **Visitor Attraction Quality Assurance Scheme** (see page 6) which recognises high standards in all aspects of the visitor experience.

ENTERTAINMENT & CULTURE

British Golf Museum
St Andrews, Fife, KY16 9AB
(01334) 460046
www.britishgolfmuseum.co.uk
Colourful history of golf in Britain and abroad from the Middle Ages to the present.

Clydebuilt (Scottish Maritime Museum Braehead)
Glasgow, Renfrewshire, G51 4BN
(0141) 886 1013
www.scottishmaritimemuseum.org
Bringing to life the story of Glasgow's development, from 1700s tobacco lords to the 21stC.

Gordon Highlanders Museum
Aberdeen, Aberdeen, AB15 7XH
(01224) 311200
www.gordonHighlanders.com
Regimental collection of the Gordon Highlanders housed in former home of artist Sir George Reid.

Museum of Transport
Glasgow, Glasgow, G3 8DP
(0141) 287 4350
www.Glasgowmuseums.com/
Collection of vehicles and models covering land and sea transport, with a special Glasgow flavour.

HERITAGE

Isle of Arran Distillery Visitor Centre
Brodick, North Lanarkshire, KA27 8HJ
(01770) 830264
www.arranwhisky.com
Witness the making of Arran Single Malt, then savour a dram in the tasting bar.

Talisker Distillery Brand Home
Isle of Skye, Highland, IV47 8SR
(01478) 614308
www.whisky.com/distilleries/talisker_distillery.html
The island's only distillery, in an Area of Outstanding Natural Beauty. Guided tours, exhibition and shop.

Balmoral Castle
Balmoral, Aberdeenshire, AB35 5TB
(01339) 742534
www.balmoralcastle.com
Scottish holiday home of the royal family. Audio tours through the grounds, gardens and exhibitions.

Caerlaverock Castle
Dumfries, Dumfries and Galloway, DG1 4RU
(0131) 668 8600
www.historic-scotland.gov.uk
Awe inspiring moated castle noted for its twin-towered gatehouse and tales of wartime siege.

Culzean Castle & Country Park
Maybole, South Ayrshire, KA19 8LE
0844 493 2100
www.nts.org.uk
Romantic 18th-century castle perched on a rocky promontory with superb panoramic views over the Firth of Clyde, situated in approximately 600 acres of woodland, formal gardens and boasting three miles of varied coastline.

Edinburgh Castle
Edinburgh, EH1 2NG
(0131) 225 9846
www.Edinburghcastle.gov.uk
Battlemented castle dominating the capital. View the Honours of Scotland and huge Mons Meg cannon.

Maes Howe
Orkney, Orkney Islands, KW16 3HA
(0131) 668 8600
www.historic-scotland.gov.uk/
World famous pre-2,700 BC tomb incorporating a passage and burial chamber with cells in the walls.

Palace of Holyroodhouse
Edinburgh, EH8 8DX
(0131) 556 5100
www.royalcollection.org.uk
The official residence of the Queen in Scotland. Royal apartments reflect different monarchs' tastes.

Paxton House and Country Park
Berwick-upon-Tweed, Scottish Borders, TD15 1SZ
(01289) 386291
www.paxtonhouse.com
18thC neo-palladian country house with Adam plasterwork, Chippendale and Trotter furniture. Picture gallery, riverside walks and adventure playground.

Scone Palace
Perth, Perth and Kinross,
H2 6BD
(1738) 552300
www.scone-palace.net
Palace and site of the ancient crowning place of Scottish kings. Outstanding objets d'art collections.

Skara Brae and Skaill House
Stromness, Orkney Islands,
W16 3LR
(131) 668 8600
www.historic-scotland.gov.uk/
Superbly preserved Stone Age houses present a remarkable picture of life in neolithic times.

Stirling Castle
Stirling, Stirlingshire, FK8 1EJ
(131) 668 8600
www.historic-scotland.gov.uk/
Highlights at this grand castle range from James IV's Great Hall to 16th–18thC artillery fortifications.

The Official Loch Ness Monster Exhibition
Drumnadrochit, Highland,
V63 6TU
(01456) 450573
www.loch-ness.scotland.com
Journey through seven themed areas and 500 million years as you investigate the mysterious loch.

The Scotch Whisky Experience
Edinburgh, EH1 2NE
(0131) 220 0441
www.scotchwhiskyexperience.co.uk
Take a memorable barrel ride through whisky history. Complimentary dram, or a treat for children.

NATURE & WILDLIFE

Logan Botanic Garden
Stranraer, Dumfries and Galloway, DG9 9ND
(01776) 860231
www.rbge.org.uk
Explore a plantsman's paradise, where many rare and exotic plants from temperate regions flourish outdoors.

Events 2010

Aberdeen International Jazz Festival
Aberdeen
www.jazzscotland.com/jazzaberdeen
June

Blair Castle International Horse Trials & Country Fair
Pitlochry
www.blairhorsetrials.co.uk/
August

Edinburgh International Film Festival
Edinburgh
www.edfilmfest.org.uk/
October

Edinburgh Military Tattoo
Edinburgh
www.edinburgh-tattoo.co.uk/
6th–28th August

Edinburgh's Hogmanay
Edinburgh
www.edinburghshogmanay.com/
29th December–1st January

Glasgay!
Glasgow
www.glasgay.co.uk/
October-November

Glasgow Jazz Festival
Glasgow
www.jazzfest.co.uk/
June

Inverness Highland Games
Inverness
www.invernesshighlandgames.com/
July

Lanark Medieval Festival
Lanark
www.lanarkmedievalfestival.co.uk/
August

Largs Viking Festival
Largs
www.largsvikingfestival.com/
August-September

Off the Page - Stirling Book Festival
Stirling
www.stirling.gov.uk/offthepage
September

Perth Races - The City of Perth Gold Cup Day
Perth
www.perth-races.co.uk
May

Piping Live! Glasgow International Piping Festival
Glasgow
www.pipingfestival.co.uk/
August

RAF Leuchars Airshow
St Andrews
www.airshow.co.uk/
September

Return to the Ridings
Selkirk
www.returntotheridings.co.uk/
June–August

Scottish Traditional Boat Festival
Banff
www.stbf.bizland.com
July

Stonehaven Folk Festival
Stonehaven
www.stonehavenfolkfestival.co.uk/
July

T in the Park
Kinross
www.tinthepark.com
9th–11th July

The Open Championship 2010
St Andrews
www.opengolf.com
15th-18th July

Up-Helly-Aa
Lerwick
www.uphellyaa.org/
26th January

Where to Eat

Scotland has great places to eat. The restaurant reviews on these pages are just a small selection from the highly respected **The Good Food Guide 2010**. Please see pages 20-21 for further information on the guide and details of a Special Offer for our readers.

BORDERS

Burt's Hotel

Market Square, Melrose, TD6 9PL
Tel no: (01896) 822285
www.burtshotel.co.uk
Modern British

The whitewashed building on the market square dates from 1722 and is still laden with period character. In the green dining room, a refined style of country-house cooking is offered, with fixed-price dinner menus of two courses (£28.50) or three (£33.75). Expect grilled red mullet with melon and feta couscous in port syrup, followed by saddle of lamb with garlic butter fondants, creamed Savoy cabbage and redcurrant and rosemary jus, and then warm treacle tart with whisky and ginger ice cream and créme anglaise. House wines are £14.95. Open all week.

EDINBURGH

David Bann

Vibrant veggie food and good puds
56-58 St Mary's Street, Edinburgh, EH1 1SX
Tel no: (0131) 5565888
www.davidbann.co.uk
Vegetarian | £21

Just off the Royal Mile, in Edinburgh's old town, David Bann's vegetarian restaurant offers sexily-lit surroundings – and a menu that will prove exotically diverting to both veggies and meat-eaters. Dishes are described in detail: roasted squash, pine nut and basil ravioli with homemade organic curd cheese and herb oil might preface udon noodles with pak choi, shiitakes and home-smoked tofu, in a sauce of red pepper, ginger, garlic, lime, chilli, soy, mirin and coriander. And topped with mooli. Oh, and cucumber. It all represents a vibrant, healthily inventive approach to flesh-free cooking, and ends with conventionally luscious desserts like dark chocolate soufflé with vanilla ice cream and white chocolate sauce. A thoughtfully chosen wine list with good notes opens with Argentinian Viognier and Cabernet Sauvignon at £12.50, or £2.95 for a standard glass.

Chef/s: David Bann. **Open:** all week L 11 to 5, D 5 to 10 (10.30 Sat, Sun). **Closed:** 25 and 26 Dec, 1 and 2 Jan. **Meals:** alc (main courses £10 to £13). **Service:** not inc. **Details:** Cards accepted. 80 seats. Air-con. Separate bar. No music. Wheelchair access. Children allowed.

GRAMPIAN

at on the Green

ottish favourites with a modern spin

dny Green, AB41 7RS

l no: (01651) 842337

ww.eatonthegreen.co.uk

cottish | £42

he dining area has been extended into what was
e old post office at this former inn overlooking the
lage green, yet the place still feels homely. Traditional
cottish modes are given a modern spin in dishes that
splay great clarity of flavour. Start with something like
n array of seafood hors d'oeuvres with lemon and lime
ème fraîche, before going on to chargrilled Angus
loin with roasted shallots, pink peppercorn cream
nd chips, or steamed halibut teamed with scallops
nd langoustines in a cognac-spiked shellfish bisque.
ne British cheeses are the alternative to desserts like
aramelised lemon tart with raspberry sorbet. The wine
st is full of dependable names at prices that shouldn't
sturb, opening at £14.

hef/s: Craig Wilson. **Open:** Wed to Fri and Sun L 12 to 2,
ed to Sun D 6.30 to 8.30 (9 Fri and Sat). **Closed:** Mon and
ue. **Meals:** alc (main courses £19 to £24). Set L £18.95 (2
ourses) to £21.95. Set Sat D £42. Sun L £19.95 (2 courses)
o £24.95. **Service:** not inc. **Details:** Cards accepted. 70
eats. Wheelchair access. Music. Children allowed. Car
arking.

HIGHLANDS & ISLANDS

bstract at Glenmoriston Town House

Minimalist chic, aspirational cuisine

0 Ness Bank, Inverness, IV2 4SF

el no: (01463) 223777

ww.abstractrestaurant.com

Modern French | £43

itting pretty beside the banks of the River Tay,
lenmoriston Town House is not only one of Scotland's
op luxury hotels, it's also home to Abstract – a fashion-
onscious restaurant with a good line in minimalist
hic. Occupying part of the ground floor, its sleek style
s matched by cooking with aspirations, intricacy and
oguish gastro trademarks. Chef Geoff Malmedy has
departed, to take over the kitchen at the Edinburgh
branch of Abstract. We were notified about the arrival

of his replacement, William Hay, too late to respond
with an inspection. New menus are unavailable as we
go to press, but previously, complex embellishments,
meat/fish combos and jokey contrasts defined the
contemporary French-inspired repertoire. Reports
please. The wine list puts its faith in luxurious drinking
from the French regions and beyond. Prices start at £18.

Chef/s: William Hay. **Open:** Tue to Sat D only 6 to10.
Closed: Sun, Mon, one week Jan. **Meals:** alc (main courses
£15 to £28). Tasting menu £50. **Service:** not inc. **Details:**
Cards accepted. 45 seats. No music. No mobile phones.
Wheelchair access. Children allowed. Car parking.

TAYSIDE

The Apron Stage

Small is beautiful

5 King Street, Stanley, PH1 4ND

Tel no: (01738) 828888

www.theapronstage.co.uk

Modern British | £25

Shona Drysdale and Jane Nicoll used to be part of
the team that put Let's Eat in Perth on the map and in
this new venture, an evocative and unusual 18-seater
restaurant, their passion for food is vividly celebrated.
A mix of trompe l'oeil mirrors, pale colours and painted
furniture gives a masterful illusion of space, while
a simple counter separates diners from a miniscule
kitchen. Given such limitations, the short blackboard
menu makes sense. It offers, perhaps, a light potato
pancake topped with goats' cheese, rocket and two
thin slices of Parmesan 'perfect in its flavour, freshness
and simplicity', then a just-pink trio of lamb cutlets
with lyonnaise potatoes. The 20 or so wines are a
knowledgeable selection, with bottles from £13.75 (or
£3.50 a glass).

Chef/s: Shona Drysdale. **Open:** Fri L 12 to 2, Wed to Sat
D 6.30 to 9.30. **Closed:** Sun, Mon, Tue. **Meals:** alc (main
courses £13 to £18). Set L £13 (2 courses) to £15.75.
Service: not inc. **Details:** Cards accepted. 18 seats.
No mobile phones. Wheelchair access. Music. Children
allowed.

Content brought to you by **The Good Food
Guide 2010**. Please see pages 20–21 for
further details.

Tourist Information Centres

When you arrive at your destination, visit a Visitor Information Centre for help with accommodation and information about local attractions and events. Alternatively call **0845 22 55 121** to receive information and book accommodation before you go.

Aberdeen	01224 288828	23 Union Street, Aberdeen, AB11 5BP
Aberfeldy	01887 820276	The Square, Aberfeldy, PH15 2DD
Aberfoyle	01877 382352	Trossachs Discovery Centre, Main Street, Aberfoyle, FK8 3UQ
Abington	01864 502436	Welcome Breaks Services, Junction 13, M74 Abington, ML12 6RG
Alford	01975 562052	Old Station Yard, Alford, AB33 8FD
Anstruther	01333 311073	Scottish Fisheries Museum, Harbourhead, Anstruther, KY10 3AB
Arbroath	01241 872609	Harbour Visitor Centre, Fishmarket Quay, Arbroath, DD11 1PS
Ardgartan	01301 702432	by Arrochar, G83 7AR
Aviemore	01479 810930	No 7 The Parade, Grampian Road, Aviemore, PH22 1RH
Ayr	01292 290300	22 Sandgate, Ayr, KA7 1BW
Ballater	01339 755306	The Old Royal Station, Station Square, Ballater, AB35 5RB
Balloch	01389 753533	The Old Station Building, Balloch, G83 8LQ
Banchory	01330 822000	Bridge Street, Banchory, AB31 5SX
Banff	01261 812419	Collie Lodge, Banff, AB45 1AU
Biggar	01899 221066	155 High Street, Biggar, ML12 6DL
Blairgowrie	01250 872960	26 Wellmeadow, Blairgowrie PH10 6AS
Boness	01506 826626	Bo'ness Station, Union Street, Bo'ness, EH51 9AQ
Bowmore	01496 810254	The Square, Bowmore, Isle of Islay, PA43 7JP
Braemar	01339 741600	Unit 3, The Mews, Mar Road, Braemar, AB35 5YL
Brechin	01356 623050	Pictavia Centre, Haughmuir, Brechin DD9 6RL
Brodick	01770 303774	The Pier, Brodick, Isle of Arran, KA27 8AU
Callander	01877 330342	Ancaster Square, Callander, FK17 8ED
Campbeltown	01586 552056	Mackinnon House, The Pier, Campbeltown, PA28 6EF
Castle Douglas	01556 502611	Market Hill Car Park, Castle Douglas, DG7 1AE
Castlebay	01871 810336	Main Street, Castlebay, Isle of Barra, HS9 5XD
Craignure	01680 812377	The Pier, Craignure, Isle of Mull, PA65 6AY
Crail	01333 450869	Crail Museum, 62 Marketgate, Crail, KY10 3TL
Crieff	01764 652578	High Street, Crieff, PH7 3HU
Daviot Wood	01463 772971	Picnic Area (A9), Daviot Wood, by Inverness, IV1 2ER
Drumnadrochit	01456 459086	The Car Park, Drumnadrochit, Inverness-shire, IV63 6TX

Dufftown	01340 820501	The Clock Tower, The Square, Dufftown, AB55 4AD
Dumbarton Milton	01389 742306	Milton, A82 North Bound, G82 2TZ
Dumfries	01387 253862	64 Whitesands, Dumfries DG1 2RS
Dunbar	01368 863353	143A High Street, Dunbar, EH42 1ES
Dundee	01382 527527	Discovery Point, Riverside Drive, Dundee. DD1 4XA
Dunfermline	01383 720999	1 High Street, Dunfermline, KY12 7DL
Dunkeld	01350 727688	The Cross, Dunkeld, PH8 0AN
Dunoon	01369 703785	7 Alexandra Parade, Dunoon, PA23 8AB
Dunvegan	01470 521581	2 Lochside, Dunvegan, Isle of Skye, IV55 8WB
Durness	01971 511368	Sango, Durness, Sutherland IV27 4PZ
Edinburgh	0131 473 3820	Princes Mall, 3 Princes Street, Edinburgh, EH2 2QP
Edinburgh Airport	0131 344 3120	Main Concourse, Edinburgh International Airport, EH12 9DN
Elgin	01343 562608	Elgin Library, Elgin IV30 IHS
Elgin	01343 562614	Elgin Library, Elgin IV30 IHS
Eyemouth	01890 750678	Auld Kirk, Manse Road, Eyemouth, TD14 5HE
Falkirk	01324 620244	The Falkirk Wheel, Lime Road, Tamfourhill, Falkirk, FK1 4RS
Fort William	01397 701801	15 High Street, Fort William, PH33 6DH
Fraserburgh	01346 518315	3 Saltoun Square, Fraserburgh, AB43 9DA
Glasgow	0141 204 4400	11 George Square, Glasgow G2 1DY
Glasgow Airport	0141 848 4440	International Arrivals Hall, Glasgow International Airport, PA3 2ST
Grantown-on-Spey	01479 872242	54 High Street, Grantown on Spey, PH26 3EH
Gretna	01461 337834	Unit 38, Gretna Gateway Outlet Village, Glasgow Road, Gretna, DG16 5GG
Hawick	01450 373993	Tower Mill, Heart of Hawick Campus, Kirkstile, Hawick, TD9 0AE
Helensburgh	01436 672642	The Clock Tower, Helensburgh, G84 7PA
Huntly	01466 792255	9A The Square, Huntly, AB54 8BR
Inveraray	01499 302063	Front Street, Inveraray, PA32 8UY
Inverness	01463 252401	Castle Wynd, Inverness, IV2 3BJ
Inverurie	01467 625800	18 High Street, Inverurie, AB51 3XQ
Jedburgh	01835 863170	Murray's Green, Jedburgh, TD8 6BE
Kelso	01573 228055	Town House, The Square, Kelso, TD5 7HF
Kirkcaldy	01592 267775	The Merchant's House, 339 High Street, Kirkcaldy, KY1 1JL
Kirkcudbright	01557 330494	Harbour Square, Kirkcudbright DG6 4HY
Kirkwall	01856 872856	The Travel Centre, West Castle Street, Kirkwall, Orkney KW15 1GU
Lanark	01555 661661	Horsemarket, Ladyacre Road, Lanark, ML11 7QI
Largs	01475 689962	The Railway Station, Main Street, Largs, KA30 8AN
Lerwick	01595 693434	Market Cross, Lerwick, Shetland, ZE1 0LU
Linlithgow	01506 775320	County Buildings, High Street, Linlithgow EH49 7EZ
Lochboisdale	01878 700286	Pier Road, Lochboisdale, Isle of South Uist, HS8 5TH
Lochgilphead	01546 602344	Lochnell Street, Lochgilphead, PA31 8JL
Lochinver	01571 844373	Main Street, Lochinver IV27 4LT
Lochmaddy	01876 500321	Pier Road, Lochmaddy, Isle of North Uist, HS6 5AA
Melrose	01896 822283	Abbey House, Abbey Street, Melrose TD6 9LG
Moffat	01683 220620	3 Churchgate, Moffat, DG10 9EG
Newton Stewart	01671 402431	Dashwood Square, Newton Stewart DG10 9JU
Newtongrange	0131 663 4262	Scottish Mining Museum, Newtongrange, EH22 4QN
North Berwick	01620 892197	1 Quality Street, North Berwick, EH39 4HJ
North Kessock	01463 731836	Picnic site A9 North Kessock IV1 1XB
Oban	01631 563122	Argyll Square, Oban, PA34 4AN
Paisley	0141 889 0711	9A Gilmour Street, Paisley, PA1 1DD
Peebles	01721 723159	23 High Street, Peebles, EH45 8AG
Perth	01738 450600	Lower City Mills, West Mill Street, Perth, PH1 5QP
Pitlochry	01796 472215	22 Atholl Road, Pitlochry, PH16 5BX
Portree	01478 612992	Bayfield Road, Portree, Isle of Skye, IV51 9EL
Rothesay	01700 502151	Winter Gardens, Victoria Street, Rothesay, Isle of Bute, PA20 0AH
Selkirk	01750 20054	Halliwells House, Selkirk, TD7 4BL

Southwaite	01697 473445	M6 Service Area, Southwaite, CA4 0NS
St. Andrews	01334 472021	70 Market Street, St. Andrews, KY16 9NU
Stirling (Dumbarton Road)	01786 475019	41 Dumbarton Road, Stirling, FK8 2QQ
Stirling (Pirnhall)	01786 814111	M9 Motorway Services Area, Pirnhall Roundabout, Stirling FK7 8ET
Stonehaven	01569 762806	66 Allardice Street, Stonehaven, AB39 2AA
Stornoway	01851 703088	26 Cromwell Street, Stornoway, Isle of Lewis, HS1 2DD
Stranraer	01776 702595	28 Harbour Street, Stranraer, DG9 7RA
Stromness	01856 850716	Ferry Terminal Building, Pier Head, Stromness, Orkney, KW16 3BH
Strontian	01967 402382	Strontian, Acharacle, Argyll, PH36 4HZ
Sumburgh (Airport)	01595 693434	Wilsness Terminal, Sumburgh Airport, Shetland ZE3 9JP
Tarbert (Harris)	01859 502011	Pier Road, Tarbert, Isle of Harris, HS3 3DG
Tarbet (Loch Fyne)	01880 820429	Harbour Street, Tarbet, PA29 6UD
Tarbet (Loch Lomond)	01301 702260	Main Street, Tarbet G83 7DE
Thurso	01847 893155	Riverside Road, Thurso, KW14 8BU
Tobermory	01688 302182	The Pier, Tobermory, Isle of Mull, PA75 6NU
Tyndrum	01838 400324	Main Street, Tyndrum, FK20 8RY
Ullapool	01854 612486	6 Argyle Street, Ullapool, Ross-shire, IV26 2UB

Regional Contacts and Information

For more information on accommodation, attractions, activities, events and holidays in Scotland, contact the regional tourism organisation below. The website has a wealth of information and you can order or download publications.

The following is a selection of publications available online from VisitScotland.com or by calling the information and booking service on 0845 22 55 121:

Where to Stay Hotels & Guest Houses £8.99

Over 3,000 places to stay in Scotland – from luxury town houses and country hotels to budget-priced guesthouses. Details of prices and facilities, with location maps.

Where to Stay Bed & Breakfast £6.99

Over 2,000 Bed and Breakfast establishments throughout Scotland offering inexpensive accommodation – the perfect way to enjoy a budget trip and meet Scottish folk in their own homes. Details of prices and facilities, with location maps.

Where to Stay Caravan & Camping Parks and Self Catering £6.99

Over 280 parks and 3,400 cottages, apartments and chalets to let, many in scenic areas. Details of prices and facilities including caravan homes for hire. Easy to use map locations.

Where to Stay Self Catering £5.99

Over 3,400 cottages, apartments and chalets to let – many in scenic areas. Details of prices and facilities, with location maps.

Touring Guide to Scotland £7.99

A fully revised edition of this popular guide which now lists over 1,700 things to do and places to visit in Scotland. Easy to use index and locator maps. Details of opening hours, admission charges, general description and information on disabled access.

Touring Map of Scotland £4.99

An up-to-date touring map of Scotland. Full colour with comprehensive motorway and road information, the map details over 20 categories of tourist information and names over 1,500 things to do and places to visit in Scotland.

Never has a rose meant so much

Everyone has a trusted friend, someone who tells it straight. Well, that's what the Enjoy England Quality Rose does: reassures you before you check into your holiday accommodation that it will be just what you want, because it's been checked out by independent assessors. Which means you can book with confidence and get on with the real business of having a fantastic break.

The **Quality Rose** is the mark of England's official, nationwide quality assessment scheme and covers just about every place you might want to stay, using a clear star rating system: from caravan parks to stylish boutique hotels, farmhouse B&Bs to country house retreats, self-catering cottages by the sea to comfy narrowboats perfect for getting away from it all. Think of the Quality Rose as your personal guarantee that your expectations will be met.

**Look no further. Just look out for the Quality Rose.
Find out more at enjoyEngland.com/quality**

Where to Stay

Entries appear alphabetically by town name in each region. A key to symbols appears on page 6. Maps start on page 394.

BRAEMAR, Aberdeenshire Map ref 7C3

SAT NAV AB35 5YQ

Scottish
TOURIST BOARD
★★★★
TOURING
PARK

(97)   £12.20–£25.10
(97)   £12.20–£25.10
97 touring pitches

SPECIAL PROMOTIONS
Special member rates mean
you can save your
membership subscription in
less than a week. Visit our
website to find out more.

The Invercauld Caravan Club Site
Glenshee Road, Braemar, Ballater AB35 5YQ
t (01339) 741373

THE
CARAVAN
CLUB

Set on the fringe of the village of Braemar, 110 feet above sea level. An ideal centre for walkers and mountain bikers. Herds of red deer roam freely and you may also glimpse capercaillie, red squirrels and badgers, golden eagles and heron. The site opens in December for the Winter Sports season.

open December 2010 to October 2011
payment credit/debit cards, cash, cheques

directions On A93 on southern outskirts of village.

General 🅾 🐴 ⚡ 📱 📷 ☼ 🔌 🔄 🛁 📶 🚐
Leisure ▶ 🏊 ⛰

Thistle Holiday Homes are top-quality caravan holiday homes on VisitScotland 4 or 5 star graded caravan parks.

ORDOUN, Aberdeenshire Map ref 6D1

SAT NAV AB30 1SJ

Brownmuir Caravan Park
Fordoun, Laurencekirk AB30 1SJ
t (01561) 320786 e brownmuircaravanpark@talk21.com

(11)	£13.50–£15.00
(11)	£15.00
(6)	£7.00–£10.00
(3)	£230.00–£250.00

11 touring pitches

A quiet park set in the Howe-of-the-Mearns not far from Royal Dee Side, ideal for cycling and fishing. Top golf courses are nearby. Children's play area on site. Toilet block with all amenities. **directions** 4 miles north of Laurencekirk turn left at junction signposted Fordoun/Auchenblae, then after 200 yards turn left over bridge, park is 1 mile on right. **open** April to October **payment** cash, cheques

General Leisure

OBAN, Argyll and Bute Map ref 6B1

SAT NAV PA34 4QH

Oban Caravan & Camping Park
Gallanachmore Farm, Gallanach Road, Oban PA34 4QH
t (01631) 562425 e info@obancaravanpark.com

(150)	£15.50–£17.50
(150)	£15.50–£17.50
(150)	£13.00
	£230–£520
	£230–£520
(15)	£230.00–£520.00

150 touring pitches

A beautiful coastal tourist park in a very attractive location. Close to the ferries to the Isles. This family park is an ideal boating centre, and offers two large rally areas in addition to the touring pitches, one with hardstandings and many electric hook-ups. **directions** From Argyll Square in Oban town centre follow signs to 'Gallanach'. Drive past the entrance to the ferry terminal and continue along Gallanach Road. **open** March to October **payment** credit/debit cards, cash

General Leisure

DUMFRIES, Dumfries & Galloway Map ref 6C3

SAT NAV DG2 9SQ

Barnsoul Farm
Shawhead, Dumfries DG2 9SQ
t (01387) 730249 e barnsouldg@aol.com
w **barnsoulfarm.co.uk** ONLINE MAP

(10)	£14.00
(10)	£14.00
(10)	£14.00
	£200–£280
	£230.00

30 touring pitches

Barnsoul is one of Galloway's most scenic farms. Acres of meadows, ponds, woodlands and heath. Two 3,500-year-old hill forts. Caravan camping and famous timber wigwam bunkhouses. **directions** Off A75 at sign for Shawhead. At Shawhead take right, then within 50 m bear left. After 1.5 miles Barnsoul is on left. **open** March to October **payment** cash, cheques

General Leisure

KIRKPATRICK FLEMING, Dumfries & Galloway Map ref 6C3

SAT NAV DG11 3AT

King Robert the Bruce's Cave
Cove Estate, Kirkpatrick Fleming DG11 3AT
t (01461) 800285 or 07779138694 e enquiries@brucescave.co.uk

(12)	£12.50
(6)	£10.00
(10)	£12.50–£16.00
(3)	£380–£600

80 touring pitches

The lovely wooded grounds of an old castle and mansion are the setting for this pleasant park. The mature woodland is a haven for wildlife, and there is a riverside walk to Robert the Bruce's cave. Luxury holiday apartments available to let. **directions** Please contact us for directions **open** All year **payment** credit/debit cards, cash, cheques

General Leisure

LOCKERBIE, Dumfries & Galloway Map ref 6C3   SAT NAV DG11 1A

Hoddom Castle Caravan Park
Hoddom, Lockerbie DG11 1AS
t (01576) 300251 e hoddomcastle@aol.com

🚐 (100)   £9.00–£19.00
🚐 (100)   £9.00–£19.00
▲ (30)   £8.00–£16.00
130 touring pitches

Part of 10,000-acre estate. Beautiful, peaceful, award-winning park. Own 9-hole golf course. Salmon, seatrout and coarse fishing. Nature trails and walks in surrounding countryside. **directions** Please contact us for directions **open** April to October **payment** credit/debit cards, cash, cheques

General 🔲 🐕 🛠 ⬛ 🁢 ☼ 🔌 🚿 📷 ⚲ 🚽 📺 ✕   Leisure ▶ ∪ ⚲ ♪ 🍴 🎣 ⛰

PARTON, Dumfries & Galloway Map ref 6C3   SAT NAV DG7 3NI

Loch Ken Holiday Park
Parton, Castle Douglas DG7 3NE
t (01644) 470282 e penny@lochkenholidaypark.co.uk
w **lochkenholidaypark.co.uk** ONLINE MAP

🚐 (31)   £16.00
🚐 (6)   £16.00
▲ (50)   £12.00–£16.00
🏠 (10)   £270.00–£480.00
87 touring pitches

Popular park in beautiful spot on shores of Loch Ken opposite RSP reserve. Excellent fishing, sailing, water-skiing. Family-owned, uncommercialised, peaceful place for relaxing family holiday. David Bellamy Gold Conservation Award. **directions** Take the A713 from A75 at Castle Douglas. 7 m to Loch Ken Holiday Park. **open** March to November **payment** credit/debit cards, cash, cheques, euros

General 🔲 🐕 🛠 🁢 ☼ 🁢 📷 🚿 🚽 📺   Leisure ▶ ∪ ⚲ ♪ ⛰

PORT LOGAN, Dumfries & Galloway Map ref 6B3   SAT NAV DG9 9NX

New England Bay Caravan Club Site
Port Logan, Stranraer DG9 9NX
t (01776) 860275
w **caravanclub.co.uk**

THE
CARAVAN
CLUB

🚐 (158)   £10.60–£23.60
🚐 (158)   £10.60–£23.60
158 touring pitches

SPECIAL PROMOTIONS
Special member rates mean
you can save your
membership subscription in
less than a week. Visit our
website to find out more.

Situated on the edge of Luce Bay and carefully landscaped into seven intimate pitching areas with sea views. Direct access from site to a safe clean and sandy beach – ideal for sailing, watersports and sea angling. Great for exploring the Forests and Rhins of Galloway.

open March to November
payment credit/debit cards, cash, cheques

directions From Newton Stewart take A75, then A715, then A716. Site on left 2.7 miles past Ardwell Filling Station.

General 🔲 🐕 🁢 🁢 ☼ 🔌 🁢 🚽 📺
Leisure ∪ ♪ 🎣 ⛰

DIRLETON, East Lothian Map ref 6D2

Yellowcraig Caravan Club Site

Dirleton EH39 5DS
t (01620) 850217
w **caravanclub.co.uk**

THE CARAVAN CLUB

🚐 (116)   £14.00–£26.90
🚐 (116)   £14.00–£26.90
116 touring pitches

SPECIAL PROMOTIONS
Special member rates mean you can save your membership subscription in less than a week. Visit our website to find out more.

This is a great choice for family holidays with acres of golden sands and rock pools close by. Pitching areas separated by sandy dunes, shrubs and roses. Nature lovers will enjoy the birds and wildlife around the dunes. It's promontory harbour location also affords exceptional views of the Bass Rock and other islands.

open March to November
payment credit/debit cards, cash, cheques

directions From North Berwick take A198, signposted Edinburgh. Turn right off bypass for Dirleton, then right again at International Camping sign.

General 🔲 🐕 🛁 🏬 ☀ 🔌 🔄 🚽 🛎 🚐
Leisure ► 🏕

DUNBAR, East Lothian Map ref 6D2

Thistle

Belhaven Bay Caravan and Camping Park

Edinburgh Road, West Barns, Dunbar EH42 1TU
t (01368) 865956 e belhaven@meadowhead.co.uk
w **meadowhead.co.uk** ONLINE MAP GUEST REVIEWS LAST MINUTE OFFERS

🚐 (52)   £13.75–£23.50
🚐 (52)   £13.75–£23.50
🏕 (52)   £7.00–£22.00
🏠 (7)   £280.00–£610.00
52 touring pitches

SPECIAL PROMOTIONS
Please see our website for special offers.

Located in the John Muir Country Park in the sunniest and driest part of Scotland, but only 30 minutes to Edinburgh's city centre! Perfect for a quiet and relaxing break and to explore Dunbar and East Lothian with its boutique shopping, castles, golf courses and spectacular countryside and sandy beaches.

open March to October and weekends up to and including Christmas
payment credit/debit cards, cash, cheques, euros

directions From A1 north Thistly Cross roundabout take A199 then A1087 at Beltonford roundabout (signposted Dunbar). Continue through West Barns. Belhaven Bay on left.

General 🔌 🔲 📶 🐕 🛁 🏬 ☀ 🔄 🛎 🚐
Leisure ► ∪ ⚓ 🏕

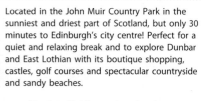

NORTH BERWICK, East Lothian Map ref 6D2   SAT NAV EH39 5N

Tantallon Caravan and Camping Park

Dunbar Road, North Berwick EH39 5NJ
t (01620) 893348   e tantallon@meadowhead.co.uk
w **meadowhead.co.uk** ONLINE MAP GUEST REVIEWS LAST MINUTE OFFERS

🚐 (127)	£13.50–£28.00
🚃 (127)	£13.50–£28.00
▲ (40)	£7.00–£26.00
🏕 (10)	£310.00–£625.00
127 touring pitches	

SPECIAL PROMOTIONS
Please go to our website for special offers.

Spectacular views to Bass Rock and Firth of Forth greet visitors to Tantallon. Situated on the East Lothian Coast, North Berwick is a bustling seaside town with a lively harbour, fine beach, fabulous boutique shopping and many golf courses. Edinburgh is a short drive or 30 minutes by train.

open March to October and weekends up to and including Christmas
payment credit/debit cards, cash, cheques, euros

directions From North Berwick, A198 towards Dunbar. From the south, turn off at A1 north Dunbar and follow signs for North Berwick and Tantallon Park.

General 🔥📻💧🐕🏪🛒☀️📞🛁🚽 WP
Leisure 🚩🏊🎣🏛

EDINBURGH, Edinburgh Map ref 6C2   SAT NAV EH21 8JS

Drummohr Caravan Park

Levenhall, Musselburgh EH21 8JS
t (01316) 656867   e bookings@drummohr.org
w **drummohr.org** LAST MINUTE OFFERS

🚐	£17.00–£25.00
🚃	£17.00–£25.00
▲	£17.00–£25.00
🏠	£350–£995
108 touring pitches	

Premier park is on the outskirts of Edinburgh and the coast of East Lothian. Excellent bus service and park and ride to city with many retail outlets in the area. **directions** From south (A1), take A199 Musselburgh, then B1361. Follow park signs. From west (A1), come off at Wallyford slip road and follow Park and Mining Museum signs. **open** 1 March to 31 October **payment** credit/debit cards, cash, cheques

General 📻💧🐕🛒🏪☀️📞🛁🚽 WP   Leisure 🏛

EDINBURGH, Edinburgh Map ref 6C2   SAT NAV EH53 0HT

Linwater Caravan Park

West Clifton, East Calder EH53 0HT
t (01313) 333326   e linwater@supanet.com

🚐 (50)	£13.00–£17.00
🚃 (50)	£13.00–£17.00
▲ (10)	£11.00–£15.00
60 touring pitches	

A peaceful park seven miles west of Edinburgh. Excellent facilities. Ideal for visiting Edinburgh, Royal Highland Showground, Falkirk Wheel, or as a stop-over on your way north or south. Try our new timbertents, a warm and dry alternative to camping. **directions** Signposted from M9, junction 1 - Newbridge, or from Wilkieston or A71, along B7030. **open** 13 March to 1 November **payment** credit/debit cards, cash, cheques, euros

General 📻🐕🏪☀️🍴🔌📞🛁   Leisure ∪ 🎣

EDINBURGH, Edinburgh Map ref 6C2

Edinburgh Caravan Club Site

Marine Drive, Edinburgh EH4 5EN
t (01313) 126874
w caravanclub.co.uk

(197) £14.00–£26.90
(197) £14.00–£26.90
197 touring pitches

SPECIAL PROMOTIONS
Special member rates mean you can save your membership subscription in less than a week. Visit our website to find out more.

Situated to the north of the city on the Firth of Forth, the site provides easy access to Edinburgh. It's a historic setting - yet Edinburgh is a friendly, modern, cosmopolitan city with something for everyone. Visit the castle which clings dramatically to the rock, walk down the Royal Mile or enjoy the green expanse of Princes Street Gardens.

open All year
payment credit/debit cards, cash, cheques

directions From A901 turn left at traffic lights; at roundabout turn right into Marine Drive. Site on left.

General 🔲 🍴 ♨ 🦽 🌐 📞 🚿
Leisure ▶

EDINBURGH, Edinburgh Map ref 6C2

Mortonhall Caravan and Camping Park

38 Mortonhall Gate, Frogston Road East, Edinburgh EH16 6TJ
t (0131) 664 1533 e mortonhall@meadowhead.co.uk
w meadowhead.co.uk ONLINE MAP GUEST REVIEWS LAST MINUTE OFFERS

(250) £13.00–£28.50
(250) £13.00–£28.50
(250) £10.00–£24.25
(20) £280.00–£810.00
250 touring pitches

SPECIAL PROMOTIONS
Please see our website for all our current special offers.

Situated in a 200- acre country estate and only 4 miles from Edinburgh's city centre. Mortonhall has beautifully maintained and landscaped parkland, with views to the Pentland Hills. Only a short bus trip or drive, the Capital's shopping, walking, arts, history and other leisure activities are all on our doorstep.

open March to January, including Christmas and New Year
payment credit/debit cards, cash, cheques, euros

directions From the north or south, Exit the city bypass (A720) at Straiton or Lothianburn Junctions and follow the signs to Mortonhall.

General 🚿 🔲 ♨ 🍴 🛒 🦽 ☀ 🌐 📞 🚿 📶 ✕
Leisure ▶ ∪ 🚲 ♪ 🍷 🎣 ⛰

CRAIL, Fife Map ref 6D1 — SAT NAV KY10 3XJ

Sauchope Links Caravan Park
warsea road, Crail KY10 3XJ
t (01333) 450 460 e info@sauchope.co.uk
w **largoleisure.co.uk** ONLINE MAP

(33)	£16.00–£25.00	
(33)	£16.00–£25.00	
(14)	£14.00–£20.00	
(6)	£20–£35	
(6)	£275.00–£520.00	
47 touring pitches		

Beautifully located on the Fife coastal path between St Andrews and Anstruther. Spectacular views across the Firth of Forth to the Isle of May. **directions** from the A917 to crail turn left onto Marketgate and follow the road for 1 mile.Turn right into Warsea Road and follow to the end **open** 21st March to 31st October touring 1st March to January 4th holiday homes **payment** credit/debit cards, cash, cheques

General Leisure

LEVEN, Fife Map ref 6C2 — SAT NAV KY8 5NT

Letham Feus Caravan Park
Cupar Road, Nr Lundin Links, Leven, Fife KY8 5NT
t 01333 351900 e info@lethamfeus.co.uk
w **lethamfeus.co.uk** ONLINE BOOKING

(100)	£30.00–£60.00	
(3)	£185.00–£410.00	

In an idyllic setting with stunning views of the Forth Estuary, Letham Feus Park is the perfect holiday location to relax and unwind. **directions** Please contact us for directions **payment** cheques

General Leisure

MARKINCH, Fife Map ref 6C2 — SAT NAV KY7 6NR

Balbirnie Park Caravan Club Site
Balbirnie Road, Markinch, Glenrothes KY7 6NR
t (01592) 759130
w **caravanclub.co.uk**

THE CARAVAN CLUB

(76)	£23.60–£27.90	
(76)	£23.60–£27.90	
76 touring pitches		

Attractive site set in 400 acres of parkland. Thirty golf courses, including one on site. Swimming pool, ice rink, ten-pin bowling, children's farm close by. **directions** From A92, follow signs to Markinch, then signs to Balbirnie Park Craft Centre. Site entrance is just inside park on right, 0.5 mile west of Markinch. **open** March to November **payment** credit/debit cards, cash, cheques

General Leisure

BALMACARA, Highland Map ref 7B3 — SAT NAV IV40 8DH

Reraig Caravan Site
Balmacara, Kyle of Lochalsh IV40 8DH
t (01599) 566215 e warden@reraig.com

45 touring pitches

Small family-run site, 4 miles from bridge to Isle of Skye. Booking not necessary. No awnings during July and August. Tents: only small tents permitted. No youth groups. Prices on application, or see our website. **directions** Please contact us for directions **open** May to September **payment** credit/debit cards, cash, cheques

General

BOAT OF GARTEN, Highland Map ref 7C3

SAT NAV PH24 3BY

Loch Garten Caravan Park
Loch Garten Road, Boat of Garten PH24 3BY
t (01479) 831769 **e** m.ireland@totalise.co.uk
w lochgarten.co.uk ONLINE MAP

◀ (3)   £275–£400

Close by the ospreys on the outskirts of Boat of Garten. A quiet location with squirrels, deer and bird life, luxury in wilderness setting. Self catering at its most comfortable. **directions** Please contact us for directions **open** All year **payment** cash, cheques

General ▢ 🏇 ⛗ ☼   Leisure ▶ ♒ ⚲ ♪

BRORA, Highland Map ref 7C2

SAT NAV KW9 6LP

Dalchalm Caravan Club Site
Brora KW9 6LP
t (01408) 621479
w caravanclub.co.uk

◀ (52)   £12.20–£25.10
▦ (52)   £12.20–£25.10
52 touring pitches

A sheltered site on the east coast of Sutherland, where you can play golf or relax on the nearby sandy beach. Marvellous walking, bird-watching, sea and loch fishing. The single track rail journey to Wick is a scenic must. **directions** 1.25 miles north of Brora on A9, turn right at Dalchalm. **open** April to October **payment** credit/debit cards, cash, cheques

General ▢ 🏇 ⛗ ⌂ ☼ ▤ 📞 🛁 ☎ CWP   Leisure ▶ ♪

CULLODEN, Highland Map ref 7C3

SAT NAV IV2 5EF

Culloden Moor Caravan Club Site
Newlands, Culloden Moor, Inverness IV2 5EF
t (01463) 790625
w caravanclub.co.uk

THE CARAVAN CLUB

◀ (97)   £12.20–£25.30
▦ (97)   £12.20–£25.30
97 touring pitches

A gently sloping site with glorious views over the Nairn Valley. Inverness, with impressive castle, great shops and fascinating museums, is 6 miles away. **directions** From A9 south of Inverness, take B9006 signposted Croy, site on left 1 mile past Culloden field memorial. **open** March 2010 to January 2011 **payment** credit/debit cards

General ▢ 🏇 ⛗ ⌂ ☼ ▤ 📞 🛁 ☎ CWP   Leisure ♪ ⛰

DUNBEATH, Highland Map ref 7C2

SAT NAV KW6 6EH

Inver Caravan Park
Houstry Road, Dunbeath KW6 6EH
t (01593) 731441 **e** rhonagwillim@yahoo.co.uk
w inver-caravan-park.co.uk ONLINE MAP

◀ (12)   £11.00–£16.00
▦ (8)   £8.00–£16.00
▲ (8)   £8.00–£16.00
▤ (1)   £175.00–£295.00
15 touring pitches

Small, friendly site with beautiful views over Moray Firth. Smooth grass, hard standings, shop and pub serving food within easy walking distance. Convenient location adjacent A9 **directions** Take road signposted 'Houstry 3', from A9 just north of Dunbeath. Park entrance immediately on left. **open** All year **payment** cash, cheques

General ▢ 📞 🏇 ⌂ ☼ ⛽ 📞 🛁 CWP   Leisure ♪ ⛰

FORT WILLIAM, Highland Map ref 6B1   SAT NAV PH33 6S

Glen Nevis Caravan and Camping Park
Glen Nevis, Fort William PH33 6SX
t (01397) 702191 e holidays@glen-nevis.co.uk
w **glen-nevis.co.uk** ONLINE MAP ONLINE BOOKING LAST MINUTE OFFERS

🚐	£13.00–£19.00
🚃	£13.00–£19.00
⛺ (300)	£10.20–£15.50
🏠 (22)	£235.00–£525.00
250 touring pitches	

Our award-winning touring caravan and camping park has a magnificent location in one of Scotland's most famous highland glens at the foot of mighty Ben Nevis, Britain's highest mountain.

open 15th March to end October   **directions** Please contact us for directions
payment credit/debit cards, cash, cheques, euros

General 🔲 🐕 🛁 🏪 🏧 ☼ ⊟ 🚽 💧 🚿 ⊕ ✕   **Leisure** ▶ 🚵 🎣 🏐 ♟ ⚓

FORT WILLIAM, Highland Map ref 6B1   SAT NAV PH33 7NL

Linnhe Lochside Holidays
Corpach, Fort William PH33 7NL
t (01397) 772376 e relax@linnhe-lochside-holidays.co.uk

🚐 (65)	£13.00
🚃 (65)	£10.50–£12.50
⛺ (15)	£6.00–£10.50
🏠 (60)	£250.00–£899.00
80 touring pitches	

Almost a botanical garden. Winner of 'Best Park in Scotland 1999' award. Free fishing. Colour brochure sent with pleasure. Also self-catering. **directions** On A830 1.5 miles (3 km) west of Corpach village, 5 miles from Fort William. **open** 15 December to 31 October **payment** credit/debit cards, cash, cheques

General 🔲 ♿ 🐕 🛁 🏪 🏧 ☼ ⊟ 🚽 💧 🚿 ⊕   **Leisure** 🚵 🎣 ⚓

GLENCOE, Highland Map ref 6B1   SAT NAV PH49 4HP

Invercoe Caravan & Camping Park
Invercoe, Glencoe PH49 4HP
t (01855) 811210 e holidays@invercoe.co.uk

🚐	£20.00–£24.00
🚃	£20.00–£24.00
⛺	£15.00–£20.00
🏠 (4)	£350.00–£470.00
55 touring pitches	

Situated on the shores of Loch Leven and surrounded by spectacular scenery, Invercoe is a small, award-winning, family-run park and is an excellent base for exploring the West Highlands. Booking advisable during high season (minimum three nights). **directions** Site is 0.25 miles from Glencoe crossroads (A82) on the Kinlochleven road (B863). **payment** credit/debit cards, cash, cheques

General 🔲 ♿ 🐕 🛁 🏪 🏧 ☼ 🚽 💧 🚿 ⊕   **Leisure** ▶ 🎣 ⚓

NCHCREE, Highland Map ref 6B1

Bunree Caravan Club Site

Onich, Fort William PH33 6SE
t (01855) 821283
w **caravanclub.co.uk**

🚐 (99)   £14.00–£29.90
🚏 (99)   £14.00–£29.90
99 touring pitches

SPECIAL PROMOTIONS
Special member rates mean
you can save your
membership subscription in
less than a week. Visit our
website to find out more.

This site must be one of The Club's loveliest in
scenic terms - It is quite literally breathtaking.
For a day out you can explore Ben Nevis, you
can take a cable car to the upper terminal of the
Aonach Mor Mountain for fabulous views of the
whole mountain range, the Great Glen and the
islands of Skye and Rhum.

open March 2010 to January 2011

directions From A82 turn left 1 mile past Onich
at Club Site sign into narrow track. Site in 0.25
mile.

General 📺 ♿ 🐕 ⛽ 🏪 🔌 🕒 🚻 ♿P
Leisure 🎣 ⛺

JOHN O' GROATS, Highland Map ref 7D1

John O'Groats Caravan Park

John O'Groats KW1 4YR
t (01955) 611329 **e** info@johnogroatscampsite.co.uk
w **johnogroatscampsite.co.uk**

🚐 (90)   £13.00–£15.50
🚏 (90)   £13.00–£15.50
⛺ (90)   £11.00–£13.00
90 touring pitches

On seashore overlooking Orkney Islands (day trips available). Hotel
restaurant 400 m, harbour 150 m, sea birds 3 km. Cliff scenery.
directions At end of A99 on seafront beside last house in Scotland
overlooking Orkney Islands. **open** April to September **payment**
cash, cheques

General ♿ 📺 🐕 ⛽ 🏪 ☼ 🔌 🕒 🚻 ♿P   **Leisure** 🎣

For **key to symbols** see page 6

KINLOCHEWE, Highland Map ref 7B3   SAT NAV IV22 2PA

Kinlochewe Caravan Club Site
Kinlochewe, Achnasheen IV22 2PA
t (01445) 760239
w **caravanclub.co.uk**

🚐 (56)   £9.30–£20.20
🚐 (56)   £9.30–£20.20
56 touring pitches

SPECIAL PROMOTIONS
Special member rates mean
you can save your
membership subscription in
less than a week. Visit our
website to find out more.

A small and intimate site at the foot of the
rugged slopes of Ben Eighe, a magic place
where the world slows down to walking pace
and you with it. A paradise for both climbers
and walkers alike. The first British national natu
reserve is just 2.5 miles away.

open March to October
payment credit/debit cards, cash, cheques

directions Just north of Kinlochewe at junction
of A832 and A896. Signposted.

General 🔲 🐕 📳 📶 ☼ 🔌 💬 🛢 🚽 🔳

SHIEL BRIDGE, Highland Map ref 7B3   SAT NAV IV40 8HQ

Morvich Caravan Club Site
Inverinate, Kyle IV40 8HQ
t (01599) 511354
w **caravanclub.co.uk**

🚐 (106)   £12.20–£25.30
🚐 (106)   £12.20–£25.30
106 touring pitches

SPECIAL PROMOTIONS
Special member rates mean
you can save your
membership subscription in
less than a week. Visit our
website to find out more.

Morvich has all the amenities for an ideal family
holiday base for those who enjoy the great
outdoors. The site is on the level valley floor,
while all around there are hills and mountains
and the most dazzling scenery. Great for walkers
- so take your boots and binoculars.

open March to November
payment credit/debit cards, cash, cheques

directions Turn right off A87 1.25 miles past
Shiel Bridge. In 1 mile turn right into road to site
entrance. Site on left in 150 yds.

General 🔲 🐕 📳 📶 ☼ 💬 🛢 🚽 🔳
Leisure 🎣 🔍

THURSO, Highland Map ref 7C1

SAT NAV KW14 8XD

Dunnet Bay Caravan Club Site
Dunnet, Thurso KW14 8XD
t (01847) 821319
w **caravanclub.co.uk**

🚐 (57) £12.20–£25.10
🚎 (57) £12.20–£25.10
57 touring pitches

SPECIAL PROMOTIONS
Special member rates mean
you can save your
membership subscription in
less than a week. Visit our
website to find out more.

A good place for those who like to be solitary,
you can look out over clean washed sands to
Dunnet Head, the northernmost point of
mainland Britain. Take a day trip over to Orkney
from John o'Groats or Scrabster. Good for birdwatching and fishing.

open April to October
payment credit/debit cards, cash, cheques

directions From east (John O'Groats) on A836.
Site on right past Dunnet village.

General 🔲 ⛺ 🏕 🍴 📶
Leisure 🎣

STEPPS, North Lanarkshire Map ref 6B2

SAT NAV G33 6AF

Craigendmuir Park
Craigendmuir Park Business Centre, Stepps, Glasgow G33 6AF
t (01417) 792973 e info@craigendmuir.co.uk
w **craigendmuir.co.uk** ONLINE MAP LAST MINUTE OFFERS

🚐 (15) £15.50–£17.50
🚎 (15) £15.50–£17.50
⛺ (20) £12.25–£14.25
🏠 (17) £160.00–£530.00
30 touring pitches

Craigendmuir Park offers substantial touring caravan and camping
areas, together with fully equipped chalets, static caravans and
holiday homes. **directions** From the M8 exit junction 12 for approx
3 miles, through Stepps 1st lights turn right into Cardowan Road,
3rd turn on right into Clayhouse Road, continue to next
roundabout, park is on left- hand side, take 3rd turn on left into
holiday park. **open** All year **payment** credit/debit cards, cash,
cheques

General 🔲 ⛺ 🏕 ☼ 🍴 📶 Leisure ▶ ∪ 🎣

CRIEFF, Perth and Kinross Map ref 6C1

SAT NAV PH7 4DH

Braidhaugh Park
South Bridgend, Crieff PH7 4DH
t (01764) 652951 e info@braidhaugh.co.uk
w **braidhaugh.co.uk** ONLINE MAP GUEST REVIEWS LAST MINUTE OFFERS

🚐   £20.50–£23.00
🚎   £20.50–£23.00
⛺ (2) £20–£30
🏠 (3) £255.00–£450.00
40 touring pitches

Peaceful, riverside park, outskirts of Crieff, in the heart of Perthshire.
Wigwams, hire caravans and hard-standing, level, fully serviced
touring pitches. Information area, play park, games room and shop.
directions On 822. From Stirling follow A9 to Greenloaning and
take A822. From Perth follow A85 through Crieff, turn left onto
A822, turn right after bridge. **open** All year **payment** credit/debit
cards, cash, cheques

General 🔲 ⛺ 🏕 ☼ 🍴 📶 Leisure ▶ ∪ 🚲 🎣 🎣 ⛰

DUNKELD, Perth and Kinross Map ref 6C1 SAT NAV PH8 0JR

Invermill Farm Caravan Park

Inver, Dunkeld PH8 0JR
t (01350) 727477 e invermill@talk21.com
w **visitdunkeld.com/perthshire-caravan-park.htm** ONLINE MAP

£15.00–£16.00
£15.00–£16.00
(15) £13.00–£15.00
50 touring pitches

We are situated in a very tranquil setting, scenic and beautiful pa of Perthshire beside the river Braan, an ideal location to explore a large part of Scotland. **directions** Turn off A9 signposted A822 to Crieff turn right follow signs to Inver. **open** end of March to end October **payment** cash, cheques, euros

General **Leisure**

MELROSE, Scottish Borders Map ref 6C2 SAT NAV TD6 9RY

Gibson Park Caravan Club Site

High Street, Melrose TD6 9RY
t (01896) 822969
w **caravanclub.co.uk**

(60) £14.00–£26.90
(60) £14.00–£26.90
60 touring pitches

SPECIAL PROMOTIONS
Special member rates mean that you can save your membership subscription in less than a week. Visit our website to find out more.

Peaceful site on edge Melrose overlooked by three hills which gave rise to its Roman name Trimontium. Children will enjoy the adjacent tennis courts and playing fields. Melrose, famou for its ruined Abbey, where Robert the Bruce's head is buried, is within walking distance.

open All year
payment credit/debit cards, cash, cheques

directions Site adjacent to main road (A6091) close to centre of town. Approx 6 miles (10 km) from A68 Edinburgh/Newcastle road.

General
Leisure

AYR, South Ayrshire Map ref 6B2 SAT NAV KA7 4LD

Heads of Ayr Caravan Park

Dunure Road, Ayr KA7 4LD
t (01292) 442269 e stay@headsofayr.com
w **headsofayr.com** ONLINE MAP

(20) £13.50–£20.00
(8) £12.00–£18.00
(8) £11.00–£18.00
(1) £300–£595
(8) £180.00–£550.00
36 touring pitches

Situated 5 miles south of Ayr on the A719. Facilities include bar, shop, laundry, play area and beach. Seasonal entertainment. Caravans to hire. Tourers and tents welcome. **directions** Please contact us for directions **open** March to October **payment** cash, cheques

General **Leisure**

AYR, South Ayrshire Map ref 6B2

SAT NAV KA8 0SS

Craigie Gardens Caravan Club Site

Craigie Road, Ayr KA8 0SS
t (01292) 264909
w **caravanclub.co.uk**

🚐 (90)   £12.20–£25.30
🚐 (90)   £12.20–£25.30
90 touring pitches

SPECIAL PROMOTIONS
special member rates mean
you can save your
membership subscription in
less than a week. Visit our
website to find out more.

Set in a beautiful park, a short walk from Ayr. This area, known as 'The Golf Coast', has 40 golf courses! Learn about 'Rabbie Burns', the greatest Scottish poet, with the Burns Heritage Trail nearby. History fans will enjoy Vikingar at Largs.

open All year
payment credit/debit cards, cash, cheques

directions A77 Ayr bypass to Whitletts roundabout, then A719 via racecourse. Left at lights into Craigie Road. 0.5 mile, then after right-hand bend left into Craigie Gardens. Site 400 yds on right.

General 🗔 🐕 🏕 🛗 ☼ 🖳 💬 🕾 🕿 🆚
Leisure ► ✦ ⚲

ABINGTON, South Lanarkshire Map ref 6C2

SAT NAV ML12 6RW

Mount View Caravan Park

Station Road, Abington ML12 6RW
t (01864) 502808   e info@mountviewcaravanpark.co.uk

🚐 (50)   £13.00–£17.00
🚐 (50)   £13.00–£17.00
🛆 (10)   £8.00–£17.00
🚐 (3)   £160.00–£350.00
50 touring pitches

A developing park, surrounded by the Southern Uplands and handily located between Carlisle and Glasgow. It is an excellent stopover site for those travelling between Scotland and the South. The West Coast railway passes beside the park. **directions** Please contact us for directions **open** March to October **payment** credit/debit cards, cash

General 🗔 🐕 🏕 ☼ 🚐 💬 🕾 🕿   Leisure ✦ ⚲

CALLANDER, Stirling Map ref 6B1

SAT NAV FK17 8LE

Gart Caravan Park

Stirling Road, Callander FK17 8LE
t (01877) 330002   e enquiries@theholidaypark.co.uk

🚐 (128)   £20.00
🚐 (128)   £20.00
128 touring pitches

A peaceful and spacious park maintained to a very high standard with modern, heated shower block facilities. The ideal centre for cycling, walking and fishing. **directions** Leave jct 10 of the M9, west to Callander. **open** 1 April to 15 October **payment** credit/debit cards, cash, cheques

General 🗔 🐕 🏕 🛗 ☼ 🖳 🚐 💬 🕾 🕿 🆚   Leisure ► ∪ ⚿ ✦ ⚲

CALLANDER, Stirling Map ref 6B1 — SAT NAV FK17 8L

Keltie Bridge Caravan Park
Keltie Bridge Caravan Park, Callander FK17 8LQ
t (01877) 330606 e stay@keltiebridge.co.uk

🚐 (50) £11.50–£13.50
🚐 (50) £11.50–£13.50
⛺ (50) £9.50–£11.50
50 touring pitches

Flat, grassy park in Scotland's new Loch Lomond and The Trossa
National Park. Top-quality shower block. Easily accessible from
central Scotland's motorways. **directions** Well signposted off A84
outside Callander. **open** Easter to October **payment** cash, cheque

General 🔲 🐕 📱 🌣 🔊 🚰 Leisure ⚑ 🚲

KILLIN, Stirling Map ref 6B1 — SAT NAV FK21 8TN

Maragowan Caravan Club Site
Aberfeldy Road, Killin FK21 8TN
t (01567) 820245
w **caravanclub.co.uk**

CARAVAN CLUB

🚐 (100) £14.00–£26.90
🚐 (100) £14.00–£26.90
100 touring pitches

SPECIAL PROMOTIONS
Special member rates mean
you can save your
membership subscription in
less than a week. Visit our
website to find out more.

An ideal family holiday base, set on one bank
the River Lochay and within walking distance
the shops and restaurants of the little holiday
town of Killin. There is a 9-hole golf course jus
0.25 mile away or you can fish for trout in the
river on site. Walkers will find plenty to
challenge them and mountain bikes can be
hired in the village.

open March to November
payment credit/debit cards, cash, cheques

directions Site on right of A827 (Killin-Kenmor
0.5 mile past end of village.

General 🔲 🐕 📱 🌣 🔊 🚰 🚰
Leisure ⚑ 🚲 🎣

BALLOCH, West Dunbartonshire Map ref 6B2 — SAT NAV G83 8QP

Thistle

Lomond Woods Holiday Park
Balloch, Loch Lomond G83 8QP
t (01389) 755000 e lomondwoods@holiday-parks.co.uk
w **holiday-parks.co.uk** ONLINE MAP GUEST REVIEWS ONLINE BOOKING LAST MINUTE OFFERS

🚐 (120) £18.00–£22.00
🚐 (120) £18.00–£22.00
🏠 (8) £295–£895
🚐 (6) £195.00–£550.00
120 touring pitches

Beside Loch Lomond and at the gateway to the National Park, this
superbly appointed, family-run park offers pine lodges and caravan
for holiday hire and sunny, secluded pitches for touring caravans
and motor homes. **directions** Sat Nav G83 8QP and directions
available www.holiday-parks.co.uk **open** All year
payment credit/debit cards, cash, cheques

General 📶 🔲 🐕 🌣 🔊 🚰 🚰 Leisure ⚑ ∪ 🚲 🎣 🎣 🎢

LINLITHGOW, West Lothian Map ref 6C2 · **SAT NAV EH49 6PL**

Beecraigs Caravan and Camping Site
Beecraigs Country Park, Nr Linlithgow, West Lothian EH49 6PL
t (01506) 844516 **e** mail@beecraigs.com
w beecraigs.com

🚐 (36)	£14.00–£17.00	
🚐 (36)	£14.00–£17.00	
⅄ (20)	£12.50–£20.40	

56 touring pitches

SPECIAL PROMOTIONS
Range of promotions -
please contact for further
details.

Open all year. Situated near historic Linlithgow town & within the Beecraigs Country Park. Onsite facilities include electric hook-ups, barbecues, play area, modern toilet facilities with privacy cubicles, baby-change & laundrette facilities. Pets welcome. Leaflets available. Great for exploring central Scotland & the Lothians. Advised to book in advance.

open All year
payment credit/debit cards, cash, cheques

directions From Linlithgow, follow Beecraigs Country Park and International Caravan Park signposts. Park is 2 miles south of Linlithgow. From M8, follow B792. From M9, follow A803.

General 🗄 🐕 ♿ 🎦 ☼ 🔌 🛁 🍴 ✕
Leisure ► ∪ ♨ ♪ 🛝

Ffestiniog railway, Ffestiniog, Gwynedd, Wales.

Wales

Wales

Wales is a small country with colourful history and spectacular landscapes, including 3 National Parks and 5 Areas of Outstanding Natural Beauty. At only 170 miles from north to south and 60 miles east to west, it is no surprise that you're never far from a mountain or the sea. Wales is rich in history, culture, myth and legend. Now home to 2 UNESCO World Heritage Sites. Welsh, the native language, is one of the oldest languages in the world and is still spoken by many people; road and public signs are bilingual. Croeso i Cymru (Welcome to Wales)

Cardiff

The capital city dates back to Roman times, but it is actually Britain's youngest city. Extensive re-development has given Cardiff world-class sporting and entertainment complexes. The Millennium Stadium (a major attraction) is home to Welsh football and rugby and for golf fans, the Celtic Manor Resort, just 20 minutes from Cardiff, will host the Ryder Cup tournament in 2010. Other 'must see' attractions are Cardiff Castle and National Museum. On the outskirts of the city are Techniquest Science Discovery Centre, fun with 160 interactive exhibits; and the fairytale Castell Coch.

Aberystwyth

Aberystwyth is an established holiday resort, which is home to many of Wales' cultural institutions. Situated on spectacular coastline it makes an ideal base for exploring the striking and unspoilt countryside on its doorstep. The town is at the mouth of the Rheidiol and Ystwyth valleys, which offer secluded walks. Steam trains ride along the Vale of Rheidol railway from Aberystwyth up to the mysteriously named Devils Bridge. Passing through some of the most rugged terrain of any railway in the United Kingdom, this trip offers spectacular views.

Carmarthen

Carmarthen is an ideal base to explore, including The National Botanic Garden of Wales, the largest single span glass house in the world, housing many endangered plant species and, in contrast, Aberglasney Gardens, a historical garden whose past secrets are only now being rediscovered through a restoration project of the house and gardens.

Llangollen

Located between the River Dee and the Berwyn Mountains is Llangollen, a picturesque, bustling market town. Famous for the Llangollen International Musical Eisteddfod held in July each year, worldwide visitors attend to watch or compete in poetry, dance and music competitions.

Take the 45-minute walk to Castell Dinas Brân, perched on a hill 800 ft above the town, the Holy Grail is said to be buried here, and there are fantastic views of the town. For long distance walks there's Offa's Dyke Path and the Precipice Walk. Alternatively, for those seeking less strenuous activities, the Llangollen Railway, operates nostalgic trips, on restored steam engines, between Llangollen and Carrog. Canal trips start from Llangollen Wharf, take a horse drawn boat or a narrow-boat ride over Thomas Telford's magnificent Pontcysyllte Aqueduct, 126 ft above the River Dee.

Pembrokeshire

Pembrokeshire Coast National Park is the only coastal park in Britain. Much of the coast line is owned and managed by the National Trust, ensuring that these stunning landscapes are protected. Some of the best beaches in Britain can be found here. Walkers are well catered for, the Pembrokeshire Coast Path is 186 miles by a coastline that is famed for its magnificent bays and headlands, and there are plenty of options from a full trek to an easy stroll.

Swansea

A city perfectly situated on the edge of a five-mile bay, Swansea is a vibrant multi-cultural destination. Birthplace and long-standing inspiration of poet Dylan Thomas, Swansea boasts award-winning parks and gardens, fantastic shopping, world class cultural and sporting facilities – including the Dylan Thomas Centre, the Wales National Pool (50 m long!) the 20,000 seat Liberty Stadium and Wales' largest indoor market, where you can sample freshly harvested cockles and laverbread – a local delicacy.

Do not miss a visit to the National Waterfront Museum in the award-winning Maritime Quarter. This £30 million attraction pushes the boundaries of technology in an interactive interpretation of Welsh industry and innovation in science, manufacturing and medicine. With high-impact graphics and interactive opportunities through the displays, it really is a must-see!

Further along Swansea Bay is the beautiful Victorian seaside resort of Mumbles, where you can browse for local pottery and hand-carved lovespoons.

And if golden sands and clear blue waters are what you need, look no further than the stunning Gower Peninsula, Britain's first Area of Outstanding Natural Beauty. From family-friendly sandy bays to secluded coves, award-winning beaches are plentiful. Do not miss the view from Worm's Head at Rhossili Bay, reputedly the ninth most photographed sunset in the world.

Where to Go

 Attractions with this sign participate in the **Visitor Attraction Quality Assurance Scheme** (see page 6) which recognises high standards in all aspects of the vistor experience.

ENTERTAINMENT & CULTURE

Big Pit National Mining Museum of Wales
Blaenafon, Torfaen, NP4 9XP
(01495) 790311
www.museumwales.ac.uk/en/bigpit/
Big Pit is the UK's leading mining museum. It is a real colliery and was the place of work for hundreds of men, women and children for over 200 years – a daily struggle to extract the precious mineral that stoked the furnaces and lit houses

Museum of Welsh Life, St Fagans
St Fagans, Cardiff, CF5 6XB
(029) 2057 3500
www.museumwales.ac.uk/en/
stfagans/
Experience centuries of Wales' social history gathered together in 100 acres of beautiful countryside.

National Museum & Gallery Cardiff
Cardiff, CF10 3NP
(029) 2039 7951
www.museumwales.ac.uk/
Gallery Cardiff is unique among British museums and galleries in its range of art and science displays. The Art Galleries provide magnificent settings for works by some of the world's most famous arti.

The Dylan Thomas Centre
Swansea, SA1 1RR
(01792) 463980
www.dylanthomas.com/
Exhibition on the life of Swansea's world famous son. Literature programme.

Wales Millennium Centre
Cardiff, CF10 5AL
0870 040 2000
www.wmc.org.uk
Wales Millennium Centre is at the heart of the performing arts in Cardiff and a key attraction in the city. If you want to see theatre, dance, opera, ballet and more, the Centre is the place to head.

FAMILY FUN

Go Ape! High Wire Forest Adventure – Margam Country Park
Port Talbot, Neath Port Talbot, SA13 2TJ
0845 643 9215
www.goape.co.uk
Take to the trees and experience an exhilarating course of rope bridges, tarzan swings and zip slides...all set high above the forest floor.

HERITAGE

Cardiff Castle
Cardiff, CF10 3RB
(029) 2087 8100
www.Cardiffcastle.com/
Come and see how an Anglo-Norman castle was transformed into a breathtaking Neo-Gothic fantasy.

Carew Castle & Tidal Mill
Tenby, Pembrokeshire, SA70 8SL
(01646) 651782
www.carewcastle.com
Visit Carew, one of the few castles to display the development from Norman fortification to Elizabethan country house. See the archaeological evidence of a much earlier settlement, dating back perhaps 2,000 years.

Gower Heritage Centre
Gower, Swansea, SA3 2EH
(01792) 371206
www.gowerheritagecentre.co.uk
Set in the heart of the beautiful Gower peninsula, Britain's first designated area of outstanding natural beauty, the Gower Heritage Centre is based around a working 12th century water-powered corn mill, with a museum of rural life, as well

Harlech Castle
Harlech, Gweynedd, LL46 2YH
(01766) 780552
www.harlech.com/
Edward I's mighty 13thC castle with twin-towered gatehouse. World Heritage Site.

King Arthur's Labyrinth
Machynlleth, Gweynedd, SY20 9RF
(01654) 761584
www.kingarthurslabyrinth.com/
An underground adventure deep inside the spectacular caverns of the Labyrinth, and far into the past. Hear Welsh tales of King Arthur and other ancient Welsh legends as you explore the dramatic underground setting.

Pembroke Castle
Pembroke, Pembrokeshire, SA71 4LA
(01646) 684585
www.pembroke-castle.co.uk
Pembroke Castle is situated within minutes of beaches and the breathtaking scenery of the Pembrokeshire Coast National Park. This mighty fortress is birthplace of Henry VII, father to the infamous Henry VIII and grandfather to Elizabeth I.

Powis Castle and Garden
Welshpool, POWYS, SY21 8RF
(1938) 551944
www.nationaltrust.org.uk/main/w-
owiscastle_garden
Wander the world-famous terraced
garden. Admire paintings, furniture and
treasures from India in the medieval
castle.

Talyllyn Railway
Gweynedd, Gweynedd,
LL36 9EY
(1654) 710472
www.talyllyn.co.uk/
The Talyllyn Railway is a historic
narrow-gauge steam railway, set in
the beautiful Mid-Wales countryside.
Running from Tywyn to Abergynolwyn
and Nant Gwernol, the line passes the
delightful Dolgoch Falls and there are
excellent forest walks at Nant Gwernol.

NATURE & WILDLIFE

Felinwynt Rainforest
Centre
Felinwynt, Ceredigion, SA43 1RT
(1239) 810882
www.butterflycentre.co.uk
Mini rainforest with glasswing, blue
peacock, scarlet swallowtail and other
tropical butterflies.

Great Orme Tramway
Llandudno, CONWY, LL30 2HD
01492) 879306
www.greatormetramway.co.uk/
Opened in 1902 the only cable-hauled
tramway still operating on British roads.

National Botanic Garden
of Wales
Llanarthney, Carmarthenshire,
SA32 8HG
(01558) 668768
www.gardenofwales.org.uk
View plants from Mediterranean
climates in the Great Glasshouse.
Diverse garden attractions in 500 acres.

Snowdon Mountain
Railway
Llanberis, Gweynedd, LL55 4TY
0871 720 0033
www.snowdonrailway.co.uk/
Pinion mountain railway running from
Llanberis to the summit of Snowdon, the
highest mountain in England and Wales.

Events 2010

Abergavenny Food Festival
Abergavenny
www.
abergavennyfoodfestival.com/
September

Beyond The Border Wales
Llantwit Major
www.beyondtheborder.com/
2nd–4th July

Brecon Jazz
Brecon
www.breconjazz.org.uk/
August

Cardiff Iris Prize Festival
Cardiff
www.irisprize.org
October

Dylan Thomas Festival
Swansea
www.dylanthomas.com
October–November

Gower Festival
Swansea
www.gowerfestival.org/
July

**Great British Cheese
Festival**
Cardiff
www.cardiffcastle.com/
September

Hay Festival of Literature
Hay-on-Wye
www.hayfestival.com
September

**National Transport Festival
of Wales**
Swansea
www.freewebs.com/
ntfwswansea/
June

Royal Welsh Show
Builth Wells
www.rwas.co.uk
July

Swansea Bay Film Festival
Swansea
www.sbff09.com/
8th–15th May

The 2010 Ryder Cup
Newport
www.rydercup.com
29th September–3rd October

**The Admiral Cardiff Big
Weekend**
Cardiff
www.cardiffbay.co.uk/
July-August

The Big Cheese
Caerphilly
www.caerphilly.gov.uk/
bigcheese
July

The Green Man Festival
Crickhowell
www.greenman.net
August

The Laugharne Weekend
Laugharne
www.thelaugharneweekend.
com/
April

Urdd Eisteddfod 2010
Ceredigion
www.urdd.org/eisteddfod
31st May–5th June

**World Bog Snorkling
Championships**
Llanwrtyd Wells
www.green-events.co.uk
August

Where to Eat

Wales has great places to eat. The restaurant reviews on these pages are just a small selection from the highly respected *The Good Food Guide 2010*. Please see pages 20–21 for further information on the guide and details of a Special Offer for our readers.

ABERGAVENNY

The Hardwick
Intelligent food in a welcoming setting
Old Raglan Road, Abergavenny, NP7 9AA
Tel no: (01873) 854220
www.thehardwick.co.uk
Modern British | £30

Stephen Terry's welcoming roadside gastropub has plenty of admirers, including one who ranks the triple-cooked chips as 'better than Heston's'. The

interior – 'warm and cosy, with a roaring log fire' – is a mix of barewood and reclaimed furniture. The menu is built on stunning ingredients such as Black Mountain Smokery hot and cold smoked salmon with salted cucumber and crème fraîche, followed by braised shoulder and roast loin of local, organic lamb with fried polenta, roast winter vegetables and salsa verde. Desserts continue along traditional lines, with an upmarket take on bread-and-butter pudding or rhubarb-and-custard crumble. While the friendly, attentive staff please most visitors, 'erratic service' has been noted when this popular pub is packed. The cosmopolitan wine list is divided by style, making it easy to tell oaked from unoaked, full-bodied from light. Bottles start at £14.50.

Chef/s: Stephen Terry. **Open:** Tue to Sun L 12 to 3, Tue to Sat D 6.30 to 10. **Closed:** Mon, 25 and 26 Dec. **Meals:** alc (main courses £12 to £20). Set L £17.95 (2 courses) to £21. Set Sun L £18.95 (2 courses) to £22.50. **Service:** not inc. **Details:** Cards accepted. 70 seats. 20 seats outside. Separate bar. No mobile phones. Wheelchair access. Music. Children allowed. Car parking.

BROAD HAVEN

The Druidstone
Bohemian rhapsody
Broad Haven, SA62 3NE
Tel no: (01437) 781221
www.druidstone.co.uk
International | £30

In contrast with the modern-rustic styling that has become de rigueur for restaurants of a certain type, this rambling country house has a gorgeously authentic, rough-round-the-edges bohemian air. A family affair that has evolved through decades of ownership, it

:cupies one of the most heart-stoppingly beautiful :ations in the UK. The sea sparkles below you; watch from the terraces, or walk down to the secluded bay. ▪ck in the warm, the simple, hearty food ranges from ok-fried chicken with cashew nuts and oyster sauce pork fillet with bacon, Puy lentils and cider. Finish ith banoffee pie. Wines start at £11.80.

hef/s: Angus Bell, Andrew Bennett and Matt Ash. **pen:** all week L 12.30 to 2.30, D 7 to 9.30. **Meals:** alc ain courses £14 to £19). **Service:** not inc. **Details:** Cards ccepted. 36 seats. 50 seats outside. Separate bar. No usic. Wheelchair access. Children allowed. Car parking.

CAERNARFON

hiwafallen
tylish restaurant-with-rooms
andwrog, Caernarfon, LL54 5SW
l no: (01286) 830172
ww.rhiwafallen.co.uk
ritish | £35

eaders enjoy the 'welcoming' atmosphere and 'varied hoice of food' in this stylish former farmhouse set two acres of grounds. Renovated using natural aterials such as wood and slate, it retains its aditional charm, albeit with a contemporary edge. he menu skips with flair and imagination through xcellent Welsh ingredients, from a Pant-Ys-Gawn goats' heese and coconut fritter with peppered pineapple nd toasted brioche to a main course of twice-ooked belly of Anglesey pork with celeriac purée, ed cabbage, roast pears and star anise jus. Finish with arte Tatin and rum-and-raisin ice cream. House wine £14.95.

hef/s: Rob John. **Open:** Sun L 12.30 to 2, Tue to Sat D 7 o 9. **Closed:** Mon, 25 and 26 Dec, 1 and 2 Jan. **Meals:** Set Sun L £19.50. Set D £35 (3 courses). **ervice:** not inc. **Details:** Cards accepted. 20 seats. Air-on. Separate bar. No mobile phones. Wheelchair access. Music. Car parking.

MACHYNLLETH

Ynyshir Hall
Smart dining with frills and thrills
Eglwysfach, Machynlleth, SY20 8TA
Tel no: (01654) 781209
www.ynyshir-hall.co.uk
Modern British | £65

A 'charming, modest country house' that once belonged to Queen Victoria, Ynyshir Hall sits in a wooded valley surrounded by a glorious 14-acre garden. Beautiful at any time of year, the grounds are resplendent in April and May with rhododendrons and azaleas. Next door is a 1,000-acre RSPB reserve, originally part of the estate. Owned by Von Essen Hotels since 2006, Ynyshir is still run by owners-turned-shareholders Joan and Rob Reen. Rob (an artist) is

responsible for the pictures on the walls and the jewel-like colour schemes, which reflect the blaze of colour outside. Equally artful is chef Shane Hughes' exact and adventurous cooking. Described as 'sensational' and 'stimulating', this is dining with frills ('delicious' cheese straws and a 'wonderful' beetroot mousse among canapés in the bar) and thrills – notably one reader's 'spectacular' vanilla soufflé into which passion fruit sauce was poured at the table. In between come refined, beautifully balanced dishes with deceptively simple descriptions: perhaps crab lasagne with tomato fondue, followed by Welsh lamb with thyme and garlic potato, aubergine and tomato. The lengthy, international wine list kicks off at a reasonable £16 a bottle. Ask the 'excellent sommelier' to recommend some of the 25 wines by the glass.

Chef/s: Shane Hughes. **Open:** all week L 12.30 to 1.45, D 7 to 8.45. **Meals:** Set L £25 (2 courses) to £32. Set D £65 (5 courses). Sun L £32. Tasting menu £80. **Service:** not inc. **Details:** Cards accepted. 30 seats. Separate bar. No mobile phones. Wheelchair access. Music. Children allowed. Car parking.

Content brought to you by **The Good Food Guide 2010**. Please see pages 20–21 for further details.

Tourist Information Centres

When you arrive at your destination, visit an Official Partner Tourist Information Centre for quality assured help with accommodation and information about local attractions and events, or email your request before you go. To search for attractions and Tourist Information Centres on the move just text INFO to 62233, and a web link will be sent to your mobile phone. To find a Tourist Information Centre visit www.visitwales.co.uk

Aberaeron	The Quay	01545 570602	aberaerontic@ceredigion.gov.uk
Aberdulais Falls	The National Trust	01639 636674	aberdulaistic@nationaltrust.org.uk
Aberdyfi *	The Wharf Gardens	01654 767321	tic.aberdyfi@eryri-npa.gov.uk
Abergavenny	Swan Meadow	01873 853254	abergavenny.ic@breconbeacons.org
Aberystwyth	Terrace Road	01970 612125	aberystwythtic@ceredigion.gov.uk
Bala *	Pensarn Road	01678 521021	bala.tic@gwynedd.gov.uk
Bangor *	Town Hall	01248 352786	bangor.tic@gwynedd.gov.uk
Barmouth	The Station	01341 280787	barmouth.tic@gwynedd.gov.uk
Barry Island *	The Promenade	01446 747171	barrytic@valeofglamorgan.gov.uk
Beddgelert *	Canolfan Hebog	01766 890615	tic.beddgelert@eryri-npa.gov.uk
Betws y Coed	Royal Oak Stables	01690 710426	tic.byc@eryri-npa.gov.uk
Blaenau Ffestiniog *	Unit 3	01766 830360	tic.blaenau@eryri-npa.gov.uk
Blaenavon *	Blaenavon World Heritage Centre	01495 742333	Blaenavon.tic@torfaen.gov.uk
Borth *	Cambrian Terrace	01970 871174	borthtic@ceredigion.gov.uk
Brecon	Cattle Market Car park	01874 622485	brectic@powys.gov.uk
Bridgend	Bridgend Designer Outlet	01656 654906	bridgendtic@bridgend.gov.uk
Caerleon	5 High Street	01633 422656	caerleon.tic@newport.gov.uk
Caernarfon	Oriel Pendeitsh	01286 672232	caernarfon.tic@gwynedd.gov.uk
Caerphilly	The Twyn	029 2088 0011	tourism@caerphilly.gov.uk
Cardiff	The Old Library	08701 211 258	visitor@cardiff.gov.uk
Cardigan	Theatr Mwldan	01239 613230	cardigantic@ceredigion.gov.uk
Carmarthen	113 Lammas Street	01267 231557	carmarthentic@carmarthenshire.gov.uk
Chepstow	Castle Car Park	01291 623772	chepstow.tic@monmouthshire.gov.uk
Conwy	Castle Buildings	01492 592248	conwytic@conwy.gov.uk
Dolgellau	Ty Meirion	01341 422888	tic.dolgellau@eryri-npa.gov.uk

Fishguard Harbour	Ocean Lab	01348 872037	fishguardharbour.tic@pembrokeshire.gov.uk
Fishguard Town	Town Hall	01437 776636	fishguard.tic@pembrokeshire.gov.uk
Harlech *	Llys y Graig	01766 780658	tic.harlech@eryri-npa.gov.uk
Haverfordwest	Old Bridge	01437 763110	haverfordwest.tic@pembrokeshire.gov.uk
Holyhead	Stena Line	01407 762622	holyhead@nwtic.com
Knighton	Offa's Dyke Centre	01547 528753	oda@offasdyke.demon.co.uk
Llanberis *	41b High Street	01286 870765	llanberis.tic@gwynedd.gov.uk
Llandovery	Heritage Centre	01550 720693	llandovery.ic@breconbeacons.org
Llandudno	Library Building	01492 577577	llandudnotic@conwy.gov.uk
Llanelli	Millennium Coastal Park Visitor Centre	01554 777744	DiscoveryCentre@carmarthenshire.gov.uk
Llanfairpwllgwyngyll	Station Site	01248 713177	llanfairpwll@nwtic.com
Llangollen	Y Chapel	01978 860828	llangollen@nwtic.com
Merthyr Tydfil	14a Glebeland Street	01685 727474	tic@merthyr.gov.uk
Milford Haven *	94 Charles Street	01646 690866	milford.tic@pembrokeshire.gov.uk
Mold	Library Museum & Art Gallery	01352 759331	mold@nwtic.com
Monmouth	Market Hall	01600 713899	monmouth.tic@monmouthshire.gov.uk
Mumbles	The Methodist Church	01792 361302	info@mumblestic.co.uk
New Quay *	Church Street	01545 560865	newquaytic@ceredigion.gov.uk
Newport	Museum & Art Gallery	01633 842962	newport.tic@newport.gov.uk
Newport (pembs) *	2 Bank Cottages	01239 820912	NewportTIC@Pembrokeshirecoast.org.uk
Oswestry Mile End	Mile End Services	01691 662488	oswestrytourism@shropshire.gov.uk
Oswestry Town	The Heritage Centre	01691 662753	ot@oswestry-welshborders.org.uk
Pembroke	Visitor Centre	01437 776499	pembroke.tic@pembrokeshire.gov.uk
Penarth *	Penarth Pier	029 2070 8849	penarthtic@valeofglamorgan.gov.uk
Porthcawl *	Old Police Station	01656 786639	porthcawltic@bridgend.gov.uk
Porthmadog	High Street	01766 512981	porthmadog.tic@gwynedd.gov.uk
Presteigne *	The Judge's Lodging	01544 260650	presteignetic@powys.gov.uk
Pwllheli	Min y Don	01758 613000	pwllheli.tic@gwynedd.gov.uk
Rhyl	Rhyl Childrens Village	01745 355068	rhyl.tic@denbighshire.gov.uk
Saundersfoot *	The Barbecue	01834 813672	saundersfoot.tic@pembrokeshire.gov.uk
St Davids	Visitor Centre	01437 720392	enquiries@stdavids.pembrokeshirecoast.org.uk
Swansea	Plymouth Street	01792 468321	tourism@swansea.gov.uk
Tenby	Unit 2	01834 842402	tenby.tic@pembrokeshire.gov.uk
Welshpool	The Vicarage Gardens Car Park	01938 552043	ticwelshpool@btconnect.com
Wrexham	Lambpit Street	01978 292015	tic@wrexham.gov.uk

*seasonal opening

Regional Contacts and Information

For more information on accommodation, attractions, activities, events and holidays in Wales, contact the national tourism organisation below. The website has a wealth of information and you can order or download publications.

t: 0845 010 3300
www.visitwales.com and
www.visitwales.co.uk

Where to Stay

Entries appear alphabetically by town name in each region. A key to symbols appears on page 6. Maps start on page 394.

LLANDOVERY, Carmarthenshire Map ref 8B3

Erwlon Caravan & Camping

Brecon Road, Llandovery SA20 0RD
t (01550) 721021 e peter@erwlon.co.uk
w **erwlon.co.uk** GUEST REVIEWS LAST MINUTE OFFERS

(75)   £12.00–£13.00
(75)   £12.00–£13.00
(35)   £4.00–£13.00
75 touring pitches

Erwlon is an award- winning park with a warm welcome and excellent facilities including a heated amenity block, family rooms and landscaped super-pitches. Within easy walking distance of Llandovery at the foothills of the Brecon Beacons Erwlon is an ideal base for touring, walking or cycling in South - West Wales.

open All year
payment cash, cheques

directions 1 mile East of Llandovery (towards Brecon) off A40.

General Leisure

LLANELLI, Carmarthenshire Map ref 8A3

Pembrey Country Park Caravan Club Site

Pembrey, Llanelli SA16 0EJ
t (01554) 834369 f (01342) 410258
w **caravanclub.co.uk**

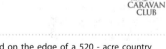

£14.00–£26.90
£14.00–£26.90
130 touring pitches

SPECIAL PROMOTIONS
Special member rates mean you can save your membership subscription in less than a week. Visit our website to find out more.

Situated on the edge of a 520 - acre country park with a vast range of outdoor sporting activities including use of a 7 mile stretch of safe, sandy beach a mile away. Bird and butterfly watchers will find the area a delight and there are a whole series of guided walks. Little ones will love the miniature railway.

open March 2010 to January 2011

directions From Pembrey follow signs to Country Park.

General

LLANGADOG, Carmarthenshire Map ref 8B3 SAT NAV SA19 9NG

Cymru Wales Touring & Camping Park ★★★★

(60) £10.00–£12.00
(60) £10.00–£12.00
(28) £10.00–£12.00
88 touring pitches

Abermarlais Caravan Park

Abermarlais Caravan Park, Llangadog, Carmarthenshire, Wales SA19 9NG
t (01550) 777868 **e** aberma@tiscali.co.uk
w abermarlaiscaravanpark.co.uk

A tranquil site in a beautiful woodland valley at the western end of the Brecon Beacons National Park, ideal for nature lovers and bird-watchers. The site's facilities are of the highest standard with excellent shower and toilet block. Camp shop and reception with comprehensive selection of groceries, gas, etc.

open 16 March to 16 November
payment credit/debit cards, cash, cheques

directions Situated on A40, 6 miles west of Llandovery or 6 miles east of Llandeilo. Signposted.

General **Leisure**

ABERAERON, Ceredigion Map ref 8A2 SAT NAV SA46 0JF

Cymru Wales ★★★★

£14.00–£24.00
£14.00–£24.00
£14.00–£24.00
100 touring pitches

SPECIAL PROMOTIONS
Rallies welcome outside school holidays. £9 per night per unit.

Aeron Coast Caravan Park

North Road, Aberaeron SA46 0JF
t (01545) 570349 **e** enquiries@aeroncoast.co.uk
w aeroncoast.co.uk ONLINE MAP ONLINE BOOKING

We are privileged to be part of Aberaeron with its picturesque harbour, shops and restaurants. River and coastal walks. Quiet out of high season but good leisure provision for families in school holidays including entertainment every evening. Apart from laundry, all facilities on-site including entertainment are free of charge.

open March to October
payment credit/debit cards, cash, cheques

directions On the main coastal road A487. Northern edge of Aberaeron. Brown signposting. Filling station at entrance.

General
Leisure

BORTH, Ceredigion Map ref 8A2

SAT NAV SY24 5LS

Cymru
Wales
Parc Gwyliau
Holiday Park
★★★

£7.00–£28.00
£198–£729
£153.00–£849.00

Brynowen Holiday Park
Borth, Aberystwyth SY24 5LS
t (01970) 871366 f (01970) 871125
w park resorts.com ONLINE MAP ONLINE BOOKING

Close to the beach and scenic inland areas. All facilities available on park including private club with nightly entertainment. **directions** From the north turn right onto the B4353 and follow the road through Borth. Just after the road turns left, the Park entrance is on your right. **open** March to October **payment** credit/debit cards, cheques

General Leisure

OAKFORD, Ceredigion Map ref 8A2

SAT NAV SA47 0RN

Cymru
Wales
Parc Teithio
Touring Park
★★★★★

£12.20–£25.10
£12.20–£25.10
50 touring pitches

Shawsmead Caravan Club Site
Oakford, Llanarth SA47 0RN
t (01545) 580423
w caravanclub.co.uk

THE
CARAVAN
CLUB

Situated about 4 miles from the coast which is dotted with lovely little bays and beaches ideal for the family. Llangranog is ideal for swimming and other water sports. **directions** From A487 into road signposted Ystrad Aeron, in 0.5 mile at cross roads continue onto road signposted Oakford. Site on right. **open** March to October

General

TOWYN, Conwy Map ref 8B1

SAT NAV LL22 9HG

Cymru
Wales
Parc Gwyliau
Holiday Park
★★★★

£8.00–£35.00
£7.00–£32.00
£171.00–£809.00

Ty Mawr Holiday Park
Towyn Road, Towyn LL22 9HG
t (01745) 832079
w parkresorts.com ONLINE MAP ONLINE BOOKING

A very large coastal holiday park with extensive leisure facilities including sports and recreational amenities, and club and eating outlets. The touring facilities are rather dated but clean. **directions** Take A55 to North Wales, exiting at junction 24, towards Abergele town centre, turn right at the lights signposted Rhyl. Park is three miles on the right. **open** March to October **payment** credit/debit cards, cheques

General Leisure

RHYL, Denbighshire Map ref 8B1   SAT NAV LL18 5NA

Parc Gwyliau
Holiday Park
★★★★

🚐 (420)   £59.00–£79.00
🚐 (5)   £129–£399
🚐 (55)   £129.00–£724.00

Golden Sands Holiday Park

Voryd, Rhyl LL18 5NA
t (01745) 343606 f (01745) 343549 e bookings@goldensandsrhyl.co.uk
w **goldensandsrhyl.co.uk**

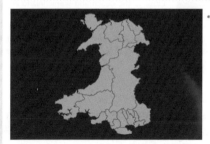

3 nights (weekend) from only £90.00, 4 nights (midweek) from only £77.00, 7 nights (week) from only £129.00. Prices are inclusive of facility passes, all bed linen, gas & electric. Newly refurbished entertainment complex.

open Easter through 31st October   **directions** Please contact us for directions
payment credit/debit cards, cash, cheques

General 🅿 ⚲ 🏊 📶 ☼ ✕   Leisure ∪ ⤵ ✎ 🍷 🎵 🔍 ⛰

BALA, Gwynedd Map ref 8B1   SAT NAV LL23 7SS

Parc Teithio a Gwersylla
Touring &
Camping Park
★★★★

🚐 (70)   £16.00–£20.00
🚐 (15)   £16.00–£20.00
⛺ (80)   £12.00–£16.00
🏠 (1)   £250–£550

Glanllyn Lakeside Caravan and Camping Park

Llanuwchllyn, Bala LL23 7SS
t (01678) 540227 e info@glanllyn.com
w **glanllyn.com** ONLINE MAP

Sixteen acres of level parkland with mature trees, and a meandering river, situated on the shore of Wales' largest natural lake in the Snowdonia National Park. **directions** Please contact us for directions **open** Mid-March to mid-October **payment** credit/debit cards, cash, cheques

General 🔥 🅿 ⚲ 🐾 🏊 📶 ☼ 🖥 🚲 🔌 🎦 ☎ 🚐   Leisure ► 🐎 ⤵ ⛰

CAERNARFON, Gwynedd Map ref 8A1   SAT NAV

Cymru
Wales

Parc Teithio
Touring Park
★★★★

THE
CARAVAN
CLUB

Coed Helen Caravan Club Site

Coed Helen Road, Caernarfon LL54 5RS
t (01286) 676770
w caravanclub.co.uk

£10.60–£23.60
£10.60–£23.60
45 touring pitches

SPECIAL PROMOTIONS
Special member rates mean
you can save your
membership subscription in
less than a week. Visit our
website to find out more.

A slightly sloping open site only ten- minutes
walk from the historic town of Caernarfon, with
views of the famous castle as you approach.
There's plenty to do here – walk Snowdon under
your own steam or take the Mountain Railway to
the top. Enjoy water-based activities on Llyn
Pedarn.

directions From A487 turn right into Fford Pant
Road, in 20 yards from right into Coed Helen
Road, in 0.5 mile turn left. Site on left in 200
yards.

General 🔲 🐕 🏔 🔌 🚻 💾
Leisure 🍷

LLANABER, Gwynedd Map ref 8A2   SAT NAV LL42 1RR

Cymru
Wales

Parc Teithio a Gwersylla
Touring &
Camping Park
★★★★★

Trawsdir Touring Caravans and Camping Park

Llanaber, Barmouth, Gwynedd LL42 1RR
t (01341) 280999 **e** enquiries@barmouthholidays.co.uk
w barmouthholidays.co.uk ONLINE MAP GUEST REVIEWS

£23.00–£30.00
£23.00–£30.00
(30) £15.00–£25.00
70 touring pitches

SPECIAL PROMOTIONS
Special Offer: September 7th
to 6th January Camping =
£10 per Night Camping with
electric = £15 per
NightTourers = £15 per
Night

Trawsdir is a luxury site situated on the mid-
Wales coast with magnificent views over
Cardigan Bay and the Lleyn Peninsula. £500,000
upgrade in 2007. Just a few minutes' walk from
miles of beautiful sandy beach. Ideal for families
and couples. Booking required.

open 1st March to 6th January
payment credit/debit cards, cash, cheques

directions 2.5 miles north of Barmouth on the
A496 on the mountain side of the main road.
Access for all sizes of vehicle. American RV's
catered for

General 🔲 🐕 🛒 🏔 ☀ 🗜 🚗 🔌 🚻 🚽 💾
Leisure 🎣 ⛺

BENLLECH, Isle of Anglesey Map ref 8A1   SAT NAV

Cymru Wales
Parc Teithio
Touring Park
★★★★

Penrhos Caravan Club Site
Brynteg, Benllech LL78 7JH
t (01248) 852617 f (01342) 410258
w **caravanclub.co.uk**

THE
CARAVAN
CLUB

🚐 £12.20–£25.30
🚏 £12.20–£25.30
90 touring pitches

SPECIAL PROMOTIONS
Special member rates mean
you can save your
membership subscription in
less than a week. Visit our
website to find out more.

An ideal site for a family holiday with views of
Snowdonia, 5 minutes drive from a safe and
sandy beach. A farm trail, bird sanctuary, 5 supe
beaches and the Sea Zoo will suit families with
young children. A trip on Snowdon's rack and
pinion mountain railway is a must for
breathtaking views.

open March to October

directions From B5110 (sp Llangefni) in about
1.75 miles continue straight on at cross roads
with California Public House. Site on right in
about 0.5 mile.

General 🔲 🐕 🅿 🔄 💡 🚻 🚐
Leisure ⛺

BRYNSIENCYN, Isle of Anglesey Map ref 8A1   SAT NAV LL61 6TX

Cymru Wales
Parc Teithio a Gwersylla
Touring &
Camping Park
★★★★★

Fron Caravan & Camping Park
Brynsiencyn, Llanfairpwllgwyngyll, Anglesey LL61 6TX
t (01248) 430310 e mail@froncaravanpark.co.uk
w **froncaravanpark.co.uk** ONLINE MAP

🚐 (39) £20.50–£26.50
🚏 (4) £20.50–£26.50
⛺ (35) £17.50–£26.50
74 touring pitches

Beautiful family- run park exclusively for touring caravans and tents.
Modern toilets including a disabled facility, swimming pool and
adventure playground. Ideally situated for beaches, tourist
attractions and walking/sighseeing. **directions** Please contact us for
directions **open** Easter-end September **payment** cash, cheques

General 🔲 🐕 🚲 🏕 🅿 ☼ 🔄 🚿 💡 🚻 🚻 🚐   Leisure ▶ ♻ ♪ 🎣 ⛺

LLANFECHELL, Isle of Anglesey Map ref 8A2   SAT NAV LL68 0RG

Cymru Wales
Parc Gwyliau
Holiday Park
★★★★

Waen Farm Caravan Park
Llanfechell, Cemaes Bay, Ynys Mon LL68 0RG
t (01407) 711561 e enquiries@waenfarm.co.uk
w **waenfarm.co.uk**

🏠 (9) £160.00–£350.00

Caravan Park, small pretty family- run farmland site in Llanfechell,
Anglesey, North Wales 2 miles from the beach town of Cemaes Bay.
5 static caravans for hire 4, 6 and 8 berths. **directions** From the
A5025 either from Valley (junction 3 A55) or A5025 via Amlwch. At
Cemaes Bay roundabout Llanfechell is signed. **open** 1 March to 31
October **payment** cash, cheques

General 🐕 ☼   Leisure ♪

MARIANGLAS, Isle of Anglesey Map ref 8A1

SAT NAV LL73 8NY

Cymru Wales
Parc Teithio Touring Park
★★★★★

Cae Mawr Caravan Club Site

Llangefni Road, Marianglas, Ynys Mon LL73 8NY
t (01342) 336842
w **caravanclub.co.uk**

CARAVAN CLUB

 (76)   £9.30–£21.00
£9.30–£21.00
76 touring pitches

A sheltered site with cheerful hydrangeas at the entrance and within a short drive of Anglesey's excellent beaches. The beaches are great for the family and nearby Traeth Bychan offers boat launching faclilties. **directions** From Marian - Glas (signposted B5110, Llangefri) site entrance on right in about 0.5 mile. **open** March to October

General 🐕 📶 🖰 📷

ABERGAVENNY, Monmouthshire Map ref 8B3

SAT NAV NP7 8DR

Cymru Wales
Parc Teithio Touring Park
★★★★

Pandy Caravan Club Site

Pandy, Abergavenny NP7 8DR
t (01873) 890370 f (01342) 410258
w **caravanclub.co.uk**

CARAVAN CLUB

(53)   £12.20–£25.10
(53)   £12.20–£25.10
53 touring pitches

SPECIAL PROMOTIONS
Special member rates mean you can save your membership subscription in less than a week. Visit www.caravanclub.co.uk to find out more.

The river Honddu runs on the western boundary and the majestic Skirrid rises in full view of the site. Visit the fine castle in Abergavenny or walk the Offa's Dyke Path. The area is littered with historical buildings which speak of the unsettled and sometimes battle-torn history of the borders.

open March to October
payment credit/debit cards, cash, cheques

directions From south do not go into Abergavenny, continue onto A465 (signposted Hereford). In 6.25 miles turn left by The Old Pandy Inn, onto minor road. Site on left after passing under railway bridge. Signposted.

General 📶 🐕 🖰 📷
Leisure 🎣

NEWPORT, Newport Map ref 8B3   SAT NAV NP10 8TW

Cymru Wales
Parc Teithio Touring Park
★★★★★

THE CARAVAN CLUB

Tredegar House & Park Caravan Club Site

Tredegar House, Coedkernew, Newport NP10 8TW
t (01342) 326944 f (01342) 410258
w **caravanclub.co.uk**

🚐 (80)   £12.20–£25.10
🚃 (80)   £12.20–£25.10
80 touring pitches

SPECIAL PROMOTIONS
Special member rates mean you can save your membership subscription in less than a week. Visit our website to find out more.

Seven acre site bordering one of the ornament lakes ideally located within a mile of the M4 ar only 7 miles from Cardiff. The beatutiful park with its ornamental lakes, 17th C orangery and garden, woodland, walled gardens and adventure playground opens throughout the year.

open All year
payment credit/debit cards, cash, cheques

directions M4 jct 28 via slip road. At roundabout turn onto A48 (signposted Tredega House). Roundabout 0.25 miles, turn left. Next roundabout, turn left into Tredegar House.

General 🔲 📶 🐕 🐾 ☼ 🔌 🚿 🚐
Leisure ▶ ⚓ ⛰

AMROTH, Pembrokeshire Map ref 8A3   SAT NAV SA67 8PR

Cymru Wales
Parc Gwyliau Holiday Park
★★★★★

Pendeilo Leisure Park

Amroth, Narberth SA67 8PR
t (01834) 831259 e pendeiloholidays@aol.com
w **pendeilo.co.uk** ONLINE MAP

🏠 (15)   £210.00–£730.00

SPECIAL PROMOTIONS
10% reduction on fortnightly bookings. Parties of 2 or less including senior citizens on selected weeks during low season 30% discount.

This is an award-winning park set amid the beautiful countryside of the Pembrokeshire Coast National Park and yet five minutes' drive from the wide expanse of Amroth's clean, golden sands. Choose from cosy cottage for 2, or luxury caravans. Central heating and double glazing available on top-of-range homes.

open March to October
payment credit/debit cards, cash, cheques

directions From Camarthen take A40 to St Clears (9 miles). Take A477 (signed Pembroke Dock). At Llanteg (8 miles) follow signs to Colby Woodlands. Park 0.5 miles on right.

General 🔲 🐕 🛁 📱 ☼
Leisure ∪ ⚓ 🎣 ⛰

FISHGUARD, Pembrokeshire Map ref 8A2

SAT NAV SA65 9ET

Fishguard Bay Caravan & Camping Park

Garn Gelli, Fishguard SA65 9ET
t (01348) 811415 f (01348) 811425 e inquiries@fishguardbay.com
w **fishguardbay.com**

(20)	£15.00–£18.00
(20)	£15.00–£18.00
(30)	£14.00–£21.00
(11)	£230.00–£525.00

20 touring pitches

Enjoy your stay on this beautiful stretch of Pembrokeshire National Park coastline. Ideal centre for walking and touring. Quiet, family-run park. Beautiful location, and superb views towards Fishguard harbour. **directions** Please contact us for directions **open** 1 March to 10 January **payment** credit/debit cards, cash, cheques

General Leisure

FISHGUARD, Pembrokeshire Map ref 8A2

SAT NAV SA65 9TA

Gwaun Vale Touring Park

Llanychaer, Fishguard SA65 9TA
t (01348) 874698 e margaret.harries@talk21.com
w **gwaunvale.co.uk** ONLINE MAP

(19)	£16.00–£18.00
(2)	£16.00–£18.00
(8)	£12.00–£18.00
(1)	£180.00–£350.00

29 touring pitches

Situated in the beautiful Gwaun Valley, overlooking Pembrokeshire National Park. Ideal for walking, sightseeing or just relaxing. Close to Irish ferry. **directions** Follow signs for B4313 from Fishguard for just over a mile. We are on right hand side. **open** April 1st to October 31st **payment** cash, cheques, euros

General Leisure

PEMBROKE, Pembrokeshire Map ref 8A3

SAT NAV SA71 5LN

Freshwater East Caravan Club Site

Freshwater East, Lamphey, Pembroke SA71 5LN
t (01342) 326944 f (01342) 410258
w **caravanclub.co.uk**

THE
CARAVAN
CLUB

	£12.20–£25.30
	£12.20
	£25.30

130 touring pitches

SPECIAL PROMOTIONS
Special member rates mean you can save your membership subscription in less than a week. Visit our website to find out more.

Only a few minutes from a beautiful stretch of beach and located in the Pembrokeshire Coast National Park this hill bottom site is flanked by treess on one side. Walk along the coastal paths with magnificent cliff top views or head to the walled town of Tenby with its colourful harbour, sandy beaches and boat trips.

open March to October

directions From A4139 signposted Tenby turn right onto B4584 and then right onto Trewent Hill. In 0.25 mile turn right into lane at Club sign.

General
Leisure

ST DAVIDS, Pembrokeshire Map ref 8A3   SAT NAV SA62 6QT

Cymru
Wales

Parc Gwyliau, Teithio a Gwersylla
Holiday, Touring & Camping Park
★★★★

🚐 (26)   £12.50–£16.50
🚃 (14)   £10.50–£16.50
⛺ (72)   £10.50–£14.50
🏠 (9)   £225.00–£440.00
112 touring pitches

SPECIAL PROMOTIONS
Senior Citizens discount
during low season (caravan
field only)

WALKERS / CYCLISTS
WELCOME

Caerfai Bay Caravan & Tent Park

St Davids, Haverfordwest, Pembrokeshire SA62 6QT
t (01437) 720274 **e** info@caerfaibay.co.uk
w caerfaibay.co.uk

A quiet family-run park, situated within the
Pembrokeshire Coast National Park. Caerfai Bay
sandy bathing beach within 200 metres and St
Davids within easy walking distance. Park
situated at end of Caerfai road on the right. No
dogs in tent fields during school summer
holidays.

open March to mid-November
payment credit/debit cards, cash, cheques

directions From Haverfordwest: A487 to St
Davids. Turn left at Visitor Centre, Caerfai
signposted. From Fishguard: A487 to St Davids.
Turn right at visitor centre.

General 🔲 📠 🏠 ☼ 🚿 🔌 🛗 🚽 ⚽
Leisure ▶ 🚲 🏊

ST DAVIDS, Pembrokeshire Map ref 8A3   SAT NAV SA62 6PR

Cymru
Wales

Parc Teithio
Touring Park
★★★★

🚐 (120)   £12.20–£25.30
🚃 (120)   £12.20–£25.30
120 touring pitches

SPECIAL PROMOTIONS
Special member rates mean
you can save your
membership subscription in
less than a week. Visit our
website to find out more.

Lleithyr Meadow Caravan Club Site

Whitesands, St Davids, Haverfordwest SA62 6PR
t 01437 720401
w caravanclub.co.uk

THE
CARAVAN
CLUB

A marvellous holiday site, open to the sun and
the scudding clouds nestled by three headlands
of the stunning Pembrokeshire Coast. Great for
energetic families, you can swim, surf, windsurf
and sail from Whitsands Bay which is just over a
mile from site. Anglers can fish in reservoir or
sea.

open April - October
payment credit/debit cards, cash, cheques

directions M4 to Carmarthen, A40 to
Haverfordwest, A487 towards St Davids. Before
entering St Davids turn right onto B4583,
crossroads. Turn sharp right opposite entrance
to St Davids golf club. Signposted.

General 🔲 🐕 📠 🏠 🔌 🛗 🚽 ⚽
Leisure ▶ 🏊 🏛

BRECON, Powys Map ref 8B3   SAT NAV LD3 0LD

Cymru Wales
★★★★

Anchorage Caravan Park
Bronllys, Brecon, Powys LD3 0LD
t (01874) 711246
w **anchoragecp.co.uk**

🚐 (60)	£12.00–£18.00
⛺ (10)	£12.00–£18.00
⚑ (40)	£12.00–£15.00

110 touring pitches

High-standard family-run park. Panoramic views of the Brecon Beacons National Park. Ideal for touring and walking mid and south Wales. **directions** Midway between Brecon and Hay-On-Wye. In centre of Bronllys village **open** All year **payment** cash, cheques

General 🅿 🐕 ♿ 🏪 📶 ☼ 🔌 🚻 🚿   Leisure ∪ ⛰

BRECON, Powys Map ref 8B3   SAT NAV LD3 7SH

Cymru Wales
Parc Teithio Touring Park
★★★★★

Brynich Caravan Park
Brecon LD3 7SH
t (01874) 623325
w **caravanclub.co.uk**

THE CARAVAN CLUB

🚐 (144)	£14.00–£26.90
⛺ (144)	£14.00–£26.90

144 touring pitches

SPECIAL PROMOTIONS
Special member rates mean you can save your membership subscription in less than a week. Visit our website to find out more.

Situated near the foothills of the Brecon Beacons, Brynich is well located with excellent facilities. It boasts some of the best views of the central Beacons, including Pen-y-Fan, Cribyn and Corn Du and is the ideal base for touring the towns and countryside of Mid and South Wales.

open March to November
payment credit/debit cards, cash, cheques

directions On A470 (Brecon - Builth Wells) 200 yards past roundabout junction A40 (eastern end Brecon By- pass).

General 🅿 🐕 🏪 📶 ☼ 🔌 🚻 🚿 ✕
Leisure ▶ ⛰

LLANBRYNMAIR, Powys Map ref 8B2   SAT NAV SY19 7EB

Cymru
Wales

Parc Teithio
Touring Park
★★★★

(37)   £8.10–£18.80
(37)   £8.10–£18.80
37 touring pitches

SPECIAL PROMOTIONS
Midweek discount: pitch fee
for standard pitches for
stays on any Tue, Wed or
Thu night outside peak
season dates will be
reduced by 50%.

Gwern Y Bwlch Caravan Club Site
Llanbrynmair SY19 7EB
t (01650) 521351
w **caravanclub.co.uk**

CARAVAN
CLUB

A gem of a site in a lovely setting, lost in Mid
Wales between Snowdonia and
Montgomeryshire. A great site for country
pursuits like birdwatching or fishing. Don't forget
your binoculars – the RSPB has reserves at Lake
Vyrnwy and Ynys-Hir. For anglers, try your luck
at Llyn Clywedog reservoir.

open April to October
payment credit/debit cards, cash, cheques

directions From A470 in 4 miles turn left at
Club Site sign.

General 🐕 📶 💬 🚻 ♿ 🅿
Leisure 🎵

SWANSEA, Swansea Map ref 8B3   SAT NAV SA4 3QP

Cymru
Wales

Parc Teithio
Touring Park
★★★★

(135)   £12.20–£25.30
(135)   £12.20–£25.30
135 touring pitches

Gowerton Caravan Club Site
Pont Y Cob Road, Gowerton SA4 3QP
t (0792) 873050 f (01342) 410258
w **caravanclub.co.uk**

CARAVAN
CLUB

A level, well-designed site within an easy drive of the whole range
of superb beaches on the Gower Peninsula, such as Oxwich and
Caswell Bay. **directions** From B2496 turn right at traffic lights. In
0.5 miles turn right at traffic lights into Pont-y-Cob road. Site on
right. **open** March to November **payment** credit/debit cards, cash,
cheques

General 🔲 🐕 📶 💬 🚻 ♿ Leisure ⛰

2010

The definitive guide to Britain's finest

Historic Houses & Gardens
Castles and Heritage Sites

HUDSON's

Open to visitors

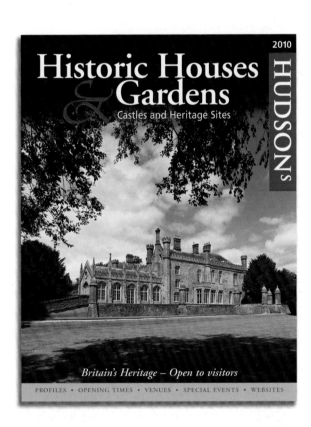

Map 1

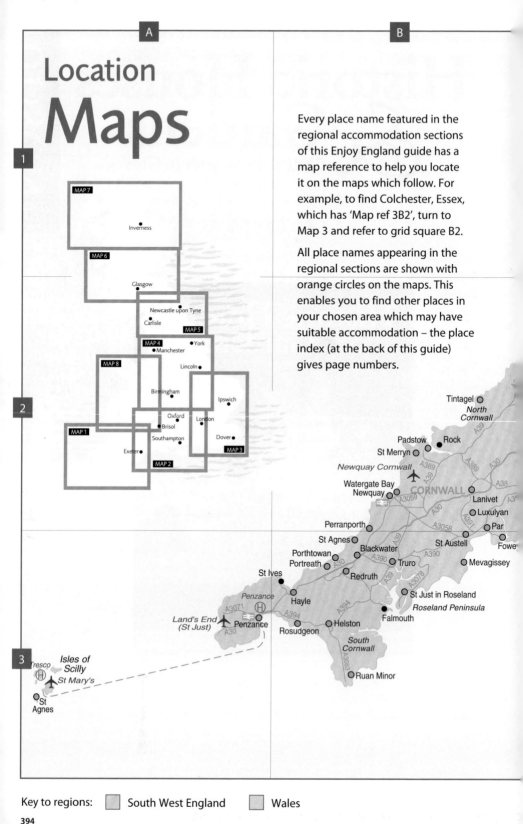

Location
Maps

Every place name featured in the regional accommodation sections of this Enjoy England guide has a map reference to help you locate it on the maps which follow. For example, to find Colchester, Essex, which has 'Map ref 3B2', turn to Map 3 and refer to grid square B2.

All place names appearing in the regional sections are shown with orange circles on the maps. This enables you to find other places in your chosen area which may have suitable accommodation – the place index (at the back of this guide) gives page numbers.

Key to regions:　South West England　　Wales

Map 1

ENGLISH CHANNEL

0   25 Miles

0   40 Km

N

Map 2

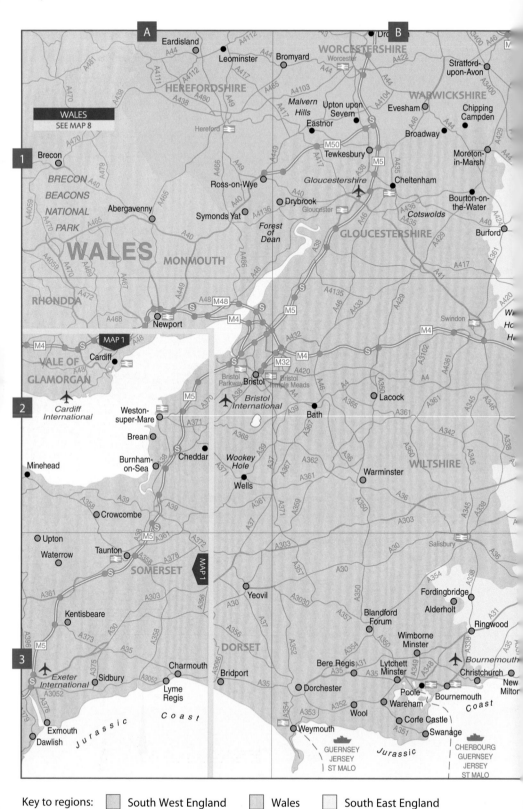

Key to regions: ⬛ South West England ⬛ Wales ⬜ South East England

Map 2

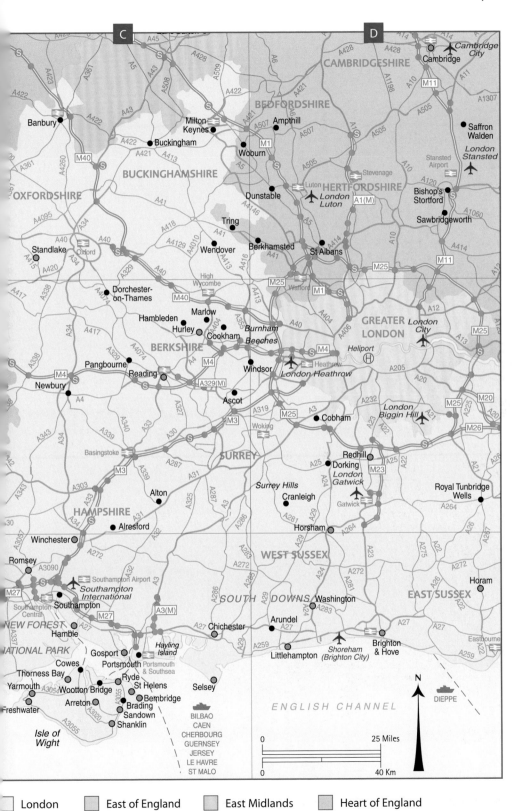

London   East of England   East Midlands   Heart of England

Orange circles indicate accommodation within the regional sections of this guide

Map 3

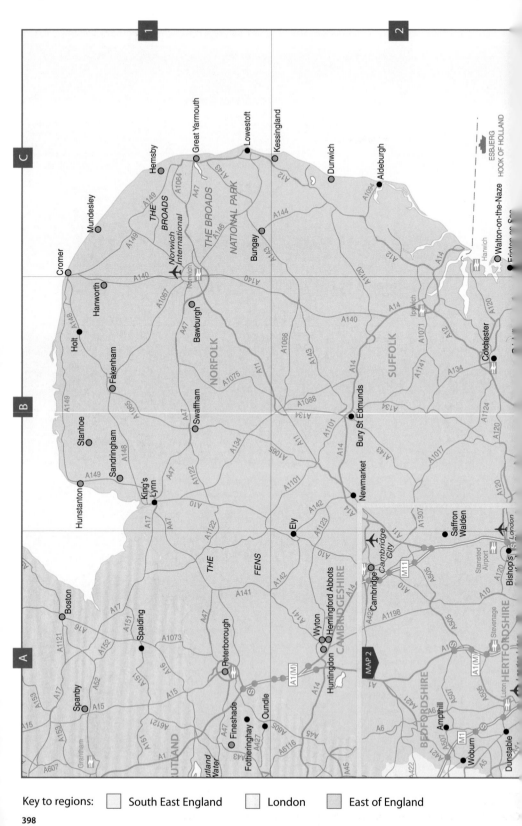

Key to regions: ☐ South East England ☐ London ☐ East of England

Map 3

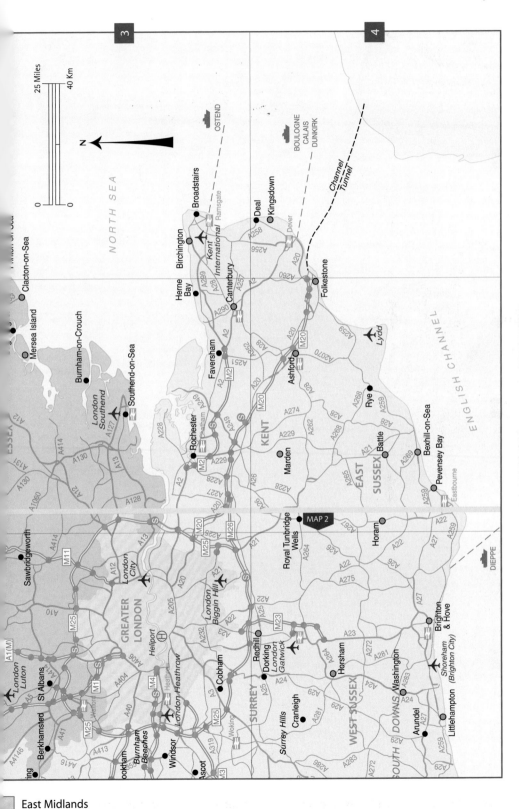

East Midlands

Orange circles indicate accommodation within the regional sections of this guide

Map 4

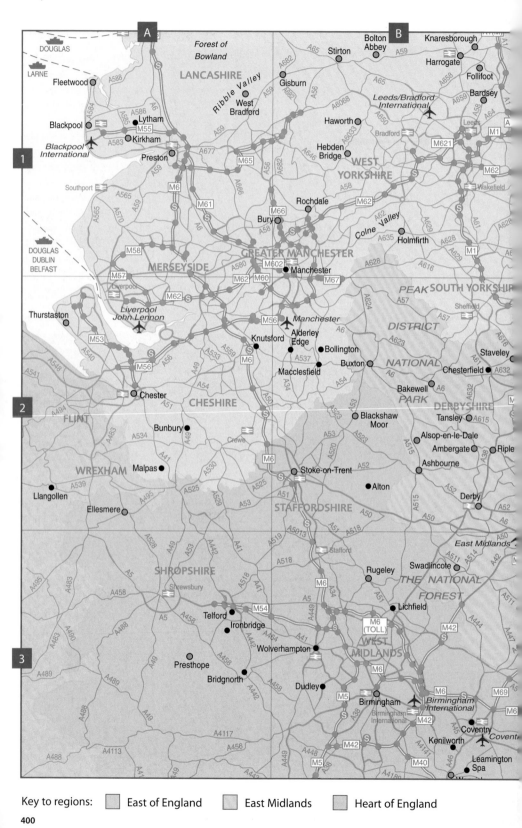

Key to regions: ▢ East of England ▢ East Midlands ▢ Heart of England

Map 4

C   D

0   25 Miles
0   40 Km

N

Claxton
York
A59
A166
A614
A165
Skipsea
EAST RIDING
OF YORKSHIRE
Brandesburton
A1079
Yorkshire
Wolds
A164
A163
A1079
A164
Little
Weighton
A63
A64
A19
A182
A1041
A63
A614
M62
A63
Hull
Roos
Yorkshire Coast
A1033
M)
S
M62
M18
A161
NORTH
LINCOLNSHIRE
A1077
Thorne
M181
A15
A180
Humberside
International
Grimsby
Cleethorpes
ROTTERDAM
ZEEBRUGGE
A19
M180
Scunthorpe
A18
A1084
A46
A16
Doncaster
A635
Robin Hood
Doncaster
Sheffield
A161
Brigg
A1173
S
A159
A18
M18
A1(M)
S
A631
A631
A631
A1031
A57
A620
A156
A15
A46
A157
A153
A16
A157
Mablethorpe
A619
Worksop
A1
Retford
A1500
A158
A153
A52
A158
A1133
Scarle
A158
Lincoln
Horncastle
A158
A158
A46
Skegness
A607
A16
Burgh-le-Marsh
NOTTINGHAMSHIRE
A6075
A617
A616
A15
LINCOLNSHIRE
Mansfield
Newstead Abbey
A617
Southwell
A46
Newark
A17
MAP 3
A52
A60
A612
A1
A153
Hunstanton
Eastwood
A607
A153
A17
A1121
Boston
A149
Stanhoe
S
A606
A46
Nottingham
A52
A15
A52
A152
Sandringham
A148
Melton Mowbray
A607
A151
A151
Spalding
A17
King's
Lynn
M1
A6
A607
A606
A151
A16
A1073
A47
A47
LEICESTERSHIRE
RUTLAND
A612
A15
A10
A1122
M69
A50
Leicester
A47
Rutland
Water
A47
THE
A1122
A134
M6
A5199
A6
A47
Fineshade
Peterborough
FENS
A6
Market
Harborough
A427
MAP 3
Fotheringhay
A605
Oundle
A141
A142
A101
A11
A5
A14
A4304
A427
A6116
A45
Ely
A1065
M45
Rugby
A5199
A5208
A1(M)
A14
Wyton
A141
A1123
A142
A10
NORTHAMPTONSHIRE
A43
A45
Huntingdon
Hemingford Abbots
A14
M4
Earls Barton
CAMBRIDGESHIRE
A14
A64
Doncaster
A1
A17
A58
Grantham
Spanby
A607
A151
A1

☐ Yorkshire   ☐ North West England   ☐ Wales

Orange circles indicate accommodation within the regional sections of this guide

Map 5

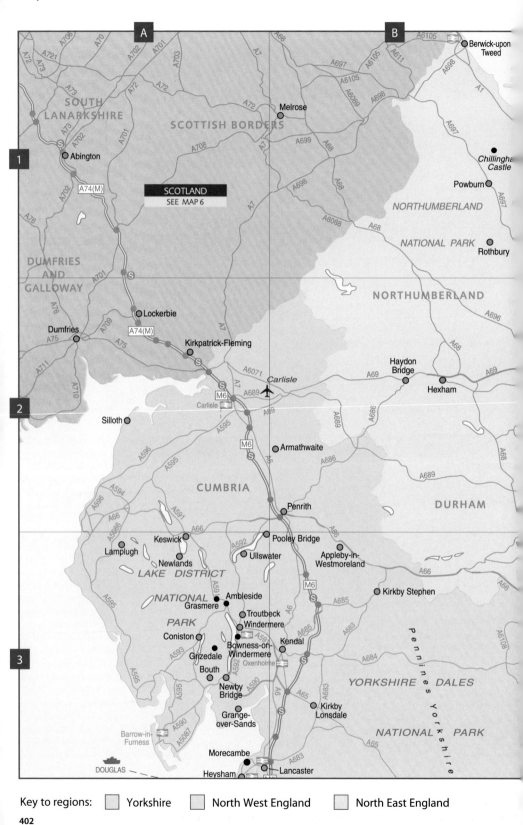

A **B**

Berwick-upon-Tweed

SOUTH LANARKSHIRE

SCOTTISH BORDERS

Melrose

1

Abington

Chillingha Castle

Powburn

SCOTLAND
SEE MAP 6

NORTHUMBERLAND

NATIONAL PARK

Rothbury

DUMFRIES AND GALLOWAY

NORTHUMBERLAND

Lockerbie

Dumfries

Kirkpatrick-Fleming

Haydon Bridge

Hexham

Carlisle

2

Silloth

Carlisle

Armathwaite

CUMBRIA

DURHAM

Penrith

Keswick

Pooley Bridge

Lamplugh

Ullswater

Appleby-in-Westmoreland

Newlands

LAKE DISTRICT

NATIONAL

Ambleside

Grasmere

Troutbeck

Kirkby Stephen

Coniston

Windermere

PARK

Bowness-on-Windermere

Kendal

Grizedale

Bouth

Oxenholme

3

Newby Bridge

YORKSHIRE DALES

Barrow-in-Furness

Grange-over-Sands

Kirkby Lonsdale

NATIONAL PARK

DOUGLAS

Morecambe

Heysham

Lancaster

Key to regions: ☐ Yorkshire ☐ North West England ☐ North East England

402

Map 5

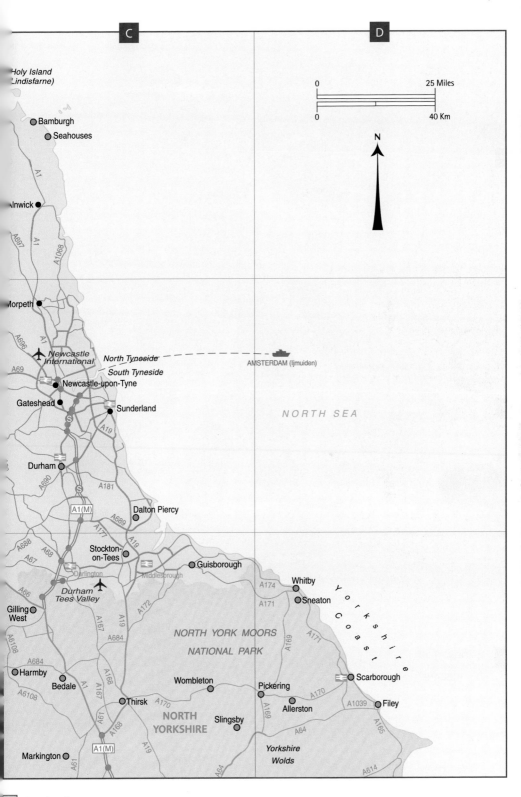

C

D

Holy Island
(Lindisfarne)

0   25 Miles

0   40 Km

N

Bamburgh

Seahouses

Alnwick

A1

A697

A1068

A1

Morpeth

A696

Newcastle
International

North Tyneside

AMSTERDAM (Ijmuiden)

NORTH SEA

South Tyneside

A69

Newcastle-upon-Tyne

Gateshead

Sunderland

S

A19

Durham

A690

A181

S

A1(M)

Dalton Piercy

A689

A177

A19

A688

A68

Stockton-
on-Tees

A67

Darlington

Middlesbrough

Guisborough

Whitby

A174

Durham
Tees Valley

A66

A172

A171

Sneaton

Yorkshire Coast

Gilling
West

A167

A19

A6108

A684

NORTH YORK MOORS

A169

A171

NATIONAL PARK

A684

Harmby

A168

Bedale

A1

A167

Wombleton

Pickering

Scarborough

A6108

Thirsk

A170

A170

Allerston

A1039

Filey

A169

Markington

A168

NORTH
YORKSHIRE

Slingsby

A64

A165

A61

A1(M)

A19

Yorkshire
Wolds

A64

A614

Scotland

Orange circles indicate accommodation within the regional sections of this guide

Map 6

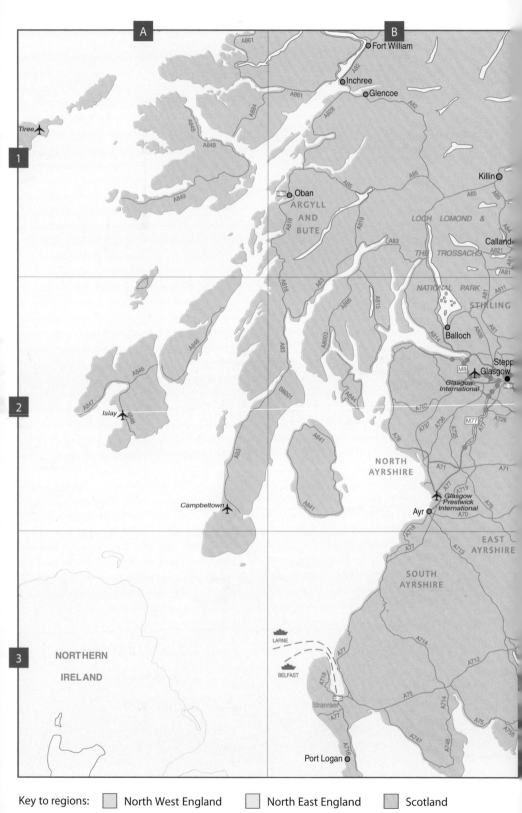

Key to regions: ☐ North West England ☐ North East England ☐ Scotland

Map 6

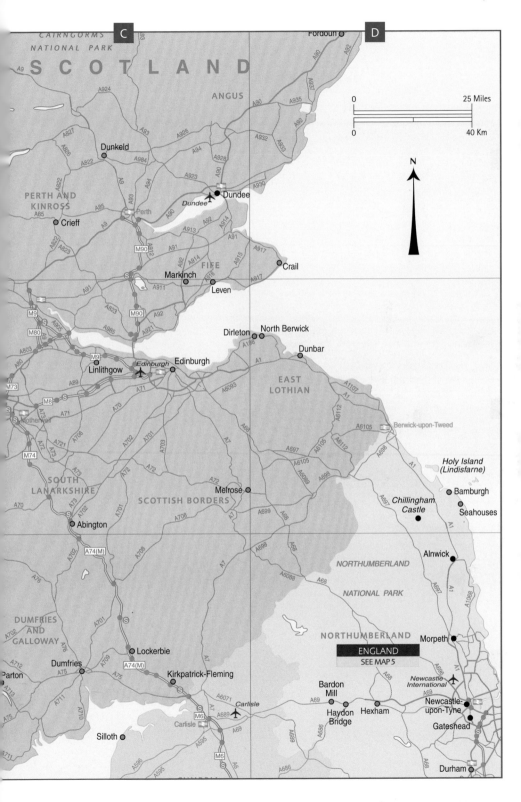

Map 7

A

B

1

2

WESTERN ISLES

Isle of Lewis

A857

A858

A859

✈
Stornoway

A896

Harris

A859

A838

A834

A837

A837

A837

A835

A832

A832

North Uist

A867

✈
Benbecula

A865

South Uist

3

✈
Barra

A865

A851

A850

A851

A87

A855

A863

A87

Skye

A832

Kinlochewe ⊙

A896

A890

A896

A890

A832

HIGHLAND

🚂 Kyle of Lochalsh

A890

Balmacara ⊙

A87

Shiel
⊙ Bridge

A87

A887

A87

A830

A830

Key to regions: Scotland

Map 7

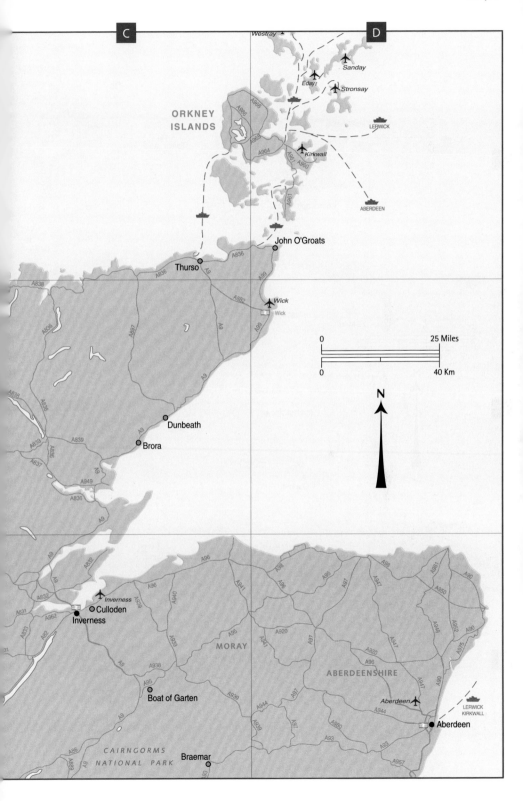

Map 8

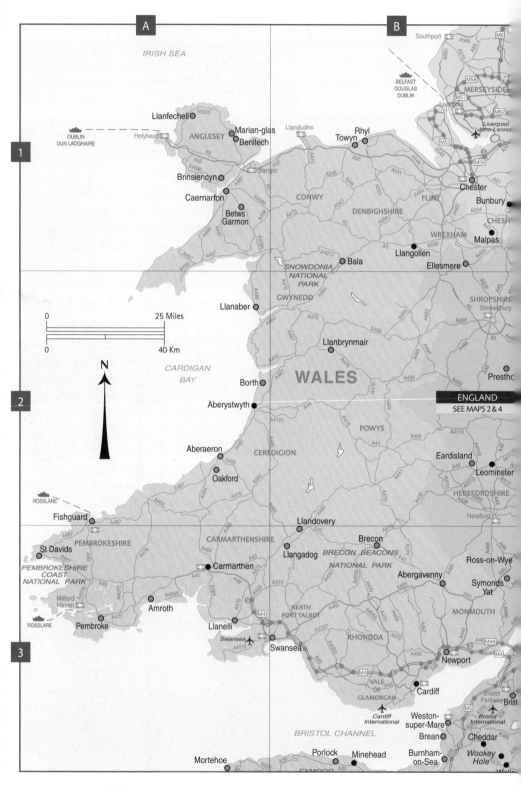

Key to regions: [ ] Wales

Orange circles indicate accommodation within the regional sections of this guide

Map 9

London

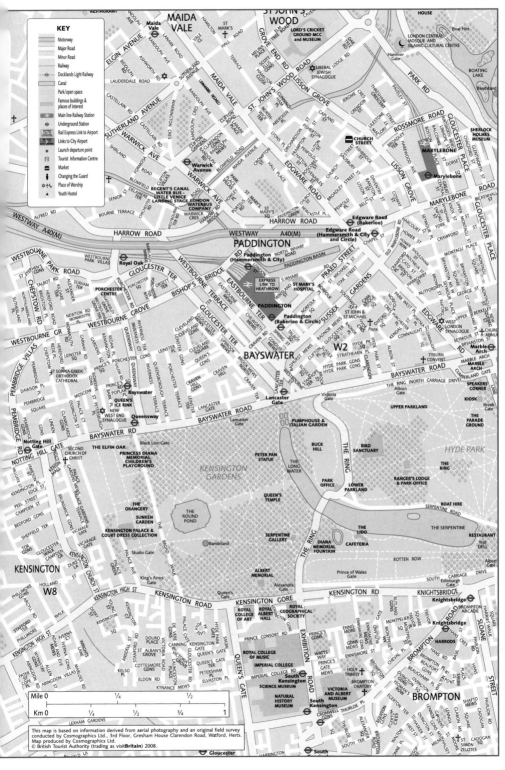

Map 10

London

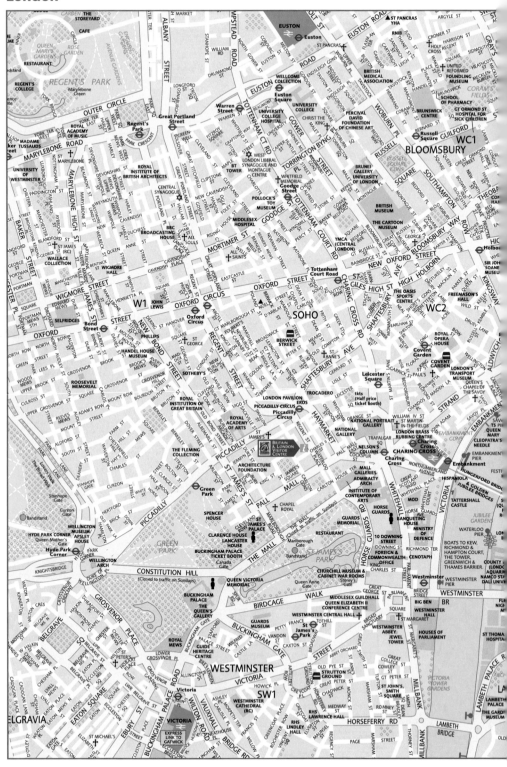

Map 10

London

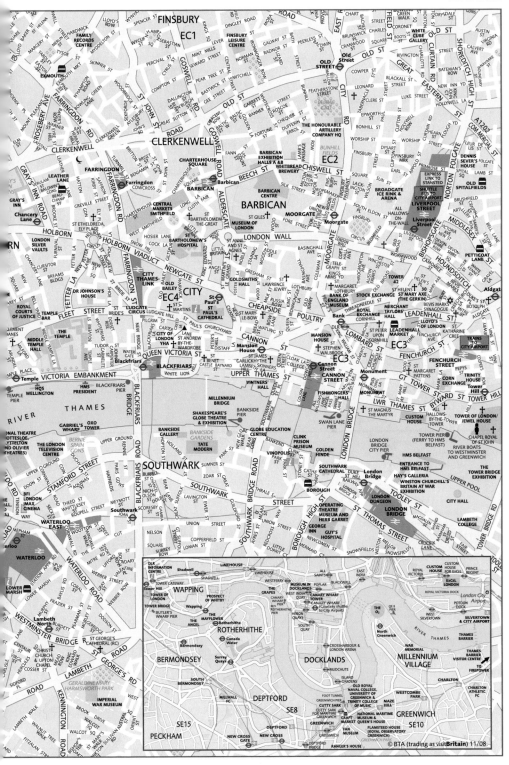

Here are just some of the most popular long distance routes on the 12,000 mile Sustrans National Cycle Network. To see the Network in it's entirety and to find routes near you, **visit www.sustrans.org.uk**

Sustrans is the UK's leading sustainable transport charity working on practical projects to enable people to choose to travel in ways which benefit their health and the environment.

68 National Cycle Network Route Number

Long Distance Routes

1. Aberdeen to John O'Groats
2. Lochs & Glens North
3. Oban to Campbeltown
4. Forth to Clyde
5. Lochs & Glens South
6. Coast & Castles Cycle Route
7. Pennine Cycleway - North Pennines
8. Hadrian's Cycleway
9. Sea to Sea
10. Pennine Cycleway - South Pennines & the Dales
11. Derby to York
12. Hull to Fakenham
13. East of England
14. South Midlands Cycle Route
15. Thames Valley Cycle Route
16. Garden of England
17. Downs & Weald Cycle Route
18. Devon Coast to Coast
19. The Cornish Way
20. The West Country Way
21. The Severn & Thames
22. Celtic Trail East
23. Celtic Trail West
24. Lon Las Cymru South
25. Lon Las Cymru North

Map reproduced from Ordnance Survey material with the permission of Ordnance Survey on behalf of the Contoller of Her Majesty's Stationery Office © Crown copyright. Unauthorised reproduction infringes Crown copyright and may lead to prosecution or civil proceedings.
Licence number 100020852 (2009)

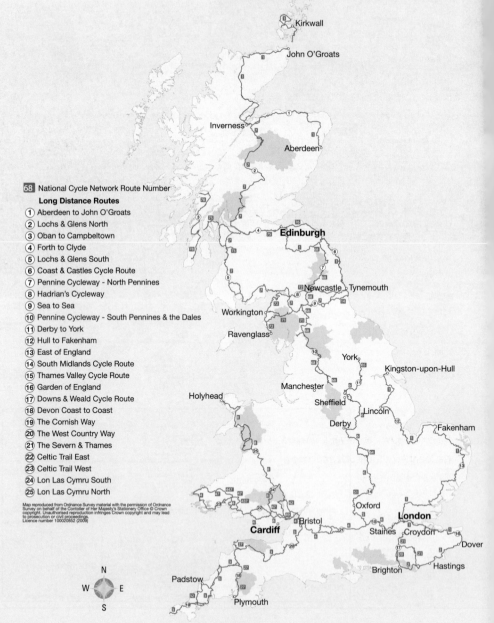

Further Information

Advice and information

Making a booking

When enquiring about a place to stay, make sure you check prices, the quality rating, and other important details. You will also need to state your requirements clearly and precisely.

Booking by letter or email

Misunderstandings can easily happen over the telephone, so do request a written confirmation together with details of any terms and conditions.

Deposits and advance payments

In the case of caravan, camping and touring parks, and holiday villages the full charge often has to be paid in advance. This may be in two instalments – a deposit at the time of booking and the balance by, say, two weeks before the start of the booked period.

Cancellations

Legal contract

When you accept a booking that is offered to you, by telephone or in writing, you enter a legally binding contract with the proprietor. This means that if you cancel or fail to take up your booking or leave early, the proprietor may be entitled to compensation if he or she cannot re-let for all or a good part of the booked period. You will probably forfeit any deposit you have paid and may well be asked for an additional payment.

At the time of booking you should be advised of what charges would be made in the event of cancelling the accommodation or leaving early. If this is not mentioned you should ask so that future disputes can be avoided. The proprietor cannot make a claim until after the booked period, and during that time he or she should make every effort to re-let the accommodation. If there is a dispute it is sensible for both sides to seek legal advice on the matter. If you do have to change your travel plans, it is in your own interests to let the proprietor know in writing as soon as possible, to give them a chance to re-let your accommodation.

And remember, if you book by telephone and are asked for your credit card number, you should check whether the proprietor intends charging your credit card account should you later cancel your booking. A proprietor should not be able to charge your credit card account with a cancellation fee unless he or she has made this clear at the time of your booking and you have agreed. However, to avoid later disputes, we suggest you check whether this is the intention.

Insurance

A travel or holiday insurance policy will safeguard you if you have to cancel or change your holiday plans both abroad and in the UK. You can arrange a policy quite cheaply through your insurance company or travel agent.

Finding a park

Tourist signs similar to the one shown here are designed to help visitors find their park. They clearly show whether the park is for tents or caravans or both.

Tourist information centres throughout Britain are able to give campers and caravanners information about parks in their areas. Some tourist information centres have camping and caravanning advisory services that provide details of park availability and often assist with park booking.

Electric hook-up points

Most parks now have electric hook-up points for caravans and tents. Voltage is generally 240v AC, 50 cycles. Parks may charge extra for this facility, and it is advisable to check rates when making a booking.

Avoiding peak season

In the summer months of June to September, parks in popular areas such as North Wales, Cumbria, the West Country or the New Forest in Hampshire may become full. Campers should aim to arrive at parks early in the day or, where possible, should book in advance. Some parks have overnight holding areas for visitors who arrive late. This helps to prevent disturbing other campers and caravanners late at night and means that fewer visitors are turned away. Caravans or tents are directed to a pitch the following morning.

Other caravan and camping places

If you enjoy making your own route through Britain's countryside, it may interest you to know that the Forestry Commission operates campsites in Britain's Forest Parks as well as in the New Forest. Some offer reduced charges for youth organisations on organised camping trips, and all enquiries about them should be made, well in advance of your intended stay, to the Forestry Commission.

Bringing pets to Britain

Dogs, cats, ferrets and some other pet mammals can be brought into the UK from certain countries without having to undertake six months' quarantine on arrival provided they meet all the rules of the Pet Travel Scheme (PETS).

For full details, visit the PETS website at
w defra.gov.uk/animalh/quarantine/index.htm
or contact the PETS Helpline

t +44 (0)870 241 1710

e quarantine@animalhealth.gsi.gov.uk
Ask for fact sheets which cover dogs and cats, ferrets or domestic rabbits and rodents.

What to expect at holiday, touring and camping parks

In addition to fulfilling its statutory obligations, including having applied for a certificate under the Fire Precautions Act 1971 (if applicable) and holding public liability insurance, and ensuring that all caravan holiday homes/chalets for hire and the park and all buildings and facilities thereon, the fixtures, furnishings, fittings and decor are maintained in sound and clean condition and are fit for the purposes intended, the management is required to undertake the following:

- To ensure high standards of courtesy, cleanliness, catering and service appropriate to the type of park;

- To describe to all visitors and prospective visitors the amenities, facilities and services provided by the park and/or caravan holiday homes/chalets whether by advertisement, brochure, word of mouth or other means;

- To allow visitors to see the park or caravan holiday homes/chalets for hire, if requested, before booking;

- To present grading awards and/or any other national tourist board awards unambiguously;

- To make clear to visitors exactly what is included in prices quoted for the park or caravan holiday homes/chalets, meals and refreshments, including service charge, taxes and other surcharges. Details of charges, if any, for heating or for additional services or facilities available should also be made clear;

- To adhere to, and not to exceed, prices current at time of occupation for caravan holiday homes/chalets or other services;

- To advise visitors at the time of booking, and subsequently if any change, if the caravan holiday home/chalet or pitch offered is in a different location or on another park, and to indicate the location of this and any difference in comfort and amenities;

- To give each visitor, on request, details of payments due and a receipt if required;

- To advise visitors at the time of booking of the charges that might be incurred if the booking is subsequently cancelled;

- To register all guests on arrival;

- To deal promptly and courteously with all visitors and prospective visitors, including enquiries, requests, reservations, correspondence and complaints;

- To allow a national tourist board representative reasonable access to the park and/or caravan holiday homes/chalet whether by prior appointment or on an unannounced assessment, to confirm that the VisitEngland Code of Conduct is being observed and that the appropriate quality standard is being maintained;

- The operator must comply with the provision of the caravan industry Codes of Practice;

- To welcome all guests courteously and without discrimination in relation to gender, sexual orientation, disability, race, religion or belief.

Advice and information

The operator/manager is required to undertake the following:

- To maintain standards of guest care, cleanliness, and service appropriate to the type of establishment;

- To describe accurately in any advertisement, brochure, or other printed or electronic media, the facilities and services provided;

- To make clear to visitors exactly what is included in all prices quoted for accommodation, including taxes, and any other surcharges. Details of charges for additional services/facilities should also be made clear;

- To give a clear statement of the policy on cancellations to guests at the time of booking, i.e. by telephone, fax, email as well as information given in a printed format;

- To adhere to, and not to exceed prices quoted at the time of booking for accommodation and other services;

- To advise visitors at the time of booking, and subsequently of any change, if the accommodation offered is in an unconnected annexe or similar, and to indicate the location of such accommodation and any difference in comfort and/or amenities from accommodation in the establishment;

- To give each visitor, on request, details of payments due and a receipt, if required;

- To register all guests on arrival;

- To deal promptly and courteously with all enquiries, requests, bookings and correspondence from visitors;

- To ensure complaint handling procedures are in place and that complaints received are investigated promptly and courteously and that the outcome is communicated to the visitor;

- To give due consideration to the requirements of visitors with special needs, and to make suitable provision where applicable;

- To provide public liability insurance or comparable arrangement and to comply with applicable planning, safety and other statutory requirements;

- To allow a national tourist board representative reasonable access to the establishment, on request, to confirm the Code of Conduct is being observed;

- To welcome all guests courteously and without discrimination in relation to gender, sexual orientation, disability, race, religion or belief.

Comments and complaints

Information

The proprietors themselves supply the descriptions of their establishments and other information for the entries (except ratings). They have all signed a declaration that their information conforms to The Consumer Protection from Unfair Trading Regulations 2008. VisitEngland cannot guarantee the accuracy of information in this guide, and accepts no responsibility for any error or misrepresentation.

All liability for loss, disappointment, negligence or other damage caused by reliance on the information contained in this guide, or in the event of bankruptcy or liquidation or cessation of trade of any company, individual or firm mentioned, is hereby excluded. We strongly recommend that you carefully check prices and other details when you book your accommodation.

Problems

Of course, we hope you will not have cause for complaint, but problems do occur from time to time.

If you are dissatisfied with anything, make your complaint to the management immediately. Then the management can take action at once to investigate the matter and put things right. The longer you leave a complaint, the harder it is to deal with it effectively.

In certain circumstances, VisitEngland may look into complaints. However, VisitEngland has no statutory control over establishments or their methods of operating. VisitEngland cannot become involved in legal or contractual matters or in seeking financial compensation.

If you do have problems that have not been resolved by the proprietor and which you would like to bring to our attention, please write to:

England
Quality in Tourism, Security House, Ashchurch, Tewkesbury, Gloucestershire GL20 8NB

Scotland
Customer Feedback Department, VisitScotland, Cowan House, Inverness Retail and Business Park, Inverness IV2 7GF

Wales
VisitWales, Ty Glyndwr, Treowain Enterprise Park, Machynlleth, Powys SY20 8WW

Useful contacts

British Holiday & Home Parks Association

Chichester House, 6 Pullman Court,
Great Western Road, Gloucester GL1 3ND
t (01452) 526911 (enquiries and brochure requests)
w parkholidayengland.org.uk

Professional UK park owners are represented by the British Holiday and Home Parks Association. Over 3,000 parks are in membership, and each year welcome millions of visitors seeking quality surroundings in which to enjoy a good value stay.

Parks provide caravan holiday homes and lodges for hire, and pitches for your own touring caravan, motor home or tent. On many, you can opt to buy your own holiday home.

A major strength of the UK's park industry is its diversity. Whatever your idea of holiday pleasure, there's sure to be a park which can provide it. If your preference is for a quiet, peaceful holiday in tranquil rural surroundings, you'll find many idyllic locations.

Alternatively, many parks are to be found at our most popular resorts – and reflect the holiday atmosphere with plenty of entertainment and leisure facilities. And for more adventurous families, parks often provide excellent bases from which to enjoy outdoor activities.

Literature available from BH&HPA includes a guide to over 600 parks which have this year achieved the David Bellamy Conservation Award for environmental excellence.

The Camping and Caravanning Club

Greenfields House, Westwood Way,
Coventry CV4 8JH
t 0845 130 7631
t 0845 130 7633 (advance bookings)
w campingandcaravanningclub.co.uk

Discover the peace and quiet of over 100 award-winning Club Sites. Experience a different backdrop to your holiday every time you go away, with sites in the lakes and mountains, coastal and woodland glades or cultural and heritage locations.

The Club is proud of its prestigious pedigree and regularly achieves awards for spotless campsites, friendly service and caring for the environment – a guarantee that you will enjoy your holiday.

Non-members are welcome at the majority of our sites and we offer special deals for families, backpackers, overseas visitors and members aged 55 and over. Recoup your membership fee in just six nights and gain access to over 1,300 Certificated Sites around the country.

For more details please refer to our entries listed at the back of this publication or if you require any more information on what The Friendly Club can offer you then telephone 0845 130 7632. Or call to request your free guide to The Club.

The Caravan Club

East Grinstead House,
East Grinstead,
West Sussex RH19 1UA
t (01342) 326944
w caravanclub.co.uk

The Caravan Club offers 200 sites in the UK and Ireland. These include city locations such as London, Edinburgh, York and Chester, plus sites near leading heritage attractions such as Longleat, Sandringham, Chatsworth and Blenheim Palace. A further 30 sites are in National Parks.

Virtually all pitches have an electric hook-up point. The toilet blocks and play areas are of the highest quality. Friendly, knowledgeable site wardens are on hand too.

Most Caravan Club Sites are graded four or five stars according to The British Graded Holiday Parks Scheme, run by VisitBritain, so that you can be assured of quality at all times. Over 130 sites are open to non-members, but why not become a member and gain access to all sites, plus a further 2,500 Certificated Locations – rural sites for no more than five vans. Tent campers are welcome at over 60 sites.

Join The Club and you can save the cost of your subscription fee in just five nights with member discounts on site fees!

Forest Holidays

Heart of the National Forest, Bath Yard, Moira, Derbyshire DE12 6BA

t 0845 130 8223 (cabins)
t 0845 130 8224 (campsites)
w forestholidays.co.uk

Forest Holidays, a new partnership between the Forestry Commission and the Camping and Caravanning Club, have over 20 camping and caravan sites in stunning forest locations throughout Great Britain in addition to three cabin sites. Choose from locations such as the Scottish Highlands, the New Forest, Snowdonia National Park, the Forest of Dean, or the banks of Loch Lomond. Some sites are open all year and dogs are welcome at most. Advance bookings are accepted for many sites.

For a unique forest experience, call Forest Holidays for a brochure on 0845 130 8224 or visit our website.

The Motor Caravanners' Club Ltd

FREEPOST (TK 1292), Twickenham TW2 5BR

t (020) 8893 3883
f (020) 8893 8324
e info@motorcaravanners.eu
w motorcaravanners.eu

The Motor Caravanners' Club is authorised to issue the Camping Card International (CCI). It also produces a monthly magazine, Motor Caravanner, for all members. Member of The Federation Internationale de Camping et de Caravanning (FICC).

The National Caravan Council

The National Caravan Council, Catherine House, Victoria Road, Aldershot, Hampshire GU11 1SS

t (01252) 318251
w thecaravan.net

The National Caravan Council (NCC) is the trade body for the British caravan industry – not just touring caravans and motorhomes but also caravan holiday homes. It has in its membership parks, manufacturers, dealers and suppliers to the industry – all NCC member companies are committed continually to raise standards of technical and commercial excellence.

So, if you want to know where to buy a caravan, where to find a caravan holiday park or simply need advice on caravans and caravanning, see the website thecaravan.net where there is lots of helpful advice including:

- How to check whether the caravan, motorhome or caravan holiday home you are buying complies with European Standards and essential UK health and safety regulations (through the Certification scheme that the NCC operates).
- Where to find quality parks to visit on holiday.
- Where to find approved caravan and motorhome workshops for servicing and repair.

Caravan holidays are one of the most popular choices for holidaymakers in Britain – the NCC works closely with VisitBritain to promote caravan holidays in all their forms and parks that are part of the British Graded Quality Parks Scheme.

Help before you go

i When it comes to your next break, the first stage of your journey could be closer than you think.

You've probably got a Tourist Information Centre nearby which is there to serve the local community – as well as visitors. Knowledgeable staff will be happy to help you, wherever you're heading.

Many Tourist Information Centres can provide you with maps and guides, and it's often possible to book accommodation and travel tickets too.

You'll find the address of your nearest centre in your local phone book, or look in the regional sections in this guide for a list of Tourist Information Centres.

About the accommodation entries

Entries

All the sites featured in this guide have been assessed or have applied for assessment under The British Graded Holiday Parks Scheme. Assessment automatically entitles sites to a listing in this guide. Start your search for a place to stay by looking in the 'Where to Stay' sections of this guide where proprietor have paid to have their site featured in either a standard entry (includes photograph, description, facilities and prices) or an enhanced entry (photograph(s) and extended details). If you can't find what you're looking for, turn to the listing sections which appear at the back of each region for an even wider choice of accommodation.

Locations

Places to stay are generally listed under the town, city or village where they are located. If a place is in a small village, you may find it listed under a nearby town (providing it is within a seven-mile radius). Within each region, counties run in alphabetical order. Place names are listed alphabetically within each county, along with information on which county that is and their map reference.

Map references

These refer to the colour location maps at the back of the guide. The first figure shown is the map number, the following letter and figure indicate the grid reference on the map. Only place names under which standard or enhanced entries (see above) feature appear on the maps. Some entries were included just before the guide went to press, so they do not appear on the maps.

Telephone numbers

Booking telephone numbers are listed below the contact address for each entry. Area codes are shown in brackets.

Prices

The prices shown are only a general guide and include VAT where applicable; they were supplied to us by proprietors in summer 2009. Remember, changes may occur after the guide goes to press, so we strongly advise you to check prices when you book your accommodation.

Touring pitch prices are based on the minimum and maximum charges for one night for two persons, car and either caravan or tent. (Some parks may charge separately for car, caravan or tent, and for each person and there may be an extra charge for caravan awnings.) Minimum and maximum prices for caravan holiday homes are given per week.

Prices often vary through the year, and may be significantly lower outside peak holiday weeks. You can get details of other bargain packages that may be available from the sites themselves, regional tourism organisations or your local Tourist Information Centre (TIC). Your local travel agent may also have information, and can help you make bookings.

Opening period

If an entry does not indicate an opening period, please check directly with the site.

Symbols

The at-a-glance symbols included at the end of each entry show many of the services and facilities available at each site. You will find the key to these symbols on page 6.

Pets

Many places accept visitors with dogs, but we do advise that you check this when you book, and ask if there are any extra charges or rules about exactly where your pet is allowed. The acceptance of dogs is not always extended to cats, and it is strongly advised that cat owners contact the site well in advance. Some sites do not accept pets at all. Pets are welcome where you see this symbol 🐕.

About the accommodation entries

The quarantine laws have changed in England, and dogs, cats and ferrets are able to come into Britain from over 50 countries. For details of the Pet Travel Scheme (PETS) please turn to page 415.

For details of the Pet Travel Scheme (PETS) please turn to page 415.

Payment accepted

The types of payment accepted by a site are listed in the payment accepted section. If you plan to pay by card, check that your particular card is acceptable before you book. Some proprietors will charge you a higher rate if you pay by credit card rather than cash or cheque. The difference is to cover the percentage paid by the proprietor to the credit card company. When you book by telephone, you may be asked for your credit card number as confirmation. But remember, the proprietor may then charge your credit card account if you cancel your booking. See under Cancellations on page 414.

See under Cancellations on page 414.

Awaiting confirmation of rating

At the time of going to press some parks featured in this guide had not yet been assessed for their rating for the year 2010 and so their new rating could not be included. Rating Applied For indicates this.

Country ways

The Countryside Rights of Way Act gives people new rights to walk on areas of open countryside and registered commonland.

To find out where you can go and what you can do, as well as information about taking your dog to the countryside, go online at countrysideaccess.gov.uk.

And when you're out and about...

Always follow the Country Code

- Be safe – plan ahead and follow any signs
- Leave gates and property as you find them
- Protect plants and animals, and take your litter home
- Keep dogs under close control
- Consider other people

Getting around

London transport

London Underground has 12 lines, each with its own unique colour, so you can easily follow them on the Underground map. Most lines run through central London, and many serve parts of Greater London.

Buses are a quick, convenient way to travel around London, providing plenty of sightseeing opportunities on the way. There are over 6,500 buses in London operating 700 routes every day. You will need to buy a ticket before you board the bus – available from machines at the bus stop – or have a valid Oyster card (see below).

London's National Rail system stretches all over London. Many lines start at the main London railway stations (Paddington, Victoria, Waterloo, Kings Cross) with links to the tube. Trains mainly serve areas outside central London, and travel over ground.

Children usually travel free, or at reduced fare, on all public transport in London.

Oyster cards

Oyster cards can be used to pay fares on all London Underground, buses, Docklands Light Railway and trams; they are generally not valid for National Rail services in London.

Oyster cards are very easy to use – you just touch the card on sensors at stations or on buses and it always charges you the lowest fare available for your journey. You buy credit for your journey and when it runs out you simply top up with more.

Oyster is available to adults only. Children below the age of 11 can accompany adults free of charge. Children between the ages of 11 and 15 should use the standard child travel card. You can get an Oyster card at any underground station, at one of 3,000 Oyster points around London displaying the London Underground sign (usually shops), or from www.visitbritaindirect.com, or www.oyster.tfl.gov.uk/oyster.

London congestion charge

The congestion charge is an £8 daily charge to drive in central London at certain times. Check whether the congestion charge is included in the cost of your car when you book. If your car's pick up point is in the congestion-charging zone, the company may pay the charge for the first day of your hire.

Low Emission Zone

The Low Emission Zone is an area covering most of Greater London, within which the most polluting diesel-engine vehicles are required to meet specific emissions standards. If your vehicle does not, you will need to pay a daily charge.

Vehicles affected by the Low Emission Zone are older diesel-engine lorries, buses, coaches, large vans, minibuses and other heavy vehicles such as motor caravans and motorised horse boxes. This includes vehicles registered outside of Great Britain. Cars and motorcycles are not affected by the scheme.

For more information visit tfl.gov.uk/roadusers/lez.

Britain's rail network covers all main cities and smaller regional towns. Trains on the network are operated by a few large companies running routes from London to stations all over Britain, and smaller companies running routes in regional areas. You can find up-to-the-minute information about routes, fares and train times on National Rail Enquiries (nationalrail.co.uk). For detailed information about routes and services, refer to the train operators' websites (see page 426).

Railway passes

BritRail offers a wide selection of passes and tickets giving you freedom to travel on all National Rail services. Passes can also include sleeper services, city and attraction passes and boat tours. Passes can normally be bought from travel agents outside Britain or by visiting the Britrail website (britrail. com).

Bus and coach travel

Public buses

Every city and town in Britain has a local bus service. These services are privatised and run by separate companies. The largest bus companies in Britain are First (firstgroup.com/bustravel.php), Stagecoach (stagecoachbus.com), and Arriva (arrivabus.co.uk), which run buses in most UK towns. Outside London, buses usually travel to and from the town centre or busiest part of town. Most towns have a bus station, where you'll be able to find maps and information about routes. Bus route information may also be posted at bus stops.

Tickets and fares

The cost of a bus ticket normally depends on how far you're travelling. Return fares may be available on some buses, but you usually need to buy a 'single' ticket for each individual journey.

You can buy your ticket when you board a bus, by telling the driver where you are going. One-day and weekly travel cards are available in some towns, and these can be bought from the driver or from an information centre at the bus station. Tickets are valid for each separate journey rather than for a period of time, so if you get off the bus you'll need to buy a new ticket when getting on another bus.

Domestic flights

Flying is a time-saving alternative to road or rail when it comes to travelling around Britain. Domestic flights are fast and frequent and there are 33 airports across Britain operating domestic routes. You will find airports marked on the maps at the front of this guide.

Domestic flight advice

Photo ID is required to travel on domestic flights. It is advisable to bring your passport, as not all airlines will accept other forms of photo identification.

There are very high security measures at all airports in Britain. These include restrictions on items that may be carried in hand luggage. It is important that you check with your airline prior to travel, as these restrictions may vary over time. Make sure you allow adequate time for check-in and boarding.

Cycling

Cycling is a good way to see some of Britain's best scenery and there are many networks of cycling routes. The National Cycle Network offers over 10,000 miles of walking and cycling routes connecting towns and villages, countryside and coast across the UK. For more information and routes see page 412 or visit Sustrans at sustrans.co.uk.

Think green

If you'd rather leave your car behind and travel by 'green transport' when visiting some of the attractions highlighted in this guide you'll be helping to reduce congestion and pollution as well as supporting conservation charities in their commitment to green travel.

The National Trust encourages visits made by non-car travellers. It offers admission discounts or a voucher for the tea room at a selection of its properties if you arrive on foot, cycle or public transport. (You'll need to produce a valid bus or train ticket if travelling by public transport.)

More information about The National Trust's work to encourage car-free days out can be found at nationaltrust.org.uk. Refer to the section entitled Information for Visitors.

By car and by train

Distance chart

The distances between towns on the chart below are given to the nearest mile, and are measured along routes based on the quickest travelling time, making maximum use of motorways or dual-carriageway roads. The chart is based upon information supplied by the Automobile Association.

To calculate the distance in kilometres multiply the mileage by 1.6

For example: Brighton to Dover
82 miles x 1.6 =131.2 kilometres

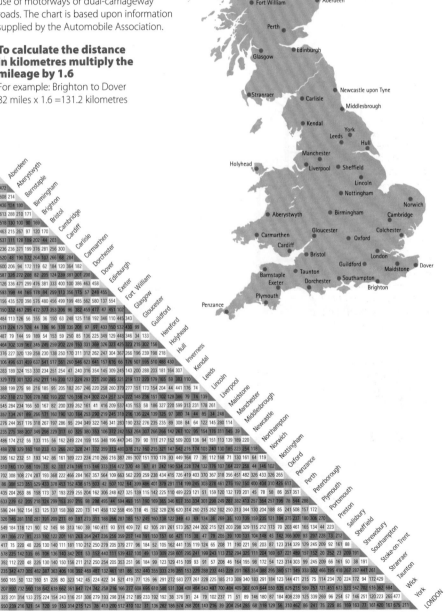

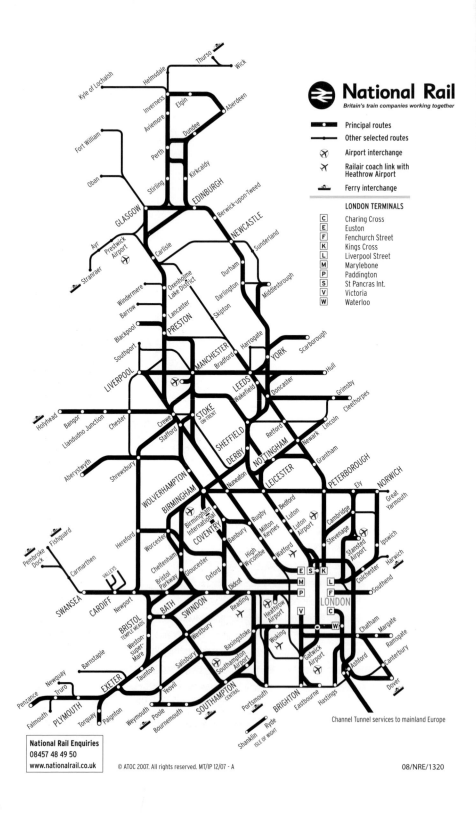

National Rail
Britain's train companies working together

▬▬●▬▬	Principal routes
▬▬●▬▬	Other selected routes
✈	Airport interchange
✈	Railair coach link with Heathrow Airport
⛴	Ferry interchange

LONDON TERMINALS

C	Charing Cross
E	Euston
F	Fenchurch Street
K	Kings Cross
L	Liverpool Street
M	Marylebone
P	Paddington
S	St Pancras Int.
V	Victoria
W	Waterloo

Channel Tunnel services to mainland Europe

National Rail Enquiries
08457 48 49 50
www.nationalrail.co.uk

© ATOC 2007. All rights reserved. MT/IP 12/07 - A

08/NRE/1320

Travel information

General travel information

Streetmap	www.streetmap.co.uk	
Transport Direct	www.transportdirect.info	
Transport for London	www.tfl.gov.uk	020 7222 1234
Travel Services	www.departures-arrivals.com	
Traveline	www.traveline.org.uk	0871 200 2233

Bus & coach

Megabus	www.megabus.com	0900 610 0900
National Express	www.nationalexpress.com	0870 580 8080
WA Shearings	www.washearings.com	0844 824 6355

Car & car hire

AA	www.theaa.com	0870 600 0371
Green Flag	www.greenflag.co.uk	0845 246 1557
RAC	www.rac.co.uk	0870 572 2722
Alamo	www.alamo.co.uk	0870 400 4562*
Avis	www.avis.co.uk	0844 581 0147*
Budget	www.budget.co.uk	0844 544 3407*
Easycar	www.easycar.com	0871 050 0444
Enterprise	www.enterprise.com	0870 350 3000*
Hertz	www.hertz.co.uk	0870 844 8844*
Holiday Autos	www.holidayautos.co.uk	0871 472 5229
National	www.nationalcar.co.uk	0870 400 4581
Thrifty	www.thrifty.co.uk	01494 751500

Air

Air Southwest	www.airsouthwest.com	0870 043 4553
Blue Islands (Channel Islands)	www.blueislands.com	0845 620 2122
BMI	www.flybmi.com	0870 6070 555
BMI Baby	www.bmibaby.com	0905 828 2828*
British Airways	www.ba.com	0844 493 0787
British International (Insles of Scilly to Penzance)	www.islesofscillyhelicopter.com	01736 363871*
Eastern Airways	www.easternairways.com	0870 366 9989
Easyjet	www.easyjet.com	0871 244 2366
Flybe	www.flybe.com	0871 700 2000*
Flyglobespan	www.flyglobespan.com	0871 271 9000*
Jet2.com	www.jet2.com	0871 226 1737*
Manx2	www.manx2.com	0871 200 0440*
Ryanair	www.ryanair.com	0871 246 0000
Skybus (Isles of Scilly)	www.islesofscilly-travel.co.uk	0845 710 5555
Thomsonfly	www.thomsonfly.com	0871 231 4787
VLM	www.flyvlm.com	0871 666 5050

Train

National Rail Enquiries	www.nationalrail.co.uk	0845 748 4950
The Trainline	www.trainline.co.uk	0870 010 1296
UK train operating companies	www.rail.co.uk	
Arriva Trains	www.arriva.co.uk	0845 748 4950
c2c	www.c2c-online.co.uk	0845 601 4873
Chiltern Railways	www.chilternrailways.co.uk	0845 600 5165
CrossCountry	www.crosscountrytrains.co.uk	0870 010 0084
East Midlands Trains	www.eastmidlandstrains.co.uk	0845 712 5678
Eurostar	www.eurostar.com	0870 518 6186*
First Capital Connect	www.firstcapitalconnect.co.uk	0845 026 4700
First Great Western	www.firstgreatwestern.co.uk	0845 700 0125
Gatwick Express	www.gatwickexpress.com	0845 850 1530
Heathrow Connect	www.heathrowconnect.com	0845 678 6975
Heathrow Express	www.heathrowexpress.com	0845 600 1515
Hull Trains	www.hulltrains.co.uk	0845 071 0222
Island Line	www.island-line.co.uk	0845 600 0650
London Midlands	www.londonmidland.com	0121 634 2040
Merseyrail	www.merseyrail.org	0151 702 2071
National Express East Anglia	www.nationalexpresseastanglia.com	0845 600 7245
National Express East Coast	www.nationalexpresseastcoast.com	0845 722 5333
Northern Rail	www.northernrail.org	0845 000 0125
ScotRail	www.firstgroup.com/scotrail	0845 601 5929
South Eastern Trains	www.southeasternrailway.co.uk	0845 000 2222
South West Trains	www.southwesttrains.co.uk	0845 600 0650
Southern	www.southernrailway.com	0845 127 2920
Stansted Express	www.stanstedexpress.com	0845 850 0150
Translink	www.nirailways.co.uk	(028) 9066 6630
Transpennine Express	www.tpexpress.co.uk	0845 600 1671
Virgin Trains	www.virgintrains.co.uk	0845 722 2333*

Ferry

Ferry Information	www.sailanddrive.com	
Condor Ferries	www.condorferries.co.uk	0845 609 1024*
Steam Packet Company	www.steam-packet.com	0871 222 1333*
Isles of Scilly Travel	www.islesofscilly-travel.co.uk	0845 710 5555
Red Funnel	www.redfunnel.co.uk	0870 444 8898
Wight Link	www.wightlink.co.uk	0871 376 1000

Phone numbers listed are for general enquiries unless otherwise stated.
* Booking line only

David Bellamy Conservation Award

"These well-deserved awards are a signpost to parks which are making real achievements in protecting our environment. Go there and experience wrap-around nature....you could be amazed at what you find!" says Professor David Bellamy.

Many of Britain's holiday parks have become 'green champions' of conservation in the countryside, according to leading conservationist David Bellamy. More than 500 gold, silver and bronze parks were this year named in the David Bellamy Conservation Awards, organised in conjunction with the British Holiday and Home Parks Association. These parks are recognised for their commitment to conservation and the environment through their management of landscaping, recycling policies, waste management, the cultivation of flora and fauna and the creation of habitats designed to encourage a variety of wildlife onto the park. Links with the local community and the use of local materials are also important considerations.

Parks wishing to enter for a David Bellamy Conservation Award must complete a detailed questionnaire covering different aspects of their environmental policies, and describe what positive conservation steps they have taken. The park must also undergo an independent audit from a local wildlife or conservation body which is familiar with the area. Final assessments and the appropriate level of any award are then made personally by Professor Bellamy.

Parks with Bellamy Awards offer a variety of accommodation from pitches for touring caravans, motor homes and tents, to caravan holiday homes, holiday lodges and cottages for rent or to buy. Holiday parks with these awards are not just those in quiet corners of the countryside. Amongst the winners are much larger centres in popular holiday areas that offer a wide range of entertainments and attractions.

The parks listed on the following pages all have a detailed entry in this guide and have received a Gold, Silver or Bronze David Bellamy Conservation Award. Use the park index to find the page number.

For a free brochure featuring a full list of award- winning parks please contact:
BH&HPA,
6 Pullman Court, Great Western Road,
Gloucester GL1 3ND
t (01452) 526911
e enquiries@bhhpa.org.uk
w davidbellamyconservation.org.uk

Churchwood Valley Holiday Cabins	GOLD	Wembury	South West Engl
Cofton Country Holidays	GOLD	Dawlish	South West Engl
Croft Farm Holiday Park	GOLD	Luxulyan	South West Engl
Dolbeare Caravan & Camping Park	SILVER	Landrake	South West Engl
Dornafield Touring Park	GOLD	Newton Abbot	South West Engl
Forest Glade Holiday Park	GOLD	Kentisbeare	South West Engl
Golden Cap Holiday Park	GOLD	Bridport	South West Engl
Halse Farm Caravan & Tent Park	GOLD	Winsford	South West Engl
Harford Bridge Holiday Park	GOLD	Tavistock	South West Engl
Hendra Holiday Park	GOLD	Newquay	South West Engl
Highlands End Holiday Park	GOLD	Bridport	South West Engl
Holiday Resort Unity	SILVER	Brean	South West Engl
Mother Ivey's Bay Caravan Park (Camping)	GOLD	Padstow	South West Engl
Padstow Touring Park	SILVER	Padstow	South West Engl
Porlock Caravan Park	GOLD	Porlock	South West Engl
Porthtowan Tourist Park	SILVER	Porthtowan	South West Engla
Rowlands Wait Touring Park	GOLD	Bere Regis	South West Engla
Silver Sands Holiday Park	GOLD	Ruan Minor	South West Engla
Tehidy Holiday Park	GOLD	Portreath	South West Engla
Treloy Touring Park	SILVER	Newquay	South West Engla
Warcombe Farm Camping Park	GOLD	Mortehoe	South West Engla
Watergate Bay Touring Park	BRONZE	Watergate Bay Newquay	South West Engla
Waterrow Touring Park	GOLD	Waterrow	South West Engla
Whitehill Country Park	GOLD	Paignton	South West Engla
Wilksworth Farm Caravan Park	GOLD	Wimborne Minster	South West Englar
Wooda Farm Holiday Park	GOLD	Bude	South West Engla
Bay View Park Ltd	GOLD	Pevensey Bay	South East Englar
Cheverton Copse Holiday Park Ltd	GOLD	Sandown	South East Englar
Crowhurst Park	GOLD	Battle	South East Englar
Heathfield Farm Camping	GOLD	Freshwater	South East Englar
Hurley Riverside Park	GOLD	Hurley	South East Englar
Lower Hyde Holiday Park	GOLD	Shanklin	South East Englar
Nodes Point Holiday Park	GOLD	St Helens	South East Englar
Riverside Holidays	BRONZE	Hamble	South East Englar
Shamba Holidays	SILVER	Ringwood	South East Englar
Tanner Farm Park	GOLD	Marden	South East Englar
Thorness Bay Holiday Park	GOLD	Thorness Bay	South East Englar
Whitefield Forest Touring Park	GOLD	Ryde	South East Englar
Wicks Farm Camping Park	GOLD	Chichester	South East Englar
Breydon Water Holiday Park (Bure Village)	SILVER	Great Yarmouth	East of Englar
Cliff House Holiday Park	GOLD	Dunwich	East of Englar
Deer's Glade Caravan and Camping Park	GOLD	Hanworth	East of Englar
Highfield Grange Holiday Park	SILVER	Clacton-on-Sea	East of Englar
Heathland Beach Caravan Park	GOLD	Kessingland	East of Englar
Naze Marine Holiday Park	GOLD	Walton-on-the-Naze	East of Englar
Sandy Gulls Caravan Park	GOLD	Mundesley	East of Englar
Searles Leisure Resort	GOLD	Hunstanton	East of Englar
Waldegraves Holiday Park	GOLD	Mersea Island	East of Englar
Wyton Lakes Holiday Park	SILVER	Wyton	East of Englar
Ashby Park	GOLD	Horncastle	East Midlands Englar
Lowfields Country Holiday Fishing Retreat	GOLD	North Scarle	East Midlands Englar
Orchard Park	GOLD	Boston	East Midlands Englar
Rivendale Caravan & Leisure Park	GOLD	Alsop-En-le-Dale	East Midlands Englar
Skegness Water Leisure Park	GOLD	Skegness	East Midlands Englar
Arrow Bank Holiday Park	SILVER	Eardisland	Heart of Englar
Fernwood Caravan Park	GOLD	Ellesmere	Heart of England
Ranch Caravan Park	GOLD	Evesham	Heart of England

er Trees Holiday Park - Static Vans	GOLD	Rugeley	Heart of England
Star Caravan & Camping Park	SILVER	Stoke-on-Trent	Heart of England
rton Park Caravan Park	GOLD	York	Yorkshire England
ton Village Caravan Park Ltd	GOLD	Scarborough	Yorkshire England
sewood Holiday Park	GOLD	York	Yorkshire England
me Valley Camping and Caravan Park	GOLD	Holmfirth	Yorkshire England
ycross Plantation Touring Caravan Park	GOLD	Whitby	Yorkshire England
berston Touring Park	GOLD	Scarborough	Yorkshire England
dlewood Farm Holiday Park	GOLD	Whitby	Yorkshire England
ketts Mill Leisure Park	GOLD	Guisborough	Yorkshire England
ding Holiday Park	GOLD	Harrogate	Yorkshire England
wood Holiday Park	GOLD	Haworth	Yorkshire England
e of Pickering Caravan Park	GOLD	Allerston	Yorkshire England
r Caravan Park	SILVER	York	Yorkshire England
tlerigg Hall Caravan & Camping Park	GOLD	Keswick	North West England
ke Valley Holiday Park	GOLD	Coniston	North West England
barrow Park	GOLD	Windermere	North West England
sco Wood Caravan Park	GOLD	Penrith	North West England
der Wood Country Park	GOLD	Rochdale	North West England
of Oaks Park	GOLD	Windermere	North West England
efitt Park	GOLD	Windermere	North West England
rton Mere Holiday Village	GOLD	Blackpool	North West England
ean Edge Leisure Park, Heysham	BRONZE	Heysham	North West England
rk Cliffe Camping & Caravan Estate	GOLD	Windermere	North West England
gent Leisure Park, Morecambe	BRONZE	Morecambe	North West England
ree Rivers Woodland Park	GOLD	West Bradford	North West England
dber Park	SILVER	Gisburn	North West England
aterfoot Caravan Park	GOLD	Ullswater	North West England
ld Rose Park	GOLD	Appleby-in-Westmorland	North West England
oodclose Caravan Park	GOLD	Kirkby Lonsdale	North West England
afield Caravan Park	GOLD	Seahouses	North East England
aren Caravan and Camping Park	GOLD	Bamburgh	North East England
lhaven Bay Caravan and Camping Park	GOLD	Dunbar	Scotland
tham Feus Caravan Park	GOLD	Leven	Scotland
nnhe Lochside Holidays	GOLD	Fort William	Scotland
nwater Caravan Park	GOLD	Edinburgh	Scotland
ch Ken Holiday Park	GOLD	Parton	Scotland
mond Woods Holiday Park	GOLD	Balloch	Scotland
rtonhall Caravan and Camping Park	GOLD	Edinburgh	Scotland
auchope Links Caravan Park	GOLD	Crail	Scotland
rynowen Holiday Park	GOLD	Borth	Wales
y Mawr Holiday Park	GOLD	Towyn	Wales

National Accessible Scheme index

Establishments participating in the National Accessible Scheme are listed below - those i
colour have a detailed entry in this guide. At the front of the guide you can find
information about the scheme. Establishments are listed alphabetically by place name.

🦽 Mobility level 1

Little Tarrington Heart of England	**Hereford Camping and Caravanning Club Site ★★★★★**	2
Pakefield East of England	**Pakefield Caravan Park ★★★★**	1
Saltwick Bay Yorkshire	**Whitby Holiday Park - Touring Park ★★★★**	2

🦽 Mobility level 2

Bishop Auckland North East	**Cromer House Camping Barn**	3

Welcome Schemes

ablishments participating in the Walkers Welcome and Cyclists Welcome schemes ovide special facilities and actively encourage these recreations. Establishments rticipating in the Families Welcome or Welcome Pets! schemes are listed below. They ovide special facilities and actively encourage families or guests with pets. commodation with a detailed entry in this guide is listed below. Place names are listed ohabetically.

Walkers Welcome and Cyclists Welcome

guard Wales	Fishguard Bay Caravan & Camping Park ★★★★	389
drake South West	Dolbeare Caravan & Camping Park ★★★★★	49
Davids Wales	Caerfai Bay Caravan & Tent Park ★★★★	390
istock South West	Harford Bridge Holiday Park ★★★★ rose	68
istock South West	Langstone Manor Holiday Park ★★★★ rose	69
mbury South West	Churchwood Valley Holiday Cabins ★★★★	70
vil South West	Long Hazel Park ★★★★	87

Walkers Welcome

Agnes South West	Beacon Cottage Farm Touring Park ★★★★	57

Families and Pets Welcome

lmfirth Yorkshire	Holme Valley Camping and Caravan Park	267

Families Welcome

ckpool North West	Newton Hall Holiday Park	311
uth North West	Black Beck Caravan Park rose	302
ngsby Yorkshire	Robin Hood Caravan Park rose	271
ke-on-Trent Heart of England	The Star Caravan & Camping Park rose	247

Pets Welcome

mburgh North East	Waren Caravan and Camping Park rose	336
nworth East of England	Deer's Glade Caravan and Camping Park	187
lsworthy South West	Noteworthy Caravan and Campsite	62
rth Scarle East Midlands	Lowfields Country Holiday Fishing Retreat rose	218
arborough Yorkshire	Cayton Village Caravan Park Ltd	269
ahouses North East	Seafield Caravan Park rose	338
egness East Midlands	Skegness Water Leisure Park	218
anby East Midlands	Highfields Country Holiday Fishing Retreat rose	219
rk Yorkshire	Allerton Park Caravan Park rose	275
rk Yorkshire	Weir Caravan Park rose	276

Quick reference index

If you're looking for a specific facility use this index to see at a glance detailed accommodation entries that match your requirement. Establishments are listed alphabetically by place name.

⌘ Indoor pool

Battle South East	**Crowhurst Park ★★★★★** rose	
Bembridge South East	**Whitecliff Bay Holiday Park ★★★**	
Birchington South East	**Two Chimneys Caravan Park ★★★★★**	
Blackpool North West	**Marton Mere Holiday Village ★★★★**	
Blackpool North West	**Newton Hall Holiday Park ★★★★**	
Blackpool North West	**Windy Harbour Holiday Park ★★★★**	
Borth Wales	**Brynowen Holiday Park ★★★**	
Brean South West	**Holiday Resort Unity ★★★★**	
Bridport South West	**Highlands End Holiday Park ★★★★★** rose	
Bude South West	**Sandymouth Holiday Park ★★★★★** rose	
Clacton-on-Sea East of England	**Highfield Grange Holiday Park ★★★★**	
Dawlish South West	**Welcome Family Holiday Park ★★★★** rose	
Filey Yorkshire	**Orchard Farm Holiday Village ★★★★★**	
Fordingbridge South East	**Sandy Balls Holiday Centre ★★★★★** rose	
Great Yarmouth East of England	**Breydon Water Holiday Park (Bure Village) ★★★★**	
Great Yarmouth East of England	**Summerfields Holiday Village ★★★★**	
Harrogate Yorkshire	**High Moor Farm Park ★★★★★**	
Hayle South West	**St Ives Bay Holiday Park ★★★★**	
Hemsby East of England	**Hemsby Beach Holiday Village ★★**	1
Heysham North West	**Ocean Edge Leisure Park, Heysham ★★★**	3
Hunstanton East of England	**Searles Leisure Resort ★★★★★**	1
Kentisbeare South West	**Forest Glade Holiday Park ★★★★** rose	
Kingsdown South East	**Kingsdown Park Holiday Village ★★★★★**	1
Looe South West	**Tencreek Hoilday Park ★★★★**	
Morecambe North West	**Regent Leisure Park, Morecambe ★★★★**	3
Morecambe North West	**Venture Caravan Park, Morecambe ★★★★**	3
Mundesley East of England	**Mundesley ★★**	1
Newquay South West	**Hendra Holiday Park ★★★★★** rose	
Newquay South West	**Riverside Holiday Park ★★★★**	
Paignton South West	**Beverley Holidays ★★★★★**	
Redruth South West	**Lanyon Holiday Park ★★★★**	
Rhyl Wales	**Golden Sands Holiday Park ★★★★**	3
Ringwood South East	**Shamba Holidays ★★★★**	1
Rugeley Heart of England	**Silver Trees Holiday Park - Static Vans ★★★★** rose	2
Scarborough Yorkshire	**Crows Nest Caravan Park ★★★★** rose	2
Scarborough Yorkshire	**Flower of May Holiday Parks Ltd ★★★★★**	2
Seahouses North East	**Seafield Caravan Park ★★★★★** rose	3
Selsey South East	**Green Lawns Holiday Park ★★★★★** rose	1
Selsey South East	**Warner Farm Camping & Touring Park ★★★★★**	1
Selsey South East	**West Sands Holiday Park ★★★★** rose	1
Selsey South East	**White Horse Holiday Park ★★★★** rose	1
Shaldon South West	**Coast View Holiday Park ★★★★**	6
Shanklin South East	**Landguard Holidays ★★★★**	12
Shanklin South East	**Lower Hyde Holiday Park ★★★★** rose	12
Skegness East Midlands	**Richmond Holiday Centre ★★★**	21
Skipsea Yorkshire	**Skipsea Sands Holiday Village ★★★★** rose	27
St Helens South East	**Nodes Point Holiday Park ★★★★**	12

🏊 Indoor pool continued

🏊 Outdoor pool

Establishments listed here have a detailed entry in this guide

Index by property name

Accommodation with a detailed entry in this guide is listed below.

Official tourist board guide **Camping, Caravan & Holiday Parks**

Index to display advertisers

Establishments listed here have a detailed entry in this guide

Index by place name

The following places all have detailed accommodation entries in this guide. If the place where you wish to stay is not shown, the location maps (starting on page 394) will help you to find somewhere to stay in the area.

Published by: Heritage House Group
Ketteringham Hall, Wymondham, Norfolk, NR18 9RS
Tel: 01603 813319 Fax: 01603 814992

On behalf of: VisitBritain, Thames Tower, Blacks Road, London W6 9EL

Production: PDQ Digital Media Solutions Ltd
Printing: Burlington, part of BPC Ltd

Photography credits: © Britain On View: Adrian Houston,
Alan Chandler, Andy Sewell, Angus Bremner, Britain On View, Chris Coe,
Co Durham Tourism Partnership, Damir Fabijanc, Daniel Bosworth,
David Lake, David Noton, Dennis Hardley, Eric Nathan, Grant Pritchard,
Howard Sayer, Ingrid Rasmussen, James McCormick, Jasmine Teer,
Joanna Henderson, Jon Spaull, Jonathan Crabb, Liz Gander, Martin Brent,
Natalie Pecht, Pawel Libera, Pete Seaward, Rod Edwards, Simon Kreitem,
Simon Winnall, Tim Fox, Tony Pleavin.

© British Tourist Authority (trading as VisitBritain) 2009
ISBN 978-0-7095-8462-9

A VisitBritain guide